FREEDOM:

GIVE ME LIBERTY OR GIVE ME DEATH!

Only In Jesus— The True Liberator!

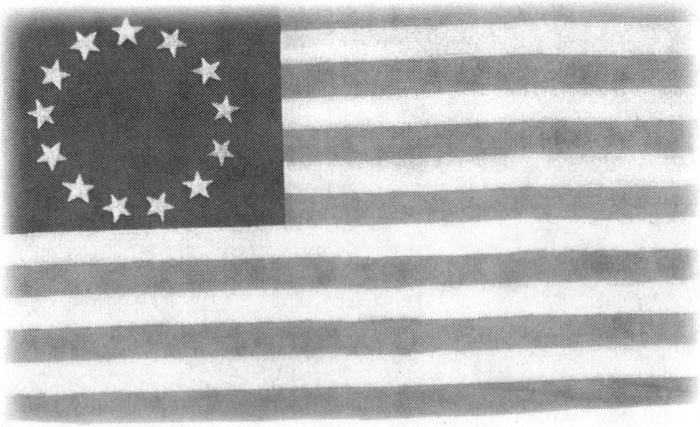

FREEDOM:
GIVE ME LIBERTY OR GIVE ME DEATH!
Only In Jesus— The True Liberator!

MARK KIRCHBERG AND PHYLLIS KIRCHBERG

VANTAGEPress

Scripture taken from the HOLY BIBLE,
New International Version ®. Copyright ©,
1973, 1978, 1984 by International Bible Society. Used by permission of
Zondervan Publishing House. All rights reserved.

The "NIV" and "New International Version" trademarks are registered
in the United States Patent and Trademark Office by
International Bible Society. Use of either trademark requires
the permission of International Bible Society.

Cover & interior design by Neuwirth and Associates

Vantage Press and the Vantage Press colophon
are registered trademarks of Vantage Press, Inc.

FIRST EDITION
All rights reserved, including the right of
reproduction in whole or in part in any form.

Copyright © 2012 by Mark and Phyllis Kirchberg

Published by Vantage Press, Inc.
419 Park Ave. South, New York, NY 10016

Manufactured in the United States of America
ISBN: 978-0-533-16404-2

Library of Congress Catalog Card No: 2010910669

0 9 8 7 6 5 4 3 2 1

This book is dedicated to our Lord Jesus, our Messiah, and for His glory. It is also dedicated to past, present, and future generations of Americans; those who have been, are, and will be willing to lose their lives, even shed their blood to serve God, our Lord Jesus, in order to maintain God-given rights, as revealed in the Holy Scriptures and American documents, for all individuals, including the unborn in the United States of America.

> "All who go down to the dust will kneel before him—those who cannot keep themselves alive. Posterity will serve him; future generations will be told about the Lord. They will proclaim his righteousness to a people yet unborn—for he has done it."
>
> (Ps 22:29-31)

ACKNOWLEDGMENT

All thanks and praise, honor and glory belong to Almighty God, our Lord Jesus Christ, and to the Holy Spirit who is working in us in a mighty way to bring forth the messages, the warnings, the divine truth of our Heavenly Father and our Lord Jesus Christ. He has continued to pour out His kindness, His love—to a country, a people who have blatantly disdained the one true God—to serve the "god of this world." With gratitude and deep humility, we thank Him for the privilege and honor of allowing us to be a ready pen for this book on Freedom! A special thanks to our children for their encouragement, for their love of American history, for their time spent with us visiting historical landmarks, for their patriotism.

CONTENTS

Preface   xi

Introduction   xv

[PART I]
AMERICA: PAST   1

1. It Had Its Foundation on the Rock, Jesus Christ in America!   3

2. To Purify for Himself a Peculiar People   18

3. Give Me Liberty or Give Me Death! Only in Jesus—The True Liberator!   39

4. Forceful Men Lay Hold of the Kingdom of Heaven!   60

5. And the Government Will Be on His Shoulders   82

6. Proclaim Freedom for the Slaves   102

7. Make Straight in the Wilderness a Highway for Our God   132

[PART II]
AMERICA: PRESENT 159

8. To See from Shining Sea	161
9. If You Forsake Him, He Will Forsake You!	184
10. Thou Shalt Not Kill!	213
11. God Gave Them Over to Shameful Lusts!	239
12. Train a Child in the Way He Should Go!	267
13. I Will Betroth You to Me Forever!	304
14. You Cannot Serve God and Mammon	330

[PART III]
AMERICA: FUTURE 371

15. And a Great Storm Arose	375
16. What Will Be the Sign of Your Coming?	402
17. A Shelter from the Storm	440
Epilogue	470
Freedom Proclamation	472
Notes	473

PREFACE

When my wife and I began courting in 1984, we had no idea that the places we desired to visit during our courtship, and after our marriage, would be so important to us in this book. In August 1994, when my wife and I were living in an apartment in Haifa, Israel, the Lord Jesus gave us a vision that would have future ramifications for this book. In the vision, I saw an airplane flying out of the Tel-Aviv Airport in Israel towards the United States. In the next vision, my wife and I landed feet first in front of Mount Rushmore in South Dakota. At Mount Rushmore are the carved images in rock of George Washington, Thomas Jefferson, Abraham Lincoln, and Teddy Roosevelt. We have yet to visit Mount Rushmore, but we believe the Lord Jesus was giving us a foreshadowing of His desire for us to write a book about America. Since our courting years, the Lord Jesus has kept our hearts focused on the Americans, who founded this great nation. We believe, they covenanted with our Lord Jesus for His providential care of this country (Gen 9:8-17; 17:4-9; Lk 21:20).

On the morning of April 16, 2008, my wife heard these words from our Lord Jesus, "The state of Virginia." That morning the Lord Jesus revealed that, "The state of Virginia has many historical sites, that providentially, you desired to spend much time visiting." On our first "official" date together, we spent several hours sharing with each other at George Washington's birthplace in Westmoreland County, Virginia. His birthplace became a favorite recreational site for us where we swam, fished, picnicked, and toured the grounds there, and at times, we shared it with our children and grandchildren.

In Fredericksburg, Virginia, we visited George Washington's boyhood home often. Several times we walked the peaceful grounds there, and heard the voice of the Lord Jesus speak to us about George Washington, and other matters (Jn 10:27, 28). We often visited a park in the city of Fredericksburg, where George Washington's mother prayed for her son during the Revolutionary War on a hill that overlooked the park (Mt 14:23). My wife and I have often prayed there with our grandchildren, holding hands together. We lived in the city of Fredericksburg for about five years. While we courted, and after we were married, George Washington's home at Mount Vernon was another site we were drawn to visit.

Within a month after our first "official" date together, my wife and I visited the home of Thomas Jefferson at Monticello in Charlottesville, Virginia. We have also walked the grounds, where there are the remaining ruins of homes and buildings of the original site of the town of Jamestown, Virginia. On a sunny day in the spring of 1985, we were content just spending time together, where those early settlers attempted to establish their first community in America.

We loved to visit Stratford Hall in Westmoreland County, Virginia, the birthplace and first home of Robert E. Lee. It has been reported that General Robert E. Lee was a strong believer in Jesus Christ[1] (Jn 4:41; Ac 2:47). We enjoyed touring the grounds there, as well as eating lunch at the Stratford Hall restaurant, at times with our children. During the times my wife and I taught in Christian schools, Stratford Hall, George Washington's birthplace, and Mount Vernon were sites where we would take field trips with our students. We attended many other historical sites in Virginia, while we were dating and after we were married.

After our wedding in 1987, we went on our honeymoon to Plymouth, Massachusetts. We toured the "Mayflower," and the Plimoth Plantation to become more familiar with the early founders of America, and to learn more about our American Christian heritage. Men and women there, who were dressed in Pilgrim outfits, often spoke about their faith in God during our visit. On one of our anniversary trips, we visited Abraham Lincoln's boyhood, log cabin home in Kentucky, and we also toured the grounds at the Battle of Gettysburg, where Lincoln gave his famous, "Gettysburg Address."

On April 17, 2008, my wife heard these words from the Lord Jesus, "Use the Carolina scene." When we lived in North Carolina for over four years, 1994-1998, we often spent time at the settlement of Bethabara, "House of Passage," the first Moravian settlement founded in 1753, in Winston-Salem, North Carolina. The Moravians were followers of John Huss, a Bohemian, who protested against the Roman Catholic Church. The Moravians are considered the first Protestants,[2] those who protested against the teachings of the Catholic Church (Mt 15:7-9). The village was so peaceful, and living there was simple. Every person served the Lord Jesus in their own specific occupation (1 Co 12:27,28; 1 Th 4:11).

We have always enjoyed visiting American historical sites. Yet, we were not aware that the Lord Jesus would have us write about our past Christian "Founding Fathers" of America, who lived at those sites. Their influence in establishing liberty in this country through faith in the One, True Liberator, Jesus Christ our Messiah, is God's main purpose for this book (Jn 8:31,32,36; Heb 11:1,2).

INTRODUCTION

We believe this country was established by men and women, who desired to ensure that all God-given rights were granted to every human being. Over the years, we believe those rights have been eroding for certain individuals, and specific groups in the United States of America. Legislators and Court justices have promoted their own causes apart from the rights that our "Founding Fathers" established in the Declaration of Independence, the Constitution, and the Bill of Rights. This country, we believe, has lost the vision of our Founding Fathers. (Dt 30:15,16; Pr 29:18 [KJV]; Gal 4:4,5).

We believe our Founding Fathers would be appalled at the moral condition of this country, and the decisions that legislators and justices have made in the twentieth and twenty-first century. What would the Founding Fathers of this country, and the soldiers who fought in the Revolutionary War, who died for the cause of freedom and independence, say to the "leaders" of our country today? We believe, that they would still say, "Give me liberty, or give me death." We believe that they would share, that what plagues America today is the lack of patriotism, the lack of American unity, the lack of one nation under God's leadership under the Lordship of Jesus Christ. We also believe, that they would say today, "We did not shed our blood for America's future to deny Americans their privileges of freedom and rights, and to grant certain rights to those who oppose the one, true living God, and His Words. Where are the men and women in America today, who have the character, fortitude, boldness and unswerving faith in God, to fight for this country's honor?" (Ps 15:1-5; Pr 31:8,9; Isa 10:1-3; Jer 34:15,16 [KJV]; La 3:34,35; 1 Co 8:6; 2 Pe 2:19 [KJV]).

On October 23, 1995, my wife saw a vision of a reddish, burgundy barn in New England. It was the kind of barn that we would see in Connecticut, Pennsylvania, or even New Jersey. The barn was on a solid, cement rock foundation. Seed was being stored up in that barn to be used for food later. A farm animal (pig) was drinking milk in a bottle in the vision. Then she heard the words, "Pony Express." The Lord Jesus then said, "This is the end-time farming. Farming began in this country, and farming will become very valuable in the last days. For the farming of My seed, (the Word of God), 'shall not return to Me void.' It is the Word of God, planted on a firm foundation, the Rock. Let them feed on the 'milk' of the Word. If you sow sparingly, you will reap a sparse harvest. If you sow generously to the kingdom of God, you will reap generously, souls. This barn is to be a house used for ministry. Ride like the 'Pony Express,' and express and warn with this message" (Dt 28:8; Isa 55:11 [KJV]; Mt 7:24,25; Mk 4:3,8,14,20; I Co 2:13; Gal 6:7-10; Heb 5:12).

On April 3rd, 2008, the Lord Jesus "connect"-ed the visions and words my wife received on October 23, 1995, with further visions and revelations. On the morning of April 3, 2008, I saw a vision of a man in a colonial outfit wearing a three-cornered hat. This man was working in a 1700's carpenter's shop drilling into wood with one of my own colonial augurs. Then I saw the same man standing next to Revolutionary War rifles, that were leaning upright onto other rifles in a circle. Then the Lord gave me an aerial vision of a map of Connecticut along the Atlantic coast. In the map were small coastal inlets and townships. In addition, I saw the closet and bedroom of a Christian Bed and Breakfast, that my wife and I had stayed at off the coast of Connecticut, celebrating our anniversary the year before. The Lord then began to reveal to me, that we will be drilling deeper into our country's foundation, and into the things of God in this book (Job 12:22,23; Da 2:22; 1 Co 2:10).

The Lord said, "The same principles that applied to the early settlers, the Pilgrims, Puritans, apply to the United States today. The lessons learned from the early founders of America, are similar to the messages that God has spoken to you regarding the future of America. The past, present, and future of America come together as 'living and active,' now, for 'Jesus is the same yesterday, and today and forever.' What held this country together? What did Americans stand for? (Dt 28:1,2,15; 2 Ch 7:14,15; Heb 4:12; 13:7,8).

"You are embarking on a journey, a journey through America, a journey to a 'New land.' This journey has taken you to different places in America, to New England, to Connecticut . . . Connecticut's constitution was used by the Founding Fathers to form the Constitution of the United States. (In the original Constitution of the state of) Connecticut, they (the Americans of Connecticut) based their constitution on covenant promises made with one another, and their covenant with the Lord Jesus Christ. (Even the license plate for Connecticut is the "Constitution State.") Connecticut today, in some areas, is a cleaner state, which based its original personal relationships (among the Connecticut people) with Jesus Christ. It is a state to 'Connect' with one another, and to 'cut' off the old, familiar ways, the ways today in America that are trampling down this country. They, (those first colonists), chose to follow 'the Way, the Truth, and the Life' of Jesus. A 'hot fire' burned in the hearts of men and women in New England, a 'hot fire' in Connecticut for Jesus (Mt 3:10; 25:14; Lk 3:16,17; Jn 14:6; Ac 2:44; Heb 8:6; 9:15).

"Your honeymoon was providentially ordained by God, (as we spent time in New England: Connecticut, Plymouth Rock, Massachusetts, and traveled at the outskirts of the city of "Providence," Rhode Island. For my wife heard these words on April 4, 2008, "Massachusetts and Providence"). I will go with you to a 'New land.' You are strangers in a strange land. America is a strange land today. But, America must again be founded on the principles established by the Pilgrims and Puritans (farming, sowing seed, the Word of God). Those times will come to pass through a shaking of this country, through a breaking down of other 'gods,' through a smashing of 'sacred poles' of material possessions, and a turning back to the one true God (Gen 12:1; Ex 2:22[KJV]; 34:12-14; Lk 8:5,11,15; Ro 8:28-30; Heb 12:26; 1 Pe 2:11).

"God made a covenant with His people, with the Pilgrims and Puritans, (including the Connecticut colonists), just as He made a covenant with Israel. He will fulfill that covenant when this country comes to its knees, seeks forgiveness, and turns from their wicked ways. 'Then I will hear from heaven, forgive their sins, (heal their land),' and raise them up again to love and honor Me. This is the introduction for your book. I have given you a sign from heaven to show you the 'Way' to 'Connect' with each other in everything you do together, and to 'cut' off the old familiar 'ties' (to the world)" (Gen 17:1,2,7; 2 Ch 7:14; Isa 40:3; Jer 31:33,34; Lk 3:9; Ac 4:32).

In this book, we will reveal how this country has lost the vision of our Founding Fathers, their love for God, their patriotism, and their willingness to die for freedom and liberty in this country, to establish their personal and inalienable rights. We will reveal what plagues America today, and will plague America in the future. We will examine the United States of America through personal experiences and revelations, visions and dreams, Scriptures, references, historical accounts, and words received from our Lord Jesus. We believe, that if we truly seek Him, the Lord Jesus desires to communicate with us, just as we talk and share with each other (2 Ch 6:28-31; Lk 10:39; Jn 10:3-5,27; Ac 2:17; 17:11; Rev 1:1).

When hearing from the Lord, regarding the work on this book, we praise the Lord, study His word, and fast every morning from food. We kneel on the floor, and write down what He reveals to us. We wait for His words, not ours. At times, His words may be considered controversial by both believers and non-believers in Jesus the Messiah. Still, we write down what God shares with us. Then the Lord has us confirm His messages with Scripture verses.

Unless otherwise noted, the Scripture verses for this book will be taken from the NIV (New International Version) Study Bible, and the KJV (King James Version) of the Bible. The selected Bible verses are not all inclusive. Come and join us, as we examine America's past, present, and future.

[PART I]

★

AMERICA: PAST

THE MAYFLOWER COMPACT

★

"In the name of God, Amen. We, whose names are underwritten, the Loyal Subjects of our dread Sovereign Lord, King James, by the Grace of God, of England, France and Ireland, King, Defender of the Faith, etc. Having undertaken for the Glory of God, and Advancement of the Christian Faith, and the Honour of our King and Country, a voyage to plant the first colony in the northern parts of Virginia; do by these presents, solemnly and mutually in the Presence of God, and one of another, covenant and combine ourselves together into a civil Body Politick, for our better Ordering and Preservation, and Furtherance of the Ends aforesaid; And by Virtue hereof to enact, constitute, and frame, such just and equal Laws, Ordinances, Acts, Constitutions and Offices, from time to time, as shall be thought most meet and convenient for the General good of the Colony; unto which we promise all due submission and obedience. In Witness whereof we have hereunto subscribed our names at Cape Cod the eleventh of November, in the Reign of our Sovereign Lord, King James of England, France and Ireland, the eighteenth, and of Scotland the fifty-fourth. Anno Domini, 1620."[3]

1

IT HAD ITS FOUNDATION ON THE ROCK, JESUS CHRIST IN AMERICA!

"Dearly Beloved, I beseech you as strangers and Pilgrims, abstain from fleshly lusts, which war against the soul."

As we embark on our journey through America in this book, we must begin with the earliest settlers in this country. We must depend on past historical accounts, and the revelations and words of our Lord Jesus, the Messiah, to discover the origins of the strong Christian roots of this country. With that information, we will discover that faith in our Lord Jesus is inseparable from the moral character, which is essential for America's people and leaders to govern, and legislate properly and righteously in America (Ac 2:17,18; Tit 2:11-14; Heb 11:6; Rev 1:1).

One Christmas our daughter and her husband gave us a bird house. We put up the bird house on a wooden pole outside our home. For three years, a male and female sparrow had made a nest, a home there. "Even the sparrow has found a home, . . . where she may have her young—a place near your altar, O Lord Almighty, my King and my God" (Ps 84:3). Those two sparrows had raised up little babies in that bird house. On May 15, 2008, the Lord Jesus gave me a vision of a mail box in the place where the bird house is located. The flag on the mail box was an American flag. In the vision, the two sparrows, male and female, are my wife and me. We were inside the outer end of the mail box looking inside it. The Lord said that morning, "Just as the two sparrows are looking in the mail box, so I have given you (both) messages ("letters") from heaven for this book, which you are to include in this book about America. This is your message today" (Hab 2:2,3; Ac 5:20; 10:36; 17:11; 1 Co 2:4).

In the sixteenth century, certain European groups of people attempted to settle on the eastern coast of the United States. One of those groups were the French Huguenots. The Huguenots had protested against the teachings and doctrines of the Roman Catholic Church in Europe. They were one of the first Protestant groups. The Huguenots suffered severe persecution from the "leaders" and followers of the Roman Catholic Church in Europe. Many Huguenots were murdered. Several French Huguenots traveled to America to escape persecution. "On June 30, 1564," they established "a small colony" near Jacksonville, Florida. Reportedly, their leader said, "We sang a psalm of Thanksgiving unto God, beseeching Him that it would please His grace to continue His accustomed goodness towards us"[4] (Ps 34:8; 95:2-5; Mt 5:10; Heb 11:36-39).

In our book, *The Great Cover-up: Living in the Shadow of a Lie, The Roman Catholic Church*,[5] we revealed a more in depth understanding of the Huguenots, their faith in our Lord Jesus, their belief in the inspired Word of God, their strong opposition to the false teachings of the Roman Catholic Church, and their horrendous persecution. The group of Huguenots that landed in Florida in the sixteenth century, we believe, were called by God to America to escape persecution from Satan's henchmen in Europe. The Lord Jesus, we believe, convicted those men and women's hearts to leave the clutches of the enemy, Satan, God's adversary, in their "homelands." They traveled to a "New land" to obtain freedom in Jesus Christ. The Huguenots were willing to risk their lives to proclaim the truth of the Word of God, and their Living Lord, Jesus, in this country (Mt 5:11,12; 10:27; Lk 9:60-62; 2 Co 11:14,15; Rev 12:10,11).

In the early seventeenth century, a group of settlers from England landed in what is now Virginia in May 1607. They established what was considered "the first permanent English colony in America at Jamestown." Some of those settlers developed the "First Charter of Virginia," in which was written, "by the Providence of Almighty God, . . . to the Glory of His Divine Majesty, in propagating of the Christian Religion to such People, as yet live in Darkness and miserable Ignorance of the true Knowledge and Worship of God." God used men in the First Charter of Virginia for His purposes to deepen America's roots in faith in Jesus Christ. It was reported in the nineteenth century, that the First Virginia Colony was rooted in the Christian faith[6] (Ac 5:42; Col 1:23,28; Rev 4:11).

Yet, only one minister by the name of Robert Hunt was sent to the First Virginia Colony. Reportedly, many were saved through his ministry, when they received Jesus Christ into their lives, and developed a personal relationship with the Lord. Robert Hunt, it was noted, "preferred the service of God to every thought of ease at home . . . He planted the first Protestant Church in America, and laid down his life in the foundation of Virginia." [7] The only building that has remained standing today is the Old Jamestown Church built in the seventeenth century. We believe, that the Lord Jesus strengthened Robert Hunt's faith to help build the Lord's church in America on the Rock, the Cornerstone, the foundation of this country's believers in Jesus Christ (Mt 16:15-18; 19:29,30; Jn 15:13; Ro 10:8-13; Eph 2:19-22; 5:23).

Satan, we believe, who had controlled the North American continent, was determined to keep Jesus Christ out of America. Unfortunately, it was reported that many Jamestown settlers were not willing to surrender "their wills to Christ" with the exception of Robert Hunt,[8] and because of their lack of faith, the Jamestown Colony suffered serious failures and setbacks after their founding. The Jamestown Colony's foundation was not firmly founded on the Rock, Jesus Christ. So when the winds blew and the rains fell on that Colony, many collapsed (Mt 6:24; 7:26,27; Mk 3:34,35; Lk 4:9-13).

The Pilgrims

In November 2000, my husband and I were teaching in a Christian school in Virginia. During the week before Thanksgiving, each class participated in skits that applied to that holiday. The skits were presented before families and friends of the students and teachers. At that time, my husband and I had been reading the book, *The Light and the Glory*,[9] which revealed the strong faith of the Pilgrims in Jesus Christ. One of our students presented the following as part of our Thanksgiving program from that book.

> "With winter storms howling around the tip of the Cape, 'whichever way they turned their eyes (save upward to the heavens) they could have little solace or content in respect of any outward objects.... What could now sustain them but the Spirit of God and His grace'..." The Pilgrims endured many hardships. But, "Something special had been born among them in the midst of all the dying—they had shared the love of Jesus Christ in a way that only happens when people are willing to suffer together in His causes. This was what they had come to the wilderness to find, and none of them wished to leave it....
>
> "Thus, they did enter into their own starving time that winter of 1621-22 (with all the extra people to feed and shelter), and were ultimately reduced to a daily ration of five kernels of corn a piece. (Five kernels of corn—it is almost inconceivable

how life could be supported on this). But as always, they had a choice either to give into bitterness and despair or to go deeper into Christ. They chose Christ. And in contrast to what happened at Jamestown; not one of them died of starvation."

The following Thanksgiving they had plenty of food. "The first course that was served: on an empty plate in front of each person were five kernels of corn . . . lest anyone should forget. . . . These Pilgrims were a mere handful of Lightbearers, on the edge of a vast and dark continent. But the light of Jesus Christ was penetrating further into the heart of America." [10]

Who were these Pilgrims? Let us discover their deep faith in Jesus Christ, and their call by God to America by referring to past historical accounts. Satan, who was controlling the Northern American continent, would make every effort to prevent the Pilgrims from establishing a foundation in Jesus Christ in this country! (Ac 2:38,39; Rev 12:17).

When we were children growing up in the 1950's in elementary school, the Pilgrims were the most honored, loved, and respected group of people in America. We drew pictures of them in their Pilgrim outfits. Yet, we had no idea of the depth of their character, and their deep faith in Jesus Christ, which God gave them to endure their hardships in Europe and America.

The Pilgrims were English men and women, who believed in the Lord Jesus, and who desired to live according to the Word of God, the Bible. In the early seventeenth century, the Pilgrims believed that the Church of England, the Anglican Church, was not proclaiming and practicing the truths in the Bible. For that reason, the Pilgrims chose to separate themselves from the Church of England, and they established their own church of believers. They were called "Separatists" at first, protesting against the practices of the Church of England, that were opposed to the Word of God[11] (Mk 4:14,18-20; Lk 8:21; 2 Co 6:14-18; 2 Pe 2:1,2).

Satan despises the Word of God, the true followers of Jesus, those separated from the world's ways. Satan would not relinquish his control over the Church of England. The "leaders" and followers of the Church of England despised and persecuted the Separatists, those men and women, who were separated from the trappings of the world. King James declared an "edict" that the "fanatics," the "Separatists" leave England, if those men and women would not submit to the Church of England. Queen Elizabeth believed that the Separatists were heretics[12] (Mt 4:8-11; 5:11,12; Lk 8:11,12; Ac 8:3; 9:1,2).

The Separatists believed that the Church of England was deeply entrenched in corruption, and "beyond any . . . purification." The Separatists believed that only Jesus Christ could be the "Head of the Church," not a man or woman. A group of Separatists chose together to travel to another country, Holland, to escape demonic persecution in England. The Lord Jesus was calling His faithful witnesses to another land. Yet, in Holland the Separatists were encountered with "worldly" allurements. Some were enticed to the "lures of the world" in Holland. Their children were suffering from those enticements. Satan would not stop his assaults on that small group of people in Europe, who desired to serve the will of God[13] (Job 1:9-11; Mt 10:23; Ac 1:8; Eph 5:23; Ja 1:14,15; 1 Jn 2:15-17).

The Separatists, their minister, John Robinson, and their elder, William Brewster, because they based "everything they did on the Bible," trusted that the Lord Jesus "was with them." It was reported that they were "knit together as a body and a most strict and sacred bond and covenant of the Lord." As a covenanted group of believers in Jesus, they adopted the name Pilgrims from 1 Peter 2:11. "Dearly beloved, I beseech you as strangers and Pilgrims, abstain from fleshly lusts, which war against the soul." John Robinson wrote about the Pilgrims, " . . . for we are the sons and daughters of Abraham by faith." [14] Satan hates a people who are covenanted together with Jesus Christ, because it is so difficult for the devil to deceive, to divide and conquer a committed group of believers in Jesus (Gen 17:3-7; Pr 3:5,6; Mt 12:25,26; Ac 4:32; 17:11; 2 Co 3:4-6).

William Bradford, who would become the second governor of Plymouth in Massachusetts wrote, "It is well-known unto the godly and judicious, however, since the first breaking out of the light of the gospel in our Honorable nation of England . . . what wars and opposition ever since, Satan hath raised, maintained and continued against the saints (those true believers in Jesus Christ, who were trying to follow God's will) . . . Sometimes by bloody death and cruel torments, otherwise imprisonments, banishments, and other hard usages . . . "[15] (Jn 8:43-45; 2 Co 4:1-6; Heb 11:35,38).

The Pilgrims, motivated by the Holy Spirit within their hearts, believed by faith that God was calling them to a "New land," to live according to the Bible, and to advance "the Christian faith." They "lifted their eyes to the heavens," sought God's favorable winds, and together set their sails in a small ship, the Mayflower for a dangerous journey across the Atlantic Ocean. Elder Brewster left for the "New land" as the acting pastor of the Pilgrims, while John Robinson remained in Europe. William Bradford wrote, "They knew they were Pilgrims. So they committed themselves to the will of God and resolved to proceed." . . . "With God's help," former President Ronald Reagan reported, "they believed that they might find a New world, a city upon a hill, a light unto the nations"[16] (Mt 5:14-16; 28:18-20; Mk 4:41; 14:36[b]; Col 3:1-3; 2 Pe 1:10,11).

The Pilgrims gave up their lives, their homeland, "their homes, their jobs, . . . to live as Jesus had called them."[17] By the grace of God, the Pilgrims made the journey that would become the Lord Jesus' great plan to bring His people and His Word to the "New land" of America, having its foundation on Jesus Christ, the Rock, (Plymouth Rock) (Mt 16:15,18; Mk 10:29-31; Eph 2:8-10; Heb 11:40).

The Lord said, "The Pilgrims desired to live according to the Scriptures, and separate themselves from false religion, false teachings from the Church of England. They refused to compromise with the world, refusing to become 'lukewarm' Christians. They desired to separate themselves from the world of unbelievers, those who attended church, but lived unholy lives. They desired, as the Puritans did, to purify their hearts from that which contaminated them in their country. ("Come out from them and be separate . . . Touch no unclean thing, and I will receive you" (2 Co 6:17)). They chose to take their separateness to America (Mt 15:8,9; 2 Co 7:1; 2 Pe 2:1,2; Rev 3:15-18).

"Their hope was to raise up a nation of people, generationally committed totally to the Scriptures in the way they lived, conducted business, worshiped and served God, and eventually to establish a government based on the Holy Scriptures separate from men's thinking or reasoning. In this way, they believed that they could be free men (and women), liberated from the doctrines of demons in Europe. They were willing to be given 'liberty or death' to serve their Lord Jesus Christ according to His Words, His commandments, His truths, and His love (Jn 14:6; Ac 2:42-47; Gal 5:1; 1 Ti 4:1; Rev 12:11).

"It was the Father's plan from the beginning to place in the hearts of the Pilgrims, and other faithful Christian groups, a desire to come to a 'New land,' to separate themselves from the compromised Church, 'and to purify for Himself a people that' were and 'are His very own.' The founding 'Cornerstone' of the United States of America was Jesus Christ. It was the Father's plan to bring Him (Jesus) to a 'New World,' to spread the gospel through every village, town, and city in America; so that Americans would be a people set apart on a 'hill,' to be a light to the world and an example for other nations to follow (Ps 15:1; Mk 16:15; Jn 6:44; Ac 11:23[KJV]; Ro 11:28-30; Tit 2:11-14; 1 Pe 2:6).

"As the Pilgrims left their 'Mother country,' England, their old habits, their 'old nature,' their families, so today you must leave your father and mother (familiar spirits), and cleave to one another, so you both can rule and reign together over the dark powers and principalities of Satan. Be willing to follow Me as the Pilgrims did to unchartered lands, for My paths lead to the Rock, to the Son of God (Gen 1:27,28; 2:24; 12:1; Isa 26:13[KJV]; Jer 20:10[KJV]; Eze 36:34; Mt 16:16,17; Ro 6:6; 2 Co 10:4; Eph 4:22).

"The Pilgrims chose to be alone, set apart from their false teachers, not clinging to their ungodly neighbors. They knew that the 'Pearl of great price' was of greater value to them, than belonging to the compromised Church of England, or with their worldly neighbors. They chose to die, to be 'alone' with Jesus, rather than to have all 'the treasures of Egypt.' I went to lonely and solitary places to pray. I chose to be alone, apart from needing men's recognition or praise. Being 'alone' with Jesus is a willingness to suffer (Dt 14:2[KJV]; Mt 13:45,46[KJV]; 14:23; Mk 6:31; 9:2; Heb 11:25,26).

"When you choose to be 'alone' with Jesus, you can receive God's love for the little lonely boy, and the little lonely girl (within yourselves). His love sets you free to weep for the lonely child (within). You then know how priceless it is to be 'alone' with Jesus. Only His love can drive out that fearful feeling of being alone. Receive your comfort from God, not from men and women. Jesus will heal you of this wound, this pain from childhood." The Pilgrims clung to Jesus, and chose to "participate in the sufferings of Christ" by themselves, in order that they would "be overjoyed when His glory" was "revealed" in America (Mt 11:28-30; 18:2-4; Mk 10:14[KJV]; 2 Co 1:3,4; 1 Pe 4:12,13; 1 Jn 4:18). (Messages received from the Lord Jesus on June 1, 1998, February 19, 2008, and March 24, 2008).

The Mayflower Compact

Prior to arriving off the coast of Plymouth in Massachusetts after an arduous journey, the Pilgrims wrote and signed the Mayflower Compact. That Compact is cited at the beginning of this chapter. The significance of this Mayflower Compact, we believe, was God's purpose to establish one nation under God in this "New land," America. The Pilgrims were compelled by the Lord Jesus, as former President Ronald Reagan reported, to "create a new Heaven and a new Earth" in what "we call America . . . to establish their city of God." The Mayflower Compact "would become the cornerstones of American Democracy," ("a precious Cornerstone"). It was the first document "in recorded history that free and equal men had voluntarily covenanted together to create their own new civil government, . . . a charter for self-government"[18] (Ps 33:12; Isa 26:1-4; 61:8,9; 1 Pe 2:4-6; Rev 21:1-2).

We believe, that the Compact was our Lord Jesus' "Way" to advance faith in Jesus Christ in this "New land," in a "New" continent, in North America. It was a charter to chart the Lord Jesus on the map of America as the foundational Cornerstone of liberty for all men and women to worship God freely without being subject to persecution. We believe, the Lord Jesus covenanted together with those Pilgrims for America to be founded under the one true God. William Bradford wrote that the Pilgrims were inspired by God "for the propagation and advance of the gospel of the kingdom of Christ in the remote parts of the world, even though they should be stepping stones to others in the performance of so great a work." The Pilgrims "risked all they owned to establish a colony at Plymouth and further the gospel of Jesus Christ"[19] (Jer 31:33; Eze 37:14; Mt 3:3; Ac 1:8[KJV]; Eph 2:19,20; 4:16[KJV]).

It was reported by William Bradford in November 1620, when the Pilgrims set foot on land in America, they "fell upon their knees and blessed the God of heaven who had brought them over the vast and furious ocean."[20] After all the Pilgrims survived a long journey, they surely knew God was with them, that He navigated them into a safe haven, Cape Cod Harbor. Having nothing but each other, and what they carried with them on the Mayflower, the Bible, the Word of God, they could only give thanks to the Lord for seeing them safely into this "New land." When God calls, He provides along the "Way"

(Gen 49:13; Neh 9:3; Job 1:20; Ps 95:6,7; Jn 17:14-19; Ac 9:2-6; 27:8; Eph 3:14; 1 Th 5:16-18).

Faith in God

After landing in America in the late fall of 1620, the Pilgrims were not prepared for the harsh winter that lay before them. Many Pilgrims died that winter. Satan was determined to destroy those Pilgrims, who had covenanted with our Lord Jesus for the "propagation" of their faith, and for their welfare in America. The Pilgrims "were in a life-or-death struggle with Satan himself." The Pilgrims trusted in God, turned to their Bibles, the Word of God for comfort, and prayed. As a "civil body" joined together, they endured their grave hardships without caving "in to despair." They understood about man's "sinful nature," and as a covenanted community, they knew they had to be cleansed through "daily repentance and forgiveness"[21] (Ro 2:4; 3:22-24; Eph 4:32; Php 4:11-13; Heb 11:35; Rev 12:10,11,17).

The Lord disclosed, "Those who first came to Massachusetts were founded on the 'Rock' at Plymouth, the 'Rock of Salvation,' the 'Rock of Revelation,' Jesus, the Cornerstone. Who were the first founders in America? Who were the ones who lived before the 'Founding Fathers'? Were not they the Indians, who worshiped another 'god,' a 'god' of hatred, a 'god' of death, a 'god' of murder, one who steals, kills, and destroys. This was their 'god.' It was Satan. The first in this country were Indians with savagery, butchery, as their 'god's' language, and they passed their 'god' to other states. They planted Indian relics of wickedness in the land to destroy the white man and his God. Spirits from the 'murderer,' Satan, were passed down generationally in America. They manifested themselves throughout the founding of America, and in centuries after its founding (Dt 7:26; 32:15[b]-18; Jn 8:44; 10:10[a]; 1 Co 10:4; Ja 5:6; Rev 1:1,2).

"The Pilgrims knew the key to freedom, and how to overcome the evil one. The world (of men and women) seeks self-sufficiency. Freedom comes at a price, the loss of yourself, your idols in the land, those persons, places, or things that take more precedence than Me in your life. Anyone or anything that takes more precedence in your life is an idol. In fact, the real idol is your self. You can take precedence over Me in your life and heart. Yet, My purpose for you is complete denial of self, so you can receive complete freedom in Me. When a man (or a woman) recognizes his state of helplessness, and knows that I placed him in that 'state,' then he may learn to totally rely on Me for help (Mt 9:36; 10:37-39; Lk 9:23-25; Jn 14:1; 2 Co 3:17; Php 2:3-8; Ja 3:14-16).

"When you are weak and not depending on flesh for your strength, you become stronger in Me. You become less self-sufficient, self-reliant. You then become more able to give to others. Real freedom comes by forgiving another. Practice the gift of forgiveness, and you will see nations of love, peace, power, and freedom overcome and conquer the tyranny of Satan, the oppressor, who attempts to oppress you into unforgiveness. My servants, (the Pilgrims), learned that when you truly become humble, stripped of any sense of self-importance, than you can give to Me more glory and praise. As My servants, when you learn this truth, the world (of men and women) will know that there is a God, who helps those in trouble and is able to respond to their every need" (Isa 14:4,5; Jer 17:5[a],7; Mt 6:14,15; 18:23-35; Lk 18:13,14; Jn 14:27; 2 Co 12:9,10). (Messages received from God on December 23, 24, 1996, June 1, 1998, and February 22, 2008).

After that winter, they were blessed beyond measure. For the Lord Jesus provided them a friendly tribe of Indians, the Wampanoags, under the leadership of their Chief, and the English-speaking Squanto. Those Indians were used by God for the Pilgrims to learn to survive in America on fishing, hunting, and vegetable and herb gardening.[22] Satan was meeting his match through the Pilgrims, who were willing to risk their lives to advance our Lord Jesus in America (Ps 111:5,6,9; 1 Ti 6:17[b]; 1 Pe 5:8-11).

In October 1621, the then Governor Bradford held a Pilgrim's three-day "feast" with the Indians as a way to give "thanks to God for His many blessings." It has been considered "the first Thanksgiving." The Indians "heard the Bible read publicly," and our Lord Jesus was making Himself known to the earliest settlers in America. During the winter of 1621-1622, which we cited earlier in this chapter, that on a ration of five kernels of corn a day per Pilgrim, they all survived.[23] The Lord Jesus was gaining spiritual territory in the Pilgrim's "New land" (Ps 95:2; Jn 10:10[b]; Php 4:12; 1 Ti 4:13).

The "Puritans," who were to follow after the Pilgrims, learned from that God-given covenanted group to "stand together as a body." The "body of Christ" was standing against the wicked schemes of the devil. The foundation of America stood on the Rock, Jesus Christ through His people, the Pilgrims. They were able to weather the falling rains and the blowing winds in the upcoming years. For we believe the Pilgrims' spiritual battle cry was, "Give me liberty or give me death, only in Jesus the One, True Liberator" (Mt 7:24,25; Lk 4:18[KJV]; Jn 8:36; Eph 6:10-14[a]).

"Poverty of soul" held the Pilgrims together against the devil's tactics, and any worldly influences. The Lord Jesus said, "For I will speak to you about the 'poverty of the soul.' The soul that is reduced to nothing is a soul that can be used for My glory. For when men and women are 'poor in spirit, . . . theirs is the kingdom of (heaven') of God. For the poor, the lowly in spirit, the ones who do not have the possessions of the world, who have given up holding on to something; it is those souls that will be honored (in My Kingdom). It is better to be with the poor, the needy, and 'the oppressed, than to share plunder with the proud.' Humility in men and women can change a nation, a country. Humility is being humble before God, acknowledging within your heart that God is God, and you are only man and woman created in God's image. (Such were the Pilgrims) (Pr 29:23; 16:19; Mt 5:3; Mk 12:42-44; Jn 15:5; 1 Co 1:27-29; Php 2:5-7; Ja 4:7-10).

"When your soul is parched, when you seek God with all your heart, like a 'deer pants for the water,' then you shall be filled with My 'living water.' You become free to thirst for the 'Living one,' Jesus. Be willing to lay down the world's drink and the world's food, (like the Pilgrims). For real food and real drink are My flesh and blood. For it is in suffering pain, that you shed the outer covering of self, and become freer in your inner self. Enduring pain is your ticket to freedom. Do not say to yourselves, 'What a price to pay to get to freedom.' Instead, look at pain as God's way of healing you on the inside, so your outside, the covering of self, won't hurt so much. Inner freedom comes when physical pain has no more foothold in your life. Freedom is a state of being in Christ Jesus, and in no others, free to enjoy the love of Jesus in your hearts (Ps 42:1,2; 143:6; Mt 5:6; 10:8; 23:25,26; Lk 4:18; Jn 4:10; 6:54,55; 15:9; 1 Pe 2:20-23; 4:1,2).

"For the delicacies and luxuries of the world can taint those in 'high' places. Whereas, 'poverty of spirit' can give growth to him or her in the 'low' place. It is not in titles or names or talents that men are rewarded. It is in walking humbly, acting justly, and loving mercy that men are brought into the Kingdom of God." The Pilgrims learned these truths from their Master, Jesus (Pr 23:1-8; Mic 6:8; Lk 14:7-11; Eph 1:18-21). (Received these words from our Lord Jesus on August 8, 1997, May 2, 1998, January 21, 1999, and August 21, 1999).

The Pilgrims weathered their storms, we believe, on their knees before God, asking the Lord Jesus to forgive them of any sinful motives in their hearts. They were a humble people, God's people, to set America's foundation on the Lord Jesus, the Messiah. America "was founded on Christian . . . and Biblical principles." The Pilgrims "brought with them the English Bible." The Pilgrims were Christians who tried to live a righteous life "both privately and publicly" in Jesus Christ. We believe, it was God's plan to use the Pilgrims and the Puritans to "reflect Christian" beliefs in "home, church, school, and state" for all future generations of Americans[24] (Dt 5:10; Mt 13:43,49; Ac 4:32-35; 1 Co 4:5; Eph 4:12-15; 1 Pe 4:16).

In the next chapter, we will look at a similar group like the Pilgrims, the Puritans, who followed the Pilgrims in to America. The Puritans were God's next stepping stone to deepen His foundation on the "Rock" in America. For the Lord Jesus revealed to us, that in this first chapter, He was setting the foundation for the remainder of this book. For those able to hear the Word, like the Pilgrims, from the "Sower" of the "seed," the Living Word, Jesus, and are able to "retain it," they will "produce a crop, . . . (a) hundred fold" as the Pilgrims did in the "good soil" of America today. That "seed" that the Pilgrims planted was taking deeper and stronger roots in America.

2

TO PURIFY FOR HIMSELF A PECULIAR PEOPLE

"Dearly Beloved, Let us purify ourselves from everything that contaminates body and spirit, perfecting holiness out of reverence for God."

As the Israelites were placed by God in an "iron-smelting furnace" to refine them in a "furnace of affliction" in Egypt, so a group of people from England called the Puritans had learned the value of needing to be refined by our Lord Jesus. The Puritans followed the foundational steps of the Pilgrims to establish the true gospel in America. The Puritans lived their lives according to the Word of God, for in the last days the Lord has revealed that, "Many will be purified, made spotless and refined." The Lord Jesus desires all of His believers to be purified before His return, and the Puritans understood their need to be pure (Dt 4:20; Ps 51:10; Isa 48:10; Da 12:10).

My wife and I have revealed throughout our book, *The Profound Mystery: Marriage—The First Church*,[25] the importance of daily repentance before God. As we begin to draw closer to God, the Holy Spirit within, reveals to us the deep sinful motives of our hearts. When we truly desire to be conformed in the image of Jesus Christ, we will genuinely repent of the evil and deception in our hearts. The Puritans understood this. Who were the Puritans? We must rely again on past historical accounts and personal revelations from our Lord Jesus (Lk 3:8; Jn 16:7-9; Ro 2:4; 8:29; 1 Co 2:10-12).

The Puritans, like the Pilgrims, protested against the corruption in the Church of England, the Anglican Church. They were a group of people in England, "who had entered into a deep covenanted relationship with God, through the person of His Son, Jesus Christ." The Puritans desired to live for Jesus, instead of their own self-interests. The Puritans believed that the Church of England in many ways was like the Roman Catholic Church. They believed the Church of England needed purification within itself[26] (Lk 9:23; Ac 17:28-31; Heb 9:15; Ja 4:8).

Satan hounded the Puritans, just like he did the Pilgrims. King James "vowed," as he did the Pilgrims, to rid the Puritans, those "fanatics" from England, if they did not accept the practices of the Church of England. Queen Elizabeth also believed, that the Puritans were "heretics." Satan was determined to keep England's Church impure, unclean; for the "bishops" of the Church of England believed that their Church was already pure enough[27] (Mt 5:11; Lk 6:22; Rev 2:20-22; 18:2,3).

Initially, the Puritans were not interested in "separating" themselves from the Church of England, unlike the Pilgrims. The Puritans had more friends in "high places" in England than the Pilgrims. They had "more education," . . . "more money,"[28] more than their spiritual relatives, the Pilgrims. Yet, if the Puritans truly wanted to follow their Lord Jesus, and His Words, they would have to be willing to give up their lives for Him, just like their predecessors, the Pilgrims (Jn 15:13,14; Ja 5:1-5; 1 Jn 3:16; Rev 3:17).

The Lord revealed, "America, from its inception began with a suffering people, a people who had been wounded by others.

Wounded because of their true faith based on the Word of God, contrary to the dictates of religion in England, Spain, and other countries. They were not accepted by men and their demonic traditions (in their own countries). They were wounded because of their faith; the Pilgrims, the Puritans, the Quakers, the Anabaptists, etc. (Ac 5:40-42; 1 Ti 4:1; Heb 11:35-40).

"Yet, the reality of their Lord Jesus was greater in them to seek freedom from their inner emotional pain, (which they) received for their beliefs in their own country. Traveling to a 'New country,' America, allowed them freedom to worship God in the way they believed was right, according to the Scriptures. Yet, they suffered hardships and death in a 'New land,' but found that their true selves were able to be healed by Jesus. The cost of finding their true selves in Jesus Christ was to sacrifice their lives for a cause, for freedom, (for liberty) (Ps 50:5; Mt 8:13-16; 10:39; Jn 4:23,24).

"Beginning with the first settlers in America up until today, the real pioneers are those who do not necessarily have to be free in a 'New land,' but seek their King Jesus to rule over their land, their lives. To be in His presence is to be in His healing touch, that heals the wounds suffered for believing the truth, the Word of God. The wounders have chosen their own way, their own 'gods,' their ways apart from the truth, apart from the Lord Jesus. They have chosen sin over repentance. They have chosen to wound those, who choose today to be healed by their God, Jesus, in a 'New land,' (as a "new creation")" (Ps 24:7-10; Mt 26:67; Mk 15:16-20; Lk 19:37,38; Ac 3:6-8,16; Ro 8:35-39; Gal 6:15). (Words from our Lord Jesus on February 7, 2008).

God had a plan for His people, the Puritans, that they would establish a purer Church by choosing to journey to America. For God honors those who honor Him. The Puritans chose to travel to America to escape religious persecution, just like the Pilgrims. God was again making His "Way" to establish America as a stronger nation founded on the Rock, our Lord

Jesus Christ. The Puritans would solidify God's purpose for America to be founded "as a Christian nation," stepping off the Pilgrim's foundational "stones" for "the Kingdom of God"[29]. The Puritans would strengthen the establishment of the Cornerstone in America, Jesus Christ (1 Sa 2:30; Ps 24:3,4; Isa 26:4; Mt 10:23; Jn 14:6; Eph 2:20; 1 Pe 2:4,5).

The Puritans received their name from their desire to be pure in living out the gospel of Jesus Christ. They covenanted with each other and with our Lord Jesus to practice "chastity before marriage, modesty in decorum and apparel." They legislated "against immorality," etc. The Puritans believed that God would be with them traveling to a "New land," because they understood their own "sinful natures," and a need to come to "daily repentance," so that their sins would not influence "their covenanted life"[30] (Ps 119:9; Mt 5:8; 2 Co 7:1,10; Eph 2:12,13[KJV]; 1 Ti 2:9; 1 Jn 1:9).

Satan again met his match with this covenanted group coming to America. Yet, Satan would try to subtly discover ways to divide the "house" that God was building in America on the firm foundation of Jesus Christ (Mt 12:25,26; Eph 2:19-22).

The Lord said, "In the United States, as well as in other countries, Satan knows that a 'house' divided against itself cannot stand. If Satan could divide the covenanted relationships the Pilgrims and Puritans had with their own group, he could divide the country from the Lordship of Jesus Christ. If Satan could convince Pilgrims or Puritans that it was not completely necessary to purify themselves from the influence of the world of men and women around them, then he (Satan) could prevent the United States from being united together with Jesus Christ for their guidance in governing America. All Satan had to do was distort the truth of the Word of God to those people. Once Satan was able to pit men and women against those true Christians, who needed to survive physically, emotionally, (and spiritually), in a 'New land,' America, he could divide the United States from their covenanted relationship with Jesus Christ, (the Messiah). For men and women, who were not Puritans helped them survive against their enemies; Indians, pestilence, disease, starvation, sin, their own selfish interests, etc. (Gen 3:1-5; Mk 3:23-26; Jn 8:44; 13:27,30; Ro 2:8; 1 Co 1:13; 2 Co 11:26,27).

"Once one puts one foot in the world, compromising his or her true belief in the Word of God, then very gradually the devil is able to tempt them to other things, to violate their marital covenanted relationship, to choose unclean relationships, fornication, adultery, to steal, to murder, etc. When a 'house' is divided, beginning with the marriage, then division can spread to a family, community, and church, the effects of that division will take down a nation, eventually. The United States today is being taken down internally through spiritual and moral compromising with the world against the Word of God (by men and women), who desire to enhance their own lusts and self-interests" (Pr 2:16-19; Mal 2:14; Lk 11:17,18; Jn 10:10[a]; 2 Co 6:9,15,16; Ja 1:14,15; 1 Jn 2:15,16; Rev 2:20-22; 3:15,16). (Message received from the Lord on February 21, 2008).

Yet, an undivided "house" of a covenanted group of believers in a covenanted life together with their Lord Jesus could stand against Satan's schemes. The Puritans gave up their "Mother country," their homes, their money, their "friends" in "high places" to follow God's plan for them to advance the true Gospel of Jesus Christ in a "New land," New England. The Lord Jesus was with them providentially from the beginning for only "one of the 198" sailing "vessels" that left England for America in the early "seventeenth century was ever lost"[31] (Ps 116:6; Isa 52:11; Mk 10:29-31; 16:15; Eph 6:11).

The Puritans' Covenant in America

What we believe held the Puritan community together, after they arrived and survived in America, was their covenant with God and themselves, and their call to spread the gospel, "the good news to all creation" and "to the ends of the earth." Puritan John Winthrop reported, "[It would be] a service to the Church . . . to carry the Gospel into those parts of the world . . . We here enjoy God and Jesus Christ, and is not this enough." He made that statement after many lives were lost in America following a "harsh winter."[32] He wrote further, "This love among Christians is a 'real thing,' not imaginary . . . as absolutely necessary to the being of the Body of Christ . . . We are a company, professing ourselves fellow members of Christ, we ought to account ourselves knit together by this bond of love . . . Thus stands the cause between God and us: we are entered into covenant with Him for this work . . . He (the Lord, Jesus) ratified this Covenant and sealed our Commission . . . We shall find that the God of Israel is among us, when ten of us shall be able to resist a thousand of our enemies, when He shall make us a praise and glory . . . For we must consider that we shall be as a 'City upon a Hill' . . ." [33] (Gen 17:7; Isa 30:17; Mt 5:14; 28:19,20; Jn 13:34,35; Ac 1:8; Ro 12:5; Col 3:14; 2 Ti 2:9).

The Puritan, Edward Johnson, shared that the "poor New England people" were the "forerunners of Christ's army" in America. This was an army headed by their Commander-in-Chief, Jesus Christ, to take charge of the American people. Concerning the "gathering" of the "first Puritan church" in America, the Puritans covenanted together to "obey Him," to "love God," and to "love one another" . . . [34] The Lord Jesus was strengthening the spiritual bonds of commitment among the Puritans to stand up against the devil's plans to thwart and destroy God's plan for America. The early seventeenth century Christians chose "God's will," rather than their own self-wills (Dt 29:12-15; Joel 2:11; Mk 3:35; Eph 6:13; Php 2:21; 1 Pe 5:4; Rev 19:14).

Satan would have a difficult time dividing God's "house" in America. For the Puritans made everlasting promises together before God of denying themselves, and taking up their cross daily. This powerful covenanted group of people would deepen the "sure foundation," . . . "the precious Cornerstone" in America, grounded firmly in Jesus Christ (Isa 28:16; Lk 9:23-25).

In 1643, it was written in "The New England Confederation," that "We all came into these parts of America with one and the same end, namely to advance the kingdom of our Lord Jesus Christ."[35] The people of New England came together in unity, in oneness, in covenant with one another to spread the gospel of our Lord Jesus. A Puritan minister, Thomas Hooker, in the seventeenth century, wrote further about how to become a covenanted people with brothers and sisters in Jesus Christ in his books, *The Christian's Two Chief Lessons*, and *The Soul's Humiliation*. Thomas Hooker believed, "that a man be driven out of self before he came to Christ, that a sinner must be humbled before he could be saved." In order to be "a genuine Christian," Thomas Hooker believed that you had to "deny (your) self and take up your cross daily." He "was able to come to (Jesus) Christ daily with openness and humility"[36] (Dt 30:20; Ps 50:5; Mt 16:24; 19:14,29,30; 28:19; Ac 2:42-47; Php 2: 3,7,8).

Today in America, we have many denominations. We do not believe that the American people are able to be covenanted to one another and with their God. Denominations set up divisions in the body of Jesus Christ. Divisions exist among members of the same denomination, the same church, and the same home. These are divisions in which Satan can divide the "house of God," so that it will not be able to stand against the wiles of the devil (Ro 16:17; 1 Co 1:10; 11:18; Eph 4:3-6).

In the early eighteenth century, a preacher, George Whitefield said, "Father Abraham, whom have you in heaven? Any Episcopalians? . . . No! . . . Any Presbyterians? . . . No! . . . Any Independents? . . . No! . . . Any Methodists? No! No! No! Whom have you there, then, Father Abraham?" "We don't know those names here! All who are here are Christians—believers in Christ, men who have overcome by the blood of the Lamb and the word of His testimony."[37] Covenanted communities among believers in Jesus Christ were essential in keeping away Satan's devious and divisive schemes among the people of God (Ro 10:9,10; 1 Co 3:23; 1 Pe 4:16; Rev 12:11).

The Puritans and Their Bible

The Puritans, a covenanted community, read the Word of God daily, a mighty spiritual weapon against Satan. The Bible was the daily spiritual meal the Puritans fed upon in America. The Word of God was their "Rock" solid foundation to proclaim the living God, Jesus. The Puritan children of New England were taught reading, writing, arithmetic, and the Bible. The "Horn-book," which was "a paddle-shaped board," contained Scripture verses and the "Lord's prayer." The Horn-book and the "New England Primer" were read by the Puritan children. The Primer, one of the first school text books in New England, included "prayers, Bible stories." The Bible was read daily by children at school.[38] The Puritan children were taught to build their character on Jesus Christ. The foundational "stones" of the Bible were being passed down generationally among the Puritan and other Christian groups, that had come to America (Neh 9:2-4; Mt 6:9-13; 16:16-18; Jn 6:56-58; 1 Co 2:13; Eph 6:11,17; 2 Ti 2:15[KJV]; 1 Pe 2:5,6).

For the early American Puritans, "the primary education" was to grasp an "understanding of the Bible." "The Massachusetts Bay Colony" in 1647, passed the law, the "Old Deleuder Satan Act." The Puritans believed that the "old deleuder Satan" would prevent children and adults from reading "the Scriptures," and following Jesus Christ. In New Haven, Connecticut, following that "Act," in the "New Haven Code of 1655," it was proclaimed that "children, and apprentices" were "to read the Scriptures" that were "necessary to salvation"[39] (Pr 22:6; Mt 4:3,4; Mk 4:14,15; Jn 1-5).

The New England Primer has been considered "the single most influential Christian textbook in history." It was reported "that most, if not all the Founding Fathers were taught to read and write from *The New England Primer*." *The New England Primer* combines "the study of the Bible with the alphabet, vocabulary, and reading of prose and poetry." The *Primer* emphasized the Scriptures and following Jesus Christ. For over a century that Primer was the American "textbook." "More than five million copies" were sold in America "in the 19th century." Of the first "123 colleges," they were established to advance the study of Scriptures and the Christian faith, and to know Jesus Christ, personally. Harvard and Yale, two of the first and notable universities in New England, proclaimed Jesus Christ. Their main goal was to produce "ministers of the gospel." In 1636, it was written in the rules of Harvard, "Every one shall so exercise himself in reading the Scriptures twice a day." Yale had similar requirements in their rules, "The Scriptures, . . . morning and evening are to be read by the students at the times of prayer in the school." From elementary school through college, the "knowledge of Jesus Christ was the ultimate objective of all education in early America"[40] (Ezr 7:10; Mk 10:13-16; 2 Ti 2:15[KJV]; 3:16,17).

Puritan parents entrusted their children to God, understanding that "their children did not belong to them; they belonged to God." The Puritan children were raised at home, church, and school in the "way" God would have them go. Because the Puritans emphasized "modesty in decorum and apparel," as well as "chastity before marriage," according to the Scriptures, temptations between the opposite sexes were almost negligible[41] (1 Sa 1:27,28; Ps 22:9,10; Pr 22:6; 1 Co 7:2; 2 Co 6:17,18; 7:1; 1 Ti 2:9).

Cotton Mather, a Puritan minister shared, "Well-ordered families naturally produce a good order in society."[42] The caring love of Jesus Christ in the Puritan parents toward their children, we believe, kept the enemy, Satan, from infiltrating the Puritan community. We believe that Satan has subtly moved into families today, to destroy order, to destroy marriages, and to destroy children. Children today, we believe, are not given to God, but given to everything but God. They are, we believe, given "high positions" in many families to do whatever they want to do. At times, we believe children are given the role of the spouse. Often, unholy and ungodly parents, we also believe, control and possess their children today (Pr 13:24; 29:15; Mt 14:6-11; Lk 15:18-24; Jn 10:10[a]; 1 Co 11:3; Col 3:18-21; 1 Ti 3:4).

As little birds become able to fly, godly parents encourage them to leave the "nest." Today, however, many parents, we believe, encourage their children to never leave their parents' "nests," emotionally. Their children stay crippled, never really learning to "fly" away on their own. Many parents, we believe, need their children to continue to meet their (parents') emotional needs. Those parents need to be "idolized" by their children. In turn, the children become the parents' "idols." Those real parents, who are true believers in our Lord Jesus, encourage their children to leave their parents' emotional "nest," and teach them to "fly," "soar on wings like eagles" with Jesus together, (parents with children), spiritually (Ps 55:4-8, 12-14; Isa 40:31; Eze 23:39; Mt 6:26; Mk 3:35; 10:29, 30; Lk 9:61,62; Eph 5:5; 1 Jn 5:21).

Satan, who masquerades as an "angel of light," we believe, has been given an elevated, a "high position" in families to destroy and break them down today. Satan's effects on children are prevalent in sexual immorality, viewing pornography, unwanted pregnancies, aborted babies, sexually transmitted diseases, juvenile delinquency, capital crimes, gangs, excessive cigarette, drug and alcohol use, suicide, etc. We will share more on this later in our book. The Puritans however, read and lived the Bible, training up their children, right, "in the way" they "should go" (Ps 119:9; Pr 20:11; 22:6,15; Zep 3:13[KJV]; 2 Co 11:13-15; 2 Ti 3:16,17; Tit 3:3).

The Puritan's Spiritual Struggles

Still, would "succeeding generations" of Puritan families stand up against Satan's deceitful tactics to keep the Lord Jesus out of America? It was reported that in the seventeenth century, future Puritan generations did not have to struggle physically and emotionally to survive as their ancestors experienced in the past. Those Puritans were becoming more self-sufficient, instead of trusting in God for their sufficiency. Those Puritans began to compromise with the world of other men and women, not desiring to be fed daily through the Word of God. They "were not coming into a saving relationship with Jesus Christ." [43] The Puritan parents were not training their children in the way God wanted them to go (Ecc 10:18; Jn 3:17-21; 17:15; Ja 5:5; Rev 3:15,16).

The covenanted way of life was slipping away from the Puritans, since they were not faced with persecution and death, as were prior Puritan generations. Even the words from God from the Puritan ministers were not being taken seriously.[44] Satan had discovered a weakness in the Puritan's covenanted relationship with God and each other. Satan would use his evil arsenal, his "flaming arrows" to stop this group of people, the Puritans, from establishing a firm foundation in America on the "Rock." Satan was determined to divide that "house of God" to get them off the "narrow road," so that he would maintain his reign over America (Dt 29:24; Mt 7:14; Mk 4:14,15,18,19; Lk 11:17,18; 1 Co 3:10,11; Eph 6:16).

The Lord said, "Satan's tactics were to get (the Puritans), and today, to get you off the right road, the 'narrow road,' and put you on another road. That road, Satan disguises as the 'right road.' Many believers in Jesus believe they are on the 'right road.' Yet, it begins slowly to veer you right away from God's road, His Way. That 'broad road' that they travel on for a time, subtly follows close to the 'Road' that I chose for you. The road I chose for you is called, 'The Living Way.' My road is called 'humility.' There are several exits off this road, which include: 'Pridesville,' . . . 'Judgement Town,' . . . 'Pleasureland,' . . . and 'Jezebel City.' There are many other detours to other towns, that can take you off My Way. Unfortunately, signs to 'Pleasureland' have taken many believers off the right road. Two of those signs include 'Invest for the Future,' and 'Get it while you can,' which are schemes and gimmicks for you to look to man's ways (Ps 52:7; Pr 2:12,13; Isa 59:7,8; Jer 18:15; Ob 3; Mt 3:3; 7:13; Lk 8:11,12,14; Eph 4:14; 2 Ti 3:4; Heb 10:19,20; Ja 4:11,12; Rev 2:20).

"Those signs find many of My followers taking detours down 'Deceit,' and deceptively wicked alternatives. Along My road, are the signs of 'Suffering along the Way,' 'Deny thy Self,' 'Painful Rocks Ahead,' 'Hold onto the hands of Sorrow and Suffering.' The road I chose you to follow is to become the least, not the greatest. To know the least of man's ways on his road, and to know the most of God's ways, is the Shepherd's path through the valleys and hills of life. The less you are in the flesh, the greater distance you can make on the Way. My familiar road is the one I took on earth. It included 'Sorrow and Suffering.' I carried a cross along My Way (Gen 3:13; Ps 23:1-4; 55:11[KJV]; Isa 35:8-10; 53:3; Mk 8:34; Lk 7:28; 9:48; 20:18; Jn 19:17; 2 Co 11:23,26; 2 Ti 3:12[KJV]).

"When you are handed a cross along the Way, do not say, 'Why me?' Do not look at how large your cross is, but be willing to receive it, for it will humble you and help you stay lower to the ground on God's road. By walking low to the ground, you will not be able to see the signs of 'Pride' and 'Arrogance' that lead in the direction of 'Self-glory.' No, you will find yourself moving quickly up the mountains and through the valleys to the Promised Land, the real home of My believers. Follow My Way instead of the way of 'Pleasure' and. 'Self-righteousness,' because that road is filled with deeper pain and tragedy at the end. It is a 'Dead End,' and leads only to complete death and destruction to the human soul. That 'broad road' may seem good for a time, but it leads you to the 'spirits of the dead' (Dt 9:23; Pr 7:24-27; 8:13; 9:13-18; Mt 9:12,13; Mk 14:35; Lk 3:5; 14:27; Jn 7:18[KJV]; Ac 9:2; Php 2:8-11; Heb 11:25[KJV]).

"'My people, who are called by My Name,' must 'humble themselves and pray' and 'turn from their wicked ways' off the 'broad road,' to the road that leads to life. Then I 'will heal their land,' . . . 'forgive their sin,' and 'bind up the broken hearted,' for those who have chosen the way of death, the way of Satan, the way of 'Pleasure,' the way of unhappiness, and the ways of depression and oppression. Those who choose the 'Way of Life,' the 'Way of Holiness,' the 'Way of Love,' the 'Way of Suffering,' will find Jesus walking with them. He will help you carry your cross, and lift your burdens and worries off your shoulders. The Way of God is liberating, free, and carries no 'extra baggage' from childhood, removing shame and guilt along the Way. The Way of God leads you in the 'path of the righteous' (2 Ch 7:14; Ps 23:3; 139:24; Pr 14:12; 21:17; Isa 9:4; 35:8; 54:4; 61:1; Mt 7:14; 11:28-30; 13:22; 22:16; Jn 13:34,35; 14:6; 2 Co 4:2; Tit 3:3; Rev 7:17).

"The 'narrow road' seems long, arduous, and hard at times, especially when you face your selfishness, self-pity, resentments, laziness, hatred, bitterness, fears, greed, sexual immorality, deceit, lies, falsehoods, guilt, shame, and timidity. They will greet you on God's road either subtly or by coercion. Their greetings will appear as if they are good and not evil. It may seem that by abiding in them, you will be better off than abiding in My thoughts and My Words. Surely, 'Selfishness' will say, 'You need your self to survive on that hard, difficult road and world.' Yet, 'Selfishness' does not care for you or for others (Job 31:16-21; Pr 18:1; Ro 1:29-32; 3:11-18; 1 Co 11:20,21; Gal 5:19-21; Col 3:5-8; 2 Ti 3:1-5).

"I've called you to love your neighbor as yourself. Yet, the self that I've called you to love is 'self-lessness.' Apart from Me, you can do nothing in your own self. If 'selflessness' greets you on the 'narrow road,' 'Selfishness' will mock, judge, and condemn 'self-lessness' out of an envy, hatred, and a jealousy.

'Self-lessness' is persecuted, but would rather be persecuted than receive approval for selfish acts (Ps 1:1; 119:36; Mk 12:31; Jn 15:5; 1 Co 4:12,13; 13:4,5; 1 Jn 3:16,17).

"Know that your salvation is worked out by both of you walking on the road to My kingdom. The one who sees the other on another road, must look first at what road he or she is on. For you may have deceitfully allowed your mate to get on another road. You may have judged the other one for being off God's road. Then you will find yourself on another road yourself. Help keep each other together on My Way; that is why I have joined you together. The 'unholy road' is any road that separates the two of you. Training on My Road can be rigorous and painful at times. Yet, it will bring a 'harvest of righteousness,' fruit that will not perish with God's power to destroy all the devil's schemes on his 'broad road.' Training equips My army with the weapons from heaven to overcome the 'self.' My Word abiding in your hearts will help you in staying on the road to My kingdom (Ps 119:11; Pr 18:1[KJV]; Isa 12:2; Mt 7:1-5; 19:4-6; Jn 15:4,5[KJV]; Ac 24:14; 2 Co 9:10; 11:3; Eph 6:10,11; Php 2:12; 2 Ti 3:16,17).

"Make preparations for the meal on My road. Make preparations to sit and listen to My voice first, for it is the 'better portion.' For a time is coming when the voice of the Lord will be heard throughout the land on God's road. Had Martha listened to Me first, like her sister Mary, she would not have been frustrated at the preparations for the meal. Instead, she would have welcomed her company. Welcoming guests comes through spending time with Jesus off the 'broad road.' The visitors, the guests have been out in the world. They need a place of rest, to refresh themselves once again. That is what a 'Way station' is, a place where visitors, guests can rest along the Way from the dangers outside in the world (Mt 11:28-30; 22:1-6; Lk 10:39-42; 15:21-24; Ac 3:19,20; 1 Co 10:13).

"My ways are not your ways. Your world is not My world, the world's ways are not My ways. Can you give love to those who reject you, or who use you for their own gain along their own road? Can you bend your knees, turn to your Father in heaven, who sees all and knows the hearts of men and women, and believe that He will reward you? (On God's road), come out fighting against the tyranny of the oppressor, Satan. Your adversary is wicked! His wicked ways are to divide and conquer every household in America. He babbles untruths to a world on the brink of destruction, (on the "broad road"). Stand firm, and plant your cross in the land" (Isa 55:5; Mt 6:6; Mk 3:23-26; Lk 6:27-36; Jn 8:44; 17:14,15; Eph 6:10-13; Heb 4:12,13; 12:2; 1 Jn 2:15; Rev 12:9,12). (Words received from the Lord Jesus on February 4, 1997, December 19, 1998, January 19, 1999, and October 1, 2001).

The Puritans would again have to learn how to "plant their cross in the land," for God sent "droughts," sent "plagues" of insects, "small pox epidemics," and many other tribulations including "sickness, poor crops, and shipping losses" upon the Puritans. The Lord Jesus was drawing the Puritan's hearts back to repentance to restore their covenanted community once again. Satan was given an opportunity to destroy the Puritan community through the Indian tribes in the New England area. Indians were butchering, scalping, and murdering Puritans, burning their homes down with "flaming arrows." The Indians were "inflicting mental torture," as well "as physical torture" on the Puritans.[45] Satan, the "murderer," was manifesting himself through cruel, barbaric demonic forces in some Indian tribes (Ex 8:16,17,24; Jdg 9:49; Jer 50:38; Jn 8:44; 1 Co 15:32; 2 Co 11:26; Eph 6:16; 1 Th 5:3; Heb 11:35; Ja 5:17; Rev 13:4).

Yet, "Greater is He that is in me, than he that is in the world." Our Lord Jesus moved in mighty power through the ministers, "Increase Mather and his son Cotton" Mather. The Mathers were preaching with great fervor to the Puritans about the need to repent from their sins, and return completely back to their Lord and Savior Jesus Christ. By "April 1676," almost all the Puritan men and women were seeking the face of God once again, and asking Him to remove all sinful motives from their hearts[46] (Ps 27:9; Mt 3:2; Lk 13:3; Ro 2:4; 12:11; 1 Co 4:5; 1 Jn 4:4).

The Lord Jesus was moved by the Puritans' prayerful, repentant, and humble hearts. The military in New England was moving the Indians out of their area. A number of Indians became believers in Jesus Christ. They were called the "Praying Indians." Those Indians taught the Puritans how "to fight like Indians." The Indian tribes under Satan's control began turning against each other. "Satan's house" was divided and he could not stand against the Lord Jesus and His army, the Puritans.[47] The Lord Jesus, the Cornerstone in America, was prevailing as the Puritans stood on the Rock despite the blowing winds and falling rains that came against the Puritan and Pilgrim communities (2 Ch 20:20-23; Isa 57:15; Mt 7:24,25; 11:29; Mk 3:25,26; Ac 28:1,2; Eph 2:20; 1 Pe 3:4,12).

Before the end of the seventeenth century, Satan would manifest himself again, "prowling around like a roaring lion, looking for someone to devour," the Puritans. He would try to stop the Lord Jesus Christ from taking over the American people. For the occult was spreading in New England then, as it has in America today. Satan's dark, evil wickedness was affecting the Puritans. Several people reportedly were "possessed." Others reportedly were casting "hexes," spells on others. Witchcraft trials were held in Salem, and ended before the turn of the century[48] (Dt 18:10,11; Isa 47:12; Mk 1:23; Gal 5:20[a]; 1 Pe 5:8).

Cotton Mather, the Puritan preacher, boldly stood up against the devil's schemes, and the "witchcraft hysteria" that existed then among the Puritans. He proclaimed, "that the exceptional destiny of New England had been under siege by the Devil, operating through his agents, to destroy God's chosen people and their promised land"[49] (Lk 4:2-13; Ac 8:7; 2 Co 12:7; 2 Th 2:9).

God would not be mocked. The Lord Jesus hates evil. Through bold and faithful praying Puritans, who were willing to stand up "against the powers of this dark world" by putting on their "full armor of God"; they overcame the "flaming arrows of the evil one" with "the sword of the Spirit, which is the Word of God." Satan lost his last ditch effort then to prevent Jesus Christ from being "rooted" in the Puritan people of New England. "For the Puritans were built up in Him, strengthened in the faith." America's territory was recaptured by the Lord's mighty army, the Puritans (Dt 29:18; 2 Ch 32:17-22; Ps 1:1; Pr 8:13; Isa 26:13-15; Gal 6:7; Eph 6:10-17; Col 2:6,7).

In the early morning of June 5, 2008, my wife heard these words, "You think of yourself more highly than you ought . . . Be willing not to be accepted, not to be valued, not to be included, not to be important, but to be less." The Puritans learned that by becoming "less," selfless, by totally depending on God, instead of compromising with the world's ways, that the Lord Jesus would bless them. When they repented and turned from their wicked ways, in order to again become "refined, purified, and made spotless," God healed them, forgave their sin, and healed their land (2 Ch 7:14; Da 11:35; Lk 6:22,23; 7:28; 9:23; Jn 3:30; Ro 12:2; Php 2:3; Heb 11:24-27).

They were taught by the Lord Jesus to stay on the "narrow road," and to stay off the 'broad road' that leads to destruction. The Puritans were taught to "be willing not to be accepted, not to be valued, not to be included, not to be important, but to be less." When they were again in covenant together to follow the Word of God, and His ways, they could cry out, "Give me liberty or give me death, only through the one true Liberator, Jesus Christ" (Mt 7:13,14; Lk 4:24; Jn 8:36; Ro 8:21; Rev 12:11).

On June 5, 2008, the Lord Jesus gave me some visions. My wife and I were sitting with our arms resting on a table. On the table was a map/chart of Puritan New England. The Lord Jesus was holding a compass, making a circle around New England. Then little lighthouses appeared on the coast of New England. The light in those lighthouses increased in intensity, becoming brighter. A vision followed of a green vine, and a large oak tree full of green leaves spread out over the New England area.

As Jesus made a circle around New England, He said, "This area was Mine. The center of the compass was Jesus. In the days to come, 'lighthouses' would be stationed on the coast of New England to warn the Americans, to warn and to protect the people; to warn them of invaders that would come from another land, from England, those who would try to take over their country; they, (the "lighthouses"), would be lights shining in the dark days ahead. The Puritans, when they abided in the 'Vine,' knew that without Jesus they could 'do nothing.' They returned to the Vine so that they could bear fruit for the Kingdom of God in America. When they abided in the Vine in the 'New land,' the Puritans were able to trample on Satan, united in the Word of God, united in worship, united with believers, those believers in Jesus Christ. When they became 'nothing' in New England, they could become something in Me. They became a mighty army, able to trample down their enemy, Satan" (Isa 30:17[KJV]; 40:22; 44:13; Eze 16:8; Joel 2:11; Mk 3:33-35; Lk 10:18-20; Jn 1:4; 15:1,5; 17:22,23; 2 Co 8:9).

The Lord Jesus then gave us the words to the song, the "Battle Hymn of the Republic,"[50] which would apply to the Puritans, as well as the Americans in the days ahead.

> *"Mine eyes have seen the glory of the coming of the Lord;*
> *He is trampling out the vintage where the grapes of wrath are stored;*
> *He hath loosed the fateful lightning of His terrible swift sword;*
> *His truth is marching on!*
>
> *Glory! glory, hallelujah! Glory! glory hallelujah!*
> *Glory! glory hallelujah! His truth is marching on."*

The Lord said further, "The 'Tree of Righteousness' was planted in New England by Almighty God through his people, the Puritans and the Pilgrims. That 'Tree' took deep root in God's country, spreading its branches (and green leaves) over

New England. It provided a protection and covering over God's people from their enemy, Satan" (Ps 5:11; Pr 11:30; Isa 61:3[b]; Jer 33:15,16; Zec 6:12; Lk 23:31; Ro 11:18; Eph 3:17).

The Puritan Example

Today we can learn from the Puritans what is right living before God. The Puritans wanted to live a pure Christian life apart from the trappings of the world. They were set apart as a simple, humble, prayerful, and covenanted people together in Jesus Christ. They desired to live by the Word of God, the Bible, and to freely worship Him, according to the Scriptures. How America has turned away from the example of the Puritans and the Pilgrims. The future colonists in America could only be blessed by following their forefathers, the Pilgrims and the Puritans. Stepping off the foundational "stones" of those early settlers in America, the true Christian colonists could follow the lead of their predecessors standing together on the Rock, Jesus Christ for America! (Ps 19:7; 116:6; 119:9; Jer 1:5,10; Mic 6:8; Jn 4:23,24; 15:19; Gal 1:15; 1 Pe 2:4-8).

On August 28, 2008, after fasting and worshiping before the Lord Jesus, the Lord gave me a vision of a cotton boll on a plant. A man then reached out and picked the cotton boll from that plant. The Lord Jesus then said, "God picked out Cotton Mather, (the Puritan preacher) to give the Americans a message; a message that they (Americans) needed to stand up against and fight the enemy to bring freedom to the land. His message spread openly like 'cotton' in a field. His message was pure and white. That message burned in the hearts of the American people, which they would take with them into the Revolutionary War" (Lk 24:32; Jn 4:35[KJV]; Ac 13:2; 17:11; Eph 6:11-13).

Cotton Mather, it was reported, "fearlessly proclaimed God's Word." That Puritan minister "hungered after God's righteousness and holiness." His message about the English and "European churches" would be fuel for the "fire" in the American's cause for liberty. For "one day Americans might be the salvation of the mother country that was seeking to oppress them . . . " That "outer darkness that the providence of God, in bringing His Pilgrims to America bearing golden candlesticks, has irradiated in order to allow a new beginning (through) our Lord Jesus Christ, carried some thousands of reformers into (America) . . . to give . . . many good things which He would have His churches elsewhere aspire and arise unto." Cotton Mather wrote, "here (in America) hath risen light in darkness."[51] The light of Jesus Christ had come to America out of the dark spiritual world of England. Believers in Jesus Christ would be willing to stand up and fight against that spiritual darkness in the days ahead manifested from Satan himself through King George III (Isa 9:5; Mt 5:6; Jn 1:4,5; 3:19-21; 8:12; 2 Co 11:13-15; Eph 6:19,20; 1 Ti 6:12).

The cry for liberty, "Give me liberty or give me death!" only in Jesus, the true liberator, would increase in volume until it reached a crescendo among the American people! Americans would stand up and fight for their God-given rights and freedoms against tyrannical England. The American colonists would deepen their roots of faith in the one true God as they faced the inevitable—A War for Independence!

AMERICA, THE BEAUTIFUL

★

"O beautiful for heroes proved In liberating strife,
Who more than self their country loved, And mercy more than life!
America! America! May God thy gold refine
Till all success be nobleness And ev'ry gain divine!

O beautiful for patriot dream That sees beyond the years
Thine alabaster cities gleam, Undimmed by human tears!
America! America! God shed His grace on thee,
And crowned thy good with brotherhood From sea to shining sea!"[52]

(Verses 3 and 4)

3

GIVE ME LIBERTY OR GIVE ME DEATH! ONLY IN JESUS— THE TRUE LIBERATOR!

> "Stand fast therefore in the liberty wherewith Christ hath made us free, and be not entangled again with the yoke of bondage."

As we move from the seventeenth and into the eighteenth century, we believe the "light" of Jesus Christ, though a flicker at times, would shine brightly over America into the 1800's. On November 4, 2007, while attending a Sunday service at a youth home, God gave me a vision of old wooden picture frames, one inside another. Those frames appeared to be going backwards in time to the seventeenth century. The vision inside the frames ended with a portrait of a young toddler with brown hair in a lower, middle-class home. On a table next to that toddler was a lighted candle stick in an American colonial home. The vision of the home was dark except for the light that was coming from the candle (Ps 103:14[KJV]; Jer 25:10[KJV]; Lk 8:16[KJV]; Eph 2:21[KJV]).

The Lord then said, "This country was 'framed' in the 'light,' the candlelight on the stand during a dark time, prior to and during the Revolutionary War. God's 'light' gave meaning to life for the new immigrants, the new settlers, the Americans. Many of them had desired to establish their lives in the 'light' of the Word of God. That 'light' was passed through generations of Americans, 'framed' in the 'light' of their forefathers despite the darkness in the midst of America's background (leading up to the) war. My 'light' still shines in many of My faithful ones in America today!" (Mt 5:15; Jn 1:1-5; 3:21; Heb 11:3[KJV]).

That 'light' shone brightly when in the fall of 2002, my husband and I (Phyllis) team-taught a seventh and eighth grade class at a Christian school in Virginia. We were studying early American History then during the colonial times. We decided to have a Colonial Day in our class. The Holy Spirit moved in a powerful way during the weeks of preparation for that day. Each student in our class chose to represent a colonial character. Students wore costumes depicting the early settlers, Pilgrims, Puritans, and various leaders of that time. They wrote an article on the history of their character. Several students reported on their Christian faith. For Colonial Day, we decided that only foods made with colonial recipes would be brought into class. Colonial pots, utensils, tools, and wares were displayed that day. The students were very excited about our Colonial Day (Lk 11:36; Ac 1:8; 2:32,33; 2 Ti 2:15).

The entire school was invited to attend our class. Throughout the day students from other classes sampled colonial foods, and participated in crafts of that time period. One student brought in "hard tack," which the soldiers during the Revolutionary War ate in hard times. We played colonial music from that time period. Teachers were amazed at the "joy of the Lord" that filled our classroom. God blessed our day in so many ways. God was turning our hearts toward the way of life of the Pilgrims, the Puritans, and the Founding Fathers. We admired their deep faith in Jesus Christ, and spoke about it openly in class that day. That class would be a "stepping-stone" for this book, which we would be writing in the future (Neh 8:10; Jn 15:11; Ac 4:13; 1 Pe 2:4,5; 4:16).

Passing the Lighted Torch, the Light, the Living Word of God

At the turn of the century, the Bible, the Living Word of God had been rooted deep in the hearts of the American colonists in the 1700's. The 'torch,' the Living Word of God, the flaming 'Sword of the Spirit,' was passed from the Pilgrims and Puritans to the succeeding generations of the Founding Fathers'. Former President Ronald Reagan said, "The Bible and its teachings helped form the basis for the Founding Father's abiding belief in the inalienable rights of the individual . . . The guide for our Founding Fathers and every generation of Americans (following was) the inspired Word of God"[53] (La 3:33-36; Zec 12:6; Jn 1:14; Eph 6:17; 2 Ti 3:16[KJV]; Heb 4:12).

In a *Newsweek* magazine in 1982, there was an article, "How the Bible Made America." It was reported, "that the Bible, perhaps even more than the Constitution, is our Founding document."[54] The true Founding Father of the United States of America, we believe, was our Heavenly Father with His Son, Jesus Christ. The Lord Jesus was establishing Himself in America as the only Lord of those first colonies. The Bible was the "foundational book" for "all the colonies." In "the First Charter of Virginia in 1606," . . . "to the Pennsylvania Charter of Privileges" . . . "in 1701," it was necessary for "all persons who . . . (professed) to believe in Jesus Christ, the Savior of the World, (that they) shall be capable . . . to serve this Government in any capacity"[55] (Mt 1:21; 28:18,19; Jn 10:29,30; 1 Pe 2:9,13).

Faith in Jesus Christ was essential for all state "government officers" in Delaware, and in other states. The officers in Delaware had to "profess faith in God the Father, and in Jesus Christ, His only Son, and the Holy Ghost, one God, blessed forevermore;" and they had to "acknowledge the holy scriptures of the

Old and New Testament to be given by divine inspiration"[56] (Ps 67:4; Isa 9:6,7; Jn 16:15; Ac 17:11; 1 Ti 6:12; 2 Pe 1:20,21).

The Holy Spirit moved with great power in the 1700's among true believers in Jesus Christ especially during the "Great Awakening." That "Awakening" woke up the American people to liberate themselves from the bondage of Satan represented from England's monarchy at that time. The Holy Spirit set ablaze a "lighted torch," a "fire" of passion among the "Americans" to establish "true liberty . . . (only) under God." A British "appointed governor in New England" during that time wrote a letter sharing that the Americans only "master" was "Jesus Christ." So deeply rooted in the hearts of Americans was their Cornerstone, the Rock Jesus Christ. Their "rallying cry" was, "No King but King Jesus!"[57] (Ps 119:45[KJV]; Isa 50:4; 51:9; Na 2:4; Mt 3:11; Lk 19:37-40; Jn 13:13[KJV]; Eph 2:20; 5:14; 1 Th 5:19).

Freedom in Jesus

At the turn of the century, the Puritan ministers understood that America was to be under the Lordship of Jesus Christ, and not under Great Britain. The American people were to be dependent "on God" for their liberty. The Puritans were aware of the spiritual battle between Satan and Jesus Christ for America from their experiences in the 1600's. They believed that it was God's will "that resistance to tyranny was obedience to God." Jonathan Mayhew, a Puritan minister, proclaimed in 1754, that "divine favor" was given to "God's chosen people, so they might be delivered out of bondage,"[58] the bondage from England. "The rod of their oppressor," Great Britain, was preventing the Americans from receiving their freedom (Pr 3:5,6; 28:16[a]; Mt 4:8-11; Jn 8:36[KJV]; 14:1; 2 Co 3:17[KJV]; Ja 4:7).

The Lord Jesus confirmed this on June 19, 2006, when my wife and I were watching part II of the video series, *Liberty*.[59]

A leader for the colonists in the video made the statement, "When England was using force against the American colonists, the Americans had a choice to either submit to, and become slaves of England, or to establish their own freedom and independence from England." The colonists willingly chose not to submit to England's tyrannical rule over them. Early the following morning, my wife heard these words, "War breaks out . . . When you cease fire! . . . Good soldiers . . . Connecting . . . Know who he is . . . and that he can't be trusted, your enemy, Satan . . . Everybody sings at the Lord's command . . . Be willing to go to jail . . . That's your only hope, . . . and Coming home."

The Lord Jesus then revealed these words to us. "Many men and women in the latter part of the 1700's knew that England, their 'Mother Country,' was a tyrannical ruling 'power' over the American people. England, the 'Mother Country,' had her own self-interests at heart. If you were a 'Loyalist' then you sided with the enemy country. You did not wash your allegiance away from the enemy. In the spiritual realm, when you decide, as the Revolutionists did in the 1770's, to 'fire' on their tyrannical enemy, Satan, and 'cease fire' on each other, then you can gain a victory (Pr 28:28; Lk 4:5-8; 10:17; Ja 1:26; 5:1-6).

"Satan tries to wear you down in a battle (in order for you) to give up and say, 'I'm too tired to fight.' Yet, 'good soldiers' in God's army 'fight the good fight of faith' against Satan. When 'war breaks out,' the army of believers need to uphold each other. Believers who are under the leadership of Jesus are aghast at the enemy's tactics. The enemy's demonic 'powers' may seem impenetrable at times. Your task, 'connecting' together with Jesus, is to 'destroy the works of the devil' (Eph 6:11; 1 Ti 1:18; 2 Ti 2:3; Ja 4:8; 1 Pe 5:8-10; 1 Jn 3:8).

"There is a deep sadness leaving your 'Mother Country'; your homes, your father and mother, and their Church. But you must fight for freedom for your marriage and family. Your enemies, like those among the colonists, were members from their (your) own households. Great Britain was like a

'Mother,' which would not give her (children) subjects up without a fight. The British aristocracy despised the American 'commoners, farmers, peasants.' Yet, the Americans, once they knew who they were in God's plan, knew that they could not be treated as subjects and slaves to a tyrannical 'Mother Country' (Gen 12:1,2; 1 Sa 30:1-5, 16-18; Jer 7:17-19; 29:11-14; Mic 7:6; Mk 10:29,30; Gal 4:1-7; Eph 5:25).

"You must fight for your lives, for your marriage, and for your children to be freed from the 'slave woman,' the 'Mother,' like the 'Mother Country.' When you are able to do this, then 'everybody sings at the Lord's command.' When you fight, you choose not to tolerate aristocracy, those demonic 'powers' that tried to rule over you. You must not tolerate her ways anymore. You must 'be willing to go to jail,' if need be, if that is 'your only hope' against the tyranny of being subject to that 'Mother' (Gen 21:10; Ps 30:4; Ac 12:3,4,7-11; 1 Co 15:19; Gal 4:30,31; Col 1:27; Rev 2:20-23).

"Yet, today the leaders for freedom in America are dying out. As believers in Jesus Christ, you can choose to submit to the tyrannical 'powers' of darkness, that oppose the Word of God and Jesus Christ. You can choose to submit to the liberal 'Mother Country' of America today. Or you can choose, like the Revolutionists, to fight for freedom against sin, that God has graciously given to you by accepting His Son, and following His Words (Dt 30:19,20; Jos 24:15; Lk 8:21; Jn 1:12; Ro 6:11-14; 2 Co 10:4,5).

"The 'world' of men and women, like the 'Mother Country,' are in opposition to the Living God. They are putting the Church to 'sleep.' Rather than offend that 'Mother,' many choose to submit to her as her slaves. Where are the 'Colonists' today, the believers in Jesus who are willing to shed their blood? The Revolutionists are becoming fewer in number today, unwilling to risk their lives for the cause of freedom in Jesus. They are not willing to 'Declare their Independence' from that 'Mother,' the 'world of opposition' to God, Satan. Today, believers are subjecting themselves to the 'world system' that says, 'Christians are not equal. They have lost their rights.' Must you submit to a tyrannical 'power' of liberal opposition to God. No! You can 'hold to these truths, that are self-evident that all men are created equal' (Pr 6:9; Jer 1:5; Mt 7:26,27; Mk 4:16,17; 13:36; Jn 3:9; 8:31,32; 1 Co 12:22-27; Gal 4:3; Heb 12:3; Rev 12:11).

"Then, like General George Washington's men under his care, you can 'come home'; home to a country free from that 'Mother's' rule. The military might that George Washington and the colonists displayed, is what you need to display spiritually in your own life to overcome the enemy's 'wicked schemes'" (Mt 11:28-30; Jn 14:1-4,23; Rev 19:11-16).

On the evening of the fourth of July, 2006, my wife and I were again watching part II of the *Liberty* video series, while fireworks were being shot off into the sky near our home. God began revealing to me how the times we live in today could be compared to the times prior to and up through the Revolutionary War. The Lord then said, "The colonists chose not to submit to England's tyrannical rule over them. In a similar way, Jesus, the Son of God, set His 'Revolutionists' free by 'declaring independence' from the tyrannical 'powers' of darkness and sin. For those who receive Him, believe in Him, invite Him in their hearts, and follow Him, they can be set free" (Isa 61:1,2; Ro 6:6,7,19-23; 10:8-13).

Early in the morning on March 1, 2008, my wife heard these words from the Lord Jesus, "Before the war," and "Get it over the wall." That day, the Lord shared, "The Pilgrims, followed by the Puritans, prepared 'before war' against the Church of England by providing themselves with adequate spiritual (prayer, worship, and the Word of God) and with adequate physical (men and women's assistance), reinforcements, to overcome the enemies of God, (i.e. the Church of England, the Indians, the heathens, the weather, the sicknesses, diseases, pestilence, etc.) They were the forerunners of those who were to prepare for the eventual War against tyrannical England. They chose to 'get over the wall' of obstacles from Satan. (For the devil's scheme was) to prevent them from spreading the Gospel of Jesus Christ into this 'New land,' America! (Mt 4:10; 6:6; 7:7,8,24,25; Mk 13:33-37; Ac 5:29-42; Eph 2:14).

"'Before the war,' the saints need to use that time to prepare for battle. They need essential support both physically and spiritually. They need adequate reinforcements. The patriot 'saints' need a God-given strategy to overcome the enemy, just like the Colonists. Yet, the Church in times of preparation, chooses not to prepare, chooses to wait, chooses not to need support from others, and does not choose proper (assistance), reinforcements" (Ps 149:4-9; Mt 3:3[b]; Rev 2:4; 3:1-3).

The Lord Jesus said further on July 19, 2000, "Spiritually speaking, America prayed night and day to establish a nation conceived under God 'with liberty and justice for all.' For they did not know where their next meal would come from. Britain tried to control America, but God cannot be controlled. Traitors were more interested in saving their flesh, rather than saving their souls, by joining ranks with Britain, believing that they would become victorious. But God fights for the innocent, the poor, the oppressed. God raised up a mighty spiritual army during the Revolutionary War to fight against the demons of 'possessiveness' and 'greed' that Britain manifested against the American people (Ps 82:3,4; Isa 9:7; Joel 2:11; Mt 23:25; Lk 4:18; Jn 12:25; Ro 8:21 [KJV]).

"It was honorable to fight for a country's freedom and take up arms. God took America up in His arms to stand against a tyrannical ruler. A real patriot would be on the front lines ministering to the sick, healing their wounds, raising them up from the dead. Those patriots fought for liberty! (Ps 35:1-3; Isa 40:11; Mt 10:7,8; Mk 10:16).

"You are a patriot when you stand fast wearing God's armor, having all His weapons of warfare in place. America needs you today. America is being run by many tyrannical 'rulers' (who embody) impurity and cowardice. American 'troops' have broken ranks today. Americans are retreating because of the demon of 'liberalism.' They say, 'It is too big,' just as many thought Great Britain was 'too big' to overcome (Ex 14:10-12; Jdg 7:2,3; Jn 6:65-67; Eph 2:2; 6:11,12; Rev 21:8).

"As God was with America's independence in her earlier years against a 'Great' Britain, so He will take up arms with you against Satan. Stand with Him. Many retreat without 'firing the first shot.' Do not retreat! The visions, the revelations, hearing My voice are given to you to warn My militia, God's army; so there are no surprise ambushes by the enemy, Satan, so as not to catch you both off guard. Be willing to warn, and build up my end-time army of warriors, who are being trained in God's 'boot camp.' My troops must be willing to die on the battlefield, to stand up for righteousness, to hate evil, to give up their lives for the cause, to spread the Gospel of truth in the dark places where people do not know Me (Ex 15:3; 2 Ch 20:22,23; Ps 18:32-42; Pr 31:8,9; Joel 2:1,2; Mk 16:15; Lk 9:62; Jn 10:27; Ac 2:17; Eph 6:13; 2 Ti 2:14; Rev 12:11).

"Pray in the trenches, in the valleys, play the 'flute,' sing joyfully as you encounter various tests and trials. For as you learn to stand as 'one' in a test, and not retreat or retaliate, the flag of liberty and freedom will fly daily in your lives and from your house" (Ex 17:15; Ps 150:4; SS 2:4; Lk 18:1; Ro 8:21; Ja 1:2-4).

The Lord Jesus revealed more to us on June 12, 2008, when I received a vision from God. In that vision, the night sky was full of dark, billowing clouds. Colonists were digging ditches, digging deep until they discovered water. The water was flowing like a stream, then it began to gain momentum moving like a river, flowing throughout the original thirteen American colonies. The colonists were then putting down their "plowshares" and pitch forks. The colonists were walking together in line, in unison making their "plowshares" into weapons of war. Then I saw a vision of hundreds of individual grave sites. Each grave site was piled up with dirt, and each had a white cross.

The Lord Jesus then said, "When England put tyrannical pressure on the American colonists to submit to England's rule over them, the colonists began to dig deeper into their hearts. They were seeking out the sinful motives in their hearts, (in order) to repent before God and seek His will for America. God had made a covenant with the Pilgrims and Puritans for America to be one nation under the one true God, the Lord Jesus. So God honored their hearts and prayers. The 'Living Water,' the Holy Spirit moved like a river through America strengthening the American people to fight demonic tyranny (1 Sa 2:30; 2 Ch 7:14,15; Da 2:22; Jn 4:10; 7:37-39; Heb 4:12,13; Ja 4:8-10).

"The colonists, in their own way, covenanted together to put down their farming equipment, their 'plowshares,' and join as one nation fighting under God. ("Beat your plowshares into swords and your pruning hooks into spears. Let the weak say, 'I am strong'!" Joel 3:10) Many crosses would be spread throughout the land of America for those who shed their blood for righteousness, for those who did not 'shrink from death' knowing the true God of heaven was with them" (Ps 72:14; Isa 41:10; Lk 22:20; Rev 12:10).

Give Me Liberty or Give Me Death!

In the 1770's, as the inevitable War for Independence grew closer, Satan, we believe, was using the King of England, George III at that time, to enslave the American people in the "chains" of England's own sins; "chains" of submission to a "ruler" against the "King of Kings and Lord of Lords," Jesus, the Son of God. Yet, our Lord Jesus was raising up men to speak up boldly for the cause of liberty; liberty found only in our Lord Jesus. The War, a battle in the heavens, we believe, would "pit" our Lord Jesus against His rival Satan for America (Isa 14:12,15; Gal 4:9; Php 1:7,14; 1 Ti 6:15; Jude 6).

The Puritans believed that the "law placed liberty under the guidance of the God of Scripture," King Jesus. They believed that their King (Jesus) would "guard (their) sovereign rights . . . from the whims of a tyrannical government." [60] The character John Adams was a delegate from Massachusetts in the DVD series, *John Adams*, who proclaimed, "Many of our rights are inherent and essential . . . We have a right to them derived from our Maker. Our forefathers have earned and bought liberty for us at the expense of their ease, their estates and their blood . . . Liberty . . . stands on . . . the inalienable and indefensible laws of God"[61] (Job 36:3; Mt 19:21; Gal 4:4-7; Php 4:8; Rev 19:13,16).

Perhaps one of the most passionate speakers for liberty was Patrick Henry. On "March 23, 1775," at "St. John's Church, Richmond, Virginia," he said, "We must fight! An appeal to arms and to the God of Hosts is all that is left us . . . Three millions of people, armed in the holy cause of Liberty . . . are invincible by any force our enemy can send against us . . . There is a just God who presides over the destinies of nations, and who will raise up friends to fight our battles for us . . . Is life so dear, . . . as to be purchased at the price of chains and slavery? Forbid it, Almighty God! . . . As for me, give me liberty or give me death!"[62] (Jn 12:25; Ro 6:16; 1 Co 6:19,20; 2 Co 3:17[KJV]; Gal 4:3).

The Lord Jesus spoke more about liberty to us on January 17, 2008, when I saw a vision of the old oak tree in the Walt Disney movie, *Johnny Tremain*.[63] That oak tree was located in Boston, Massachusetts prior to and during the Revolutionary War. The oak tree appeared to be deeply rooted in the ground. It represented an "oak of righteousness." A light shone out from the branches of that tree. Then I saw my wife and I hanging lit lanterns in the branches of that tree. In that vision, we are part of the group, "The Sons of Liberty" as portrayed in the movie. Then I saw an oil lamp sitting on a table. A vision followed of the old North Church steeple in Boston in April of 1775 with two lit lamps shining in the steeple, which was also shown in the movie. Following those visions, I saw myself laying down on a haystack, just like the character Johnny Tremain at the end of the movie. My wife came over to the haystack to talk with me. There were camp fires all around us at night. On July 17, 2008, I saw another vision in the movie, in which the character Johnny Tremain was invited to a rich man's (his uncle's) house. In the movie, Johnny refused to go back to England with his uncle to receive a "proper" upbringing. He chose instead to fight for freedom and liberty with his fellow Americans.

The Lord said, "The sons and daughters of Jesus, who stand as 'oaks of righteousness,' stand firm in those branches in the Branch, Jesus, holding My light for America and the world. You (Mark) were an apprentice growing up in your home, like (the character) Johnny Tremain, but you got hurt because of the messages given to you by your parents. You tried to go back to serve the 'rich,' but you chose to leave that home. You are finding your worth, not in the things of the past, but in the things of liberty and of freedom. Johnny Tremain (in the movie) took a woman in his arm, while walking through the streets of Boston singing, 'We are the Sons of Liberty.' So are you growing more confident in your cleanliness in your marriage, and you can sing (also) with your wife, 'We are the Sons of Liberty' (Isa 61:3[b]; Hos 1:10[b]; Zec 3:8; 6:12; Mt 16:29; Mk 3:35; Lk 18:22-24; Jn 8:12; Ro 8:21 [KJV]; 2 Co 6:18).

"Your oil lamps are lit in the 'Tree of Righteousness' and on My table, for I am changing the old into the new, the former things into the new things! This 'is marvelous in' your 'eyes' as you see it unfolding, the 'Proclamation of Freedom.' 'One if by land, two if by sea,' not one, but two will go together 'to spread the alarm to every middlesex village and farm.' These words will go out, not only in the New England area, but throughout the United States and to countries beyond. 'Two if by sea, and I' will be there 'on the opposite shore,' as you cross over the seas (Dt 30:12-14; Ps 92:12; Pr 11:30; Isa 62:11; Mt 19:5; 25:4,7; Mk 12:10,11; 2 Co 5:17).

"As you find true liberty (in Jesus), you will learn to express your God-given emotions and cover and protect your wife properly in the days ahead. Your wife says to you, (while you are laying on a haystack), 'Are you awake?' You respond, 'I was just resting,' for you are getting ready for the great spiritual battle ahead," (while the "fire" of God's Spirit is around you!) (Isa 52:1-3; Mt 11:28; 1 Co 11:3,7,8; 1 Th 5:19; Heb 4:9-11).

> *"I have seen Him in the watch-fires of a hundred circling camps;*
> *They have builded Him an altar in the evening dews and damps;*
> *I can read His righteous sentence by the dim and flaring lamps;*
> *His day is marching on. Glory! glory, hallelujah!*
> *Glory! glory, hallelujah! Glory! glory, hallelujah!*
> *His day is marching on."* [64]
>
> (Battle Hymn of the Republic: Verse 2)

Bells Ringing for Liberty

When we began writing this book, the Lord Jesus told us to go to Philadelphia. On September 12, 2008, we were obedient to that call to Philadelphia, the "City of Brotherly Love." We were writing this chapter at that time. We were impressed with the lack of commercialism at the historical sites in that Old City; compared to other historical places we have visited that would charge, what we believe were excessive entrance fees. Almost all the historical sites we visited were free: Carpenter's Hall, where the First Continental Congress met; Independence Hall, which was the meeting place for the Second Continental Congress, and where those men created, ratified, and signed the Declaration of Independence and the Constitution of the United States; and the Center, which housed the Liberty Bell. Each historical site maintained their original authenticity of the 1700's. We experienced the people of Philadelphia, and the park rangers of the Old City, expressing the same kindness, practicality and freedoms that our Founding Fathers exemplified in Philadelphia.

Though we experienced the kindness and practicality that we believe our forefathers expressed and lived by, while in Philadelphia, we, however, were hurried at times, walking through the the Old City. We were not able to thoroughly enjoy ourselves, or reciprocate kindness and friendliness to the people in Philadelphia, because we wanted to "beat" the evening traffic out of Philadelphia. We also desired to eat at one of our favorite restaurants in Lancaster County, Pennsylvania before it closed that evening. Our own worries and self concerns were a "driving" force, that kept us, and probably others from being with Jesus there, and with the people of Philadelphia that day (Ps 106:7; Mt 6:25; Lk 10:38-42).

While we have been writing this book, the "Liberty Bell" stamp had been offered through the United States Postal Service to the American people. It is called the "Forever Stamp." We are able to purchase those stamps at a lower price before the Postal Service increases their price at a later date during any given year. The "Liberty Bell" stamp continues to be used by Americans, "forever," just as God has been ringing His "bells" to proclaim liberty in the United States "forever," and throughout this book.

When we visited the Old City in Philadelphia, we observed the symbol of Americans' freedom, "The Liberty Bell." On that bell is inscribed the Scripture verse from the Book of Leviticus, chapter 25:10 [KJV] with the words "Proclaim Liberty throughout All the land unto All the Inhabitants Thereof." Our Forefathers' faith in their Living God and His Word are not hidden, for His Scriptures are openly engraved on America's "Liberty Bell" (Isa 49:16; Mk 4:22; Ac 20:21).

On February 15, 1998, I (Mark) saw a vision of the crack in "The Liberty Bell." The crack appeared larger than the original "Bell's" crack. On November 8, 2004, the Lord Jesus gave me a vision of church bells ringing louder and louder. He said, "I move in cracked vessels, imperfect vessels, (like those Americans who were oppressed prior to and during the Revolutionary War). Let freedom ring! May it be proclaimed in the heavens and the earth, that the battle has already been rung, won. Satan is being taken down in that 'ring' today. The true 'Church' bells are ringing for liberty. The 'word of your testimony' must go forth ringing the 'Bells' of freedom once again in America!" (Ps 150:5; Zec 14:20; 2 Co 4:7[KJV]; Gal 5:1; 1 Jn 5:4,5; Rev 12:7-12[a]; 20:10).

A Mighty Leader for Liberty!

Who would God choose to be a mighty leader for liberty in America, to deepen the roots of faith in the only true Liberator, our Lord Jesus? The Lord chose George Washington to carry the "torch" in battle and in government, to follow the Pilgrims and the Puritans' faith in their foundation on the Cornerstone, Jesus. George Washington would be a "lamp" on a "stand" to give "light to everyone in the house" of America during a dark time in our history (Isa 28:16; Na 2:3,4; Zec 12:6; Mt 5:15).

It was reported that George Washington was "born into" a Christian family. When he was a child, "he was taught the Scriptures," the Word of God. At the age of "eleven," George Washington's "father died." After that, it was noted that he led the family's daily devotionals "every morning"[65] (Dt 6:4-7; Isa 50:4; Ac 2:42; 2 Ti 3:15).

On September 4, 2008, after fasting and worshiping before the Lord Jesus, I saw a vision of the movie theater at George Washington's birthplace in Westmoreland County, Virginia. The Lord Jesus recalled to us the time when we were there with two of our grandchildren. They were three and five years old at that time. During the movie, which was about his birthplace, both children shared out loud, "That's sad, all those people dying." Then a vision followed of George Washington in a Virginia colonial military uniform leaving another home in Virginia. The Lord Jesus said, "George Washington experienced several deaths in his family, and many among his soldiers. Blood was shed to firmly establish the Kingdom of God in America" (Mt 23:35; Col 1:19,20; Rev 16:5,6).

On November 13, 1994, while my wife and I were walking on the grounds of George Washington's boyhood home in Fredericksburg, Virginia, the Lord Jesus spoke to us about George Washington. The Lord disclosed, "This was his boyhood home. He played here as a boy. George loved butter. There was a 'churning' in this nation then, when lives would be lost. Yet, the sweetness of the Lord prevailed, (sweetness compared to butter). He was a man after My own heart. He was raised with the knowledge of who he would become in America (1 Sa 13:14; Pr 30:33; Isa 7:15,22[KJV]; 2 Co 2:15[KJV]).

"George received a prophetic utterance, that he would become the President of the New Republic. He exemplified the leadership qualities that I desire in a man, which I molded into him. Those qualities of character were: fortitude, strength, boldness, unswerving faith, solidness, and godly (servanthood). George Washington stood 'tall' for the truth. He did not back down from adversity. Pray that you receive those qualities of character in your life. Rewards come through a repentant heart in a 'refiner's fire.' Fight for freedom, (like George Washington)" (1 Sa 17:45; 2 Ki 9:4-6; 2 Ch 11:11[KJV]; Ps 138:3; Jer 16:19; Mt 20:26-28; 1 Co 7:35; 2 Co 10:4; Heb 11:24-26; Rev 3:18,19).

(On July 29, 2010, after we fasted and praised the Lord Jesus, I saw a vision of my wife in a colonial outfit. She was churning butter in a wood churn at a house in New England. The Lord shared, "There is a churning again in America; a 'churning' for righteousness against tyrannical 'leaders' in this country. It is a 'churning' in the spiritual realms. That 'churning' is taking place in your lives, in your homes, today") (2 Co 6:14-18; 10:3-6; Heb 1:9[a]).

After leaving his home, George Washington joined up as an officer in the Colonial Army of Virginia. It was reported that George Washington "read the Scriptures, . . . the Bible and prayed regularly" every evening from "9 till 10 p.m.," and each "morning" from "4 to 5 a.m." He led the "worship service for his armies for two years." George Washington became "a Colonel in charge of the forces of Virginia." His troops fought in the French and Indian War[66] (Lk 4:8; 1 Th 5:17; 1 Ti 4:13).

In one of those battles in July 1755, all his officers were "killed." It was reported that General Braddock was shot and killed during a battle with the French and Indians. The Indians were bearing down on the troops. The troops wanted to leave, to flee! George Washington ordered that General Braddock have a "proper ceremony, and he pulled out his prayer book" and conducted a funeral service. George Washington ordered his men to dig a hole in the middle of the road. The men shuttered, "Oh, No!" George Washington knew that if the Indians found the grave site, they would dig up the body, desecrate it, and steal the uniform. As Washington and his troops were leaving, he had their wagon wheels run over the grave site, so the Indians would not find General Braddock's body. George Washington had "great compassion, great love and prayer" for his men. George Washington wrote that he had "been protected beyond all human probability" by "Providence," by God. Although he was shot "four" times through his "coat," and had "two horses shot under" him, George was never harmed. In all of his battles, it was reported that George Washington was "never" . . . "wounded."[67] The Lord Jesus was sovereign in choosing and protecting our first General and President of the United States for His purposes (Pr 2:8; Isa 54:17[a]; Ac 24:2[KJV]).

Several years later, before the War of Independence took place, the Indian Chief, who led the battle against George Washington and his military troops shared about that leader. He was quoted as saying, "Quick, let your aim (rifles) be certain, and he dies. . . . T'was all in vain, a power mightier than we shielded you . . . He can never die in battle . . . The Great Spirit protects that man . . . He will become a ruler of a great people and nation."[68] The Lord Jesus spoke through an Indian chief, who witnessed the miraculous protection the Holy Spirit, ("The Great Spirit") provided for George Washington, who prophetically would become the "chief of nations" (1 Ch 7:40[KJV]; Job 30:25; Isa 55:4,5; Ro 8:26-28).

On March 1, 2008, the Lord Jesus spoke further about George Washington. "Each battle or war can find the patriot 'saints' either alert and ready, or blinded and asleep. God chose an alert and ready man spiritually and morally to prepare the United States 'before the War.' It was George Washington, who set a precedence for future military leaders and Presidents; that if you want to win the war, you must be prepared, spiritually. George Washington, through his disciplined and Christian moral life, brought freedom to the 'White House' for future Presidents, who would choose to follow in his steps!" (Nu 32:16; Na 2:3; Mt 24:44; Mk 1:1-3; 13:33,36; 1 Pe 2:21).

George Washington, a man of humility and honorable spiritual character, wrote about his faith in Jesus Christ in his "prayer diary." He wrote, "Accept me for the merits of thy son, Jesus Christ . . . I have called on thee for pardon and forgiveness of sins . . . Cover them all [my sins] with the absolute obedience of thy dear Son . . . in and for the sacrifice of Jesus Christ offered upon the cross for me . . . Wash away my sins in the immaculate blood of the lamb, and purge my heart by the Holy Spirit . . . Daily frame me more and more into the likeness of thy Son Jesus Christ . . . Thou gavest Thy Son to die for me."[69] George Washington was indeed picked by God "for such a time as this," to bring the new colonies of America under the banner of liberty through Jesus Christ (Est 4:14[b]; Ps 51:10; Jn 16:7-10; Ro 4:7; 2 Co 3:18; Heb 12:2,3; Rev 12:1 [a]).

On August 2, 2008, the Lord Jesus said, "George Washington was 'washing' the country from men's fears to fight the enemy. The 'washing with water through the Word,' through the Holy Spirit, was cleansing men and women in America from sin. They (Americans) were given a purpose to fight against sin, to fight against submitting to an evil ruler. They resisted the devil, (who "prowls around like a roaring lion looking for someone to devour"). Americans humbled themselves, sought to be washed of their sins; so they could stand on God's 'holy hill' and 'fight the good fight of faith' with 'clean hands.' Those Americans, through repentant hearts before the Lord Jesus, were 'Washing tons' of sins away. They were preparing for battle both spiritually and physically" (Ps 24:3,4; Lk 7:47; Jn 13:8; Eph 5:26; 1 Ti 1:18; Tit 3:5; Ja 4:7-10; 1 Pe 5:8,9).

Early in the morning on September 17, 2008, my wife heard these words from the Lord, "Get back to David Hogan . . . Compare each chapter . . . Washington, D.C.." David Hogan, the leader of Freedom Ministries in Mexico today, shared in Part IV of the video series, *Faith To Raise The Dead*[70] about the characteristics of a true leader, a leader like George Washington. Referring to the Book of Daniel, Chapter 6 in the Bible, he talked about how to "shut the lions' mouths," the devil. Three characteristics of Daniel's heart were emphasized: "an excellent spirit," . . . "faithfulness," . . . and "innocence before God."

In the King James version of the Bible, the Scriptures indicated that, "Daniel was preferred above the 'presidents' and princes, because an 'excellent spirit' was in him . . . The 'presidents' and princes . . . could find (no) fault (in him) forasmuch as he was 'faithful,' neither was their any error or fault found in him . . . Forasmuch as before him (God) 'innocency' was found in me," God "shut the lions' mouths" (Da 6:3,4,22[KJV]).

Those characteristics of true leaders today are necessary to achieve victories over the devil's wicked schemes in America. Only through genuinely repentant hearts before the Lord Jesus, like George "Washington who had a 'D'irect 'C'urrent to the Living God through his prayers," can one obtain those true leadership qualities (Da 6:10,11; Ac 9:17; Ro 2:4; Ja 5:16,20).

In preparation for American independence, "Delegates from 12 of the original colonies" gathered together at "The First Continental Congress" . . . "in the fall of 1774" at "Carpenter's Hall" in Philadelphia. They met to address "their grievances against the 'mother country.'"[71] It was reported that during "the first prayer" of the Continental Congress, George "Washington was kneeling there, . . . bowed in reverence, (with) the Puritan patriots of New England."[72] The men there reportedly "prayed fervently for America, for Congress." The Lord Jesus through the Holy Spirit was using American patriots to pray for our country and future generations. Those prayers, like the Pilgrims and Puritans, were meant to establish America under the freedom, guidance, protection and leadership of the Lord Jesus Christ (Ps 95:6; Ro 12:11; 1 Co 6:19; Php 2:10; Ja 5:17,18).

That "first prayer" included these words. "O Lord our Heavenly Father, high and mighty King of kings, and Lord of lords, . . . look down in mercy, we beseech Thee, on these our American States, who have fled to Thee from the rod of the oppressor and thrown themselves on Thy gracious protection, desiring to be henceforth dependent only on Thee. . . . To Thee do they now look up for that countenance and support, which Thou alone canst give . . . All this we ask in the name and through the merits of Jesus Christ, Thy Son and our Savior, Amen."[73] Those laborers on their knees prayed "three hours."

In a letter that John Adams sent to his wife, Abigail, it was shared, "that God spoke to them, (while in prayer), in such a way out of Psalm 35, that they believed for the first time they could defeat the British."[74] Psalm 35 reads: "Plead my cause, O Lord, With them that strive with me: Fight against them that fight against me. Take hold of shield and buckler, and stand up for mine help." They were not building the "house" in America "in vain." For the Lord Jesus was building a spiritual "house" in America on the prayers and faith of the patriot "saints" in the one true God, our Lord Jesus. The Foundational Rock, we believe, was firmly embedded in the hearts of those American patriots. Their faith would be the "stepping stone" that would take the colonies into the War for Independence (2 Ch 7:14,15; Ps 127:1; Isa 14:4,5; 26:4; Lk 18:13,14; Jn 17:12,15; 1 Co 10:4; Heb 12:12; 1 Pe 2:4-6).

Where are the leaders in Congress who are willing to pray on their knees together for this country, and for her deep troubles and problems today? Many of us would rather complain and find fault with our government, rather than pray for America to turn back to Jesus, to repent for our sins, and turn away from our own wicked ways. Our only hope is in Jesus, our true Liberator!

WASHINGTON'S PRAYER FOR THE UNITED STATES OF AMERICA

★

"Almighty God; We make our earnest prayer that Thou wilt keep the United States in Thy holy protection; that Thou wilt incline the hearts of the citizens to cultivate a spirit of subordination and obedience to government; and entertain a brotherly affection and love for one another and for their fellow citizens of the United States at large.

And finally that Thou wilt most graciously be pleased to dispose us all to do justice, to love mercy, and to demean ourselves with that charity, humility, and pacific temper of mind which were the characteristics of the Divine Author of our blessed religion . . . Grant our supplication we beseech Thee through Jesus Christ Our Lord. Amen."[75]

4

FORCEFUL MEN LAY HOLD OF THE KINGDOM OF HEAVEN!

"To the general assembly and church of the firstborn, which are written in heaven, and to God the Judge of all, and to the spirits of just men made perfect."

While we visited Independence Hall in Philadelphia on a cool and cloudy September day, a park ranger shared about the important meetings where delegates of the original thirteen colonies met to discuss their eventual independence from Great Britain. There had already been "armed" conflicts when the "Second Continental Congress" met in May 1775 in that "Hall." At that meeting, "George Washington" was appointed as "commander in chief of the Continental forces."[76] Those prophetic words for George Washington came true as he became a "chief" of a new nation called by God to bring American patriots from different colonies together to fight against tyrannical England under the leadership of his Savior, Jesus (Mt 3:14,15; Lk 1:13-17; Jn 3:30,31; Ac 9:15).

Concerning the Continental forces under the command of General George Washington, there was a struggle to finance, support, and keep the American colonial military troops together at the outset of the Revolutionary War. Could this Continental Army be representative of the Lord Jesus' Army? As the War for Independence drew closer "98.4%" of that army were Protestant professing Christians. Only "1.4%" were Roman Catholics, and ".2%" were Jewish/others. Those Christians would fight "for freedom of their land," and fight "for religious freedom."[77] The Lord Jesus was amassing a mighty army for His purposes for America to overcome Satan's attempt to keep the United States for himself. As commander in chief of the Continental forces, George Washington and his troops struggled initially in skirmishes with Great Britain (Ps 37:28,29; Isa 61:1; Joel 2:4,5; Jn 8:31,32; Ac 2:44-47).

The Declaration of Independence

The cry among the colonists for freedom was increasing in volume, while "armed" conflicts were increasing between the American colonists and the British military troops. In 1773 "the men of Marlborough" declared, "Death is more eligible than slavery. A free-born people are not required by the religion of Jesus Christ to submit to tyranny, but make use of such power as God has given them to recover and support their laws and liberties . . . [we] implore the Ruler above the skies, that he would make bare His arm in defense of His Church and people, and let Israel go."[78] "Patriots," as well as ministers of the gospel, were proclaiming freedom under the banner of our Lord Jesus (Ps 2:9; 98:1,2; Lk 10:17-20; Ac 26:17,18; Rev 1:4,5).

In 1776, John Witherspoon, a signer of the Declaration of Independence, and a minister of the gospel of Jesus Christ, preached a sermon that propelled the delegates of the thirteen states to reconvene at Independence Hall. In the spring of 1776, the delegates gathered together to create a document, which would establish American independence from Great Britain. John Witherspoon cited I Samuel 17:45,46[KJV] in his sermon. "Thou comest to me with a sword, and with a spear, and with shield: but I come to thee in the Name of the Lord of Hosts, the God of the armies of Israel, whom thou hast defied." In that sermon, John Witherspoon shared "that resistance to oppression was sanctioned by God." Other pastors and ministers of the gospel of Jesus Christ believed the same way as John Witherspoon[79] (Isa 14:4,5; Lk 4:18[b]; Ja 4:7; 1 Pe 5:8,9).

The delegate to the Continental Congress from Massachusetts, the second president of the United States, John Adams, believed that "the political revolution of America, the American Revolution, was predated by the spiritual revolution." That revolution, that our Lord Jesus spread among the colonists was "The Great Awakening," which we previously reported. John and his wife Abigail Adams often wrote letters to each other. In a letter from Abigail to her husband, she shared that she believed in the God of the Bible, who was with them in their cause for the country's independence[80] (Lk 20:9; Jn 11:24-27; Ac 5:14; Ro 13:11,12).

The Spirit of the Living God was igniting passion among the delegates from the original thirteen colonies to meet again and choose to declare independence from Great Britain. The Continental Congress on "May 16," 1776 proclaimed, "The Congress, . . . Desirous . . . to have people of all ranks . . . devoutly to rely . . . on his aid and direction, . . . Do earnestly recommend . . . a day of humiliation, fasting, and prayers; that we may, with united hearts, confess and bewail our manifold sins and transgressions, and, by sincere repentance . . . and, through the merits and mediation of Jesus Christ, obtain His pardon and forgiveness"[81] (Isa 59:6; Mt 6:17,18; 26:28,29; Jn 16:7-15; Ro 2:4; 1 Ti 2:5; Heb 12:24).

Former President Ronald Reagan shared that, the "Continental Congress proclaimed the first National Day of Prayer" to be undertaken for "every colonist." "Congress, in 1952" ... "revived" ... the "annual observance" of "the National Day of Prayer." Ronald Reagan said, "Prayer unites people ... (and) heals and brings us together as a nation." "From 1776 to 1783" ... "the Congress of the United States" held a National Day of Prayer. In 1952, a "senator" shared that the people of the United States "join in this service of prayer in the spirit of the Founding Fathers who believed that God governs in the affairs of men and who based their Declaration of Independence upon a firm reliance on the protection of Divine Providence." Today, the President of the United States is "to set aside and proclaim a suitable day each year as a National Day of Prayer"[82] (2 Ch 30:27; Pr 2:8; Isa 56:7[b]; Ac 1:14; 12:5; Ro 15:30; Heb 4:13).

After summoning the nation for a day of repentance and forgiveness, the Continental Congress could return on solid footing, anchored on the Eternal Rock, Jesus Christ, to proceed with their endeavor to establish an American document that would be a covenant between Almighty God and the American people. For King George III of Great Britain was proclaiming that America was in "rebellion," and that "rebellion" must be eradicated. "The penalty for instigating rebellion was death." Protestant ministers were comparing "George III" to Pharaoh in the Book of Exodus.[83] It was time to "Let My people go!" (Ex 5:1,2; Mt 26:3,4; Jn 8:58,59; 1 Co 10:4; Rev 12:11).

"Henry Lee of Virginia" was the first to propose that the Continental "Congress make a declaration of independence, stating that these united colonies are, and of a right ought to be, free and independent states." John Adams "seconded the proposal." Some members of the Continental Congress then began to draft the Declaration of Independence, "appealing to the Supreme Judge of the World for the Rectitude of our Intentions," and "a firm Reliance on the Protection of divine Providence"[84] (Ps 37:5,6; 116:4-9; Jn 5:26,27; Ac 10:42; Gal 5:1).

Thomas Jefferson, the third President of the United States, helped to draft the Declaration of Independence with the assistance of other Congressional delegates. They would proclaim that "all men are created equal, that they are endowed by their Creator with certain inalienable rights, . . . that to secure these rights, governments are instituted among men." Therefore, the government is there "to secure the rights that flow . . . solely from our Creator," and "not from men or documents."[85] That reference to the Creator, to the Supreme Judge of the World, and to Divine Providence, was referring to our Lord Jesus Christ (Pr 31:9; Hab 2:2,3; Jn 1:1-3; Ac 17:31; Ro 13:1; 1 Co 12:22-27; Gal 3:28; Col 3:10).

Of the "fifty-six signers of the Declaration of Independence," 24 "were active ministers," and they had obtained Christian "seminary degrees." Their dependence was on the God of the Bible for their cause of liberty. Of the 250 men considered the Founding Fathers, two-fifths of them "held offices in Bible societies." At the most, only "5%" of those men were not considered Christians, true believers in Jesus Christ[86] (Ac 11:26[b]; Ro 13:4[KJV]; 2 Ti 2:15[KJV]; 3:16,17).

John Witherspoon declared in 1776, that "If your cause is just—you may look with confidence to the Lord and intreat Him to plead it as His own."[87] "Many of the nation's leaders" were trained under John Witherspoon, a delegate to the Continental Congress, who became the "president" of Princeton University. Witherspoon believed that "Cursed be all learning that is contrary to the cross of Christ!" Under the guidance of the Holy Spirit and his Lord Jesus, John Witherspoon trained several "Supreme Court Justices," . . . "Cabinet members," . . . "Governors," . . . "Senators," . . . "Representatives," . . . and "many members of the Constitutional convention and many state Congressmen," as well as a "President" and a "Vice-President"[88] (Gen 14:14; Ps 37:6; 1 Co 3:18-21; 8:1).

Those men who would sign the Declaration of Independence, though they struggled among themselves, finally came to a unanimous decision. They made a pledge, a covenant with God together for the independence of the United States. They would be sworn to "mutually pledge to each other our

Lives, our Fortunes, and our sacred Honor." Their "sacred Honor" was protected, for not one of the "signers betrayed their cause." "None of them backed down" on their covenant pledge to the Lord nor to one another[89] (Isa 61:8,9; Jer 11:5; Mt 18,19; Ac 4:32; Ro 12:1; 2 Pe 2:21).

We believe that those who signed the Declaration of Independence had God's complete support. The eleven apostles/disciples of Jesus Christ who lived with Him, were willing to die for Him after He rose into heaven. They knew the truth that Jesus was the Son of God, the Messiah. In like manner, the signers of the Declaration of Independence were willing to sign their lives away, and die if they were forced to for the truth of their cause. We believe our Lord was completely behind the Declaration of Independence both physically and spiritually to free the colonists from the slavery of sin and Satan's oppression (Mt 16:15-17; Jn 8:31,32,34-36; 21:18,19; Ac 12:1,2; Rev 12:10).

On a morning in October 2008, before we typed this story, my wife heard these words from the Lord Jesus, "An angel unawares." Former President Ronald Reagan shared this story that, "was found in the writings of (Thomas) Jefferson" concerning the signing of the Declaration of Independence. It seems that God sent a messenger, an "angel" which those Founding Fathers "entertained . . . unawares." A man rose up in Independence Hall and said, "Sign that parcement . . . If my hands were freezing in death, I would sign that parchment with my last ounce of strength. Sign, sign if the next moment the noose is around your neck, sign even if the hall is ringing with the sound of the headman's axe, for that parchment will be the textbook of freedom, the bible of the rights of man forever." The "fifty-six delegates," moved by that man's statements, signed the Declaration of Independence. When the delegates looked for that elderly man in their midst, "he could not be found nor were there any who knew who he was or how he had come in and gone out through the locked and guarded doors"[90] (Dt 30:19; Gal 4:3,4; Heb 1:14; 13:2[KJV]).

The Lord Jesus revealed more to us regarding those Founding Fathers. On one afternoon, when we lived in North Carolina in 1998, my wife was looking out of a window in our kitchen. She saw a huge majestic eagle flying in the air with a long snake in its beak. The eagle flew into a group of trees on the right side of our yard. A fierce struggle ensued between the eagle and the snake in the trees. Leaves and branches were shaking and snapping. Finally, the eagle flew out from those trees victoriously with the snake still hanging from the eagle's beak. We believed then, that God had given us a sign that He was giving us His victory over Satan in our lives (Ps 103:2-5; Jer 48:40-44; Lk 10:19).

On May 29, 2008, I saw a vision of a man in a colonial outfit. He was wearing a lengthy gray wig, and appeared to be Ben Franklin. That man was holding the handle of a cane, and he was walking into what appeared to be Independence Hall in Philadelphia, Pennsylvania. Then I saw someone kick the cane out from that man's hand. Another vision followed of a bald eagle. The eagle initially had a huge V-shaped (victory) wing span. The eagle's wings were then lowered from a V-shape to something more open, like an open window to heaven. Then that eagle was flying over Independence Hall. A vision followed of a thirteen star American flag with a bald eagle's head in the center of the flag. Finally, I saw a fountain of water flowing in front of Independence Hall.

The Lord Jesus then spoke, "I want to speak more to you about the Founding Fathers of America. The 'Loyalists' and the Tories were trying to cripple the thirteen colonies from declaring independence from England. They were used by Satan to keep Americans from becoming free, so they could continue to serve him, (Satan), under a tyrannical ruler in England. The enemy was trying to cripple the faithful ones (Ps 55:12-14; 78:8; Heb 2:14,15; 1 Jn 2:19).

"The eagle was representing a messenger of God, one like the four 'living creatures' sent to bring Jesus Christ to America. As the men prayed in Independence Hall for God's intervention in the cause of liberty and freedom in the land, a window was opened to heaven. The eagle represented America, a nation flying away from its 'Mother Country' to establish its pinions, its roots in America. America would begin to 'soar on wings like eagles.' Many grew 'tired and weary,' and began to 'stumble and fall.' But God gave them strength to write the Declaration of Independence and later the Constitution, and to sign those contracts as established covenants with each other, the people, and their Lord Jesus (Dt 32:11,12; Ps 55:6-8; Isa 40:29-31; Eze 1:10-12; Mt 21:22; Rev 3:7; 4:6,7).

"Those documents were ordained by the Lord God Almighty for America to establish freedoms in the land. On that great day, (July 4, 1776), those men at Independence Hall 'mounted up on wings like eagles' and signed the Declaration of Independence. Those men, like eagles, stood alone as leaders willing to sacrifice their lives for the truth, for liberty, for their great Lord and Savior, their Providential God, Jesus! (Job 39:27,28; Isa 40:31[KJV]; Eze 17:7,8; Ro 12:1,2; Eph 6:13).

"And yet, in years to follow, many so-called 'leaders' and even believers would turn their backs on their faith, and follow 'doctrines of demons.' But those contracts, those documents were 'Rock' solid, guided by the Holy Spirit to proclaim the truth in the land, that God 'governs in the affairs of men,' that God was Lord over all their declarations of freedom, the God of the Bible, Jesus! That fountain of water, the 'fountain of life,' the Holy Spirit was flowing in those men, guided by 'the Spirit of Truth' that would cover the land (of America). That is what I want you to put in the book!" (Ps 36:9; Pr 14:27; Isa 9:7[a]; Mt 7:24,25; Jn 7:37-39; 16:13; 1 Ti 4:1; 2 Ti 4:3,4).

The Lord disclosed more on July 17, 2008, when I saw a vision of a judge in a black robe wearing an English wig. The wig appeared to be of the latter part of the eighteenth century. The judge was slamming a gavel down. On July 30, 2008, my wife heard these words in the early morning from our Lord Jesus, "John Adams." That morning, after fasting and worshiping our Lord Jesus, the Lord revealed to me some visions.

In the first vision, I saw the British parliament as shown in the movie, *Amazing Grace*, during the time of the Revolutionary War.[91] The parliament was supporting the King's War against the colonists in America. Then I saw a vision of John Adams and his wife Abigail writing letters to each other. Finally, I saw a vision of fireworks bursting in the air at night.

The Lord Jesus disclosed, "The English parliament chose to please their wicked king, their tyrannical ruler, and sacrificed many English men's lives to support their king's decision to rule over America. There were men however, leaders like George Washington and John Adams, who desired to declare their independence from the 'ruler of the king of the air,' who manifested himself in England at that time through King George III (Jer 17:5,7,8; Jn 5:44; 2 Co 11:13-15; Gal 1:10; Eph 2:2).

"John Adams was so deeply concerned about his freedom, his independence, his becoming a free man, free from the 'Mother Country,' that he signed the Declaration of Independence. He (John Adams), like his wife Abigail, expressed their deep concerns for freedom to one another. Abigail wrote him letters sharing her same concerns for independence, for freedom from England. They had compassion for one another, just as you, Mark and Phyllis, write letters to one another on special occasions in your lives. You both have a similar compassion for your inner freedom, for freedom from your childhood fears, your 'Mother countries,' your families of origin (Ps 27:10; 119:32; Ro 8:15,16; 2 Co 3:3; Gal 4:26,31; 5:1).

"John Adams proclaimed that the Day for signing the Declaration of Independence should be a day to remember for future generations. A Day when bombs burst in the air and 'fireworks' were displayed in the sky at night. A Day of freedom and liberty for all Americans; God-given freedoms and privileges, the freedom of religion, the freedom of speech, the freedom of the press, the freedom not to be censored by religious demons represented in liberal men and women today in America. 'Bombs' were bursting in John Adams' heart, the 'fire' was working in his life to establish liberty in the United

States of America among the thirteen colonies. So must that 'fire' burst in your hearts for the cause of liberty in the land today! (Isa 55:12; Mt 3:11; Lk 19:37-40; 24:32; 2 Co 3:17; 1 Th 5:19; Ja 1:25).

"(Some) judges today are like the former tyrannical England. They are taking away the freedoms of Christians, true believers in Jesus. They are pronouncing Christians, 'guilty,' just as England pronounced Americans guilty of rebellion against their 'Mother Country.' Those judges are pronouncing Christians guilty in the liberal courts of America today! The soldiers of the Revolutionary War fought for the freedoms you have today. Those judges are taking away those freedoms!" (Jn 7:24; Ac 4:18-21; 5:12-20, 27-29, 40-42; 9:1,2; 1 Co 10:29; 15:32).

The Battlefield: American Patriots' Hearts vs the Schemes of the Evil One

After the Declaration of Independence, the battle lines were now clearly drawn. The Americans were depending on their Lord Jesus to aid General George Washington and his Continental Army to ultimately defeat Great Britain's military might. In the late summer of 1776, a remarkable intervention of Almighty God saved "nearly eight thousand men (who) had escaped from certain death or imprisonment without the loss of a single life"[92] (2 Ch 20:15-17, 22-24; 32:20-22; Ps 37:5,6; Pr 3:5,6; Lk 4:28-30).

While George Washington and his Army were fighting the British in New York City, much of his Army were trapped in Brooklyn by the British military. George Washington "had decided to take the entire army off Brooklyn by small boat" at night. George Washington "needed" . . . "boats and men to handle them" to bring his Army across the Delaware River. He was able to get those boats. At night the "oarsmen" were able to scurry much of the Continental Army across the river to safety. A heavy fog rose early in the morning, settling over the

Delaware River. "The fog remained intact until the last boat, with Washington in it, had departed."[93]

Not a "soul" was taken by the British that night. All of George Washington's Army had been "saved." The Lord Jesus, who we believe is in charge of the weather, divinely provided protection for those American patriots. Satan, who would have desired to imprison, "to steal, to kill, and to destroy" those American patriots, lost those men to the One who brought them "life," and "it more abundantly," to their Lord Jesus (Mt 10:28; Mk 4:35-41; Jn 10:10[KJV]; 1 Ti 2:3,4; 1 Pe 3:18-20).

It was a foggy Sunday morning on November 25, 2007, when my wife and I drove to work at a Youth Home. The fog was so heavy, that we had to drive below the speed limit to see just a few yards ahead of our car. At about 11:45 a.m., my wife and I were sitting in that Home during the Sunday church service. While my eyes were closed, the Lord Jesus then gave me a vision. The vision was of George Washington looking over the Delaware River in the fog. In this vision, it was as if George Washington could see far beyond what others normally see. His face then changed into Thomas Jefferson's face.

The Lord then spoke to me, "Though the air was 'foggy,' George Washington could see far beyond time. He could see what the enemy could not see. Great Britain, their enemy then, could not see George Washington and his military troops crossing the Delaware River. God gave him a 'way of escape,' while the enemy had trapped him in. George Washington was given spiritual insight to see an opportunity to overcome the enemy's entrapment against America's future freedoms (Jn 9:24,25, 39-41; 1 Co 10:13; 2 Co 4:18; Col 3:1,2; 2 Ti 2:25,26).

"Like George Washington, you will see a 'way of escape,' when the enemy surrounds you. You will see beyond yourselves. Jesus will help you see the Son above the 'fog,' the Son of God, when others cannot see Him. As He (Jesus) covered George Washington and his troops with a blanket of fog, so God's love will cover you (Ps 27:2,3; Ac 7:55-58; 9:3-7; 1 Pe 4:8); April 20, 1999.

"George Washington's face changed into Thomas Jefferson's face for they were working together on the same pages to declare independence from their enemy, England. As you and your wife work together on composing the pages of this book, so Jesus will be declaring independence from sin in your lives and in others. This will be for those who 'fight the good fight' for their freedom in Jesus Christ" (Eze 37:16,17; Mk 16:20; 1 Ti 1:17,18).

The Lord Jesus revealed more to us about the American patriots. On August 28, 2008, after fasting and worshiping before the Lord Jesus, the Lord gave me some visions. In a vision, I saw English soldiers during the time of the Revolutionary War. The soldiers in the front line were kneeling down. Another line of soldiers was standing up behind them. All those soldiers were shooting their muskets at American patriots, who were hiding behind trees, shrubs, and bushes. Then I saw a vision of the wall that surrounds the Old City of Jerusalem.

The Lord Jesus then said, "'When the wicked rise to power, the people go into hiding.' The American soldiers were not hiding from God, they were hiding behind God's creation to 'fire' their muskets on their enemy. (You might ask), 'How could a God, the Lord Jesus Christ, who said, 'Do not kill, and do not murder,' support the war against England?' Because it was a war, a spiritual war, Satan against Jesus. It was a war that took the Pilgrims and Puritans out from England, out from a corrupt religious government, to establish the Kingdom of God under the Lordship of Jesus in the United States of America (Jos 8:4,7,12,13,19; 1 Sa 14:22; Pr 28:28; Mt 4:8-10; Mk 1:15; 2 Co 10:3,4; 1 Ti 6:3-5; Rev 12:7-11).

"Those true American believers in Jesus had the right 'to tread on serpents and scorpions,' for God gave them that authority over the dark 'powers' of England. They had the right to shed their blood, as Jesus did, to set (them) free from the slavery of sins, from the tyrannical ruler, Satan, manifested from England. They had the right to 'not shrink from death,' and take America by force, so the Kingdom of God could reign in America. 'And from the days of John the Baptist until now, the kingdom of heaven suffereth violence, and the violent take it by force.' The American soldiers were called to 'fight the good fight of the faith' in the Lord's Army (Joel 2:25; Mt 11:12[KJV]; 23:35; Lk 10:18,19[KJV]; Ac 22:20; Ro 13:4; 1 Ti 6:12; Rev 12:11).

"They were not to be intimidated by men, but to stand their ground firmly with all of the armor of God worn proudly. For the armor is a protective shield 'against the wiles of the devil.' The Sword of the Spirit is a weapon of warfare against Satan, the weapon is the Word of God (Lk 4:3-8; Eph 6:10-17); June 4, 1998.

"God's plan was to establish America under the shed blood of Jesus; for if Jesus shed His blood, surely the saints were willing to shed their blood for the advancement of the Kingdom of God, for freedom, for liberty, which could only come through Jesus Christ (Ps 116:15; Mt 26:28[KJV]; Jn 3:36; 14:6; Rev 16:6[a]).

"Just as Nehemiah built a 'wall of protection' around God's people in Jerusalem, so God was building a 'wall' around His people in America. It was a 'wall' from the world, a 'wall' from worldly things, a 'wall' around His 'temple' being built in America, just as He did in Israel. The 'temple' being Jesus the Christ. It was not a 'wall' to separate Church and state, but a 'wall' to separate the unbelievers from the believers, a 'wall' to separate the light from the darkness, a 'wall' to separate the true God from the liar, Satan, and a 'wall' to separate an anti-christ spirit from the Holy Spirit. It was being built to bring true believers together, to bring the Church in fellowship, in common, in harmony, in agreement, in 'union' with all of the United States (Ne 4:6,21-23; 6:15,16; Jn 2:19-22; 8:44-47; 2 Co 6:14-18; Tit 2:12-14; 1 Jn 2:18,19).

"It was a 'wall' supporting the cause for freedom from sin, freedom from Satan, freedom from religious demons, and freedom from the tyrannical rulers of the world. Within that 'wall of protection,' Americans could serve their Lord Jesus in government, in politics, in public and private enterprise, in their homes and churches throughout the nation" (Ezr 9:9; Mt 20:25-28; Jn 17:12,15; Ro 6:6,7).

The Lord revealed more information on the patriot soldiers on December 13, 2007, when I saw a vision of American Revolutionary War soldiers in their uniforms. The soldiers were standing on a hill shooting their cannons down on the enemy. Then I saw a vision of a man like in the movie about Johnny Tremain, who was hammering and working on copper, silver, and gold vessels.

The Lord then said, "'A city on a hill cannot be hidden.' Your place together is on a hill, (our last name translated in English is Churchill), so you will have a better ad-'vantage' against the enemies that would oppose your books, and the books to come. God has given you a 'vantage' point. As the vessels of different worth were hammered into refined forms, so the 'Maker of vessels,' has been molding His people, (His vessels) for His purposes to establish freedom from sin in America. Those patriots had a determination, a fervor, a zeal, a commitment, a loyalty, a steadfastness to serve the purposes of God, to fight for the truth, to fight for the freedoms they cherished, that the Lord still cherishes for His people today" (1 Ch 29:18; Ps 37:5; Jer 23:29; Mt 5:14,15; Ro 9:21[KJV]; 12:11; 2 Co 4:7[KJV]; 10:4; 2 Ti 2:20,21[KJV]; 1 Pe 5:10).

As the intensity of the War increased, the Continental Congress gathered together again in the fall of 1777 to petition Almighty God for His Sovereign intervention and protection for America and the patriots fighting for this country. They proclaimed, "It is the indispensable duty of all men to adore the superintending providence of Almighty God; to acknowledge with gratitude their obligation to Him, ... to offer humble and earnest supplication that it may please God, through the merits of Jesus Christ, mercifully to forgive and blot out our sins ... for the promotion and enlargement of that kingdom which consisteth 'in righteousness, peace, and joy in the Holy

Ghost'"[94] (2 Ch 6:14,39,40; Ps 51:1,2,9; Mt 28:18-20; Ro 14:17[KJV]; Php 4:6,7).

Our Founding Fathers were in unity together in calling upon their Lord Jesus Christ, who is "an ever-present help in (times of) trouble." Those men knew that Jesus, America's "precious Cornerstone," was the only salvation for the country. Backed up by prayer, George Washington chose to move the Continental Army to an encampment at Valley Forge during the winters of 1777 and 1778. Valley Forge is located outside Philadelphia, Pennsylvania (Ps 46:1-3; Isa 28:16; Ac 4:12; 1 Th 5:17).

Valley Forge

That first winter in 1777, "disease" took "a fearful toll of their numbers; they would lose one in four that winter . . . Men were literally naked, because they did not even have rags to wrap around them . . . Exposure to the elements combined with . . . starvation . . . were optimum conditions for the diseases, which . . . ravaged the camp."[95] Even rotten food had been shipped to that Army at Valley Forge.

Those horrible conditions at Valley Forge were revealed in the video, *The Winter of Red Snow*.[96] As the Continental Army was walking in the snow to Valley Forge, bloody red footprints were left in the snow. For many of those patriots did not have adequate clothing or footwear. Their bloody feet left red footprints. Men were coughing, and their bodies were freezing from the cold weather, having no blankets to warm them.

Martha, George Washington's wife shared, "These are ordinary men; farmers, craftsmen, laborers, representing each of the thirteen colonies. They left their homes two years ago as strangers, bound only by one common goal, independence from the tyranny of British rule. It has not been easy. Redcoats greatly outnumber us, and have many more weapons at their disposal, but we must not give up, not ever!"[97] Martha Washington shared similar sentiments as her husband, George.

General George Washington, under the guidance of the indwelling Holy Spirit, understood the battle for the hearts of those colonial patriots was a spiritual battle. That battle was again pitting their Lord Jesus against the ravaging wolf, Satan. "Washington made no secret of his Christian faith." The Continental Army "endured" and was "delivered" by God through George Washington's faith in His Lord Jesus. Some ministers of the gospel of Jesus Christ were comparing "Washington to Moses," for George Washington chose "to suffer affliction with the people of God," (his Army) . . . covenanting "himself with his men in the suffering of Valley Forge"[98] (Mt 24:13; Mk 8:38; Jn 10:11-16; Ac 20:29-31; 1 Co 6:19; Heb 11:24-26[KJV]).

Former President Ronald Reagan shared that, "George Washington knelt in prayer at Valley Forge and in the darkest days for our struggle for independence said that 'the fate of unborn millions will now depend, under God, on the courage and conduct of this army'"[99] (Dt 5:10; Ps 45:17; Lk 22:41; Ac 21:5).

It was reported that a Quaker overheard George Washington praying out in the woods at Valley Forge. The Quaker and his wife, were both opposed to the American Revolution. The Quaker ran and told his wife, "Our cause is lost. God cannot help but hear and answer such prayers as I have just heard." George Washington had stated that, "For an American to not believe in God's providence would make him worse than an infidel."[100] Through George Washington's, as well as the Americans and patriots' prayers, the Lord Jesus convinced France to join the "Colonial army" as American "allies" for the American cause for independence from Great Britain[101] (Mt 7:7,8; Jn 9:31; Ro 15:30; Ja 5:16-18; 1 Pe 3:12).

On December 20, 2007, I received a vision from the Lord Jesus of a scene in the video, *The Winter of Red Snow*. In the vision, the beleaguered Army at Valley Forge were out in the cold winter. They were blowing on their hands to keep them warm. In the vision, a cast-iron pot filled with food was hanging from an iron tripod over a fire. Then I saw a vision of a huge bonfire. Men and women were burning up books and papers. A man was also lifting up his hands to heaven.

Then the Lord said, "Those that are out in the cold, fighting for freedom in this country, the United States, are mistreated, abandoned, and discarded today. George Washington and his (Continental) Army were put out in the cold at Valley Forge. His heart and his message are becoming more extinct in this country, (today). But, just like God provided for the soldiers at Valley Forge, He will provide for those that are being put out in the cold. Women and children will nurse the 'freedom fighters' back to Himself. He will feed them warm food, and provide warm blankets for their bodies to cover them from the enemy's attacks (Gen 22:14; Ps 91:4; Na 1:7; 2 Co 11:27; Eph 5:29; Php 4:3; 2 Ti 4:3,4; Heb 11:36-38).

"Those that are fighting for the freedom of the unborn, (freedom to live), for the freedom of right relationships in marriages, fighting for a cleaner lifestyle, for right relationships (heterosexual) with men and women, for those who would stand up for the Name of Jesus in this country, in the government, are being put out in the cold. The United States has been putting the 'freedom fighters' out in the cold, as they did at Valley Forge when the support for the military was waning. But God will feed them a warm 'stew.' He will make provision for them. A warm 'stew' is stewing up today's 'freedom fighters' (2 Ki 4:38,41; Pr 31:8,9; Eze 36:29,30; Mt 24:12; Mk 6:17-19; Ac 5:28-32, 40-42; Ro 1:16; 5:17; 1 Co 6:9-11; Eph 5:22-33).

"In the first century, men and women were burning up scrolls, their witchcraft books. At that time, the first century believers were being put out in the cold by the enemies of Jesus Christ. But they warmed themselves by the fire, a bonfire, the 'fire' of the Holy Spirit to burn up that which was not of God, sin in their lives, in order to follow Jesus. Those who would fight against the occult, the dark powers, the witchcraft and magic in the land of the United States are being put out in the cold in this country today (Mt 3:11,12; Mk 14:54; Ac 9:1,2; 16:16-24; 19:18-20; 26:17,18; 28:2-5).

"But you have been given authority through the power of the Holy Spirit, who dwells within you, the Spirit of the Living God; to put out in the cold, the enemies of Jesus Christ, to put out in the cold, dark powers, the witchcraft in this country (USA), by putting a fiery 'torch' to the scrolls, sorcery, witchcraft and wizardry of that past age, and of today (Isa 47:9-14; Eze 13:18-23; Lk 10:18-19; Jn 14:16,17; Eph 6:10-13; Rev 18:8; 21:8).

"Those that would fight for freedom against God's enemies are My 'freedom fighters' today. You will speak up and write boldly about this in these last days in this book on freedom. For in the last days, the hearts of many 'will grow cold' to the truth, to the Word of God, and to the Sovereign Power of Jesus Christ. It will be like taking 'away a garment,' a blanket from a believer, a 'freedom fighter' . . . 'on a cold day' in the dark days ahead. But I will provide you water, Living Water, and meat that will sustain you, the meat of the Word of God" (Ps 35:1-3; Pr 25:20; Zec 10:5; Mt 24:45[KJV]; Jn 4:10,14; 6:54-56[KJV]; 2 Ti 4:3,4; Heb 11:32-34; 2 Pe 2:1,2).

To affirm the call by God on George Washington's life, to keep America under the Lordship of Jesus Christ, God revealed to him visions, while he was encamped at Valley Forge. There was a "well-documented" account of those visions.[102] Anthony Sherman, an officer with General George Washington at Valley Forge, spoke to a Mr. Wesley Bradshaw at "Independence Square" on July 4, 1859. Mr. Bradshaw published an article on Washington's vision "in the *National Tribune*" for the "December, 1880" issue.

Anthony Sherman shared with Mr. Bradshaw that, "I have often seen the tears coursing down our dear commander's care-worn cheeks, . . . about the conditions of his poor soldiers . . . He used often to pray in secret for aid and comfort from God, the interposition of whose Divine Providence brought us safely through the darkest days of tribulation." One day, Mr. Sherman was requested to meet with George Washington after dusk. George Washington shared this story with him. A "mysterious visitor" appeared in the room where he was sitting. "I felt strange sensations spreading through me . . . My tongue had become useless. Even thought itself had become paralyzed. . . . I now began to feel as one dying, . . . I did not reason, I did not move; all were alike impossible, I was only conscious of gazing fixedly, vacantly at my companion."

George Washington then told Mr. Sherman, "I heard a voice saying, 'Son of the Republic, look and learn,' . . . at the same time the visitor extended her arm eastwardly . . . I looked upon a strange scene. Before me lay spread out in one vast plain all the countries of the world—Europe, Asia, Africa and America. I saw rolling and tossing between Europe and America, the billows of the Atlantic, and between Asia and America lay the Pacific . . . At that moment I beheld a dark, shadowy being, like an angel, . . . floating in the mid-air, between Europe and America. . . . A cloud raised from these countries, and joined in mid-ocean . . . and then moved slowly westward, until it enveloped America in its murky folds . . . I heard the smothered groans and cries of the American people . . . The dark cloud was then drawn back to the ocean, in whose heaving billows it sank from view."

This peril which "George Washington saw took place on American soil." This first peril was "the Revolutionary War." . . . "There was much suffering," men shedding their blood to obtain freedom and independence from Great Britain. George Washington saw two other perils that day that take place on American soil, that we will reveal in later chapters.

George Washington chose to suffer with his people, like Moses did, being touched by their "groans and cries." Just like Moses, he was called by God to be their "deliverer" from their Egypt of tyranny. We believe that the "dark, shadowy being, like an angel," was Satan, who was behind the killing of both British and American soldiers on American soil (Ex 2:23-25; 3:10; 18:10; Pr 4:19; Jn 10:10[a]; Ac 26:18; 2 Co 11:14,15; Heb 11:25).

George Washington, like the prophet Daniel, was called "Son" by an angel. George was so valued by the Lord Jesus, that God sent a messenger, an angel who prophesied to him about the future of America. Just like Daniel and the apostle John, who were given visions of the end times, George Washington was given a vision of "peril" in the future of the United States of America. He was called, "Son of the Republic." Under the Lord Jesus, he was one of "the sons of God," sent to establish the Republic of the United States of America. America would become a nation in which the people elect their country's leaders to represent them in government, a democratic form of government. America would be a nation at that time under the guidance of the Holy Spirit, and under their Master, the Lord Jesus. "As God's spokesman," George Washington had "Ezekiel's 'son of man' status," as "Son of the Republic," which testified "to the sovereign God he was commissioned to serve"[103] (Ps 127:1; Eze 2:1; 21:2; Da 8:15-17; Jn 13:13,14[KJV]; 16:13; Ac 2:17; Rev 2:9,10; 10:8-11; 17:15-18).

Early in the morning, on October 16, 2008, my wife heard these words from the Lord Jesus, "Patient endurance . . . They fought on . . . Light-bearers, carrying the good—unseen . . . to drive the stakes of freedom deep into the soil (soul) of a new nation; deeply rooted and grounded in (Jesus) Christ, . . . Onward Christian soldiers."

That day the Lord gave me a vision after prayer and fasting, of the Valley Forge encampment. The Valley Forge vision was during the end of the winter near springtime. Soldiers were sitting around in a circle studying the Bible, the Word of God. Ministers were there helping the soldiers study the Bible. Then I saw an iron tripod with a pot of meat and stew hanging from it over a fire.

The Lord Jesus then said, "The soldiers were studying the Word of God. Ministers from the local area came to Valley Forge to pray for the Army, and assist them in studying the Bible. The stew, the meat of the Word that the patriot soldiers were eating gave them 'patient endurance,' so they would not sink into despair. The patriot saints knew that they had to rely on the one, true God for their sustenance. There was an outpouring of the Holy Spirit, there, a type of revival at the camp (Isa 61:3; Joel 2:11.28.29; Ac 17:11; 2 Co 1:5,6; 2 Ti 2:3,4,15[KJV]; Heb 6:5; Rev 1:9).

"Those soldiers understood that God was with them, despite the tragedies that occurred in the Valley Forge encampment. With the power of the Holy Spirit, they could go forth from that camp with the zeal of the Lord in their hearts, with a fervor to do His will, pressing on with the upward call 'in Christ Jesus,' the Lord! So they could 'fight on' with a new strength to continue the War for independence. They were 'light-bearers, carrying the good—unseen to drive the stakes of freedom deep into the soil/soul of a new nation; deeply rooted and grounded in Jesus Christ'" (Mt 5:16; Ro 12:11; 2 Co 4:18; Eph 3:16-19; Php 3:14; 1 Ti 1:18; 2 Ti 1:7; Ja 1:2-4; 1 Pe 4:12,13). And so we say on their behalf and for the soldiers today in the Lord's Army:

> "*Onward, Christian soldiers! Marching as to war, With the cross of*
> *Jesus Going on Before; Christ, the royal Master,*
> *Leads against the foe; Forward into battle, See, His Banner Go!*
> *Onward, Christian soldiers! Marching as to war,*
> *With the cross of Jesus Going on before.*"[104]

ONWARD CHRISTIAN SOLDIERS

"Like a mighty army Moves the Church of God; Brothers we are
treading Where the saints have trod; We are not divided,
All one body we; One in hope and doctrine, One in charity.
Onward, Christian soldiers! Marching as to war,
With the cross of Jesus Going on Before.

Crowns and thrones may perish, Kingdoms rise and wane;
But the Church of Jesus Constant will remain; Gates of hell
can never 'Gainst that Church prevail; We have Christ's own
promise, Which can never fail.
Onward, Christian soldiers! Marching as to war,
With the cross of Jesus Going on Before."[105]

(Verses 2 and 3)

5

AND THE GOVERNMENT WILL BE ON HIS SHOULDERS

"For the Lord is our judge, the Lord is our lawgiver,
the Lord is our King; He will save us."

The War for Independence would continue for three more years after George Washington and his Army left the Valley Forge encampment. The Lord Jesus spoke more to us about those fighting patriots in the Continental Army. On April 17, 2008, I saw a vision of the cover of this book. A thirteen-star flag was flying from a flag pole on the right side of the vision. Then I saw the flag on the flag pole move from the right to the left. The flag then appeared to be a boundary on the left side of a map of the original thirteen colonies. A vision followed of a colonial schoolroom in which Revolutionary War patriot soldiers were praying at night. They were looking up into the sky. The sky was lit up with "bombs bursting in air," like at the Fourth of July. The facial expressions of those patriots exuded excitement. After that I saw a vision of my wife and me with others holding a lighted torch at night. The torch was being held by runners moving from the east coast to the west coast. Finally, I saw the American flag move from the left, back to the right side. On October 22, 2008, after praying and worshiping before our Lord Jesus, I saw a vision of a faded, thirteen-star flag. Then I saw the flag magnified several times larger.

The Lord then revealed that He was with the American people establishing a border on the left side of the thirteen colonies. "From the west side of the colonies, the Americans were protected. For God's purpose and plan was to contain the enemy, (Great Britain) on the inside, and move the Americans eastward to drive their enemy out into the sea (Atlantic Ocean) back to England. The patriots' prayers were answered when the English returned back to their homeland, (their "Mother Country") (Nu 34:6; 1 Ch 5:20; Mt 21:21,22).

"You are moving to the right side of the land of America. America has been moving to the left, to the liberal side, as if that was the solution to the troubles in America. But I say, 'Stay on the right side. Stay on the conservative side. Stay on the side of (Constitutional) rights and freedom for all in America including the unborn. Stay on the righteous side with the Word of God, with the Lord Jesus. Be willing to carry the banner of freedom, (the American flag), and the torch, the light of God on the right side, so the left can see it.' It will move from the east coast to the west coast. For right is better than wrong. Right in the Word of God. 'Write these words down that I tell you,' says the Lord (Isa 11:10; Na 2:4; Hab 2:2,3; Mt 25:33; Ac 7:56; 2 Co 8:21).

"The Lord Jesus has called you to live a simple life, like the early Moravians did in Winston-Salem, (North Carolina). The Moravians separated the men from the women, and the boys from the girls until they were married for purer purposes. So God is using this book to separate the right from the wrong in America for purer purposes. A more simple lifestyle involves removing from the American homes the electronic trappings of this world that draw Americans away from taking up their cross daily, taking up the Word of God, and following Me.

Separate yourself from the left, the leftist viewpoints, and stay right with Me (Gen 4:7; Ps 116:6; Lk 9:23,24; Ac 2:44,45; 1 Co 6:18,20; 2 Co 6:17,18).

(In 1753, fifteen "Moravian settlers" sang a song to their "Savior," Jesus, after they settled in Winston-Salem, North Carolina. They sang, "We hold arrival Lovefeast here in Carolina land, A company of Brethren true, A little pilgrim Band, Called by the Lord to be of those Who through the whole world go, To bear Him Witness everywhere, And naught by Jesus know")[106] (SS 2:4; Mk 16:15; Ac 1:8).

"You have been writing about the liberty of the thirteen original colonies. My desire is to set you free from your 'Mother countries,' from your families of origin, to magnify liberty and freedom in your walk together, in your marriage together, in your ministry together. It is going to be magnified. It will be exposed to the world, so expose yourselves, show yourselves true to one another!" (Mk 10:29,30; Lk 12:2,3; Eph 5:13,14; 1 Th 3:12); October 22, 2008.

The Lord Jesus spoke more about America's leader for freedom and liberty, George Washington. The Lord shared, "George Washington persevered with his Army despite many enemy attacks. George stood strong with God, and would not surrender to the enemy. Press on with your God together like the Americans did in the late 1700's, in order for you to obtain a victory for your marriage, your family, and your nation, never surrendering to your enemy, Satan!" (2 Ch 20:15-17; Php 3:14; 2 Ti 4:17,18); June 19, 2006.

On May 27, 2007, my wife and I were attending a Sunday morning service at a Youth Home. During the service, the Lord Jesus gave me a vision of George Washington riding on a horse in front of his patriot soldiers. In the vision, men cheered General Washington, waving their hats at him.

The Lord then spoke to me, "George Washington was a man's General, a man's President. When he trotted on his horse in front of his military troops, his men cheered him. For he was with his men in their defeats, in their victories, in their pain and woundedness, and in their faith. He stood a head taller than his men; tall in stature, tall in his heart for his faith in his Father in Heaven, tall in his heart for God's purpose for the United States of America; a country founded on the shed blood of Jesus, on the shed blood of the American people, who were willing to die for freedom. The oppressed, the down-trodden, the less, the weak, the poor confounded the 'strong,' the wisdom of the world, Great Britain (at that time). The poor in the eyes of the world, America, inherited a great victory" (1 Sa 13:14; Jn 12:12-16,24,25; 1 Co 1:26-29; Col 1:19,20; Heb 10:33; 11:24-26; Ja 2:5).

The War finally came to an end at Yorktown in Virginia, when General Cornwallis of Great Britain surrendered to George Washington. George "Washington ordered a thanksgiving service to be held the day after the surrender," a thanksgiving in honor of God's "Providence" with the Continental Army's victory over Great Britain's military force. When George Washington disbanded the Continental Army,[107] he prayed to his Lord Jesus, "Wilt most graciously be pleased to dispose us all to do justice, to love mercy, and to demean ourselves with that charity, humility and pacific temper of mind which were the characteristics of the Divine Author of our blessed religion . . . Grant our supplication, we beseech Thee, through Jesus Christ our Lord. Amen"[108] (Ps 95:2; Mic 6:8; Col 1:9-13; 1 Ti 2:5,6; Heb 12:2).

The Treaty of Paris in 1783 was the official end of that War. In the opening lines of that Treaty, it was written, "In the Name of the Most Holy, and Undivided Trinity, Amen."[109] Jesus is the Name referred to in that Treaty, when He gave "The Great Commission" to His disciples stating, "Go and make disciples of all nations, baptizing them in the name of the Father and of the Son and of the Holy Spirit," which is "the Most Holy, and Undivided Trinity." The War began in prayer and recognition of our Lord Jesus, and ended in recognition of Almighty God (Mt 3:16,17; 28:18,19; 1 Co 7:35; Eph 4:4-6).

We believe our Lord Jesus was preeminent in the hearts of

George Washington and the American signers of the Treaty of Paris for liberty for the American colonists from England. It was God's will to use His believers to re-establish the Cornerstone foundation of the United States of America under the Banner of our Lord Jesus (Ex 17:15; 2 Ti 2:19; 1 Pe 2:6).

The Constitution

In 1787, following their faith and the spiritual framework of the Founding Fathers, delegates from the original thirteen colonies would gather again at Independence Hall, to frame "a new constitution in May and sign it in September."[110] It would become "The Constitution of the United States of America," created, we believe, under the guidance of the Spirit of God, and the Lordship of Jesus Christ to aid in governing the American people (Isa 9:7; Mt 12:18; Jn 16:13).

Regarding the document, the Constitution of the United States, "Our founding fathers were . . . Christians, (and) their purpose in carefully constructing the laws governing the nation was motivated by their belief that 'the Christian religion must be the basis of any government intended to secure the rights and privileges of a free people' (Noah Webster)"[111] (Mt 28:18-20; Gal 4:4,5; 5:1; Heb 10:16).

"The Preamble to the U.S. Constitution" affirms the Founding Fathers' Christian beliefs, that they were to "secure the blessings of liberty." In order to "secure those blessings," our Founding Fathers knew that they would need to depend on "Almighty God." For those men understood that neither they, "nor the government, . . . could create the blessings of liberty"[112] (Ps 62:7,8; Pr 10:6[a]; 14:26; Ro 10:12; Heb 6:18-20).

Peter Marshall, an historian and author, revealed that "In 1787," George Washington, who presided over the delegates forming the U.S. Constitution, "ordered a copy of the Fundamental Orders of Connecticut," which had been "written in 1639." That document "was the first complete constitution on

American soil." George Washington ordered that document "to be read by every delegate," who was involved in "forming" up the United States Constitution. "The Fundamental Orders of Connecticut" were "rooted in the Holy Scriptures and the Word of God," and were based on a sermon by the "Puritan preacher, . . . Thomas Hooker." In that sermon, Thomas Hooker shared, "We enter into combination and confederation together to maintain and preserve the liberty and purity of the Gospel of our Lord Jesus, which we now profess"[113] (Mk 4:20; 16:16; Ac 2:44-46; 2 Co 4:5; Col 2:6,7).

Our founding documents, the Declaration of Independence, and the United States Constitution, we believe, were rooted and founded on the Living Word of God, the Lord Jesus to "secure the blessings of liberty" from Almighty God, from Him. The Lord Jesus, we believe, was present with the "framers" of the U.S. Constitution. In the Word of God, Almighty God establishes His relationship with men and women through covenants. Our Lord Jesus, we believe, was in covenant with the "framers" of the U.S. Constitution (Gen 9:8-17; Jer 31:31-33; Mt 7:24,25; 16:15-18; 26:27,28; Eph 2:19-22).

Donald Lutz, a professor at the University of Houston, revealed that just like the Declaration of Independence, the Constitution was a "covenant" signed again "by those making a covenant agreement." It was an agreement between God Almighty and the delegates representing each of the thirteen colonies in America. "Rabbi Daniel Lapin," an "orthodox" Jewish rabbi shared that, "Only two nations have been governed by constitutions, ancient Israel and modern America." Those "two nations are based on the Biblical idea of covenant contract constitution." For in the U.S. Constitution, it ends with "In the year of our Lord"[114] (Gen 17:1-7; Ex 28:21; 1 Co 11:25,26; 2 Co 3:6; Heb 8:6-10).

While forming the U.S. Constitution, the delegates struggled among themselves, which they had previously experienced when they drafted the Declaration of Independence. Satan again, we believe, was pitting men against men, attempting to divide those delegates from establishing a Constitution under the guidance of the Holy Spirit. Benjamin Franklin spoke to those delegates on "June 28, 1787," . . . "In the beginning of the contest with Great Britain, . . . we had daily prayer in this room for Divine protection. Our prayers . . . were heard and they were graciously answered, . . . and have we now forgotten that powerful Friend, or do we . . . no longer need His assistance? . . . I have lived . . . a long time, and the longer I live, the more convincing proofs I see of this truth—that God Governs in the affairs of men. And if a sparrow cannot fall to the ground without His notice, is it probable that an empire can rise without His aid? We have been assured . . . in the Sacred Writings, that 'except the Lord build the house, they labor in vain that build it!' I firmly believe this; and I also believe that without His concurring aid we shall succeed in this political building no better than the builders of Babylon"[115] (Gen 11:5-9; Ps 9:19; 46:1,2; 127:1 [KJV]; Mt 12:25-28; 21:22; Rev 18:2).

Those daily prayers were to their "powerful Friend," Jesus, who calls us His "friends if (we) do what (He) command(s)." It was our Lord Jesus who said, "Not one of them (sparrows) will fall to the ground apart from the will of your Father." After Congress returned to "daily prayer," those men were able to come to a unanimous agreement and sign the Constitution. James Madison, one of the framers of the Constitution, introduced a "proposal" . . . "dividing the government into three separate branches—an idea that mirrored the three functions of governance ascribed to the Lord in Isaiah 33:22: 'For the Lord is our Judge [judicial], the Lord is our lawgiver [legislative], and the Lord is our king [executive]'"[116] (Mt 10:29; Jn 15:12-15; 1 Th 5:17,18).

On October 24, 2008, my wife heard these words, "America is on its last leg." On October 30, 2008, after fasting and worshiping before the Lord Jesus, I saw a previous vision that I had of picture frames going back in time, back to the seventeenth century. A young boy was standing near a lighted candle in a darkened colonial home. Then I saw a vision of a candle glowing on a table next to Benjamin Franklin in Independence Hall. The candle changed into a fiery torch, which lit up that Convention Center. On July 18, 2008, the Lord Jesus gave me a vision of the renowned kite that Benjamin Franklin flew in the sky. A golden key was at the base of the string attached to the kite. In the vision, the weather was stormy, the clouds were billowy, dark and gray.

The Lord Jesus then said, "Going back in time, one of the 'framers' of the Constitution was Ben Franklin. The Holy Spirit convicted Ben Franklin to speak up at the Constitutional Convention. A lighted candle on a table next to Ben Franklin changed into a powerful 'light' in that room when Ben Franklin spoke about his Friend, Jesus. Benjamin Franklin was My friend that day, and a friend to the delegates at that meeting. They knew that many men 'fell' on the battlefield, shedding their blood for freedom. They knew that a 'sparrow' does not 'fall to the ground apart from the will of (their) Father' in Heaven (Ps 72:14; Mt 5:15,16[KJV]; Lk 12:6; Ja 2:23).

"The Holy Spirit moved upon those men that day to work together in unity, in their prayers to the Lord. Their Rock, that held them together during the Revolutionary War, was the Lord Jesus. This time Satan did not kick out Benjamin Franklin's 'cane,' when that robust and balding man spoke on My behalf that day. The 'cane' being the 'measuring rod,' the 'canon' of freedom with the Constitution's 'checks and balances,' was to keep sinful man under the discipline of Almighty God, under His law and order. A wave of Holy Spirit 'fire' ministered through the men that day. It would continue moving in those early days of the nation. Those men would willingly sign the Constitution, covenanted together for the future posterity of America. It was a jubilant year of our Lord! (Lev 19:35,36; Ps 96:12,13; Pr 23:14; 29:15[a]; Mt 3:11; 7:24,25; Ro 15:5,6; Heb 12:10).

"Yet your wife heard, 'America is on its last leg,' for Americans today have turned their backs on the Lawgiver, the Judge, the King, Jesus, and turned their backs on those men who framed the United States Constitution. For America does not even have a 'cane' to support its other leg. Americans have allowed wicked sinful men and women to interpret the Constitution according to man's self-elevated will, unknowingly under the direction of the evil one, Satan. This is in direct opposition to the Word of God (Isa 33:22; 1 Ti 6:20,21; 2 Ti 4:3,4; Ja 3:14,15; 4:12; Rev 2:14,15).

"Congress today chooses to seek 'praise from men,' rather than 'praise from God.' Congress needs their own self 'checks and balances' to check their sinful natures in repentance before God, so they can present to America a nation 'balanced' under the weight of the Holy Scriptures, the Word of God. The Founding Fathers sought 'praise from God,' who they recognized as the One who secured their 'blessings' for their new nation (Eze 18:30,31; Jn 5:44; 12:43; 2 Co 13:5; 1 Th 2:6; 2 Ti 3:16,17).

"The 'key' to healing the land of America is to forgive the wounders, those who have wounded Jesus, in believing men and women. As you let God's light shine on your shameful, (wounded) memories, and allow Jesus to come into those memories, (to heal you and bring His truth), you can forgive those who shamed you"[117] (Isa 54:4; Mt 6:14,15; 16:19; Ac 9:3-6; Eph 5:13,14; Heb 13:8; Rev 2:4,5); July 18, 2008.

Those Founding Fathers understood man's sinful nature and they established a "proper government" based on a "checks and balances against tyrannical exercises of power." A properly balanced government would help prevent Satan from interfering with God's people in establishing law and order in America. George Washington "proclaimed an annual day of prayer and fasting to Almighty God,"[118] after the Constitution had been signed and ratified. For George Washington and the delegates understood that "without the strong check and balance of an awareness of the dangers of self-righteousness, it can soon become an instrument for the gratification of self, not God," which is "Satan's prime harvesting grounds"[119] (Neh

9:1-3; Est 4:15,16; Isa 2:4; 9:7; Mt 4:8-10; 9:11-13; 23:25,26; Jn 9:40,41; Ro 3:23; 13:1-7; 1 Co 14:40).

George Washington valued the importance of a prayer to Almighty God in forming up a governing document that would ensure that America's "government (would) be on His shoulders," the Lord Jesus. The Lord Jesus would prevail again in developing an America under His guidance, direction, and leadership through the faith of our Founding Fathers. The Pilgrims in their covenant with one another and God in the Mayflower Compact, and our Founding Fathers with their covenanted documents in the Declaration of Independence, and the U.S. Constitution, were stepping stones to help solidify an American people deeply rooted in their faith in our Lord Jesus. The Cornerstone from which all future generations of Americans would be built upon, was and is the Rock, Jesus Christ! (Ps 67:4; Isa 9:6; Hab 2:2; Mt 28:18-20; Lk 22:20; Jn 16:13; Col 2:6,7; 1 Pe 2:4-8).

The First Amendment to the Constitution

In September of 1789, the First Amendment to the Constitution of the United States was approved by Congress. In that Amendment it states, "Congress shall make no law respecting an establishment of religion, or prohibiting the free exercise thereof; or abridging the freedom of speech, or the press; or the right of the people peaceably to assemble . . . "[120]

Former President Ronald Reagan shared, "The American people have long recognized that the liberty we cherish must include the freedom to worship God as each of us pleases . . . In the First Amendment is the protection of religion and conscience from government interference . . . The Founders realized that we must guard freedom of religion . . . against tyranny and bigotry . . . The First Amendment was not written to protect American people from religion; the first amendment was written to protect the American people from government tyranny"[121] (Est 3:8-10; Pr 29:2; Ac 5:27-32,40-42; 8:1-3; 18:2).

The "U.S. Constitution's Establishment Clause and the Free Exercise Clause 'were adopted by the framers for the explicit purpose of promoting, not suppressing religious freedom.' The Establishment Clause only restricted the federal government, not the states. It was the Supreme Court 'in a series of abhorrent decisions that ruled that the First Amendment Establishment Clause was applicable to the states' . . ."[122]

It was our Lord Jesus who said, "Seek 'first' his kingdom and his righteousness, and all these things will be given to you as well," food, "drink," and clothing. The Founding Fathers, who established the 'first' amendment to the Constitution, we believe, were seeking His Kingdom 'first' in America; so future Americans could enjoy the blessings of "life, liberty, and the pursuit of happiness," which can be represented by food, "drink," and clothing, among other blessings (Ps 68:3; Mt 6:31-33; Lk 12:31; 2 Co 3:17[KJV]).

When Jesus tells a man to "Follow Me" in the Scriptures, the man responds by saying, "I will follow you, Lord; but 'first' let me go back . . . to my family." Jesus responds to the man by saying, "No one who puts his hand to the plow and looks back, is fit for service in the kingdom of God." When you put your family of origin, your "Mother country," your own self-interests first before God, we believe, that you are not "fit" to serve Almighty God. The United States government, we believe, is not "proclaiming the kingdom of God" first, today, contrary to our Founding Fathers, who were willing to follow God, first. Congress, we believe, has chosen first, to "bury their own dead" by choosing the world's familiar ways and putting the Living God, Jesus, behind them, so they can follow their own self-interests. Jesus "has no place to lay his head," as the "head of the church" among men and women today, who legislate laws and policy for the United States of America (Mt 10:34-38; Mk 10:29-31; Lk 9:57-62; Ro 2:8; Eph 1:22).

Separation of Church and State

Thomas Jefferson, the third President of the United States, is referred by men and women, today, for the use of his words, "a wall of separation between church and state." Thomas Jefferson's phrase is being used to protect the American government from religion, and to prohibit the free exercise of one's religious beliefs on government property and in government facilities.

Why did Thomas Jefferson use the words, "a wall of separation between church and state"? And was this included in the United States Constitution? Thomas Jefferson was overseas "when the Constitution was written and when the Bill of Rights" was approved and ratified. "Separation of church and state" has never been included in the Constitution. Thomas Jefferson sent a letter back to the "Danbury Baptist Association" in Connecticut on "January 1, 1802." It was reported, the Christians from that "association," were concerned that "the federal government would become a great danger to their Christian faith and to their churches"[123] (Jn 9:22; 12:42; Ac 8:1-3; 16:16-24).

Daniel Dreisback, a professor at American University, revealed that in Thomas Jefferson's letter, he was assuring those Christian men and women that a "national religion" or a "nationally established church" were not being built, . . . "thus building a wall of separation between church and state." This was written to inform them "that the federal government was (not) going to intrude on their religion." That "wall" was "to protect them . . . against federal government." Thomas Jefferson never suggested that there should be a separation "between God and state," and he ended the "letter with a prayer." Two days after that letter was sent to the Danbury Baptist Association, Thomas Jefferson attended church "in the chambers of the House of Representatives," which he attended "weekly," when he was the President of the United States[124] (Ezr 6:7; Neh 2:4-9; Ac 16:13; 1 Co 14:26).

That letter was not a part of the Constitution, nor was it a legal document. Thomas Jefferson never intended that expressing faith in God, in Jesus Christ be separated from governmental officials and legislatures. It was reported that Thomas Jefferson said, "The religion of Jesus Christ is the best religion the world has ever been given, and that the ethics and teachings of Christ are incomparable." "As President, Thomas Jefferson supported government involvement in: Legislative and Military chaplains, . . . Official Days of Fasting and Prayer, . . . Granting land to Christian churches, . . . and Christian schools, . . . Allowing government property and facilities to be used for worship, . . . and requiring the Bible to be taught in our public schools," etc.[125] (Jn 8:31,32; Ac 2:46; 17:19-34; 18:28; 20:20; 2 Ti 2:15[KJV]).

The Lord Jesus spoke to us on the "wall of separation between church and state" on March 3, 2008, and September 10, 2008. On September 10, 2008, I received a vision from the Lord Jesus of men blowing trumpets at the Old City of Jericho in Israel. Then I saw a vision of closed blinds on a window in our living room, and a shade was being pulled down at the window.

The Lord Jesus then said, "The 'wall of separation between church and state' came tumbling down, as did the wall in Jericho, for the Founding Fathers blew their trumpets on that so-called 'wall.' For they believed that their Creator, their Divine Providence, their Supreme Judge, Jesus, would rule over the government. That He would lead them as a nation, undivided in 'union' with one another. That was God's plan for this country, your country. The 'wall' would be against the establishment of a national church. Satan has 'blinded the minds of unbelievers' today about the 'wall of separation between church and state.' Satan has pulled his dark shade down on this country, so that the nation's government would not be led by the Creator, Divine Providence, the Supreme Judge, Jesus (Gen 22:14; Jos 6:15,16,20; Ecc 12:1; Eze 11:19; Jn 5:27; Ro 1:20; 2 Co 4:4; Eph 6:12).

"Americans today have been blinded to the 'self-evident'

truths of their forefathers. For they have chosen another 'god,' the 'god' of anti-christ, the 'god' of liberalism opposed to the Word of God. God will break down the 'wall of separation between church and state.' Those 'walls' will come tumbling down. You have a country with no national religion, a country that has accepted all religions. Yet, Christianity is becoming unacceptable in government today, while Islam is becoming more acceptable (Mt 24:9-11; Lk 20:18; Jn 15:18-21; 2 Co 4:4[KJV]; Col 2:8; Heb 11:30; 1 Jn 2:18,19).

"Today, the saints must get over the 'wall of hostility' from their enemies, Satan's henchmen, (who are) opposed to the Gospel of Jesus Christ being spread in the United States. (Those masquerading as "servants of righteousness" are) united, not in unity with fellow believers, but united against Christians, true believers in Jesus. There is a 'wall' that the American 'opposition' uses today, the 'wall of separation between church and state.' They strive to separate Jesus Christ from being united with the states of America. Their 'wall' is based on a complete misinterpretation of Thomas Jefferson's letter to the Danbury Baptist ("Association") community. Jefferson never intended to separate the Lord Jesus Christ from the states, states united under His care and providence. That 'wall' was to separate federal government from influencing the church in state matters. (Each state) developed its own faith, belief and churches. Federal government was to embody the Christian virtues of their forerunners, the Pilgrims and Puritans, which was freely followed by America's first President" (Isa 2:12,15; Mt 23:13-15; 2 Co 11:13-15; Eph 2:4; 4:18; Php 2:1,2; Col 3:12-17; Heb 12:3; Rev 12:17; 13:10[b]).

> "*He has sounded forth the trumpet that shall never sound retreat;*
> *He is sifting out the hearts of men before His judgement seat.*
> *O be swift, my soul, to answer Him! be jubilant, my feet!*
> *Our God is marching on!*"[126]
>
> ("Battle Hymn of the Republic": Verse 3)

The First President of the United States

George Washington followed his American Pilgrim and Puritan forerunners in exemplifying Christian virtues. We believe that his faith in Jesus Christ was deeply rooted within his heart, as we have previously written in this book. Almighty God had called George Washington to that leadership position, calling him the "Son of the Republic." The prophetic words from an Indian chief came true again, when he was elected the first President of the United States of America, becoming a "ruler of a great people and nation" (Gen 27:29[a]; Eze 2:1,2; Da 8:17; Ac 21:10,11; Ro 13:1-4; Col 2:6,7).

As a "deeply committed" . . . "Christian," George Washington wrote a letter to the "Delaware Indian Chiefs." He said, "You do well to wish to learn our arts, and ways of life, and above all the religion of Jesus Christ . . . Congress will do everything they can to assist you in this wise intention"[127] (Mt 4:18-20; 7:24,25; 11:28-30; Jn 13:13; 14:6; 15:9,10).

President George Washington "took the oath of office" in "April . . . 1789." He set a precedent for future Presidents, when he placed his hand on the Bible, while taking his "oath." George Washington ended that "oath" with the phrase, "so help me God," which has continued to be practiced today, when a President takes the "oath of office"[128] (Isa 41:10; Ac 26:22; 2 Ti 2:15; Heb 13:6).

In his "first Inaugural Address," George Washington stated, " . . . it would be peculiarly improper to omit, in this first official act, my fervent supplications to the Almighty Being who rules over the universe, who presides in councils of nations and whose providential aids can supply every defect[129] . . . We ought to be no less persuaded that the propitious smiles of Heaven can never be expected on a nation that disregards the eternal rules of order and right which Heaven itself has ordained"[130] (Dt 28:1,2,15; Job 29:23-25; Ps 103:19; 111:5-9; Heb 1:2,3).

In his first act as President, George Washington gave honor to Almighty God. The Scriptures state that, "Those who honor me (God Almighty) I will honor." George Washington was honoring his Father in Heaven, when he placed his hand on the Bible, the Word of God. The Lord Jesus, in the New Testament Scriptures, reveals the "eternal rules of order and right," which George Washington highly regarded as necessary in order for the United States of America to prosper as a nation. For the next eight years of George Washington's Presidency, a "New nation," the United States of America, would be founded on the leadership of a man appointed by God under the guidance of his Lord Jesus and the Word of God, so that "the government (would) be on His shoulders." Those next eight years would be a relatively peaceful time for the American people (1 Sa 2:30; Isa 9:6,7; Mt 13:23; Mk 12:28-31; Jn 15:16; Heb 4:12; 1 Jn 1:1).

George Washington understood that "the way and the truth and the life" was found in the Living Word of God, Jesus. For he said, "True religion affords government its surest support. The future of this nation depends on the Christian training of our youth. It is impossible to govern without the Bible."[131] As we shared earlier, George Washington was raised up reading the Scriptures as a youth, leading devotionals, and even presiding as a preacher for his Army soldiers. He knew how valuable the Word of God was in his life, and for the success of his country. As we reported earlier, the Bible was the school text book for our Founding Fathers. George Washington set a precedent for future government leaders when he said, "It is impossible to rightly govern the world without God and the Bible"[132] (Mt 7:26,27; Mk 4:20; Jn 1:14; 10:10; 14:6; Ac 17:11; 2 Ti 3:16,17; 4:2).

"In 1790, Moses Seixas, warden of the Hebrew Congregation of Newport, Rhode Island," wrote a letter "to newly elected President, George Washington." In that letter he wrote, "This Federal Union, . . . we cannot but acknowledge to be the work of the Great God, who ruleth in the Armies of

Heaven, and among the Inhabitants of the Earth, doing whatever seemeth Him good . . . For all these Blessings of civil and religious liberty which we enjoy under an equal benign administration, we desire to send our thanks to the Ancient of Days"[133] (Dt 28:1-14; Isa 61:1 [KJV]; Da 7:9,13,14; Joel 2:11; Rev 19:11-16).

Under the leadership of George Washington, "we were almost the only country on earth to provide equal rights and protections to the Jewish people."[134] God's "Chosen people" were considered by George Washington as "all men . . . created equal." The Lord Jesus, we also believe, blessed the United States of America for blessing the children of Abraham, the Jewish people in this country (Gen 12:1-3; Dt 7:6; Ps 33:12; Ro 10:12,13).

In 1797, George Washington had decided to step down from the Presidency of the United States, and return to his more "simple life" at his home in Mount Vernon. On June 12, 2008, and on September 4, 2008, the Lord Jesus said, "After the War, the Colonists put their weapons down for a time. Many returned to farming like George Washington. (The scriptures state, "They will beat their swords into plowshares and their spears into pruning hooks.") (Isa 2:4).

"When George Washington returned to his home at Mount Vernon, the people struggled then, as they do today. They toiled and labored 'against flesh and blood,' and not against their enemy, Satan. Satan has moved the world into a busyness, into a 'desire for other things' to keep even believers from living a 'simple life' today, from spending time with Jesus, resting in His presence (Ps 19:7; Mt 11:28; Mk 4:14,15,18,19; Lk 10:38-42; Eph 6:12).

"The United States will come back to that 'simple life,' that time of rest enjoyed by the early Colonists. But it will come at the price of many lives lost, because they (Americans) refuse to choose that 'simple life.' They have chosen Satan's world of things, of idols, and of busyness. They will suffer for that in the days ahead, because they refuse the truth that Jesus is their Sabbath rest. He is their peace, and He is their joy. They (Americans) will suffer because they seek joy from 'other things,' from other people and other places, instead of the real joy that comes from Jesus! Choose the 'simple way,' the way of Jesus, and follow Him" (Isa 30:15; 35:8; Mt 7:13,14[KJV]; 11:28,29; Lk 8:11,14; Jn 15:11; 2 Th 2:10; Heb 4:1-11).

Early in the year 2008, the Lord Jesus had asked us to visit Mount Vernon in Virginia. On May 29, 2008, my wife and I again visited the grounds at Mount Vernon, and we walked through the "mansion." We thoroughly enjoyed the beautiful gardens and the landscape there. We understood why George Washington enjoyed being at home. However, we were disappointed that no one mentioned God. In fact, it seemed that George Washington was elevated to a "god-like" status at a "new" museum on the grounds. We also saw a "new" movie depicting a segment of George Washington's life. In the movie, the character representing George Washington used the word "luck," instead of putting his trust in God, in Divine Providence for his victory over the Hessians on a Christmas Eve. At the Mount Vernon "mansion," the elegant furniture, china, and numerous bedrooms revealed a proud showiness like the English people exhibited during the time of the Revolutionary War (Dt 8:17,18; Jer 17:5; Da 3:7; 4:28-30; 6:6,7).

Early in the morning on May 30, 2008, my wife heard these words, "Mount Vernon is an empire . . . You went to England yesterday . . . Brought this country down . . . George Washington was a planter, farmer . . . He did not beat them. He set them free."

The Lord Jesus then said, "Mount Vernon is its own empire, an empire of show and elegance from the England of George Washington and his wife's past. 'You went back to that England yesterday,' which in times past 'brought this country down.' George Washington was a sinner, like all men and women. He was a planter, farmer, who chose to honor his God, his Lord Jesus, trusting in Him for his provision. On his plantations were slaves. 'He did not beat them,' as many slave owners did during that time, but 'set them free' in his own way (Pr 3:5,6; Jer 34:8-10; Mt 23:5-7; Mk 4:14; Lk 9:62; Ac 12:21,22; Ro 3:23).

"George Washington was a man's man, a leader, because he put his faith in God's Divine Providence for his welfare, his family's welfare, and the welfare of his military troops, (and his country). Today, men and women in your society have taken out of Mount Vernon and other historical places, the man, (George Washington), that desired to serve his God. Satan's desire is to elevate men, and discredit any relationship a man or woman has with his and her true God" (Mt 24:9; Jn 14:1; 2 Th 2:3,4,9; 1 Ti 4:1; Rev 12:10,17).

It was reported that, George "Washington was the only prominent, slaveholding Founding Father to emancipate his slaves . . . After the war, Washington often privately expressed a dislike of the institution of slavery." George Washington, in a letter "to a friend," wrote, "I never mean . . . to possess another slave by purchase, it being among my first wishes to see some plan adopted, by which slavery in this Country may be abolished by slow, sure and imperceptible degrees"[135] (Jn 8:34-36; Gal 4:30,31; 5:1; Rev 5:9,10).

George Washington was given a vision at Valley Forge of another War on American soil, the Civil War, which we will share in the next chapter. It was primarily a War regarding slavery. George Washington surely struggled within himself over the issue of slavery, after he received that vision at Valley Forge, and having tolerated slavery up until his death at Mount Vernon. The Civil War would again be a battle between Jesus Christ and Satan over the souls of the American people in the nineteenth century.

AMERICA

☆

"My country, 'tis of thee, Sweet land of liberty,
Of thee I sing: Land where my fathers died,
Land of the pilgrim's pride,
From every mountain side
Let freedom ring!"[136]

                (American slave children during the Civil War sang this song in the movie, *Glory*).

6

PROCLAIM FREEDOM FOR THE SLAVES

"All the officials and people who entered into this covenant agreed that they would free their male and female slaves and no longer hold them in bondage."

Our Lord shared about returning to the "simple life," which many early colonists chose to do after the War for Independence. My wife experienced that simple lifestyle at George Mason's Gunston Hall Plantation in Northern Virginia. Returning to the "simple life," while we were living in Manassas, Virginia, I (Phyllis) signed up for a Community college course on Open Hearth Cooking at Gunston Hall. Early in the morning, I arrived at the kitchen house at that plantation. It seemed as if I stepped back in time to another world, to early colonial times, to a world, we believe, we will experience again in the "End-Times." The Lord Jesus had convicted me to be a part of that class, and to learn how to cook like the early colonial women.

It was so peaceful and quiet that day. There were not any sounds from automobiles, radios, televisions, telephones ringing, nor cell phones. There were no evidences of the "electronic age" there. When I entered the kitchen, there were three other students. Our instructors were all dressed in colonial outfits. The colonial kitchen had a huge fireplace, and there were cast iron pots, black iron tools, and a dutch oven. Our first assignment was to bring in firewood that had already been split and stacked outside. We then filled up buckets of water from the well. We were given a tour of the herb garden, and we actually picked the herbs we would be using for the meal preparation that day.

Our main dish was "Welsh Rabbit." A rabbit had been purchased from the local butcher. At the bottom of a deep cooking pot hanging over a roaring fire, we sauteed leeks, herbs, and bacon. Then we added rabbit that was seasoned and cut up in cubed pieces. When it was cooking over the fire, we covered it with fresh cream, and added flour to thicken the gravy base. We grated oranges and vegetables, beat eggs, shaved sugar, etc. It took us all day to prepare the various dishes for a late afternoon meal. We also made a carrot souffle, which we cooked in the dutch oven. We placed it in the fire, and occasionally we piled hot coals over it.

Finally, we were invited to sit down together and enjoy the meal. The food tasted delicious, and it was worth all of our efforts that day. Returning to a colonial lifestyle has many benefits. It is hard work, but the simplicity of life with neighbors helping neighbors, and living off the land is something we believe God will rebirth within us in America in the "last days." After returning home that evening, I felt so good having spent a day working in a colonial kitchen experiencing that "simple life" style. That lifestyle, we believe, many of the early colonists were able to choose, because they chose to follow Christianity, to follow Jesus Christ, to follow their Bibles, the Word of God (Dt 30:19,20; Mk 1:16-18; 4:14,20; Ac 2:44-46).

When we lived in Whiteville, North Carolina, my husband and I often visited Poplar Grove Plantation outside Wilmington, North Carolina. That plantation was built in 1850, just prior to the Civil War. It was another place where we could walk the grounds, and experience the "simple life" of that past time period. On the grounds was a former slave tenant quarters. In that quarters were a table, benches, and chairs of that Civil War period. My husband, using the same dimensions of that primitive wood furniture, was able to build a sturdy table, bench and two chairs similar to those in the tenant quarters. A blacksmith at the plantation made a cast iron tripod for us to hold cast iron pots of food that could be cooked over a fire. We were again preparing for the days, when we would need those items, when America, we believe, will return to the "simple life" style. The Words in the Bible, and their love of Jesus helped the former tenant slaves endure severe hardships and brutality from many slave-owners (Ps 119:130; 123:2; Jn 14:21; Eph 6:5-8; 2 Ti 2:3; Phm 14-16).

Spreading the Word of God

Our "founding fathers of this nation agreed on the importance of the Bible and faith toward God as the only good foundation for a good education." The Bible was always to "remain" as "the principle text in school" by our Founding Fathers.[137] A Founding Father, John Adams, the second President of the United States, following his predecessor George Washington, shared "in 1813," that "The general principles of which the fathers achieved independence were . . . the general principles of Christianity"[138] (Mt 7:24,25; Gal 4:3-7; 2 Pe 1:1).

John Adams' son, John Quincy Adams, the sixth President of the United States, affirmed his father's sentiments, as well as George Washington's and the Founding Fathers'. In 1825, when John Quincy Adams "was inaugurated as President," he shared in "his inaugural address," . . . "Knowing that 'except the Lord keep the city, the watchman waketh but in vain,' with fervent supplications for His favor, to His overruling providence, I commit, with humble, but fearless confidence, my own fate, and the future destinies of my country." John Quincy Adams had said, "I have myself for many years made it a practice to read through the Bible once a year . . . My custom is, to read four or five chapters every morning." He also shared that, "A man to be a Christian must believe in God, in the Bible, in the Divinity of the Savior's mission"[139] (Dt 17:18,19; Ps 127:1 [KJV]; Pr 3:5,6; Jn 3:16-18; 1 Ti 2:1-3[KJV]; 4:13; Heb 11:6; Rev 1:3).

Our Lord Jesus used those early leaders of our country, we believe, to spread the Gospel, His Word throughout America in the early nineteenth century. Our Founding Fathers believed that following the Bible was essential for the "future survival" of the American colonies. A "committee" of "the Continental Congress" reported on "September 11, 1777," . . . "that the use of the Bible is so universal, and its importance so great," they ordered that the "Committee of Commerce" . . . "import 20,000 Bibles from" countries overseas for use in the American colonies. Immediately, those Bibles were ordered for the "inhabitants of the United States." In 1782, Congress approved a petition for printing "Bibles in America." Founding Father, James McHenry, a signer "of the federal Constitution" stated, "[T]he Holy Scriptures . . . can alone secure to society, order and peace, and to our courts of justice and constitutions of government, purity, stability and usefulness"[140] (Ps 119:9; Pr 29:4[a]; Mt 7:26,27; Ac 6:7; 2 Ti 3:15-17).

The "American Bible Society," which still exists today as a strong Christian organization, began "in 1816." That Bible Society sends Bibles to millions of people throughout the world in their "native language." Through that Christian agency "hundreds of thousands of Bibles" were delivered to "frontier families (who were) hungry" for the Word of God, and for "daily Bible reading." The Cherokee Indian tribe was able to read the Bible "in their native language," and many became believers in Jesus Christ, which helped to sustain them during their trying times in America during the nineteenth century[141] (Mt 5:6; Lk 1:53; Jn 6:27,51; Ac 2:6; 12:24; Rev 5:9,10).

Many Indians, we previously shared, who had served another 'god,' Satan, were turning their hearts over to Jesus. Satan was losing control over millions of souls in America. "The American Tract Society," which began in "1825," delivered millions of Bible "tracts and Christian books" throughout the American states and into "the West." The Word of God was being sent by God's missionaries and preachers into the new frontier[142] (Pr 11:30; Mk 16:15; Ac 19:20; 26:17,18).

Founding Father, Benjamin Rush, a "signer of the Declaration of Independence," shared that, "[T]he Bible . . . should be read in our schools in preference to all other books." From the beginning of our nation, "up to the 1940's and 1950's," . . . "the first book in the classroom was the Bible" . . . "In the public schools of America," . . . "the Bible was required reading." Much of a student's "school day was devoted to memorizing and reciting passages from" . . . "the Bible." We have previously shared about the "New England Primer." The school classroom textbook that followed the "Primer" was the "'McGuffey Readers' series." That series also had stories about the Bible, and revealed biblical "allusions"[143] (Ps 45:1; 119:11; Gal 3:24[KJV]; 2 Ti 2:15[KJV]; 3:15-17).

Since 1836, the McGuffey Reader "was filled with biblical principles and religious instructions."[144] Those school text books were read by "five generations of Americans and sold about 130 million copies." William McGuffey was a teacher and "he preached" as a servant of the Bible, the Word of God.[145] Using the "New England Primer" and the "McGuffey Readers," teachers throughout the United States, we believe, were able to share openly among their students the Word of God, and their faith in Jesus Christ. God was using teachers and preachers to raise up generations of Americans on the "tested stone, a precious cornerstone, for a sure foundation," on Jesus Christ, well up into the twentieth century. The United

States of America would still continue under the Lordship of Jesus through the nineteenth century. Our Lord Jesus would be, we believe, the central figure in the abolishment of slavery as the "War between the States" drew near (Isa 28:16; Jn 8:34-36; 13:13; Eph 4:11-13; 6:4; 2 Ti 4:2; Heb 5:12-14).

The Courts would confirm that the United States was built on the foundational Rock, Jesus Christ prior to the Civil War. In 1811, in the case of "The People v. Ruggles," the New York Supreme Court held that blaspheming the name of "Jesus Christ" was a criminal offense. The Court determined "[that blasphemy against God . . . and profane ridicule of Christ or the Holy Scriptures, are offenses punishable at the common law, whether uttered by words or writings]." The Court stated that, "We are a Christian people, and the morality of the country is deeply engrafted upon Christianity . . . [We are] people whose manners . . . and whose morals have been . . . inspired . . . by means of the Christian religion"[146] (Dt 5:11; Mt 12:30-32; Ac 11:26[b]; 1 Co 10:4; 1 Pe 4:16).

In 1844, the Supreme Court of the United States," in a case between "Vidal v. Girard's Executors" affirmed the Bible and the Christian faith in the United States. In their decision it was proclaimed that, "The Christian religion is as much a part of the public law as any of these guarantees . . . That Christianity is a part of the public law . . . , if there were no other source of authority, the churches, meeting-houses, spires, . . . over the face of the country all show" men's faith in the God of the Bible. It was further stated that, "Why may not the Bible, and especially the New Testament . . . be read and taught as a divine revelation in the college? . . . Where can the purist principles of morality be learned so clearly or so perfectly as from the New Testament? Where are benevolence, the love of truth, sobriety, . . . so powerfully . . . inculcated as in the sacred volume?"[147] (Mt 7:28, 29; Lk 4:15; Jn 14:6; 18:37; Ro 13:1-10; 1 Jn 1:7-9).

Even the highest Court in the land upheld Christianity, upholding faith in the Lord Jesus as a standard of "public law

... over the face of the country." We believe that the Courts, Christian Bible societies, the teachers in public schools, and the preachers were powerfully influential for the Gospel of Jesus Christ to be spread like "fire" throughout America, which kindled the "Second Great Awakening" in America (Mt 28:20; Lk 12:49; Ac 18:28; 20:20).

"The Second Great Awakening" was the "second great . . . revival in United States History, and consisted of renewed personal salvation, (receiving Jesus in their hearts to save them from their sins), (which was) experienced in revival meetings." "Camp" meetings were held in different parts of the country lasting "several days . . . with multiple preachers." The Methodist Church established "ministers known as circuit riders, who sought out people in remote frontier locations . . . The Awakening influenced numerous reform movements, especially abolitionists," as well as "temperance," and "women's rights"[148] (Ps 85:6; Isa 57:15; Mk 16:15,16; Ac 2:40,41; 16:30,31; Ro 10:9,10; Rev 19:14; 20:9).

The "circuit riders" were "preachers" who rode on horses, and spread "the Gospel." They rode "basically (in) the first half century following the War" (Revolutionary War). Those "travelling ministers" distributed "Bibles and tracts." Their influence was to "form one of the roots of the public education movement that was originally intended to get everyone to read the Bible." The "circuit riders" goal was "to speak to the heart and win souls to Jesus"[149] (Dt 17:19; Pr 11:30; Jer 22:2; Mt 10:11-13; 16:24-27; 1 Co 9:19-23; Eph 2:7; 3:16,17; 1 Ti 4:4-6,13).

During that "Second Great Awakening," the "Sword of the Spirit," the Word of God was cutting through the enemy's territories in America through the ministry of the "circuit riders." The Word was like "fire" burning up patches of Satan's darkness over the land, and sending light into the new frontier. It was sweeping like a "consuming fire" in the "camp meetings." The Lord Jesus was also moving with the "fire" power of the Holy Spirit into the hearts of the abolitionists throughout America, those strongly opposed to slavery, those willing to fight for freedom from the bondage of Satan. The abolitionists understood that their Founding Fathers declared independence for "all men, (because they) are created equal," and that skin color had nothing to do with dividing or segregating God's creation of mankind from one another (Gen 2:7; Jer 23:29; Lk 4:14; 24:30-32; Jn 8:34-36; 1 Co 12:25; 2 Co 8:13; 10:3,4; Gal 3:28; 2 Ti 2:25,26; Heb 12:28,29).

Let My People Go!

Early in the morning on November 18, 2008, my wife heard this word, "Moses." As we previously shared, George Washington was compared to Moses in the Bible. George Washington, the Christian leader of the American people, was recognized as the People's deliverer from King George III and tyrannical England. King George III, like Pharoah of Egypt, "hardened" his "heart" to the cries of the American people, who desired to be free from English tyranny. George Washington, like Moses, was used by our Lord Jesus to "Let My People Go"! (Ex 3:9,10; 7:3; 8:1; Ac 7:35).

In a "well-documented" account, as reported by Anthony Sherman, an officer with George Washington at Valley Forge, George Washington shared with him another vision of the United States of America.[150] A "voice" said, "Son of the Republic, look and learn." George Washington then saw a vision of America's "villages, towns and cities" springing up over "the whole land from the Atlantic to the Pacific . . . That mysterious voice" said, "Son of the Republic, the end of the century cometh." Then George Washington saw "a dark shadowy angel turned his face southward, and from Africa." He saw an evil "spectre approach" America moving "slowly over every town and city" (Ex 10:21,22; Dan 8:17; Lk 23:44).

George Washington then saw the American people "set themselves in battle array against each other." Then he "saw a bright angel, on whose brow rested a crown of light. On" that brow was written "the word, 'Union,' bearing the American flag." The flag was "placed between the divided nation." The angel stated, "Remember ye are brethren." Then George Washington saw the American people removing "their weapons" and becoming "friends" again, "united under the National Standard" (Isa 2:4; Rev 10:5,6).

The second peril that George Washington saw on American soil was the Civil War. The slaves in America, who originally came "from Africa," were revealed in that vision. The "issue of a terrible civil conflict" over slavery, in which "brothers fought brothers," was a cause of a "divided nation." The third peril on American soil that George Washington saw that day had to do with America in the very last days. We will share that vision later in this book in America's Future.

We believe the "shadowy angel" that George Washington saw was of the devil, who brought an evil "spectre" to America, slavery. Satan used his evil wickedness to elevate men as slave owners over the African-American race. That, we believe, caused a great division in the once "united" states. A battle ensued between the Northern and Southern States over primarily the issue of slavery. It was a battle, instigated, we believe, by Satan the "murderer." No other battle had ever occurred on American soil, in which thousands of American people killed each other. However, our Lord Jesus would prevail over Satan in America, regaining this country under His banner, "the National Standard" united in "Union" with one another as a Christian nation. Our Lord Jesus in His sovereign power removed the devil's "weapons" of warfare over slavery in America (Ps 133:1; Pr 4:19; Isa 62:10[KJV]; Mt 12:26; Jn 8:44; Ac 26:17,18; Ro 16:17,18; 1 Jn 2:9,10; Jude 6).

The Nation of Israel

The Lord Jesus compared slavery in America to the enslavement of the modern nation of Israel. We believe our Lord plans to remove the devil's "weapons" of warfare against Israel. George Washington was considered a deliverer, a "Moses" for the American people, and was victorious in letting God's "people go." In like manner, the Lord Jesus spoke to us about delivering the modern nation of Israel. After fasting and worshiping before the Lord, I saw a vision of jet planes flying over Jerusalem in the direction of Iran. Then I saw a vision of the character of Jesus in the video series, *Jesus of Nazareth*.[151] Jesus was pointing in an angry manner in the direction of Iran, and calling them a "brood of vipers." He was pointing at the jet planes, sending them in the direction of Iran. Then I saw an aerial view of what appeared to be Iran. Bombs were dropping down on that land, and the explosions were spreading out, destroying specific targets.

The Lord Jesus then said, "The Iranian leaders are preparing to destroy the temple of God, the temple is My people. Just as I hardened Pharoah's heart against My people, so I have hardened the President of Iran's heart against My People to show forth My glory, to show forth My signs and wonders. The Israelites are crying out, 'When Lord? When will you let your people go from the enslavement of the Muslim nations around us? And who will support us?' God said, 'I will be your God in this battle against Satan. Just as I was in Egypt with My people against Pharoah and the Egyptians.' This war will influence the whole world. There will be a great conflagration in the Middle East" (Ex 3:7-9, 12, 20; 4:21; 1 Co 3:16,17; Rev 12:7-11); (November 20, 2008).

Harriet Tubman

Another deliverer of the American people prior to and during the Civil War was an African American slave, Harriet Tubman. Harriet Tubman was also called, "Moses." She was "a devout Christian," a strong believer in Jesus Christ. When she was a child, her mother told her "Bible Stories." Harriet Tubman was "born into slavery in Dorchester County, Maryland." When she was a child, Harriet Tubman "was beaten and whipped by various (slave) owners." "In 1849," Harriet Tubman was able to escape to freedom in Pennsylvania following "the Underground Railroad." The "Underground Railroad" was an underground "network," a "well-organized system" . . . "of free blacks, white abolitionists, and Christian activists." Those people utilized different ways to "hide and protect" slaves, so they might gain freedom in the Northern states of America[152] (Ex 2:1-3; Jos 6:17; 1 Ki 18:13; Pr 28:12; Jn 3:16; Ac 5:40-41).

Harriet Tubman believed that the Lord Jesus was calling her to return to the Southern states to free her people from slavery, and bring them home to the "promised land." She made several "missions" and rescued many "slaves." Harriet Tubman was proud that she "never lost a passenger" on "the Underground Railroad." She had "a passionate faith in God." Harriet Tubman found her "guidance" from the Lord Jesus, and "in the Old Testament" stories of "deliverance"[153] (Gen 50:24; Ex 3:8-10; 15:1-21; Isa 35:4; Jn 16:13; Heb 11:23).

The Lord Jesus used an African American woman to "Let My People Go." The slave owners were like Pharoah of Egypt, whose hearts were "hardened" from letting the American slaves free from their bondage. Yet, Satan was losing territorial ground in America through the efforts of another "Moses" (Ex 5:1,2; 2 Ti 2:26; Heb 3:7,13).

The Negro Spiritual

Many slaves believed in the Lord Jesus. They had the "faith" to understand that Almighty God would eventually set them free from slavery. Many slaves understood that true "freedom" was found only in their "Savior," Jesus Christ, "freedom from the bondage of sin" and Satan. On the other hand, the slave owners and their supporters, we believe, were slaves to Satan, slaves to evil brutality and hatred towards a people with a darker skin color. The "Christian slaves" sang "Negro" spirituals[154] to overcome the torments of enslavement and strengthen their faith (Jn 8:31,36; 10:10[a]; Ac 26:17,18; Ro 6:16-18; 8:21; 2 Co 11:14,15; Gal 4:3-7; 5:1; Eph 5:19).

One of those spirituals was "Go Down Moses." This was the first verse of that spiritual.

"Go down Moses
Way down in Egypt land.
Tell Ole Pharoah
To let my people go"[155]

The Lord Jesus heard the "groans" and cries of His people, and He would set the slaves free from the bondage of Satan. In this way, the African-Americans could truly sing the "American Negro" song, "Free at Last." These are the first and fourth verses of that "Negro spiritual" (Ex 2:23-25; Mk 10:31; Jn 6:40; 1 Th 4:16,17).

"Free at last, free at last
I thank God I'm free at last
Free at last, free at last
I thank God I'm free at last

Some of these mornings, bright and fair
I thank God I'm free at last
Goin' meet King Jesus in the air
I thank God I'm free at last"[156]

Setting Our Hearts and Souls Free

In a deeper sense, the Lord Jesus has revealed to us ways in which we can set our hearts free by "Letting go and Letting God" have His way in us. On June 9, 1999, the Lord Jesus shared this story with us, which He compared to the War between the States. The Lord Jesus said, "Let Me tell you a story. 'There was a man who had two sons.' One son wanted to follow Jesus, while the other son chose to go his own way. The son who chose his own way lost all the worldly goods he had obtained, selfishly. He was left destitute without a penny to his name. His face was covered with shame (Lk 15:11-19).

"The other son, who followed Jesus, though he was angry at his brother at first for going his own way, learned by sitting with Jesus, that he was called to help his lost brother. This son wept as Jesus did for the other son who chose to go his own way. Rather than walk past his brother, he went to care for him. The son that lost everything was so ashamed, that he did not want his brother's help, initially. But when he saw that his brother really loved him, he allowed his brother to help him walk again and find Jesus. This story is about two parables, 'The Prodigal Son' and 'The Good Samaritan.' The man and woman who follow Jesus learn that God's love is what motivates a man or woman to change." (This was an example of how we believe the Americans in the free states came to help the Americans in the Southern states after the War) (Lk 7:44-50; 10:30-35; 15:20-31; Jn 8:33-36).

The Lord shared more about freedom, about setting our hearts free. He said, "Freedom is (embodied in) forgiveness. Forgiveness sets you free from the ones who originated pain on you. Freedom is not having to worry about being hurt again. You are free to endure the pain for another's salvation. When you are free, you can share your love without becoming defensive, when someone opposes Jesus in you. You can then see the darkness of opposition in a new light, and love those who opposed you by being honest and forthright with them. Freedom is what the slaves began to experience after the Civil War (Lev 19:17,18; Mt 6:14,15; 18:21,22, 32-35; Lk 6:27,35,36; Eph 4:15,25,26; 2 Ti 2:25; Heb 12:2,3).

"Slave owners were too proud to let their slaves go free, free to be picked up in the arms of Jesus. Like Pharoah, the slave owners would not 'let My people go.' Slave owners possessed their slaves like parents possess their children. They, (the slave owners) said, 'They are our slaves,' not yours, not Jesus' (Ex 5:2; Jer 34:11; Mt 19:13,14; Gal 4:30,31; 5:13).

"Being abandoned as an infant (has been) a core issue for you, (others, and many slaves). For an infant emotionally is not able to know how to cope with that abandonment, so the child unknowingly splits off from its true self. That emotional split displays the false self, while the real self goes into hiding within the soul. Throughout your life you seek not to be abandoned, alone ever again. So the false self in the child learns to find comfort in being false, in pleasing others, in unclean relationships, and in all kinds of dependencies and addictions. Those comforts, they believe unconsciously, keep them from ever experiencing that fear of abandonment again. It is a fear that runs deep to the soul, back into infancy (Ex 1:16,22; Pr 28:12[b]; Isa 55:12-14; Eze 16:3-5,15,20,21; Lk 9:61,62; Jn 12:42,43; Gal 1:10).

"Remember that Jesus picks up infants, holds them close in His arms, and does not let them go until they do not feel abandoned from their real self anymore, not alone. In the arms of Jesus, you can feel safe and you can be healed. Jesus will hold you in His arms, so your real self won't be split off emotionally, hidden, but rather loved and comforted by the Comforter, who will never abandon you. Stay in My arms until your true self feels protected, then I will let you walk by My side, holding My hand. Let Me be your shield against 'all the fiery darts of the evil one,' that come against My true witnesses (Ps 27:10; 139:1-18; Isa 40:11; 54:4; Mt 9:25; Mk 9:36,37; 10:13-16; 2 Co 1:3-5; Eph 6:16[KJV]).

"That abandonment in infancy is (when parents) never allow their infant to come into the arms of Jesus. The parents are too proud to let this happen. The parents have to keep the 'little ones' in their arms, in their wicked ways apart from Me. 'These are our children,' they say, 'Not yours'! The infant's false self chooses the comfort of his or her parents' arms, never knowing that Jesus' arms can free their real self. This was and is like a slavery, (like the slave owners possession of slaves) (Isa 30:15,16; Jer 7:18; Mt 18:6,7,10; Gal 4:30,31).

"When a man is willing to stand up in Jesus against the devil, he helps a people, a nation, so they may no longer live in tyranny, in a slavery. When a man stands up against those who control and intimidate, he overcomes timidity. But if a man chooses timidity in order to be accepted by those who intimidate him (or her), it will keep you from ever finding your real self. You will receive a false respect, a disrespect, for you have submitted to demons of intimidation, insults, and threats. I have called you to live a fruitful life free in Jesus. Many Americans, Christians, abolitionists, and slaves chose courage over timidity prior to, during, and after the Civil War" (Jos 1:1-9; Ps 27:1-3; 35:1-4; Lk 2:48-50; Jn 15:16; Eph 6:13; 2 Ti 1:7; 4:16-18; 1 Pe 5:8-10). (Messages received from God on October 2, 1998, July 19, 2003, and October 31, 2008).

While the American people were about to fight over the issue of slavery, who would be the mighty leader the Lord Jesus would raise up to deliver and free the American slaves? That man would be Abraham Lincoln, the sixteenth President of the United States.

Abraham Lincoln

Prior to the Civil War, the "issue of slavery" was "of great division and disagreement" among the men in the Northern and Southern states. "In 1854," the House of Representatives "turned to Jesus Christ and the God of the Bible for comfort and strength." In the "H. Res. 397" in 1854, "the U.S. House of Representatives" declared, "Christianity; in its general principles, is the great conservative element on which we must rely for the purity and permanence of free institutions." [157] With that "great division" becoming wider between the Northern and Southern states, the Senator from Illinois, Abraham

Lincoln, was elected President of the United States. When he gave his farewell address to his constituents in Springfield, Senator Lincoln put his trust in Almighty God (Ps 22:27; Mk 3:23-27; Lk 1:16; Ac 26:20).

He gave that address in February 1861, prior to becoming the President of the United States on "March 4, 1861." In that address, he stated, "With a task before me greater than that which rested upon (George) Washington. Without the assistance of the Divine Being whoever attended him, (George Washington), I cannot succeed. With that assistance, I cannot fail. Trusting in Him (Jesus) who can go with me, and remain with you, and be everywhere for good."[158] President Lincoln understood that he was just a man, and that his reliance on God was essential in his Presidential position of leadership in the United States (Ps 32:7; Pr 3:5,6; Jn 14:1; 15:4).

Just prior to the Civil War in Abraham Lincoln's "First Inaugural Address," he stated, "If the Almighty ruler of Nations, with His eternal truth and justice, be on your side of the North or on yours of the South, that truth, and that justice, will surely prevail . . . Christianity, and a firm reliance on Him; (Jesus), who has never yet forsaken this favored land, are still competent to adjust, . . . all our present difficulty."[159] Abraham Lincoln, just like George Washington, was putting his trust in the Lord Jesus Christ for the outcome of that "great division" between the States. President Lincoln shared, "It's more important that we pray to be on God's side rather than pray for Him to be on our side."[160] We know that God was on President Lincoln's side (Ps 5:11; 26:3; Mic 6:8; Mt 6:9-13; 2 Co 1:10,11; 3:4; Heb 13:5).

In his "Annual Message to Congress" on "December 1, 1862," President Lincoln shared, "We know how to save the Union . . . In giving freedom to the slave, we assure freedom to the free—honorable alike in what we give and what we preserve, . . . and God must forever bless."[161] We believe God's blessings fell completely on the "Union." We believe that Abraham Lincoln was called by the Lord Jesus "to save the Union." To follow God's calling "to save the Union," on New Year's Day, January 1, 1863, President Lincoln issued "the Emancipation Proclamation," which proclaimed freedom for all slaves in all the States fighting against the Union[162] (Dt 15:12-15; Jer 34:10; Ac 13:47,48).

"The U.S. Senate endorsed legislation" calling upon "Jesus Christ" for His assistance in the War.[163] President Lincoln responded to that legislation, and proclaimed a "National Day of Humiliation, Fasting, and Prayer" on "March" 13, 1863, to take place in "April 1863." In that "Proclamation," Abraham Lincoln wrote, "The Senate of the United States: devoutly recognizing the Supreme authority and just government of Almighty God in all the affairs of men and nations, has, by a resolution, requested the President to designate and set apart a day for National prayer and humiliation . . . It is the duty of nations, as well as of men, to owe their dependence upon the overruling power of God, to confess their sins and transgressions, in humble sorrow, yet with the assured hope that genuine repentance will lead to mercy and pardon, and to recognize the sublime truth announced in the Holy Scriptures and proven by all history, that those nations only are blessed whose God is the Lord (Jesus) . . . But we have forgotten God, . . . we have become too self-sufficient to feel the necessity and preserving grace, too proud to pray to the God that made us . . . It behooves us, then, to humble ourselves before the offended Power, to confess our national sins, and to pray for clemency and forgiveness"[164] (2 Ch 7:14,15; Neh 1:4; Ps 10:4; 33:12; Isa 30:15; Ac 4:29-31; Ro 2:4-8; 1 Jn 1:8-10).

President Lincoln put his trust in the Lord Jesus, and the "Holy Scriptures." Former President Ronald Reagan shared that, "Abraham Lincoln had steeped himself in the Bible during the most dire days of the Civil War . . . Lincoln relied on the Bible and Judeo-Christian principles to defend the abolitionists . . . Should Moses have told the children of Israel to live in slavery rather than dare the wilderness? Should (Jesus) Christ have refused the cross? . . . Abraham Lincoln called the Bible 'the best gift God has given to man . . . But for it, we would not know right from wrong' . . . Abraham Lincoln said, 'I have been driven many times to my knees by the conviction that I have nowhere else to go!' . . . No one can serve in this office without understanding and believing exactly what he said . . . (President Lincoln had the) faith to walk with Him (Jesus) and trust in His word"[165] (Ps 138:2[b]; Pr 4:4; Isa 35:8-10; Lk 8:21; 24:15; Jn 19:16,17; Ac 17:11; Heb 3:7,8[KJV]).

Former President Ronald Reagan stated further, "On the eve of the Battle of Gettysburg, in November 1863, Abraham Lincoln . . . (said), 'I went into my room and got down on my knees in prayer.' He had 'never before' prayed 'with as much earnestness."[166] A clergyman from Illinois, who talked with President Lincoln, asked him, "Mr. President, Do you love Jesus?" . . . President Lincoln then responded, "When I went to Gettysburg and saw the graves of thousands of our soldiers, I then and there consecrated myself to Christ . . . Yes, I do love Jesus" . . . Even a "long-time friend of Abraham Lincoln," a Mr. "Noah Brooks" said, "He freely expressed himself to me as having a hope of blessed immortality through Jesus Christ."[167] President Lincoln followed the precedence set by George Washington for future Presidents, and set by our Founding Fathers. He put his trust in the Bible, the Living Word of God, and his Lord Jesus! (Lk 22:40-44; Jn 3:16; 6:51; 21:16,17; Col 3:16; 2 Ti 1:10; Heb 2:13).

President Lincoln gave his "Second Inaugural Address" on "March 4, 1865," about a month prior to the end of the War, and prior to his assassination by John Wilkes Booth. In that address, President Lincoln said, "Both (the Union and the Confederacy) read the same Bible, and pray to the same God; and each invokes His aid against the other . . . The prayers of both could not be answered . . . The Almighty has his own purposes. 'Woe unto the world because of offences! For it must needs be that offences come; but woe to that man by whom the offence cometh!' If we shall suppose that American Slavery is one of those offences . . . He now wills to remove, . . . this . . . (being) the woe due to those by whom the offence came, shall we discern therein any departure from those divine attributes which the believers in a Living God always ascribe to Him? . . . It must be said 'the judgments of the Lord, are true and righteous altogether' . . . With malice toward none; with charity for all; . . . as God gives us to see the right, let us . . . bind up the nation's wounds; . . . and cherish a just and lasting peace, among ourselves"[168] (Ps 19:9[KJV]; 147:3; Isa 55:8,9; Mt 18:7[KJV]; Jn 1:12-14; Col 3:15).

Abraham Lincoln proclaimed that the Living God, Jesus Christ, would have His way in the War primarily against slavery. He, like a prophet and wise man in the Bible, was called by God, we believe, to proclaim righteousness to all men and women. As we recall the words George Washington heard, "Remember, ye are brethren," so President Lincoln summoned the American people to "bind up their wounds," and provide brotherly love to all the people in the United States. In the Bible, Jesus said, "I am sending you prophets and wise men and teachers. Some of them you will kill." And so that mighty leader and wise man, Abraham Lincoln, who believed in Jesus, was killed. Yet, he was providentially influential in setting all men free regardless of their skin color (Mt 23:34[a],35; Lk 10:34[KJV]; Jn 13:35; 14:6; 1 Pe 2:17).

The Lord Jesus said of Abraham Lincoln, "That Senator from Illinois, Abraham Lincoln, was sent by God to set the African Americans, the slaves free, and men free from sin, and free from the sin of slavery. Abraham Lincoln was given a vision of the Founding Fathers. Abe Lincoln saw that the United States was 'a new nation conceived in liberty and dedicated to the proposition that all men are created equal.' Abe Lincoln saw the 'light,' to 'fight the good fight (of faith)' against enslavement to sin. He saw the storm coming on the (American) land that would eventually bring freedom to all men. (George Washington had been given a similar vision of that storm) (Ex 3:10; Ps 107:25[KJV]; Isa 6:8,9; 61:1; Jn 8:12; Ro 8:2; 1 Ti 6:12).

"Abe Lincoln was thirsty for the Word. Abe knew about Jesus early in his life. 'Honest Abe' was a humble man, a man of principles, a man who loved God. Abe suffered death for standing up for My principles, that 'all men are created equal,' no matter what color, race, nationality, or tongue. He turned to Jesus for his hope, and I raised him up to be a 'man of God' during the Civil War. In those days, 'men of God' were still respected men, who followed the Word of God" (Gen 1:26,27; Pr 12:7[a]; Mt 5:6; Jn 7:37; Ro 3:23; 2 Ti 3:15-17; Ja 4:6-10; Rev 5:9). (Messages received from the Lord Jesus on November 16, and 19, 1994, February 12, 1999, and November 4, 2008.)

The 54th Massachusetts Infantry

During the Civil War, President Lincoln commissioned a regiment of "negro soldiers," "the 54th Massachusetts Infantry." A "Robert Gould Shaw," a young Army officer, was promoted to Colonel and assigned to become the commanding officer of that regiment, as reported in the movie, *Glory*.[169] During the Civil War, Colonel Shaw wrote letters to his parents, who were abolitionists. Those letters are kept at a library at Harvard University. The movie, *Glory*, was based on those letters.

In that movie, an African American infantry man from South Carolina, who was in "the 54th Massachusetts Infantry," played the character, "Jupiter." He shared his faith in the Lord Jesus. The regiment of African American soldiers sang a song to the Lord Jesus before going into battle at Fort Wagner, which was held by the Confederate troops. In the middle of that song, "Jupiter" said, "Lord, Tomorrow we go into battle, so Lordy, let me fight with the rifle in the one hand and the Good Book, (the Bible, which he was holding) in the other.

Then if I should die at the muzzle of the rifle, die on water or on land, I know that you, Blessed Jesus, Almighty, are with me, and I have no fear!" That regiment shared, like "Jupiter," the same faith in Jesus Christ, when they sang that song to the Lord (2 Ch 20:20-24; Ps 149:6-9; Mt 28:20; Jn 14:27; Ac 22:6-10; Php 1:20-23).

President Lincoln "credited those men of color with helping turn the tide of the war." After "the 54th Massachusetts Infantry" displayed such courage at Fort Wagner, Congress authorized the enlistment of many more "black troops." Those men were fighting for their "brothers'" freedom from slavery. We believe their faith in the Lord Jesus gave them the courage to "fight the good fight of faith" for the Union and for freedom (Php 1:14; 1 Ti 6:12).

The United States Christian Commission

Another organization working under the authorization of President Lincoln was "The United States Christian Commission." The "purpose" of that "Commission" . . . "was to care for the spiritual and physical needs of Union soldiers." That "Commission" . . . "sent almost five thousand volunteers to the battlefields and military hospitals of the Civil War" in both the Northern and Southern States. Those volunteers also ministered to "wounded confederates."[170] Volunteers "distributed millions of salvation tracts and thousands of Bibles to the soldiers," and "pastors volunteered to preach in the camps"[171] (Mt 25:35,36; Lk 10:33-35; Jn 21:16; Ac 15:35; Tit 1:3; 1 Pe 5:2).

On one occasion, a "chaplain, Rev. Willie Ragland preached very faithfully the gospel of Christ" to the Confederate troops in November 1863, off the banks of the "Rapidan River" in Virginia. A new believer in Jesus, a Confederate soldier named "Goodwin," wanted "to be baptized in the Rapidan River." The Union soldiers had camped on the other side of the River.

The Confederate soldiers sang "that grand old hymn, 'There is a Fountain Filled with Blood.'" Many soldiers from "the Northern army joined in the song. Both armies were at peace as they witnessed the death of the old man into the resurrection of the new man through Jesus Christ our Lord"[172] (Mk 16:16; Ac 16:30-33; Ro 6:4-6; Eph 4:22-24; Col 3:16; 1 Pe 1:12).

When the army troops from both the Northern and Southern States honored the one true Living God, Jesus Christ, they experienced His presence of peace. George Washington experienced a similar presence of peace when he heard a "voice" say, "Remember, ye are brethren." In 1865, shortly after the war had ended, the United States Congress approved the 13th Amendment to the United States Constitution, abolishing slavery in all the States in America. Under the leadership of President Abraham Lincoln, once again, the people of the United States of America developed deeper roots into the Living God, the Lord Jesus. America's foundation was on the Rock, built from the Cornerstone, Jesus, to love the "brethren" their neighbors as themselves. We believe the blessings produced by "The Second Great Awakening," resulted in the peace that followed the Civil War. With the assistance of "The United States Christian Commission," the Word of God spread like "fire" in the "camp meetings" for both the Union and Confederate soldiers. Satan, the "murderer," again lost territorial ground in the hearts of many of the American people (Jer 20:9; Mt 13:23; Mk 4:39,40; 12:31; Lk 6:47,48; Jn 13:34,35; 16:33; Eph 2:20; 4:3; Col 2:6,7).

More On Slavery

On September 10, 2008, I, (Mark) received a vision of our blinds being shut on a window in our living room, and a shade was being pulled down at the window. The Lord then reminded me of a vision my wife received several years ago. In that vision, a white board was being stained. Then a young

African American girl was crying in deep pain. Then I saw a vision of a hallway at a Christian middle school where my wife and I team-taught middle school students. That hallway was outside our classroom.

(My husband and I team-taught a history class in the school year 2002-2003. The Christian school was in the building of a Baptist Church. In the fall, we prepared a display of notable American people on the bulletin board outside our classroom. A few days after I, (Phyllis) placed those pictures on the bulletin board, we were approached by a church member advising us to remove a picture of Phillis Wheatley, an African-American woman. Phillis Wheatley's poetry influenced the abolitionists during the Civil War. It was apparent to us, that the Church still held prejudices against the African-American race.)

Phillis Wheatley

Phillis Wheatley was "born in 1753 in Africa." When she was seven years old, Phillis Wheatley was sold at a slave auction to the "Wheatley family," who lived in "Boston," Massachusetts. The "Christian compassion" of that family encouraged her to read "the Bible," and learn the "English" language. The Lord Jesus gave Phillis Wheatley the gift of writing "poetry." A "theme . . . throughout her poetry, is the salvation message of Christianity—that all men and women, regardless of race or class, are in need of salvation"[173] (Gen 37:28; Ac 13:26; 1 Co 12:4-8; Heb 5:7-9; 2 Pe 3:9; Jude 1-3).

In one of her poems, she wrote in the second stanza,

"And mark the systems of revolving worlds.
Still more, ye sons of science ye receive
The blissful news by messengers from heav'n,
How Jesus blood for your redemption flows.
See Him with hands outstretched upon the cross;
Immense compassion in His bosom glows;

He hears revilers, nor resents their scorn:
What matchless mercy in the Son of God!
When the whole human race by sin had fall'n,
He deigned to die that they might rise again,
And share with in the sublimest skies,
Life without death, and glory without end."

"Phillis Wheatley received her freedom . . . in 1778 . . . Her life was an inspiring example to future generations of African-Americans. In the 1830s, abolitionists reprinted her poetry and the powerful ideas contained in her deeply moving verse stood against the institution of slavery."[174] As a strong African-American believer in Jesus, Phillis Wheatley gave a "Second Great Awakening" to the abolitionists prior to the Civil War.

Regarding the visions on September 10, the Lord said, "The nation of the United States of America was blinded to the wickedness and evil of slavery prior to, during, and even after the Civil War, blinded by Satan. The Lord Jesus looks at the heart, not one's skin color. What God created as beautiful, man has stained. He had stained the African-American race through slavery. The anguish and pain of being treated as slaves, less than human, had been the result of that stain (Ex 3:9; 1 Sa 16:7; Eze 16:15; 28:17; 2 Co 4:4; Heb 11:36-38).

"A 'wall' was set up by Satan through men (causing separation) between blacks (African-Americans) and whites. That 'wall,' though not as pronounced today, continues into the twenty-first century. A dark 'wall of hostility' still existed between white and black (African-Americans) at that Baptist Church, where you both taught students in school" (1 Co 11:18; Eph 2:14; Tit 3:10; Ja 2:1-7).

Senator from Illinois

On November 4, 2008, "Election Day," I received some visions from our Lord Jesus around 10:30 a.m. to 10:45 a.m.

In the first vision, I saw what appeared to be the African-American President-elect floating in the air about four feet off the ground. He was wearing a white garment. People were looking up to him as if he was an "angel." In the next vision, I saw his arms outstretched with light around him. He appeared to be a "Messiah" in that vision. On December 4, 2008, the Lord Jesus gave me further visions, after we fasted and worshipped before the Lord. In the first vision, I saw a dark-skinned man in Africa holding a shield. That man was only wearing a pair of ragged shorts. Then I saw a vision of the recently elected President of the United States dressed in what appeared to be an affluent suit. Finally, I saw a vision of a man shooting a gun at other people in one of the "big" cities in America.

The Lord Jesus then said, "It is not a coincidence that you are ready to write on the chapter on slavery; for it is 'Election Day' and the United States is about to choose an African-American President. He is the new black, African-American 'Messiah,' appearing to be like an 'angel' in 'sheep's clothing.' What many Americans learned during the days of slavery and after the Civil War, was that God Almighty does not look at skin color, but the heart of a man and a woman (Jer 17:9,10; Mt 7:15; 24:24-27; 1 Co 4:5).

"Today, many are looking at the skin color of a man to lead the country. The color of the man does not make the man. It is the heart of man after My heart that makes the true man; the man that follows the truth, one that follows the Word of God. This is America's new 'Messiah,' but there is only one Messiah (1 Sa 13:14; Mt 4:4; Mk 1:16-18; Ac 13:22; Eph 4:4-6).

"As President of the United States, the Senator from Illinois has a calling on his life, as have all the Presidents of the United States. It is a call to the Word of God to unite the American people under one banner, the banner of Jesus Christ. However, that Senator has been choosing his own call, the call to those special interest groups, who violate and oppose the Word of God, who oppose the true Lord Jesus. When a President forsakes his true calling, he will quickly see the demise and fall of this country. George Washington set a godly precedence for all Presidents. (For he understood,) 'Unless the Lord builds the house,' the 'House' of the United States of America, (including) the House of Representatives, the House of Senators, the 'White' House, the 'House' of the Supreme Court, (etc.), 'its builders labor in vain' (Ps 127:1; Isa 11:10; Lk 5:31; 6:49; Jn 17:23; Heb 2:2; 12:3); received November 13, 2008.

"Your Bible speaks clearly about My warnings for the 'last days.' Many have 'itching ears,' today, and do not want to hear the truth. They want 'what their itching ears want to hear' . . . They have turned 'their ears away from the truth.' In this recent election, they have turned away from the truth, to hear what they want to hear, and to see what they want to see; so I am blinding their eyes. I will send 'them a powerful delusion,' for they are turning to other 'gods' in America. They are turning to the 'gods' of this world; the 'god' of abortions, the 'god' of homosexuality, and to the 'god' of murders. They are turning to Satan, who is a 'god' of outward appearances, a 'god' opposed to the heart after Jesus. Open your eyes and see that the end is near. It is knocking at your door!" (Da 11:35; Jn 8:44; 12:31; Ro 1:25-27; 11:8; 2 Co 11:14; 2 Th 2:9-11; 1 Ti 4:1; 2 Ti 4:3,4; Rev 12:9,12,17); received November 20, 2008.

(James Dobson, Founder and Chairman of the Focus on the Family, Christian organization, reported in a newsletter of October 2008, the beliefs of the Senator from Illinois on abortion, who was recently elected President of the United States.[175] James Dobson wrote that the Senator from Illinois' "record is more liberal than that of any other Democrat in the Senate . . . He voted four times in three years against legislation that would have saved the lives of babies that managed to survive the abortion process, . . . when he was a state senator . . . (He) was chairman of the committee that opposed (the) protection of babies . . . In 2001 and 2002, (he) was the only legislator who rose to argue against the Illinois Born Alive Act" (Ps 139:13-16; Lk 18:15-17; Rev 12:17).

Dr. Dobson shared more about the Senator of Illinois' "radical devotion to abortion rights." The Senator said, "'The first thing I do as president' would be to sign the Freedom of Choice Act." That "Act," James Dobson reported, "would overturn nearly every local, state, and federal anti-abortion law past in the last 40 years . . . What the Senator believes and the policies he would seek to implement are on a collision course with the biblical principles and beliefs I have fought to defend for more than 35 years"[176]) (2 Ki 17:17; Ps 119:73; Isa 44:2,24; Jn 10:10[a]).

The Lord Jesus disclosed, "Thousands were killed in your country in what they call the Civil War. Demonic spirits of "murder" passed from one generation to another, manifesting themselves during the Civil War. Those murdering spirits found a place to manifest again on the innocent, in an attempt by Satan to destroy a belief in man's true God, in destroying those innocent 'little ones' made in His image, (the unborn). Satan, leading organizations with his own henchmen, has been seeking to destroy mankind (through) the 'abortion industry' today. Millions of lives (have been) lost. Many men and women in America turn their heads aside, and say nothing. The message they have given to the 'abortion industry' is, they have the right to murder the innocent, despite the (appalling) violation of God's commandments (Gen 1:26,27; Ex 20:13; Job 1:9-12; 2:4-7; Pr 6:16-18; Mt 18:6-10; Ro 3:10-18; 2 Co 11:14,15; 1 Jn 3:12).

"(In this country), the works of Satan are manifested by removing Jesus out of America through legislative 'leaders.' It is a principality of liberalism that is destroying the very 'fiber' of the American people today, for the American people have become slaves to Satan's practices, kindled by the demonic practices of murder and savagery of many Indian tribes in the beginning of this 'new nation,' passed from generations long ago. These words are to be placed in this book. America covers itself with a veneer of prosperity, affluence, and wealth (Gen 4:7; Lk 12:15-21; Eph 6:12; 2 Pe 2:19; 1 Jn 2:18,19; 3:8-11).

"The African people, as well as the Christians in Africa, have suffered from diseases, famines, pestilence, poverty, (homelessness), murders, (etc.), because many there have served and worshipped other 'gods.' In contrast, the American people have chosen a President representing a veneer of affluence, wealth, and prosperity in America. Even the elected President has had a relative living in Africa. That veneer covers over another 'god,' the 'god of murder,' Satan, who working through men and women, kill the unborn. The veneer of affluence and wealth in tyrannical England covered over the 'slave trade' and slavery in Great Britain. England obtained their 'affluence' from the practice of the slave trade. The unborn are marketed in the 'slave trade,' the 'abortion industry,' today, slaves of the 'prosperous and wealthy slave-owners' (Dt 19:10; Ps 49:12,13; Lk 21:11; Jn 8:44; Ja 2:11; Rev 18:11,13[b].); received December 4, 2008.

"Many are murdering God's creation, the unborn, for those Americans were all unborn at one time. The 'little ones,' the unborn, are created in the image of God, 'male and female He created them.' Those that support and conduct abortions are destroying My image, destroying My commandment, 'You shall not murder,' destroying the Lord Jesus in this country and throughout the world. So do not be deceived by the veneer of wealth, affluence, and prosperity; for this country will suffer similar consequences like Africa for serving another 'god'; diseases, poverty, murders, especially in the 'big' cities, (etc.)" (Gen 1:27; 9:6; Lev 24:17; Dt 5:17; Ps 10:2,4,8-10; Mt 18:10; 1 Ti 6:9,10; Ja 5:1-6); received December 4, 2008.

"America will suffer tremendously for its degradation of human rights, degrading the unborn, and for supporting Satan's butchering henchmen (abortionists) for years. Unless this country repents (of this wickedness), this nation will suffer severe consequences, many losing their lives. For there is a hatred of the 'Cornerstone,' the 'Rock,' the true Founders of America, those who believed in Jesus, and His believers today, who are being mocked and vilified in the public square for their faith in the one true God!" (Eze 18:30; Mt 5:10-12; Mk 13:13; Jn 15:18,19; Ac 7:19; Ro 2:4-9; Ja 5:5,6; Rev 12:17); received February 22, 2008.

Ruby Bridges

On November 4, 2008, I saw a vision of a blue police officer's cap like a cap worn in the movie, *Ruby Bridges*.[177] (*Ruby Bridges* is the true story of a young African-American girl, who was placed at a white public school in New Orleans, Louisiana in the fall of 1960). In the next vision, my wife and I are children holding hands and carrying lunch pails in our other hands. We are walking up the steps of a school that was shown in the movie about Ruby Bridges. Police officers were standing beside barricades set up on the right and left side of us, just like in the movie.

Hecklers were behind those barricades, and the Lord revealed to us who these hecklers will be. Some were "Christians," some were African-Americans, some were white people, some were abortionists, some were homosexuals, lesbians, and some were judges in black robes, etc. We turned around as Ruby Bridges did on the steps of the school in the movie, and we prayed that God would forgive them. I then heard the words Ruby Bridges' mother shared with her daughter, "Jesus loves you. God will protect you." In the next vision, we were walking into a classroom, sitting down at a school desk, and opening up our Bibles. An African-American couple were in that classroom. They were our teachers, who were supportive and with us.

The Lord then said, "In the days ahead, police will set up barricades to protect true believers in Jesus Christ. Those hecklers will treat true Christians in a similar manner as Ruby Bridges was mistreated when she was desegregated into a white public school. Those hecklers will oppose the truth of the Word of God, and oppose the real Jesus. Yet, Jesus loves and protects His 'little ones.' You will forgive them, for they will 'not know what they are doing'" (Ps 22:7,8,11-18; Lk 18:15-17; 22:63,64; 23:34-37; 1 Pe 2:20-23).

Yet, after the Civil War, many American men and women turned their hearts back to the Lord Jesus. The "fire" of the Holy Spirit's "Second Great Awakening" was rekindled, burning with "fervor," traveling from the East and deeper into the West, the "new" frontier. Many believers in the Lord Jesus, in the nineteenth century and the early twentieth century, had learned the value of freedom in Him, so as not to become slaves to Satan, slaves to men, nor slaves to sin.

7

MAKE STRAIGHT IN THE WILDERNESS A HIGHWAY FOR OUR GOD

"They were longing for a better country—a heavenly one. Therefore God is not ashamed to be called their God."

Moving from the latter half of the nineteenth century into the twentieth century, the sovereign Lord Jesus would keep the Bible presses turning, spreading the Word of God through men and women in Christian organizations like the one we wrote about earlier, The American Bible Society. The lighted "torch," the "fire" of the Holy Spirit would travel by men and women from the Eastern United States of America to the Western frontier.

Mount Rushmore

On June 11, 1995, my wife saw a vision of a white bird flying around a covered wagon. On May 22, 2008, the Lord Jesus gave me a vision I had received when we lived in Israel in the summer of 1994. In that vision, which we briefly shared about at the beginning of this book, my wife and I were in an airplane flying out of Tel-Aviv, Israel from the International Airport back to the United States. We then landed feet first in front of Mount Rushmore. On November 18, 2008, my wife received a vision of the Presidents' faces at Mount Rushmore. The four faces of the Presidents that were carved in the rock were rising up with outstretched necks. Their faces appeared angry, troubled, and fearful.

The Lord said, "(Those early settlers), they had hoped to soar; they sought freedom, they sought a 'new' land. Those freedoms for which they sought, have eventually been taken away, today, enslaved and covered over by men's and women's choices, apart from God." (Received June 11, 1995.) "Those Presidents at Mount Rushmore would be aghast at the recent choices this country has made that violate the Word of God, and the Lord Jesus." (Received November 18, 2008.) "So repent! Come back to your 'first love,' to Jesus, to love each other with an 'agape love,' an unconditional love, a love of the brethren, a love of the children (Eze 22:26[KJV]; Gal 3:8,9; Tit 3:3; Heb 2:2,3; 1 Pe 1:22[KJV]; 1 Jn 3:14[KJV]; Rev 2:4; 3:19).

"I will be 'Rush-ing more' information to you about the Founding Fathers. You are to 'Rush-more' information to America through this book, 'Rush'-ing before this great tribulation hits the United States of America. Whether they knew it or not, those Presidents at Mount Rushmore had God's call on their lives for His purposes to set captives free, captives who were slaves; slaves to sin, slaves to tyranny, slaves to Satan, slaves to a corrupt government, slaves to a corrupt people, that they might be freed through the One who could liberate them, Jesus, who is the King of the whole world. He still reigns as King over the United States of America" (Ex 15:18; Ps 24:10; Pr 19:21; 28:16[a]; Jn 8:34; Ro 6:6,20; 8:28; 1 Ti 2:7; 2 Pe 2:19). (Message received from the Lord Jesus on May 22, 2008).

We have written in this book about three of those Presidents, whose faces are carved in rock at Mount Rushmore, George Washington, Thomas Jefferson, and Abraham Lincoln.

Theodore Roosevelt served as the twenty-sixth President of the United States from 1901 through 1909.[178] Theodore Roosevelt affirmed God's call on his life when he said, "There are those who believe that a new modernity demands a new morality. What they fail to consider is the harsh reality that there is no such thing as a new morality. There is only one morality. All else is immorality. There is only one true Christian ethics over against which stands the whole of paganism . . . "[179] (Mt 6:32; 1 Co 5:9,10; Eph 5:5; 1 Pe 2:12; 4:3).

President Roosevelt understood that the Bible, the Word of God, as revealed by the Lord Jesus, was the only standard by which to govern the country morally. His statement followed the precedence of former Presidents of the United States. Shortly after the Presidency of Theodore Roosevelt, the twenty-eighth President of the United States, (Thomas) Woodrow Wilson served as President from 1913 through 1921[180] during the outset of World War I (Isa 62:10[KJV]; Jer 51:12[KJV]; 1 Co 6:13[b],19,20).

President Wilson shared, "A nation which does not remember what it was yesterday, does not know what it is today, nor what it is trying to do. We are trying to do a futile thing if we do not know where we came from or what we have been about . . . America was born a Christian nation. America was born to exemplify that devotion to the elements of righteousness which are derived from the revelations of Holy Scripture"[181] (Nu 18:14; 1 Ch 28:9; Ezr 7:10; Ac 2:42; Gal 1:15; Rev 4:8[b]).

President Woodrow Wilson honored the Holy Scriptures and our Founding Fathers' faith in the Lord Jesus, when he proclaimed, "America was born a Christian nation." He understood the importance of governing this country in "the elements of righteousness." Those "elements" would aide the United States and President Wilson in yet another war, the first World War (Mt 5:20; 6:33; Ac 11:26[b]; 17:11).

Spreading the Word of God to the New Frontier

The Lord Jesus, the Cornerstone and foundational Rock of liberty and freedom for all Americans, would send His missionaries westward in the latter part of the nineteenth, and early part of the twentieth century. On September 18, 2008, the Lord Jesus gave me some visions. In the first vision, I saw several covered wagons led by horses traveling from east to west. Then I saw a vision of a family inside a covered wagon. The father of that family was reading the Bible to his wife and children in the wagon. A vision followed of Michael Landon, who played the character of Charles Ingalls in the television series *Little House on the Prairie*.[182] He was standing up and speaking to his congregation at his church in Walnut Grove, Minnesota. This vision was the ending of a *Little House on the Prairie* television show. Then I saw a vision of Circuit Riders, preachers, riding their horses from the eastern part of the United States to the west. A vision followed of gold miners panning for gold. Finally, I saw farmers planting seeds in the western part of the United States.

The Lord Jesus shared, "Travel with Me, if you will, to that country, a virgin wasteland of forests and mountains, and a land with food in abundance. For I was traveling with those early settlers through a land filled with 'milk and honey,' the United States of America! The true believers were covered in the 'blood of the Lamb' to spread the gospel, the Word from the east to the west (Ex 3:8; Nu 14:8; Ac 5:42; 1 Th 3:2; Rev 12:11 [a]).

"Many of those early settlers sought to find gold instead of Jesus. Those settlers were not willing 'to buy from Me gold refined in the fire.' That is why I called families who believed (in Jesus,) to move west to bring the 'gold nuggets' of the Word of God to the Indians, and the pioneers moving westward. 'The Great Spirit,' the Holy Spirit, was bringing the truth, the 'Spirit of Truth' to the Indians, as well as the early pioneers.

Families, like the Ingalls' family,[183] who lived according to the Word of God, traveled west seeking a 'new' land" (Job 22:21-23,25; 31:24,25,28; Ps 119:9,105; Jn 14:16,17; 16:13; Rev 3:18).

(At the ending of one of the shows in the series, *Little House on the Prairie,* "Charles Ingalls" shared in his church pulpit, "I think it's time we begin to practice what we preach inside this church, outside this church, on the streets of Walnut Grove, on our farms, and our homes with our friends, our neighbors, and our loved ones with every human being everywhere. In the Name of God think about it . . . Shall we rise and sing, 'What a Friend'" (Mt 23:3; Lk 8:21; 10:29,33-37; Jn 15:13-15). "Charles Ingalls" and the congregation then sang:

> "*What a friend we have in Jesus, All our sins and griefs to bear!*
> *What a privilege to carry Ev'rything to God in prayer!*
> *Oh, what peace we often forfeit, Oh, what needless pain we bear,*
> *All because we do not carry Ev'rything to God in prayer!*"[184])

The Lord revealed, "It was God's plan that the new territories, (states), would be united under one God, the God of love, the God of righteousness, the God of mercy, the God of compassion, the God of hope for the American people. This was not the 'god' of gold, nor the 'god' of the Indians. Farmers sowed the Word, like Charles Ingalls, planting seeds in the hearts of men and women throughout the land of America, that living 'Seed,' the Living Word of God, Jesus" (Ex 34:6; Dt 13:6-8; 32:7; Isa 40:41; Lk 8:11,15; Gal 3:16; Eph 4:1-4; 1 Jn 4:16; Rev 9:20).

The Lord Jesus used families like the Ingalls family to minister the Word of God to the American people at the latter part of the nineteenth century, as well as today through the *Little House on the Prairie* television series. However, Satan, the 'god of this world,' was turning many away from God, who were searching for riches and wealth, searching for gold (Mt 6:31,32; Lk 4:5,6; 2 Co 4:4[KJV]).

On December 11, 2008, my wife received these visions from the Lord Jesus early in the morning. She saw an American flag with dark red narrow stripes, that appeared to be the color of blood. Then she saw a huge American flag unfurling, that appeared to be a quilt covering of a large land area. The flag had many different designs representing freedom and liberty.

That morning, after fasting and worshiping before the Lord Jesus, He gave me, (Mark) some visions. In the first vision, I saw our black, antique iron. Then I saw a woman ironing clothes with that iron, and hanging laundry outside on a line. That vision was from the Walt Disney movie, *Old Yeller*.[185] In the vision, the oldest son was hugging "Old Yeller," their dog. A vision followed from the original movie, *Little House on the Prairie*.[186] From that movie, the Lord showed me some of the dangers families encountered during that time: Indians, weather, fires, wild animals, and dangers from some of the early settlers.

In addition, I saw saloons with dancing girls spring up in the western part of the United States. Churches were also being established in the west, though some appeared not to be of God. Then I saw a vision of the American flag that was like a quilt covering a map of the United States. Finally, the Lord Jesus gave me a vision of the Mississippi River running from North to South on an American map. Another river was flowing from East to West forming a cross at the Mississippi River with branches of that river moving out into villages, cities, and towns in the west.

The Lord Jesus then said, "As the early settlers, the pioneers moved westward into a 'new frontier,' Satan was attempting to stop Americans from spreading the Word of God in the western territories for fear that the Lord Jesus would take over those territories, the future states. The enemies of God were used by Satan to try to prevent Christians from staying in that 'new' land. Those enemies were wild animals like the one in the movie who killed "Old Yeller,"(poor) weather conditions, fires, Indians, bandits, sickness and diseases, fellow countrymen, and religious cults (Hos 13:8; Mk 4:14,15; Ac 20:19; 2 Co 11:3,4,26; 1 Ti 4:1; 2 Ti 4:3,4).

"The demons from alcoholism and immoral dancing girls were used by Satan in the western saloons and other places to destroy many men and women, turning them away from the one, true God, and following the wicked schemes of the devil. Amidst villages, towns, cities, and churches springing up in the west, (which George Washington saw in his vision of the future of America), Satan used men and women to establish cults, religious doctrines contrary to the Word of God. Cults sprang up like Mormonism, Jehovah's Witnesses, Unitarianism, (etc.) (Job 30:21; Pr 6:23,24; 7:10-13; 20:1; 31:4,5; Jn 10:10[a]; Eph 6:11; 1 Ti 6:20; 2 Pe 2:1-3).

"Still, the Lord Jesus would have His way moving His people westward through the Midwest and Western territories, states, establishing the foundational Rock, (Jesus), throughout America. The Lord was removing barriers and obstacles set by Satan in the West, obstacles to deter pioneers who believed in Jesus from moving West. For that is the (meaning of the) vision your wife received of the American flag with narrow 'blood,' red stripes. For people were shedding their blood to establish the Cornerstone, the Word of God, Jesus in the western territories. For 'by His stripes (they were) healed.' The American flag was like an unfurling quilt covering the United States, for believing men and women were sowing, embroidering the Word of Truth in the hearts of men and women throughout America, establishing freedom and liberty from being enslaved by Satan and his evil tactics (Ex 28:39; Ps 103:12; Isa 28:16; 53:5[KJV]; Eze 16:10; Mt 7:25; Jn 20:1; 1 Co 3:11; Col 1:20; 2 Ti 2:26; Heb 9:20).

"A River flowed in America from the North to the South, and a spiritual River flowed from the East to the West of the United States. It was a 'River of Living Water,' the Holy Spirit moving from North to South and East to West. That River moved into cities and the countryside of America, into the western cities in California. That is the message you are to put in this chapter of this book" (Jn 7:38,39[KJV]; Rev 22:1).

To confirm those words from our Lord Jesus, it was reported, "The Principle Approach to American Christian history developed as the chain of Christianity moved westward in a liberating mission, internal and external. The Biblical principles of government that appeared with the Pilgrims in America established the world's first Christian republic and enabled us to extend the gospel into all fields"[187] (Gen 12:2,3; Isa 9:6; Mk 16:15[KJV]).

The Third Great Awakening

That "chain of Christianity moved westward" in "The Third Great Awakening." That Christian awakening "in American history (occurred) from the late 1850s to the 1900s . . . The Social Gospel Movement gained its force from the Awakening . . . Protestant denominations all sponsored growing missionary activities inside the United States"[188] (Ac 4:4; 5:14; 6:2-4; 2 Co 8:1-5).

"From 1840 until the 1870s numerous preachers entered the ranks of traveling evangelists . . . The concept of large campaigns led by preachers who were not pastors of specific churches was generally accepted . . . All over the country, in small towns as well as in great cities, . . . people . . . gathered together daily . . . to pray" during the Third Great Awakening[189] (Ac 2:42; 12:5; Eph 5:14; 1 Th 5:16-18).

The Lord Jesus called men and women to travel westward to spread the gospel of Jesus Christ. The Holy Spirit's "fire" was convicting men and women, "all over the country," to pray and trust in the one true God. God's missionaries were being sent out to proclaim the Lord Jesus (Mt 3:11; 28:19,20; Ac 19:20; Eph 4:4-6; 1 Th 5:19).

Dwight L. Moody

One of the Christian leaders during "The Third Great Awakening" was Dwight L. Moody, "also known as D. L. Moody." The Lord Jesus raised up a man after His own heart to preach His Word to thousands in America, to win souls to Jesus. D. L. Moody was born in "1837 . . . in Northfield, Massachusetts . . . In April 1855," D. L. Moody had a born-again experience, accepting Jesus into his heart. This happened "when his . . . Sunday school . . . teacher . . . talked to him about how much God loved him. His conversion sparked the start of his career as an evangelist"[190] (1 Sa 13:14; Pr 11:30[b]; Jn 3:3; Eph 4:11,12; 2 Ti 4:2).

D. L. "Moody moved to Chicago, Illinois in . . . 1856," and there, he took "an active part in . . . prayer meetings." From those meetings "his work led to the largest Sunday School of his time . . . The average attendance at his school was 650 . . . President Lincoln visited and spoke at a Sunday School meeting on November 25, 1860" . . . D. L. Moody also "was involved with the U. S. Christian Commission" during "the Civil War," which we previously reported. He "founded the Moody Church, (and) the Moody Bible Institute," which still exists in Chicago, Illinois today[191] (Mt 21:13 [a]; Ac 16:5).

"In the late 19th century," D. L. Moody returned "to his birthplace in Northfield, MA," which "became an important location in evangelical Christian history." He "organized summer conferences (there), which were led by prominent Christian preachers and evangelists from around the world." Prior to the turn of the century in "November . . . 1899, . . . he preached his last sermon"[192] (Ac 18:5; 21:8; 2 Ti 4:5).

It was reported that D. L. Moody "had the joy of hearing literally thousands give testimony to the fact that he had led them to (Jesus) Christ." D. L. Moody "believed that men were lost without (Jesus) Christ . . . No one this side of Heaven can ever estimate the number of people he won to (Jesus) Christ in his evangelistic services. It has been estimated that he preached to millions . . . He must, under the power of God, have led hundreds of thousands to a decision" of accepting Jesus Christ into their hearts and to take up their Cross and follow Him, Jesus[193] (Lk 9:23,24; 15:3-7; 19:10; Jn 1:12,13; Ac 16:29-34; Rev 3:20).

In D. L. Moody's "work of . . . evangelism," he utilized "The Wordless Book," a Christian "teaching tool . . . In 1875, he added a fourth color to the" . . . "book" . . . , "gold—to 'represent heaven.'" That "'book' has been and is still used to teach uncounted thousands of . . . people—young and old— around the globe about the Gospel message"[194] (Pr 10:19; Mt 28:19,20; Rev 21:10,18,21[b]).

My husband and I were introduced to "The Wordless Book," when we taught at a Christian school during the school year 2002-2003. At that time we took a Christian accredited course, "Teaching Children Effectively,"[195] in which we were required to use "The Wordless Book" for Christian evangelist purposes. We shared "The Wordless Book" with our students, and two of our young grandchildren. At times, we still utilize "The Wordless Book" in our Youth Bible studies (Ro 2:21; 1 Co 2:13; 1 Ti 4:13; 1 Pe 3:1).

The spiritual "River of Living Water," the Holy Spirit was beginning to flow across America. The Lord Jesus would raise up another Christian leader, an African-American man to take the lighted "torch," the "fire" of the Holy Spirit to the western coast of the United States.

William Seymour

William Seymour was born in "1870" in "Centerville, Louisiana . . . William was born into a world of horrible racial violence." He "taught himself primarily through reading the

Bible." William "Seymour found his identity in Jesus Christ, believing that the Lord was the only liberator of mankind. He was . . . hungry for the truth of God's Word." Traveling north to "Indianapolis," Indiana when he was a young man, William Seymour joined a church there. He understood, "that there was no class or color line in the redemption of Jesus Christ"[196] (Mt 5:6; Lk 6:21[a]; Jn 8:31-36; Gal 3:26-29).

Moving "to Cincinnati, Ohio," William Seymour "began traveling as an itinerant evangelist." Eventually, William Seymour moved to "Los Angeles," California "in early 1906 . . . to start a new Pentecostal church." Charles Parham, considered "The Father of Pentecost," ministered at the turn of the century up through "1929 . . . His ministry contributed to over two million conversions, both directly and indirectly. His crowds often exceeded seven thousand people." Charles "Parham . . . pioneered" the Pentecostal Movement and "the truth of tongues as the evidence of the baptisms of the Holy Spirit." Charles Parham at times assisted William Seymour in his ministry[197] (Mk 1:8; Ac 2:1-12; 10:44-46).

In the spring of "1906," William Seymour purchased "an old Methodist church" on "Azusa Street" in Los Angeles. That old church was a "humble . . . setting" in a "lower class area" for which an "international . . . revival" would take place. "Soon, all classes of people began attending Azusa Street meetings . . . The power of God could be felt at Azusa, even outside the building. Scores of people were seen dropping into a prostrate position in the streets before they ever reached the mission"[198] (Lev 9:24; 1 Ki 18:38,39; 2 Ch 7:1-3; Lk 1:48; 2:6,7).

During the summer of 1906, "crowds had reached staggering numbers, often into the thousands." Each "day trains unloaded numbers of visitors who came from all over the continent." Thousands "received the baptism of the Holy Spirit," many received the call to the mission field. "No one could possibly record all the miracles that occurred there"[199] (Ac 19:4-7; Ro 8:28; Heb 2:4).

It was said of William Seymour that "doctors, lawyers and professors, listened to the marvelous things coming from his lips . . . It was what he said from his spirit to my heart that showed me he had more of God in his life than any man I had ever met." William Seymour desired to restore "camp meetings, revivals, missions, (and) street" evangelism. William Seymour wrote, "There is no Jew or Gentile, bond or free, in the Azusa Mission. No instrument that God can use is rejected on account of color or dress or lack of education"[200] (Lk 10:21; Ac 3:19,20; 16:14; 1 Co 12:13[KJV]; Ja 2:1-7).

"Throughout 1909 and 1910, (William) Seymour continued his ministry at Azusa" Street. "The fire of God . . . (had) spread . . . throughout Southern California." William Seymour traveled "across America" in his "ministry" campaigns up through "1922." It was reported that "his efforts . . . produced and exploded the Pentecostal Movement around the world." William Seymour was considered the "catalyst" and springboard from which "many denominations (today) attribute their founding to the participants of Azusa," for "the power of the Holy Spirit . . . was poured on their ranks"[201] (Lk 12:49; Ac 2:33; 6:4; 10:45).

During "The Third Great Awakening," the "fire" of the Holy Spirit moved upon men like Charles Parham and the African-American, William Seymour. The wave of the "River of Living Water" was flowing across the United States through men and women that God was raising up to proclaim the power of God in Jesus Christ! They experienced the "baptism of the Holy Spirit" on Azusa Street. The Holy Spirit was no respecter of persons, for the "gifts of the Holy Spirit" moved upon every person regardless of their lack or level of education, race, nationality, socio-economic class, and whether they were Jews or Gentiles. Thousands of souls were being won for Jesus Christ (Jer 5:14; 23:29; Mk 1:8; Jn 7:37-39[KJV]; Ac 2:3,41 [KJV]; 1 Co 12:4-11; Col 3:11).

The Outpouring of the Holy Spirit

The prophet Joel and the Apostle Peter, as recorded in the Bible, shared about the outpouring of the Holy Spirit in the last days. Out of powerful movements of Almighty God, "new" denominations were established in America, following the Pentecostal and Charismatic Movement of the Holy Spirit. Many in those denominations are still flowing in "the river of the water of life" today. We have experienced a number of times the Holy Spirit "fire" poured out on us through our Lord Jesus, and especially at a Rodney Howard-Browne Revival in February/March 1994 at a church in Oxford, Maryland (Joel 2:28-32; Ac 2:14-21; Tit 3:5-7; Rev 22:1).

Prior to attending that Revival, I, (Phyllis) was coughing, and I had a fever and chills in my body. Yet, when I entered the church among the numbers of people at the Revival from many Christian denominations, within a short amount of time, I felt fine. During those days at work, while the Revival was taking place, I felt sick again. But at the Revival, that sickness left me until I was completely healed (Mt 8:15,16; Ac 5:16; 8:6-8).

My husband and I attended several evening services at that Revival, staying well into the night. We sensed spiritually that the presence of the power of the Holy Spirit was there. Yet, we were cautious since we observed so many different manifestations taking place among the participants, some of the manifestations were of the "flesh," manifestations that were not from God. But, by the third day at the Revival, the Holy Spirit began to take over our inner spirits (Lk 24:49; 1 Co 12:7; 2 Th 2:9).

My husband began to experience "holy laughter" from the Spirit of God, as he broke out into uncontrollable laughter. We both experienced that "laughter," which was heavenly and freeing within our spirits, souls, and bodies. We stayed late into the nights hungering for more of God, more of the outpouring of the Holy Spirit. While we stood in line, men and women, who were anointed by the Lord Jesus, laid hands on us, the power of God came upon us, and we would be on the floor filled with the Holy Spirit (Gen 21:6; Ps 126:2; Isa 61:1-3; Lk 6:21; Ac 2:15; 4:31; 13:2).

On one evening, my husband and three other men at the Revival were filled with "holy laughter." The power of God came upon them and instantly they were taken to the floor. They rested in the powerful presence of Almighty God. That power was so great, that it took my husband about twenty minutes to crawl back to a seat in the church, that was about twenty feet away from him. The power of the Holy Spirit was so strong, that when my husband was lying on the floor, he knew that Jesus was healing him from past childhood pain. It had taken years for my husband and I to work through our pain in Christian classes and counseling, but God was healing him in minutes. At times the Holy Spirit would move upon people around us, in which they would break into deep repentance with holy sobbing, and weeping (Ps 51:5-10; Ecc 3:4[a]; Mk 3:10; Lk 6:21; Ac 8:7; Ja 4:9).

The second week of that Revival, after a powerfully anointed time of praising Jesus, a young woman was kneeling on the floor at the church, weeping deeply. She was crying out to the Lord, and praising God in the English language as the Holy Spirit flowed through her. After she praised God, my husband and I wanted to talk with her, but we discovered that she could not speak a word of English. We were told by her friends that she was from Russia, and had only arrived in the United States a week earlier. All of the heavenly praises that sprang forth from her heart were in English, and given to her freely by the Holy Spirit (Lk 23:27,28; 1 Co 12:4,10,11; 14:15; 1 Jn 2:20).

Although we had previously received an immersed water baptism, we chose to get into the "River" at the Revival. Near the end of the Revival, we received a Holy Spirit baptism in a large tank of water along with over 500 people. On the last night of the meeting, seven people at a time would step down into the tank of water in order to be baptized. Rodney Howard-Browne was on a platform outside the pool of water. He lifted up his right arm and prayed anointed prayers, baptizing us in the Name of Jesus. When he dropped his right arm, the power of God came upon us and we were taken down forcefully, fully immersed into the water without anyone touching us. After many people were baptized in this manner, they were lying on the floor weeping and crying. Many people were being healed of deep-seated pain. We were touched by God in a mighty way, soaring "on wings like eagles" to prepare us for our ministry of marriage, and our calling to Israel that summer (Isa 40:31; Lk 19:40,41; Ac 8:34-40; 19:2-7; 2 Ti 1:7; 1 Jn 2:27).

One of the praise songs Rodney Howard-Browne sang was, "There is a River."

> "There is a River, That flows from deep within.
> There is a fountain, That frees my soul from sin.
> Come to these waters, There is a vast supply.
> There is a River, That never shall run dry."[202]

The "River of Living Water," the Holy Spirit had been flowing freely in our hearts during that Revival. At that time, we had been working at a Juvenile Court Service Unit in Prince William County, Virginia. The Supreme Court of the United States would confirm that America was a Christian nation, flowing in the Spirit during "The Third Great Awakening" (Ps 36:8,9; 46:4,5; Jn 7:37-39).

The Supreme Court of the United States of America

In "1892," the "U. S. Supreme Court" heard the case of "Church of the Holy Trinity v. United States." In the majority decision, the Supreme Court Justice David Brewer reviewed many American documents which included: "The first charter of Virginia, (and) various charters granted to the other colonies, . . . The Mayflower . . . compact, . . . The fundamental orders of Connecticut, . . . the Declaration . . . of independence, . . . constitutions of the various states, . . . the Constitution of the United States, . . . (the case of) People v. Ruggles (from) the Supreme Court of New York, . . . the famous case of (Vidal v. Girard's Executors)," and other court cases and charters, etc.[203]

Supreme Court Justice Brewer declared on "February 29, 1892" that, "We are a Christian people, and the morality of the country is deeply engrafted upon Christianity . . . We find every where a clear recognition of the same truth, . . . the custom of opening sessions of all deliberative bodies in most conventions with prayer; . . . the laws respecting the observance of the Sabbath, . . . the churches and church organizations which abound in every city, town, and hamlet; the multitude of charitable organizations existing every where under Christian auspices; and the gigantic missionary associations, . . . aiming to establish Christian missions in every quarter of the globe. These, and many other matters which might be noticed, add a volume of unofficial declarations to the mass of organic utterances that this is a Christian nation"[204] (Gen 2:2,3; Ex 20:8-11; 2 Ch 7:1; Neh 1:4; 2:4; Ac 11:26[b]; 2 Co 8:7-15; 11:28).

Supreme Court Justice Brewer researching many of our Founding Fathers' documents, and prior Court cases, could only come to the right conclusion that our country was founded on the Cornerstone of America, the Foundational Rock, Jesus Christ. Justice Brewer maintained "justice in the courts." The Supreme Court of the land by honoring the Holy Scriptures, honored God by hating "evil," and loving what is "good." Justice Brewer was "not ashamed of the gospel" of Jesus Christ "for the salvation of everyone who believes," declaring it "in every city, town, and hamlet" (Pr 8:17; Am 5:15[a]; Mt 16:15-18; Ro 1:16; 1 Pe 2:6).

In the U. S. Supreme Court case of "U.S. v. MACINTOSH" of "(1931)," the Supreme Court Justice George Sutherland came to a similar conclusion stating, "We are a Christian people, . . . according to one another the equal right of religious freedom, and acknowledge with reverence the duty of obedience to the will of God."[205] Justice Sutherland supported the Supreme Court case of "Holy Trinity v. United States" (Mk 3:31-35; Jn 7:17; 1 Pe 2:9; 4:16).

Well into the twentieth century, the Supreme Court honored the truth that the Foundational Rock for this country was and is Jesus. As it is written in the book of Judges in the Bible, "the Lord raised up judges who saved them out of the hands of raiders," Satan's "servants of righteousness." God raised up judges in the United States to save America from Satan's evil tactics (Jdg 2:16; Mt 7:25; 1 Co 3:11; 2 Co 11:14,15; Rev 4:8 [b]).

Beginning with the "first Supreme Court chief justice ... John Jay" and "America's longest serving chief justice (1801-1835)" of the Supreme Court, "John Marshall"[206] up to the former Chief Justice of the Supreme Court, Earl Warren, the Lord Jesus had given those men a "sound mind" to "make a right judgment." For in a "February ... 1954, ... Time magazine (interview), Chief Justice Earl Warren" shared about his Christian faith[207] (Jn 7:24; Ac 26:23-29; 2 Ti 1:7[KJV]).

Former Chief Justice Warren shared, "I believe no one can read the history of our country ... without realizing that the Good Book and the spirit of the Savior have from the beginning been our guiding geniuses ... Whether we look to the first Charter of Virginia ... or to the Charter of New England, ... or to the Charter of Massachusetts Bay ... or to the Fundamental Orders of Connecticut, ... the same objective is present: a Christian land governed by Christian principles"[208] (Php 1:19; 2 Ti 3:16,17; Heb 5:12[KJV]; 1 Pe 1:11).

Justice Warren stated, "I believe the entire Bill of Rights came into being because of the knowledge our forefathers had of the Bible and their belief in it ... I like to believe we are living in the spirit of the Christian religion. I like also to believe that as long as we do so, no great harm can come to our country."[209] Former Justices of the Supreme Court understood from America's court cases, charters, compacts, covenants, constitutions, declarations, and the faith of millions of believers in Jesus Christ, that the Lord Jesus established the United States under His guidance, under His banner for His honor and glory; so that "The (American) government (would) be on his shoulders" (Ex 17:15; Pr 9:10; Isa 9:6[a]; 11:10; Jer 29:11; Ro 8:9-11; Rev 7:11,12).

Nation Will Rise Against Nation

The United States' involvement in two World Wars and the "Great Depression" would draw the American people continually to their knees to ask the Lord Jesus for His aid, support, and protection over the country of the United States, and the American military troops at home and overseas. For "Churches grew as Christians and non-Christians looked to God in their hard times. Revivals, camp meetings, and Bible conferences flourished. Evangelists and Bible speakers traveled up and down the country preaching."[210] The Lord's modern day "Circuit riders" were not traveling by horseback, but by automobiles, trains, and airplanes to spread the gospel of Jesus Christ across America (2 Ch 7:14,15; Isa 35:8; Ac 5:42; Ro 16:3-5; 2 Co 8:19; 1 Th 3:2; 2 Th 2:1; 1 Ti 5:17).

The people of the United States during World War II, did as they had done before, they put their faith in the one true God, the Lord Jesus Christ. The Axis powers consisting of Germany, Italy, and Japan, put their faith in other "gods," and in their dictatorial leaders. In the DVD, *The League of Greatful Sons*[211] it was reported that, "World War II was understood by both sides to be a fight between two things, Christendom and Statism. The Axis powers were committed to the elimination of Christianity. Nazi officials demanded that Protestant . . . churches must vanish from the life of our people . . . The Japanese population was no less committed to the destruction of Christendom. The religious warriors of Imperial Japan were told that those who died for the (Japanese) Emperor would live forever . . . They fought with suicidal determination" (Dt 32:16,17; Jn 10:10; Ac 9:1,6; 2 Co 10:3-5; Eph 6:10-12; Col 2:15).

The Lord Jesus was with the American people again to overcome Satan's attempt to destroy true Christians, God's faithful followers. For Satan was using men and women in the Nazi regime, and the Japanese "population" and their "religious warriors" to carry out his wicked schemes. The United States, as we know, prevailed in victory over the Axis powers, for God heard the prayers of His people in America. The Lord Jesus was again victorious. America, under the leadership of the Lord Jesus Christ, would stand as the strongest nation in the world at the end of the War (Dt 28:13; Job 1:8-12; 2:1-7; Ac 20:29; Eph 1:19-23; 6:11; 1 Pe 3:12; 1 Jn 2:19).

Many Americans at that time believed that the Second Coming of the Lord Jesus would take place to gather His faithful believers to Himself and into heaven. For "Nation (rose) against nation, and kingdom against kingdom," which was one of the signs Jesus gave to His disciples prior to His imminent return. Yet, those were just "the beginning of birth pains," birthing His return, foreshadowing the soon coming King's return for His people. Apparently, His believers did not take into consideration that the nation of Israel did not exist at the end of World War II. Who would be the leader from the United States, whom God would appoint to spearhead the establishment of Israel becoming a nation? (Eze 39:28; Mt 24:2,3,6-8,30,31; Heb 10:1; Rev 22:7,20).

Harry S. Truman

Harry S. Truman was the thirty-third President of the United States, from "(1945-1953)."[212] He was a soldier in World War I, and a Vice-President and President of the United States during World War II. Former President Truman was used by Almighty God to fulfill Biblical prophesy. For President Truman was the American leader, who voiced his strong support that Israel should become a nation. The nation of Israel, which has been revealed since the beginning in the Bible in the Book of Genesis, and through the prophets in the Old Testament, would be reestablished as a nation in its own right in 1948. The United States of America was blessed by God for blessing the "new" nation of Israel (Gen 12:1,2; Ezr 1:1-4; Isa 11:11,12; 66: 7,8; Jer 31:10; Eze 37: 21,22; Ac 1:6,7).

The American people would be blessed by God after World War II, and through the 1950's, for the Lord Jesus, and the Bible, His Word would still be honored privately and publicly in government and schools. Almighty God, who honors His Word, has, and is having His Chosen people "the Israelites (taken) out of the nations where they (had) gone. (The Lord has and will)) gather them from all around and bring them back into their own land. (God has made) them one nation in the land, on the mountains of Israel." The Lord Jesus' imminent return for His people was now fulfilled by Scripture since Israel had become a nation (Dt 6:4-7; Isa 33:22; Eze 37:21,22; Mt 28:19,20; Gal 3:24[KJV]).

The American leader for the establishment of the nation of Israel, Harry "Truman, grew up in . . . a devout Christian home." At eighteen years of age, "he joined the Baptist church by baptism and remained a Southern Baptist the rest of his life." We have attended Baptist churches. In order to be baptized in that Church, you must believe that Jesus Christ died to save us from our sins. That baptism was a public acknowledgement that Jesus was in your life, was washing away your sins, and that you would follow Him "the rest of (your) life." Before Harry Truman was "14" years old, he "read the Bible through four times." He even "considered entering the ministry for a time," having a "fundamentalist reverence for the Bible"[213] (Ps 119:11,105; Mk 16:16; Jn 3:26; Ac 8:34-38; 16:30-34; 22:16; Ro 6:3,4; 10:9).

Harry Truman said, "Divine Providence has played a great part in our history . . . God has created us and brought us to our present position of power and strength for some great purpose . . . It is given, (our great purpose), to defend the spiritual values, . . . the moral code—against the vast forces of evil that seek to destroy them"[214] (Dt 28:7,12[b]; 1 Sa 17:45-51; 2 Ch 20:15-23; Ps 68:5; Eph 6:10-13).

President Truman, despite opposition from his "most trusted foreign policy advisors," and other legislative "leaders" announced that, "The United States recognizes the provisional government . . . of the new State of Israel." President Truman "believed in the historic justification for a Jewish homeland," calling himself, "Cyrus." King Cyrus of Persia "in the Old Testament . . . enabled the Jews to return to their land in the sixth century B.C. after their 70-year captivity"[215] (2 Ch 36:22,23; Ezr 4:3; Jer 25:11,12).

"Increase Mather (1639-1723)," who we reported on previously, supported "the national restoration of Israel to her land in the future, (which) was typical of American Colonial Puritans and was generally widespread . . . From the earliest times, American Christianity has always (moved) toward support of the restoration of national Israel in the Holy Land."[216] Following the prophetic words from God's prophets, Isaiah, Jeremiah, Ezekiel, Amos, and other prophets, to bring the Israelites back to their homeland, and following our forefathers' faith in the prophets, in the Scriptures, as well as President Tru(e)man's God-given beliefs, the American people blessed Israel and God's people, and in turn for blessing Israel, the United States was blessed (Gen 12:2,3; Ex 23:22; Isa 49:5,8,12; Jer 31:10; Eze 37:21,22; Am 9:15).

It is significant to note, that "at the time of the (Revolutionary War), it is estimated that only 2,500 out of 2.5 million Americans (or 0.1 percent) were Jewish . . . There were hundreds of . . . Jewish soldiers and sailors who fought in the Revolution and patriots who supported it . . . Many had sacrificed their lives for their new country," just as they did in two World Wars. After the Revolutionary War, one of those fighting "patriots . . . Benjamin Nones" received "a personal anti-Semitic attack in a Philadelphia paper." Mr.

Nones responded to that attack, "But I am a Jew . . . and so were Abraham and Isaac and Moses and the prophets, and so too were (Jesus) Christ and his apostles. I feel no disgrace in ranking with such society."[217] We believe that we all need to be "ranking with such society" in Jesus, the Jewish and Gentile Messiah (Gen 14:13; Ex 2:1-10; 3:6,15,16; Neh 4:1-3; Est 3:6,7; Mt 1:1,2,6,20; 23:34-38; Jn 1:41; 4:25,26).

"In 1790, . . . President George Washington delivered a (letter) to the Synagogue in Newport, RI." President Washington reported that "happily the government of the United States . . . gives to bigotry no sanction, to persecution no assistance." From that letter the Jewish people "were at least guaranteed religious freedom."[218] From the first President of the United States up through Harry Truman, the American people blessed the descendants of "Abraham and Isaac," offering them freedom to worship God in America, and freedom to worship God in the "new" nation of Israel in the twentieth century (Gen 47:1-6; Est 7:3-10; 8:11; Da 3:28,29; 6:26,27; Zec 14:16,17; Mt 4:10; Jn 4:23,24).

On December 19, 2008, my wife heard these words from the Lord Jesus, "I can go to Woodrow Wilson." In the twentieth century, President Woodrow Wilson, in a "New York Times" article in "May . . . 1920," which was during World War I, stated to a Rabbi Stephen Wise, "Dr. Wise, . . . when the war will be ended, . . . Jewish Palestine . . . will never go back to the Mohammedan apache" . . . "President Woodrow Wilson's" reference to the Turks as "the Mohammedan apache" was compared to ("the Apaches," who had "the image of being perhaps the most mindlessly violent Native American tribe.") . . . "The devoutly Christian Woodrow Wilson, as a preacher's son, maintained an anti-Turkish prejudice rivaling that of many missionaries"[219] (Gen 49:17; Eze 37:22,25-28; Joel 3:19-21; Jn 8:44; 16:2,3).

That promise by President Wilson would be fulfilled by President Truman later in the twentieth century, when the Jewish people would be able to worship God freely in their "new" nation of Israel. The United States was blessed because of their support of the Jewish people and the nation of Israel, as America had become the "head," the leader of all the nations in the world (Dt 28:7,13; Isa 66:8-10).

On December 18, 2008, after fasting and worshiping before the Lord Jesus, He gave us some visions: In a vision, my wife and I were gazing into the sky through a window on our front door. We saw a stained glass "Star of David," that we had received as a gift, lit up in the sky at night. This is the time of year, when we remember that the "Wise men" followed the "Star" to the child, Jesus. Then I saw a vision of a large Colonial canister that we received as a gift on my birthday. That canister has pictures of American flags surrounding it from the 1700s to today. It also has portions of the Declaration of Independence, the Constitution of the United States, and statements about freedom and liberty from our Founding Fathers in America.

The Lord Jesus said, "Follow that 'Star,' the 'Star' that came 'out of Jacob,' . . . 'the bright Morning Star.' Follow Jesus. Look up, 'because your redemption draweth nigh.' As you both are birthing Jesus in your hearts on (Mark's) birthday, so you are establishing more freedom and liberty in Me. You both were sent a canister representing freedom and liberty, representing the faith of your Founding Fathers in Jesus Christ. As you wrote about the birth of the nation of Israel for this book, you and your wife, as well as your family members will be blessed. For he who blesses Israel will be blessed by God." . . . Who would God call to carry the "torch" for Him in America following World War II? (Gen 12:3; Nu 24:17; Isa 66:8; Mt 2:1,2; Lk 21:28[KJV]; 1 Pe 1:3; Rev 14:4; 22:16).

Dwight David Eisenhower

"Dwight David Eisenhower," a "U.S. general" and "commander of Allied forces in Europe" during and after World War II, became the thirty-fourth President of the United States, "(1953-1961)."[220] Former President Eisenhower, following his predecessor Harry Truman, said, "Without God there can be no American form of government, nor an American way of life. Recognition of the Supreme Being is the first—the most basic—expression of Americanism. Thus the Founding Fathers of America saw it, and thus with God's help, it will continue to be"[221] (February 20, 1955) (Isa 9:7[a]; Mt 6:33; Mk 12:29,30).

"From the very beginning of our nation, . . . President . . . Eisenhower (understood that) our American way of life is firmly rooted in our belief in God," in the one true God, our Lord Jesus Christ. Under President Eisenhower's leadership, "Congress voted to incorporate the phrase 'under God' into the Pledge of Allegiance, . . . (as well as) to make 'In God We Trust' the national motto of the United States," which is still printed on our currency[222] (Ps 56:4; Jn 14:1; 1 Co 15:23-28; Eph 1:22,23; Col 2:6,7; 1 Pe 5:6).

The former President of the United States put his trust in the one true God for the welfare of this country, just like his predecessor, George Washington. So this country would endure a relatively peaceful period of time under the guidance of the "Prince of Peace," Jesus. However, prior to his Presidency, the Supreme Court of the United States, in 1947 made "a landmark decision" in the case of "Everson v. Board of Education," declaring "the Constitution required a sharp separation between government and religion."[223] This decision, we believe, would mark one of the major schemes by Satan to remove the Lordship of Jesus Christ from America . . . Our Lord Jesus wanted us to include the story of the pioneer man and woman from our book, *The Profound Mystery: Marriage—The First Church*,[224] as we finish up this chapter.

Pioneers on the Narrow Road

The Lord disclosed, "Men and women are made in the image of God. Male and female, He made them. They are made in My image to be helpmates, to help one another. (They are) to forge out a life together as 'one,' spiritually, (emotionally, physically, and mentally). Even as man pioneered the land in the early days of America, so man must pioneer ahead in his relationship with his wife on the land he lives on. He must be the provider, (like the pioneer), who fished and hunted food for the family, and planted a field of crops (Gen 1:26-28; 2:18,24; 30:29,30; Lev 17:13; Jer 16:16; Mk 4:2,8; 1 Pe 1:13).

"Man dug wells to provide water for the family to make it on a dry and barren land. Today, man must be able to provide his wife 'living water.' (He needs) to provide 'a cup of cold water' to refresh her. After an attack of the enemy on their land, in their marriage, (this "living water" can) restore them to wholeness (Gen 21:30; 26:18-22; Nu 21:17,18; Pr 11:25; 25:25; Jn 4:3-13; 1 Pe 5:8-10).

"You see the pioneers faced many enemies; Indians, bandits, thieves, weather, sickness and disease, famines, (etc.). The ones (pioneers) who followed Me, worked with their wives, so that they would be safer together against the threat of attacking enemies. Even today, the world becomes an enemy to a marriage and family. The lack of a foundation on the 'Word of God' allows the 'words of the world,' and the 'rains of immorality,' to reign over, and against a house, a marriage, and a family. Pioneers today are in the minority, as they were in the times of finding new land in America. The man must learn to split, and cut his own wood; to split himself away from the world's answers; their wood, their judgments, their answers, and their immorality (Mt 3:10; 7:24,27; Lk 10:2; Jn 15-19; Ro 8:35,36; 1 Co 3:9; 4:12; 2 Co 11:26; Eph 4:16).

"Where are the pioneers; the forgers for a new land, a new nation, and a 'new creation'? They are the few who try, and walk on the 'narrow road' to freedom. They walk with a Bible in their hands. They 'walk the walk,' and 'talk the talk' of the real men (and women) of God. They choose not to compromise with the world, nor have one foot in the world, and one foot with God. They have split the wood, burning up the chaff in themselves in their 'furnaces of repentance.' They have chosen, like real pioneers, to keep only the food that God gives them. Their food is the 'bread of life,' the food of the 'Word of God,' that lasts and sustains the family (Dt 6:4-7; 11:18,19; Isa 58:4; Mt 3:12; Jn 6:35,51; 2 Co 5:17; Gal 5:1; 6:15; 1 Jn 1:6,7).

"(Those pioneers) have chosen to keep out of their homes, detestable idols, and things that will tear the very fabric out of a marriage and family. They have chosen to follow Jesus, and leave the wasteful things behind. The television, (they realize) can be a source of great chasm between themselves and God. The source of evil springs up eternal in the media; in written form, in audio form, in video form, (in DVD's), and (in) computers and television (Dt 7:26; Est 3:8-14; Mt 4:19,20; Lk 16:26; Php 3:8).

"You see a man loses his ability to pioneer his land, when he becomes the prey to the 'schemes of the devil.' For man, rather than hunt and fish for prey, becomes ensnared in the devil's alluring trap. So rather than pray, man consumes himself in those electronic contraptions. (In so doing), he loses the fiber, the strength he needs to try to build his house on the 'Rock' (Pr 28:19; Mk 4:18; 16:18; 1 Co 3:10-15; Eph 6:10; 2 Ti 2:26).

"The woman, wife in turn, begins to become ensnared in the broader 'road of destruction' that her husband has chosen. She begins to feel that the man she married is choosing other things over her. Since she is not being attended to by her husband as before, she begins to lose her sense of being secure (in their relationship). They, (the husband and wife), gradually begin to lose their God-created need to be helpmates. Since he has chosen the world's answers for help, he is not as willing to pioneer his land together with his wife (Mal 2:14; Mt 7:13; Lk 11:46; 2 Pe 3:17; Rev 3:16,17).

"(The wife) gradually becomes lonelier, and more despondent. She finds other things, relationships to replace the loss of the God-given love in their marriage. The man has chosen to split off from his wife, to the world. Thus, Satan deceitfully destroys what God created in His image, male and female. Destruction can come on this 'broad road,' unless they repent and return to their 'first love.' (When you choose to return to your "first love"), God will pour out more love on your 'narrow road' together, than He ever could do on the world's 'road'!" (Ps 25:16; Mal 3:10; Mt 12:25,26; 19:4; Lk 6:38; 8:14; Ro 5:5; Rev 2:4,5). (Words received from the Lord on or about January 2003).

Would the American people follow the faith of their forefathers, their Founding Fathers, and believing patriots in the true Liberator, Jesus into the twenty-first century? Would the American people take heed to the prophetic utterance of General George Washington to his Continental Army in 1776? An utterance that caused the Army to fight for, and shed their blood for, freedom from a tyrannical ruler.

"The fate of 'unborn' millions will now depend on the courage . . . of this Army . . . We have, therefore, to resolve to conquer or die."[225]

For as "the Pony Express . . . used a relay system of horseback riders" to carry the mail and a "Bible . . . in the Western U.S." in the nineteenth century to "more than 160 stations along the route, . . . each "having a copy of the Bible";[226] so let us carry the "mail," the messages from heaven, the Word of God into the twentieth century, and discover that George Washington's prophetic utterance would fall on deaf ears.

[PART II]

★

AMERICA:
PRESENT

GOD SAVE AMERICA

"God save America! New world of glory,
New born to freedom and knowledge and pow'r,
Lifting the tow'rs of her lightning lit cities
Where the flood tides of humanity roar!

God save America! Bearing the olive,
Hers be the blessing the peacemakers prove,
Calling the nations to glad federation,
Leading the world in the triumph of love!

God save America! 'Mid all her splendors,
Save her from pride and from luxury;
Throne in her heart the Unseen and Eternal;
Right be her might and the truth make her free!"[1]

. 8 .

TO SEE FROM SHINING SEA

"The land you are . . . to possess is a land polluted by
the corruption of its peoples.
By their detestable practices they have filled it with
their impurity from one end to the other."

When my husband and I were teenagers, almost everyone older or slightly younger than us can remember where we were when President John F. Kennedy was shot and killed in Dallas, Texas. That incident happened in November 1963. It was a sad day for many of us. Yet, many of us had no idea that just prior to his death, the Supreme Court of the United States would make two decisions from the Bench, that would drastically change for the worst, the morality of the United States of America. Those decisions would directly oppose the faith of our forefathers, our Founding Fathers, our founding American documents, and prior decisions of higher Courts, in which it was accepted that the Lord Jesus Christ was and is the foundational Rock and

Cornerstone of this country. Sadly, a President of the United States would be assassinated shortly after those two Supreme Court decisions.

The Supreme Court of the United States of America

As we reported earlier, the First Amendment to the Constitution of the United States, states, "Congress shall make no law respecting an establishment of religion, or prohibiting the free exercise thereof; or abridging the freedom of speech, or of the press."

The Case of Engel v. Vitale

In the state of "New York," the "Board of Education of Union Free School District," . . . "under state law, directed the School District's principal" to recite a "prayer to be said aloud by each class . . . at the beginning of each school day." That prayer was "Almighty God, we acknowledge our dependence upon Thee, and we beg Thy blessing upon us, our parents, our teachers and our Country." The "state officials" of New York believed that this prayer would be beneficial to "all men and women of good will." The "state court" of New York "permitted the use of the prayer as long as it was not forced."[2] The prayer was challenged up to the Supreme Court (Pr 3:5,6; 11:27; Lk 2:14[KJV]; Ro 10:12).

In "1962," in the Supreme Court case of "Engel v. Vitale," Supreme Court "Justice Black" reported that the prayer was "a violation of the Establishment Clause" of the First Amendment to the Constitution for "government officials" were furthering "religious beliefs." Justice Black reported further that, "the constitutional prohibition against laws respecting an establishment of a religion must ... mean that in this country it is no part of the business of government to compose official prayers for any group of the American people"[3] (Lk 11:2-4; Ac 1:14; 2:42; 8:20-23; 1 Th 5:17).

Unfortunately, Supreme Court Justice Black did not take into consideration that the Establishment Clause applied to "Congress" establishing a "religion," a national religion like the Church of England in the seventeenth century. The Pilgrims and Puritans left their "Mother country" to "exercise" their freedom to worship God much more in line with the Scriptures. Supreme Court Justice Black must not have recognized that the individual states in America had at times established their own Christian denomination, for the state governmental officials were not members of Congress (Ac 11:26[b]; 24:7[KJV]; 1 Ti 4:7[KJV]; Heb 5:14[KJV]).

The states had free reign to freely "exercise" their Christian beliefs. Further, Justice Black must not have examined the numerous American documents from our forefathers and Founding Fathers, which were established under the direct guidance and Lordship of Jesus Christ, the one true liberator of the American people. In addition, Justice Black did not take into account the prior Supreme Court decisions that proclaimed the United States was a "Christian" people, and a "Christian nation" (Pr 1:5; Mt 7:24-27; 11:28-30; Jn 10:26,27; 1 Pe 4:16).

That landmark decision has removed public prayer in public schools even up to today. In no way, do we believe that the prayer offered in the state of New York, surely inspired by Almighty God, Himself, would be offensive to the majority of school officials, parents, and students in the state of New York, and throughout the states of this nation. On the contrary, seeking the Lord's blessings, as our forefathers and Founding Fathers sought earnestly, could not in any way harm the American people, but bless their school district and this country. To our extreme dismay, the removal of prayer in public schools, we believe, has fostered deplorable consequences among the children, youth, and adults, today (Dt 28:15,16; 2 Ch 7:14,19,20; Da 6:10-16; Ac 7:55-60; 2 Co 7:11).

Satan, using more liberal Supreme Court judges, as his "servants of righteousness," was allowed to "strike" the "heel" of Jesus Christ in America, striking at the foothold "Almighty God" had held for centuries in the United States. That case would be the "stepping stone" of further Court decisions that would spiral the morality of this country downward through the removal of public prayer and Bible readings in schools (Gen 3:15; Pr 22:28; 2 Co 11:14,15; Eph 4:27).

The Case of School District of Abington Township, Pennsylvania v. Schempp

Just months prior to the assassination of President Kennedy, the Supreme Court of the United States made another landmark decision on "June 17, 1963," which would "piggyback" off the case of Engel v. Vitale in 1962. It was recorded that, "The Commonwealth of Pennsylvania, by law, . . . as amended (on) December 17, 1959," required that, "'At least ten verses from the Holy Bible shall be read, without comment, at the opening of each public school on each school day. Any child shall be excused from such Bible reading, or attending such Bible reading, upon the written request of his parent or guardian'" . . . "On each school day at the Abington Senior High School between 8:15 and 8:30 a.m., while the pupils (were) attending their home rooms, . . . selected students" . . . read "10 verses of the Holy Bible," . . . which was "followed by the recitation of the Lord's prayer." Those readings were "broadcast to each room in the building." Students were "asked to stand and join in . . . the prayer" . . . "As directed by statute," the morning exercise was "voluntary." Students could choose to be "absent from the classroom," or choose "not" to "participate in the exercises"[4] (Dt 6:4-7[KJV]; Neh 8:8; Mt 6:9-13; 2 Ti 2:15[KJV]; 3:16,17).

"The Schempp family, husband and wife and two of their three children," who were "of the Unitarian faith," brought a "suit" against their School District in Pennsylvania. The "reading of the Bible" was "contrary to the religious beliefs which they, (the Schempp family), held." The "suit" was brought forth "contending that their rights under the Fourteenth Amendment to the Constitution of the United States . . . (had) been . . . violated."[5] The Fourteenth Amendment states that, "No state shall make or enforce any law which shall abridge the privileges or immunities of citizens of the United States." The case was challenged up to the Supreme Court (Gal 1:6-9; Col 2:8; 2 Pe 2:1,2).

Supreme Court Justice Clark "delivered the opinion of the Court." It was reported that, "In light of the history of the First Amendment, . . . we hold that the practices at issue and the laws requiring them are unconstitutional under the Establishment Clause, as applied to the States through the Fourteenth Amendment . . . No state law or local school board may require that passages from the Bible be read or that the Lord's Prayer be recited in the public schools of a State"[6] (Jer 36:13-27; Lk 4:21-30; Jn 15:19; Ac 9:1,2).

Supreme Court Justice Stewart in his dissenting opinion reported, "I cannot agree that, on these records, we can say that the Establishment Clause has . . . been violated . . . As a matter of history . . . of our free society, . . . religion and government must necessarily interact in countless ways. . . . The Establishment Clause leads to irreconcilable conflict with the Free Exercise Clause . . . The First Amendment was adopted solely as a limitation upon the . . . National Government, (so) that Congress . . . would be powerless to establish a national church, but would also be unable to interfere with existing state establishments . . . The right of free exercise of religion (is) protected by the First Amendment, (and is) embrace(d) . . . by the States (in) the Fourteenth Amendment . . . Freedom to adhere to (a) religious organization or form of worship as the individual may choose cannot be restricted by law . . . It safeguards the free exercise of. . . . religion . . . A refusal to permit religious exercises thus is seen . . . as the establishment of a religion of secularism . . ."[7] (Ps 67:4[KJV]; Isa 9:6,7; 33:22; 1 Ti 6:20,21).

Justice Stewart declared further, "There is no constitutional bar to the use of government property for religious purposes . . . (Yet,) a different standard has been applied to public school property . . . The Constitution does not require extirpation of all expression of religious belief . . . It could hardly be contended that the exercises . . . provide(d) an opportunity for the voluntary expression of religious belief, . . . and which contained (an) excusal provision . . . Our Constitution . . . protects . . . the freedom of each of us . . . to believe or disbelieve, to worship or not worship, to pray or keep silent, according to his own conscience, uncoerced and unrestrained by government . . . What (they) allege as the basis for their causes of action are . . . violations of religious liberty . . . (There is) no constitutional requirement which makes it necessary for government to be hostile to religion . . . (The) public school system (is) to aid religious groups to spread their faith . . . "[8] (Mt 28:18-20; Ac 13:45-49; Ro 8:21; Gal 5:1; 2 Th 3:1).

Supreme Court Justice Stewart, we believe, was of a "sound mind" maintaining "justice in the Courts," when he courageously dissented from the majority of his associate justices. In following the decisions and Christian beliefs of our forefathers and Founding Fathers, as well as America's founding documents, the national government had no right to impose a national religion on the American people. Yet, American students and school officials had a constitutional right to express their Christian beliefs in any government facility. According to the First Amendment, it is a right, and not an abridgement of the Fourteenth Amendment, as long as it was voluntary and not coerced (La 3:34,35; Am 5:15; Gal 4:4,5; 2 Ti 1:7[KJV]).

Unfortunately, Satan was able to elevate certain men's thoughts and opinions in the Supreme Court over the truths of the Lord Jesus Christ and His Word, the Bible. We believe from those Supreme Court decisions, that the elevation of men's beliefs over God's Word, is like men and women becoming their own "gods." A "secular humanism" began to strip away the foundations of this country on the Rock, Jesus Christ (1 Co 3:18-21; Gal 4:9; 1 Ti 4:1,2; 2 Ti 4:3,4).

"The New England Primer" and "the McGuffey" reading series would be replaced with school text books void of Scriptures, Bible verses, the Lord's Prayer, and any recognition of the Founding Fathers' faith and compassion towards their Lord Jesus Christ in the founding of our Country, following those two Supreme Court decisions. The Lord Jesus said, "But everyone who hears these words of mine and does not put them into practice is like a foolish man who built his house on sand. The rain came down, the streams rose, and the winds blew and beat against that house, and it fell with a crash!" The United States, we believe, is and has become "foolish" crashing before our very eyes, because of the decisions made by men and women apart from the God of the Bible (Mt 7:26,27; Lk 10:33[KJV]; 1 Co 1:18-20; Eph 5:17).

Jesus was tested by Satan, "Bow down and worship me, (Satan)." The Lord Jesus responded, "Away from me, Satan! For it is written: 'Worship the Lord your God and serve him only.' Then the devil left him." In the early 1960's, we believe men of the "high" Court chose to "bow down and worship (Satan)," giving the devil a "stronghold" in America that continues up through this day. The devil has not left America, because we believe many "leaders" in governmental positions have said by their actions, "Away from me, Jesus! Worship men's thoughts, not God's Word. Serve us, serve our 'god,' (Satan)" (Mt 4:8-11; 12:25-29; 26:63-68; 2 Co 11:3,4,14,15).

Through the voice of one man, an unbeliever, "a foolish man" in the eyes of the Lord Jesus, and through the voices of his family members, the United States of America would find itself on a collision course with the God of the Bible, the one and only true God, Jesus, and change the course of American history. The free exercise of religion, the freedom of speech and of the press in the Constitution of the United States allows us to write this book. Sadly, this book and others like it, that mention God, Jesus Christ, would most likely be forbidden reading in the public schools throughout America today, as a consequence from those two Supreme Court rulings (Pr 18:7; Mt 7:26; Ac 4:17,18; 5:28; 9:1,2).

In affirmation of this, it was noted that, "The courts of the land, primarily the U.S. Supreme Court, originally thought to be the least powerful branch of government, bears grave responsibility for ignoring the original intent of the U.S. Constitution, disregarding the history of our nation, and orchestrating the movement of our nation from its religious foundation onto the . . . path of anti-Christian, secularism/humanism"[9] (Ac 18:6; 20:30; 26:28; Col 2:2-4; 1 Jn 2:18).

In a newsletter received on May 31, 2007, from Alan Keyes, Chairman of Declaration Alliance, he reported that, "Our Constitution is being violated when the First Amendment guarantee for Americans to freely express their religion is voided . . . Liberal judges (are declaring) 'Freedom of religion' means freedom from religion . . . The Constitution does not give the federal government any power to address issues of establishment of religion, it explicitly forbids it to do so . . . The Constitution of the United States did not give the judiciary the right to establish law. Laws are passed by legislatures that represent the people . . . We are witnessing a raw exercise of judicial power against people of faith."[10] Since the 1960's rulings of the Supreme Court, we have seen the evil manifestation of the antichrist spirit in America, gloating even today (Pr 28:28[a]; Mt 5:10-12; Lk 6:22,23; Ac 8:1; 1 Jn 4:3).

The Fourth Great Awakening

It was reported that "since 1963, our nation has seen a sharp increase of violent crime, drug abuse, unwed teen mothers, sexually transmitted diseases, divorce, suicide, single-parent homes, abortion, homosexual relationships, and pornography."[11]

When prayers to the Lord and His Word were taken out of the public schools in America, the morality, the righteous moral code of many Americans spiraled downward. "For lack of guidance a nation falls." The United States was falling because they chose to be guided by men and women, rather than trusting in the guidance of Almighty God, the Lord Jesus. We reported earlier, that our forefathers and Founding Fathers trusted in God for their guidance. No longer did "righteousness" exalt the "nation" of America, rather the acceptance of "sin" was becoming "a disgrace to" the "people" of the United States (Pr 11:14[a]; 14:34; 16:18; 29:26; Isa 2:12-17; Jn l4:1; Ro 1:22-25).

Yet, the battle between Jesus Christ and Satan over the Lordship of the United States of America was and is not over. A "Fourth Great Awakening," many believe, occurred "in the late 1960s" through "1980." "Secularism" was growing in America, which was the belief that faith in Almighty God and His Word was to be removed from public schools, government, and their "officials." Despite the "growth" of secularism, "most conservative religious denominations, (and) . . . evangelical and fundamentalist denominations . . . grew rapidly in numbers, (and) spread across the United States . . . [12] (Ps 10:4,5; Ecc 4:13-16; Isa 50:4; 51:9; Lk 4:2-13; Ac 4:4).

"There was a new emphasis on a personal relationship with Jesus from . . . 'non-denominational' churches and 'community faith centers' . . . A charismatic awakening occurred between 1961 and 1982 . . . From (the) Pentecostal movement . . . emphasis (was) placed . . . on experiencing . . . the gifts of the spirit, . . . the Holy Spirit, . . . (which included) speaking in tongues, healing, and prophesy . . . The Jesus Movement (was) considered . . . to be part of the Fourth Great Awakening"[13] (Joel 2:28-32; Mk 1:41 [KJV]; Ac 4:13; Eph 5:14; Php 2:1,2; 1 Jn 1:3).

The Jesus Movement

It was noted that, "The movement arose on the West Coast of the United States in the late 1960s . . . and spread primarily through North America, . . . before dying out by the early 1980s . . . The Jesus movement . . . greatly influenced contemporary Christian . . . and . . . Jesus music." Many "hippies" during that time were tired of "the hippie lifestyle and became 'Jesus people' . . . (They had a) zeal for Christ and love of others . . . Secular and Christian media exposure in 1971 and 1972 caused the Jesus movement to explode across the United States . . . "[14] (Mt 4:24,25; 8:1; Ro 12:9-11; Eph 5:19).

"Some of the fastest growing US denominations of the late 20th century, such as Calvary Chapel, Hope Church and the Vineyard Churches, trace their roots directly back to the Jesus movement, . . . as well as (the organization), . . . Jews for Jesus, (the) contemporary Christian music industry, (and) evangelical Christianity"[15] (Mt 16:18; Ac 6:7; Ro 1:16; 2 Ti 4:5).

As early as 1967, it was reported "among the hippies (that) many (had) an encounter, the experience of faith in Jesus Christ." They proclaimed "Their lives had undergone a radical spiritual transformation. Addicts spoke of freedom from drugs, (and there) was a fanatic-like allegiance to the person of Jesus Christ . . . Most of these street Christians (believed that they were) . . . walking through similar events as those outlined in the Book of Acts." In an article in *Look* magazine in 1971, the headline proclaimed, . . . "'The Jesus Movement is Upon Us' . . . Many of today's largest church congregations and most well-known contemporary leaders trace their origins to this time," as well[16] (Mk 16:19,20; Ac 2:42-47; 4:32-35; 9:17-22).

Our Lord Jesus, we believe, was reaching out to those who were "sick" and in "need" of "a doctor." Jesus was touching men and women, adults and youth in a profound way during the Fourth Great Awakening. Radical changes were taking place among many Christian Americans. It was during this time, that my husband and I accepted Jesus Christ into our hearts and lives. We both would say, that our lives were radically changed, as we daily developed a deeper personal relationship with our Savior and our Lord Jesus (Mt 9:12; Jn 1:12; 10:4,5,9,29; Ro 10:9,10; Rev 3:20).

We have benefited from the origins of the Jesus movement, as we have enjoyed attending some of the churches and congregations that trace their roots to the movement. We have been blessed by some of the contemporary Christian music, the evangelical leaders in the church, as well as experiencing the "gifts of the Spirit." Many Christian schools began and were established after the Supreme Court's decisions in the early 1960's. We have been blessed to teach at two Christian schools, and have had the privilege to pray, read the Bible, and share openly about Jesus Christ freely with our students. Still, the effects of the Supreme Court rulings would cause destructive consequences on the morality of many Americans in the United States. What leader would God call to the Presidency to stem the tide of immorality in America? (Ac 2:42; 5:42; Ro 12:7; 1 Co 12:28; 14:1).

We believe that prayers offered on behalf of former President Ronald Reagan, the "40th president of the U.S., . . . (1981-1989),"[17] prior to and during his Presidency, were from many of those Americans who were impacted during the Fourth Great Awakening. It is significant to note, that our Lord Jesus Christ fasted 40 days at the outset of His ministry, and Moses also fasted 40 days. At the outset of his Presidency, Ronald Reagan would begin his tenure as the 40th President of the United States (Ex 34:28; Mt 4:1,2; Ac 12:5).

Ronald Reagan

Ronald Reagan "was raised (in a) . . . Christian Church . . . (His) mother . . . was a devout Christian, (and they were) members of Dixon Christian church," that Ronald Reagan grew up in. It was reported, while in "grammar" school, "Reagan led Sunday school classes, Bible Studies and prayer sessions . . . 'The Bible was a daily and vital part of his life.'" He went to "Eureka College," which had "a reputation for being an 'old-timey' . . . Bible school." Ronald Reagan claimed that he had "received a 'prophesy,' that he would become president" "ten years before he was elected." Shortly after Ronald Reagan became President of the United States, an assassination attempt (was made on his life). Following that attempt on his life, President Reagan wrote, "Whatever happens now I owe my life to God and will try to serve him in every way I can"[18] (Ps 119:9,11; Lk 2:42,46,47; Jn 16:13; 2 Ti 1:5; Heb 9:14).

Ronald Reagan "believed in the Bible as the inspired Word of God (for) he . . . said, ' . . . of the many influences that have shaped the United States of America, . . . none may be said to be more fundamental and enduring than the Bible' . . . If we'd only read and believe . . . God is the center of our lives . . . I was motivated to proclaim or designate 1983 as the Year of the Bible . . . When Americans reach out for values of faith, . . . they're saying, 'We want the Word of God. We want to face the future with the Bible.'" In 1984, some time after reading Scripture verses to participants at an "annual National Prayer Breakfast," . . . "(. . . Mt 22:36-40)," Ronald Reagan said, "Can we resolve to reach, learn, and try to heed the greatest message ever written—God's Word and the Holy Bible"[19] (Ps 138:2[b]; Mt 5:6; 21:22; Jn 1:1,14; Ac 17-11; 2 Ti 2:15; 3:16,17).

Ronald Reagan "believed Jesus was . . . the actual incarnate Son of God." He shared, "His name alone, Jesus, can lift our hearts, soothe our sorrows, heal our wounds, and drive away our fears. He gave us love and forgiveness. He taught us truth." It was reported that, "aides closest to President Reagan would occasionally see him get down on his knees and pray . . . 'Belief in the dependence of God,'" he said, "'is essential to our state and nation'"[20] (Mt 18:20; Lk 10:17; 23:34; Jn 1:12,14; 3:16; 14:13,16; Php 2:10).

In a letter, Ronald Reagan wrote, "Christ's own statements foreclose, in my opinion, any questions as to his divinity . . . Either he was what he said he was, or he was the world's greatest liar. It is impossible for me to believe that a liar or charlatan could have had the effect on mankind that He has for 2,000 years . . . Would even the greatest of liars carry his lie through the Crucifixion when a simple confession would have saved him?"[21] (Mt 16:15-17; 26:63,64; Lk 23:33).

Ronald Reagan said, "Can you name one problem that would not be solved if we had simply followed the teachings of the man from Galilee? . . . If the Lord is our light, our strength, and our salvation, whom shall we fear? . . . Believing in Him, we need never be afraid . . . And, by dying for us, Jesus showed how far our love should be ready to go: all the way . . . We are enjoined by Scripture and the Lord Jesus to oppose it, . . . sin and evil . . . with all our might"[22] (Ps 27:1,2; Mt 4:12-15; Jn 14:27; Ac 2:23,24,33; Eph 6:13-17).

Former President Reagan, we believe, was called by the Lord Jesus to lead our country. He had an understanding of how the United States had lost its "moral compass." President Ronald Reagan "believed . . . that America had deserted the moral roots upon which it was founded . . . As a result of breaking its moral covenant with God, America was plagued by a host of societal and economic problems: the breakdown of the family, . . . the spread of atheism, . . . immorality and legalized abortion, . . . a disintegrating economy, secularism in education, (etc.) . . . The constitutional concepts of individual freedom and limited governmental powers constituted America's covenant . . . (However), the people had been misguided by leaders who violated, the covenant, and the nation was suffering"[23] (Dt 28:15-19; Eze 16:8,15,43; Ac 20:30; Ro 8:28; 2 Ti 4:3,4; Jude 4).

Former President Reagan shared further, "In the 1960's, . . . we began to make straight steps towards secularizing our nation and removing religion from its honored place . . . (This happened through banning) the compulsory saying of prayers, (and) . . . the Court (banning) the reading of the Bible in our public schools . . . Now our children are not allowed (to participate in) voluntary prayer . . . Suits were brought to abolish the words 'under God' from the Pledge of Allegiance and to remove 'In God We Trust' from public documents and from our currency . . . Those who are attacking religion claim they are doing it in the name of tolerance . . . Isn't it the real truth that they are intolerant of religion? . . . You may forbid the name of Jesus to pass their (the American people's) lips. But you will never destroy the love of God and freedom that burns in their hearts"[24] (Ps 55:4; Lk 24:32; 1 Co 2:9,10; 2 Ti 2:25,26; Tit 1,9; Heb 12:3; 1 Pe 5:6).

President Reagan declared, "When men try to live in a world without God, it's only too easy for them to forget the rights that God bestows—too easy to suppress freedom of speech . . . Standing up for America also means standing up for God who has so blessed this land . . . The wall of separation between church and state in America was erected by our forefathers to protect religion from the state, not the other way around . . . Politics—legalization of abortion; attempts to fund abortion with taxpayers' money; prohibition of voluntary prayer in public schools; weakening of laws against pornography; failure to enforce civil rights legislation on behalf of helpless, severely ill infants—has moved across the barrier of church and state."[25] God gave former President Ronald Reagan and other Presidents in the past, wisdom, "To see" the need for Almighty God to govern our country "from shining sea" (Pr 29:16,27; Isa 2:12,15,17; 9:7; Jer 7:1-11; Mt 13:15; Ac 5:28,29; 2 Th 2:15).

An Antichrist Spirit of Rebellion in America

In direct opposition to Ronald Reagan's statements, a woman stated before a Justice of the Court, "I stand for separation of church and state, for the same reasons our forefathers did. It's not to protect religion from the grasp of government; it is to protect our government from the grasp of religious fanaticism." This statement was from the movie, *The Contender*, a Dream Works Production in 2000. In support of Ronald Reagan, Rabbi Lapin, who we reported on previously, responded, "The reality today is that we still have a choice. The choice is between a benign America based on Judeo-Christian principles, and on the other side is a very aggressive, sinister, and power-hungry secular fundamentalism that wishes to inject its tentacles into every aspect of American life!"[26] (Ps 10:2-11; Lk 6:27-31; Ac 9:1,2; 2 Co 6:14-18; 2 Ti 3:1-5).

Some Christian men and women today are speaking up about the moral decline of values in America. We need to listen to them on this matter, and to the voice of the Good Shepherd, Jesus. Alan Sears, President, CEO & General Counsel for the Alliance Defense Fund, shared in a newsletter that we received on March 1, 2008, that, "We now live in a country where our Christian faith and Biblical values are openly attacked; . . . where parental authority is undermined and children have less protection from pornography, . . . (where) advocates of dangerous sexual behavior (prevail), . . . and where the value of human life has been cheapened—from the moment of conception . . . The American Civil Liberties Union (ACLU) is actively striving to eliminate the freedoms of millions of Americans"[27] (Ps 106:37-39; Pr 31:8,9; Mt 24:9-12; Jn 15:18-21; Ac 4:18; 8:3).

Alan Sears reported, "The ACLU has . . . threatened politicians, cities and towns, and even entire legislatures with lawsuits for official prayer . . . In South Carolina and Virginia, the ACLU used the threat of a lawsuit against local government entities to silence prayer 'in Jesus name' . . . In another lawsuit in Virginia, the ACLU demanded that a Wiccan priestess be allowed to open a town meeting with her own humanistic prayer . . . The message is clear—Christianity . . . (is) out, but everything else is fine . . . The ACLU . . . works to prevent Christians and ministries from publicly sharing the Gospel at various times and places"[28] (Dt 18:10-12; Pr 29:10; Ac 5:28; 16:16-19; 18:5,6; 1 Pe 2:23; 3:14,15).

David Wilkerson, pastor and founder of Teen Challenge ministries worldwide, reported in 1998 at Times Square Church in New York City, "Fifty million Americans . . . smoke pot, and millions more are hooked on heroin, crack and other hard drugs . . . Disney has become one of the world's most corrupt media systems. Its movies are rife with homosexuality, violence and the occult . . . Jesus' day was very similar to ours . . . Jesus described his society as a generation of vipers: priests who robbed widows, scoffers, blasphemers, adulterers, child offenders, (etc.)"[29] (Pr 20:1; 23:20,21,25,29; Mt 23:33-36; Mk 8:38; Lk 20:42; Jn 10:33-39; Ro 1:26-32; Rev 9:21).

In May and September 2008, David Wilkerson shared that, "Right now, there is an all-out attack on Christ and his Word . . . We are slowly pushing God completely out of our courts, our schools, our society. We refuse to acknowledge his blessing on our nation, saying instead, 'We have accomplished everything in our own strength. We are the greatest, mightiest, wealthiest nation on earth, and we have achieved it on our own' . . . This nation has stuck up its nose at God, shaking our fist at him and daring him to act"[30] (Dt 8:17,18; Ps 10:4; Isa 65:2,5; 1 Co 2:14; 2 Jn 7).

In a "national survey from the Culture and Media Institute," that was "newly released," (2008), it was reported that: "74% of Americans . . . say they believe moral values in our country are weaker than they were 20 years ago . . . 68% say the media—entertainment and news—are having a detrimental effect on moral values . . . 51% describe themselves as 'pro-choice,' (and) . . . 36% believe people should live by God's principles."[31]

On January 16, 2009, after worshiping before the Lord Jesus, I received a vision of a man lifting up his left arm in a defiant manner against God. Then the man was sweeping his arm in the air, moving all that had to do with God away from him. He appeared to be a person in government. On March 6, 2008, I saw a vision of a thirteen-star flag with bullet holes shot through it. The flag was old and shredded at its fringes.

The Lord Jesus said in January, "Many in government have this attitude, saying to God, 'Keep away! Don't come near me. We are too good for you! You (God) are smoke in our nostrils. We have no room for God in our house, the White House, the House of Representatives, the House of the Senate. Look at how prosperous we are. We have done this ourselves without your help. We don't like your Jesus. We have our own 'Jesus,' one who loves all regardless of their beliefs and actions. We love the homosexuals and their love for each other. We love those women who choose to get an abortion. We want to protect them, protect their lives. We love those who have committed capital crimes. We don't want to offend them. We love those who have the courage to speak out against God, against your Jesus, for they are our heroes! We love ourselves, just as God intended it to be. God created us to love our neighbors as ourselves. Don't tell us about sin, judgements and eternal fire, for our 'god' is a 'god' of love, and he loves all' (2 Ch 7:14; Ps 10:5; Pr 6:16-19; 27:5,6; Isa 65:5; Mt 25:41-46; Lk 2:7; 9:58; Jn 3:18; 16:7-11; Ro 3:23; 2 Co 11:4; Heb 12:5,6).

"But this is not the God of the Bible, this is not the God of the Word of God. This is not the God, Jesus. This is the testimony of another 'god,' one who elevates men and women who violate God's laws. The first commandment is this, 'Love the Lord your God,' first. 'If you love Me, you will obey' My commandments; to love one another, to hear My Words and put them into practice, and to repent from sin, and to speak up against it in your homes, neighborhoods, and in the private and public sector. As a God of love, I discipline those who love Me and My Words. For their other 'god' is Satan, the deceiver, who 'loves' evil, who deceitfully has led many away from the truth, from faith in the one true God, from faith in Jesus" (Pr 3:11,12; Mt 4:17; 7:24; 12:43-45; 22:37,38; 28:20; Lk 13:3; Jn 15:10-12[KJV]; Ac 7:51-53; Rev 12:9[KJV]).

A House Divided

In March, the Lord said, "The American patriots, who suffered at the hands of tyrannical England, were able to bring freedom to this land through the shedding of their own blood. They were United in their States together, undivided with one cause, one purpose. Therefore, they could defeat their enemy. Today, the enemy, Satan, has a stronghold of division in this land with disunited people. They are no longer States that once said, 'United We Stand.' This country is disunited for Satan knows that a 'kingdom divided against itself' cannot 'stand.' A family divided cannot stand. America is divided on (the issues of) allowing abortions of the unborn, accepting homosexual marriages, school prayer, and having God recognized in public settings. This country is divided on honoring Jesus Christ (Eze 11:19; Mk 3:23-27; Ro 16:17,18; Col 1:20; Heb 9:22).

"The States are not united, but divided, because they have chosen other 'gods.' They have chosen the 'god' of separation of church and state. What a division it has caused between the Church, and the people in each state. As long as this country is divided, it will not stand very long. For God needs to bring this country to its first purpose, to its first cause; the United States, united in Jesus Christ, united in the Word of God. God must tear down before He can build up. God must destroy the bastions of evil before He can restore this land. A kingdom, a nation divided against Jesus will not stand (Ecc 3:3; Jer 1:10; Mt 12:25,26; Jn 17:23; Ro 1:22,23,25; Php 2:1,2; 1 Jn 3:8; Rev 2:4,5).

"Today, houses, married partners are not united in their state of mind. For they do not have one purpose and one call together. So you see the breakdown in families. Satan has been attacking the foundation of families, marriages. After the breakdown of a marriage, especially one joined together as believers, Satan can drive deeper wedges between families, communities, states, and the nation. His wedges are manifested in preventing prayer in public settings, in the acceptance of abortion as a legal practice, and in leading men and women away from normal heterosexual relationships toward marriages with same sex relationships. For many men and women today are not following the same cause and purpose of the Founders of America, who chose to follow the one true God, Jesus, and His Words (Mt 19:4-9; Lk 11:17,18; 1 Co 11:18; 1 Ti 4:1,2; 2 Pe 1:2).

"The United States had been divided over slavery during the Civil War. Only by the grace of God, after the death of thousands, was America able to stand after that War. The real slaves during the Civil War were the slave owners, who were enslaved to the bondage of their own human possessions. When those who are slaves to sin submit their sins at the altar of Jesus, the one true God, they can be set free. They can stand together against the so-called 'rights' to sin that come from the enemy, Satan. Those sins include the 'rights' of women to choose to abort children, the 'rights' of homosexuals to be given the same privileges as married couples, the 'rights' of students in public schools not to be offended by the Christian God, by Scripture readings, or by prayer at their schools. Those 'rights' have been separating Jesus from the private and public sector. Their 'rights' have enslaved them to sin, burdened by a 'yoke of slavery,' instead of finding real liberty in Jesus. For only the Son can set them free" (Mt 23:13-15; 25-28; Jn 8:34-36; Ro 2:8; 1 Co 13:5; Gal 4:3,9; 5:1; 1 Ti 1:9,10).

On February 13, 2008, my wife heard these words, "Our own ill country." And the Lord shared, "Your country is ill in sin. Your country is becoming sicker, more diseased, because they act as if they are not ill, that they are well. The 'ill' ones are considered by those who are truly sick, as religious 'fanatics.' Those who are truly ill, see those seeking Jesus to heal them from their sickness of diseased sin, as out of touch with reality, holding on to the 'crutch' of religion. They see those seeking Jesus, as being 'blind' to the truth. The really ill ones see themselves having their own truth (Mt 4:24; 9:12,13; 24:16[a]; Jn 8:42-47; Ac 20:30).

"Those truly ill, value illness in your country as something acceptable, and deserving honor, such as 'reproductive rights,' the 'right' to abort babies, or 'gay rights,' the right to have America accept gay/lesbian relationships as 'normal.' The truly ill ones cover over the disease of sin in their own lives, and how their disease has contributed to the murder of innocent victims, fetuses in the womb, as well as the murder of persons who have chosen the 'gay lifestyle,' a major contributor to the AIDS disease and other sexually transmitted diseases. The truly ill ones approve of unclean, immoral sexual relations between men and women. They despise those who seek to follow Jesus Christ and His Words. They despise those who avoid sexually immoral thoughts and acts, and those who stand up against the ills in your country. Satan has deceived the truly ill ones, diseased by sin, to hate the healthier ones in your country (Lev 20:13; Ps 106:37-39; Pr 29:10; Isa 53:3; Ro 1:24-27,32; 2 Pe 2:10).

"The truly ill ones have murdered many innocent victims by choosing to take out prayer in schools, in public places, and in the government. They call it, 'separation of church and state.' The really ill ones perceive the followers of Jesus, as the really sick, religious ones for trying to bring prayer back in public schools. Some of the 'fruits' of the truly ill ones, the unrighteous, are seen in the illness in your country today; growing criminal activity, gangs, drugs, sexual immorality, prostitution, and hatred towards the few standing up for righteous acts. What makes your country ill is that the truly sick ones choose not to seek the true Physician, who could heal them of their illness, diseased sin in their lives. 'I have come for the sick, not for the righteous' (in their own eyes)" (Da 6:11-16; Mt 9:12[KJV]; 24:9-13; Gal 5:17-21; Ja 5:6; 3 Jn 10[KJV]).

On the day after September 11, 2001, (9/11), the Lord said, "Satan plots to destroy mankind through wicked and devious schemes. This destruction was done by men led by the darkness of demons which scared the American public. The United States has been weakened by its own sinful ways. This was a beginning of an assault on America. America is not as strong or pure in its faith in God as it once was" (Pr 14:34; Mt 8:28-34; Jn 10:10[a]; Eph 6:11; Rev 2:20-22).

Loss of America's Foundation on the Word of God

According to the voice of the Good Shepherd, Jesus, and others who are speaking up about the loss of spiritual direction in our country, *America* has lost its foundation on the Rock, on the Word of God! Some leaders for Jesus are able, "To see from shining sea," between the Atlantic and Pacific Oceans, the damage that Satan has afflicted in America. We seem to be traveling on murky, dark, cold, unchartered waters without a "magnetic moral compass" to guide us, without the Holy Spirit. For many Americans are no longer pulled toward Jesus and His Words to guide this nation. We believe that many of our "leaders" are "poles" apart from the true liberator, Jesus (Isa 57:20; Mt 7:26,27; Jn 10:14; 16:13; 2 Co 4:18; 11:26; Heb 12:3).

The pilot guiding the "ship" of the United States, the "USS *America*," has become man, not the Son of God, not the Living Word, not the Lord Jesus Christ. Our country has begun to become spiritually adrift without an anchor on the Rock, Jesus, to steady, stabilize, and prosper this country. We believe America is about to run aground on the "shoals" and "sandbars" of men and women's thoughts (that are) apart from God, for we believe that our country's foundation has moved off the Rock onto sand. We believe that the steering, the helm of our country is being given over to Satan, to the antichrist spirit, who, when given the opportunity, will take America "down to the grave," . . . "to the depths of the pit," through self-elevation of men and women over God (Isa 14:12-15; 55:8,9; Eze 27:27-30; Mt 7:26; Ac 27:29,30,39-41; Heb 2:1; 6:19).

It was noted that, "The Bible gives us both the Mosaic legal code—a detailed set of civil laws designed for ancient Israel, but with clear applications for modern states—as well as a set of principles to guide our . . . civil government . . . The Bible indicates that God's people have a duty to confront political authorities who stray from God's moral standard . . . The Founders (of our nation) designed a government filled with safeguards against human evil . . . (They understood) that the Bible offer(ed) political wisdom and guidance . . . to provide order and justice, (and) to . . . restrain the wicked acts of men"[32] (Lev 19:1-37; Dt 4:44,45; 5:1-21; 28:1-19; Pr 16:11; 23:10; 29:25; Mt 23:13; Mk 6:17,18; Ac 5:28,29; Ro 13:2-5).

The Lord Jesus shared with "the Pharisees" and "the Herodians," . . . "Give to Caesar what is Caesar's," when referring to a Roman coin, "and to God what is God's." When the laws of the land reject Biblical moral laws, God calls us to give to God what is God's, His Living Word. Peter and John in the Book of Acts were "commanded . . . not to speak . . . at all in the name of Jesus." They responded, "Judge for yourselves whether it is right in God's sight to obey you rather than God . . . (For) we must obey God rather than men." Just as our forefathers resisted the tyrannical government of England in order to follow the Scriptures, the Lord Jesus, so today true believers in Jesus are being called by God to speak up about the laws in the land that oppose the Living God and His Word (Mt 5:14-16; 22:15-22; Lk 9:26; Ac 4:18,19; 5:29; Ro 1:16; Heb 4:12; 10:28).

As we come to the end of this chapter, Paul Harvey, well-known radio broadcaster and "commentator," aired Evangelist Billy Graham praying the "Prayer for Our Nation." His prayer was from an original version of that prayer "written in 1995 by Bob Russell." Evangelist Billy Graham's prayer sums up the moral degeneration of America.[33]

"Heavenly Father, we come before You today to ask Your forgiveness and to seek Your direction and guidance. We know Your Word says, 'Woe to those who call evil good,' but that is exactly what we have done. We have lost our spiritual equilibrium and reversed our values. We confess that:

> We have ridiculed the absolute truth of Your Word and called it Pluralism.
> We have worshipped other gods and called it multiculturalism.
> We have endorsed perversion and called it alternative lifestyle.
> We have exploited the poor and called it the lottery.
> We have rewarded laziness and called it welfare.
> We have killed our unborn and called it choice.
> We have shot abortionists and called it justifiable.
> We have neglected to discipline our children and called it building self-esteem.
> We have abused power and called it politics.
> We have coveted our neighbor's possessions and called it ambition.
> We have polluted the air with profanity and pornography and called it freedom of expression.
> We have ridiculed the time-honored values of our forefathers and called it enlightenment.
> Search us, Oh, God, and know our hearts today; cleanse us from every sin and set us free, . . . (we) ask it in the name of Your Son, the living Savior, Jesus Christ. Amen"

9

IF YOU FORSAKE HIM, HE WILL FORSAKE YOU!

"Behold, ye trust in lying words, that cannot profit.
Will ye steal, murder, and commit adultery, and swear
falsely, and burn incense unto Baal, and walk
after other gods whom ye know not; and come and
stand before Me in this house, which is called by
My Name, and say, We are delivered to do
all these abominations?"

In the spring of 1978, shortly after I (Mark) became a "born again" believer in Jesus Christ, I attended several different Christian denominational churches. On one occasion, I attended a United Methodist Church. The "pastor" prayed and "preached" a sermon, but I never heard the name of Jesus in his message. The Holy Spirit convicted me at that time, to approach the "pastor" about never mentioning the name of Jesus. At the door of the Church, as I was leaving, I shared with the "pastor," that I never heard him say the name of Jesus. The "pastor" replied, "It was implied in my message."

Implied or not, no one knew about the name of Jesus in his message or prayers (Mt 21:42; Jn 3:3; 1 Pe 2:4).

After becoming a believer, I began to realize that some pastors did not want to say the name of Jesus. What was happening in churches? The name of Jesus was not important, and not mentioned among so-called "believers" in Jesus Christ. What was taking place, we believe, was a movement by Satan of an antichrist spirit in the Church, which was influenced by the world of unbelieving men and women to discredit our Lord Jesus (Isa 53:3; Jn 15:20,21; 2 Co 4:4; 1 Jn 2:18,19).

Jesus Seminar

Renowned author and radio commentator, Dr. James Dobson of the Focus on the Family Christian organization, wrote a "Family News" article in March 2008. In that article he wrote about "the so-called 'Jesus Seminar.'" It was noted, that a "group of very liberal scholars . . . assembled in 1985 to 're-evaluate' the person of Jesus Christ and to deconstruct the biblical accounts surrounding Him . . . A leading figure in the Jesus Seminar" reportedly said, "'I do not think anyone, anywhere, at any time brings dead people back to life'" . . . "Another fellow of the Seminar" shared that, "Jesus, regardless of where his corpse ended up, is dead and remains dead"[34] (Mt 28:1-15; Ro 10:9; Col 2:8-12; 2 Pe 2:1).

Dr. Dobson reported further that "in 1993, the Jesus Seminar released . . . the following conclusions: The resurrection of Jesus did not involve the resuscitation of a corpse . . . The body of Jesus decayed as do other corpses . . . It is not necessary to believe in the historical veracity of the resurrection narratives." An "influential New Testament scholar of the twentieth century," reportedly said, "It is impossible to . . . believe in the New Testament's world of demons and spirits" . . . "Bodies do not rise from the dead, and it is high time Christians stopped making such claims." Another critical scholar shared, "The tomb of Jesus was not empty, but full, and his body did not disappear, but rotted away"[35] (Isa 53:10-12; Ac 2:22-28, 31-33; 1 Co 1:18-21; 2 Co 2:6-10,14).

Dr. Dobson wrote further that those, "who do not even see themselves as sinners—want . . . nothing to do with Jesus Christ as our sinless substitute, who shed his blood for the remission of our sins . . . The tomb was really empty . . . He is risen. He is risen indeed . . . That will be the faith of the true Church when the risen Christ returns to claim his own"[36] (Mk 16:5-7; Ro 3:22-26; Col 1:15-20; Heb 4:15).

Attempts made to discredit our Lord Jesus through the "wisdom" of men and women, we believe, have influenced both believers in Jesus and non-believers. Yet, those who have been "born-again" by accepting Jesus into their hearts, know the real truth through the indwelling Spirit of Truth, the Holy Spirit. The real truth, that Jesus is the Son of God, the Christ, the Messiah, is known by true believers, because it is spiritually discerned. "The man without the Spirit does not accept the things that come from the Spirit of God, for they are foolishness to him." Still, Satan is at work through his "servants of righteousness" to dethrone Jesus Christ in America (Mt 16:15-17; Jn 1:13; 1 Co 2:7-10, 14-16; 2 Co 11:14,15; 1 Ti 4:1).

The Media

Another tactic of Satan to destroy the credibility of Jesus is through the media. In a Coral Ridge Ministries' news magazine, *Impact*, it was reported in "a recent PBS documentary, . . . 'The Bible's Buried Secrets,'" that "the Scriptures are not historically accurate." Also, in a "documentary film, *Religulous* (a play on the words 'religion' and 'ridiculous'), . . . God and Christianity (were) . . . mocked."[37] Dr. D. James Kennedy and Jerry Newcombe reported on an article that "Barbara Reynolds wrote . . . in

USA Today . . . She asked, 'What does the press have against Jesus? Is there a bias against Christianity? . . . By concluding that God isn't important, the press is trying to play God itself'"[38] (Ps 22:6,7; Jn 15:18-20; Ac 4:17,18; 2 Ti 3:16).

Dr. Kennedy and Jerry Newcombe wrote further, "Bernard Goldberg, a . . . CBS—veteran . . . in 1996," shared, "I'm more convinced than ever, . . . that our viewers simply don't trust us . . . The networks and other 'media elites' have a . . . bias, (which) is so blatantly true." In a "Lichter-Rothman report on the 'media elite,'" it was "found that 93 percent seldom or never attend religious services." In a "George Gallup" poll, it was noted that only a little "more than 40 percent of the population attend church every week, . . . (and) only about seven percent of the media elite" attend a church. It was noted that, "Bias in the media is reflected . . . in their . . . denigrating the Christian faith, promoting sexual perversion, profanity, blasphemy, and obscenity"[39] (Mk 7:20-23; Ac 20:30; Ro 1:22-27; 1 Ti 4:1).

Anti-Christian and Antichrist Spirit in America

Unfortunately, we believe that the media has a powerful influence on the beliefs of Americans through television, radio, the movie industry, newspapers, magazines, books, billboards, etc. We believe the consequences of watching and listening to various forms of the media will subtly remove Jesus out of the minds and hearts of Americans. In "New York, NY— City officials (took) down a pastor's billboard with Bible verses on it, labeling it 'hate crimes' rhetoric . . . 'Hate crimes' (are) crimes committed against favored groups of people . . . Preaching that Christ is the only way to Heaven can be seen as 'hate speech' against other religions . . . (A) pastor's sermon could potentially be considered a 'hate crime' . . . Children will be indoctrinated and pressured to keep silent"[40] (Mt 5:10; 21:15,16; Mk 13:13; Jn 14:6).

Even "in Louisiana, government officials ordered a church to shut down its dinners for victims of Hurricane Katrina—because the church invited victims to voluntarily stay after dinner to hear about Jesus Christ."[41] There is a movement by Satan that seems to be gaining momentum in America to persecute American Christians. A movement that Jesus, Himself spoke about, that would happen in the last days. The Lord Jesus said, "You will be hated by all nations because of me. At that time many will turn away from the faith" (Mt 5:11,12; 24:9,10; Mk 4:14,15; Rev 12:17).

"Author and pastor David Wilkerson wrote . . . in the early 1970's . . . that the current trends in the culture, the education system, and the workplace would be so directly opposed to a Christian's beliefs and values" . . . Further, author David Limbaugh wrote that "Christians are not merely treated as antiquated outcasts; sadly, we are finding that our constitutionally guaranteed religious rights have been seriously eroded and our right to speak the truth is not only limited, but increasingly denounced as 'hate speech' . . . Christians are often subjected to scorn and ridicule and denied their religious freedoms"[42] (Lk 6:22; Ac 5:28-32,40-42; 2 Ti 4:3,4).

In addition, removing "under God" from the Pledge of Allegiance is another warning to Americans, that Satan's, anti-God, antichrist spirit is moving across America. In "2002," Judges in California, Satan's "servants of righteousness," declared the words "under God" in the Pledge of Allegiance, "unconstitutional" . . . "Judge Alfred Goodwin of the 9th Circuit Court of Appeals wrote that the words 'under God' in our Pledge of Allegiance were unconstitutional"[43] (2 Co 11:14,15; Eph 1:20-22; 2:2; 1 Jn 2:22).

Michael Reagan, son of former President Ronald Reagan, reported that there is a "campaign . . . to remove 'In God We Trust' from all U.S. coins, . . . (to) shut down the U.S. Senate Chaplain's office, . . . and repeal my father's National Day of Prayer." Michael Reagan noted what President Ronald Reagan shared in "1984," . . . "If we ever forget that we are

One Nation Under God, then we will be a Nation gone under." Michael Reagan reported further that, "Our nation is more morally 'going under' as . . . judges, politicians, and educators systematically strip away our country's biblical foundations." Michael wrote, "The greatest thing he, (his father, Ronald Reagan) passed on to me is a faith in Jesus Christ"[44] (Ps 56:11; Pr 14:34; Mk 15:29,30; Jn 14:1; Heb 2:7-11; 12:2,3).

Another reason that the name of Jesus and Christianity have suffered in America is because of the American Civil Liberties Union, the "ACLU," which we mentioned earlier. The ACLU has used bullying tactics against "the Church" filing "thousands of law suits each year." The ACLU "is the nation's largest public interest law firm." The campaign "of the ACLU" is "1. Erasing Our Christian Heritage. 2. Attacking Religious Liberties, (and) 3. Silencing the Church."[45] Satan, the "murderer," the one who "comes only to steal and kill and destroy," is going after true believers in Jesus in these last days, "those who obey God's commandments and hold to the testimony of Jesus" (Jn 8:44,45; 10:10[a]; Ac 8:1; Rev 12:17).

While we had been working at a Christian Youth Home for over twelve years, the word "Christian" at the Home had been joined together with Roman Catholics and Muslims. At a recent graduation ceremony, (2008), the name of Jesus was used sparingly, once at the end of a prayer. This Christian Youth Home was founded by a notable, strong Christian believer in Jesus Christ. When the home first opened its doors to residents, only Christians were employed at this Youth Home. Today, in the Youth Home's "Employee's Handbook," it is reported that the home does not discriminate in their employment of staff members on the basis of one's religion, or on one's sexual orientation. Any individual from other religious beliefs can, and have been hired at the "Christian" Youth Home. Homosexuals and lesbians can be hired at the Home regardless of their sexual orientation (Ac 4:18; 1 Co 6:9,18-20; 2 Co 6:14-18; 1 Pe 4:14).

Today, the Youth Home "yokes" with unbelievers, those having other "gods." The founder of this Christian Youth Home built the home from a vision given to him by God. We believe, that God's vision is not being followed today, for the Home is not being built on the foundation of the Lord Jesus Christ. Even a "leader" of the Youth Home reported at a recent graduation ceremony, that "We are a faith-based institution." He shared that the Home takes "Protestants, Catholics, and Muslims," and that the staff members do not "evangelize or proselytize" at the Youth Home. What happened to taking in true Christians? Why has Jesus Christ been minimized at a Christian Youth Home? (Dt 13:6-8; Ps 127:1; 1 Co 3:11; 2 Co 6:14; 1 Ti 4:1).

We believe, it is the spirit of antichrist infiltrating "Christian" organizations. The name of Jesus, we believe, has become offensive to some "Christian" ministries, as well as to the public. We believe, like former President Ronald Reagan, that America is "going under." Many Americans are choosing to go under the dictates of the devil, and not choosing to submit under Almighty God! (Mt 4:8,9; Lk 8:11-14; 2 Ti 2:25,26).

On January 25, 2008, early in the morning, my wife heard this word, "America." The Lord said that morning, "America is becoming a nation of self-interests, self-indulgence, self-centeredness, selfishness. It is becoming a 2 Timothy 3 country. ("But mark this: There will be terrible times in the last days. People will be lovers of themselves, lovers of money, boastful, proud, abusive, disobedient to their parents, ungrateful, unholy, without love, unforgiving, slanderous, without self-control, brutal, not lovers of the good, treacherous, rash, conceited, lovers of pleasure rather than lovers of God"). Demonic opponents of the truth are bullying the Church into submission to secular humanism, to a belief in, and trust that man has the answers to America's problems, not God. Believing in the God of the Bible is considered foolish, a crutch, and in some places, fanatical. So, out of fear of being considered foolish, pastors are choosing church services, (sermons), that blend in with the world (Dt 8:17,18; Isa 2:22; Da 4:28-32,37; 5:20-23; 1 Co 1:27-31; 2 Ti 3:1-4; 2 Pe 2:2).

"Men and women have an answer to every problem in America. Every answer is an answer without God, without Jesus, without the Word, the 'real thing.' A 'real thing' in the world's eyes is a 'coke'! Men and women say, 'I have the answer.' With their own intellect, with their own man-made ways to solve problems in America, they have become their own 'gods.' With their own rhetoric, (men and women), believe that they can convince America, that they have the 'answers.' Yet, behind the scenes are the murderous deaths of unborn children; adults sacrificing their children on the altar of materialism, children discarded because of men and women's answers. Men and women's answers will never resolve America's problems. The 'real thing,' the 'real' answer is Jesus!" (Ps 10:4,11; 106:37,38; Jn 6:54,55; Ac 12:21-24; 1 Co 1:20). (Words received from Jesus Christ on May 27, 2008).

On October 26, 2007, my wife had previously heard the word, "America." The Lord disclosed, "America has to do with your grandson, 'Noah.' While in kindergarten class, he proudly said the 'Pledge of Allegiance' with his hand over his heart. (That incident was reported to my wife by our daughter over the telephone). 'One nation under God' is sadly not becoming the case for America. For there are groups that desire to remove the name 'God' from the Pledge, today. Some Americans are offended, when Christians give the names 'God' or 'Jesus Christ' to anything related to America. They believe that 'creative minds' brought the United States to where it is today. They do not believe God, and His Son, Jesus, have anything to do with America's prosperity (Isa 45:7; Jn 1:1-3; 15:20,21; 1 Pe 4:16; 5:6-9; 1 Jn 2:22,23).

"The 'proud mocker,' Satan, has blinded many of those groups of unbelievers over the years from the truth about America's foundation. America was founded on the Word of God, and on the shed blood of many believers in Jesus Christ. Satan, using self-elevated pride in men and women's hearts in America, has deceived Americans into believing that, 'We can do it ourselves. We don't need God, Jesus.' But, they fail to realize that they serve their own 'god,' Satan, the 'prince of the world,' who has desired to be above God from the very beginning of time!" (Gen 3:1-5; Pr 21:24; Isa 14:12-14; Mt 24:24,25; Jn 14:30; 2 Co 3:5; 4:4; Rev 12:11).

The Church in Laodicea

Many true Christians believe that "the Church in Laodicea," as revealed by our Lord Jesus in the Book of Revelation, is representative of the Church in the last days. We have shared how Satan is using government officials, private organizations, and certain groups of people to silence the Church of true believers in Jesus from spreading the gospel. We believe that many in the Church are blending in with the world today, so as not to be persecuted for their faith in Jesus. Many Christians in America, we believe, have "itching ears" to hear what they "want to hear," as they "turn their ears away from the truth." We believe that many in the Church have become "lukewarm," as revealed in the Church of Laodicea. "On the inside (they) are full of dead men's bones and everything unclean" (Mt 13:18-21; 23:27,28; Ac 9:1,2; 2 Ti 4:3,4; Rev 3:14,17).

One Christian man reported in an article about politics, "Conservatives who profess the Christian faith . . . (are chasing) God out of the public square, . . . (because of their) . . . ignorance of the biblical history of this nation . . . The majority of Christians have rebelled against obeying the Great Commission. The lack of the church's obedience to the cultural mandate imbedded in the Great Commission is the main reason for the present deplorable condition of the nation . . . It is when Christians fail to fulfill their civic duty that they turn their back on the blessings God longs to shower upon this nation . . . Christians (have been) . . . keeping . . . away from the political arena, which has (allowed) . . . men and women who despise the absolutes of God, to take control of the government, universities, courts, legislation, media, the world of entertainment, science and the economy"[46] (Mt 22:21; 28:18-20; Mk 4:16,17; Ro 13:1-5; 1 Co 11:22; Heb 4:11).

Satan, we believe, has been subtly putting the Church of true believers in Jesus to sleep. Rather than waking up from their slumber, we believe, many believers are turning their heads back on their "pillows." They are not giving Jesus a "place to lay His head" in their hearts. David Wilkerson, as we reported previously, has spoken openly about the condition of the Church today at Times Square Church in New York City. We believe that David Wilkerson has an understanding of the "heartbeat" of the Christian Church (Pr 26:14; Lk 9:58; Ro 13:11,12; Heb 4:12).

In his messages in 1998, Pastor Wilkerson disclosed, "I believe America's rejection of Christ's lordship is the reason behind all the bloodshed, violence, racial hatred, moral decay, drug abuse and outbreak of deadly sexual diseases in our society. Lawmakers, educators and the media have made God an unspeakable subject . . . Rejection of Jesus' authority (is) . . . happening in his church! . . . Jesus, our exalted Lord and king, is being dethroned in churches throughout the land and in the lives of a multitude of believers"[47] (Isa 53:3; Lk 10:16; Ro 1:21-27; 1 Ti 6:15; 1 Jn 2:19).

He shared "Our society no longer trusts God, turning instead to the government, the President, the educational system, Social Security . . . We have dethroned God—rejecting the Bible and prayers—and enthroned science, psychology and education instead . . . It has given us a plague of AIDS, a deluge of drug abuse, (and) . . . absolute chaos among our youth . . . The White House is embroiled in a sex scandal . . . Sin is seen (as) . . . a 'disease.' A drug addict is said to have a 'weakness' . . . Prophets of holiness have been replaced by psychologists and social workers . . . The church has slowly but surely dethroned Christ and enthroned the wisdom of the world"[48] (Hos 9:17; Mt 23:34,35; Ac 7:52,53; Gal 6:3; 1 Ti 4:1; 2 Ti 3:1-7; 2 Pe 2:1,2,10).

Pastor Wilkerson said, "The American church today is the most blatant 'feel good' church in all of history . . . Believers who have been devoted to Jesus for years now turn (to) their television sets . . . (Even) books and magazines you find in Christian bookstores . . . are casting (away) the yoke of Christ . . . (Some) pastors . . . believed God would use rock-and-roll and rap music to bring in the next great revival . . . No— never! . . . There is an unwillingness to hear the true word of God . . . People are . . . hardening their hearts"[49] (Ex 32:18,19; Ps 2:1-4,12; 4:2; Am 8:11; Mt 24:10; Mk 10:21,22; Heb 3:7,8,12,13; 1 Pe 4:3).

In a message in 2005, Pastor Wilkerson shared further, "Christ warned that many imposters would come representing themselves as him . . . He's describing deceived ministers who preach a different gospel and a different christ . . . These articulate teachers depart from the authority of Scripture . . . They pose as angels of light to introduce new, 'enlightened' concepts they say reflect Jesus . . . (They are) deceitful workers, transforming themselves into the apostles of Christ . . . A Barna Group survey found that some 10 to 12 million 'born again' Christians have stopped going to church in the U.S. . . . I see it as the enemy's last assault on the church before Jesus returns"[50] (Mt 24:3,5,23; Mk 13:22; 2 Co 11:3,4,13; Gal 1:6,7; 1 Ti 4:1).

In a message in 2006, Pastor Wilkerson stated, "Our nation's courts . . . are mocking Christianity . . . In thousands of churches . . . there is never any mention of sin, the Cross, sacrifice, judgment or hell. Godly watchmen aren't allowed to speak . . . The whole focus is on success, . . . (and) prosperity . . . with every sermon designed to make people feel good . . . (The) self-serving, get-rich gospel . . . (is) all cursed . . . All the hireling shepherds are going to face bankruptcy"[51] (Jer 6:17; Da 6:7-12; Jn 10:12,13; Ac 26:28; 1 Co 1:18; 1 Ti 6:3-5, 9,10; 2 Ti 4:4).

In another message in 2008, David Wilkerson reported that, "A recent poll shows that atheism is spreading rapidly across America . . . Some 30 percent of Americans now say they no longer believe in the God of the Bible . . . His Word warns that the heathen will rage, secular powers will try to outlaw Christianity, and fast-growing, anti-Christ movements will boast they'll rule the world and destroy Jesus' followers"[52] (Lk 2:16-19; Ac 20:29,30; 2 Th 2:11,12; Jude 4; Rev 12:7).

He disclosed, "I see . . . (the) separation today between the church and God . . . in the soft-pedaled gospel of post-modern churches . . . Many have become lovers of pleasure more than lovers of God, . . . having a form of religion with no power, . . . despising the gospel of their fathers, . . . (and) changing God's infallible Word to suit the times . . . False religions grow in great numbers while Christ's church seems so few in number"[53] (Pr 13:13[KJV]; Mt 24:24; Lk 16:13[KJV]; 1 Co 11:22; 2 Ti 3:4,5).

Further, he shared, "Backslidden theologians are redefining Jesus, attacking his divinity, heaping ridicule on the Bible . . . The fact is the world will never accept Jesus as the answer . . . (When) those powers of the world . . . come whispering, 'Let us help,' . . . worldly offers to assist ministries can be Satan-inspired . . . When a ministry relies on the world's resources, . . . it's dangerous . . . For any Christ-centered ministry to be dependent on government funds, (will lack) the power of Christ to truly set free"[54] (Jer 5:6[b]; 2 Co 6:14,15; 11:4,13-15; 2 Th 2:4; 2 Ti 3:5).

It is significant to note, that the Christian Youth Home, where we had worked for several years, has been relying "on the world's resources" for years. The Home has received funds and grants from state government officials. We could see that the "power of Christ" at that Home had not set many youth "free" through Jesus Christ (1 Co 1:17; Gal 4:9; 1 Jn 2:15).

The Lord Jesus disclosed, "Devils are spreading lies in the pulpits (through men and women) under the guise of Christianity. The American Church has become 'lukewarm.' My children, do not listen to the falseness preached in the pulpit today, as they compromise with evil, and display a lack of compassion for the Son of God. I am not into performances. I want hearts dedicated to the real Jesus. Performances will not save the poor, the hungry, nor the destitute. Have you not performed in your faith towards others, which has become an outward appearance of life, but inward deadness. You know the difference (Mt 23:5-7,27; Mk 13:22,23; Lk 20:45-47; 2 Pe 2:1,3; Rev 3:16).

"In countries who want a Savior, many listen to My voice, for they want the One who helps them. In countries like the United States, many have grown tired of My presence in their lives. Some hear My voice, but most do not. They choose to stay in their worldly mansions, watching their worldly programs like the rich man, (Lazarus, as told by Jesus in the Bible). They will enjoy their luxuries on earth, rejecting those who have nothing but Jesus (Mt 7:26,27; Mk 4:18,19; Lk 8:21; 10:39; 16:19-21; 25; Jn 10:4,5,27; Ja 5:1-6).

"As you see the world falling down beside you, who is going to pick up the fallen pieces? Only Jesus can do that. When the world was falling apart, I came to rescue the world of men and women from eternal punishment through suffering for the sake of saving all mankind. All the ways of the world of men and women have fancy terminology or phrases, but the Way of God is real, not false, and goes right to the heart in love. Do not lean on man for your understanding. It is not in man's studies that behavior changes, but it is in being a man for God, who learns how to rightly handle the Word of God, (that changes a man's heart). It is in denying self in humility, so as not to need to please man, that you can hear the Words of God and put them into practice (Isa 53:10-12; Mt 7:24; 18:2-4; Lk 9:23; Jn 3:16-18; Ro 5:5; Gal 1:10; 2 Ti 2:15; 3:16; 1 Jn 4:14).

"Change comes through Jesus, who went to desolate places to pray, so that He could reveal to the world, God's answers for peace. It was and is His peace that can come to you in those desolate places in your heart. You can learn to live and survive without the worldly comforts. Set your heart, set yourself apart like on a desolate island, so you can learn to 'walk on water' with Jesus" (Mt 11:28,30; 14:27-29; Mk 1:35; Jn 14:27; 2 Co 3:18[KJV]; 6:17,18; Php 3:21[KJV]). (Messages received from the Lord Jesus on January 19, 1999, March 29, 30, 1999, April 10, 15, 2002, and January 25, 2008).

As true believers in Jesus, we are witnessing the signs that Jesus spoke about that would occur in this generation before His return. The Church, we believe, is becoming "lukewarm," and our Lord Jesus is about to vomit us out of His mouth. We must stand "firm to the end (so we) will be saved" from the "great distress" coming to America. We believe that the true Church will experience "a great persecution" in the days ahead. We must "hold" fast "to the testimony of Jesus." With our Lord Jesus to "strengthen" us, "help" us, and "uphold (us) with (His) righteous right hand," we will be victorious over "the evil one," "the dragon," who is "enraged at the . . . offspring" of Jesus, "those who obey God's commandments" (Isa 41:10; Mt 24:13,21,24; Ac 8:1; Rev 3:16; 6:9[KJV]; 12:17).

On January 28, 2009, after fasting and praising Almighty God, the Holy Spirit "fire" came upon me and such a way that my body was trembling. The Lord gave me some visions, and then spoke to me. In the first vision, I saw myself (with my wife) hiding behind what appeared to be wheat stacks that Ornan hid behind in the Book of 1 Chronicles, Chapter 21 in the Bible. Then I saw what appeared to be a 1950's neighborhood with homes fairly separated from one another, and built during that time period. Then a vision followed of a young man, a Pilgrim looking out of a bubble-glass window up to heaven. In the sky were many clouds, and there appeared to be a "whirlwind" in the clouds.

Then the Lord disclosed, "We don't need to hide behind those wheat stacks out of a fear of God. We need to step out on faith! Step out on the Word of God, which has been like 'fire shut up in (your) bones.' Step out in confidence, knowing that Almighty God is with you together, as one. So you step out of your house, and walk on those streets proclaiming the kingdom of God. Your neighborhood will be like the time in the 50's, when people could step out of their houses and speak about Jesus openly. There will be a freedom in your neighborhood (Jos 1:9; 1 Ch 21:20; Jer 20:9; Ac 4:13; 5:42; Ro 4:12).

"You have been given freedom to see what you see, and

hear what you are hearing today, that Jesus is coming soon. I am giving you a voice to speak up and warn America in this book! These Words come from heaven above, and are not to be hidden behind those wheat stacks. My Words must be proclaimed from the 'rooftops,' for I am taking out of you both, the silence that held you captive as children, (perpetrated) by your parents, to serve their world of demons (Pr 31:8,9; Isa 61:1-3; Mt 10:27; Lk 10:23,24; Ac 26:25[KJV]).

"Jeremiah (in the Bible) said, 'But I'm only a child.' But I say to you, 'Do not say that you are only a child anymore, for I have given you Words to speak; to uproot, to tear down, to destroy, and to build up.' Your sins have been atoned for on the Cross. The inner guilt (from your childhood) has been atoned for, that guilt, that if you speak up, you will be punished, that if you speak up, you will be abandoned. As a child, how could you live without that guilt. But you are not children anymore. I have called you to speak up together, for love, for your marriage, for your oneness, for your book, whether you are punished or not, whether you are abandoned or not (Isa 6:6,7; Jer 1:6-10; Ac 18:26; 1 Co 13:11; Eph 4:15,16; Heb 10:23; 12:2; 1 Jn 4:18).

"Those lies that have been embedded so deeply in your memories, 'Do not speak about evil. Close your eyes,' (to the evil around you). That is what you were taught as little children. But I am removing those lies, and I have given you eyes to see and ears to hear, to speak not only to your neighbors and your community, but to the nations! The enemy, (Satan), has thwarted your attempts to speak up in the past, but I have given you 'gold refined in the fire' in the 'furnace of affliction' in these last days. This is My day of salvation" (Ps 12:2; Isa 48:10; Mt 13:15; 2 Co 6:2; Eph 4:25; Rev 3:18; 12:10).

Then the Holy Spirit came on me in such a way, that I began to sob and weep deeply. Finally, I felt compelled by the Holy Spirit to throw up, to vomit out of my mouth, sin within me. Then I said, "Forgive me Father for my sins, my wretchedness." The Lord then said, "I am weeping through you for the wickedness of this nation. I am spitting out of My mouth, through your mouth, (the "lukewarm") Church, the Church of Laodicea" (Jer 7:28; Mt 6:14,15; Lk 6:21; Jn 16:7-9; Ac 10:44-46; Rev 3:14-16).

The Earth Was Full of Violence

In the days of Noah, "the earth was corrupt in God's sight and was full of violence." A sign of Jesus, "the Son of Man's" imminent return would be, "as it was in the days of Noah." We believe that God sees the earth "corrupt" today, and "full of violence." Pastor David Wilkerson revealed in a message in 2008, that, "All around us in the world today, there is terrorism, senseless violence, mounting financial crises and panic . . . Satan's powers of darkness have been sent expressly to wage battles that will wear down the confidence of God's saints. This assault from hell is about to become so devastating, so terrifying, we are going to need supernatural power to sustain us. Human will and intelligence will be no match for the demonic manifestations we're going to face"[55] (Gen 6:11; Lk 17:26; Ac 26:18; Ro 1:29-31; Eph 6:12; 2 Ti 3:1-4; 4:16-18; 1 Pe 5:8,9; Rev 6:9).

In a message in 1998, David Wilkerson disclosed, "Teenage crime in this country is the highest in the free world . . . Our children have been robbed of all moral standards, denied all access to God—and they're reacting by becoming more violent and rebellious"[56] (Pr 13:24; Eze 18:10-13; Mt 18:6-9; 19:13).

It is significant to note, that on "March 2, 2005, . . . The Supreme Court . . . abolished the death penalty for convicted killers who committed their crimes before the age of 18 . . . Executions for those 15 and younger when they committed their crimes were outlawed in 1988 . . . Justice Anthony Kennedy wrote in the majority opinion, . . . 'The age of 18 is the point where society draws the line for many purposes between childhood and adulthood.'"[57] Those court decisions, we believe, have contributed to a more violent, murderous number of juveniles and adults in the United States. (Gen 9:5,6; Mk 13:12; Ro 13:3,4; 1 Jn 3:12,13).

Gangs

At a Juvenile Court Service Unit and at a Youth Home where we had worked for years, we had noticed an increase in violent crimes among juveniles. Many of the male teenagers that we had worked with had belonged to gangs. We found that they had a difficult time turning their lives over to Jesus Christ. Gang members, we had experienced, maintained their loyalty to their gang, even when they were residents at a Christian Youth Home. At times, they instigated gang-related activity at the Home. There seemed to be a legitimate fear, that if they chose to leave their gang, they would have been severely harmed by their gang members, or possibly murdered (Pr 1:10-19; Ro 1:29-31; 1 Jn 2:19).

It has been reported that, "The early adolescent years (12-14 years of age) are a crucial time when youths are exposed to gangs and may consider joining a gang . . . Research indicates that parents play a pivotal role in keeping young people out of gangs. Negative influences within the family—including domestic violence, child abuse, harsh or inconsistent parenting practices, and/or drugs/alcohol abuse by family members—can increase the risk that a youth will join a gang . . . Parents can protect their children from gang activity (by) . . . using positive discipline strategies . . . (and setting) firm limits with (their) children and teens . . . Do not rescue your children from the consequences of their decisions . . . Talk to your children about ways to deal with pressure from friends"[58] (Dt 6:4-7; Pr 20:1; 22:6; Eze 18:2; Mal 2:16; Col 3:21; Heb 12:5-11).

"The days of Noah," we believe, are upon us, which must draw true believers closer to our soon coming King, Jesus! For our Lord Jesus did not preach violence, but love. It is our experience, that it is difficult to bring youth to Jesus Christ in a violent atmosphere. Scripture validates our experience, "In repentance and rest is your salvation, in quietness and trust is your strength, but you would have none of it." Another type of violence moving throughout the world has come to America in the bombing of the World Trade Center in 1993, and in the destruction of the Twin Towers in New York City, as well as the attack on the Pentagon on September 11, 2001, (9/11) (Isa 30:15; Mt 24:37; Lk 6:27-36; 21:28; Gal 6:8[a]; Ja 4:8).

They Sacrificed to Demons, to Foreign "gods"

Radical Islamic followers have attacked Americans on the shores of the Continental United States at the end of the twentieth century, and into the twenty first century. President George W. Bush declared on television after the attack on 9/11, that those who attacked America's buildings were terrorists. Our country was suddenly at war with terrorist organizations. We believe that Almighty God had lifted His grace of protection over our country then, because many Americans had rejected the faith of our forefathers and Founding Fathers in God, in Jesus. What type of murderous violence consumed those terrorists? We believe they were serving their 'god,' a 'god' of murder, killing, and destruction, described as Satan by Jesus in the Bible (Ps 2:12; Isa 24:17,18; Mt 24:6; Lk 21:26; Jn 8:44; 10:10[a]).

In a *Family News* letter in October 2006, Dr. James Dobson reported that, "millions of . . . Muslim . . . extremists do exist, . . . and they hate us with a vengence . . . There are, according to several estimates, (over one) billion Muslims in the world . . . 120 to 180 million people, (extremists), are committed to our destruction. These extremists have been promised from childhood that they will be rewarded in paradise with endless glory and 72 virgins for sacrificing their lives in the Jihad (holy war) . . . (Even if their numbers were less, millions of) people

... would give their lives, if required, to murder Christians, atheists and members of other religious faiths, (and) . . . bomb our homeland . . . This is a threat of enormous proportions"[59] (Pr 29:10; Jn 3:20; Ja 5:6; 1 Jn 3:10; Rev 21:8).

Dr. Dobson shared, "That threat takes on new meaning when we consider the convincing evidence that Iran . . . (is) working feverishly to develop nuclear capabilities, (building) . . . weapons of mass destruction . . . Confrontations with wicked rulers are coming . . . As long as we are pledged to defend Israel and its 'covenant land,' we will be targeted by Muslim terrorists . . . Trying to negotiate with those who want to kill us is ridiculous . . . There are politicians whose . . . plan for national defense (is to) 'talk' (with terrorist "leaders") . . . They are . . . foolish and dangerous . . . In 2004, . . . (almost) 21 million evangelical Christians did not bother to vote,"[60] for politicians that stand up against terrorism. The Lord Jesus proclaimed in the gospel of John, "In fact, a time is coming when anyone who kills you will think he is offering a service to God" (Ps 10:2,3,7-11; Pr 6:9-11; 12:10[b]; 21:10; 28:4; Jn 16:2,3).

There is No Other Rock

In an article in the *Jewish Voice Today* magazine, March/April 2008, it was asked, "What is Written on the Dome of the Rock about Jesus?" Reportedly, it is written on that site in Jerusalem, that, "There is no God but Allah, He has no-copartner . . . The messiah Jesus, son of Mary, is but a messenger of Allah . . . So believe only in Allah and his messenger but do not say three (trinity) . . . Allah is only one God, far be it from his glory, that he should have a son . . . The religion in Allah's sight is Islam." Kamal Saleem, a believer in Jesus, reported that the Muslims believe, according to what is written on the dome of the Rock about Jesus, that, "There is allah only and Christ is a messenger of allah only—Christ is a muslim—there is no Father, Son, and Holy Spirit . . . There was never any other religion but Islam. The rest are made up—Judaism and Christianity." Mr. Saleem shared his beliefs, "Satan declared himself the only god—allah—and humanity is not of his level of glory. Humans are satan's enemies"[61] (Mt 17:1-8; 26:63,64; Mk 12:29-31; Lk 3:21,22; Jn 3:16-18; 14:16,17; Eph 3:4-6; 2 Th 2:4,9; Rev 12:9; 13:4).

That is why we believe that true Christians are in a spiritual war against Satan and his murderous henchmen, who are attacking the founding Rock of our country, the Cornerstone, Jesus in the United States. In a letter by Gary Kreep, Executive Director of the United States Justice Foundation, which we received in 2008, he reported that "Keith Ellison, Democrat of Minnesota, was sworn in as the first Muslim to serve in the United States Congress . . . Keith Ellison . . . planted . . . his hand . . . firmly on a Qur'an instead of the time-honored traditional Bible . . . To Muslims like Keith Ellison, Sharia law . . . is Allah's revealed law . . . and it overrides everything, including the U.S. Constitution"[62] (Gen 3:14,15; Lk 4:2-13; Jn 13:27-30; Ac 19:26-40; Eph 2:20; 6:10-12).

Mr. Kreep disclosed, "The Qur'an . . . says 'take neither Jews nor Christians for your friends' . . . Ellison has addressed the Muslim American Society and the Islamic Circle of North America, both said to be terrorist front groups . . . Sharia law demands revenge under the guise of justice . . . Any Muslim . . . could be executed for renouncing his or her faith. And any non-Muslim . . . —faces the same fate for merely criticizing Islam, . . . and women are the major victims of Sharia law."[63] For the United States Congress to allow a new member of Congress to be sworn in on the Qur'an, instead of the Bible, we believe, says to the American people that another 'god' is to be honored in government, not the God of our forefathers and Founding Fathers (Dt 32:15-18; Mt 5:21,38-42; Ac 9:1,2; 18:2; 1 Co 4:9,10; 2 Co 1:8-10).

Pastor David Wilkerson shared in a message in September 2006, his views on "Radical Islam." He reported, "Radical

Islam is unleashing its angry wrath against all who refuse to bow to Allah . . . Islamic clerics are calling for worldwide fatwah against all who refuse to worship their false god. In a demonic rage, the enemies of Christ are literally lifting weapons and commanding the masses, 'Bow to our god, or die' . . . The wrath of those who loathe and despise the name of Jesus is intensifying . . . The Bible is despised, mocked and cursed by ungodly men"[64] (Isa 5:20-24; Da 6:6-16; Mk 13:13; Jn 15:18-20; Ro 12:19; Rev 12:17; 13:15).

Pastor Wilkerson said, "Today, Islam is a kind of Babylon with mad leaders like King Nebuchadnezzar (in the Bible). This religion is threatening . . . with the demand to worship its deity, Allah. Terrorist organizations with Islamic support are demanding: 'Bow to Allah, or we will blow up your airplanes. We'll bomb your towns, trains, buses and tunnels. We'll kidnap you, torture you and behead you. Allah will rule the world. Islam is going to prevail.'"[65] We believe that we are living "in the days of Noah," where Satan is intensifying violence throughout the world, and bringing it ever closer to the American people (Gen 6:5,11,12; Da 3:1-30; 7:7,23,25; 11:36,37; Rev 9:20,21).

On October 22, 2008, after fasting and worshiping before the Lord Jesus, the Lord spoke to us just prior to the election for the President of the United States. And, after the election, in the early morning of January 23, 2009, my wife heard these words, "Hussein," which is the middle name of the President, and "He's going to cause problems." After worshiping before the Lord that day, I received some visions. In the first vision, I saw a fish outside our fish bowl looking into the water in the bowl. Then that fish swam away in the air. In the next vision, I saw what appeared to be the Vice President of the United States reaching his hand into an empty fish bowl pulling out pieces of paper and reading each piece. A vision followed of the prophet Jonah in the Bible, who was inside the belly of a "great fish." Then I saw an outdoor water faucet dripping drops of water. After that, the water flowed forcibly out of the faucet. Finally, I saw a white toaster. One slice of bread popped up out of the toaster, toasted brown.

The Lord Jesus said prior to the election, "This election will reveal what America is concerned about, a disdain of the name of Jesus in government, in politics, in schools, in public and private enterprise. The name of Allah has been elevated in those same places. (Allah) is a monstrous 'god' of hate, a hatred of Jesus and His people. So be sober and alert" (Ps 2:2; Eze 28:16,17; Mt 2:16; Lk 21:17; Ac 7:52-58; 12:2; 1 Pe 5:8,9).

After the election, the Lord Jesus revealed, "The President (of the United States) is 'like a fish out of water.' He looked into the bowl where the 'fishers of men' once had been, your forefathers, the Founding Fathers, who founded this country on the Bible, on the Rock, on the Lord Jesus, living in the water of the Holy Spirit. But rather than join them, the President chooses to survive outside the guidance of the Holy Spirit. And so, you have a President and a Cabinet, who have compiled their own thoughts and placed them in a 'fish bowl' to run the country each day. The advice of men and women is this country's guidance, for they are not turning to the God of Heaven above for direction! (Jer 17:5; Mt 4:19,20; 16:15-18; Jn 7:38; 1 Co 2:14).

"The President of the United States has a calling to serve Almighty God. He is not to act like Jonah, who was called by God to preach repentance to the people of Nineveh, but ended up in the belly of a 'great fish.' Unless the people of America repent of their ways, this country will find itself in the 'belly of a whale.' Ronald Reagan understood this when he quoted, 2 Chronicles 7:14. Because the President (of the United States) is rejecting the flow of water from the Holy Spirit, true believers; Christians will be just like a 'drip of water.' However, when the President ("Hussein") and his staff speak about (the religion of) Islam, water will flow out of their 'faucet,' but it will not be My water (2 Ch 7:14; Ps 137:1-4; Jer 2:13,18; Jnh 1:1-3,15-17; Mt 12:40).

"The President and many 'leaders' of this nation believe that the First Amendment of the United States Constitution was designed to give free expression and free exercise of religious beliefs to all religions in America. Yet, they will say to Christians, 'Your freedom to exercise your religious beliefs violates the Constitution, if you speak up against Islam and against their 'god,' Allah. You are offending their religious beliefs. You are restricting their freedom of speech, and because of that restriction, we must restrict you, evangelical Christians.' The President and other 'leaders' in America are forsaking the beliefs of their forefathers and the Founding Fathers of this country, who chose to leave a tyrannical England because of the restrictions placed on true believers in Jesus (Dt 11:16,17; Da 3:16-23; Ac 4:17,18; 17:21-23; 19:26-36; 22:4,5).

"This attitude is (prevailing) in America, and true Christians say, 'We are toast.' But God wants us to 'pop up' after we have been 'toasted' in the 'fire' to speak up against tyrannical America. For My people must become like 'toast' refined in 'the furnace of affliction,' toasted, warm bread, 'hot' for the kingdom of God in America. 'Hot,' in order to speak up against the violations of the First Amendment of the Constitution. For this country was founded by Christian men with Christian principles under the guidance of the Holy Spirit, the Lord Jesus Christ. This was done to welcome all into the kingdom of God, and to love all men and women, so that salvation might be for all in America (through Jesus Christ)" (Isa 48:10; Da 3:22; Mal 3:2; Mt 3:11,12; 11:28; Lk 6:35,36; Jn 16:13; Ac 4:19,20; Ro 12:11; 2 Pe 3:9,15).

It is also significant to note, that the Words of our Lord Jesus were validated in a fact report, which we received on January 30, 2009. It was indicated in that report, that the President's appointed "U.N. Ambassador, . . . gave (the President) an interview on (his) faith . . . She noted that although he is a Christian, his religion would not influence his policies. Obama would not highlight the 'Jesus factor,' because, as a 'secular Christian' he will not pursue foreign policy initiatives that are similar to President Bush. Second, unlike the

Republican Party, the Democratic Party does not allow conservative Christians to influence the president"[66] (2 Co 11:3,4; 2 Ti 4:3,4; 1 Jn 2:18,19).

Salvation is Found in No One Else but Jesus!

In 1995, my husband and I were working in a girl's cottage at a Baptist Children's Home in North Carolina. One of the twelve female youths, that we were serving there, was the highlight of this testimony. This girl, in order to survive emotionally in that cottage, displayed a tough, masculine, defiant demeanor towards us and her fellow female residents. That young woman could "body slam" girls to the floor. Around her neck, she wore chains with other "gods," idols hanging down from those chains. On three different chains were shark's teeth, amulets, and an image of Buddha (Dt 16:21,22; Isa 44:9,10,15,17,18; Eze 13:18-20).

"gods" Our Forefathers had not Known

As time went by, that young girl slowly began to ponder about believing in Jesus Christ. She purchased a large, heavy cross on a silver chain, and added it to the other "gods" hanging around her neck. On one day, while she stood standing in the cottage kitchen, a chain broke off around her neck. The heavy cross and chain came clanging down on a table. That night as we slept, the Lord spoke to us about that young girl. The Lord said, "I will not share Myself with any other 'god'" (Ex 20:3-5; Dt 5:7-10; 1 Co 1:18).

After this girl began to develop a trust with us, she shared many stories about her being abused, physically and sexually. We became very close with her, and she let us pray with her one evening. We then were able to share with her what the Lord Jesus had revealed to us about her cross. A few days later, this young girl purchased another large cross and chain. She again placed it with those other "gods" around her neck (Mt 4:8-10; Lk 4:5-8).

About a month later, we were driving the girls to our cottage in a van at night from a beach in North Carolina. When we were about twenty minutes away from the Baptist Children's Home, a back tire blew out. We managed to pull over to the side of the road. My husband took my hand in front of the girls, and we began to pray that God would help us. The girls then got out of the van. Some of them were emotionally upset, threatening to run away down the woods, and other girls were crying. To add to the tension all around us, we could not locate the emergency tool box, in order to remove the old tire and mount a new tire.

Suddenly, a white car pulled up. Two men, one younger than the other, got out of the car dressed in white clothes. Those men asked if they could help us. Within what seemed to be only five minutes, those men found the necessary tools, and had the tire changed. Then as quickly as they arrived, they drove off in the night. We hardly had a chance to thank them. While the tire was being changed, the young girl with the other "gods" hanging around her neck, was standing next to the van. Her cross and chain broke again, falling to the ground. After that incident, she was convicted by the Holy Spirit not to wear any other graven images around her neck. We felt that God answered our prayers by sending His angels "unawares" to help us. And at the same time, God's Words and His authority came to bear on her heart, that "You shall have no other 'gods' before me" (Ex 20:33; 2 Ki 17:35; Ps 44:20,21; Heb 1:14; 13:2[KJV]).

A few weeks later, that young woman gave her life over to Jesus Christ. We believe that the Lord Jesus was healing her of deep, shameful scars from her childhood. She was happier, and she received "A" marks in her high school subjects. That young woman applied to, and was accepted at a college. On our last day of employment at the Baptist Children's Home, she brought us a beautiful bouquet of flowers and a card that brought tears to our eyes. The Lord Jesus was able to change the life of that young woman. He pulled that young woman's heart away from other "gods," and turned her heart to the one true God (Jn 1:12-14; Ac 3:19,20; 26:17,18; Rev 3:20).

In the fall of 1998, my wife and I were working at a Boys and Girls' Home in North Carolina. At that Home, I was the coach of the varsity basketball team. One afternoon, during a varsity basketball practice, one resident wore what appeared to be an African idol carved in wood around his neck. This concerned me, so I questioned the young man about wearing an idol. Responding positively to my question, he seemed willing to remove the idol, which was hanging around his neck. Then he asked my wife and me, if we would buy him a wooden cross. We agreed to do that (Ps 135:15-18; Isa 41:7; 44:13; Rev 9:20).

A few days later, we gave him a wooden cross that we bought at a Christian book store. The following day at basketball practice, he wore that cross around his neck. An amazing "miracle" happened. When that young man began shooting "three-point" shots on the basketball court, my wife and I, and the Assistant Recreation supervisor witnessed something awesome. That young man shot a record number of "three-point" shots in a row, somewhere in the low thirties. He could not miss. Finally, in total amazement, he threw the ball down and left the basketball court area.

We are not saying that wearing a cross enabled that young man to score all those "three-point" shots in a row. For after that practice, he did not shoot baskets as well as he did that afternoon. We believe God was revealing to him, that because he chose to get rid of that African idol, and wear a cross instead, God blessed him in an unbelievable way. The Lord Jesus made himself known to that young man, when all of us witnessed a "miracle"! The Lord Jesus will have no other "gods" before Him (Dt 7:25,26; Jer 35:15[a]; Lk 9:23; Jn 14:12).

Dr. Rich Hobson, Executive Director of the Foundation for

Moral Law, wrote, that on "July 12, 2007, . . . (on) the floor of the United States Senate, . . . Senate Majority Leader Harry Reid (D-NV) had . . . invited a Hindu, Rajan Zed, to open that day's Senate session with a prayer to a Hindu god . . . Mr. Zed sprinkled water from India's Ganges River around the Senate rostrum and (then spoke) his 'prayer' . . . Not one United States Senator objected. Three Christian (family members), visitors to the Senate that day . . . began to pray aloud to God to have mercy on our nation and proclaimed Jesus Christ as the only way for our sins to be forgiven . . . All three were arrested by Capitol police and charged with a criminal offense"[67] (Ex 32:1-10,19,20; 1 Ki 11:4-11; Neh 9:30,31; Mk 2:10-12; Jn 14:6).

Former Judge Roy S. Moore, the President for the "Foundation for Moral Law" reported, concerning those three Christians, that they "demonstrated the bravery of the great Christian patriots that founded this country as one nation under God. Our Founding Fathers, who instituted the practice of praying everyday in Congress to the God of Holy Scriptures, would be appalled to see a prayer to a Hindu god in the Senate. It is the one, true Creator God that has endowed each of us with our inalienable rights, not a Hindu god . . . It took three humble Christians in the visitor's gallery to remind our Senators which God they should be trusting"[68] (Gen 1:26,27; Neh 9:1-3; La 3:33-36; Da 6:10,11; Mt 6:9-13; Jn 14:1).

It was "reported . . . in mid-November (2008) . . . (by) the United Bible Societies, . . . that Christian communities (in India) . . . were suffering extreme violence at the hands of Hindu extremists. Stories tell of the destruction and burning of Christian villages, churches and orphanages, murders, (etc.) . . . More than 100 Christians (had) been killed, including 30 pastors—in front of their families, wives and children. Thousands more have fled their homes to hide"[69] (Pr 28:12[b]; Mic 2:2; Lk 13:34; Jn 16:2; Ac 8:1,3; Heb 11:36-38).

Hindus believe in other "gods" apart from Jesus, the Son of God. There are Hindu extremists on the other side of the world opposed to Christianity. We have allowed a Hindu and a Muslim to dishonor the God of the Bible in the Congress of the United States of America. Jesus said of Himself, "I am the way and the truth and the life. No one comes to the Father except through me." The apostle Peter proclaimed that, "Salvation is found in no one else, for there is no other name under heaven given to men by which we must be saved," but by "the name of Jesus Christ." The Lord spoke through the prophet Isaiah and declared, "Is there any God besides me? No, there is no other Rock; I know not one!" Moses recited these words, "They sacrificed to demons, which are not God—gods they had not known" (Dt 32:17; Isa 44:8; Jn 14:6; Ac 4:10-12; 1 Jn 2:22,23).

We believe that government officials are welcoming "gods" that our forefathers and Founding Fathers "had not known," . . . "which are not God." Some "leaders" in government are giving honor, we believe, to "foreign gods." According to the Word of God, this angers our Almighty God "with their detestable idols, (for) they sacrificed to demons." Government officials, along with public and private organizations, we believe, are dishonoring our Lord Jesus, the name of Jesus, the Living Word of God, by giving honor to other "gods." Satan's dark, antichrist spirit is unfortunately moving throughout America in the last days (Dt 32:16,17; 1 Sa 2:30; 1 Ki 16:30-33; Isa 29:13,15,16; Eph 6:12; 1 Jn 4:3).

The Lord Jesus revealed more. On May 1, 2008, my wife heard the Lord say these Words, "Senate chambers." On May 7, 2008, the Lord spoke to us, "In 'Senate chambers,' Senators have chosen to seek their own interests from ungodly interest groups to further their terms in office. Behind 'Senate chambers,' political dealings have been destructive to this nation; dealings with foreigners, dealings with other countries, who serve other 'gods,' dealing this nation away from the faith and beliefs of this country's Founding Fathers" (Ps 10:11; Isa 29:15; Eze 11:2; Da 2:22; 1 Ti 4:1).

The Lord said further, "The world is blind, for they do not see the pain that they cause against God. The United States is a 'lukewarm' country, because the voices of opposition, the voice of Satan has been given too much voice in the land. So the land will oppose itself and become divisive. For this country will literally be divided in half; men choosing to serve God through Jesus Christ, and other men serving mammon, their 'god' of riches and worldliness. The United States negotiates by selling their country out to other countries out of fear and a need to please men (Ezr 9:10,11; Pr 12:5[b],6[a]; Mt 6:24[KJV]; 12:25,26; Mk 4:18,19; Jn 12:42,43; 2 Co 4:4).

"I will turn over the tables in America violently, because America refuses to repent and honor the one, true God. They dishonor the one, true God, when they choose to accept other 'gods': the Islam 'god,' the Hindu 'gods,' the 'god' of murder, the 'god' of the antichrist, the 'god' of hatred toward the unborn, the 'god' of hatred toward purity in marriage, the 'god' of hatred toward Jesus, and His righteousness and His Word; they are the enemies of God (Ex 34:15,16; Ps 106:37-39; Mt 21:12; Jn 8:44; Ro 2:5; Ja 4:4; 1 Jn 3:10; Rev 2:20-22).

"Many are not willing to speak out against those other 'gods' for fear of threats on their lives, for fear of being rejected and excluded, and for the fear of being called religious 'fanatics.' God is giving you a passion to speak up on these issues in your nation. The passionate will hear your cry. They will follow the true leaders, the patriots today, who will hold up the 'National Banner,' the standard on which America was founded, the 'National Standard,' the foundation of which is Jesus Christ!" (Ex 17:15; Pr 29:25; Isa 11:10; Jer 5:14; Mt 7:24,25; Jn 9:22). (Messages received from God on June 9, 1999, March 14, 2008, and May 7, 2008).

Since we believe that many in America are rejecting the faith of our forefathers and Founding Fathers in Jesus Christ, the only Cornerstone and Foundational Rock of this nation, the loss of untold millions of unborn children is a horrendous consequence of this country's rejection of Jesus!

10

THOU SHALT NOT KILL!

"They sacrificed their sons and their daughters
to demons.
They shed innocent blood, the blood of their
sons and daughters,
... and the land was desecrated by their blood."

We had remained in hiding for months; yet, our hearts were beating rapidly. We were innocent, hopeless, and helpless. Would this be the day that we would be caught by terrorists and murdered? Who would come to our rescue? Who would save us from being tortuously and violently exterminated? How could this be? What happened to the real heroes in America? What happened to those, who had faith in Jesus Christ like our forefathers and Founding Fathers? What happened to those who believed in securing "the Blessings of Liberty to ourselves and our Posterity?" Where are those that believed that "all men are created equal," and that we "are endowed by (our) Creator with certain inalienable rights, . . .

life, liberty, and the pursuit of happiness," the right to life? (Gen 2:7; 6:5,11; Dt 30:20; Pr 10:6; Jn 14:6; Heb 11:1,2,6,37).

Who will save us from men and women ready and armed to kill us, ready to puncture our brains or poison our hearts? Do we have to be Prisoners of War, "POW's" in Satan's "medical" death "camps"? Yes! For this, we believe is the fate of many of the unborn children in America today; those that are "created . . . in the image of God, . . . male and female." We believe that our Lord Jesus weeps deeply in painful anguish over the unborn, because the American people have become so desensitized to sin, the sin of murder! (Gen 1:27; 6:6; Eze 22:25; Mt 12:7; Gal 3:22; Eph 4:18,19; 1 Pe 5:8). This introduction was a revelation from our Lord Jesus Christ on February 9, 2009.

Medical Death "Camps"

The "executioners" in this case are not the ones who pulled the cord on the guillotine during the French Revolution, beheading thousands, nor are they the German Nazi "medical" doctors who "experimented" on body parts of living Jewish people, and aborted Jewish children in the concentration camps. These executioners, we believe, are Satan's "servants of righteousness," which includes, "Licensed physician(s), . . . Nurse practitioner(s), . . . Resident assistant(s), . . . (and) Registered nurse(s)"[70] (Ps 41:9; Mk 5:26; 2 Co 11:14,15; Php 3:19).

Dr. James Dobson wrote in a *Focus* on the *Family Action* newsletter in May 2007, that "There is no constitutional right to slay a healthy, nearly-born baby by stabbing it in the back of the head and vacuuming out its brains, all without even anesthetizing the child . . . We . . . (need to put) an end to the Nazi-esque barbarism known as partial-birth abortion . . . (Either done by) injecting poison into their hearts, (or by) . . . collapsing the head of a viable baby and extracting his brains . . . How could so many Americans have come to this point of brutality and callousness? . . . Legislation to ban . . . partial-birth abortion . . . was first introduced in Congress in 1995. It was . . . twice vetoed by then-President Clinton"[71] (Eze 34:4,5; 1 Ti 4:1; 2 Ti 3:1-4; 2 Pe 2:12).

A nurse for over "eighteen years," . . . Brenda Shafer shared in an interview that "a partial-birth abortion starts at twenty weeks and continues until full term." The abortionist pulls out the baby outside the mother's womb, legs first, leaving the "baby's head" inside the mother's body. "He (the abortionist), then takes a pair of scissors and stabs the baby in the back of the neck; this leaves a "hole in back of the neck." The abortionist then takes a "suction catheter . . . to suction out the baby's brain . . . The baby goes limp and it's dead."[72] If the baby comes completely out of the mother, and is aborted in this manner, it is considered "murder" (Ps 106:37-39; Jer 2:34,35; 22:17; Mk 7:21,22).

Dr. Bernard Nathanson, former "co-founder of NARAL (National Association for the Repeal of Abortion Laws)," a former abortionist, showed through ultra-sound technology in his documentary, "The Silent Scream," the extreme fear and pain an unborn child experiences in an abortion. Dr. Nathanson pointed out in that documentary, that as the "lethal," abortion instrument moves toward the child, "The (child's) heart rate is speeding up . . . It (the child) does sense aggression . . . It is moving away . . . (from the instrument) in a pathetic attempt to escape the . . . instruments the abortionist is using to extinguish its life . . . We see the child's mouth wide open in a 'silent scream' . . . of a child imminently threatened with extinction"[73] (Ps 22:11-13; La 3:46-51; Mt 18:6,7).

Another report indicated that, "Abortion . . . subjects a living human being to a grotesque, often excruciating death." Dr. D. James Kennedy revealed that, "In the Nuremburg Trials the Nazis were denounced . . . for aborting children in their concentration camps and killing them . . . Words like 'women's rights' and 'reproductive health'—create a facade for an evil comparable to Nazi war crimes."[74] Satan "prowls around like a roaring lion looking for someone to devour." The devil has been devouring unborn children for years, as he "masquerades as an angel of light." Satan "comes only to steal and kill and destroy," which he has been doing to the unborn in horrendously evil ways. We will now examine how Satan's "medical" death "camps' were introduced to unborn children in the United States of America (Pr 9:13-18; Isa 52:14; Jer 4:19[a]; Mk 6:22-28; Jn 10:10[a]; 2 Co 11:14; 1 Pe 5:8).

The Supreme Court Case: Roe v. Wade

In the case of "(Roe), . . . a pregnant single woman . . . brought a class action challenging the constitutionality of the Texas criminal abortion laws, which proscribe procuring or attempting an abortion except on medical advice for the purpose of saving the mother's life . . . She sought a declaratory judgment that the Texas criminal abortion statutes were unconstitutional, . . . and that they abridged her right of personal privacy, protected by the First, Fourth, Fifth, Ninth, and Fourteenth Amendments."[75] The case was challenged up to the Supreme Court.

The Supreme Court "Justice Harry Blackmun wrote the Court's opinion, . . . (which was) decided January 22, 1973 . . . (He) asserted that the 'right of privacy,' . . . founded in the Fourteenth Amendment's concept of personal liberty and restrictions upon state action, . . . is broad enough to encompass a woman's decision whether or not to terminate her pregnancy." It was reported further that, "Although the Constitution does not explicitly mention any right of privacy, . . . the Court determined . . . that the right of personal privacy includes the abortion decision."[76]

It was indicated that, "The Court majority determined that the original intent of the Constitution . . . did not require protection of the unborn . . . (However, Justice) Blackmun also asserted that if the fetus was defined as a person for purposes of the Fourteenth Amendment then the fetus would have a specific right to life . . . The Court ruled that the state cannot restrict a woman's right to an abortion during the first trimester."[77]

Supreme Court "Associate Justices Byron R. White and William Rehnquist wrote . . . dissenting opinions in this case . . . Justice White wrote: 'I find nothing in the language or history of the Constitution to support the Court's judgment. The Court . . . announces a new constitutional right for pregnant mothers and, with scarcely any reason or authority for its action, invests that right . . . to override most existing state abortion statutes' . . . The Court 'values the convenience of the pregnant mother more than the continued existence and development of the life or potential life that she carries,' . . . creating 'a constitutional barrier to state efforts to protect human life and by investing mothers and doctors with the constitutionally protected right to exterminate it.'"[78]

Supreme Court Justice "Rehnquist concluded that, . . . 'the drafters (of the Constitution) did not intend to have the Fourteenth Amendment withdraw from the States the power to legislate with respect to this matter.'"[79] It was noted that, "According to the Roe decision, most laws against abortion in the United States violated a constitutional right to privacy under the Due Process Clause of the Fourteenth Amendment. The decision overturned all state and federal laws outlawing or restricting abortion that were inconsistent with (the Supreme Court's) holdings . . . Roe v. Wade centrally held that a mother may abort her pregnancy for any reason, up until the 'point at which the fetus becomes viable,' . . . (which struck) down Texas abortion laws."[80] Yet, the Fourteenth Amendment declares, "No State shall . . . deprive any person of life . . . without due process of law." What "due process of law" was held for the unborn child?

It was reported that, "Norma McCorvey, the unnamed plaintiff in Roe, confessed that her entire case 'was all based on a lie.'" Miss McCorvey "admitted lying that she was raped," and lied that she was "desperately seeking an abortion." Her attorney used Miss McCorvey "to advance her own agenda," to overturn the state's abortion laws. Miss McCorvey "has dedicated her life to overturning Roe v. Wade . . . Norma McCorvey . . . faced unimaginable burdens of guilt, . . . and despair (over) . . . her case that paved the way for (the slaughter) . . . of millions of babies . . . (An) eight-year-old girl . . . (told her), 'You can pray right now and Jesus will forgive you' . . . Norma McCorvey (went) . . . to church, . . . (and) surrendered her life to (Jesus) Christ"[81] (Gen 39:10-20; Pr 6:16,17; 7:24-27; Isa 5:20; Na 2:12; 3:1; Lk 7:37,45-50).

Dr. Bernard Nathanson, who we mentioned earlier, formerly of NARAL, shared that their organization "inflated statistics" on the dangers of abortions. Their false "statistics" claimed that there were "1 million illegal abortions . . . every year and 5–10 thousand women died per year" from those abortions. "The actual figures," he reported, were "100–200 thousand illegal abortions" each year, and "200–300 women died each year from illegal abortions." The "claims" of NARAL "went unchallenged all the way to the Supreme Court"[82] in the case of Roe v. Wade (Ex 20:16; Dt 19:18,19; Job 13:4; Ps 119:69[a]).

Satan, considered by Jesus as the "father of lies," was able to use false information through his "servants of righteousness," to pass as truth in the Supreme Court case of Roe v. Wade. The devil's "agenda," his "wicked scheme" was to pass laws justifying "murder" in America, as a constitutional right of women. "The god of this age has blinded the minds of unbelievers" to accept Satan's lie that the unborn are not worthy of life. The devil's scheme, we believe, has been to violently murder those helpless, innocent children. Where are the ones who will rescue the unborn from Satan's "medical" death "camps"? We believe "the land" of America (is and has been) "desecrated by their blood." The court case that piggybacked Roe v. Wade was Doe v. Bolton (Job 1:9-19; Ps 22:19-21; 106:38; Jn 8:44; 2 Co 4:4; Eph 6:11,12[KJV]).

The Supreme Court Case: Doe v. Bolton

In the case of Doe v. Bolton, "Mary Doe was a 22-year-old resident of Georgia, married, and nine weeks pregnant. She already had three children . . . Doe had been a mental patient at a state hospital. She had been told that an abortion would be less dangerous to her health than giving birth to the child she carried . . . (She) was denied . . . an abortion . . . in Atlanta, Georgia . . . Mary Doe and nine physicians brought a federal action . . . want(ing) the Court to declare that the Georgia abortion laws were unconstitutional in their entirety, . . . (claiming that) the Georgia abortion laws . . . denied her equal protection and procedural due process . . . The doctors in the suit alleged that the Georgia laws . . . 'deterred' them from practicing their profession and deprived them of the rights guaranteed by the First, Fourth and Fourteenth Amendments . . . (The case was) appealed directly to the Supreme Court."[83]

Supreme Court Justice "Harry A. Blackmun" wrote the majority opinion for the Court, which was also decided on "January . . . 22, . . . 1973." The Supreme Court asserted "that after the end of the first trimester of pregnancy, Georgia may adopt standards for licensing all facilities where abortions may be performed . . . 'Just as the Privileges and Immunities Clause . . . protects persons who enter other states to ply their trade, . . . so must it protect persons who enter Georgia seeking the medical services that are available there' . . . The provisions of the law ruled on in this case all violated the Fourteenth Amendment."[84]

Chief Justice Burger wrote, "under the Fourteenth Amendment to the Constitution, the abortion statutes of Georgia and Texas impermissibly limit the performance of abortions necessary to protect the health of pregnant women" . . . Justice Douglas wrote "that the Georgia abortion statute went against the idea that a woman is free to make the basic decisions of whether or not to bear an unwanted child. Childbirth may deprive a woman of her preferred lifestyle . . . The Georgia law resulted in the 'total destruction of the right of privacy between physician and patient, (which) . . . are basic to Fourteenth Amendment values.'"[85]

Again, Supreme Court "Justice White dissented" asserting that "the life or potential life of the fetus" was far less important than the "convenience, whim, or caprice of the . . . mother" . . . In both "Roe v. Wade and Doe v. Bolton the Court upheld a woman's right to abortion."[86]

Sybil Fletcher Lash, the author of the book, *Supreme Deception*, shared that the "case (of Doe v. Bolton) . . . went before the Supreme Court with no facts, . . . no evidence in the case, (and) no interrogatories were answered . . . The plaintiff Mary Doe was allegedly . . . Sandra Cano." While she was "pregnant at the time of the case," Mrs. Cano, "never wanted or sought an abortion." Mrs. Cano "went to Atlanta Legal Aid to get a divorce . . . She was told that her case would have something to do with women's rights . . . An ACLU attorney" took over her case, "seeking to overturn a Georgia law restricting abortion."[87]

Ms. Lash reported that Mrs. Cano's "affidavit (which) was submitted to the Supreme Court . . . was filled with false information and likely forged." In the affidavit, it was reported that Sandra Cano "would go crazy, . . . if she had another baby . . . That she needed this abortion and . . . she want(ed) to be sterilized." Mrs. Cano "made none of those statements . . . She will say that she is 99% sure that she never signed" that affidavit. Ms. Lash said further, "They took a woman who wanted a divorce and to place her children in a foster home, and they turned that around and it's okay to kill babies through the ninth month"[88] (Jer 9:3-6; Na 3:1; Mt 26:63-68; 1 Ti 4:2).

Again, we have a case before the Supreme Court fabricated on lies. The Lord Jesus, we believe, was not allowed in the Court room, for He is "the truth," and only "tell(s) the truth" . . . "Satan, who leads the whole world astray," the "deceiver," led the Supreme Court Justices astray into "hands that shed innocent blood." The devil, who has "no truth in him," was the voice honored in the majority of the Supreme Court Justices. Through his "servants of righteousness," the Supreme Court Justices permitted the killing of unborn infants up until their birth (Ps 8:2; Pr 6:16,17; Jn 8:44,45; 14:6; Ac 3:15; 2 Co 11:14,15; Rev 12:9[KJV]).

It was reported further that, "Both Roe and Doe were founded on a web of falsehood and deceit . . . Bernard Nathanson, Norma McCorvey, and Sandra Cano are now . . . actively working to promote the right to life of the unborn . . . Both the Declaration of Independence and the U.S. Constitution placed . . . emphasis on our God-given right to life . . . The Fifth and Fourteenth Amendments to the U.S. Constitution promise that no person shall be deprived of life without due process of law"[89] (Gen 2:7; Ps 139:13-16; Jer 1:5; Jn 1:1-4).

David Gibbs, Jr., attorney and founder of the Christian Law Association, shared in an interview that, "We have to understand that an individual within the Constitution was a life entity given by God. . . . The framers (of the U.S. Constitution) understood that to be at conception. That's why in the early days up until the times that these (Supreme Court) decisions came down, if you at any point did something to a mother carrying a baby, it was actionable for the mother and the baby, because the baby was a human life, an individual protected by the laws of our land"[90] (Ex 21:22,23; Ps 127:3; Isa 44:2,24[a]; Eze 16:3-5; 20-22).

Former President Ronald "Reagan believed in the constitutional rights of unborn children . . . (He) wrote, . . . 'The values and freedoms we cherish as Americans rest on our fundamental commitment to the sanctity of human life' . . . 'The first of the inalienable rights affirmed by our Declaration of Independence is the right to life itself, a right the Declaration, states, has been endowed by our Creator on all human beings—whether young or old, weak or strong, healthy or handicapped.'" President Reagan shared that, "Abortion has denied them the first and most basic of human rights . . . To diminish the value of one category of human life is to diminish us all . . . Can we say that abortion—which treats the unborn as something less than human, to be destroyed if convenient—will be less corrosive to the values we hold dear?"[91] (Gen 1:27; 9:5,6; Mal 2:10; Eph 3:9; Heb 11:38[a]).

Former President Reagan wrote, "It is not for us to decide who is worthy to live and who is not." He proclaimed, "We can, as is written in Deuteronomy, choose life, so that we and our descendents may live . . . How can we survive as a free nation when some decide that others are not fit to live?" President Reagan shared, "'Suffer the little children to come unto Me, and forbid them not, for such is the kingdom of God' (see Mk 10:14)"[92] (Dt 5:17; 30:19; Mk 10:14[KJV]; Ja 4:12).

Dr. James Dobson wrote in January 2008, that those two Supreme Court "decisions, . . . legalized abortion across the United States . . . 2,740 . . . innocent babies . . . (are) being killed every day . . . This is . . . our 'culture of death' . . . A woman may have an abortion . . . anytime during her entire pregnancy . . . (There are) no limitations . . . on why a woman may have an abortion . . . Parental notification before an abortion . . . is not required . . . Sex selection abortions—abortions performed because of the sex of the baby . . . (are) allowed . . . Fewer than 1 percent . . . of abortions are performed because of rape or incest . . . None . . . of our nation's founding documents contains the phrase 'right to an abortion' . . . (The) country's laws (in the) . . . United States . . . make it easiest to have an abortion, (than in any other country) . . . According to the Center for Disease Control, . . . 40–49 million . . . abortions have been performed in the United States since . . . 1973"[93] (1 Ki 18:4; 19:1,2; Ps 55:3-8,12-14; Pr 7:24-27; Ecc 7:26; Rev 17:5,6).

Former President Ronald Reagan declared the words of Jesus, "Suffer the little children to come unto Me, and forbid them not, for such is the kingdom of God." The "little ones," the unborn and little children, we believe, are so precious and loved by God. The extremely painful anguish the Lord Jesus must experience over the murder of His "little ones" is beyond human comprehension. We believe that the blood shed of these "little ones" has and will have grave consequences for this nation and many of the American people (Mt 2:17,18; 18:7-10; Mk 10:14[KJV]; Lk 18:15-17; 19:41-44).

Pastor David Wilkerson, shared that, "The Puritans had a saying: 'Our affections bribe our discernments.'" Our affections for pregnant mothers, who do not want their babies, David Wilkerson revealed, has caused "Million(s) . . . (of) babies (to be) murdered by abortionists. There is awful blood on our nation's hands. Do you think God is going to wink at that? No, he is a just God, and he will make America weep because of all the blood spilled. How? Already I see murderers spilling blood on our streets and in our schools . . . No other nation has killed more babies than the United States has through abortion. Our soil cries out with the blood of these children!"[94] (Dt 16:19; 1 Ch 22:8; 28:3; Ps 55:23; Lk 18:22-27; Ro 3:15-18).

The "Little Ones"

It was reported by Dr. Rodney Suidmak, an obstetrician, "It is an established medical fact . . . that life begins at conception, and . . . this fact is not in dispute in any reputable medical textbooks anywhere in the world." It was written in "The American College of Pediatricians in an official policy statement in 2004," that "the body of scientific evidence (has shown) that human life begins at conception—fertilization"[95] (Ru 4:13[KJV]; Isa 49:1; Mt 1:20; Lk 1:24,35,36[KJV]; Ro 9:10-12[KJV]).

It was further reported by "sixty prominent physicians . . . in the 1980s, . . . (that) 'the developing fetus is not a sub-human species . . . (T)he embryo is alive, human, and unique.'" It has been discovered that at the time of "conception, . . . the baby's DNA (a complete genetic blue print) is established . . . At 18 to 21 days, the unborn baby's heart begins to beat . . . At four weeks, . . . arms and legs begin . . . to develop . . . At six to seven weeks, the child . . . is sensitive to touch. At eight weeks, . . . the child goes from an embryo to a fetus. . . . (The) child is alive." Through "ultrasound technology," the scientific evidence is clear, that the "fetus" has limbs growing, "a face and a beating heart"[96] (Gen 38:3-5[KJV]; Ps 8:2; 22:9,10; Isa 49:1; Lk 1:44).

In the early 1960's, the Supreme Court Justices' rulings removed prayer and Bible readings from public schools. If those Justices had referred to the Bible, the Word of God, "the Word made flesh," Jesus Christ, in rendering their decisions in support of prayer and Bible readings, we believe, that the outcome of the Court decisions made in 1973, concerning the unborn would have been life at all cost. Had those Justices in the early 1960s and 1973, referred to the faith of our forefathers and Founding Fathers in Jesus Christ, who we believe is the Cornerstone and Rock of America, and referred to the American documents that revealed our Christian heritage, and prior Supreme Court decisions that the United States is "a Christian nation" and "a Christian people," then Satan's "servants" would have not been able to murder all the innocent "little ones." The Supreme Court did not "maintain justice in the courts" (Am 5:15[a]; Mt 2:16-18; Jn 1:3,4,14; Ro 10:9; 1 Co 10:4; 1 Pe 2:6,8; 4:16).

In the book of Jeremiah in the Bible, the Lord declared, "Before I formed you in the womb I knew you, before you were born I set you apart." King David in the Bible proclaimed, "You created my inmost being; you knit me together in my mother's womb . . . My frame was not hidden from you when I was made in the secret place . . . Your eyes saw my unformed body. All the days ordained for me were written in your book before one of them came to be." Elizabeth, the mother of John the Baptizer, shared with Mary, the mother who bore Jesus, "As soon as the sound of your greeting reached my ears, the baby, (John) in my womb leaped for joy" (Ps 139:13-16; Jer 1:5; Lk 1:44).

The Word of God clearly reveals how God knows before a child is even conceived, that he or she is loved and special in God's eyes, "created . . . in the image of God." Though John the Baptizer, and our Lord Jesus would suffer barbaric deaths through Satan's henchmen, we are so grateful to Almighty God that abortion was not an accepted practice back then. Unborn babies, the "little ones," as we previously revealed, still experience emotions today, as did John the Baptist (Gen 1:27; Isa 40:11; Jer 31:3; Mt 5:21,22; 14:6-11; Mk 10:13-16; 14:6-11; Lk 1:44).

Consequences: No Room for God

In the city of "Bethlehem in Judea, . . . there was no room for (Jesus) in the inn." While the people were sleeping in those "inns" and in their homes, Jesus was born. Many American people today, we believe, are sleeping in their closed off "inns." Closed off from allowing Jesus to come "in(n)" to their hearts. Those who opposed the coming Messiah, Jesus, suffered grave consequences. King Herod was a "king" over Palestine during the time Jesus was born in Bethlehem. Herod was used by Satan to attempt to "abort" the new-born King's life. Herod ordered "to kill all the boys in Bethlehem and its vicinity who were two years old and under" (Mt 2:1,16; Lk 2:7; 10:16; 1 Th 5:7).

Pastor David Wilkerson revealed that, "Herod the Great" attempted "to kill" the Son of God, Jesus, who is "the exact representation of his (God's) being" . . . Herod, "shortly after, was plagued by God with an incurable disease, (which) . . . continually torment(ed) . . . his inward parts . . . His inward bowels rotted, (and) . . . growing mad with pain, he died miserably . . . Caiphas the high priest" declared that Jesus had "spoken blasphemy" for proclaiming himself, "the Messiah, the Son of God." Caiphas shared with others that Jesus "is worthy of death." Caiphas "was shortly after put out of his office, . . . whereupon he killed himself . . . Pontius Pilate, who "had condemned our Lord Christ" to be crucified to death, "lost . . . Caesar's favor, . . . (and) fell into such misery that he hanged himself"[97] (Na 1:2; Mt 26:63-65; 27:22,26; Mk 15:15; Heb 1:3).

Those who tried to shed the blood of an innocent baby, and shed the blood of an innocent man, Jesus, were held accountable by God, the Father, for their evil, murderous actions, suffering horrendous consequences. In the book of Genesis, it is written that, "Whoever sheds the blood of man, by man shall his blood be shed; for in the image of God has God made man . . . For your life blood I will surely demand an accounting . . . from each man . . . I will demand an accounting for the life of his fellow man" (Gen 9:5,6; Isa 35:4; Ro 12:9).

Pastor David Wilkerson wrote, "America has shed the blood of multiplied millions of innocent babies. God's word says the blood of these innocents is precious in His sight (see Psalm 116:15). Scripture warns that the cries of their blood reach high into the heavens, demanding justice . . . And God promises to punish the nation that is responsible: ' . . . thou hast given them blood to drink; for they are worthy' (Revelation 16:6)"[98] (Ps 116:15; Pr 14:34[b]; Rev 6:10; 16:6).

A just God is holding men and women accountable for aborting their unborn children, those "little ones" made "in the image of God," those who had "no room . . . in (their mother's) inn(s)." While my wife was composing information on this chapter, a violent wind and rainstorm pelted our house. Our windows were rattling from the force of that storm. Yet, we knew that this chapter is founded on solid ground, on the Rock (Ps 10:4; 36:1-4; Mt 7:24,25; Jn 8:37).

According to "The National Right to Life News" in 2007, over 48,500,000 unborn babies, "such non-persons have lost their lives." In a "Southern Medical Journal," it was noted that "out of 137,000 pregnant women, women who chose abortion were 62% more likely to die . . . within eight years of the procedure, . . . than those who carried their babies to term . . . Many women experience long-term consequences" for aborting their babies, which include: "cervical damage, . . . perforated uterus, bleeding, . . . infertility, premature deliveries, . . . higher suicide rate, . . . guilt, grief and regret, . . . (and) increased . . . risk for breast cancer, some studies indicate as much as twelve fold."[99]

Dr. James Dobson reported in January 2008, that "the pro-life community has been emphasizing the fact that every abortion leaves 'one dead and one wounded' . . . The American Association of Pro-Life Obstetricians and Gynecologists (AAPLOG) conducted an in-depth study in July 2007 . . . (They discovered) 'that induced abortion in many cases is associated with significant degradation of emotional, . . . physical . . . and reproductive health' . . . (Their) study cites links between abortion and depression, substance abuse, suicide, . . . breast cancer, premature birth, (etc.)."[100]

Dr. Dobson wrote further that in a study "from California, . . . women who aborted were 929 percent more likely to use marijuana, (than) . . . women who had previously given birth . . . (Those women who aborted) were 460 percent more likely to use other illicit drugs, and 122 percent more likely to use alcohol during their next pregnancy." Dr. Dobson noted further that in "a University of Minnesota study on teen suicide, (it was) found that . . . teens who had aborted, . . . increased ten fold . . . (their attempts to commit) suicide . . . 16 . . . studies . . . conducted in America have reported data on the risk of breast cancer among women with a history of induced abortion . . . More than 50 studies have demonstrated . . . significant increase in premature birth . . . in women with prior induced abortion . . . Reading a so-called 'right to abortion' into any of our nation's founding documents is a gross deviation from the intent of our Founding Fathers."[101]

There is sufficient medical evidence to reveal that abortion is destructive to women's mental, emotional and physical condition, "The one who sows to please his sinful nature . . . will reap destruction." The "convenience, whim, and caprice of the . . . mother," and "her preferred lifestyle," as well as the father of their child, are severely harming her after the abortion of her unborn infant. Choosing a sexual lifestyle of sin; fornication/adultery is reaping destructive consequences in men and women's lives for murdering the unborn. We include men, because many men often put undue pressure on women to obtain abortions (Ro 1:24,25; 1 Co 6:9,10[KJV]; Gal 6:8; Col 3:5,6; Rev 21:8).

At a Word Alive Church service in Manassas, Virginia in June 2007, Pastor Rob Schenck of Faith and Action ministries in Washington, D.C., shared about abortion. He declared, "There is a plague in our culture today that degrades the value of human life. If you create, you don't have to take responsibility. You . . . (men) get her money to abort her baby. Abortion hurts babies not given life, hurts women, the mothers . . . There is a great injury to the soul . . . God sees their pain. He will come and heal, for there is hope of a reunion with their child in heaven. (It was reported) that 85% of women who aborted were bullied by men to do so. Many women say, 'It wasn't my choice, I was bullied by my father, or the father of the child' . . . A father needs to stand up and take responsibility to take care of the child, and mother of the child . . . Men must be guardians of life . . . respect(ing) every human life"[102] (Ex 1:15,16,22; Pr 1:10-16; Mt 1:22-25; 2:13-16; 18:6-9).

The Lord Jesus holds us all accountable for the "life blood" of the innocent ones. Yet, the great news is that if we turn from evil and turn to Jesus for genuine forgiveness, we all can be forgiven for sinning against God, for choosing to abort the unborn. We must "sin no more," and choose "life" over "death," and "blessings" over "curses," . . . "so that (we) and (our) children may live and that (we) may love the Lord (our) God, listen to his voice, and hold fast to him. For the Lord is (our) life" (Gen 9:5; Dt 30:19,20; 2 Ch 7:14; Lk 24:46,47; Jn 8:11[KJV]; Ac 26:17,18).

We believe millions of women were not properly informed of the destructive effects abortion would have on their infants, and their lives. We believe our Lord Jesus has great compassion for those women who have suffered mental, emotional, and physical consequences for their choice to abort their babies. Jesus, we believe, desires to heal those women from their painful scars (Lk 7:37,38,44-50; 8:42-48; 15:11-13,17-24; Jn 8:3-11).

A Root of All Kinds of Evil

In the Scriptures it is written, "and (let) no bitter root grow up to cause trouble and defile many." We believe that the "abortion industry" is a "bitter root" that has grown "to cause trouble and defile many" women and men, those who perform the abortions. The Scriptures also proclaim that "the love of money is a root of all kinds of evil." Those involved in the "abortion industry" are making millions of dollars from our "taxpayer money." One of those organizations making millions is Planned Parenthood. The ACLU (American Civil Liberties Union), which we shared about earlier, provides attorney support for "abortion on demand throughout pregnancy, (and) . . . supports partial-birth abortion"[103] (1 Ti 6:9,10; Heb 12:15; Ja 5:1-6).

In May 2007, we received a newsletter from the American Center for Law and Justice. It was reported that, "Public money funds more than 400,000 abortions a year—more than nine million abortions in the past 20 years. Planned Parenthood has received $3.9 billion in taxpayer money since 1987 . . . Planned Parenthood . . . received a total of $551 million in federal money alone . . . over the past two years (2005, 2006)—roughly a third of its total income . . . Technically federal funds can't be used for abortions, but funding the rest of the organization's operations enables them to continue performing abortions . . . Planned Parenthood's annual revenue . . . is $1 billion."[104]

In another report, it was indicated that "from 1997 to 2005,

Planned Parenthood's own annual reports reveal that the(ir) abortion industry . . . netted profits in excess of $469 million, . . . (of which) the organization collected $2.07 billion from American taxpayers . . . Planned Parenthood . . . is responsible for the death of more unborn children than any other organization in America." It "reported" the deaths of "289,750" unborn children "in its 2006 fiscal year."[105]

It was indicated in a letter from Dana Cody, Executive Director of Life Legal Defense Foundation, that "Planned Parenthood pulls in more than $810 Million a year of their abortion and contraception business! . . . (This is) according to their Annual Reports . . . When you multiply those . . . abortions they do every year by the average price of $400, it's (over) $91 Million a year . . . (In the state of Ohio), Planned Parenthood . . . (was) being sued for covering up a statutory rape . . . of a 13-year-old girl . . . by her . . . soccer coach, in direct violation of Ohio state laws."[106]

The American Center for Law and Justice reported that, "Planned Parenthood . . . poured enormous amounts of money into a long court battle against New Hampshire's parental notification law . . . Planned Parenthood lost (their case in) . . . the Supreme Court of the United States . . . Planned Parenthood in Indiana also fought in court to avoid releasing medical records for abortions committed on children under 14 years of age."[107] In addition, it was noted in a report that "undercover video has proven that abortion workers cover up statutory rape and advise minors to abort secretly, in spite of state laws requiring parental notification"[108] (Ps 10:2-11; Isa 28:15; 29:15; Mk 4:22; 2 Pe 2:1-3).

In still another report, it was noted that, "Planned Parenthood reportedly broke the $1 billion threshold in revenues in fiscal 2007, performing more than a quarter-million abortions in the U.S. . . . The nation's biggest abortionist operation (conducts) . . . (24% of all U.S. abortions in 287 clinics) . . . Planned Parenthood affiliates are (also) aggressively pursuing business, going so far as to distribute 'gift cards' for abortions." . . .

It was also noted, "According to a *Washington Times* story about a Government Accountability Office (GAO) report, . . . Planned Parenthood . . . received hundreds of millions of taxpayer dollars, . . . and now apparently can't account for it . . . More than 1.4 million people, . . . babies (were) killed by Planned Parenthood abortions between 2002 and 2008."[109]

The "abortion industry," which we believe is satanically driven through lies and deception, appears to be "flourishing" financially. In our country, for those who strongly oppose the killing of the unborn, we are indirectly financing the abortion organizations in the United States. Satan, through the evil in many men and women's hearts, is stealing monies from millions of taxpayers to perform barbaric murders of the unborn. Believers in Jesus Christ must be willing to stand up against that "bitter root" of all kinds of evil in America, "the love of money" in wicked aborting hearts (Pr 30:8,9; Mk 4:18,19; Jn 10:10[a]; Eph 6:13; 1 Ti 6:10).

Mathew Staver, Founder and Chairman of Liberty Council, shared that, "If you have the opportunity just on the issue of abortion of saving a human life, and you are silent on that; If you are by a crematorium in Nazi Germany, and you are silent on that—God's going to hold us, especially pastors, accountable for that silence, because He is the author of life. We know that Satan is the destroyer of life, and that's where life and death battles take place"[110] (Est 4:14; Lk 9:24; Jn 10:10; 12:25,26; Ac 3:15).

Freedom of Choice

Dr. James Dobson wrote in May 2007, "The U.S. Supreme Court handed down an . . . important ruling on . . . April 18, upholding the ban on partial-birth abortion, which had been signed into law by (former) President George W. Bush in 2003 . . . President George W. Bush, the most pro-life president in United States history—has acted to protect children from the barbarity of partial-birth abortion . . . Ending partial-birth abortion, . . . which would more accurately be named 'late-term murder,' does not (stop) . . . abortion . . . throughout nine months of gestation . . . Liberal Democrats in the Senate have introduced a bill to override the Supreme Court's decision on partial-birth abortion and to outlaw any measure designed to restrict abortion in any way . . . entitled the 'Freedom of Choice Act'"[111] (Pr 8:36; 15:11,12; Eze 18:32; Jn 17:15; 1 Co 13:7).

In a newsletter, it was reported that, "The Freedom of Choice Act: . . . will nullify any anti-abortion laws and the parental notification laws in all states, and indeed all abortion reporting requirements . . . It will nullify all parental and spousal consent laws regarding abortion . . . It will nullify the federal ban on partial-birth abortion, as well as bans on the practice (of abortion) in 38 states . . . It will nullify all state laws restricting late-term abortions . . . It will nullify 33 states' laws requiring counseling before an abortion, . . . nullify 28 states' laws requiring a waiting period before an abortion, (and) . . . nullify 16 states' laws concerning ultrasounds before an abortion . . . It will require taxpayer funding of abortions . . . (and) it will create a 'fundamental right' to abortion throughout pregnancy, (etc.) . . . Upon passage of the Freedom of Choice Act (FOCA), . . . estimates indicate the number of abortions in America could increase by 125,000 a year, or more."[112]

In another newsletter, it was indicated that, "Our new President has long supported the so-called 'Freedom of Choice' Act . . . In July 2007, (then) President-elect Barak Obama . . . told a Planned Parenthood audience, . . . 'The first thing I'd do as President . . . is sign the Freedom of Choice Act' . . . Our new President has actually talked on his website about a $1.5 billion 'bailout' for the abortion industry—including major funding for Planned Parenthood."[113]

When we were composing this chapter on abortion, we were waiting for legislators to bring forth the Freedom of Choice Act. It is utterly deplorable to us, that our nation would elect an African-American President so entrenched in the death of the unborn, who we believe is "a slave to (the) sin" of murder, a slave to the devil, according to the Scriptures. In contrast, former President Abraham Lincoln, a strong believer in Jesus, was used by Almighty God to free the African-American race from slavery, from enslavement to the "white" race. Jesus declared, "If the Son sets you free, you will be free indeed." A former President was used by the Lord Jesus to proclaim "life" to enslaved people. The current President is being used by the "murderer, . . . the devil," to "destroy" life to the disenfranchised unborn through the enslavement of a woman's choice (Jn 8:34-44; 10:10; Ro 6:16,20; Gal 4:31; Tit 3:3-7).

Ironically, "67% of Planned Parenthood clinics are in predominantly black neighborhoods . . . The African-American (women) sustain about 37% of all the abortions, . . . (while African-Americans) make up 13% of the American population . . . The African- Americans are the only minority that are declining in population. Black women are three times more likely to have an abortion than other females."[114]

Tyrannical America

On March 14, 2008, my wife heard these words from the Lord Jesus, "The whole generation is being closed up, . . . all over the United States," and she also heard "Dirty tables." While we were praising our Lord Jesus during that same morning, I saw a vision of my ear. Then I saw a blacksmith during colonial times hammering out hot, black, metal iron on an anvil. The black metal iron was then formed into a lantern with a candleholder. A candle was lit up inside the lantern. Then I saw hot metal being poured out in a steel factory. That hot metal became like a huge black iron arch extending from the east to the west coast of the United States. Then, I saw a rainbow extended over that iron arch from one coast to the other in America. After that vision, I saw what appeared

English aristocracy drinking tea in English teacups in a parlor in a colonial home in America. The English aristocrats were wearing fine, fancy clothing of that time period. Then I saw their tables being violently turned over. Following that vision, I saw a forest fire taking place in America. Finally, I saw an old oak colonial door opening, and a young boy, who was at the door, was dressed in a colonial outfit. He was inviting us into a house. It seemed that as we walked in that house, the Lord Jesus was revealing, what happened in the past, and what is and will happen in the future in America. After those visions, the Lord Jesus spoke to us.

The Lord Jesus said, "He who has ears, let him hear what the Lord says today. In these last days, many men and women's 'consciences' will have 'been seared with a hot iron,' choosing 'doctrines of demons' instead of the one true God. Choosing a 'hot iron' to extinguish the unborn, a blind denial of the gruesome brutality used to murder an unborn infant. This country is enslaved to the will of Satan, instead of being set free to follow the will of God. The sky will become like 'iron' in America in the last days, and the land like dust. For God will judge the unrighteousness in America, those who have opposed the one, true God of the Scriptures, Jesus (Lev 26:18-20; Dt 28:23,24; Mt 25:31-46; 1 Ti 4:1,2; 2 Ti 2:26; 1 Pe 4,5; Rev 12:9).

"Many of the 'leaders' in America today are like the former British aristocracy. They are similar to the tyrannical rulers in England, who ruled over the American colonists. For money, they are selling out the next generation 'all over the United States.' 'The whole generation is being closed up' from the truth. Many in that generation have been closed up in the womb through abortion. Even moral Christian taxpayers are indirectly funding money to the abortion clinics throughout the United States through federal monies allotted for such purposes. The 'leaders' of the country are destroying and selling off the next generation to a 'god' of abortion, a 'god' of money, a 'god' of sexual immorality (Mt 6:24; 22:21; Jn 2:14; Ro 1:24,25; 2 Th 2:10; 2 Ti 4:3,4; Rev 9:20,21).

"I will turn over the ("dirty") tables of the 'aristocrats,' the pompous, the antichrists, and the merchants in America, those who have traded the truth for a lie. They have traded purity for immorality, and have traded the living God for Satan. They have forsaken their Founding Fathers' purity and forsaken the Living God. They have chosen their own ways. Today, America is like tyrannical England (in the latter 1700s), for they would not listen to the voice of God. England chose to oppress the Americans, attempting to enslave them to their 'Mother country's leaders.' The so-called 'leaders' in America are enslaving the people in lies, enslaving the people in (their) tyrannical decisions, enslaving the people to a false 'god' (Ex 1:11; Dt 13:6-8; Isa 66:4; Eze 18:24-26; Da 7:25; Am 5:12; Mt 22:32; Jn 8:44-47; Ro 1:25; 1 Co 6:18-20; Gal 6:9; 1 Ti 3:7).

"A tyrannical, dark power over this nation is the 'silent holocaust' of aborted fetuses, the aborted unborn. America is enslaved under many of their so-called 'leaders' in government, in courts, in schools, even in churches. The 'aristocracy' in this country have been selling America out to the devil, choosing their own rights, and prohibiting the rights of those who cannot speak up for themselves. A fire will be burning in America, until America chooses to repent and turn from their wicked ways. You must forge out this message, as 'iron sharpens iron' in this book. Take my lanterns to the dark world today, to those who have been snuffing out the light, ("the light of the world"), Jesus, and His Words of truth" (Gen 25:31-33; Dt 4:23,24; Ps 32:3,4; 39:2,3; Pr 27:17; Mt 4:8; 5:14-16[KJV]; Jn 8:12; Eph 6:12).

Healing through Jesus

On March 25, 2008, my wife heard these words from the Lord, "Aborting our baby in us." She saw a vision of herself and her husband holding a baby out in front of both of us. The baby was dressed in white clothes wearing a little white hat. The baby was crying, and was actually gritting its teeth at us.

The Lord Jesus then spoke to me that morning about those who support abortion. "Those that kill the unborn are destroying the little child within themselves, 'aborting our baby in us.' They are carrying out the sentence, that was opposed against them as children. As little children, they were not loved with the love of Jesus. In fact, because of their fears as little children from being abused emotionally, physically, and some sexually, they were cut off from their God-given emotions during childhood. So unknowingly, they're cutting off their umbilical cords within their wombs, as they cut off the lives of the unborn. They, as the unborn, were not nurtured in their wombs by their mothers, because of the lack of the love of Jesus in their mother's hearts. However, they sensed that they were safer in their mother's wombs, after facing the cold, stark world ahead of them (Ex 20:5; 1 Ki 3:16-27; Job 8:14-19; Da 9:26; Mt 18:2-4; 21:15,16; Mk 10:13; Lk 9:25; Col 3:21).

"They were not properly cared for as infants, not taken seriously by their parents and other adult figures in their lives. They were manipulated, and some were molested by their parents, and/or others. They were infants in fear, which rooted into them a bitterness, a gritting of teeth against the parent who would not allow the 'real' child to be born in themselves. Subconsciously, they were able to get back at those who wounded them by taking out their deep hatred and resentments on the unborn (Isa 13:8; 51:13[b]; 59:5-15; Mt 18:7,23-30; Lk 18:15; Heb 12:15).

"They need to come to Me, to Jesus to be healed; to heal the deepest pain in their mother's wombs, their deep pain of woundedness as children. Jesus will heal their deep hurts, if they are willing to change, to turn from evil, to repent of their wicked ways, and allow Jesus to love them in their unborn and infant pain. They need to forgive their wounders, and seek forgiveness with a deep sense of sorrow and repentance for killing the unborn, infants (Mt 11:28-30; 18:3,4,35; Lk 18:16,17; Ac 20:21; Ro 2:4; 2 Co 7:10; 1 Pe 3:11,12).

"Jesus takes the little babies, and lifts them up to heaven like Simeon in the Bible. Simeon lifted up the baby Jesus and blessed Him. Yet, Simeon told Mary that 'a sword' would 'pierce' her heart and 'soul.' Jesus is the real, the true Word of God, the Sword of the Spirit, which pierced the falseness in His mother's heart and soul, penetrating it with the real. In the Bible, Mary and Jesus' family members were ashamed of the real in Him for speaking up publicly, even against His flesh and blood family. Yet, Jesus 'entrusted' His real pain and suffering to His Father in heaven, who loved Him. Through His Father's love, Jesus could 'scorn (the) shame (of) the cross' from those who did not take Him seriously, who insulted, mocked, beat, and killed the real man, Jesus (Mt 16:21; Mk 3:20,21; 31:35; 6:4; 10:14-16; Lk 2:25-35; Jn 1:1,2,14; 7:2-8; 15:9; Eph 6:17; Heb 4:12; 12:2; 1 Pe 2:23).

"The 'key' to being healed of your childhood shame is forgiveness. Jesus was able to 'scorn (the) shame' by forgiving those who shamed Him. As you let God's light shine on your memories of shameful (experiences), and allow Jesus to visit and expose the lies in those memories, you can forgive those who shamed you (Isa 54:4; Lk 23:33,34; Jn 1:4,5; Eph 5:13,14; Col 3:13,14; Heb 13:8).

"Jesus is smiling at the births of little girls and boys in the delivery rooms, smiling at their innocence, and total dependence on their parents. Yet, knowing with a deep sadness, that their parents will manipulate that dependence for survival on them, so that their children become emotionally dependent on their parents throughout life. Jesus is smiling, because 'down the road,' He will become Savior to many of these children. Then they will no longer need to be emotionally dependent for survival from their parents. Jesus will save them from a world of manipulation that is without real love, through His love." (Mt 7:14; Lk 19:10; Jn 3:16,17; 14:6; 1 Jn 4:10,11). (Message received from God on March 25, 2008, April 6, 2008, and July 18, 2008).

The American patriots fought during the Revolutionary War

for freedom and liberty, which we have enjoyed for over two centuries. They were willing to shed their blood, primarily for independence from tyrannical England. The American people had no voice to represent their concerns to Great Britain. Today, we are shedding the blood of the innocent, unborn children, who have no voice to represent their concerns to the President of the United States, Justices, legislators, organizations for abortion, and abortionists in America. As our Founding Fathers declared, "All men," including the unborn, "are created equal; that they are endowed by their Creator with certain inalienable rights; that among these are life," the right to life. However, this is not the case for the unborn. The American people, as well as Christian "soldiers," must stand up and continue to fight for the right of unborn children to have life (Ps 94:20,21; Pr 6:16,17; 31:8,9; La 3:35,36; Lk 21:19; Jn 10:10[b]; 1 Ti 6:2; 2 Ti 2:3; Heb 9:22).

We believe that our nation's standard of morality has been sinking into a deep morass since the Supreme Court's rulings on abortion, and the banning of prayer and Bible readings in the public schools. We believe that the standard that is prevalent today in America is "sexual immorality," which we will reveal in the next chapter. America unfortunately is not turning to the one true Liberator, Jesus for freedom!

11

GOD GAVE THEM OVER TO SHAMEFUL LUSTS !

"Therefore God gave them over in the sinful desires of their hearts to sexual impurity for the degrading of their bodies with one another"

When Jesus' ministry began on earth, He was offered "the kingdoms of the world," if He would "bow down and worship" Satan. Our Lord Jesus refused. He refused to bow down to Satan's world of "the lust of the flesh, and the lust of the eyes, and the pride of life." Those worldly lusts will pass away, "but the man who does the will of God lives forever." Our forefathers, the Pilgrims and the Puritans, as well as our Founding Fathers, we believe, understood about the sinfulness in man's nature, about the sexual lusts in men and women. We believe that the Pilgrims and Puritans left England because of those lusts in their clergy and fellow English men and women. Those lusts were contrary to the Word of God (Mt 4:8-11; Ja 1:14,15[KJV]; 1 Pe 2:11[KJV]; 1 Jn 2:16,17[KJV]).

America's founding documents were filled with the truths of Scripture, with "checks and balances" regarding man's sinful nature. Our American forefathers understood the need to deny their fleshly desires and follow Jesus in order to bless their families and their country. Those founding documents provided order and structure for the American people to place limits on their lusts for Satan's world. Yet, today we believe that many men and women in our country have chosen to bow down and worship Satan's "kingdoms of the world," so their flesh can be gratified in sexual ways, and their sin desensitized to the point of calling sin, good, and righteous living, evil (Lev 19:36[KJV]; Isa 5:20; Lk 4:5-8; 9:23; Ro 13:13,14; Tit 2:12).

Condoning legalized abortion allows a country to glorify immoral sexual activity among its people. Removing the barriers of the Bible, the living Word of God, Jesus from the public sector, gives a worldly people their entitlements to their rights to sin in the flesh. Our forefathers and Founding Fathers, we believe, understood that when a nation condones sexual immorality through the media, legislation, the courts, government officials, etc., that nation will eventually be destroyed within spiritually, morally, and economically. Satan has become America's master of worldly desires today. Still, Almighty God will not be mocked by a sexually immoral people for He has exhibited His wrath against immoral nations in the past! While we composed this chapter, we were aware that the devil would attempt to attack us with sexually impure thoughts, motives, and imaginations to discredit us, and this book (Pr 11:14[a]; 14:34; Isa 5:24,25; Jer 8:9-12; Gal 6:7; 1 Ti 4:1; 2 Ti 4:3,4,18; Jude 7).

Former President Ronald Reagan shared, "As morality's foundation is religion, religion and politics are necessarily related . . . We need it because we are imperfect, and our government needs the church, because only those humble enough to admit they're sinners can bring to democracy the tolerance it requires in order to survive . . . We poison our society when we remove its theological underpinnings . . . Those who believe must be free to speak up and act on their belief . . . If we ever forget that we're one nation under God, then we will be a nation gone under"[115] (2 Ch 7:14,15; Isa 60:12; Lk 18:13,14; 1 Co 3:11; Gal 5:1).

In the Days of Noah

Malcolm Hedding, former Executive Director of the International Christian Embassy in Jerusalem, (ICEJ) wrote in a letter in January 2009, "Paul described the days in which we live in 2 Timothy where he wrote that in the last days, fierce (perilous) times will arrive. Our world is rapidly changing and our Judeo-Christian foundations are quickly being destroyed. Marriage for many is a . . . relic of the past, and new alliances and relationships are taking its place . . . The only game in town is hedonism. That is, the preoccupation with one's self and the need to satisfy (one's) cravings"[116] (Mal 2:16; Mt 7:26,27; Eph 2:3; 2 Ti 3:1-5).

Mr. Hedding reported, "The true definition of the days in which we live is summed up in one word: 'Decadent.' For if we reject a standard . . . verified by history called the Bible, we shall end up measuring ourselves by ourselves! . . . It's as old as Sodom and Gomorrah and the fall of Rome . . . When we reject God's word in favor of new social models, we invite . . . the correction of heaven. God hands us over to our basic desires"[117] (2 Ki 17:15-20; Mt 7:2; 10:14,15; Ro 1:24-28).

Pastor David Wilkerson of Times Square Church in New York City shared in messages in 1998 and 2008, that "It is clear from Scripture that America has now out-sinned backslidden Israel, out-sinned Sodom and Gomorrah, (and) out-sinned Noah's violent and wicked society . . . Consider the mockery being made of marriage by the glorifying of sexual perversions." Pastor Wilkerson said further, "God destroyed Noah's generation, as well as Sodom, all for lesser sins than ours. What arrogance to think that while these societies were judged severely, we might be spared"[118] (Gen 6:5,13; 19:5,24,25; Lev 18:22; 1 Co 6:9; Jude 7).

Pastor Wilkerson disclosed in 2007, that "When Paul came on the scene, flesh-driven doctrines of devils were sweeping through the church . . . Meanwhile, in the outside world, homosexuality was rampant. Throughout the Roman Empire, sexual perversions and sensual pursuits were the rule of the day. The self was exalted, flesh was worshipped, and pride held reign . . . It sounds to me as if Paul (was) describing our own times"[119] (Ro 1:24,25; Eph 4:19; 1 Ti 4:1,2; 1 Jn 2:16).

Pastor Wilkerson stated further that, "Sensuality, perversion and greed are running rampant throughout our society . . . When God sent the Flood upon the earth, it was because of a worldwide eruption of violence: 'The earth also was corrupt before God' . . . Children . . . are being raped, kidnapped and forced into enslavement in the global sex trade . . . The world's largest church denomination (Roman Catholic) has spent hundreds of millions of dollars to settle the claims of those who were molested in childhood by clergy (in America) . . . How long will God endure the pitiful cries of children who are molested by those who would represent Christ?"[120] (In our book, *Living in the Shadow of a Lie: The Roman Catholic Church*,[121] we reveal the depth of sexual sin, pedophilia among the clergy in that church) (Gen 6:12[KJV]; 19:8; Jdg 19:23-30; Ps 55:4-8, 12-14; Eze 16:5,20,21; Mt 18:6,7; Eph 5:5).

Pastor Wilkerson shared in 2006, "Our ministry receives scores of letters and e-mails from grieving lovers of Christ across the nation . . . They're asking, 'What is happening to America? It once was known for carrying the light of the gospel to the world through its mission efforts. Now it's a totally different story. TV programs have become utterly filthy, mocking Christians, moral standards and Christ himself. These shows glorify homosexuality and tear down family values'"[122] (Mt 5:14-16; Jn 15:18,19; Ro 1:27,28; 2 Pe 1:19; 2:7).

In the spring of 1994, the Lord Jesus directed us not to have cable TV in our home. Television programs and commercials, as Pastor Wilkerson shared, were and are filled with worldly views apart from our Lord Jesus, and sexually immoral innuendoes, overtones, and open sexual activities. We were obedient to remove cable from our television set. By just turning on and watching those programs, we were sinning with our eyes and our ears. Satan's world is "the lust of the flesh, and the lust of the eyes." Today we only watch on our television set, family and Christian DVD's and videos. Satan has captured much of the television media to lead "the whole world" of men and women, boys and girls "astray," away from the Cornerstone of America, Jesus Christ (Pr 27:20; Jn 8:43,44; Eph 2:20; Col 3:5,6; Tit 2:12; 1 Jn 2:16[KJV]; Rev 12:9).

In the winter of 2009, we purchased the movie, *Fireproof*[123] in the DVD format. That movie addresses the issue of watching pornography on the Internet. It is revealed in the movie, that the character, Caleb Holt, (Kirk Cameron) has an "addiction" with observing pornographic material on his computer. His wife in the movie will not compete with Caleb's sexual addiction and wants out of the marriage. His wife shares how utterly worthless and humiliated she feels, that Caleb would choose pornography over her. The extremely destructive elements of pornography, an adulterous "addiction," are displayed in this movie (Mt 5:27-30; Mk 7:20-23).

Caleb ends up accepting Jesus Christ into his heart, and loves his wife back to himself through Jesus. Though he struggles with his pornographic "addiction," and said, "Why is this so hard" (to stop)? He removes his computer, physically destroying it and its effects on him and his wife. That movie clearly depicted the difference between Satan's world of sexual corruption, and righteous living for Jesus Christ in the kingdom of God. America has suffered severely destructive consequences for choosing to abide in Satan's "kingdoms of the world" (Mt 4:8-10; Jn 1:12; Ro 10:9,10; 1 Co 15:24; 2 Co 12:21).

A Standard of Sexual Immorality

The Lord Jesus said, "The land of the United States has prostituted itself out to false 'gods,' false religions, the 'god' of sexual immorality. For this country chooses sexual immorality as its standard. Sexual immorality as a standard promotes abortion as a legal practice, and acceptance of homosexuals and lesbians as legitimate relationships. This standard is destroying the United States from within, for many have been killed through abortions, AIDS, and many personal relationships have been affected (destructively) by abortion and AIDS (Lev 20:13; 1 Ki 14:22-24; Jer 4:20-22 [KJV]; Eze 16:20,21; Mt 24:23,24).

"Many in the land are united in sexual immorality, in pornography. The land is polluted with idols. Idols of men (and women) are plastered up on billboards, alluring America to the 'god' of pleasing the flesh. A man can only hide his sins so long before his sins start to show up publicly in his appearance and demeanor (Da 2:22; Na 3:4; Ro 1:22-25; 2 Ti 3:1-4; Rev 9:20).

"'Jezebel' has been tolerated in the so-called "White House." She was given a place of high honor on Capitol Hill. A 'hill' clothed in sin and unholiness. Those who call themselves righteous and holy will not see My kingdom. The eloquence of men's talk will not change a man's heart, but the love of Jesus will pierce a heart to change a man. Look at the 'tree' to see if it bears good or bad 'fruit.' Those who desperately seek for true love will choose to repent for their sins, and will be received willingly into My kingdom. Your standard must be one of purity, love, and mercy without judgments. I must transform this land back into My image, as it was when it was founded by humble men and women before God (Gen 1:27; Mic 6:8; Mt 5:8; 7:15-20; 9:12,13; Lk 2:35; 24:46,47; Ja 2:12,13; Rev 2:20).

"The world today is a cesspool of impurities and idols, full of sexual sin. So much goes on behind closed doors, reaping to the flesh, but nothing is hidden from God's sight. For in the days of Noah, sin dominated the earth, so man today is choosing sin, reaping to the flesh rather than reaping to the Spirit. Man is risking his flesh to die quickly, rather than live forever and die holy (Ezr 9:11; Mk 4:22; Lk 17:26,27; Gal 6:8).

"The sin of sexual immorality is the weapon Satan is using to destroy the United States from within, as it destroyed the former Roman Empire in the past. Has not the United States become like that former Roman Empire condoning sin in the White House, condoning sin on television for little children to view? The nation wonders why there is so much corruption. Sexual immorality reigns on soap operas where little children watch partners married and unmarried in bed with each other. It used to be that purity and holiness were regarded as honorable virtues. Today, purity is a 'by-word' among Christians (2 Ki 23:7; Pr 22:6; 1 Co 5:1,2,11-13; 2 Co 7:1; Tit 1:11; Rev 18:2,3; 19:2).

"In Jesus, through the power of God's Holy Spirit, men can be set free from demons of sin and flesh, if they choose to eat good 'fruit.' It's what you choose to listen to, the voices you hear. People desire 'bad fruit,' because they hear the voice of Satan and follow that voice. Do not listen to secular radio stations for they voice the evils of men and women's flesh. Listen to Jesus, tune in every morning to His channel of LOVE. Then the Holy Spirit will channel His love to you (Lk 6:43-45; Jn 8:43,44; 10:4,5; Ro 5:5; Gal 5:19-26; Eph 3:17-19).

"In the days of Noah, so many men and women were involved in sexual sins, that it was considered normal; so it is with this adulterous generation. There is a toleration of sin in America; sexual sin, an impure stain that has spread over this country. The righteous and pure are despised today. When you hold to My standards of decency and purity, you face much opposition. There are those who do not oppose My standards of purity, those who seek My righteousness to change their hearts, to follow Jesus (Gen 6:5; Pr 29:10; Mt 6:33; 7:7,8; 24:37-39; Lk 10:16[KJV]; Jude 23; Rev 2:20).

"There is a raging battle in the demonic world against God's purity, to disguise sexual impurity as something that is not sin, that it is just a part of natural living. But that sin has destructive consequences in the lives of married and unmarried couples, and children. A great deception, even among men and women believers, is that they have the right to find someone more suited for themselves in a 'Christian' sense, rather than stay devoted to their own spouse. Somehow, they believe that God made a mistake on choosing their partner, or they made a mistake in God's eyes by their choice of a married partner. They believe, that they are entitled to their 'rights' with another, and that God approves of their decisions (Isa 5:20,21; Mt 7:15; Ro 1:25,28; 2 Co 11:3; Eph 6:12; Ja 1:14,15; Rev 2:20-22).

"If you look to the 'bad' in your spouse, you will find it. Then, in your mind, you can court other people. Many believers today are separating from each other, and are getting a divorce. But if you look to the good in your partner, you will find Jesus there, and you will never separate or divorce yourself from Him. Marriages and families are being attacked relentlessly by Satan through many forms of the media, TV and secular radio stations. Demons run in and out of homes through television sets, newspapers, magazines, computers, video games, etc., anything to get one's eyes off Jesus, and on other worldly and fleshly things. Choose to cleanse yourselves in repentance from sexual impurities passed down through generations (Pr 2:16-19; Mal 2:14-16; Mk 4:19; Ro 2:1-10; 1 Ti 4:1,2).

"My people are pulled away, because of the problems in the world. They are pulled to the problem, and then pulled away from Jesus. Do not listen to the false teachers, who claim to be wise, for they are 'wise in their own eyes.' They are deceived from the real truth. America, 'a land flowing with milk and honey,' has become disobedient, just as Israel was disobedient. This is the state of this country. America will suffer loss because the 'shepherds' did not care for the sheep. They care for their wealth, fame, fortune, and illicit affairs to please their inner desires. What a 'state of affairs' it is to be sitting on the Supreme Court bench and choose abortion and death over life, and choose sexual immorality as their honored 'god'" (Ex 3:8; 32:1; Dt 29:19; Pr 3:7; Jer 50:6; Eze 34:2-4,10; 1 Co 10:7; 2 Pe 2:1,2). (Messages received from our Lord Jesus on January 23, 1998, February 11, 1998, March 16, 23, 1999, April 2, 1999, March 4, 2000, and October 15, 2000).

Consequences of Sexual Immorality

Former President Ronald Reagan declared in 1983, that "Three times as many families are headed by single parents today (than) in 1960 . . . Welfare dependency, and a large increase in births out of wedlock (contributed to) single parent(ing) . . . In the 1970s the number of single mothers rose from 8 to 13 percent among whites and from 31 to a tragic 47 percent among blacks . . . (Do) not . . . pay any attention to all those who say that promiscuity is somehow stylish or rewarding (1988) . . . Corrosive influences such as illegal drugs and pornography seek to substitute for the permanent bonds of family life (1986)."[124]

In a letter received in June 2007, it was reported that, "One in 10 girls aged 15 to 19 becomes pregnant each year; more than a third become pregnant by age 20 . . . About one in five adolescents has had sexual intercourse before his or her 15th birthday . . . Nearly 40% of teen pregnancies end in abortion . . . The average age of a child's first Internet exposure to porn is 11 years old . . . The largest consumer of Internet porn is 12-to 17-year-olds."[125]

The American Civil Liberties Union, (ACLU) has been defending court cases to enhance sexual impurity in our nation. It was reported in a fact sheet that we received in 2008, that "The ACLU . . . supports free access to pornography, including Internet pornography access for children . . . Supports legalized polygamy . . . Supports legalized prostitution . . . Supports nudist camps for teenagers ... Supports open homosexuality in the military ... Supports publicly funded profane art ... Supports same-sex marriages, ... (and) supports legalized child pornography ... (The ACLU) opposes medical safety reporting of AIDS cases ... (In) Loudoun County, Virginia taxpayers (paid over) $106 (thousand dollars) in legal fees to the ACLU, because public libraries were ... actually using computer software to keep little children from viewing pornography."[126]

Alan Sears, the President and CEO of the Alliance Defense Fund wrote that, the ACLU "defends the distribution of child pornography and files or supports lawsuits against laws to protect children from registered sex offenders ... The ACLU (has) sought to redefine marriage and the family in a relentless campaign to separate sexual activity from morality and responsibility."[127] The ACLU strongly supports homosexual activity, which we believe is an abomination in God's eyes.

We have addressed in more detail the issue of sexual immorality in chapters 11 through 13 of our book, *The Profound Mystery: Marriage—The First Church*[128] (Lev 18:22; 1 Co 6:9,10,18-20; 1 Th 4:3-7).

In the Days of Lot

In the early morning of March 12, 2009, my wife heard these words, "A world of sexual crime." That morning, after fasting and worshiping before the Lord Jesus, He spoke to us. "'A world of sexual crime' is not just in the United States, but throughout the world. Men and women are choosing to devalue the Bible, the Word of God, calling it just an outdated book. They are valuing their own sexual desires, which are violating; marriages, women and children through rape, statutory rape, teen rape, molestation of children, incest, pedophilia, violating through; adultery, fornication, sex trade, prostitution, pornography, homosexuality, lesbianism, transvestism, etc. From their 'sexual crimes' come jealousies and murders (2 Sa 11:2-4; 12:7-10; Am 8:11,12; Mt 24:10-12; Mk 6:17-28; 1 Ti 1:9,10; 2 Pe 2:12-14,18,19).

"In the days of Lot, men were having sexual relations with men despite the prohibition against it as revealed in the Book of Leviticus. Almighty God's hatred of that sin caused Him to destroy with sulfur and fire Sodom and Gomorrah and the surrounding towns. Today America is being compared to the sexual sins committed in the towns of Sodom and Gomorrah" (Gen 19:5,24; Lev 20:13; Lk 17:28,29).

Satan, we believe, is using spirits of unbridled lusts in men and women to destroy America and other countries. Homosexual, gay and lesbian relationships, which the Scriptures decry, are becoming more acceptable. Those who speak out against the sexual sins of same-sex intimate relations are being accused of "hate crimes." The homosexual agenda is promoted by many in the media and the educational field as an acceptable alternative lifestyle. The Courts of the land and the Supreme Court of the United States have granted homosexuals "rights" to carry on their sexually, sinful, immoral relationships, relationships that are "detested" by Almighty God in the Scriptures (Dt 12:8[KJV]; Ps 81:12[KJV]; Hos 4:12[b]; Zec 13:2; Jn 15:18; Ro 1:27; 2 Ti 4:3,4; Ja 4:1-3[KJV]).

It was reported that in England "throughout the eighteenth century and up until 1861, all penetrative homosexual acts committed by men were punishable by death."[129] It was indicated further that, "In the United States as early as the early 1800s, . . . legal punishments often included heavy fines and or long prison sentences . . . to anyone convicted of the crime of sodomy. In the late nineteenth and early (twentieth) centuries, several states imposed various . . . laws against (sodomy) . . . In the 1950s, . . . an organized American and homosexual-rights movement emerged, . . . and sought to change . . . the various criminal laws used against homosexual Americans . . . By the 1960s, attitudes toward sexual relations, marriage, (and) sexual orientation . . . began to change . . . Attitudes strongly discouraging premarital sex decreased . . . The number of unmarried partners living together . . . soared . . . The acceptance of same-sex relationships . . . increased."[130] The increased acceptance of sexually immoral relationships followed the Supreme Court's rulings in the 1960's and 1970's, which we reported earlier.

Bowers v. Hardwick

In 1986, the "Supreme Court of the United States . . . (held that) a Georgia law classifying homosexual sex as illegal sodomy was valid because there was no constitutionally protected right to engage in homosexual sex . . . (A) police officer . . . (serving an) . . . arrest warrant . . . observed . . . Michael . . . Hardwick and a male companion . . . engaged in (homosexual) . . . sex . . . Both men . . . (were) placed . . . under arrest for sodomy."[131] That case went up to the Supreme Court of the United States.

In "the majority opinion," Supreme Court "Justice Byron White, framed the legal question as whether the constitution creates 'a fundamental right upon homosexuals to engage in sodomy.'" Justice White stated, "to claim that a right to engage in such conduct is 'deeply rooted in this Nation's history and tradition' or 'implicit in the concept of ordered liberty' is, at best, facetious." "Chief Justice Warren E. Burger . . . (in his) concurring opinion . . . concluded, (that) 'To hold that the act of homosexual sodomy is somehow protected as a fundamental right would be to cast aside millennia of moral teaching.'"[132]

Supreme Court "Justice Harry Blackmun . . . (in his) dissenting opinion . . . attacked the majority opinion as having an 'almost obsessive focus on homosexual activity' . . . The Bower's decision (took place) . . . in the 1980s, (when) the . . . AIDS . . . epidemic had occasioned a large amount of press coverage about homosexuality."[133]

In 1986, we believe that the Supreme Court "maintain(ed) justice in the courts" by upholding a Georgia law prohibiting a constitutional right to homosexual sex. The opinion of the majority in the Supreme Court validated the Scriptures in proclaiming that homosexual sex is sin, and an abomination in the eyes of Almighty God. Those Justices were able to "render true and sound judgment in (their) courts" (Lev 18:22,26-29[KJV]; Am 5:15; Zec 8:16).

We believe that men and women's personal sins and sinful lifestyles are not entitled to specific "rights" in the Word of God. Rather, our sins need to be genuinely confessed to our Lord Jesus, so we can be forgiven. We believe our Founding Fathers understood when writing the Declaration of Independence and the Constitution of the United States, that men and women's sinful lifestyle, whether public or private, was not protected by the laws of the land. It is significant to note, that Supreme Court Justice "White's" decisions, that we have reported in this book, supported the Scriptures. "Though your sins are like scarlet, they shall be as 'white' as snow." Supreme Court Justice Harry "Black"mun's decisions, that we have previously reported, opposed the Scriptures, the Word of God (Ps 10:2-11; Isa 1:18; Jer 7:1-11[KJV]; Heb 12:3; 2 Pe 2:13-17; 1 Jn 1:8-10).

Lawrence v. Texas

Unfortunately, in 2003, the United States Supreme Court "struck down the sodomy law in Texas . . . The majority held that intimate consensual (homosexual) conduct was part of the liberty protected by substantive due process under the Fourteenth Amendment. (This case had) the effect of invalidating similar laws throughout the United States that . . . criminalize sodomy between consenting same-sex adults." [134]

A "sheriffs deputy . . . arrested . . . John . . . Lawrence" and his male partner, when he observed them involved in homosexual sex. He charged them with "violating Texas's anti-sodomy statute." The case went all the way to the United States Supreme Court.[135]

"Justice Anthony Kennedy wrote the majority opinion, . . . casting doubt, . . . that homosexual sodomy is a widely and historically condemned practice, (and that the case of) . . . 'Bowers v. Hardwick . . . is overruled.'" The Court held that "the Texas statute furthers no legitimate state interest which can justify its intrusion into the personal and private life of the individual." The Court concluded that "the anti-sodomy law (was) unconstitutional," which had "opened the door . . . to (the) protection of a whole host of sexual activity between consenting adults."[136]

Supreme Court "Justice Antonin Scalia wrote (the) . . . dissent, (concluding that), . . . the Court 'has largely signed on to the so-called homosexual agenda.'" Justice "Scalia also averred that, State laws . . . based on moral choices . . . against bigamy, same-sex marriage, adult incest, prostitution, . . . adultery, fornication, bestiality and obscenity are likewise sustainable only in light of (the) Bowers" case. "Judge Thomas, in a . . . dissenting opinion, wrote that . . . he could find 'no general right of privacy or relevant liberty in the Constitution.'"[137] Tom Minnery of the Focus on the Family, Christian organization, wrote that the Supreme Court of the United States decided that "morality cannot be the basis for laws." That decision is being used to support "same-sex" marriages.[138]

The Scriptures proclaim, "Woe to those who make unjust laws, to those who issue oppressive decrees." We believe that the majority decision in the Lawrence v. Texas case was an "oppressive decree" for those Americans who stand up for righteous, moral living, according to the Word of God, and choose to follow Jesus Christ. We also believe that the Court's decision was an "unjust law," since the penalty for homosexual sex, whether in public or private, in the Old Testament was "death." Almighty God considers homosexual sex "detestable" and a criminal action worthy of death (Lev 18:22; 20:13; Isa 10:1; 53:8; Lk 9:23).

The Court's ruling "opened the door" for the American people to accept and protect an abominable sin, homosexual sex, as deserving a constitutional "right of privacy." Other types of sexual sins, that we believe are "detestable" in God's eyes, may be given a similar constitutional "right"; incest, pedophilia, prostitution, same-sex marriage, etc. In the Book of Romans it is written that, "men committed indecent acts with other men, and received in themselves the due penalty for their perversion." Women committing indecent acts with other women were also included in that admonition. The Supreme Court of the United States by condoning homosexual sin has blatantly defied the Word of God and placed America in the hands of God's judgment. Sodom and Gomorrah, whose men "gave themselves up to sexual immorality and perversion, . . . serve as an example of those who suffer punishment of eternal fire," and so will many Americans, today! (Dt 1:17; Pr 28:13; Ecc 12:14; Isa 29:15; Lk 13:24-28; Ro 1:26,27; Heb 4:13; Jude 7).

The United States of America will suffer, we believe, "the due penalty for their perversion." We believe, as we reported previously, that the framers of the United States Constitution had no intention of protecting the rights of American citizens involved with homosexual sins, nor other acts of sexual immorality. Committing sinful acts was not protected by "due process," we believe, by the Founding Fathers of this country. Justice Thomas "could find 'no general right of privacy or relevant liberty in the Constitution'" (Pr 14:12; Jn 8:24,26; Ro 1:27[b]; 3:19,20; Heb 9:26,27).

Dependence on God

On March 12, 2009, after fasting and praising God, I received a vision of a Founding Father sitting in a chair in Independence Hall, Philadelphia writing on parchment with a feather pen. In the vision, he was writing by candlelight in the Hall. He was wearing a white wig, and was dressed in colonial attire of that time period.

The Lord Jesus then said, "He is writing to America's future generations. 'The Bible, the Word of God is what we live our lives by. It is what we write in these documents for all future generations in America. We believe the Bible and our Lord Jesus are the guiding forces for the future posterity of this nation. The words in the Bible are our governing principles applied to these founding documents providing 'checks and balances,' as revealed in the Bible. They are to protect the morality of men and women and children in this country. Always hold on to the statutes, the precepts, the ordinances of the Word of God founded on our Rock, our Lord Jesus Christ. Our founding documents protect the morals of the American people from the evils of the world and the devil'" (Gen 45:7[KJV]; Dt 5:6-21; Ps 119:11,44-48; Mt 7:24,25; Mk 12:29-31; Jn 3:16-18; 8:34-36; 16:8,9; 1 Co 10:4; Ja 1:21).

Authors Peter Marshall and David Manuel, who were in agreement with our Lord's revelation wrote, "Some social indicators of the lifting of God's grace—the rapidly decaying morality, the disintegrating American family, the acceptance of rebellion and violent crime (are) the norm for modern life . . . The Puritans would say, 'God's Controversy with America has begun' . . . If God continues to lift His grace, . . . it will not be long before we will be in a hell very much in our own making"[139] (Mt 23:33; Ro 1:22-26; 2 Ti 3:1-4).

The authors wrote further, "The way to deepening in Christ is the Way of the Cross: the way of self-denial—of unconditional surrender of one's own will to God's will . . . We need to re-enter the covenant relationship which our forefathers had with God and with one another . . . The Pilgrims and Puritans . . . understood that . . . freedom was not (a) license to do as they pleased, but freedom to do the will of God . . . (This) means to (deal) with the things of self and ego, to battle them, . . . (as the) Pilgrims and Puritans (did in the past)! . . . The Pilgrims . . . chose to relinquish their individual independence, and . . . established our basic spiritual and civil institutions . . . Our forefathers have broken the trail for us, and shown the way."[140] It is up to believers in our Lord Jesus to follow "the trail" of our forefathers, and show others the "way" to freedom in Christ Jesus (Da 3:28; Mt 26:27,28; Mk 14:36; Lk 9:23-26; Ro 12:1,2; Gal 5:13; Heb 8:10; Jude 4).

Same-sex Relationships

Many Americans have not chosen "the way" of our forefathers, the Pilgrims and the Puritans. In an article that we received in December 2007, it was reported that, "In recent years there have been numerous homosexual or lesbian characters on prime time network shows . . . Some 1.4 percent of women and about 2.8 percent of men are homosexuals, according to an exhaustive University of Chicago study. But if you watched prime-time television, you might think that about 30 percent of Americans were 'gay' and less than 3 percent were Christians . . . (In a) Lichter-Rothman report on the 'media elite,' (it was) found that . . . 80 percent do not regard homosexual relations as wrong; 86 percent support the rights of homosexuals to teach in public schools; 51 percent do not regard adultery as wrong; and 17 percent strongly agree that extramarital affairs are wrong." It was further disclosed in a July 2010, newsletter, "The Gay and Lesbian Institute is now actually encouraging homosexuals to 'help President Obama lead the nation.' (They have) placed nearly 100 openly homosexual people in positions . . . within the federal government, . . . which (opposes) biblical morality."[141]

Pastor David Wilkerson of Teen Challenge ministries revealed in a message in 1998, that "We have begun to glorify homosexuality and lesbianism. Our media applauds the 'bravery' of gays who declare their sexual orientation—but we ought to weep over it! . . . Yet at one time, Christians across the country would have been on their faces crying out to God for mercy over such immorality . . . Radical homosexuals cry out to society, 'In your face!' Yet what they're really saying is,

'In your face, God!'"[142] (Ps 10:4,11; 36:1-4; Isa 5:20,21; Lk 6:21; 23:28; Ja 4:6-10).

In the early morning of March 19, 2009, my wife heard these words from the Lord Jesus, "This is a Sodom against God." That morning after praising the Lord, I received a vision of a tan, stuffed animal, a lion. A man's face replaced the stuffed animal's face. That face appeared to be of a homosexual man.

The Lord then said, "Satan uses stuffed animals and toys, as well as animated shows to create an atmosphere of cuddliness, of softness for children regarding homosexuality. In the media and in public school systems, Satan is trying to create an atmosphere of appropriateness for homosexual activity as an acceptable style of living. 'This is a Sodomy against God' Almighty and the Word of God. There are many joining the ranks in the 'church' that tolerate homosexuality. That is detestable and a blatant disdain of God's creation. For 'God created man in his own image, in the image of God he created him; male and female he created them'; created 'a man' to 'be united to his wife.' It is a type of blasphemy against God! (Gen 1:27; 2:24; Job 40:8; Ro 9:29; 2 Co 11:14,15; 2 Pe 2:12; Rev 2:20; 17:1-6).

"Many in the 'church' are 'abandoning the faith' and serving 'doctrines of devils,' that promote homosexuality as a gift from God! Men in 'Sodom and Gomorrah and the surrounding towns' committed sodomy with one another, and burned in their flesh. So the 'private parts' of those involved in homosexual sex will burn in the flesh, which is a 'due penalty for their (sexual) perversions.'" We believe, that as the Lord Jesus revealed, men and women were created by Almighty God physically, emotionally, and spiritually to compliment each other's masculine and feminine nature, to be "helpmates" for one another (Gen 2:18,20[b]-24; Isa 33:12; Ro 1:27[KJV]; 1 Ti 4:1,2[KJV]).

Pastor Wilkerson shared in messages in 2005 and 2006, that "In New York State, we're seeing a 'great falling away' of the kind Scripture predicts. Some 410 pastors have enlisted for a homosexual agenda called 'Pride in My Pulpit' . . . The message is, 'We're proud of the homosexual community and we endorse it.' The numbers of these pastors are growing"[143] (Ps 10:4; Isa 2:12-18; Mt 24:10; 1 Ti 4:1,2; 2 Ti 4:3,4).

Pastor Wilkerson stated further, "A growing number of bishops and preachers are promoting homosexuality and same-sex marriages. These churches are apostate." He disclosed that, "The Episcopal church . . . has fallen into apostacy . . . The denomination is one of the first to ordain a homosexual bishop . . . The newly elected head bishop is a woman who has adopted the gay agenda . . . Sodom's primary sins were: pride and arrogance . . . New York City has an annual Gay Pride parade, which numbers up to 400,000 marchers. Marchers carry signs reading, 'God Is Gay,' 'Christ Was Gay,' 'Gay and Proud of It.' I once saw marchers leap out of the parade to attack a small group who carried signs reading, 'Jesus Loves Gays. He Only Hates Sin.' That . . . group sought only to offer love, but they were cruelly manhandled"[144] (Gen 19:5-9; Ps 22:7[KJV]; Pr 8:13; Isa 5:20,21; Mk 3:22; Ro 5:8).

Those who stand up for righteousness, and right living according to the Word of God, are being persecuted. Brian Fisher as Executive Vice President of Coral Ridge Ministries, wrote a letter in March 2007. He reported that, "In Philadelphia, a group of Christians was actually arrested—and threatened with 40-year prison terms—for peacefully sharing the Gospel with those entering a rally (who were) encouraging homosexual behavior"[145] (2004) (Mt 5:10-12; Ac 5:40-42; 9:1,2; Heb 11:36-38).

Mike Evans, in charge of the Jerusalem Prayer Team, wrote in an "Urgent Gram" in May 2006, that, "There are now homosexual churches all over America and the world, whose adherents claimed to be good Christians . . . Lesbians, gays, bisexuals and transgenders (were involved in) organizing WorldPride in 2006, an international parade in the city of Jerusalem . . . The majority of the organizers and funds for WorldPride (came) from the United States . . . The majority of these people . . .

profess to be... Christians... My heart aches that the Jewish people (may have thought that) the majority of Gays, Lesbians, Bisexuals, and Transgenders are Christians... (It) is an attempt to disgrace everything that true Christians consider to be pure and holy"[146] (Ac 20:30; 1 Ti 6:1[KJV]; 2 Pe 2:1,2,15; 1 Jn 2:19).

In the last days, "They will gather around them a great number of teachers to say what their itching ears want to hear. They will turn their ears away from the truth," thinking that our Lord Jesus approves of same-sex sexual relationships. In the book of Isaiah in the Bible, the Scriptures declare, "Woe to those who call evil good and good evil. Who put darkness for light and light for darkness." Woe to those who believe homosexual sin is of God! (Isa 5:20; Mt 18:7; 1 Ti 6:3-5; 2 Ti 4:3,4).

Boy Scouts of America v. Dale

From first through third grades, I (Mark) was a cub scout, and I am thankful that my cub scout leaders were not homosexuals. However, the Boy Scouts have recently come under "fire" for refusing to allow homosexuals to become scout leaders. In the Supreme Court case of Boy Scouts of America v. Dale, "James Dale,... position as assistant Scoutmaster of a New Jersey troop was revoked when the Boy Scouts learned that he (was) openly gay... Dale... filed (a) suit in the New Jersey Superior Court, alleging,... that the Boy Scouts had violated the state statute prohibiting discrimination on the basis of sexual orientation in places of public accommodation."[147] That case went all the way up to the Supreme Court.

In 2000, the "Supreme Court of the United States (held that)... a private organization is allowed, under certain criteria, to exclude a person from membership through their First Amendment right to freedom of association... Chief Judge William Rehnquist wrote the majority opinion... 'Forcing a group to accept certain members may impair the ability of the group to express (their) views, and only those views, that it intends to express.' Thus 'freedom of association . . . presupposes a freedom not to associate.'"[148]

That was a victory for the Boy Scouts organization, and for those that honor moral heterosexual relationships. However, Mathew Staver, Founder and Chairman of Liberty Counsel reported that, "The Boy Scouts teach young boys . . . to be honorable and show respect. When they take their oath, they acknowledge God and pledge themselves to a moral life. Revealing their disdain for the Scouts, . . . the ACLU sued San Diego to force the city to break its lease of Balboa Park to the Boy Scouts, where for the past 50 years they had held their annual jamboree . . . The Boy Scouts were evicted and the city's taxpayers ended up paying the ACLU $950,000."[149]

NAMBLA

Mr. Staver also revealed that, "The ACLU represented the North American Man-Boy Love Association (NAMBLA), a group whose purpose is to promote sex between men and boys (pedophilia) . . . The ACLU has twisted the intent of the Founding Fathers. They have cunningly perverted the very Constitution that guarantees our freedom, in order to silence Christians, to kill innocent children and to destroy the institution of marriage!"[150] (Dt 32:5; Ps 106:37-39; Mic 3:9; Ac 4:18,19).

Don Swarthout of Christians Reviving America's Values, (CRAVE), in a newsletter which we received in 2008, wrote, "NAMBLA's website, which advocates sex between boys and adult men and the abolition of age—consent laws, incited the attempted molestation and murder of (a) . . . 10-year-old boy . . . The ACLU claimed this is a case of freedom of speech and association. 'For us, it is a fundamental First Amendment case,' said the executive director of the Massachusetts branch of the ACLU ... The ACLU ... (defended) homosexual pedophile predators after they raped and murdered a little boy."[151]

Choosing to defend and support wickedness like in the ACLU and NAMBLA organizations will eventually "reap destruction." For those who sow "to please (the) sinful nature, from that nature will reap destruction." Satan's "servants masquerade as servants of righteousness. Their end will be what their actions deserve," destruction. In the Gospel of Matthew, Jesus proclaimed, "But if anyone causes one of these little ones who believe in me to sin, it would be better for him to have a large millstone hung around his neck and to be drowned in the depths of the sea. Woe to world because of the things that cause people to sin! Such things must come, but woe to the man through whom they come!" Our Lord Jesus hates evil, especially evil done towards children (Mt 18:6,7; 2 Co 11:15; Gal 6:8).

AIDS

Some of the destructive effects of homosexual sin are exposed in the AIDS blood disease. In August 2008, it was reported in Atlanta, Georgia, through the "(AP)," Associated Press that, "The number of Americans infected by the AIDS virus each year is much higher than the government has been estimating, U.S. health officials reported, acknowledging that their numbers have understated the level of the epidemic. The country had roughly 56,300 new HIV infections in 2006—a dramatic increase from the 40,000 annual estimate used for the past dozen years."[152]

It was reported further, that "The Centers for Disease Control, ... CDC (found) that infections continue to increase in gay and bisexual men ... More than a third of those with HIV are younger than 30 ... Blacks ... account for nearly half of annual HIV infections ... The CDC focused on infections among men who have sex with men."[153]

Same-sex Marriages

We believe "God blessed them . . . male and female . . . and said to them, 'Be fruitful and increase in number; fill the earth and subdue it.'" The Lord blessed them as husband and wife in the book of Genesis to procreate, reproduce and "increase in number." We believe God does not bless same-sex sexual relationships, for God abhors that sin. Same-sex relationships do not have "natural relations," but "unnatural ones," so they are not able to bear children, naturally. We believe that our forefathers and Founding Fathers, who tried to live according to the Word of God, had no idea that many Americans today would begin to condone same-sex unions, marriages (Gen 1:27,28; 2:24; Lev 18:22; Ro 1:26,27; 1 Co 6:9,10).

Following the Supreme Court case of Lawrence v. Texas in 2003, "The Massachusetts Supreme Judicial Court ruled in Goodridge v. Dept. of Public Health that the Constitution of the Commonwealth of Massachusetts required that same-sex couples be given full marriage rights. The decision did cite Lawrence."[154]

In the state of New Jersey, it was reported in a newsletter in 2007, that "The New Jersey Supreme Court found a right in the state constitution for homosexuals to marry and ordered the legislature to rewrite the state laws to comply with its decision." It was noted that, "Courts throughout the nation will be forced to consider whether laws limiting marriage to heterosexuals are in conflict with provisions of the state constitutions."[155]

It was revealed in a newsletter in 2008, that "The Ocean Grove Camp Meeting Association, a Methodist retreat center in New Jersey, lost its tax exemption after it refused to let two lesbian couples use its facilities for their civil union ceremony. New Jersey gives homosexuals protected status (2007) . . . In 2008, "the New Mexico Human Rights Commission ruled that (a certain woman's) photo studio violated a state anti-discrimination law when, on religious grounds, she declined to let her business photograph a lesbian couple's 'commitment ceremony.'" That woman had "to pay the lesbian plaintiff's court fees . . . of more than $6,000!"[156]

In the state of California, it was reported in a newsletter in 2008, for the National Organization for Marriage that, "Four California judges . . . (repealed) Proposition 22, which defined marriage as a union between one man and one woman and was overwhelmingly approved by the voters in 2000 . . . (Those judges) extended the internationally recognized human right to marry to include same-sex marriage. Not even in Massachusetts or in New Jersey could the courts stomach the idea that same-sex marriage is deeply rooted in our foundational American traditions of human rights."[157]

It was also noted that "The California court . . . (declared that) . . . sexual orientation should be treated just like race under the California equal protection amendment . . . Hollywood, academia and some in the medical profession . . . have succeeded in shaping the minds of young people against traditional marriage, and intimidating and punishing anyone who offers a defense of marriage."[158]

Dr. James Dobson of the Focus on the Family Christian organization reported in a newsletter of June 2008, "Four members of the California Superior Court . . . intend to jettison the divine plan . . . (Former) Senator, (now President), Barak Obama (agreed) with the decision by the Supreme Court . . . The Colorado State Legislature . . . passed recently . . . Senate Bill 200 . . . It defined one's sexual inclinations as 'a person's orientation toward heterosexuality, homosexuality, bisexuality, or transgender status' . . . Colorado will no longer have two 'sexes'; it specifies a myriad of 'sexual orientations' that must be granted access to . . . public . . . facilities . . . Restrooms are not the only problem with the new law . . . A refusal to do business with someone based on a sincerely held religious belief that homosexuality is wrong would violate the law."[159]

It was written further in a newsletter in 2009, that "if Congress passes a so-called 'hate crimes' bill, reaching out in love to help a homosexual turn away from sin could land you in court . . . or in jail. In fact, under such a law, you or your pastor might be sued for reading your Bible aloud—if you read anything calling homosexual behavior a sin . . . A 'hate crime' is any offense motivated by a 'bias against' someone's 'race, color, religion, ethnicity, gender, disability, or sexual orientation.' It also increases the penalty for crimes committed against homosexuals."[160]

Sadly, it was also reported in a September 2008 newsletter, that then former Senator and now President of the United States, Barak Obama, "believes that the Sermon on the Mount justifies his support for legal recognition of same-sex unions . . . (He also) wants to 'expand adoption rights' for same-sex couples."[161] When the President of the United States of America supports "same-sex unions," and bases his belief on the "Sermon on the Mount," America is destined for fiery punishment, as were "Sodom and Gomorrah and the surrounding towns." We believe Satan has been using men and women to promote "the homosexual agenda." Since many of our country's elected, appointed "leaders" have continued to support homosexual sex, we believe this country will fall, like the Roman Empire. In our book, *The Profound Mystery: Marriage—The First Church*, we reveal in more detail on the sin of homosexuality[162] (Pr 14:34[b]; Jer 12:17; Mt 18:6,7; Jude 7; Rev 21:8).

Healing and Forgiveness

As we shared previously, we "all have sinned and fall short of the glory of God, and are justified freely by his grace through the redemption that came by Christ Jesus." The "good news" is that when you accept Jesus Christ in your life, He can heal you of your sinful habits and lusts. In 1990, we attended a

Conference for about a week at a church, that we had been attending at that time. The Revival was primarily focused on being healed from past emotional, physical, and sexual wounds from childhood. The Revival was also directed toward leading homosexuals and lesbians away from their lifestyle through Jesus Christ. Some former homosexual men, who were leaders at the Conference, shared about their homosexual background, and how Jesus Christ healed them from same-sex lusts and relationships (Mt 4:23,24; 11:28-30; Lk 7:37,47-50; Jn 1:12; Ac 3:6-10; Ro 3:23,24; Rev 3:20).

We experienced powerful deliverance by the Holy Spirit. We observed demons manifesting themselves against the spiritual leaders of the Conference, as if to try to stop them. A pastor's wife was struck a hard blow in the back by a man, who was demonized. The woman apparently was not hurt, protected by the Holy Spirit. By the end of the Conference/Revival, many openly "gay," homosexual men and lesbian women testified of being healed completely from same-sex lusts by Jesus Christ. We left that Conference hugging several who had been healed by Jesus through the power of the Holy Spirit (Lk 15:11-13,18-24; Ac 2:17,18; 4:31; 5:15,16; 8:5-8; 10:44-48; 1 Co 12:4-11; 2 Ti 1:7).

It was further reported that, "Coral Ridge Ministries and other pro-family groups, had profiled people who had found liberation from homosexuality through faith in Jesus Christ . . . (in a) 'Truth and Love' print and TV ad campaign." In the advertisement, it indicated that, "If you really love someone, you'll tell them the truth." In the ad, a woman revealed, "I'm living proof that Truth can set you free." She shared further, "Recently, several prominent people . . . have spoken out on homosexuality . . . calling it a sin. When I was living as a lesbian I didn't like hearing words like that . . . until I realized that God's love was truly meant for me"[163] (Ps 141:5; Pr 27:5,6; Jer 31:3; Eze 16:4-6,8; Jn 8:31,32).

However, "The San Francisco Board of Examiners . . . sent a . . . letter to Coral Ridge Ministries and other pro-family groups (writing that) . . . there is a 'direct correlation' . . . between calling homosexual behavior sinful and the . . . 'crimes committed against gays and lesbians'"[164] Satan has so entrenched some men and women in the homosexual lifestyle, that they have become hostile to Christians and former homosexuals, who have become Christians, those who have been healed of the sin of homosexual sex by Jesus Christ (Lk 6:22; 13:34; 2 Co 11:3; 12:21; 2 Ti 3:13; Tit 3:3).

The Focus on the Family Christian organization sent out a newsletter in 2007, in which they shared about "Media Coverage of (the) Love Won Out Conference." The Conference presented how "Gay people can become straight with support, counseling and the Lord's help." At the Conference, "The essential message is that homosexuality can be overcome through therapy and devotion to Jesus Christ." An "ex-gay . . . walked away from homosexuality" stating, "It's a difficult process . . . But . . . let the Christian community know that for those who want to walk away from homosexuality, change is possible."[165] We believe that the Lord Jesus has His arms wide open for all who have sinned (Isa 40:11; Mt 11:29,30; Jn 8:10,11; 1 Pe 4:3,4).

The Lord Jesus said on August 17, 2007, "The sins that the Lord Jesus has been setting you free from: sexual impurity, an allurement to evil, and pride, are the sins in America that have been taking her down, morally. This country glorifies sexual impurity, allurements to evil things, and self-elevation, pride. Pride in men and women in America, (is establishing its own rules of morality), instead of the rules of an Almighty God. America has been crippled spiritually, (morally), under the demonic guise of 'equal rights' (Eze 28:17,18; Ro 3:10-18; Col 3:5,6[KJV]; Tit 3:3-6; Ja 1:14,15; 1 Jn 2:16[KJV]).

"(These "equal rights" include): 'equal rights' for women desiring abortions, 'equal rights' for homosexual and lesbian relationships, and those desiring to have a same-sex marriage contract, 'equal rights' for children in public schools to learn about same-sex relationships, as a 'normal' way of life, 'equal rights' for men and women desiring to divorce their marriage partner, because they found a better 'alternative,' another man or woman, 'equal rights' for choosing other 'gods' like Allah. But not having equal rights for those desiring wholesome relationships, choosing to live their lives according to the Word of God (Gen 39:6,7, 10-20; Dt 13:6-9; Pr 7:9-12,21, 25-27; 9:16-18; Isa 10:1,2; Am 3:10; Zec 3:1; Rev 17:4-6).

"America is losing its 'moral compass' for choosing man-made 'equal rights,' instead of the rights the Lord Jesus has given to His people in His Words. (Those rights) are the right of human dignity, the right of purity, the right to have only one partner, a spouse of the opposite sex, the right to believe in the one and only true God, His Son Jesus Christ, the right to honor Him, the right to hear about wholesome relationships in public schools, and the equal right of men and women to have a personal relationship with Jesus" (Pr 8:27[KJV]; Jer 31:22[KJV]; Mt 5:8; 19:4-6; Mk 12:29,30; Jn 3:16,17; 1 Co 6:20; 1 Th 4:3).

We will reveal in the next chapter, how students in public schools have suffered over the years, because of the Supreme Court's rulings during the early 1960s, and subsequent Court decisions. We also expose how those rulings have negatively affected the United States Armed Forces.

12

TRAIN A CHILD IN THE WAY HE SHOULD GO!

"The armies of heaven were following him, riding on white horses and dressed in fine linen, white and clean."

It was Jesus who said, "Unless you change and become like little children, you will never enter the kingdom of heaven." According to our Lord Jesus, we all must change and become like little children, depending solely on our Father in heaven through His Son, Jesus Christ. Jesus also said, "Woe . . . (to those who cause) these little ones . . . to sin." As we continue to examine what our government and courts have done to children in public schools and other public settings, the United States of America will surely "have a large millstone hung around (its) neck and (will) be drowned in the depths of the sea" for causing "these little ones to sin" (Mt 18:3-7; Lk 17:1,2).

Deceptive Philosophy

As we reveal how adults in public schools today, cause "these little ones to sin," we will report on the destructive ramifications of sin in children's lives, as well as the unbelief in the one true God and His living Word among this generation of adults. It was reported that, "the (government) education establishment vigorously opposes the dissemination in schools of any value or belief that can be remotely traced to the Bible; at the same time it affirmatively endorses other values that many Christians find repugnant. Public schools are replete with 'values-laden' curricula, from sex education and sexual orientation to notions of . . . death education . . . Our children are often being inculcated with values and attitudes that conflict with or are hostile to Christianity"[166] (Jn 15:18,19; 2 Co 12:21; Col 2:8).

In the early 1960's, "secular humanism" replaced the removal of prayer and Scripture readings in the public schools. It was further reported that, "Secular humanism" is "a philosophy that teaches that 'God does not exist, and that man is . . . self-sufficient and the measure of all things' . . . The National Education Association . . . makes sure Christians don't have the right to speak biblical truth in the classrooms."[167] Satan, who has desired to be "the measure of all things" apart from God, introduced through men and women "a philosophy" in the public schools, that man's decisions are exalted and the Word of God is disdained (Gen 3:1-5; Isa 14:12-15[KJV]; Jer 17:5; Ro 2:8).

It was noted by Brian Fisher, former Executive Vice President of Coral Ridge Ministries, that "Abraham Lincoln . . . said, 'The philosophy of the classroom in one generation is the philosophy in the next.'" That philosophy that exists today in public schools and in government, reportedly was introduced by "John Dewey, (considered the) father of modern American public education." John Dewey reportedly said, "There is no God and there is no soul. Hence, there are no needs for the props of traditional religion . . . Immutable truth is also dead and buried. There is no room for fixed, natural laws or moral absolutes" . . . "The effects" of this antichrist philosophy have influenced "the ACLU and the National Education Association (NEA)—the largest teachers union in America. (The) 3.2-million member teachers union openly uses its member dues to politically support abortion, homosexuality," etc. The effects of an "anti-Christian" philosophy has significantly degenerated morality among children and youth. "Teen immorality, teen depression, substance abuse and suicides" have "increased" since the early 1960's[168] (Ps 10:4; Mk 4:14,15; Ro 1:24-28; 1 Co 1:18-20).

When the current President of the United States was a Senator in Illinois, he "voted for a bill authorizing 'comprehensive' sex education beginning in kindergarten."[169] Pastor David Wilkerson revealed in a message in 2007, that "Satan's powers of darkness, . . . (his) demonic forces have infiltrated high places of human power (in) the media, political offices, (and) high courts . . . These demonic principalities have an agenda. They work to reeducate young schoolchildren about the 'rightness' of homosexuality. They seek to erode moral values. They work to pull down the saving power of the gospel"[170] (Jdg 19:22-25; Isa 5:20; Mt 12:25,26,34; Eph 6:11,12).

Louis Sheldon, Founder and Chairman of Traditional Values Coalition wrote in a letter in 2007 that, "In schools across America, the right of parents to direct the moral upbringing of their children is being overruled by education professionals who indoctrinate children with anti-parent, anti-God, sexual permissive philosophy . . . A three-judge panel of the 9th Circuit court of appeals in San Francisco recently denied parents the right to remove their elementary school-age children from a public school sex survey . . . Children in America's public schools are being taught that the homosexual lifestyle is perfectly okay . . . Public schools are providing abortion counseling and distributing condoms and birth control devices to teens without the consent or knowledge of parents"[171] (Pr 5:3-14[KJV]; Isa 10:1,2; Jer 17:23; Mk 7:20-23; 2 Jn 7).

Don Swarthout, President of Christians Reviving America's Values, (CRAVE) in 2008, reported about the American Civil Liberties Union in a newsletter. He wrote, the ACLU "Supports pro-homosexual school curriculums, . . . (and) supports mandatory comprehensive sex education, including detailed promotion of homosexuality and condom use . . . (The ACLU) opposes 'abstinence before marriage,' sex education, . . . (and) opposes parental consent laws"[172] (Mal 2:17; 1 Co 6:9,10; Gal 5:19-21).

According to the Scriptures, according to the living Word of God, Almighty God has set moral rules to live our lives by, in order to bless and foster wholesome relationships among children and adults. However, since many American "leaders" have opposed the one true God of the Bible, Jesus, the true liberator from slavery to sin, we see the horrendous effects on American children today. Satan has come "to steal and kill and destroy" . . . "these little ones." Satan has been snatching "the Word" out of their hearts for years through "blind guides," the so-called "leaders" in the United States. Because those "leaders" have "exchanged the truth of God for a lie, and worshiped and served created things rather than the Creator, . . . Because of this, God (has given) them over to shameful lusts" (Lev 18:22; Dt 5:6-21; Mt 13:18,19; 23:16[a]; Jn 8:34-36; 10:10; Ro 1:25,26[a]).

The Homosexual Agenda

As we have revealed already, sexual promiscuity has been increasing among youth who attend public schools. The "homosexual agenda" is being pushed with force to school-age children. In a newsletter from Concerned Women for America in 2003, it was reported that "American standards of sexual morality have eroded to the point that almost nothing is off-limits in our schools. And sex education that promotes homosexual behavior as an 'alternative lifestyle' is quickly becoming the norm... Grade-school children are being taught that cross-dressing is just healthy self-expression. Graphic details of perverted sex practices are being taught to high school children, and parents are being locked out of assemblies led by radical homosexual activists"[173] (Gen 19:1-5; Dt 22:5; Ro 1:26-28; 1 Pe 4:3; 2 Pe:2:12-14).

Alan Sears, President and CEO of the Alliance Defense Fund shared in a newsletter in 2009, that the "ACLU, (and) its allies . . . (who) advocate homosexual behavior (along with) a growing number of public school officials (are aiming) to condition children—starting in kindergarten—to embrace and approve of homosexual behavior . . . The National Education Association, (NEA) and the Gay, Lesbian and Straight Education Network, (GLSEN) . . . seek an end to parents' traditional rights to raise their children with their own values . . . Some elementary schools now present: 'Family life education' and 'respecting differences,' . . . which encourage children to participate in role-play, depicting same-sex families . . . A GLSEN video, titled 'It's Elementary,' . . . trains elementary school teachers to advance the homosexual agenda in their classrooms"[174] (Pr 24:24,25[KJV]; Isa 5:20; Mt 7:15-20; 18:6,7; Jn 3:19,20; Ro 1:25).

Mr. Sears reported further that, "high school" students receive "a GLSEN questionnaire," which asks, "What do you think caused your heterosexuality? Is it possible heterosexuality is a phase you will grow out of? If you have never slept with someone of the same sex, how do you know you wouldn't prefer that? Is it possible you merely need a good gay experience?" . . . "State . . . law S.B.777 . . . in California . . . requires that homosexual behavior be presented to young people—all the way down to kindergarten—as a choice just as legitimate and even desirable as heterosexual behavior"[175] (Lev 20:13; Mt 4:8-10; Ro 6:12-14,19; 1 Co 6:9,10,18).

Alan Sears noted further that, "GLSEN wants unrestricted access to every student in America, to train them to embrace homosexual behavior, regardless of the values they were raised with at home . . . (In) April, GLSEN sponsors a nationwide day . . . called the 'Day of Silence' . . . Participating students refuse to speak during . . . part of the school day . . . to protest alleged 'unfair treatment' of those who practice homosexual behavior"[176] (Lev 18:22; Ps 32:3-5; 1 Th 4:3-7).

Our former dental assistant shared with me, (Phyllis), that her son attended a high school in Richmond, Virginia that sponsored the "Day of Silence." She reported that teachers wore red shirts, supporting gay and lesbian relationships, and opposing their mistreatment from others. Her son chose not to participate in that pro-homosexual day.

Alan Sears revealed in another newsletter in 2007, that "A health textbook for high school freshmen in Massachusetts" indicated, "'Testing your ability to function sexually and give pleasure to another person may be less threatening in your early teens with people of your own sex . . . You may come to the conclusion that growing up means rejecting the values of your parents' . . . (In) Colorado (at a) high school, students were required to attend a seminar (that shared), 'It's very natural for young people to experiment with same-sex relationships' . . . 'Now, what is healthy sexual behavior? . . . Men and men, women and women, men and women. Whatever combination you would like to put together'"[177] (2 Ti 3:1-4; 2 Pe 2:18; 3:3; Jude 16,18,19).

Brian Fisher of Coral Ridge Ministries revealed in a newsletter in May 2007, that "U.S. District Judge Mark Wolf boldly imposed the homosexual agenda on grade-school children in public schools in Massachusetts . . . Judge Wolf ruled against parents who did not want this disagreeable subject matter taught to their Christian children . . . The parents were denied the right to be notified in advance of such teaching"[178] (Mt 10:21; Ro 1:30[b]; Col 3:20).

According to the Bible, sexual relationships outside marriage are forbidden by God. Healthy sexual relationships are discovered in a devoted marital relationship. According to the Scriptures, those who participate in sexual relationships outside marriage will not "inherit the kingdom of God," unless they repent of their sins. Satan, using men and women who have embraced sexual immorality and homosexuality, are causing "these little ones to sin." We believe this an abomination to God and His Word. God opposes the "lust of the flesh, and the lust of the eyes." What our Lord Jesus reveals as an abomination in His eyes is what is portrayed as good, homosexual behavior, in children's eyes in the public schools. Woe to the man who calls "evil good and good evil"! Our Lord Jesus is a just God, and He will judge those who are harming and destroying children (Lev 20:13; Isa 5:20; Mt 18:6; Mk 7:20,21[KJV]; 1 Co 6:9; 7:2; 1 Jn 2:15-17[KJV]).

The Lord Jesus revealed more information to us on this subject. On April 23, 2009, and May 14, 2009, after fasting and worshiping before the Lord Jesus, I received some visions. In the first vision in April, I saw an eagle with its wings in a V-formation in the air. It was a vision, I had received months ago, where an eagle was hovering over Independence Hall in Philadelphia as our Founding Fathers were writing our American documents. In this vision, the eagle spread out its wings and turned into a large black raven. That raven then went and plucked out an eye of one of the thieves on the cross next to Jesus as portrayed in the movie, *The Passion*.[179] Then I saw a vision of the statue of Liberty. The torch which was held in the statue's left hand, broke off, and crashed down to the ground.

A vision followed of teachers in a public school wearing red shirts honoring a "Day of Silence" on behalf of homosexuals and lesbians. There was a vision of a high school football "sled" used during football practices for aggressive hitting by the players on the pads of the "sled." Those pads, however, were of pastel colors. Another vision followed of the current President of the United States with one end of a rope tied around his neck, while the other end of the rope was not attached to anything. The vision appeared to take place in Europe. Then I saw a vision of President Obama wiping his mouth, as were his Cabinet members.

A vision followed of a poster of "Uncle Sam" angrily pointing at President Obama stating, "The military needs you! Where are you? America needs you!" A vision followed of firemen with their hats on hoisting up an American flag at the rubble of the Twin Towers, at "Ground Zero." The flag was furled, it was wrapped around the flag pole. Then I saw a vision of rifles held by what appeared to be "red neck" type men in camouflage clothing. Finally, I saw a vision from a distance of a man sitting on a toilet.

The Lord Jesus then said, "The signers of the Declaration of Independence and the Constitution of the United States believed that Almighty God and the Bible were 'part and parcel' to who they were. Today the (torch), the 'light' of God that the Founding Fathers turned to has been 'plucked out' of the public schools. Those students are living in darkness without the Word of God to guide them. The Bible, the Word of God is despised in the public schools (Pr 30:17; Jn 1:1-5; Eph 5:11-13; 2 Ti 2:15; 1 Jn 1:6).

"Some public schools have teachers (and students) wear red shirts to honor a day of 'gay pride' at their schools. The red shirts are like the 'redcoats' of the former British army, who fought to maintain their tyrannical control over America, (and) many were covered in sin and sexual immorality. It is a mockery towards God. Football and other high school athletes are becoming effeminate in support of homosexuality. Young men in high school are losing their masculinity, and their need to be solely heterosexual (Gen 1:27; Pr 21:24; Isa 1:18; Gal 6:7,8).

"The flag is not unfurled, because the 'leaders' in government are 'furling' the American people (in lies) about Islam. The President of the United States was unleashed in Europe compromising with the 'evil one.' He was not holding on to the 'end of his rope' for he was negotiating with terrorists, those who bombed the 'Twin Towers.' He is choosing another 'god,' the Islamic 'god.' There was a war, a demonic 'War between the States' to free the African-Americans from slavery in the United States. It was a just War. But another war is 'brewing' against the government of the United States throughout this country for condoning Islam, wicked men condoning homosexuality, sexual immorality, and even abortions among (the) youth in the public schools (Dt 11:16,17; Da 9:26[b]; Mt 24:6; Eph 6:13; Rev 19:11).

"God is not with those government 'leaders.' Men will rise up with guns to fight this corruption. The country is being torn down within itself from its choices to disdain the Name of Jesus, to despise the Word of God, to choose man over God, to choose other 'gods.' They wipe their mouths and say, 'We have done nothing wrong'! This country is feeding on the 'excrement' from those American 'leaders' today, that 'good' is portrayed as 'evil,' and 'evil' is proclaimed as 'good.' The United States has become like the nation of Israel in the past, a nation that has disobeyed God's commandments" (Pr 30:20; Isa 5:20; Eze 4:12,13; Mt 24:9; Ac 4:18; Ro 1:24-26).

In the first vision in May, I saw myself (Mark) as a youngster wearing a coon-skin cap. Then I saw apples turning into applesauce. A vision followed of the "Hoggettes," men who attend Washington Redskin football games dressed up in women's clothing, wearing pig noses. Finally, I saw a young couple in a flooded area. It appeared from the vision that their house had just been washed away.

The Lord Jesus then said, "As a child growing up, your hero was a masculine, Davy Crockett. You carried a play musket and a gun powder holder (inspired by the Davy Crockett represented in the Walt Disney series).[180] Today's young boys' heroes are not images of Davy Crockett, nor of George Washington, (a General and President) representing a man's man. Most of all, there are not many men representing Jesus Christ, who is the example of perfect masculinity. Boys are becoming like soft applesauce. They are losing their masculinity in public schools with educators condoning same-sex relationships from elementary school up through the colleges. Young men are becoming more effeminate wearing earrings, wave caps, and their pants worn down below the waist. The "Hoggettes" receive their laughs (as cross-dressers), but all these things are an abomination to God (Gen 2:24; Dt 22:5; Mt 4:3,4; Mk 14:61,62; 1 Th 2:4; 1 Jn 2:14).

"When your 'house' is built 'on sand,' like in the public school system, it will come crashing down. For it is not built 'on the Rock,' the Living Word, the Lord Jesus, but on men and women's thoughts and decisions. Many homes throughout the United States have come crashing down, because they have built their lives, (and) their homes 'on sand.' You see it in the (public) schools; the cursing, the violence, the disrespect, the defiance, the drinking, the drugs, the crime, the suicides and teen depression, the abortions, the sexual activity to name just a few. These are the ramifications for living and building your 'house on sand'" (Mt 7:24-27; 22:32; Lk 6:47-49; 2 Ti 3:1-4).

Satan has been trying to sweep the "homosexual agenda" through the public school system, through radical homosexual activists. We believe that it would be appalling to our Founding Fathers, that America has turned to sexual immorality as a so-called standard or norm for students from kindergarten through college. We are disgusted by the push for the "homosexual agenda" in all school grades. We thank God, as children growing up in public schools in the 1950's and the 1960's, that we were not exposed to Satan's wicked schemes of sexual impurity and degradation of "bodies with one another," with other students. Our Lord Jesus will judge those who "committed indecent acts" with one another, "and received in themselves the due penalty for their perversion," those who caused "these little ones" to sin (Lk 17:1,2; Ro 1:24,27; 1 Co 6:18; 10:8; Eph 6:11,12).

An Antichrist Spirit in the Public Schools

We have reported previously about the landmark Supreme Court decisions in the early 1960's, that removed prayer and Bible reading from the public schools in America. Former

President Ronald Reagan shared in 1984, "From the early days of the colonies, prayer in school was practiced and revered as an important tradition. Indeed, for nearly two hundred years of our nation's history, it was considered a natural expression of our religious freedom. But in 1962 the Supreme Court handed down a controversial decision prohibiting prayer in public schools"[181] (Mt 6:9-13; 21:22; Eph 6:4; 1 Th 5:17).

He declared further, "When a group of students at (a) . . . High School in Albany, New York, sought to use an empty classroom for voluntary prayer meetings, the Second Circuit (Court) of Appeals said no . . . Then there was the case of a kindergarten class reciting a verse before their milk and cookies, . . . (thanking God) 'for the food we eat, . . . (and thanking) God, for everything.' But a federal court of appeals ordered them to stop. They were supposedly violating the Constitution of the United States . . . Up to 80 percent of the American people support voluntary prayer. They understand what the Founding Fathers intended. The First Amendment of the Constitution . . . was written to protect religion from government tyranny"[182] (Ps 8:2; Mt 18:10; Mk 9:36,37).

Former President Reagan also said that, "We're told that it somehow violates the rights of others to permit students in school who desire to pray to do so. Clearly this infringes on the freedom of those who choose to pray—a freedom taken for granted since the time of our Founding Fathers . . . A group of children, again on their own initiative and with their parents' approval, wanted to begin the school day with a minute of prayer and meditation . . . They, too, were prohibited from doing so . . . The relentless drive to eliminate God from our schools can and should be stopped"[183] (Mt 21:15,16; Lk 18:15-17; Ac 1:14).

Fortunately, when I, (Phyllis) was in elementary school, we were taught the Lord's prayer. "Our Father which art in heaven, Hallowed be thy name. Thy kingdom come. Thy will be done in earth, as it is in heaven. Give us this day our daily bread. And forgive us our trespasses, as we forgive those who trespass against us. And lead us not into temptation, but deliver us from evil: For Thine is the kingdom, and the power, and the glory, forever. Amen." We recited that prayer every day, along with the Pledge of Allegiance to the flag up through the ninth grade in public school. All the students prayed the Lord's prayer, and said the Pledge of Allegiance together. That, we believe, was the right American custom for years. We understood that the Lord's prayer and the Pledge of Allegiance honored God (Ps 33:12; 55:4; Mt 6:9-13[KJV]).

Brian Fisher of Coral Ridge Ministries reported in October 2007, that "School children learned of the Pilgrims thanking God. But not anymore. Today Thanksgiving has been secularized and squeezed out in the stores and schools by the pagan holiday of Halloween . . . Thanks to the American Civil Liberties Union (ACLU) and modern revisionists, the faith of the Pilgrims is disappearing from our textbooks . . . New York University professor Paul C. Vitz studied 90 of the most used public school history textbooks. He found up to 30 pages devoted to the Pilgrims, yet not a word about their devout faith in God. 'It is common in these books to treat Thanksgiving without explaining to whom the Pilgrims gave thanks' . . . The Bible was (the Pilgrim's) guide in creating a document, . . . the Mayflower Compact, . . . that would powerfully influence our Constitution"[184] (Ps 30:11,12; Ac 2:44; 1 Th 5:18; 2 Ti 3:14-17; Heb 11:39,40; Rev 4:9-11).

Don Swarthout, President of Christians Reviving America's Values reported in 2008 about "the ACLU's prohibitions against religious activity." Those prohibitions included: "Thou shalt not pray in public school . . . Thou shalt not pray at graduation ceremonies . . . Thou shalt not permit teachers to have even their personal Bibles in class . . . Thou shalt not pray at school sporting events . . . Thou shalt not say the words 'under God' in the Pledge of Allegiance, (and) . . . Thou shalt not distribute Bibles to students." Mr. Swarthout reported further that, "The Founding Fathers wanted to protect our religious rights . . . John Adams said, 'The general principles upon which our founders achieved independence . . . were the principles of Christianity'"[185] (Ex 20:1-17; 1 Ti 4:1; 2 Ti 4:3,4; 2 Pe 2:2).

My husband and I have had opportunities to share openly about our faith in Jesus Christ to students in our classrooms. On April 9, 2009, after fasting and worshiping before the Lord Jesus, He gave me (Mark) some visions. In the first vision, I saw a globe of the world spinning around. A vision followed of my wife teaching students about the Pilgrims and Puritans in a school classroom. In that vision, I was assisting my wife in teaching the students. The Lord Jesus then said, "What God has given you, the children and youth need to hear it in their classrooms today" (Jer 1:7,8; Mt 25:20-23).

During the winter/spring semester in 1995/1996, at a public high school in North Carolina, I (Mark) taught two classes of Physical Science. The Principal of that high school was a Christian, and I could freely share with him about Jesus Christ. During each class that I taught, I left my Bible out on the teacher's desk hoping to stimulate a discussion with students about God. In those classes, I would write a Scripture verse on the chalkboard that pertained to what we were studying in class (Ac 17:11; 2 Ti 2:15; 3:15-17).

During a class in February 1996, an African-American student commented on my Bible. He said that he carried a Bible in his backpack to school every day. After conversing with him about our Bibles, I asked him if he would be willing to read a Scripture verse at the end of each class. He willingly did this. The students in the class accepted this, and before long other students asked to read Bible verses in class. Amazingly, stimulated discussions developed among students about the Bible, about Jesus Christ, and about salvation up through the end of that school semester. The Lord Jesus protected me and the students during the rest of the semester from any offensive allegations from parents (Lk 4:16-19; Ac 13:14-16; 1 Th 5:27; 1 Ti 4:13).

During the 2000/2001 school year, my husband and I taught at a Christian school in Northern Virginia. My husband taught sixth grade students, and I taught fifth grade students in a classroom adjacent to his classroom. We shared together special events, some Bible studies, recreational activities, and lunch. In our classes, we worshiped by singing songs to our Lord Jesus every morning. At times we sang together with the fifth and sixth grade students. We were able to share openly about Jesus Christ at that school. We prayed with our students, and often used the Word of God to help resolve conflicts in our classrooms (Ps 8:2; Mt 28:19,20; Ac 2:46,47; Heb 4:12).

We both felt that we had closer relationships with out students there, then in any other places of employment. Those students were openly receptive to Jesus Christ and the Word of God. The Lord Jesus had revealed to us at that school, that He did not want children to be placed on medication for mental/behavioral problems. Two students, who had been taking prescribed medication for troubled behavior, were taken off their medication during the school year by the healing power of our Lord Jesus Christ (Mk 5:40-43; Lk 18:16,17; Ac 4:32; Eph 4:3-6).

During the 2002/2003 school year, we again taught at another Christian school. We taught together as a team, seventh and eighth grade students. Again, it was refreshing to pray, read the Word of God in class, share freely about Jesus Christ, and sing songs to Him. However, by far the majority of students in our classroom came from broken families; single-parent homes, blended families, and foster homes. The breakdown in their families, we believe, contributed to more difficult and defiant behavior among some of the students at times. Yet, there were some students who were faithfully committed to serving our Lord Jesus Christ in our classroom that year. We have been grateful for the growth of private Christian schools that sprang up rapidly in the 1980's, as well as for the growth of Christian home schooling, where Almighty God can be exalted at school and at home (Ps 138:2; Mt 12:25; Mk 16:15; Ac 3:19,20; 1 Th 3:8).

Unfortunately, an antichrist spirit has been taking over home schooling. Dr. James Dobson reported in a newsletter in June 2008, that in California, the "Second District Court of Appeals, . . . ruled that uncredentialed parents who home school their children are in violation of the law . . . Home-schooling parents would have . . . to expend the . . . time and . . . money . . . necessary to get a teaching license. This is a dramatic example of judicial tyranny in action."[186]

The Lord Jesus revealed more information to us about an antichrist spirit in America today. On May 7, 2009, after fasting and praising the Lord Jesus, I saw some visions. In the first vision, I saw the skyline over Washington, D.C. The sun was going down, and the sky became darkened. Then I saw the upper body of the Roman Catholic, "Mary." That "Mary" was dressed in a white, hooded garment. In the vision, she was hovering in the air over Washington, D.C. in the daytime. She was wrapping her arms tightly around that city. A vision followed of a knotted rope.

The Lord Jesus then said, "Spirits from the Roman Catholic Church moved (rapidly) in Washington, D.C., when John F. Kennedy became the President of the United States. Liberal spirits moved into the White House, the Capitol, (and the Courts). Their 'Jesus' opposed the reading of the Bible, prayer, and the real Jesus. Jesus was being squeezed out of Washington, D.C., the public schools and the nation (2 Co 11:4; 2 Pe 2:1-3; 1 Jn 2:18).

"At this time, President Obama has a Roman Catholic Vice-President, and several staff members who are Catholic. Many Catholics are opposed to true Christianity and the Word of God. (Our book, *The Great Cover-up: Living in the Shadow of a Lie–The Roman Catholic Church*, reveals the deceptions in that Church.[187]) Washington, D.C.'s government 'leaders,' court justices, and the public and private sector are tied tightly in knots, because they have accepted the liberal Roman Catholic spirit of 'Mary,' unknowingly. They are in darkness believing it is 'good' for the country not to believe in the real Jesus Christ, nor to allow Bible readings and prayer in the public schools, (and other government facilities). Satan has master-minded this antichrist spirit in America, which moved rapidly through the acceptance of a Roman Catholic President" (Mt 24:9-13; Ac 20:30; Ro 1:25; Gal 1:6-9; 2 Pe 2:10[a]).

We have been sharing about some examples of Satan's antichrist spirit in the public school system today. That spirit opposes God, the Bible, the Cornerstone of our faith, our Lord Jesus. That "anti-Christian" spirit has manifested itself in many ways in the public schools in America.

Grade School

It was reported in a newsletter of April 2009, that "Elementary school officials in Tennessee ordered the phrases 'God bless the USA' and 'In God We Trust' (to be) covered up on children's handmade posters . . . A fourth-grade student in Missouri was placed on detention for a week for saying grace silently before lunch."[188] In another report, "A principal in a Virginia public school barred a young girl from reading the Bible on the bus . . . In Alaska, public school students were prohibited from using the word 'Christmas' because the word 'Christ' was in it."[189] It was indicated also, that "In 2001, a federal district judge in Kentucky prohibited schools from displaying portions of the Declaration of Independence, simply because that Declaration acknowledges the existence of a sovereign Creator, God, who grants to us inalienable rights."[190]

In still another report, "Muslim students . . . at (an) Elementary School in San Diego . . . were given a dedicated room for 15 minutes of prayer each day after lunch . . . School policy has . . . (accommodated) . . . Muslim students, (and) . . . added a new lunch schedule where Muslim students can pray . . . A suburban Dallas school allows Muslims to leave class to pray . . . (At the) Byron Unified School District, (in) California . . . seventh grade students were given an 'Islam Student Guide' that specifically states: 'From the beginning, you and your classmates will become Muslim.' The program has been upheld as constitutional by the 9th Circuit Court of Appeals."[191]

It was further noted, "The Byron school program taught or asked students to . . . Recite aloud Muslim prayers that begin with 'In the name of Allah, Most Gracious, Most Merciful,' . . . (to) Memorize the Muslim profession of faith: 'Allah is the only true God and Muhammad is his messenger,' . . . (to) Chant 'Praise be to Allah' in response to teacher prompts, . . . (and to) Profess as 'true' the Muslim belief that 'The Holy Quran is God's word' . . . Students were taught this jihadist prayer: 'Believers, why is it that when it is said to you: 'March in the cause of Allah,' you linger slothfully in the land? . . . If you do not fight, He will punish you sternly and replace you with other men.'"[192]

In Oregon, "School Superintendent Don Grotting . . . (said that) the Islamic program is mandated by the State of Oregon . . . Students are taught: How to Say Muslim Prayers, . . . (to recite) The Five Pillars of Islamic Faith, . . . (and) Key Scriptures from the Koran."[193] We have already written about another "god," Allah in this book. Allah is not the one true God of the Bible. Allah is not the God of love. Yet, despite the prohibition of prayer and reading of Scriptures from the Bible in public schools, the Islam religion and prayer is permitted and encouraged to be taught in some public schools in America. Satan's dark forces appear to be gaining ground in the public school system, while Jesus Christ, the Living Word of God, the true God of love continues to be rejected (Dt 5:6,7; Isa 53:3; Eze 22:27; Mk 8:31; 12:29-31; Jn 8:44-47; 15:18-21).

High School

We believe that public high schools are inundated today with an antichrist spirit. In a public high school in South Carolina, "Students (are) required to: . . . Discuss the Five Pillars of Islam . . . Students (are) told by a guest speaker: (that) 'All religions are based on Islam' . . . Students (are) taught: (that) The United States is a 'Judeo-Christian-Muslim' nation, according to the beliefs of the founding fathers . . . Muslim students (are) allowed to use the school library for prayer each day."[194]

According to the Scriptures in the Old Testament, it is written in the first commandment that, "You shall have no other gods before me." It is also written in the book of Deuteronomy, "Make sure there is no man or woman, clan or tribe among you . . . whose heart turns away from the Lord our God to go and worship the gods of those nations; make sure there is no root among you that produces such bitter poison." It is written also that, "If (someone) entices you, saying, 'Let us go and worship other gods,' . . . do not yield to him or listen to him. Show him no pity . . . You must certainly put him to death" (Ex 20:3; Dt 13:6,8; 29:18).

In the New Testament, Jesus said, "I am the way and the truth and the life. No one comes to the Father except through me." We believe Jesus is the truth and the only true God. He is the only 'Way' to the Father. The Bible reveals that other "gods" are demons. Again, those who are leading children to other "gods," are causing "these little ones" to sin, for the adults are violating God's first commandment (Dt 32:17; Ps 106:37-39; Jn 14:6; 1 Co 10:20,21).

School "officials," we believe, are being led by the 'evil one' to turn children and teenagers away from our Lord Jesus to other "gods," to demons. Those "officials" are drawing students to a "god," who "will punish you sternly," a hostile and bitter "god." Those school educators, we believe, are encouraging children to receive a "root" of "bitter poison" at a very young age (Hos 3:1; Jn 10:10; Gal 4:8; Heb 12:15; Rev 9:20).

Other examples of an antichrist spirit occurred "in Hawaii," in which "a high school valedictorian . . . was told by her principal that she violated Department of Education policy by thanking God in her graduation speech."[195] In another state, "A Texas judge warned that any student mentioning Jesus at graduation would be jailed for six months."[196] In another example, "a class salutatorian was ordered to remove any mention of Jesus before giving his graduation speech."[197]

At a high school in Las Vegas in 2006, "School officials" reviewed the "graduation . . . speech" of the "valedictorian" of their school, "and deleted all references to Jesus Christ and the importance of God in (her) life, . . . days before (her) graduation . . . (Her) graduation speech (expressed) . . . what was in (her), . . . (which was) Christ . . . (At the graduation ceremony, as she) talked about the one thing (she had) found that actually (filled) the hole (in her life)—God's love, . . . the microphone went dead! . . . Many . . . school officials . . . (were) acting (then and afterwards), as if (she) broke the law by talking about (her) faith in Christ."[198]

In other cases, a "Federal Judge Joseph McKinley issued a restraining order preventing students from praying at high school graduation ceremonies . . . Federal Judge John Jones ruled that teaching creationism alongside evolution violated the First Amendment."[199] Our Lord Jesus revealed more information to us on the antichrist spirit in America. On April 2, 2009, after fasting and praising before the Lord Jesus, I received some visions.

In the first vision, I saw a vision of a tear coming out of the eye of the Lord Jesus. Then I saw a vision of teachers and school administrators standing outside a door of a public school classroom. There were young children in that classroom. The teachers and school administrators were laughing together in a mocking manner, and said, "We are going to give them a new one." A vision followed of the Liberty Bell, and the crack in the bell appeared pronounced. Finally, I saw a "school master" in a colonial outfit teaching a classroom of children in a one-room school house. He had the Bible open, and the students were reading their Bibles at their seats.

The Lord Jesus then said, "It is sad that children are not being loved, and are not coming to know Jesus. Parents settle for saving money having their children attend public schools, rather than investing in their children's heritage, for this country's heritage has been in Jesus Christ. Christian parents choose public colleges for notoriety, and for sports. Satan is laughing behind closed doors in the public schools using teachers and administrators to not mention God, the Bible, (Jesus) to the students. They are presenting evolution, not Creation, and alternative sexual lifestyles, instead of male/female marriages. That is why it is imperative for Christian schools and home schooling to flourish in the last days (Gen 1:20-27; Eze 16:20-22; Mt 19:13-15; Lk 23:28; 1 Co 6:9,10; 2 Co 11:14,15; Col 2:8).

"The Liberty Bell in America was a symbol to 'proclaim liberty throughout the land to all its inhabitants,' freedom coming through Jesus Christ! Yet, the Liberty Bell is cracked, (and) the United States is 'cracked,' divided from the truth. It is a nation divided by falseness, by proponents of wickedness and immorality. A nation 'divided against itself will not stand.' Children/youth are disillusioned in their early years, and will not stand up for Jesus Christ, for they know not of Him (Lev 25:10; Mk 3:23-26; Jn 8:36; 2 Co 4:4; 2 Pe 2:2).

"The American public school system is comparable to tyrannical England (in the 1600's and 1700's), for the 'leaders' of this country have taken true liberty out of the public schools. But as the Pilgrims and Puritans left England, their homes, their comforts to obtain spiritual liberty and follow Jesus, more in line with the Scriptures, so parents must be willing to let their children leave the public schools for other types of schooling, Christian and home schooling to better follow Jesus and the Word of God (Mk 10:29,30; Lk 9:23-26; Gal 4:3-5; 1 Pe 2:11[KJV]).

"The Bible was the first subject students were taught in the early public schools in America. The Bible gave them hope, gave them life, gave them truth, gave them encouragement, gave them right living, gave them Jesus. It is a sad 'state of affairs' what children are given today in the public schools apart from Jesus" (Mt 19:13-15; Jn 8:31,32; 14:6; 1 Co 15:19; Heb 3:13,14).

We learned this song, "Jesus Loves Me," when we were little children. Today, we believe that millions of little children are not taught that Jesus loves them, nor are they taught to read the Bible.

"Jesus loves me, this I know
For the Bible tells me so.
'Little ones' to Him belong,
They are weak, but He is strong.

Yes, Jesus loves me.
Yes, Jesus loves me.
Yes, Jesus loves me.
For the Bible tells me so!"

Creationism vs. Evolution

Another movement of "the god of this world" is what "the little ones" are not being taught in public schools about our Creator. It was reported in 2007, that, "Our children are taught content that directly contradicts God's Word, such as the mandated teaching of evolution while denying creation."[200] It was also noted in April 2008, that "Darwin is lionized as a champion of science in the popular high school textbook, 'Biology.' The textbook devotes a chapter to Darwin and calls him 'the individual who contributed more to our understanding of evolution than anyone.'" As a result of his theory, Tom DeRosa of Coral Ridge Ministries reported that, "'Evolutionary ideas fueled Hitler's Nazism and Stalin's communism' . . . 'Today, its consequences are evident in our society's lawlessness and immorality. No Creator means no accountability for our actions' . . . Closing the door on the existence of God liberates man . . . to become his own master and lawgiver"[201] (Ro 1:21-26; 1 Co 2:14; 3:18-20; 2 Ti 4:3,4).

Tom DeRosa shared further that, "'If our learning centers continue to shove Darwinism on students, they [students] will reap a life of confusion and purposelessness as they grow older' ... 'We're now reaping a generation who has been taught that there is no God or Creator who cares for them' ... The culture is already reaping the effects ... According to the American Association of Suicidology, suicide was the third ranking cause of death for those 15-24 in 2005"[202] (Pr 22:8; 1 Co 14:33 [KJV]; Gal 6:7,8).

When I, (Mark) served as a substitute teacher at a public high school in North Carolina, I was assigned a Biology class for a week. The subject that week in the class was "Evolution." After seeking the Lord Jesus on how I should teach that class, I began every class, writing on the chalkboard, "Creation or Evolution: Which is the truth?" We, the students and I, compared the theory of evolution to the understanding of a Creator, creating the universe, and creating all living creatures, "according to their (own) kind." This stimulated students in the class to share their personal beliefs in God. Not one student complained about those classes that week (Gen 1:1,20-27; Isa 45:18; Jn 1:1-3).

At a Christian-based youth home, where my husband and I have been employed for several years, the public school teachers at the school on campus defend Evolution over Creationism. Young men, who have attended our Bible studies have been taught ways to defend Creationism over Evolution in their classes at the public school. We believe, that it is by faith that Christians believe God created the world, and everything in it. When He spoke the Word of God, it was so. On a Christian radio program several years ago, we overheard a talk show host share that Charles Darwin denied his theory on his "death bed" (Isa 40:21,22; Col 1:16; Heb 11:3).

It was reported that a "Lady Hope, a Christian visited Darwin on his death bed ... He had confessed (to her), 'How I wish I had not expressed my theory of evolution as I have done' ... He went on, she said, to say that he 'would like to speak to them, (a congregation), of Christ Jesus and His salvation, being in a state ... eagerly savouring the heavenly anticipation of bliss' . . . Lady Hope's story was printed in the *Boston Watchman Examiner* . . . Darwin's biographer, Dr. James Moore (shared) . . . there was a Lady Hope, (who) probably did visit Charles (right before he died)." Charles Darwin's "daughter Henrietta" reported that "the whole story has no foundation."[203]

An Antichrist Spirit Influencing Colleges and Universities

An antichrist spirit is also active at many colleges and universities in America today. In 2007, at "Iowa State University, . . . tenure to (an) astronomy professor . . . (was) denied, . . . despite (his) having scientific and academic credentials that surpassed many of his colleagues. The reason, based on statements made by (his) fellow faculty members, (was) his support for the view that Intelligent Design best explains the remarkable way in which physical laws are 'fine-tuned' to support complex life" . . . "In 2005, (a) biology professor . . . was let go from George Mason University . . . (for giving) 'evidence for and against evolution' . . . (during) only one lecture . . . (At the end of) the class, . . . (she) made this final remark about origins: 'Is it evolution, Intelligent Design or Creation? Think about it' . . . She was banned from lecturing" after that class[204] (Isa 40:28; Am 5:12,13; 2 Ti 4:4; Rev 4:11).

Despite that professor's statements to her class, it was reported in 2008, that at George Mason University located in Fairfax, Virginia, "Muslim students are given a 'prayer' room when no such room is available to Christians or Jews . . . At least nine universities have prayer rooms for 'Muslim students only.'"[205] Again, we see many American educators turning young men and women away from the true liberator from sin, Jesus Christ to another 'god' (Isa 30:15; Ac 7:39,43; 1 Ti 5:15).

In another report, it was indicated that "The true agenda of America's universities is the undermining of the Christian values and standards that made our nation and its culture a moral and decent society . . . 'The idea that God might really exist is rarely seriously considered,' but 'classroom advocacy of atheism is common and everywhere assumed to be protected by academic freedom'"[206] (Ps 10:4; 14:1; 53:1; Ro 1:19,20).

Pastor David Wilkerson revealed in a message in 2006, that "Both Harvard and Yale were founded by godly preachers as Bible schools. Great revivals once swept through these colleges . . . Yet today these renowned universities are hotbeds of atheism, unabashed deniers of the divinity of Christ. They have become apostate institutions moving far from their biblical roots . . . The same is true of Columbia in New York and Princeton in New Jersey . . . Even in Christian colleges and evangelical seminaries, . . . the leaven of apostasy has become embedded . . . The new gospel they present dismisses the divinity of Christ, the reality of hell and judgment, and biblical standards of purity and morality"[207] (Lk 12:9[KJV]; 1 Ti 1:3,4; 2 Pe 2:1,2; Jude 4[KJV]).

In a message in August 2006, Pastor Wilkerson shared, "The devil has unleashed an ocean of alcohol upon young people. College and high school campuses have been flooded by a party spirit, with barrels of beer, wine and liquor fueling drunken sprees. Teenagers by the droves are entering secular rehab clinics, while others remain bound by addiction. All of this is the devil's last-ditch effort to enslave masses and 'immunize' them to the mercy message of Jesus."[208] We believe these are some of the destructive effects of a God-less America, where the living Word of God, the truth, Jesus Christ is despised in public grade schools, up through the colleges (Job 12:25; Ps 107:27; Pr 20:1; Gal 5:19-21).

The Days of Noah

Jesus informed his disciples that, "As it was in the days of Noah, so it will be at the coming of the Son of Man." Jesus was speaking about His Second coming for His people to be gathered together with Him. For it is written, that "In the days of Noah," . . . "the earth was corrupt in God's sight and was full of violence." We believe that "the days of Noah" are here today. My wife and I worked at the Juvenile Court Service Unit in Prince William County, Virginia for several years. While working there our last three years, up through April 1994, violent crimes had increased significantly among youth in that county. More teenagers were charged for bringing guns to public schools. In 1993, when I, Mark, was a Probation Counselor, I was assigned a juvenile who "accidently" shot a student in his foot in a local school's bathroom. Allegedly, the juvenile was showing his "friend" his handgun. It came out through in-depth counseling, prior to the shooting incident, that the juvenile had been sexually assaulted by his mother's brother, his uncle, over 50 times (Gen 6:11; Pr 4:17; Mic 2:1,2[KJV]; Mal 2:16; Mt 24:37-39).

Barbara Wheeler, former President of America's Prayer Network, revealed in a newsletter in May 2007, that "the Founding Fathers of our great country would be horrified if they saw that prayer was school banned . . . As a result, we have youngsters who put their faith in substances like drugs, rather than developing a 'substantial' faith in God. Since the early 1960's, when a liberal Supreme Court ruled that school prayer violated the First Amendment, our country has been morally decaying . . . It's a fact—our schools have turned out more murderers, more rapists, and more robbers than ever before. It's a fact—we see more school girls getting pregnant and either having abortions or giving birth to babies without a father in the home . . . It's a fact—we've had more schoolchildren turn to drugs to escape the realities of life"[209] (Job 4:8; Mk 7:20-23; Gal 6:7,8; 2 Ti 3:1-4).

Pastor Wilkerson revealed in a message in 2007, that "Reports of school murders no longer shock many of us but continue to terrorize our children. We may grow hardened by such reports, but God's heart is grieved by them . . . I tell you, there is no worse violence than the brutalizing of children.

Heaven is crying out, 'Woe, woe! Your judgments have no cure'"[210] (Gen 4:8; Job 24:14; Rev 21:8).

According to the words of Jesus in the gospel of John, "the devil . . . was a murderer from the beginning, not holding to the truth, for there is no truth in him . . . He is a liar and the father of lies. Yet because I tell you the truth, you do not believe Me!" America's public school officials, we believe are reaping the consequences of choosing "a murderer," Satan, "a liar," over Jesus Christ who is love and "the truth" (Ps 10:8; 94:6,7; Jn 8:44,45; 1Jn 4:16).

School Murders and Deaths

Many people are aware of some of the more recent horrific murders that occurred at different schools, because of the media and news headlines. In (an) Old Order Amish community . . . of Lancaster County, Pennsylvania, . . . on "October 2, 2006, a gunman took hostages . . . at (an Amish) school, a one-room schoolhouse, . . . and eventually killed five girls (aged 6–13) and then killed himself . . . All of the surviving Amish schoolgirls were hospitalized . . . This marked the third school shooting in less than a week . . . This was the twenty-fourth school shooting in the United States in 2006."[211]

On September 27, 2006, another shooting in that week occurred "at Platte Canyon High School in Bailey, Colorado . . . The gunman . . . took six female students hostage and sexually assaulted them, later releasing four." One of the female students was shot "in the head," and died. "The other remaining hostage escaped unharmed . . . (Afterwards), the gunman . . . had committed suicide."[212] Two days later "on September 29, 2006, in Weston High School in Cazenovia, Wisconsin," another shooting occurred. "The gunman, (a) 15-year-old, (and) a freshman at Weston High School, . . . shot and fatally wounded (the) principal . . . The gunman . . . was charged with first-degree murder, . . . (and) was sentenced to life imprisonment."[213]

During the 2002–2003 school year, when my husband and I were school teachers at a Christian school, a man was randomly shooting and killing innocent victims in the Northern Virginia area on different days. It was reported that some of those killed were school children, and children coming off of a school bus. We remember driving to school in the morning, and observing police and sheriff patrol cars blocking off exits to Interstate 95 in hopes of catching the murderer.

At times at our school, we were told to close our window blinds and turn off the classroom lights. It was a frightening time for the students. Many parents kept their children out of that school during that time. We were all relieved, when the gunman and his son were caught and arrested by the police early one morning, while they were sleeping in their vehicle.

Early in the morning on March 3, 2007, I, (Phyllis) saw a vision of an American flag blowing violently, as if it were flying in a storm, in a tornado. That day the newspaper headlines carried the story of violent tornadoes and storms that touched down in some southern states. A tornado struck a public high school, "Enterprise High School" in Enterprise, Alabama, and "killed eight students."[214]

On February 14, 2008, another murdering incident occurred, "at Northern Illinois University" in Dekalb, Illinois, where an "outstanding student . . . opened fire on a geology class. He killed five students before committing suicide."[215] In a *USA Today* report, it was disclosed that at "the Virginia Tech campus" on April 16, 2007, "32 students and teachers (were) slain in the worst mass shooting in U.S. history . . . A senior English major was the killer, . . . who killed 30 people at an engineering building, . . . and then shot himself. He (was) also suspected in the killing of two other people in a dorm room."[216]

We believe that public school educators unknowingly have allowed Satan, "The thief, . . . to steal and kill and destroy" students' lives. The effects of the antichrist spirit in America, we believe has been taking a significant toll on young people.

The removal of Jesus and His Word from public school settings, as well as other public government facilities, we believe, is, and "will reap destruction." Even in the United States military, the Armed Forces is reaping the effects of an "anti-Christian" spirit (Jn 10:10[a]; Ga 16:8[a]; 2 Jn 7).

Antichrist Spirit in the Armed Forces

When my husband and I were teachers at a Christian school during the school year of 2000–2001, at the end of the school year in May, we took a field trip to the United States Naval Academy at Annapolis, Maryland. The students were full of excitement during the tour of that Academy. The "Blue Angels" flew that day, and we took a small utility boat out on the water to tour a U.S. Navy "Cruiser." We observed the midshipmen in formation before lunch in front of Bancroft Hall. We then ate lunch in the midshipmen's "Mess Hall." Before the meal was served, a French Naval Officer gave announcements, but no one said a "blessing." Our students chose to say a "blessing" at their tables. We sensed an "anti-Christian" spirit there at that time (Mt 14:19; Jn 6:11; 1 Jn 2:18).

It is noteworthy, that in newsletters of October 2008, and February 2009, "the . . . ACLU is trying to prevent the Midshipmen at the Naval Academy from praying before noon-time meals, (this campaign is ongoing) . . . (The ACLU) announced plans to sue the Academy, and terminate the lunchtime prayer tradition which began in 1845."[217]

In another newsletter, which we received in April 2009, it was noted that at the "U.S. Air Force Academy (2006)—after years of scandals involving sex-assaults, cheating, drug use, and a rash of suicide attempts by cadets, the Air Force has told chaplains they cannot pray in the name of 'Jesus.'" It was also indicated that, "Lt. Gordon Klingenschmitt, a Navy Chaplain (was) preaching at a . . . sailor's funeral . . . aboard the U.S.S.

Anzio (in 2004), . . . (and he) was reprimanded and sent ashore for uttering the name 'Jesus.'"[218]

In other reports, "A brigade official ordered Army Chaplain Capt. John Stertzbach to 'modify' his prayers at the funeral of a slain sergeant . . . (at) 'Camp Liberty' near Baghdad, Iraq (2005) . . . (The Captain was ordered) to minimize (the) use of the name of 'Jesus.'" It was also reported that, "The ACLU and other liberal atheist groups won a lawsuit to force the Pentagon to start removing crosses formerly used as grave markers in all the nation's military cemeteries."[219]

Pastor David Wilkerson shared in a message in September 2006, that "All over the world, there is arising a red-hot hatred for God's Word. The Bible is despised, mocked and cursed by ungodly men . . . We know that Jesus' name has always been hated by wicked men. But now that hatred has turned into a demonic rage. Christ's name is slowly and subtly being erased from society, by legislative mandates . . . An attempt is being made to rule that no chaplain, . . . can mention the name of Jesus Christ. The reasoning behind this is unbelievable: 'We must have spiritual maturity in a pluralistic society.' What a deception! Think of it: first, to forbid any mention of the name of Jesus, and then to say it's a matter of spiritual maturity. This is straight out of hell!"[220] (Jn 15:18-21; Ac 5:28,29; 26:9; Eph 6:12).

Gordon Klingenschmitt, a "Former Lieutenant and Chaplain (in the) United States Navy" shared in a newsletter in 2009, that he "was involuntarily discharged as a Chaplain from the United States Navy for the 'crime' of praying 'in Jesus' name' in uniform outside chapel, and for quoting the Bible in chapel . . . When (he) took a stand, and violated the Navy's unconstitutional policy, which mandated 'non-sectarian' prayers, and restricted 'public worship' in uniform to Sunday chapel, the Navy court-martialed (him) for violating their policy."[221]

Mr. Klingenschmitt reported that, "Over 300,000 God-fearing Christians signed petitions with (him) in protest . . .

—to push Congress to rescind that bad Navy prayer policy . . . And (they) won! Congress agreed with (former Lt. Klingenschmitt) . . . When (he) took a stand against the Navy, it cost (him) a 16-year career, and (he) lost (his) . . . pension for honoring Christ . . . The day has dawned in America when it is criminally punishable to pray 'in Jesus name,' to quote Scripture passages in military chapels, and to voice messages about Jesus Christ in the public square."[222]

Mr. Klingenschmitt wrote further, that "Navy Chaplains have prayed Christian prayers in public since 1775, and since 1860 federal law and regulations protected (them) . . . (Today) the mention of God might 'offend.' Yet the ungodly care not how their anti-religious coercion hurts Christians . . . Jesus taught us to . . . shine the light of His truth and dispel the darkness, so all will see that Christ is the way to God's salvation."[223]

Former Lt. Klingenschmitt shared also that, "'Emboldened by Presidential inaction, the Navy passed the worst prayer policy in 231 years—SECNAVINST 1730.7C, which banned praying 'in Jesus' name' anywhere outside of Sunday chapel' . . . (Mr. Klingenschmitt was) punished . . . for preaching that 'Jesus is the way to heaven' . . . 68 other chaplains (are) suing the Navy for religious harassment, . . . because they preached Jesus Christ, and prayed (in) Jesus' name, without compromise . . . There is no more fundamental American principle than the inalienable right to freely worship our Creator, and . . . pray publicly in Jesus' name—without fear!"[224] (Mt 18:20; Jn 14:6,13,14; Ro 10:13).

As we revealed before in this book, our Founding Fathers established and strongly supported Chaplains in the military. We believe that our Founding Fathers recognized the importance of man's "eternal life," that men and women in the military needed to be "saved" through Jesus Christ. We also believe the Founding Fathers recognized who was giving them their victories in battle, their Lord Jesus (Jn 3:16-18; Ro 10:9,10; 1 Jn 5:4,5).

We believe Satan knows that if he can remove Jesus Christ

from the military, he can weaken and cripple the United States Armed Forces. It is written in the Scriptures, that "demons submit to" the "name" of Jesus. We believe demons and darkness flee when Christians cast them out with God's authority. According to the Scriptures, demons know that Jesus is the Son of God. That is why Pastor Wilkerson shared, "This is straight out of hell" to ban Chaplains from praying "in Jesus' name." Our American Armed Forces have called on the name of Jesus to defend and protect our country. There is power, God's power "in the name of Jesus." We believe our Founding Fathers understood this, for without His aid, our Founding Fathers believed that they would be defeated (Mt 10:7,8; Mk 1:24; 6:12,13; Lk 4:34; 10:17-20; 24:48,49; Jn 14:12-14; Ac 4:40-42).

In October 1977, while on my last cruise in the United States Navy in the Western Pacific area, I (Mark) accepted Jesus into my heart and life. A significant influence in my new "born again" life with Jesus was the ship's Chaplain. The Lord Jesus used that Chaplain in a mighty way, to turn many of the officers and enlisted men to Jesus Christ. Our ship was transformed by his boldness for the Lord Jesus. It seemed then, like the multitudes of the "loaves and fishes" had occurred on that ship, as many turned to Jesus daily (Mk 6:41-44; Jn 1:12,13; 3:3; Ac 4:29-31; 26:17,18; Rev 3:20).

God moved in an awesome way on that ship in those days, as the Lord Jesus was healing the wounded, working miracles through fellow shipmates, and creating a "holy boldness" in many of us to witness for Jesus Christ. That Chaplain helped many of us grow in our walk with the Lord Jesus. While I was on that ship, six out of the eight men in my division became "born again" Christians. We talked about Jesus in our work area, prayed together, and had much closer relationships than before Jesus came into our lives (Ac 2:42,44,46,47; 1 Co 12:7-11; Eph 4:15,16; Php 1:14).

Thank God that Chaplains could pray "in the name of Jesus." Morale was high then, and relationships were real and closer, thanks to Jesus Christ. We believe, that today, Satan has so deceived many of the military "brass," commanders, and some officers, to quench the Spirit of God by attempting to remove the name of Jesus in prayer and Word at military and public places (Ac 4:32; 5:40; 9:1,2; 1 Th 5:19[KJV]).

Rob Schenk, President of Faith and Action, wrote in a newsletter in 2007, that "Muslims in the U.S. military are allowed to worship and openly practice their faith . . . The U.S. military is bending over backwards to (accommodate Muslims) . . . But when Christians like Chaplain Klingenschmitt pray in Jesus' name, they are silenced . . . *FrontPage Magazine* recently wrote: 'Military brass dedicated the first Muslim prayer center for the Marines as a symbol of the military's 'religious tolerance' and 'respect' at the Quantico Marine Base . . . This double-standard, . . . it's an outrage! . . . Christian rights are being trampled." In another news report, "The Pentagon barred evangelist Franklin Graham from its National Day of Prayer in May (2010), saying Graham's previous remarks about Islam were 'not appropriate.' After 9/11, Graham called Islam 'a very evil and wicked religion.' (An) Army Spokesman . . . said, "We're an all inclusive military . . . We honor all faiths."[225]

One of the reasons we believe that we are in "the last days," is because the "name of Jesus," the Word of God, and Christianity is offensive to many American people and military personnel. Again, another "god," Allah, is being exalted in the military. Military personnel, we believe, do not want to offend the Muslims and their so-called "god." We believe, as we shared before, that the United States Armed Forces will not be blessed with their current policies, and they will suffer severe losses in the days ahead. For men and women, we believe, are being moved by Satan's wicked schemes to significantly impair the American military (Dt 28:15,25; Isa 44:8; Jer 8:9-12; 44:25-30; Jn 3:36; Ac 19:26,27; 1 Co 8:4[b]-6; 1 Ti 4:1,2).

Homosexual Agenda in the Military

We remember that in 1993, former President Bill Clinton attempted to allow homosexuals to have the opportunity to enter the United States Armed Forces during his first 100 days in office. In the televised news, we observed the former President and former Senator John Warner on a United States ship in enlisted men's close living quarters. Fortunately, many in Congress at that time opposed homosexuals entering the military. We recalled that former President Clinton came up with his own policy concerning that matter, "Don't ask, don't tell," when men and women enlisted in the military service.

When I, (Mark) was in the United States Navy, (1973-1978), military personnel strongly opposed homosexuals in the Armed Forces! We understood that if a President of the United States, the Commander in chief of the military, would support homosexuals in the Armed Forces, this would significantly affect the military in very destructive ways. Many men and women, we believe, would choose not to enter the military if homosexuals were permitted to enter the U.S. Armed Forces. Homosexuality, as we reported before, is a sin and an abomination to God! We believe that Almighty God would not bless America's military, as He has in the past (Lev 18:22; 20:13; Ro 1:26-28; Jude 7).

In a newsletter of May 2009, it was disclosed that, "If President Obama and Congress have their way—open, practicing homosexuals (will be) welcomed into the Army, Navy, Air Force, and Marines . . . They're threatening to repeal the longstanding law that says homosexuals are not eligible for military service . . . In this age of tolerance, many Americans—Christians included—are becoming desensitized to the problem of homosexuality . . . Section 654 of U.S. Code Title 10— . . . gives the good reasons why homosexuality is utterly incompatible with military service . . . Military personnel live in . . . an environment 'characterized by forced intimacy with little or no privacy.'"[226]

It was further noted, more than "1,000+ retired senior military officers . . . have already publicly called for the President and Congress to leave this law in place . . . (A) *Washington Post* editorial . . . says the military, (including the National Guard), would lose an estimated 228,600 people if the law is repealed . . . (This would) see our nation weakened, even crippled, . . . undermining our military force from within! . . . The President and Congress are calling wrong 'right' . . . This travesty (was stopped) during the Clinton years—now we must fight again to protect those who serve"[227] (Gen 18:25; Pr 17:15; 24:24,25[KJV]; Isa 5:20; 10:1).

Dr. James Dobson revealed in a newsletter of May 2007, that "The nation's highest-ranking military officer, Marine Gen. Peter Pace, chairman of the Joint Chiefs, (in) an interview (with members) of the *Chicago Tribune* (in) March (2007), . . . condemned homosexual behavior . . . in the military, (as well as adultery between military spouses)." Hillary Clinton, (the current Secretary of State) and Barak Obama, (the current President of the United States), . . . said (after the General's remarks that) "they didn't believe homosexuality to be immoral."[228]

We believe that since the current Commander in chief of the Armed Forces, who has not served in the military, had shared that same-sex intimate relationships are not "immoral," this country and military will be eventually led into a severely debilitating outcome. The "head" of the United States, we believe, is following "the devil's schemes." For it is written, "I ("the devil"), will give you all their authority and splendor, ("the kingdoms of the world"), . . . if you worship me, it will all be yours." The world, which the current President, we believe is bowing down to, is filled with the demonic, seducing spirits of lust (Gen 19:14-26; Dt 28:36,37,43,44; Lk 4:5-7; 1 Ti 4:1 [KJV]; 1 Jn 2:15-17[KJV]).

The Army of the Lord Jesus

The Lord Jesus revealed to us information about leaders who have fought and fight in His Army today. On August 17, 2007, my wife heard the word, "Washington." Then I saw a vision of George Washington, after my wife received the word. George Washington was in a military uniform with his chest sticking out. He appeared to be a strong leader in the vision.

The Lord Jesus then said, "George Bush (after 9/11), and George Washington, both men named George, had some similar qualities. They were men who stood up against tyrants, against terrorists on behalf of their country, their American people. They were willing to lead their nation to 'war' against the evil perpetrated in their land. Both of those men had suffered from the lack of support from certain factions of people in their own country. Yet, following their one true God, their Lord Jesus and His direction, they were leaders convicted to hate evil. They were convicted to fight against demonic, tyrannical, terrorist forces; despite the dissentions among some of the people in their home country" (Ps 138:3; Pr 28:1; Ro 12:9; Eph 6:13; Rev 12:7-9; 19:11-14).

On April 9, 2009, after fasting and worshiping before the Lord Jesus, He gave me a vision of two military swords crossed together at their blades. The Lord then said, "The Sword of the Spirit, which is the Word of God, is your weapon of warfare against 'the accuser of the brethren,' Satan. Fall back on the Word, back up your statements with the Word of God, so (men and women's) arguments are not against you, but against the Scriptures, for the Word is truth" (Jn 17:17; Eph 6:17; Rev 12:10[KJV]).

The Lord said further, "'Mine eyes have seen the glory of the coming of the Lord; He (has) trampled out the vintage where the grapes of wrath are stored; He hath loosed the fateful lightning of His terrible swift Sword; His truth is marching on!'"[229]

Take pride in being a soldier in My Army, dressed in My fine 'military' wear, dressed to destroy the enemy, 'the works of the devil' (2 Sa 22:15; Isa 42:13; 1 Ti 1:18; Heb 4:12; 1 Jn 3:8[KJV]; Rev 14:18-20).

"There is an awesome power that goes with My faithful warriors. They will not be denied 'the spoils of victory.' They shall celebrate in the King's court, for there will be much feasting and merrymaking. Great honor will be bestowed on My mighty ones in the kingdom of God. They are those who have been trained for battle, those men (and women) who long to be in My Army, to serve Me, those who fight for freedom against wickedness in the (world). The 'die' has been cast, the time is now to join ranks in the mightiest Army on the face of the earth, an Army that will not be denied (Ex 14:14; 1 Sa 2:30[b]; 2 Sa 22:35-41; Ps 84:10; Pr 6:16-19; Ecc 11:1; Joel 3:9; Lk 14:16,17).

"To become a soldier in God's Army, one must be disciplined, undivided with one mission in 'the mind of Christ,' to be 'one in Spirit.' 'One' means leaving family to serve as a soldier, a 'soldier of Christ Jesus.' Forgive and be 'ready' for your 'traveling orders,' for you are about to be 'shipped out' for battle, for God's purposes (Joel 2:25[b]; Mal 2:15; 2 Ti 2:3).

"My Army knows Me. They know My ways. They anticipate My commands before I give them. Their heart's desire is to please their Commander's orders. They are My men and women sold out and enlisted for life in My Army. They give up everything to wear My uniform, a uniform that is form-fitting for each individual. Yet, each uniform is different. A different part of the body requires a different shape and size. My Army comes in different sizes and shapes, but they all have one purpose in common, a desire to serve wholeheartedly in My 'military' service (Joel 2:11; Jn 10:3-5,14; Ro 12:4,5; 1 Co 12:12,14-27; Rev 5:9; 19:14).

"My Army is always victorious. The enemy hides from My Army. The enemy tries to persuade men and women in My Army to come away, and see what they are missing by staying in My Army. The enemy is talking My people out of joining up. Enlist in My ranks, for My Army storms the enemy's camps, setting captives/prisoners free. Freed captives willingly join up with Me, for they know the cost of what they fight for is 'eternal life' in Me. My Army is distinguished by the light of God filling their hearts, setting them on 'fire.' All the ("military") ranks must come together for the End-time battle, a battle that will be fought with honor. 'Endure hardships' as 'a good soldier of Christ.' 'Onward, Christian soldiers! Marching as to war, With the cross of Jesus Going on before!'" (Isa 55:1-4; 61:1; Joel 2:2,4-11; Zec 14:3-9; Mt 3:11; Mk 4:14-19; Lk 9:23,24; 2 Ti 2:3; 2 Pe 2:2; Rev 17:14). (Messages received from the Lord Jesus on October 31, November 4, November 11, and 12, 1995, and December 7, 2010.

As Christian Americans fight for the banner of Jesus Christ in the land, so they must fight for heterosexual marriages, which we will share about in the next chapter.

13

I WILL BETROTH YOU TO ME FOREVER!

*"So God created man in His own image,
in the image of God.
He created him; male and female He created them.
God blessed them and said to them, 'Be fruitful
and increase in number.'"*

Believers in Jesus must be willing to stand up and fight for biblical marriages in America. We believe marriage was the "first church" established by God through His creation of male and female, Adam and Eve. Marriage, according to the Scriptures, is a covenant between a man and a woman before Almighty God. Our forefathers, the Pilgrims and Puritans, understood the need to be covenanted with one another and God. Our Lord Jesus blessed and honored their covenant with which they established the foundation of this country on the Cornerstone, on the Rock, on their Lord Jesus (Gen 1:27; 3:20; Isa 28:16; Mal 2:14; 1 Co 10:4).

The Pilgrims and Puritans, as we wrote previously, wanted to live purer lives separate from worldly influences in their

"Mother country" and the "Church of England." Today, worldly influences are opposed to marriages, and we believe, this is one of the reasons why marriages are deteriorating in America for both believers and nonbelievers, in Jesus Christ (Lk 4:5-7; 2 Co 6:17,18; 7:1; 1 Jn 2:15-17).

Satan, we believe, knew that if he could divide marriages in America, he could divide this nation from the Lordship of Jesus Christ. Fortunately, Satan could not contend with the covenanted faith of the Pilgrims and Puritans in our Lord Jesus Christ, and could not divide their marriages and families. Subsequently, many of our national leaders followed the example of our forefathers and Founding Fathers' faith. The United States was able to flourish spiritually under the Lordship of Jesus Christ for many Americans up until the early 1960's (Eze 16:8; Mk 3:23-26; 1 Co 11:25,26).

Today we must "fight the good fight of the faith" for right marriages in God's eyes amidst the opposition against it in the homosexual community, the media, and many government leaders and court justices, as we reported previously. For Almighty God, we believe, will not bless a nation who allows Satan to divide and conquer marriages and families. A more detailed examination of marriages in God's eyes is revealed in our book, *The Profound Mystery: Marriage—The First Church*[230] (Gen 19:5,10,11; Pr 14:34; Lk 11:17,18; 1 Ti 6:12).

The Breakdown of Marriages

On March 2, 2008, the Lord disclosed to us, "A 'kingdom' and country 'divided against itself . . . cannot stand.' Men and women are not willing to follow Jesus and His Words, contrary to the one purpose and call of the Founding Fathers of America" (Mt 12:25,26). In a November 2006 newsletter, James Daly, President and CEO of Focus on the Family revealed that, "In America . . . 50%" of those who get married will eventually be divorced. "Polls show that among Christians, the divorce rate is actually a few points higher . . . You probably know someone very close to you who has gone through the terrible trauma of having their life and family broken by divorce . . . Divorce is not an automatic solution to marital problems . . . Women and men who have endured the disaster and pain of one divorce are very likely to face that same life trauma a second time . . . The divorce rate for couples in second marriages (is higher than in first marriages)."[231]

Mr. Daly shared that, "God calls us to be committed to our marriages for life . . . It is . . . what God wants . . . The best option is to fight for our marriages . . . Your marriage is a model for your children and others of your circle of influence . . . Children of divorce are at greatest risks of themselves divorcing because they haven't learned about commitment from their parents . . . The biblical mandate is marriage, not cohabitation, . . . living with a partner of the opposite sex outside of marriage," which exists with millions, in the United States[232] (Mk 10:6-9; Eph 5:22-30; Col 3:5,6; Heb 13:4).

Financial Costs

Dr. James Dobson and James Daly shared in a May 2008, newsletter regarding, "The financial burden . . . divorce . . . places on society" . . . "The Institute for American Values, the Georgia Family Council, the Institute for Marriage and Public Policy, and Families Northwest released statistics sharing the staggering annual taxpayer costs associated with divorce and unwed childbearing . . . That translates into more than $1 trillion . . . It literally 'pays' to strengthen the institution of the family, not to mention the impact of divorce on children and the culture at large."[233]

Dr. Dobson noted further in a November 2007, newsletter, "In 1969, . . . Congress attempted to equalize the tax burden of singles and married couples . . . Congress implemented . . . the 'marriage penalty tax' because it mandated that married parents . . . had to pay a higher share of the tax burden than men and women who were cohabiting . . . President George W. Bush . . . overturned . . . this policy . . . in 2001."[234]

Dr. Dobson wrote further, that "in the Oct. 5 issue . . . (of) *U.S. News & World Report*, . . . Editor-in-Chief Mortimer Zuckerman . . . (affirmed) the traditional family . . . (Mr. Zuckerman) reported that, 'The stable family of two biological parents—surprise, surprise!—turns out to be the ideal vessel for molding character, for nurturing, for inculcating values, and for planning a child's future. By comparison, the children of single parents or broken families do worse at school and in their career . . . Marriage, or the lack of it, is the best single predictor of poverty, greater even than race or unemployment . . . Public policy should not contribute to an a la carte menu of sex, love, and childbearing . . . It should emphasize the benefits for all from the package deal of marriage"[235] (Mal 2:16; Eph 5:5; 1 Th 4:3-7; Heb 13:5[KJV]).

Homosexual Agenda

Dr. Dobson also disclosed that Judge "Robert Hanson from Iowa, took it upon himself in August (2007), to create same-sex 'marriage' by personally nullifying the states' defense of marriage act!"[236] In a newsletter of June 2009, it was noted that, "A unanimous Iowa Supreme Court (trashed) marriage, calling it a form of 'prejudice' and (opened) the door to same-sex 'marriage.' And one day before the National Day of Prayer, Maine's legislature (approved) a homosexual 'marriage law.'"[237]

In October 2006, Dr. Dobson revealed in a newsletter that, "The result of increased efforts on the part of liberal groups, . . . funneling millions upon millions into their cause, (was) to portray pro-traditional marriage advocates as 'extremists' while suggesting that gay couples who wish to marry are victims of intolerance . . . Support for traditional marriage is seriously flagging in (several) states."[238]

Alan Keyes of the Declaration Alliance reported in an April 2007 newsletter, "Today one of the most critical issues before us is the on-going destruction of the institution of marriage. Again, this is a moral issue . . . Polls show voters in both political parties overwhelmingly oppose homosexual 'marriage' . . . Abraham Lincoln's proclamation calling for national repentance (occurred) on our first Thanksgiving Day . . . (We need to) pray (for) Mr. Bush (to) listen to the Holy Spirit and confront the evil within this nation as sin, and ask us as a people to humble ourselves and repent! Pray for spiritual revival in our land!"[239] (2 Ch 7:14,15; Jn 16:7-11; Ro 1:25-27; Heb 3:7,8).

In a Coral Ridge Ministries news article of June 2009, it was disclosed that, "An openly homosexual USA pageant judge scolded, . . . chewed out . . . Miss California in April for saying she believed marriage is 'between a man and a woman' . . . Christians applauded (Miss California's) stand for traditional marriage . . . Homosexuals backed . . . (the) homosexual . . . judge." Additionally, "The Gay & Lesbian Advocates & Defenders (GLAD) . . . declared goal is 'six by twelve,' which means redefining marriage to allow for same-sex unions in all six New England states by 2012." In another newsletter, it was noted that in August 2010, "U.S. District Judge Vaughn Walker struck down California's Proposition 8, a voter-approved constitutional amendment defining marriage as a union of a man and woman . . . He branded the biblical view of marriage and homosexuality as irrational, bigoted, . . . dangerous, and harmful."[240] (Gen 2:24; Pr 28:4,5; 29:27; Isa 5:20).

Many American people today, we believe, are not anchored on the Rock of our forefathers and Founding Fathers, Jesus Christ. It is so disheartening to us, to see many Americans call what is sin, what is evil, good. It was Jesus who said, "A man will leave his father and mother and be united to his wife, and the two will become one flesh." Marriage in America among many people is not viewed according to the Scriptures. The

Word of God reveals that a man is a male person like Adam, and a woman is a female person like Eve, for "He created them... male and female" (Gen 1:27; Pr 24:24,25 [KJV]; Mt 7:26,27; 19:5).

Satan has so deceived many Americans to accept and tolerate sexual sins in so-called same-sex "marriages" by his "servants of righteousness," by numerous government "leaders," justices of this country, and homosexual activists. A country, divided against God's Word, we believe, will not stand, and will suffer a fiery outcome, especially when the Scriptures reveal that Almighty God detests same-sex intimate relationships (Mk 4:14,15; Ro 16:17,18; 2 Co 11:13-15; 2 Ti 4:3,4; Jude 7).

We believe that, "The one who sows to please his sinful nature, from that nature will reap destruction." America is reaping the destruction from the effects of divorce, and will reap destruction for accepting same-sex unions. Satan's dark powers are moving forcefully to regain the United States from our Lord Jesus for his own wicked schemes. The New England area, the original home of the Pilgrims and Puritans, those men and women who desired to live a purer lifestyle, is gradually being taken over by so-called "leaders," who are legislating a sinful lifestyle. What can men and women, who believe in Jesus as their Messiah, do to oppose and "destroy the works of the devil" manifested in many of the American people today? (Pr 29:10; Isa 10:1; Mt 5:5; Gal 6:8[a]; Eph 6:11,12; 1 Jn 3:8[KJV]).

The Roles of Christian Men and Women

The Lord Jesus revealed to us the importance of proper men and women's roles in overcoming Satan's wicked schemes in America. The Lord said, "I called you both together to separate yourselves from Satan, to be one with Me. 'Male and female, He created them' to compliment each other, not to override each other's specific roles. The man's role is to lead spiritually by example. A woman's role is to follow his lead. Help each other to fulfil your roles together. Help and do not discourage, but give courage to one another (Gen 5:1,2; Ecc 4:10; Ro 15:5,6; 1 Co 11:3; Eph 4:29).

"There is a misconception in America (on roles for men and women). Women were not created to usurp man's authority, to take over the man's role, but to be side by side with man, to be helpmates, helpers. Women in the Bible were servants. They served the Lord by accompanying their husbands. They were not created to be the leaders of their families. When that God-given order is changed, man can become more effeminate, and the woman can become more masculine (Gen 2:20[b]-25; 1 Co 12:28; 14:33-35; 1 Pe 3:5-7).

"Women who accept their role according to the Word of God, can enjoy God's biblical plan for them much more than when they choose (the position of) authority over men. When women follow their God-given roles, men are able to treat women in a proper manner, and women are able to treat men properly. However, if a man on the other hand is placed in a subservient role to a woman, he must acquiesce his God-given authority over to her. Men consciously or unconsciously resent their more effeminate role, and resent women's more manly authority over them. Misogyny in men, a hatred toward women, despises that role change" (Pr 15:12; 21:19; Eph 5:22-33; Col 3:19; 1 Pe 3:7-9). (We received these words from God on December 19, 1996, and June 11,1998).

Men's Roles

Stephen and Alex Kendrick, in their book, *The Love Dare*,[241] wrote that, "Men—you are the head of your home. You are the one responsible before God for guarding the gate and standing your ground against anything that would threaten your wife or marriage. This is no small assignment. It requires a heart of courage and a head for preemptive action . . . This role is yours. Take it seriously" (1 Sa 30:3-5,17,18; 1 Co 16:13-15; Eph 5:23-25; 1 Ti 6:20).

On June 3, 2007, Pastor Rob Schenck, President of Faith and Action shared a message at Word Alive Church in Manassas, Virginia. Pastor Schenck reported that, "In our popular culture there is an attempt to emasculate, to take away those properties that are distinctly male in men, and in America to degrade the importance of men in our culture . . . There is a difference between testosterone in men and estrogen in women. God has balanced the two perfectly, one complimenting the other in order for two to become one . . . God calls men to be guardians, sentries!" (Jos 8:2-4)[242] (Gen 2:23,24; Isa 21:8; 1 Co 11:11,12; 1 Ti 2:9-15).

Pastor Schenck revealed further that, "The mighty men of valor were men of strength; . . . confident, (knowing) what they believe(d) . . . (They were men of) wealth; . . . (having) a wealth of knowledge knowing Jesus Christ . . . (They were men of) power; . . . the power of God (was) working through (them) . . . (They were men of) substance; . . . men of right principles, . . . men (who) honor(ed) God . . . Men . . . must love the Lord his God, first . . . A married man's love must be set right for his wife before anyone else. If you don't love your wife right, you won't get anything else right . . . You must be a guardian of these relationships, your relationship to God, to your wife, to your children"[243] (1 Sa 10:26; Mt 22:37,38; Ac 4:29-31; 1 Co 2:4; Eph 5:25-29; Heb 11:3-40; Rev 14:4,5).

The Lord Jesus revealed to us ways that a man can become a man of valor. On June 4, 2009, after fasting and worshiping before the Lord Jesus, He gave me some visions. The first vision was from a song in *The Worship DVD*,[244] in which dolphins were swimming off the southern coast of Israel. A scuba diver was holding a large circular hoop in the vision. All the dolphins swam through the hoop. A baby dolphin was wearing a child's birthday hat on his head in the water. The dolphins then moved through the water as a "school" of fish.

Then I saw a vision of George Washington's birthplace in Virginia, and the river there where my wife and I often fished. The Lord reminded me of a "school" of dolphins that came into those waters at one time, and I caught one of them on my fishing hook. The other dolphins had been making squealing noises, after I caught a dolphin on my fishing line. As I was struggling to hold that dolphin on my line, another dolphin's tail sprang up out of the water, and then came down and snapped my fishing line.

Another vision followed of a wine bottle opener removing the cork on a wine bottle. The effervescence, a mist was moving out of the top of the bottle. My wife and I were sniffing the aroma from the wine bottle.

The Lord Jesus then said, "We (humans), like dolphins, can be taught to swim in the 'living water' of the Holy Spirit through the circular ring, the wedded covenant we made with Jesus when we were 'born again,' birthed into the kingdom of God. The Shepherd holds the ring, the Good Shepherd, as we pass through to His side. We (humans) are like fish, 'dolphins' brought to Jesus by the "Great Fisherman," (the Father). Dolphins, like believers in Jesus, can be taught to defend their own kind, and have compassion for one another. Dolphins defend against the 'sharks' of the world, like believers can learn to defend their spouse and children (Pr 31:8,9; Eze 16:8; Mt 4:8-11,19; 7:15,16,20; Lk 15:22-24; Jn 3:5-8; 4:10; 10:3,4,11; Ac 20:29-31; Col 3:12).

"As you struggled with bringing a dolphin in on your line, so you have struggled in becoming 'real.' Cut the lines from the past, from the old ways, (from the "old man"), from the 'old wine,' just like the dolphin that snapped your line. Drink the 'new wine' of the Holy Spirit, the 'oil and wine' that is poured out on your past 'wounds,' the 'wine that gladdens the heart of man' in your marriage. It is the heavenly aroma of Jesus Christ, that bubbles up from your heart towards each other" (Ps 104:15; Mt 9:17; Mk 10:29-31; Lk 10:33,34; Jn 7:38; 2 Co 2:14,15; Eph 4:22).

On March 12, 2009, and May 14, 2009, after we were fasting and praising the Lord Jesus, I received some visions. On March 12, I saw a triangular "Vicks" cough drop positioned upside down, inverted. Then it positioned itself right side up. The Lord Jesus then said, "When you take a 'Vicks' cough drop, you breathe into your nostrils the 'Vicks' vapor. So as you, (Mark) take your rightful position as head of the household and breathe into your nostrils the breath of life, the Holy Spirit, so you can love your wife properly and righteously before God. You have been following the guidelines of *The Love Dare* book, breathing in new 'vapors' into your marriage. So you are breathing easier together in your love towards one another" (Gen 2:7; Job 27:3; 33:4; Jn 16:13; 20:22).

On May 14, I saw in the first vision, one of my tools, a clamp with a red top. The clamp was around my head, and it was tightening. In the vision, my head was becoming smaller, while my chest was increasing in size. Then I saw a vision of myself painting the ceiling of our utility room. As I was painting, I looked down at the recently installed new furnace in our home. The Lord Jesus then said, "As your thoughts and imaginations 'decrease,' My thoughts will 'increase' in your heart. Let the 'furnace of affliction' in repentance burn and clean out the sins inside, so that the outside can be 'painted' clear" (Isa 48:10,11; Mal 4:1; Jn 3:30[KJV]; 2 Co 7:10; 1 Pe 4:7).

In an article on the "Evangelist," Dwight L. Moody, it was reported that, he chose to set "holy boundaries" with women. A close associate revealed, that after a "service . . . (in New York City a) group of ladies, . . . prominent women of the City" wanted to shake hands with Mr. Moody. Dwight L. Moody left the women without shaking their hands. "The ladies waited for some time, and" became indignant, calling Mr. Moody "so rude." In another situation, "Some year or so after this . . . in Chicago, . . . a woman . . . want(ed) to shake hands with him," Dwight L. Moody. Again, Dwight L. Moody refused to shake her hand and left the area.[245]

At a young men's conference, "a few days later," Dwight Moody shared about "how we should guard against flattery, . . . to prevent the devil's getting a hold upon us." He shared that, "'If I had shaken hands with those women, I wouldn't have been half through before the devil would have made me believe that I was some great man, and from that time I would have to do as he bid.'" His close associate shared, "No one thing has ever helped me more to explain his closeness to God, and his humility of Spirit"[246] (Mt 4:8,9; Eph 4:1-3; 2 Pe 2:18; 1 Jn 2:15-17; Jude 16; Rev 14:4,5).

We believe that when Satan is allowed to alter men and women's, husbands and wives biblical roles in relation to each other in America, he is then able to wedge a division in marital relationships. That division, we believe, will then be wedged deeper in the family, in the community, and have destructive ramifications for the nation, eventually. However, as our hearts are open to learning from the Good Shepherd, the Lord Jesus, we, husbands and wives, can learn to live according to the Word of God, on the Rock solid foundation of our forefathers and Founding Fathers. In so doing, we can overthrow the dark powers of the devil and regain America for our God! Believing men, husbands can learn to become "men of valor" setting appropriate boundaries with the opposite sex, as they become "guardians, sentries" for their wives and children (Ps 119:9-11; Jn 10:14,27; 1 Co 10:4; 1 Jn 2:14).

Women's Roles

The Lord Jesus had spoken to us about women's roles in our book, *The Profound Mystery: Marriage—The First Church*.[247] The Lord disclosed to us, "Woman plays a lesser role than man. Man was created first, then woman; not that woman is any less than man. The woman is to take a lesser role in the ministry of teaching and preaching. It is for her own good. Besides, the least will enter the kingdom of God; those who are humble of heart, servants of the Lord (Gen 2:21-23; Mk 10:31; Lk 14:11; 1 Co 11:7-12; 1 Ti 2:11-13).

"The woman makes preparations, gets things ready for the man to speak. The women in the Bible were never given a role that they are given in the church today. So where is the order today in the church? A woman who seeks her own glory, her own recognition apart from man, will never be fulfilled. Only in God's divine order, from the creation of man, until the last days, will the woman be fulfilled (Gen 3:16; Est 1:9-12, 16-21; Mk 6:22,25-28; Lk 24:1; 1 Co 14:33-35; 1 Ti 2:15; Rev 17:4-6; 18:4-8).

"Yet the woman says, 'How can I ever be fulfilled in submission to my husband? It's boring. It's not exciting. It's silencing the Holy Spirit in me.' The Spirit is not silent. The Spirit is filling the woman to obey the Word, to prophesy the truth of the Word, to encourage, to give good gifts (Lk 2:36-39; Ac 2:17,18; Ro 13:10; 1 Ti 5:10,16; Ja 3:17; 1 Pe 3:1-6).

"'Women, don't you know you can find rest in the fulfillment of the Word?' God made a difference in men and women. Men, don't change the Word to please women, and submit to the 'god of this age,' 'Ishtar.' She has given women the authority over men (Ps 119:41,42,105; Pr 31:15-31; Jer 44:15-19; Mt 11:28-30; Lk 10:39,42; Rev 2:20,21).

"Still, God has anointed women to prophesy when God speaks to them; to heal, when God heals through them, to work miracles. They are to be modestly submissive in speech and in actions (Jdg 4:4; Ru 2:10; 3:7-10; Ac 21:9; 1 Co 12:7-11; 1 Ti 2:9-11).

"The world (of men and women) clamors after not offending women. However, 'real' women clamor to Jesus and His Words. Those women were: the woman at the well, the women at Lazarus' grave, the women helpers of the apostles, and the women at My grave. They took lesser roles, but roles of great power, love, and forgiveness. They knew their place at My feet (Lk 7:37-50; 10:39; 23:55,56; Jn 4:7-42; 11:17-37; Ac 1:14; 9:36; 12:12).

"Man does not lord (his spiritual headship) over women; but by his side, they conquer kingdoms of darkness together. Women that I have anointed to speak in churches, speak from humility to provoke men to speak up. Mary Magdalene spoke up for Jesus, when the men would not. She was angry at those men for not taking their roles as leaders, but she did not belabor it (Gen 2:21-24; Ex 15:20,21; Jdg 5; Mk 16:9-11, 14; Lk 24:1-11; Ac 18:2,3; Heb 10:33; 1 Pe 3:3; 5:3).

"The spiritual order was right when men spoke up in the book of Acts. Women were caretakers, nurses, meal preparers, helpers, givers of love, nurturers, (etc.). They were all glad to be in the kingdom of God. There was not any competitiveness to preach, nor to teach men. There was a desire to submit to the men preachers (Ac 2:14-47; 4:29-31; 6:15; 7:1-56; 13:46-49; 16:13-15; Php 4:3; 1 Ti 2:10).

"Prophesy, when given by God, is the right of a woman, when she is directed, to speak to men (and women). It is a woman's right to teach My Word, and to share her testimony with other women; the older women teaching younger. They teach about proper roles, modesty, and submission. (Even in this country), men supported by women, founded America (Ac 2:17,18; 18:26; Ro 12:7,8; Tit 2:3-5; 1 Pe 3:4-6). (One of the reasons) Rome fell, was because they gave 'gods of women,' honor. The demons of shameful lusts destroyed the rightful roles of men and women (then) (Ac 19:28,35[KJV]; Ro 1:24-27).

"Set a standard, so that when man speaks, you are there to support it. The Word is clear, 'Let women pray and prophesy.' But let it be done in submission to the Lord Jesus, in God's divine order. Even when men won't take their rightful place, let women encourage men by not choosing to take their place. It is better to be silent, and to provoke man to take his rightful place, than to try to fulfill yourself as a woman by speaking in his place" (Ac 15:32; 1 Co 11:5; 14:33-40; 1 Th 5:14; 1 Pe 3:1,2). (Words received in December 2002).

Believing women, wives can learn to fulfill their rightful roles in relation to men, to husbands by their obedience to the

Word of God. When both men and women, believers in Jesus, take their rightful role, we believe Satan will not be able to place a wedge of division in marriages, and in families, preventing deeper wedges occurring in America (1 Co 11:3; Tit 2:5; 1 Pe 3:1,2).

The Value of Marriages

The Lord Jesus spoke more to us about valuing our own marriage and marriages in America. The Lord Jesus shared, "To be united in marriage, you must be willing to submit to Jesus. You must be willing to give up your rights, your fears, your ways, your self. You must be willing to listen to your partner. Giving in is not being enslaved; on the contrary, it is freedom and liberty from yourself, your fears, your fleshly desires, your appetites. Submitting to Jesus and His Words is the way to be 'united in the states' of your mind toward each other" (Mt 19:21,22[KJV]; Ac 2:45; Gal 5:24; Eph 4:3; 5:21,22,25; Ja 4:7).

On February 5, 2009, after we were fasting and worshipping before the Lord Jesus, I received some visions. In the first vision, I was placing a wedding ring on my wife's index, pointing finger, in a marriage ceremony. My wife, in turn, placed a wedding ring on my index, pointing finger. (The night before, my wife and I had watched the movie, *Fireproof*.[248] At the end of the movie, a marital couple reaffirmed their marriage vows). In the next vision, I saw a fire hydrant with water gushing out in all directions. Then a fireman attached a hose to the hydrant, and shot a stream of water on a fire. A vision followed of the man who played the character of the father in *Fireproof*. He was leaning up against a cross.

The Lord Jesus then disclosed, "In the movie, *Fireproof*, the couple reaffirmed their marriage vows as a life-long covenant. They were covenanted together, so as not to say 'negative' words, nor to find fault, nor to point their fingers at each other.

So you, (Mark and Phyllis) must be willing to do everything you can not to say negative words about each other. Will you do that?" We both replied, "Yes." The Lord spoke further, "You must be willing to not let your tongue, your 'fire' burst forth against one another. You can extinguish, put out that 'fire' on the enemy, not on yourselves, through the Spirit of God within you, through the 'fruit of self-control' (Isa 58:9; Mal 2:14; Ro 2:1; Gal 5:22,23; Eph 6:16[KJV]; Ja 3:6; Jude 16).

"You need to turn to the cross, turn to self-denial, not turning on each other. Instead of turning to other people, turn to your Father in heaven. The Father in heaven was like the father in the movie, who so wanted to help his son come to the cross. The producers of *Fireproof* allowed Me, (Jesus), to come and be represented in that movie. They prayed that Jesus would be in that movie, a movie that honors Me, and (honors) those that 'dare' to 'love' one another. 'Dare' to 'love' by learning through Jesus to 'tame' your tongues, and seek genuine forgiveness for your sins from God. Genuinely forgive your covenanted partner, who may have sinned against you. Place this in the book in the chapter on marriages" (Mt 18:34,35; Lk 9:23; 15:19-24; Jn 6:44; 10:17; Ro 2:4; Ja 1:26; 1 Pe 2:23; 1 Jn 4:7,8).

Shortly after watching the DVD version of *Fireproof*, we purchased the book, *The Love Dare*,[249] which we recommend for all marriages. After the previous visions, my husband and I tied a band around our "pointer fingers" to remind us not to point blame on one another. In the book, the authors encouraged marital partners, on the 40th day, to: "Write out a renewal of your vows and place them in your home. Perhaps, if appropriate, you could make arrangements to formally renew your wedding vows before a minister . . . Make it a living testament to the value of marriage in God's eyes and the high honor of being one with your mate" (Ps 51:10; La 5:21; Ac 3:19; Ro 12:1; Eph 4:23,24; Heb 13:4,5).

My husband and I chose to follow the authors' recommendation, and on Sunday, April 19, 2009, an African-American minister from a nearby church conducted the ceremony in a private room at our place of employment. An African-American woman, a missionary at his church, was a witness to our ceremony, as well as the Lord Jesus, while we reaffirmed our marriage vows and placed another ring on our ring fingers. This second time, my husband and I came together to covenant with one another, forever. We were not interested in the number of witnesses, as before, but we were interested in the sincerity of our words before Almighty God (Ru 1:16,17; 4:10; Jer 32:40; Ro 1:9; 8:16; 2 Co 2:17).

This is what was spoken on that day before Almighty God.

Minister: "We gather here together today to celebrate the reaffirmation of vows for Mark and Phyllis, whereas this second time they have made a commitment to this marriage on the foundation of Jesus Christ! It is the desire of Mark and Phyllis to establish their vows from this point on as a biblical covenant. For marriage is a sacred institution established by God and one that is meant to last for life."[250]

Mark & Phyllis: (Mark and Phyllis state together,) "We must be covenanted together in all things, yoked to our Lord Jesus Christ. We must dwell together in unity—of the same mind, of the same judgment—there must be no division. We must be knit together in a love that is real. We must act justly, love mercy, and walk humbly with our God! We must delight in each other, make one another's condition our own, rejoice together, mourn together, labor and suffer together. We profess ourselves to be the Lord's free couple, joyned in love, together by a covenant of the Lord, into a church estate."

Minister: "Do you Mark and Phyllis, come today to freely and unconditionally commit to this covenanted marriage:

to have and to hold, for better—for worse, for richer—for poorer, in sickness and in health, to love, cherish, and obey till death do you part? Forsaking all others, cleaving only to each other as long as you both shall live?"

Mark & Phyllis: (We both in unison answered,) "I do!"

Minister: (He prayed for us, and then shared,) "'For this reason, a man will leave his father and mother and be united to his wife, and the two will become one flesh ... Therefore what God has joined together, let man not separate.'"

My husband and I were strongly convicted by the Holy Spirit to reaffirm our vows on the firm, Rock foundation of our Lord Jesus. The Lord Jesus revealed more to us on the value of marriages in God's eyes. On January 8, 2009, and June 11, 2009, after we were fasting and worshiping before the Lord Jesus, He gave us some visions.

On June 11, I saw a vision of my wife disembarking from a passenger plane parked off a runway at an airport. As she was walking down the stairway to the ground, I was walking towards her. We embraced and kissed each other like the characters, David and Lucia, who were married in the movie, *Miss Rose White*.[251] (David survived the concentration camps during WWII, left Eastern Europe, and met his wife at a ship's dock in New York City. Needless to say in the movie, they were deeply in love with each other, and not ashamed to show it publicly).

The Lord Jesus then said, "Mark and Phyllis, greet each other (daily) like David and Lucia. You have been 'flying' high, but you have been separate from each other, (not on solid ground). Come 'down to earth.' God wants you to come together and love each other like David and Lucia in the movie, *Miss Rose White*. That is the love I desire for you both. Let the public feel awkward, but let your love be enthroned in the kingdom of God" (SS 8:6,7; Jer 13:18; Oba 4; 2 Co 13:12; 1 Pe 5:14).

On January 8, I saw a vision of a bearded gold-miner standing outside his camping tent. He began to pan for gold in a feverish manner. After that I saw a vision of a full rubber hot water bottle. Then I saw the Lord turning the heat up on an oven. (My wife had been cooking a tasty chicken soup and a delicious Jewish cake that morning), and I saw a vision of her taking the cake out of the oven.

Following that vision, I saw a parabola on a man-made satellite in outer space. My wife and I were standing on earth talking, and radio waves were sending out our voices to the satellite, which were being reflected back to us. Then followed a vision of me wearing a lamp shade over my head.

The Lord Jesus then said, "As men mined for gold feverishly with perseverance, so persevere for 'gold nuggets' from the Word of God. 'Buy from Me gold refined in the fire' in your furnaces of repentance, seeking first the kingdom of God with all of your heart. Turn up the heat in 'the race marked out' for you, together with your wife for 'the high calling of God in Christ Jesus.' Then Jesus will turn up His heat in your lives, in your marriage. As your wife praised the Lord, she was serving Me, cooking that good 'food,' the Word of God, which you fed on this morning (1 Sa 8:13; Job 22:23,25; Ps 119:2; Mt 6:33; Lk 12:49; Jn 6:58; Php 3:14[KJV]; Heb 12:1 [b]; Rev 3:18).

"For 'My Word . . . shall not return unto Me void' in your lives, in your books, 'but it shall accomplish that which I' purposed. These books, as they go out, must reflect My Words and My light in your lives. The books will not be kept under a basket; but shall show forth My light in you both" (Isa 55:11[KJV]; Mt 5:15,16).

On August 14, 2008, my wife heard these words from our Lord Jesus early in the morning. "I will help you. Get out of yourself and help others. Feel the pain of others. Feel the pain of your spouse. The 'power' of pain is giving others the blame. In spite (of this), take up your cross by faith. Keep your mouth quiet in all circumstances." That morning, the Lord Jesus revealed to us visions after a time of fasting and worship.

In the first vision, I saw a flag flying at our place of employment. (The logo/emblem on that flag is of two adult people standing next to each other with outstretched arms.) Then I saw a vision of a man in the movie, *John Adams*,[252] getting his lower leg cut off. (That man had been fighting the British out at sea on a United States naval vessel during the Revolutionary War.) A vision followed of the man on the Quaker Oats cereal box sitting down. In the next vision, my wife and I were in a wooden ship in a storm at sea. Waves were breaking over the ship's bow. The rigging and sails on the ship were falling apart.

Then I saw a vision of my wife and me when we were little children about to be punished by our parents. In the vision, my wife, as a child, was willing to be spanked by my parents for me. She was pulling my pants up before I would have been spanked. In the vision, I, as a child, was willing to be switched by her parents for her. Outside, near her family's outhouse, I was gathering clothes for her to wear, in order to cover her shame of being alone and humiliated.

Finally, I saw a vision of my wife and me facing each other in a New England home inside the front door of that house. We were like the characters of John and Abigail Adams in the movie, *John Adams*. We were bowing down before each other, while the character of George Washington in that movie was walking through the front door.

The Lord Jesus then said, "Be with each other in that workplace, and in all other places that God sends you two, to. 'Cut' off in your lives, that which is not of God. If your leg, or your hand, or your eye, (or your "tongue") causes you to sin, cut it off, so you can enter the kingdom of heaven. Take My 'axe' at the 'root of the tree,' at the roots of your childhood, using the 'Sword of the Spirit,' the Word of God, and cut them out! (Mt 3:10; 5:29,30; Mk 9:45,46; Eph 4:32; 6:17; Ja 3:8-10).

"You feel each other's pain, when you are willing to take the punishment for the other one. As you ask Jesus to 'help you' understand the pain of punishment from your spouse's childhood, you can be willing to cover up their shame. ("Get out of yourself and help" your spouse and others.) When you are in a stormy situation, Jesus will 'help you' when you help each other in a 'fiery' trial. Be merciful towards one another without spewing blame. In spite of your pain, take your cross up and bear it for each other. 'Cut' off the 'tongue,' the 'tongue' that hurt you as children and hurts others today. The Quakers served God, not by 'tongue lashing,' but by underground action, keeping their 'tongues' quiet in all situations, 'circumstances' (Pr 10:31; 25:15; Isa 53:4,5; Eze 16:8; Da 3:22-28; Mt 5:7; Lk 23:26; Gal 6:2; Heb 12:2; 1 Pe 4:12,13; 1 Jn 4:18).

"You set 'slaves of sin' free in this manner when you are willing 'to act justly and to love mercy and to walk humbly with your God.' When you attend to each other first, honoring one another at the door, making room in the house for your spouse, then you can open the door to God's dignitaries" (Ru 2:8-13; Est 5:1-3; Mic 6:8; 2 Co 1:24[KJV]; Php 2:4; Rev 3:20).

Those revelations from our Lord Jesus were given to us as ways to help us and other married partners to honor and value their spouses. These revelations can help strengthen marital bonds and a covenant between a couple, as well as prevent Satan from destroying and breaking up families.

Almighty God's Passion for Marriages

Almighty God, we believe, has a powerfully awesome passion for marriages in the United States and worldwide. We believe that the American people can return to their allegiance to the Lordship of Jesus Christ when husbands and wives are willing to "endure hardships" together, to "be content with what you have," to follow the Scriptures on marriages, and to honor "the marriage bed." We believe that as couples willingly stand together on the Cornerstone of freedom in America, our Lord Jesus, just like our forefathers and Founding Fathers, they will be able to overthrow the dark, divisive demonic forces opposed to covenanted relationships in marriages. We must "fight" for marriages in America (Mk 10:6-9; 2 Co 10:4,5; Eph 2:20; 2 Ti 4:5; Heb 13:4,5).

Our Lord Jesus has revealed to us His desire in these last days for us and other covenanted couples to express His passion for our marriages! On April 28, 2000, May 24, 2007, November 28, 2007, December 13, 2007, April 5, 2008, December 18, 2008, March 26, 2009, and May 28, 2009, the Lord Jesus revealed His heart to us about marriages.

The Lord Jesus said, "Jesus was smiling at the birth of the little girl and boy in the delivery room, (smiling at the births of all baby boys and girls), smiling at their innocence, their total dependence on their parents. Yet, with a deep sadness (He knew) that their parents would manipulate this dependence for survival on them, so that they, (the children) would become emotionally dependent on them, (their parents) throughout their life. Jesus was smiling though, because 'down the road,' He would become their Savior (Mt 18:2-4,10; Lk 3:5,6; 18:15-17; Jn 4:42). (Message reemphasized again by our Lord Jesus).

"No longer would they need to be emotionally dependent for survival from their parents. He would save them from their world of manipulations, and lack of real love. Jesus desires to love the little child in adults, smiling on the little boys and girls, setting them free from the manipulation of guilt, fear, and over-responsibility that they experienced as children, raised without the love of Jesus (Pr 27:10; Mk 10:13-16; Jn 15:19; Heb 10:19-22; 1 Jn 4:7,20).

"Then the little boys and girls become freer to love and play with each other as adults. They are not as fearful of others' expectations. They do not feel guilty for not taking responsibility for others' emotions. They are loved as little children by a loving Father through His Son, Jesus. America needs to be reborn again, 'born-again' into the love of Jesus for the little children in adults today and in the future. That is true liberty and freedom from past emotional bondage of the enemy's making. Jesus wants to smile on all the little children in adults in America" (Isa 6:7; 11:8; Jn 3:3; 14:23; 2 Ti 2:1-4; Tit 3:5,6; Heb 11:1,2; 1 Pe 2:2). Received April 5, 2008.

On March 26, I saw a vision of the Kings Dominion amusement park in Virginia. Little children were playing and having fun together. Then I saw a vision of two flowers growing in a log. The Lord Jesus said, "On your first date, you saw two flowers growing in a log, two ducks paddling together on a pond, and two stars in the sky. As little children, I have called you both to play and have fun together in your marriage, so that the two may become 'one' under the King's 'dominion'" (Ecc 4:9; Isa 32:1; Zec 8:4,5; Mk 10:7,9; 1 Ti 6:15; Rev 19:11).

The Lord said, "You were raised up in different parts of the country to come together and become 'one' . . . 'In a thousand years, in a thousand life times, could she be the one, could he be the one?' Your search is over for God brought you together as 'one'" (Gen 2:24; 24:12-19,60,66,67; Eph 5:31). Received April 28, 2000.

On December 13, I saw a vision of myself standing beside my wife at a high school prom. The Lord Jesus was placing a jeweled tiara on her head. Her hair length was much longer, flowing down over her neck. The Lord Jesus then revealed that my wife has been given greater insight into the motives and purposes of God. My wife's life is like the "Cinderella" story of a young woman who came out of poverty and ashes, into a beautiful lady, wife, serving the Lord Jesus (Eze 16:6-8; Lk 1:48[a],53; 6:20).

The Lord Jesus disclosed, "Take your wife to the prom. Choose her as the one you want to elevate, to show off to the world. Your heart's desire would have been to take your wife to the prom as high school sweethearts. This is the woman you would be engaged to, and that your heart's desire would be to marry and live a fruitful life together. You are coming into your own romance together, to show off your wife to the world in Me, like at a 'prom' (Gen 1:27,28; Ru 2:8-17; Est 2:17; Ps 150:4; Jer 31:3,4).

"This is the 'prom' that husbands and wives need to (enjoy

with each other), just like high school sweethearts. In my love, you can stay up late after the 'prom' and share with each other late into the night. You can spend a night at the beach talking, waiting for the Son, (sun) to come up in the morning, as your hearts are dressed up for Jesus in your fanciful 'garments of righteousness' (Ru 3:7-11; SS 8:14; Isa 61:10; Lk 24:1-6).

"You can swim out into the water together without a care in the world, only caring for Jesus in each other; laughing and giggling, splashing water on each other, and running back and forth together on the beach! This is My will for your consecrated marriage. Let the Son of God rise up at the water's edge in your lives, as you pray and play freely together in the sun. Love with all your heart, soul and strength. Write these words on the door posts of your hearts, (over the door(s) of (your) lips.) This is what you take out to the world, your love for each other (Dt 6:4-6,9; Jos 19:27[KJV]; Ps 126:2; Ecc 10:19[a]; Eze 47:3-5; Hos 2:19,20; Mal 4:2; Jn 13:35; 1 Pe 5:7). Received May 24, 2007.

On December 18, I saw a vision of my wife and I looking up into the night sky. Then I saw a vision of the dawn coming up in a magenta color over New York City. Then the Lord Jesus reminded me of the television comedy show, *The Honeymooners*.[253]

The Lord Jesus then shared, "As you look to Me to sustain your life, you will travel like 'honeymooners' through New York City, through New England, as you did on your 'honeymoon.' You will be like 'honeymooners,' not like Ralph and Alice, but as Mark and Phyllis. 'Honeymooners' do not bruise and wound each other, rather their 'wounds cry, Hallelujah,' and their 'bruises honor Me.' Allow My 'stripes' to heal your wounds, bruises, your marriage" (SS 1:2,4; 3:4[a]; 5:1,2; Isa 30:26; 53:5[KJV]; Ac 7:54-60).

On November 28, I saw a vision of an Olympic torch. My wife and I were holding it up at night, and carrying it throughout the United States. The Lord then revealed that,

"The torch represents a ("flame") from God that He has kindled in us. It represents God's passion burning in us (for marriages). Too long in this land have men and women been shackled with irons (and kept) from the real truth about God's plan for marriages. For too long have the pulpits of this world been enslaved to the enemy's schemes and tactics, enslaved to sin, enslaved to unrighteousness, so that he, Satan, might divide and conquer marriages, not only in the United States, but throughout the world (Jer 28:13,14; Na 2:4; Zec 12:6; Mk 3:23-26; Lk 3:16; 12:49; Jn 8:34; Ro 6:19).

"In the movie, *Amazing Grace*,[254] (the character of) William Wilberforce displays a passion, like the one I have for My people, to set My people free, 'to bind up the broken hearted,' and 'to release prisoners' who are bound in 'darkness.' In the days ahead, stand together with your wife, with My passion for your marriage. My Words for marriages must be given to the world with 'flames of fire,' the 'fires' of freedom from slavery, from sexual sins. Open the doors to purity in marriages. May compassion like Wilberforce (in that movie), burn in you like 'fire,' an anointing 'fire,' a 'refiner's fire' (Isa 61:1; Mal 3:2; Ac 2:1-4; 2 Co 7:1; Gal 5:1; Heb 1:7).

"Feel the passion that this man had against slavery. So you can speak up with passion against divorce, against illicit affairs, against adultery, against the lies and falsehoods in marriages, today. Your wife will be your support. She will be with you as you face the onslaught and mocking of the enemy. There will be many obstacles, the obstacles of sin in men and women. God wants you to put to death whatever belongs to your fleshly nature, so that God's kingdom might reign over all the onslaughts and mocking of sin from men and women that come your way (Ps 2:2-6; 89:50,51; Mal 2:16; Mt 19:7-9; Mk 7:21; Ac 18:26; Ro 16:3,4; 1 Co 2:4; Col 3:5).

"You will be able to speak freely about your marriage and marriages publicly! God is developing in you both an unquenchable love for each other, so nothing will be able to quench My 'flames' of passion in your marriage. Those 'flames' will grow stronger in the days ahead" (SS 8:7; Isa 10:17; Da 7:9; 1 Th 5:19).

On May 28, I saw a vision of myself in the cockpit of a jet plane like in the *Dogfights*,[255] DVD series. Off the right side of that jet, I fired guns on a small passenger jet plane. The jet plane blew up in fire. Instinctively, I moved my plane to the left, in order to miss the fire debris from the passenger jet. Then I saw a vision of my wife seated in the cockpit behind me. She was navigating the plane. My wife tapped me on the shoulder and gave me a "thumbs up" sign, and said, "Good job!"

Then the Lord Jesus disclosed, "Much of the (past) passenger baggage from your families that had followed you was blown out of the air by the power of praise and deliverance. I, (Jesus), am in the cockpit of life with you. It's My power that sets captives free. As you 'fire' My Words, My praises in the face of the enemy forces, they will be taken down. Remember, you are a team in deliverance, in teaching, in working, in praying, in singing, in worshiping, and in being together. You are a team that cannot be divided by the enemy, that cannot be broken apart (2 Ch 20:21-25; Ps 8:2; 149:6-9; Ecc 4:12[KJV]; Mt 18:19,20; 28:20; Ac 2:44-47; 5:42; 10:38).

"You are strengthened by the bond of leaving family and cleaving to each other in Me. You are a team that is becoming a fighting force in the heavenlies, teamed up with Jesus, your 'Head' coach. You are teamed up 'to destroy the works of the devil,' and to enhance marriages, enhance love, enhance the real, enhance companionship, and enhance 'the fruit of the Spirit' nationwide and worldwide. Enhance your love for one another. This is My will for you as you write the chapter on marriages in this book" (Pr 16:21; Mt 19:5[KJV]; Mk 10:29,30; Ro 12:9-16[KJV]; Gal 5:22,23; Col 2:19; Heb 11:34; 1 Jn 3:8[KJV]).

God's passion of love is exemplified in the Scriptures, "For love is as strong as death, its jealousy unyielding as the grave. It burns like blazing fire, like a mighty flame" (SS 8:6). We need to take our Lord Jesus' Words to the deepest places of our hearts, for our marriage, and to help us endure the grave economic crisis in America today and in the last days.

. 14 .

YOU CANNOT SERVE GOD AND MAMMON

"The merchants of the earth will weep and mourn
over her because no one buys their . . . cargoes
of gold, silver, precious stones and pearls,
fine linen, . . . cargoes of cinnamon and spice,
of incense, myrrh and frankincense, of wine and olive
oil, of fine flour and wheat; cattle and sheep; horses
and carriages; and bodies and souls of men."

The Lord Jesus revealed to us that, the messenger, John, who was called to "Prepare the way for the Lord," Jesus on the earth, was the one who disclosed that He, Jesus would make "low" the mountains and hills. The prophet Isaiah revealed that, the Lord God had "a day in store for all the proud and lofty, . . . for all the towering mountains and all the high hills, for every lofty tower and every fortified wall, for every trading ship . . . The arrogance of man (would) be brought low, . . . (so that) the Lord alone will be exalted in that day." That lofty mountain, hill, tower, wall, ship, we believe, is related to man's master, "mammon," and/or "money" in America today, being "brought low," because of many who disdain Almighty God and His Word! (Isa 2:12-17; Mt 6:24[KJV]; Lk 3:2-5).

For many of the American people, we believe, are, and will be humbled through the loss of their "god," the "god" of "mammon," and/or "money." For Americans have chosen, we believe, to "live on bread alone," and not "on every word that comes from the mouth of God." So many Americans, we believe, as we reported earlier, have chosen to embellish a sinful, sexual lifestyle, choosing to abort babies, and choosing to despise the name of Jesus, and all references to the one true God and His Word. We believe America will come to its knees through God's judgment of this nation's sins as the economy falls. We believe there will be little to no money for sinners to flaunt their sinful choices and lifestyles (Isa 45:22-24; Mt 4:4; Ro 8:7,8; 14:10,11; Rev 6:5-8).

The American Economy

We believe that the United States of America is and has been the "wealthiest" nation in the world. Yet, many American people today are just like the rich young man in the Bible. He left Jesus and "went away sad, because he had great wealth." That young man would not "sell" his "possessions and give to the poor," and would not follow Jesus. By running after worldly "riches," we believe that the American people have become "wretched, pitiful, poor, blind and naked" in God's eyes. Until this country chooses to repent of its sins against God, and turns back to the Lord Jesus, the Cornerstone of America, the one true Liberator, we believe the American people will suffer severe losses of their possessions and "things" in the days ahead (Mt 10:39; 19:21-24; 2 Co 7:14; Eph 2:20; Rev 3:17).

America's Prosperity

In the Bible, Joseph received "a richly ornamented robe" from his father, Jacob. Joseph was "hated" by his brothers, because their father "loved" him above "them." Joseph was "stripped" of his rich "robe" by his brothers, and subsequently suffered the loss of his family, suffered as a slave, suffered false accusations, and suffered imprisonment. But "God intended it for good" later in Joseph's life. Joseph was humbled from his high position with his father, and said, "God sent me ahead . . . to save your lives by a great deliverance." America's high position in the world, wearing its "richly ornamented robe," we believe, is, and will be humbled "to save . . . lives by a great deliverance" from Satan back to our Lord Jesus (Gen 37:3,4,23,28; 39:13-20; 45:7; 50:20; Ps 37:40; Ac 26:17,18; Ja 2:2-7).

Our Lord Jesus has revealed some information to us on America's economic condition. The Lord said, "America's posterity will not inherit America's prosperity until America's austerity tightens spending in America's economy" (Ps 73:3,12,18,19; Isa 55:2; Jn 14:27). Received July 15, 2009.

On April 1, 2008, my wife heard these words, "More than this country ever had . . . One if by land, two if by sea, . . . and To the point." The Lord then said that morning, "The United States is a nation, that has been given more than any other country ever had in terms of worldly material things. This nation has been more 'prosperous' than any other country; prosperous in technology, in foods and goods, in homes, in vehicles, in monies, etc. Yet, America has turned its back on Me. They, (the American people), are not grateful for their prosperity. They take it for granted, as if they, the people in America, are solely responsible for their wealth, their cars, their technology, their homes, their shopping malls, (and much more). It is a sad thing to see that men and women's wealth in America is more important than God in their daily lives (Dt 8:17,18; Ps 14:3; Jer 12:1; Ro 3:12; 2 Ti 3:1-4; Rev 3:17,18).

"Money colors their choices. They have made money their 'god.' Their 'god of prosperity,' of wealth, will fall as it has in different times in America. This will happen in order to bring My people back to Myself, totally dependant on Me for their prosperity. Since America has been giving itself away financially to other countries, and has been choosing other 'gods,' other beliefs, it has become a debtor nation. A nation in debt to God for not heeding the warnings of the true prophets, today. That debt can only be paid back by the American people submitting their lives to the one true God, and repenting for turning away from the source of their wealth, their prosperity (Pr 3:5,6; Isa 60:12; Hab 2:6-9; Lk 16:13; Ac 3:19,20; Ro 2:4,5).

"Just like the rich man, who could not give up his material possessions in order to inherit eternal life, so many in America, including believers in Jesus, have been selling themselves out to the world, (to worldly material things). As Paul Revere knew that, 'One if by land, two if by sea,' meant that he must warn the American people that the British were coming, so God is warning America as she continues to sell herself out to countries who do not acknowledge the one true God. They (people from those other countries) are infiltrating America, not only by land and sea, but in the air also. And that's getting right 'to the point'" (Gen 25:31-33; Dt 13:6-8; Eze 2:1-7; 3:19; Mk 4:18,19; 10:17-25).

In April 1997, Pastor David Wilkerson "delivered" a "message" at Times Square Church in New York City on America "Experiencing the Calm Prior to the Greatest Storm America" will suffer. "Two days before" his message, "the stock market reached an all-time high of over 7,000. Newscasters and magazines boasted: 'America is enjoying its greatest prosperity ever. Unemployment has fallen below 5 percent . . . Profits are at an all-time high, . . . interest rates are low, and homes sales are increasing.'"[256] "The Greatest Storm America" will experience, that Pastor Wilkerson was referring to, will be an economic collapse in the United States in the upcoming days.

The Collapse of the American Economy

In 1998, Pastor Wilkerson revealed in his book, *America's Last Call*, the coming "Financial Holocaust" in the United States.[257] Pastor Wilkerson reported that he believes "America stands at the brink of an economic and social collapse . . . Sodom and Gomorrah enjoyed the same booming economy as Noah's society, (as does the United States) . . . A time comes when people sin so persistently, grieving God so deeply, that a line is crossed. God determines to bring judgment, . . . and it is happening in America right now. . . . The Bible warns that when God pours out his judgments on nations, he begins by crippling the economy!" Throughout the Bible, when the Jewish people and other ethnic groups of people had been warned about their disobedience to God, and refused to repent, Almighty God brought down judgment (2 Sa 12:7-13; Jer 52:1-13; Lk 17:26-29; 21:5,6; Jude 5-7).

Pastor Wilkerson wrote further that, "On October 18, 1987, during a Sunday morning service at Times Square Church," he "warned" their church "that the stock market was" going to fall. The next day, "the market had fallen 508 points, . . . one-fourth of its value! . . . The United States has been living far beyond its means . . . Total consumption by households, businesses and government has exceeded . . . almost $500 billion of debt . . . America is no longer in control of her economic future . . . (America is) subject to . . . financial power of world markets."[258] We believe many Americans today have chosen to satisfy their desires for possessions by buying on credit, rather than choosing to suffer without their "desires for other things," the "things" of the "world" (Dt 28:45-47; Mt 4:8,9; Mk 4:19; Lk 12:15; 1 Jn 2:15).

In 2007, Pastor Wilkerson revealed that, "In America, Satan's war against the church is in the continual flood of sensuality and materialism. His weapons in this war are love of money and addiction to pleasure" (10/15/07).[259] He shared that, "More and more preachers are urging their people, 'God wants you to get rich' . . . They are falling into the same money-focused, ("prosperity") gospel that Jesus drove from the temple in his day" (2/5/07)[260] (Lk 4:5-7; Jn 2:14-16; Eph 4:19; 1 Ti 6:5-10; 2 Ti 3:4).

While growing up in my, (Mark's) Roman Catholic family, we did not believe in the real Jesus, nor did we trust in God, so "mammon," money, we were taught, was our security, was our "god," was our proud reputation with others. Money was placed at a high value in my father's eyes. We believe wealth breeds pride, a pride that felt like I was better than others. Pride was bred in me at an early age. It is only through constant time spent with Jesus in repentance, that He has lessened my pride, lessened my need to have money, and increased my trust in the Lord Jesus to provide for my wife and me (Ps 10:2-6; Mk 10:21-25; Lk 16:13[KJV]; 1 Co 3:18; 2 Co 11:4; 1 Ti 6:17; Ja 4:6-10).

When I, Phyllis grew up in a large Roman Catholic family, we lived on a farm. Our livelihood, regarding family finances was quite different than my husband's. Survival and hard work were the driving forces in our family, in order to provide food, clothing and shelter for all of us. Planting crops, gardening, preserving food, hunting, fishing, splitting wood, etc. were carried out to maintain our family's provision year round. Rather than trusting in Jesus to provide for us, we were raised that the more we could preserve, stock pile, and accumulate, the better off we would be in the long run. Our family was constantly worried and stressed to ensure that we would have food on the table (Gen 3:17-19; Jer 17:5; Mt 6:19,25,31,33).

When I became "born again," Jesus calmed me with His love, His peace, and His Word. He gave me a gift of faith to eat less, store less, prepare less, and shop less. After several years, our kitchen cupboards have been packed with less food items. We have fewer clothes in our closets, and our home has become less cluttered with collectibles, furniture, and bric-a-brac (Mt 6:31-34; Jn 3:3,30; 4:34; 14:21,27).

As the money markets are now dwindling in the American

economy, my husband and I are living a much sweeter and calmer lifestyle, as we walk with Jesus, and trust in His love and provision for us. We have an understanding of the simplicity, the simple life of the past colonial times. We believe there was a true liberty in Jesus back then. We also believe that many Americans will experience that simple life again, and turn back to Him, when the country changes in the future (Ps 19:7; 116:6; 119:130; Lk 9:3,10-17).

Before my husband and I were married, I handled the monthly bills and expenses. Issues regarding money often increased worry, tension, and a constant unrest in my life. During our premarital counseling sessions, we were given a book by Larry Burkett, the Christian author and economist, on how to budget our finances together as a married couple. My husband encouraged me to accept the Scriptural teachings in that book. Since that time, he has managed our monthly finances. My husband's assistance has offered me a much more calming peace and assurance over money issues in our marriage. Jesus is at the helm of our "ship," and my husband keeps our "ship" steady on course. God has always taken care of our finances, as we abide in Him for our provision (Mk 4:37-41; Lk 6:38; Jn 15:4[KJV]; 2 Co 9:13; Eph 5:22,23; 1 Ti 6:19).

Yet, there was a time when my wife and I were in deep credit card debt, while we lived in North Carolina. We actually lived on credit for the most part. While renting a home, we had accumulated over $32,000 debt using six credit cards. The Lord Jesus had impressed upon us to pay off that debt, when we moved back up to Virginia in January 1999. We received a loan to pay off all six credit cards. After three years, we were able to pay off that loan. Today, we use one credit card only, usually at service stations, and for items that can only be purchased over the telephone. We use our credit card for identification purposes. Otherwise, we try to pay cash or write checks for everyday purchases.

On February 28, 2008, my wife received these words from the Lord Jesus, "Ezekiel, Chapter 3 . . . Lack of money, . . .

and bread and butter." The Lord then gave us a vision that morning of the woman in the Bible, who had crumbs falling off her table, which were eaten by dogs. In the vision, a dog was under a table eating crumbs, and catching water that was dripping down from the table. The Lord was revealing to us a time of poverty that is coming to America.

The Lord Jesus disclosed that morning, "As you have gone through and read books on the founding of America, you have discerned clearly that wealth, affluence, money, possessions, and the seeking after (those things), draws people away from their God, from the one true God, Jesus. Even in the churches today, preachers preach on wealth as being a 'good' thing, on financial contentment as a 'good' thing. They are preaching about their 'god.' Their 'god' is not the God of the Bible, but the 'god of this world,' Satan. It is Satan that influences men and women to make God into a financial 'god.' This is not the God of the Bible (Dt 8:17,18; Mt 4:8,9; 2 Co 4:4[KJV]; 1 Ti 6:9,10; Ja 5:5,6; Rev 3:17; 12:9).

"Every time the Puritans sought other things, possessions, bigger homes, more land, Satan cunningly drew them away from their real sustenance, their real 'bread and butter,' away from their dependence on Jesus and no other. They made their wealth and material things their idols. You read in the book, *The Light and the Glory*, how the Puritans began making idols of their family members, instead of turning to God. Parents became idols, children became idols, and there began a breakdown of the American family. But God had to break them down in order to build them back up, just as He did the Israelites in Babylon (Ecc 3:3[b]; Jer 1:10; 17:5; Da 1:1,2; Mt 4:3,4; 10:37,38; Lk 14:26; Jn 6:51; Rev 9:20).

"The United States of America has become like Babylon, a people who do not seek after the one true God, a people who are despising Him. So God will take America's affluence and wealth, and break it down, just as He did to the Israelites, and just as He did to the Puritans. There will be a 'lack of money.' The breakdown will be economic. It will be a financial disaster, because Americans have chosen other 'gods.' Once they are broken down, God will rebuild America up again by her roots, just like He did through the faith of the Founding Fathers, and their forefathers, the Pilgrims and Puritans, by those who follow Jesus. You can now see it in America's national debt, in the home mortgage foreclosures, in the making of paper money, and in the bartering for oil with its increased prices. These are early signs of what is to happen in the future" (Jer 28:14; 38:2; 51:6; Da 3:13-15; Mt 24:8; Lk 20:18; Eph 3:17; Rev 17:5,6).

That morning, the Lord Jesus gave us a vision of my wife and me flying in the sky in what appeared to be a "Piper cub" airplane. We were looking down on the earth. The Lord shared, "I'm giving you a vision of America. You will be given visions and revelations about this country, (the United States) in the days ahead. I will speak truths to you, that you will see come to pass in this generation. You will give My warnings to a 'rebellious house.' I'm warning America, a rebellious people, just like I warned the Israelites, who were rebellious, which was written in the book of 'Ezekiel, Chapter 3'" (Eze 3:4-14,19,21,22; Ac 2:17; 1 Co 10:6-11,14).

On January 8, 2009, after fasting and worshiping before the Lord Jesus, I was given a vision. In the vision, I saw a stuffed toy snake wrapped around a toy. The snake's colors were purple and green, like the character "Barney" in the children's television show. The snake was squeezing the insides out of that toy.

The Lord Jesus then shared, "Even children today are more preoccupied with possessions. What the world offers through 'toy makers,' are toys made apart from Jesus Christ. Although the children's television shows share some 'good' messages like 'Barney,' those messages do not refer to the Word of God. The 'toy world' is stealing the life out of generations of children. Children and youth have become more occupied with their toys, their video games, rather than with church, with Bible studies, with Christian youth groups, and with reading the

Bible. They have become idol-oriented, their idols are their toys" (Isa 44:9-11; Mt 19:13,14; 1 Co 10:18-21; 1 Jn 5:21).

Pastor Wilkerson warned further that, "The stock market we thought was so fail-proof and insulated against disaster is going to be shaken as never before . . . God is going to rise up and shake everything that can be shaken! . . . Multimillionaires will become penniless overnight . . . The stock market is going to crash, and the bond market will experience a meltdown . . . 45 million American families own some share of the bull market, . . . (and) their paper profits will disappear within days!"[261] (Hag 2:6,7; Mt 24:29; Heb 12:25,26).

On October 2, 2008, the Lord Jesus gave me visions after we fasted and praised our Lord Jesus. In the first vision, I saw a red fox looking sly and cunning, riding on a huge bull, a beast. The fox was riding in what appeared to be the area of the New York Stock Exchange, near "Wall Street." The Lord Jesus then gave me a vision in the city of Chicago, where I went on a high school field trip to the American Stock Exchange. Then I saw a vision of the logo for the Chicago Bulls, NBA basketball team. The logo is a red "bull." The fox then changed into the "woman," that sits "on a scarlet beast" (Rev 17:3).

The Lord Jesus then said, "The 'bull' has to do with the United States' economy. Satan is riding that 'bull,' which is affecting your financial system. Chicago, the state of Illinois is involved, and they are 'bullish' on America. The evildoers, the 'bullies' are going to dominate America. That woman riding the 'bull,' the beast, represents spiritual adultery with the 'bulls' of other masters, money, etc., in America. In the past, 'bulls' (issued by former Popes in the Roman Catholic Church), were declared against having personal Bibles, against Bible societies, and against Bible studies. Just like in the United States, Satan is using ungodly men and women to declare 'bulls,' against the Word of God and Jesus" (Ps 22:12; Isa 34:7; 51:20-23[KJV]; Ac 4:18; Rev 17:1-6; 18:2,3,11-17).

The Lord Jesus further said, "The world flounders on its dependence on man, on that great 'god,' the stock market; a market of thieves. There is a different market to take stock in—into heaven. The investments in that market last forever! As you 'bank' on Me, the true giver of your fortune, the giver of your wealth, you will live forever. For the man who stands on My Word of truth will not be penniless in the kingdom of God. They, My true believers, have put their trust in God and not in man, (not in the stock market), for their fortunes" (4/4/01). (Pr 29:25; Isa 2:22; Jer 17:5; Mt 7:11; 21:13[KJV]; 25:27; Lk 12:33-34; Jn 10:1,10[KJV]; 14:1; Eph 6:13,17).

Pastor Wilkerson disclosed further that, "Wall Street has completely abandoned God in its clamor for the almighty dollar . . . The big moneymakers and analysts in America have mocked God and pushed him out of sight . . . As America has grown ever richer, (they have) completely forgotten God in the process . . . America is going to see its wealth perish . . . Multiplied thousands . . . are going to lose their savings . . . Many will try to declare bankruptcy . . . (In 1997), 1.3 million individual Americans declared bankruptcy."[262]

In addition, Pastor Wilkerson wrote, "Almost every block on America's streets will be lined with 'For Sale' signs in front of homes. They will be sellers only, and very few buyers. The housing market will collapse . . . There may be a 70 to 80 percent devaluation in real estate . . . And there will be mass unemployment . . . When the financial panic strikes, . . . many common people will take their lives . . . All across the nation, the suicide rate will leap dramatically . . . God is going to act quickly to devastate America's economy—not only as judgment upon the sins of this nation, but for . . . purging of the church, . . . to deliver his redeemed children from the contagious spirit of materialism and worldly-mindedness now engulfing our nation"[263] (Da 11:35; 12:10; Jn 15:2; 1 Co 10:14; 1 Ti 6:10,11; 2 Ti 2:22; Rev 19:11-15).

What is happening to America's economy since David Wilkerson wrote his book, *America's Last Call?* In messages by Pastor Wilkerson in December 2007, in May, August, and December 2008, and in February 2009, he revealed that

America's economy is collapsing. Pastor Wilkerson disclosed, "Builders, realtors, Wall Street professionals, retailers, executives, lawyers, restaurant owners, small-business owners—they're all saying the same thing: 'It's worse than most people know' . . . Nationwide, many people have walked away from mortgage commitments . . . God is . . . causing . . . our spiritual bankruptcy (to be) turned into financial disarray . . . Our strength . . . (in the) all-surpassing . . . dollar . . . is ebbing fast"[264] (12/17/07).

Dr. James Dobson of Focus on the Family reported in December 2008, that "Businesses that have thrived for decades are staggered by the most serious economic downturn since the Great Depression in the 1930s. Individual families have lost a significant portion of their life's savings in 401Ks, or IRAs, or directly in the stock market . . . The burgeoning national debt . . . is approaching $11 trillion now, and we are spending money faster than we can print it."[265]

In December 2008, David Wilkerson revealed, that "In two weeks' time, more than $4 trillion of American wealth vanished . . . What we see happening to our economy is not only God's vengeance, (but also) . . . the very honor and glory of Almighty God" (12/8/08).[266] In February 2009, Pastor Wilkerson reported that, "In just two weeks time God . . . (shut) down (America's) mighty financial credit system . . . Many (even) in God's house are placing their hope in government bailouts—trillions (are) intended to save the economy, rescue the financial system, provide millions of jobs."[267] Pastor Wilkerson revealed in another message that "China has loaned America hundreds of billions of dollars. We have become the world's number one debtor nation . . . Politicians . . . promise all kinds of new, multibillion-dollar programs, while the Fed is" trying to keep the nation out of more debt (5/12/08).[268]

On July 14, 2009, the Lord Jesus gave me a vision of a U.S. Navy aircraft carrier, whose bow was surging through the water. On the deck of that carrier was only one World War II fighter plane. As the aircraft carrier passed by, I then saw the "tail" of the ship. The stern appeared like the "belly" of the ship, pressed down and out. The carrier, viewing it at the stern, was moving slowly, puttering through the water like a motor boat. On the back deck of the carrier, people were in bathing suits sitting in lounge chairs getting tanned.

The Lord Jesus then said, "The aircraft carrier represents the United States of America. America moved as the 'head' with great power in past military battles, (during World War II). But America has now become the 'tail'; overfed, prideful, arrogant, and disobedient to God, a debtor nation. For America is 'up to its ears' in debt ('to suit their own desires'). Although America appears to have some strength, its appearance is deceiving, for its people care more for themselves, more for their possessions, more for their immoral lifestyles, and care less for God (and His Word)" (Da 28:12,13,43,44; Eze 16:49; 2 Ti 3:1-4; 4:3,4).

Startling Headline Articles

Some headline articles in the news have disclosed America's economic downfall. In April 2008, it was concluded in "A survey of all 50-state fiscal directors" that, "The finances of many states have deteriorated so badly that they appear to be in a recession . . . The situation looks even worse for the (upcoming) fiscal year . . . in most states."[269] In August 2008, it was reported by the Associated Press, "AP," that "Consumer prices (rose) . . . at twice the expected rate, pushed higher by surging energy and food costs. The latest surge left inflation at the fastest pace in 17 years."[270]

In September 2008, the "AP" reported that, "The Dow Jones industrials plunged nearly 800 points, the most ever in a single day."[271] In another "AP" report in October 2008, it was reported that, "Wall Street suffered through another traumatic session . . . with the Dow Jones industrials plunging as much as

800 points and setting a new record for a one-day point drop as investors despaired that the credit crisis would take a heavy toll. . . . The catalyst for the selling was the growing realization that the Bush administration's $700 billion rescue plan and steps taken by other governments won't work quickly to unfreeze the credit markets."[272]

In another "AP" headline on October 15, 2008, it was reported that, "Dow plunges 733 on new disheartening economic data . . . The daylong sell-off came as retailers reported the biggest drop in sales in three years . . . The plunge in stocks put the nation's economic anxiety front-and-center."[273] Also reported by the "AP" was an article on March 2, 2009. "The Dow Jones industrial average plunged below 7,000 . . . for the first time in more than 11 years as investors (grew) even more pessimistic about the health of banks, and the turn in the economy. A staggering $61.7 billion in quarterly losses at insurer American International Group Inc. touched off fresh fears about the health of the nation's financial system."[274]

In yet another "AP" report, it was indicated that, "The number of people receiving jobless benefits exceeded 6 million for the first time, the government reported, . . . and housing construction unexpectedly plunged to its second-lowest level on record . . . Companies (are) reluctant to hire new workers until an economic recovery is well under way. And the latest housing data show the slump in that market."[275] We are witnesses of several houses with "For Sale" signs in our home town, as well as throughout America with very few buyers. Many homes have been foreclosed. These headlines were just a small sampling of the recent fall of the economy in the United States.

Pastor Wilkerson confirmed this in September 2007, when he disclosed that, "The world's most prominent idol is money, and right now America is facing a monstrous financial disaster . . . Mortgage companies are going bankrupt."[276]

Good Stewardship of Money

Today, how should the American people spend their money wisely, according to the Scriptures? Our Lord Jesus said, "It is more blessed to give than to receive." Yet, who are we to give money to, and are we to give money out, when we do not have any? The "poor widow" in the Bible, put "into the temple treasury . . . two very small copper coins." Jesus said, "She, out of her poverty, put in all she had to live on." That widow gave to her congregation, gave to God's treasury for His purposes (Lk 21:1-4; Ac 5:32-35; 20:35).

The Lord Jesus shared in the Scriptures, "Give what is inside the dish to the poor, and everything will be clean for you." In order to be clean inside, we believe, you give to those in need of food, water, clothing, and shelter. You do not give to those who are unclean, "full of greed and wickedness." You do not give money to support a sexually immoral lifestyle, homosexuality, to the abortion "industry," and to those who abhor the name of Jesus, and honor other "gods" (Lk 11:39-41; 1 Co 5:9-13; 6:9,10,18-20).

In the book of Acts, the first century believers in the Lord Jesus gave to their fellow believers, and the poor, those who were in need of food, water, clothing, and shelter. The Scriptures state, "Selling their possessions and goods, they gave to anyone as he had need." We believe God blesses those who voluntarily and "cheerfully" give to a true believing congregation, church, in Jesus, who give to true Christian organizations, and who give to those who are without the necessities of life (Dt 15:7,8; Isa 58:7,10; Mt 25:34-36; Ac 2:45; 2 Co 9:7).

An individual, a congregation, a church, a Christian organization can choose to voluntarily give money and necessities where they are needed, as they are guided by the Holy Spirit. We do not believe Almighty God will bless a nation, whose government gives out millions of dollars for "bail-outs," for "welfare" payments, for sinful/sexual relationships, for abortions, for those who oppose the Word of God, the name of Jesus, prayer and the reading of Scriptures, and for those who honor other "gods" (Dt 28:15-19; Ps 2:1-12; 110:6; Isa 40:17; Jer 46:28[a]; Jn 16:7-13; Ac 4:25).

In the early morning of June 23, 2009, my wife heard these words from the Lord Jesus, "The Founding Fathers had great rules established . . . We hold these truths to be self-evident." Later that morning, the Lord revealed, "'The Founding Fathers had great rules established' on biblical principles, on God. For Almighty God has rules to live by, which are written in your Bibles. Those rules are being torn apart, dismantled, and discarded as having no value today. There are rules about giving and stewardship toward families, goods, and property that the Founding Fathers established in their American documents, that arose from the Word of God (Dt 5:6-22; Mk 12:29-34; Lk 6:38; 16:1-8; Ac 4:32; Gal 4:3-7; Heb 4:12).

"They held 'these truths to be self-evident' by the Spirit of Truth residing in the believers in Jesus, who is the Truth, which was self-evident to them. Those rules were established so that any violation of those rules would be subject to judicial action, (a checks and balance system). Today, however, the judiciary and many government officials have not chosen those biblical rules of the Founding Fathers. For many have been granting monies for unrighteous and evil activities opposed to the Word of God (Dt 16:18-20; Jdg 2:12-18; Jn 14:6,16,17; Ro 13:1-5; Gal 4:9).

"The government has out-spent itself on wicked ploys of the enemy in the public schools and (school) textbooks opposed to God, in the funding of the welfare system, in funding abortions, in funding the gay/homosexual agenda, and in promoting other 'gods,' of other nations. This has been a wicked misappropriation of taxpayers' money through government handouts. A nation that values the funding of wickedness over the rules established by the Founding Fathers, will not be blessed" (Pr 14:34[b]; Isa 60:12; Mt 6:24; 24:10-12; Ac 1:18; Eph 6:11).

In the book of sermons from the former D. James Kennedy, *The Mortgaging of America*,[277] he reported on the troubles America is suffering economically, because of the government's distributions of money for ungodly purposes. It was noted that, "Not only is our country ignoring His commands regarding sanctity of life and marriage, but we are spending our grandchildren's inheritance to satisfy our desires for material things, and we are looking to the government—not God—to supply all our needs ... More and more, people (have been) looking to government, not God, to be America's economic savior ... (The) government, ... in effect, (has been) stealing (money) from one group ... to give it to another more favored group" (Mt 6:31,32; 19:18; Lk 3:12-14; 16:13-15; Ac 5:1-5; Ro 13:14).

Dr. Kennedy disclosed, "The overriding problem facing our nation, ... and facing the administration and Congress is the problem of the spiraling out of control national debt. ... There has been much analysis of the situation—but all of it without God ... None of it has considered His Word ... The Puritan Work Ethic, or the Protestant Work Ethic ... has been virtually forgotten in America, and as a consequence we have seen a tremendous decline in our national productivity ... We have lost the biblical concept of self-discipline—of saving and postponing the fulfillment of desires"[278] (Ro 13:8,9; Eph 4:28; 2 Th 3:10; 1 Jn 2:15-17).

Dr. Kennedy shared further, "Escalating welfare is causing a federal deficit that is absolutely going to destroy America ... Continual recipients of welfare ... has destroyed the incentive (to work) and the meaning of life for whole generations ... The federal government (is) ... subsidizing illegitimate children, ... (through their) poverty programs ... These programs have produced a whole generation of children who live in father-absent households ... As goes the family, so goes the nation."[279]

Dr. Kennedy mentioned that, "Most people in this land ... have been deluded by the Great Deceiver ... Only when the

Spirit of God so works in our hearts that the things of this world and our desire for them is limited—only when our trust no longer is in government as our shepherd, but in our God . . . —only when we get back to the Protestant (biblical) work ethic that provides for the material needs, . . . that make for a prosperous nation—only then is there any hope" (for this nation)[280] (Jer 23:1; Zec 11:17; Lk 10:7; Jn 10:14; 2 Co 1:22; 1 Ti 6:17-19).

Satan, "the Great Deceiver," "who leads the whole world astray," we believe, has been masquerading "as an angel of light" through government officials, offering many of the American people in special interest groups, monetary handouts for their ungodly actions and sinful lifestyles, that are directly opposed to the living Word of God, to Jesus. Despite the downfall in the American economy, true believers in Jesus can be "good stewards of money" by following the truth of the Scriptures (Eze 22:12; Mt 26:14-16; 1 Co 16:2; 2 Col 1:14,15; Rev 12:9[KJV]).

Jesus said, "Give, and it will be given to you. A good measure, pressed down, shaken together and running over, will be poured into your lap." We believe that you cannot out give God. The more you give with a "cheerful" heart to the church, congregation, to Christian organizations, and/or to those in need, time and voluntary donations, the more you will receive back from Almighty God in both tangible, and intangible, heavenly ways. The former Dr. D. James Kennedy learned from our Lord Jesus, the value of the gift of giving, as related in a Coral Ridge Ministry, "Commentary" (Dt 15:10; Pr 21:26[b]; Lk 6:38[a]).

Dr. Kennedy shared that, "Many people spend much of their lives worrying about money . . . Some people, . . . never learn the secret of trusting God for their finances, as I did . . . We ignore His promises, . . . that if we, 'Bring all the tithes into the storehouse . . . ' He 'will . . . open for you the windows of heaven and pour out for you such blessing that there will not be room enough to receive it' (Malachi 3:10 NKJV) . . . He is a

God who gives! His greatest gift to us is His Son, and through Him is given the gift of eternal life . . . We have to learn to give . . . to become like Him . . . We can take the strain out of our finances by tithing"[281] (Nu 18:26; Mt 6:31; Lk 22:19; Jn 3:16,17; 1 Ti 6:10).

In another message, Dr. Kennedy revealed that, "Many . . . built their worldwide enterprises on faith in God and in cheerful giving: the founders of . . . Quaker Oats, . . . Kraft Cheese and Heinz, . . . Colgate—Palmolive Company, . . . Amway, . . . United States Plastic Corp., . . . and many more. These companies were based on a firm belief in God's promise of blessings and gave millions to the cause of Jesus Christ! . . . You too, can live God's 'abundant life,' . . . as you . . . give willingly and graciously to the Lord!"[282] (Jn 10:10[KJV]; Ac 5:32-35; 2 Co 9:7).

Our Housing Market

From our own personal experiences, we have learned from our Lord Jesus, the blessings of God's giving! The Lord Jesus has made provision for us in the housing "market," since we were first married. Before we were married, my husband and I spent about six months looking for a home that would accommodate our family at that time. After searching many days, we finally found a home that would meet all of our needs in Manassas, Virginia. However, when we talked with our Christian real estate agent, she informed us that there were two pending contracts on that house.

A few days later, that house was taken off the market. The potential buyers met all the necessary requirements for buying that house. We had searched so long, so it was very discouraging for us. A few weeks later, however, we received a phone call from our real estate agent at our workplace. Miraculously, she informed us that this house was back on the market. The Lord Jesus opened a door for us to buy it. We believed that God ordained this house for us, but He wanted us to persevere in trusting Him for His provision. It is significant to note, that the word, "Manass"-eh in the Bible means, "God has made me forget all my trouble and all my father's household." We left our fathers and mothers, and began our marriage in Manassas (Gen 41:51; Mt 7:7; 19:4-6; Ja 5:11).

Israel

In the summer of 1994, we left Manassas, as God had called us to the land of Israel. In February of 1992, the Lord Jesus spoke to me, Mark one morning, while I was on my knees praying. The Lord was calling my wife and me to Israel. Three weeks later, we met at a Pastor's house of the Messianic congregation that we were attending at that time. We prayed together, and through a series of visions and revelations, that Pastor confirmed our call to Israel. We had to sell our home, resign from our jobs, leave our children, and prepare for the new cultural change in Israel. The Lord Jesus led us every step of the way (Ps 119:133; Mk 10:29,30; Ro 4:12; 2 Pe 1:10,11).

Our Lord made provision for us before we left for Israel. When I left my job in April 1994, I filed for retirement income of over $10,000. Just before receiving that income, I received a notice from the state government of Virginia. The state passed a new law that I would receive over $18,000, if I waited a month or so. We waited, and God provided over $8,000 more for our call to Israel.

In the summer of 1993, I decided to sell my baseball card collection, that I had kept hidden away in a cigar box for years. After checking a price guide for those cards, I decided to try and sell them at a yard sale. At the yard sale, I sold three cards and then packed everything up to go home. A man met us at our car and shared, "I heard you have a baseball card collection. Can I see it?" We told him that we were tired and ready to leave. But he insisted, and mentioned that he really wanted to see the cards. After we pulled out the card collection, he told us that he was an auctioneer in Manassas, Virginia. Those cards, he shared, "Might make some good money for us."

That night, my wife heard these words from the Lord Jesus, "My hand is on the baseball cards." Over a period of about four months, the auctioneer sold all of those cards, and my stamp collection. We received over $12,000 from the sale of the cards and the stamps. God made additional provision for us to go to Israel.

On June 29, 1994, my husband and I flew on a Tower Airlines jumbo jet to Tel Aviv, Israel. The plane was filled with hundreds of Jewish people. As we neared the Israeli Airport, we noticed that a woman in the seat in front of us was reading a book about the Holy Spirit. Then I told my husband, "The woman in front of us may be a Christian." After we landed, the woman stood up, turned and stared at us. Then she spoke to us and said, "I never fly at night. I never use this airline, but now I know why God had been speaking to me, to follow through on this flight. I am to help you, when you get off the plane" (Mt 3:11; Ro 16:3,4[KJV]; Heb 4:16).

What a mighty God we serve! She and her husband were believers in Jesus. That woman helped us through customs, find our luggage, exchange our money, and obtain a rental car. Her husband and some of their church members prayed for us at the Airport, gave us directions to people we knew in Israel, and invited us to their home at a later date. What a welcoming comfort that was for us in a foreign land. It was all orchestrated by our God, Jehovah Jireh, our Provider! Our Lord Jesus made miraculous provisions for us that day! (Gen 22:14; Ps 103:5).

In July 1994, while we were in Haifa, Israel, staying at a Christian guest house, a woman knocked on the door of our guest room. That woman did not know us, and asked if we could "house sit" for over two months at their apartment in Haifa. She and her husband were going to Argentina to spend time with family there over the summer. They were "born again" believers in Jesus/Yeshua. She told us that the Lord spoke to her, and wanted us to live in their apartment (2 Ki 4:8-10; Lk 10:38; Ac 18:2,3,26).

The Lord Jesus provided us a place to stay, rent free, near the Mediterranean Sea for about two months. Again, miraculously, the Lord made provision for us in a foreign country. According to the Bible, Israel means, "struggled with God." We "struggled with God" there. The Lord Jesus was stripping us of everything ungodly and sinful in our hearts through a process of repentance. He desired that we would make Him our Lord in all areas of our lives (Gen 32:28; Job 41:25[KJV]; Ro 2:4; Ja 4:8-10).

North Carolina

When we returned to America in October 1994, the Lord called us south to North Carolina. One day, after searching out several houses for rent near Greensboro, we finally found an affordable, farmhouse with a wraparound porch in the town of Asheboro, North Carolina. When we saw that house, we were so excited that we ran up to the front porch. When we inquired about that home, two other parties had already expressed a serious interest to the owner to rent that house. One party was in the process of filling out an application at that time. We also had two indoor cats, but the owner had said, "Absolutely, no pets." We called the owner, letting her know that we had two cats.

The owner was a Christian woman. By the grace of God, she rejected the other two parties' applications. The landlord/owner was very kind to us. She waived the "No pet" rule, and trusted God to let us live in that rented house. The owner became a personal friend of ours, and helped us in many ways during the time we lived there. Again, the Lord Jesus miraculously opened a door for us to live at that house through His marvelous provision. In Asheboro, we were often in repentance in "sackcloth and 'ashe'-s" for the past and present sinful motives of our hearts (Da 9:3; Ro 5:17; Rev 3:8).

We moved from Asheboro to Whiteville, North Carolina in the summer of 1996. Again, we searched in that area for a decent home to rent. After we received a list of homes in nearby Wilmington, North Carolina from a rental agency, our list actually blew out of our car window as we were driving over a bridge. God had another home in mind for us. The Lord Jesus opened another door to a home in a rural area in Whiteville. A pastor and his wife owned a home there, which they rented out to us. In Whiteville, the Lord Jesus was refining us in "furnaces" of repentance, so "though (our) sins (were) like scarlet, they shall be as 'white' as snow" (Dt 4:20; Isa 1:18; 48:10).

Virginia

In the winter of 1998, the Lord Jesus called us back to Virginia after we had lived in North Carolina for about five years. We were excited, because we would be living closer to our children again. We searched out many homes around the Fredericksburg, Virginia area. We found a house in the City of Fredericksburg that we considered renting. We discovered that house was not for rent, but it was a house up for sale. We were intending to rent a house, as we only had $500 to invest.

We contacted a real estate agent, who was supposed to represent us regarding that house. No one knew where that agent was at that time, not even his wife. So we decided to telephone the agent, whose phone number was on the "For Sale" sign outside that home. That agent was a Christian woman. She informed us later, that there was a new loan out called the "Nehemiah Loan." The loan required that we could not make over or under a certain amount in our salaries. We qualified for the loan, and received financial help to buy that house from a director, from our new employer, at a youth home. Again, God provided us a home in a miraculous way. We lived on "Wilderness" Lane at that home. The Lord Jesus was taking us through a "wilderness" there, like the Israelites experienced in the wilderness years ago, to conform us more into His image (Neh 2:7-9; 5:11,12; Ps 95:8[KJV]; Heb 3:7,8[KJV]).

After living there for over four years, the Lord Jesus called us again to relocate and move closer to our children, who were moving to another location. We found a house in Berryville, Virginia that had been taken off the housing market. After talking with the owner of that home, and later with our Christian real estate agent, we put a contract on that house, contingent on selling our home in Fredericksburg over the next weekend. In July 2003, we put our home up for sale. As our real estate agent was placing a "For Sale" sign into the ground, a car pulled up into our driveway. A woman stopped by to see our home. The woman liked it so much, that she placed a contract on it that day. It was amazing to us, to see our Lord Jesus provide for us in such a short period of time.

Before we actually moved, we were sitting down eating a Sabbath meal on a Friday evening. The Lord Jesus spoke to me, Phyllis, at the table, to call the Navy Federal Credit Union about a lower interest rate on a mortgage loan. When we called the Navy Federal Credit Union, we found that their interest rate would be much lower than with another company. We accepted the Credit Union's interest rate. Since that time, we have been able to save a great deal of money on our monthly mortgage payment at a much lower interest rate. God worked it all out. The Lord Jesus has been faithful every time to make provision for us in finding a home, that He has ordained for us. The Lord desired that we might bear ("Berr"-y) "fruit in keeping with repentance," and bury ("Berry") "our old self" in us, while we had been living in Berryville (Jer 33:3; Da 2:22; Mt 3:8; Ro 6:4-6).

Israel

In the summer of 2004, the Lord again called us back to Israel. That summer, my husband saw a vision of a three-story building in Israel near a body of water like an ocean. In that vision, on the second floor of that three-story building, was an area covered in red, His blood. In May 2005, we heard the words, "Beit Immanuel," which is a Christian guest house in Jaffa, Israel. We applied as volunteers, and we were accepted by the pastor, there. It was amazing, that our room was on the second floor of the three-story building at Beit "Immanuel," where "God (was) with us." The guest house was only a few blocks away from the Mediterranean Sea (Ex 12:7-13; Mt 1:23; Rev 12:11).

The Lord Jesus provided us a place to stay in Israel for over two months. We did not have to pay for lodging, for food, and other expenses. The CEO of the youth home that we had been working, sponsored us for our missions trip. He saw to it, that all of our traveling and miscellaneous expenses were paid for by donors of the youth home. God has continued to make provision for us in the places that he has called us to. We do not believe that it was just a coincidence, that the names of the towns and the names of some of the roads that we have lived at in America, reflected God's desire for us to become more "refined, purified and made spotless until the time of the end." It has been our personal experience, that the Lord Jesus gives back far more, than we could ever give to Him (Neh 9:15; Da 11:35; Jn 6:31-33).

Our Lord Jesus shared, "Provision comes from heaven above. It's a vision that is for you, supports you, a pro-vision. It is a vision of the future. I am your provision, providing you food from heaven to meet your needs in the days ahead (Ex 16:33; Nu 12:6; Eze 36:25-27; Jn 16:13; Ac 2:17). Received October 6, 1995.

"Those you work with, the people around you, are given you, to test your hearts before Me; so that your hearts may be refined, purified, and ready to endure the hardships coming upon the world. I need to strip My people of everything, (that is not of God), so that I am able to move with power in My people in these last days. You must be willing to stay together in the most difficult times ahead. Love each other despite the circumstances around you. Your circumstances are what molds you into the vessels I need you to become" (Jer 9:7; Mk 10:9; Ro 9:21; Php 2:3-8; 4:11-13; 2 Ti 2:3). Received July 28, 1996.

On January 7, 2010, after we fasted and praised the Lord Jesus, I was given a vision of what appeared to be Noah's ark. In the center of the ark was the face of Moses surrounded by different animals. The Lord Jesus said, "Just as Moses was placed in a basket protected by 'pitch and tar,' so Noah's ark was built and covered with 'pitch' to protect it in the turbulent waters. Your 'new' home will be like an 'ark,' covered and protected with 'pitch' for your family and others, as you 'pitch,' in, and build your home on love, mercy, compassion, humility, forgiveness, and fervor, so that you may walk with Jesus amidst the turbulent waters in the days ahead" (Gen 6:14; 7:6,7; Ex 2:1-3,10; Mt 14:28,29).

The Selling Out of America

Despite the Biblical principles of being good stewards of our money, many Americans we believe, are choosing to "sell out" America for their own personal interests apart from God. Many of the signers of the Declaration of Independence "lost their property," their homes during the Revolutionary War. Those Founding Fathers were sold out for the cause of freedom in America. They "mutually" pledged their "lives," their "fortunes," and their "sacred honor" to each other. It was reported that, "None of the signers betrayed the cause of liberty!... All 56 signers followed through on their commitment ... They gave their whole life for it ... Many of them paid a high price, so that the United States could (become) one nation under God!"[283] (Ps 33:12; Heb 2:8-10; Rev 12:11).

Today, many of the American "leaders" are not sold out for the freedom and privileges the Founding Fathers cherished in the late 1700's. Those "leaders" are selling America out, we believe, to "the evil one." On December 25, 2008, Christmas

Day, my wife heard these words from the Lord Jesus, "Bankrupt . . . No America."

The Lord Jesus disclosed that morning, that "America, when you (Mark and Phyllis), were born in the 1940's, still maintained its Biblical foundation on the Word of God, on Jesus. However, (primarily) since the early 1960s and up through today, America has been selling itself out to the devil and his wicked schemes. America has become 'bankrupt' spiritually, as well as economically. There is 'No America,' when Satan has been given authority over the good, over the truth, over the Word of God, over Jesus, over true Christians (Mk 4:14,15; 10:21-25; Lk 4:5-7; 2 Ti 2:19; Rev 13:17).

"'No America,' Why? Because America's foundation was on the Rock, the Cornerstone, Jesus Christ. American 'leaders' are choosing a foundation of 'sand'; a foundation of lies, deception, and falseness that has been portraying 'evil as good.' A foundation built on 'sand' will fall with a resounding crash, just as you see America's economy fall" (Isa 5:20[a]; Mt 7:24-27; 1 Co 10:4; Eph 2:20).

On July 9, 2009, after we fasted and worshiped before our Lord Jesus, He gave me some visions. In the first vision, a man's heart was being opened up. His skin and lungs were pulled apart. The man's heart was split in half. The heart appeared to have a diseased section in it. Then, the heart enlarged, and it appeared over a map of the United States. It appeared that the blood was clotted in many tributaries, and was not flowing to many states in America. There was not a backbone behind the heart. Then I saw a vision of a doctor placing an artificial heart in a man on an operating table.

A vision of an overweight man followed, and he had fat hanging over the sides of his body. Then I saw a vision of the "Lone Star" state flag of Texas. Finally, I saw a vision of a man in Independence Hall, Philadelphia signing with a fervor, the Declaration of Independence. He was passing a feather quill pen to another signer there.

Then the Lord Jesus revealed, "The United States, like Israel and Sodom, has been arrogant, overfed, and prideful because of everything that has been given to them from Almighty God! The United States is ballooned up in their own arrogance, in their own 'pork.' Because of this, the heart of Jesus has been diseased in America. Many are having strokes, heart attacks, and heart diseases in this country. It is symptomatic of the heart's disease in America, a heart not after Jesus, a heart that has gone astray to the world, a heart after every special interest group. It is a heart with an irregular heart beat, that is not beating with the heart of God, the heart of Jesus (1 Sa 13:14; 1 Ch 29:14; Pr 10:17; 21:24; Jer 17:5; Eze 16:49; Mt 13:15; Jn 11:33; 12:27; Ac 8:21-23).

"Those men, (the Founding Fathers) were signing their lives and their fortunes over to the will of God for freedom in the land! Yet, today, America has 'no backbone.' America is signing over the 'sacred fortunes' and 'honor' of the Founding Fathers to 'the evil one,' to other 'gods,' and to wickedness. And like Sodom and Gomorrah, this country will burn for many in leadership positions have sold out America (Mt 5:37; Mk 3:35; Lk 11:39; 2 Pe 2:21,22; 1 Jn 2:17; Jude 7).

"Those men, who willingly fought for freedom at the Alamo, were willing to sacrifice their lives. Many of them were believers in Jesus Christ fighting against the Roman Catholic nation, Mexico. It was Jesus, fighting through believers for America, against Satan. Yet, many Mexicans today, who are not believers in Jesus, are taking over territories in the United States! And America sits and watches. God is allowing this. America will suffer a major heart attack, because many Americans have chosen 'blind leaders' to serve this country" (Mt 15:14; 23:24; Ac 5:4,5; 12:23; 2 Co 10:4,5; Eph 6:11,12).

The Current Presidency and Government

In March 2009, it was reported that, "President Barak Obama" believes "'the federal government is the only entity left with the resources to jolt our economy back into life' . . . On the near trillion-dollar economic stimulus pushed by the Obama administration, . . . Sen. Tom Coburn (OK) . . . (stated that), it's 'the worst act of generational theft in our nation's history' . . . Even though President Barak Obama warned that failure to pass the massive pork-laden measure would 'turn crisis into a catastrophe,' others (argued) that adding $1 trillion to the national debt is itself catastrophic . . . As proposed, the bill pours billions of dollars to fund government pork, (and) gives transfer payments to poor Americans, (which doesn't generate jobs)." [284]

Dr. James Dobson shared in a December 2008 "Family" newsletter, that in 2004, "Senator Tom Coburn [R-OK]" had condemned "the reckless spending of his congressional colleagues and (predicted) dire consequences if it continued." Dr. Dobson wrote further that the "liberal President . . . (had) promised nearly $1.3 trillion in new spending . . . The support for this and endless liberal programs can only cause the national debt to skyrocket. We already owe China more than half a trillion dollars . . . A new administration . . . seems to believe more taxing and spending can rescue us . . . Already, the tax and spend policies have brought our economy to its knees."[285]

In a Coral Ridge Ministries' newsletter of February 26, 2009, it was reported that, "We have seen Congress and the President blithely discuss *trillions* of dollars in handouts . . . We must . . . call Americans out of a life of debt, . . . out of a life of greed, . . . out of a life of materialism and consumerism, . . . into the light of freedom, contentment in Christ, and trust in God . . . Rev. William Boetcker, an outspoken minister in the early 1900's, . . . stated, . . . 'You cannot bring about prosperity by discontinuing thrift . . . You cannot keep out of trouble by spending more than your income . . . You cannot establish security on borrowed money' . . . They are . . . biblical principles"[286] (Lk 12:14-21,33,34; 15:11-20; 1 Ti 6:6-9).

In a newsletter of April 2008, Dr. James Dobson wrote that in 2008, "Medicare (would) pay out more benefits than it takes in from taxes . . . The same thing happens to Social Security in 2017. That's when the government will have to start paying back all the money it has stolen from the people from the Social Security 'lock box' [that doesn't exist] over the years . . . By 2019, Medicare becomes completely insolvent. And by 2041, Social Security runs dry . . . By most estimates, this is a $53 trillion asteroid."[287]

Dr. Dobson noted further, "As you realized just how much of your hard-earned money will go to support the bloated bureaucracy and to an ever growing catalog of entitlements, you may have felt . . . helpless . . . Thanks to the efforts of the liberals in the Senate and the House, you will almost certainly be paying even more taxes next year . . . The 'marriage penalty' tax will return, saddling 50 million married couples with an average of an additional $3,000 in taxes, for the coming year, while those living together, (unmarried), will pay less . . . Dr. Del Tackett (believes) . . . that God did not institute governments to 'save' people, especially in a manner that intrudes on every citizen's God-given rights to life, liberty and the pursuit of happiness"[288] (Ps 146:3; Pr 18:22; Mt 16:25,26; 1 Co 6:9,10).

In another newsletter of 2011, it was indicated that America's "total federal debt has jumped 40 percent since 2008 and is now $14 trillion. Last year's federal deficit was $1.3 trillion. (From our founding to 2008, the annual deficit never topped $500 billion). ObamaCare will add another $700 billion to the deficit over ten years. The unfunded liability of Medicare and Social Security is projected to be $43 trillion over the next 75 years." In a news report of December 2010, it was revealed, "The new health care law will use your tax dollars to kill unborn children and ration health care for the elderly . . . Entitlement programs and massive debt are mortgaging our children's future at an astounding rate."[289]

Opposition to the Current Presidency and Government

When Jesus walked on the earth during His ministry, tax collectors were disdained by the Jewish people. It was reported that, "Taxes were collected for the Roman government by Jewish agents, who were especially detested for helping the pagan conqueror and for frequently defrauding their own people."[290] The American people are beginning to protest the unjustified increase in taxes in the United States, especially under the current administration and Congress.

It was reported that on April 15, 2009, the final day of sending off personal income tax forms, many protestors were involved in "tea parties," similar to the Boston Tea Party, protesting the government's excessive tax policies. Again, there is a growing disdain against those involved in collecting taxes, and taxes for unrighteous purposes (Lk 3:12,13; 19:2,8).

In an Associated Press, (AP) news article of April 15, 2009, "Demonstrators . . . organized protests across the country, including outside the White House . . . Demonstrators said they disapproved of government spending since President Barak Obama took office."[291] On July 4, 2009, again there were "nationwide anti-taxation protests . . . Flag-waving protestors (carried) signs that read 'America's no longer free' and 'Save our constitution!' . . . A bipartisan crowd, (was) brought together by a mutual feeling of American pride and disgust over policies believed to increase the burden on taxpayers . . . Tea party groups from across the nation plan to gather in Washington, D.C. on Sept. 12 for a 'unity' rally."[292]

Michael van der Galien of the PoliGazette reported on July 18, 2009, that there "was another big day for the national tea party movement . . . Turnout was robust around the country . . . The tea party-movement is really catching on. And it has succeeded in changing the dynamics in America already. Obama's approval ratings are dropping fast . . . Obama has proved to be a true liberal, a hardcore leftist, this even though he campaigned as a moderate . . . The tea party protestors—and others of course—did what the media should have done, namely to educate voters about the real nature of (the current administration's tax policies, etc)."[293]

On September 12, 2009, as revealed in the *Tea Party*, documentary film,[294] the leader of the "1.5 million" march in Washington, D.C., was dressed in an American Revolutionary War outfit. The march and rally that day were the largest ever in the nation's capital. The leader of the march is "a white pastor of a black church, . . . Maranatha Baptist Church." He shared, "My political beliefs apply only as long as they line up with the teachings of Jesus Christ . . . I believe that if Christians all over, regardless of denomination, . . .will live according to biblical principles, ultimately they will come together as one people. The Tea Party patriots are absolutely not racists, or I wouldn't be a part of them."

One of our daughters saw a protestor's sign in her hometown, which read, "Give Me Liberty, or Give Me No Debt." Our Lord Jesus has revealed more to us about what's in His heart regarding the current administration and government's policies. In the early morning of April 16, 2009, the day after income tax forms are required to be sent in, my wife heard these words from the Lord Jesus, "Crash . . . Boston Tea Party . . . The United States, (and) . . . New England."

That morning, after we were fasting and worshiping before the Lord Jesus, He gave me some visions. In the first vision, I saw men hanging lit lanterns in the "Old Oak Tree" in Boston, Massachusetts, that was portrayed in the movie, *Johnny Tremain*.[295] Those men, we previously reported, were called the "Sons of Liberty." In the movie, those men had just dumped tea from England in the Boston harbor. A vision followed of a map of the United States. A star representing the capitol of Kentucky was pronounced on that map. Then I saw a vision of the top half of the Statue of Liberty and the sky over New York City. The statue came crumbling and crashing down. Finally, I saw what appeared to be a "large statue" of a man broken into "pieces" by "a rock." It appeared to be the revelation that was given to Daniel, as revealed in the Bible (Da 2:31,34,35).

The Lord Jesus then said, "Rise up ye sons and daughters of Israel. Rise up ye sons and daughters of liberty, and live freely in the United States, free from 'taxation without representation.' The American people are taxed, but the government does not represent the American people in (financially) bailing out the wicked. This 'rings' of tyrannical England, who bailed out wicked men and exploited the poor, just like the United States today. The American government has compromised with evil. It has become like a 'police state,' policing the good and supporting the evil in men and women (Mal 4:2,3; Ac 4:17-20; Gal 5:1 [KJV]; 2 Ti 3:13; 1 Jn 5:19[b]).

"In 'New England,' the 'Boston Tea Party' took place by those who were 'Sons of Liberty.' Boston is no longer at the heart of God's freedom in America. Frankfort, Kentucky was at the heart of many American people, who had their own 'tea party' yesterday in opposition to the government's 'taxation without representation,' (in opposition) to the tyranny in this country. Be willing to throw 'tea bags' on the lawn of the White House, (as some men and women did yesterday) (Jn 8:31,32; Ac 5:28-33,40-42; Ro 8:21 [KJV]).

"Where are the 'Sons of Liberty' today? Who will stand up and speak boldly about Jesus, and the Word of God? Be 'Sons of Liberty,' willing to fight for the freedoms of the people in America. The 'voice of freedom' has come crumbling down in America. (Consequently), wealth and possessions will come tumbling down, and it will all fall with a 'crash.' The 'Rock,' the 'Cornerstone' of America's freedom, Jesus, will break the economy into 'pieces,' just like the statue that Daniel saw of the 'rock' (crushing the figure of a man). For the government taxes the American people, taxes those who oppose sin, to pay for the abortions of the unborn, to pay for sin in the United States" (Pr 16:18; Isa 6:8-10; 26:4; Da 2:44,45; Lk 20:17,18; Jn 8:36; Eph 6:19,20; Php 1:14).

On July 1, 2009, our real estate agent shared about the President working on a tax break of $15,000 for those that buy a house in America to stimulate the economy. Our agent said, "It will not help this nation." On November 13, 2008, March 26, 2009, and May 20, 2010, God gave us a series of visions and revelations after we fasted and worshiped before the Lord Jesus.

On November 13, I saw a large blue-skinned apple. The "big apple" was falling in New York City. Several years ago, my wife saw a vision of the ball falling in New York City on New Year's Eve, indicating the "fall" of the stock market. Then I saw a vision of a young man climbing up a pineapple tree. A person was pulling him down from the tree before he reached the fruit. A vision followed of my wife and me cooking hot dogs and ribs on an outdoor ground fire.

The Lord Jesus then gave me a vision of Himself drilling through a board. In that vision, my wife and I are sitting underneath the board looking up at Jesus through a drilled hole. Then I saw the Lord trying to drill through a log with an augur. It was taking Him much time to drill through the log. Then I saw Him take an axe and split the log in half. A vision followed of a drilled hole in a wine casket. Then I saw a cluster of reddish-purple grapes attached to a tree.

The Lord Jesus then disclosed, "The blue apple represents the economy, the New York Stock Exchange falling in the United States causing a 'depression,' the 'blues.' This economic 'fall out' will cause many people to drill within their hearts to repent of their sinful heart motives, and to 'become like little children,' who look up to Jesus. Others, will be like those who have 'logs in (their) own eyes.' They will try to get 'the speck out of others' eyes. They will not choose to get 'the log out of (their) own eye's, for they are so-called 'believers' in Me, who 'measure' others by the world's standards, instead of God's love (Isa 2:12-18; Mt 3:7,8; 7:1,2; 18:2; Lk 5:8; 6:41,42; Jn 13:34,35).

"But I will take the 'axe' at the 'root' of 'the tree of the knowledge of good and evil' in their hearts. This is a warning to 'believers' to come out of the 'world,' and the trappings of this world, or else I will come and 'split' their wood and burn it up in an 'unquenchable fire.' This country of hospitality, (the pineapple tree), is being pulled down by its own government, and public and private enterprise. Eventually, outdoor cooking will again take place in America. Many believers will be cooking in the 'fire' of the living God. You must be crushed like grapes, used to make wine, crushed of yourself, crushed of your flesh, so you can drink the 'new wine' of the Holy Spirit daily. For many will drink of the 'wine' of the world, and become intoxicated as a way to survive in the days ahead" (Gen 2:17; Pr 20:1; Mt 3:10-12; 9:17; Mk 14:24,25; Jn 15:6; 21:9; Ac 2:15-17; Ro 12:13; 2 Co 6:17,18; Eph 5:18).

On March 26, the Lord Jesus gave me a vision of President Barak Obama's federal budget for the year, as revealed on the Internet. Then I saw a vision of a Ferris Wheel at an amusement park. My wife and I were seated at the top of the Ferris Wheel. We were about fourteen years of age, having fun at night. We could see over a great area of land from the Ferris Wheel.

The Lord Jesus revealed, "You have been given revelations from above, to see what is happening in America. The President, his cabinet, and White House staff members are stuck at the top of America's 'Ferris Wheel.' They are not willing to come down out of their pride to see from God's eyes. Even though the American economy is sinking, Barak Obama has proposed the highest federal budget in the United States, (over 2 trillion dollars) which would increase America's debt, (significantly)! They, (the President and his staff members) think they are at the top, but God has given them a mind not to see the things of God" (Isa 14:12-15; Da 5:18,20,22,30; Hab 2:2,3; Mt 13:13-15[a]; Rev 1:1,2).

On May 20, I saw the Statue of Liberty at night. There were dark, billowing clouds above the statue, as well as thunder and lightning. The face of the statue appeared to be angry. Then I saw bats flying around the Statue of Liberty. Finally, I saw a vision of golfers at a driving range, adjacent to a golf course.

The Lord Jesus shared, "It is night time in America. The occult, witchcraft is thriving under Barak Obama, since he welcomes the Islamic religion, which has brought in another 'god' to the United States. Former President Abraham Lincoln issued the 'Emancipation Proclamation,' which proclaimed freedom for the slaves. Since 'President' Obama took office, he has issued a 'De-Emancipation Proclamation' to the American people. Instead of following 'The Declaration of Independence,' Barak Obama has declared a 'Declaration of Dependence' on the government of this nation. Americans have become 'slaves' to the whims and desires of the government 'leaders,' their 'masters.' The 'Obama Manifesto' is manifesting America to enslave the people to the government's decisions, not the people's choices (Dt 18:10-12; 32:15-17; Jer 17:5; Mt 6:24; Jn 8:34,35; Gal 4:8,9).

"The American people have a 'golfer's' mentality. (In the news, on National Prayer Day in the United States, I saw 'President' Obama playing golf). The people believe, they can come and go, as they please, spending time and money frivolously in their 'sand traps.' The American people want it this way. God is angry with America's choices and desires. He is allowing Satan to take this country down" (Dt 32:18-25; Job 1:6-19; 2:1-8; Lk 17:26-29; 2 Ti 2:25,26; 3:1-7).

Pastor David Wilkerson, in a message on September 15, 2008, warned the American people of the coming fall of the United States. He revealed, "Right now, the day of reckoning has come upon America and the world. All branches of the U.S. government—including federal banks and financial institutions—will see the crashing and burning of our economy. The old, established corporations— ... rooted in our society— will be affected, with no visible way of recovery ... Even the secular world sees America is headed for hard times. A recent issue of *The Economist* shows the Statue of Liberty sitting dejectedly with her face in her hands, (and) her flame lying on the ground. The headline reads: 'Unhappy America'"[296] (Lk 3:7,17; Rev 18:7,8,11-17).

In August 2010, it was noted, "The panic struck Wall Street in August. Severe economic pain quickly followed. Banks failed, firms closed, joblessness soared, and the stock market dropped sharply . . . It was 1857 . . . When Christians prayed in 1857, . . . at a time of economic downturn, the 1857-58 revival reached millions of Americans . . . Soon, some 6,000 men gathered daily for prayer in New York City. Some 10,000 people came to (Jesus) Christ weekly in New York City for a season. Prayer gatherings sprang up in . . . hundreds of cities and villages in (America). An estimated one million people came to (Jesus) Christ as a result of the revival—in a nation of 35 million,"[297] during "The Second Great Awakening."

We have exposed through revelations and visions from our Lord Jesus, the inevitable fall of the American economy, today. Yet, through many diligent prayers, God could eventually turn this nation around to Jesus.

The Founding Fathers

Prior to moving into the section on America's Future in this book, we again visited the Old City in Philadelphia on July 23, 2009. The Lord Jesus desired that we take a deeper examination of the cover up of the Founding Father's faith in Jesus Christ, and how their faith served God's purposes for America.

It was reported that, "Many have concluded that the Seven Churches of Revelation—found in chapters 2 and 3 —also represent the History of the Church from its inception to the present. Accordingly, Philadelphia is the sixth church named, . . . —the city of brotherly love—, . . . and would represent a time frame from approximately 1700 to 1900 AD—the Philadelphian Church Age . . . The Believers of the Philadelphian Church Age (had) only a 'little strength.' But, we should read of Philadelphia's exploits"[298] (Rev 3:7,8,10).

It was further noted on July 3, 2009, that, "Of the fifty-six signers of the Declaration of Independence, (most) . . . were motivated by their faith in Christ . . . The Founding Fathers . . . wrote sermons and creeds and hymns. They founded Bible Societies and Sunday Schools. They served God's purposes in their generation, . . . (men like) John Witherspoon, . . . Charles Thomson, . . . Charles Carroll, . . . Francis Hopkinson, . . . Benjamin Rush, . . . Roger Sherman, . . . (and many others)"[299](Eph 5:19; 2 Ti 2:15; 4:2; Heb 10:25).

Reportedly, "It was Benjamin Rush who said the Constitution was 'as much the work of Divine Providence as any of the miracles recorded in the Old and New Testament, (which) were the effects of divine power' . . . Roger Sherman . . . wrote a personal creed that was adopted by his church: . . . 'I believe that there is one only living and true God, existing in three persons, the Father, the Son, and the Holy Ghost . . . The Scriptures of the Old and New Testaments are revelation from God.'"[300] John Quincy Adams stated, "Posterity, you will never know how much it cost the present generation to preserve your freedom. I hope you will make good use of it."[301] The Founding Fathers were men of Christian principles and faith in the "one only living and true God," in Jesus (Ps 136:3-26; Mt 4:23,24; Mk 1:10,11; Lk 4:14,18; Eph 3:21; 4:4,5; 2 Ti 3:6; 2 Pe 1:20,21).

Sadly, as we have revealed in this chapter, our prosperity for our "posterity" is rapidly becoming extinct, as our government "leaders" spend America's future away.

Our Visit to the Old City

Early in the morning, prior to taking our trip to the Old City in Philadelphia, my wife heard these words from the Lord Jesus, "Do it for America . . . Coming down, the country is bloated." Our experience in the Old City this time, confirmed the sad state of the country, that it has become a faithless nation, disdaining the God of the Bible, Jesus, and the faith of our Founding Fathers.

At the Quaker Meeting House in the Old City, the tour guide there had shared with us previously, that he did not believe Jesus was the Son of God. Today, many at that meeting house, he reported to us, shared his similar beliefs in the Quaker denomination. There meetings were held monthly without men sharing messages to the congregation about Jesus.

At the Visitor's Center, we viewed the start of a movie called, *Independence*. We left the movie shortly after it began. For the term "ghosts" of the past was used for bringing back Founding Fathers; Benjamin Franklin, Thomas Jefferson, George Washington, Benjamin Rush, Thomas Paine, and others to the modern era in Philadelphia. There was no reference to their faith in Almighty God, in Providence, in the Creator, in Jesus Christ. We sensed this movie had ramifications of the occult, dark elements, consulting with the dead from the past (Dt 18:10-12; Isa 8:19,20).

The Curator at Christ Church in the Old City did not promote the Christian faith of the Founding Fathers. When we asked him about any information regarding their faith in Jesus Christ, he avoided our questions. At the National Historical Museum, there were many portraits of the Founding Fathers on display. We read the history of many of those Founding Fathers. There were not any indications in those captions, that they had a faith in Jesus Christ. Only on one caption of a man named, William White, the rector of Christ Church, was there mention of his ministry in the Old City.

At the National Liberty Museum, an elderly lady was the receptionist there. When we asked her about the faith of the Founding Fathers in Jesus Christ, she commented to us that she did not know of any information regarding their Christian faith. A middle-aged park ranger at the Visitor's Center responded in a similar way to our question. That ranger stated also, that he was not aware of any information on the Christian faith of our Founding Fathers, but he directed us over to Christ Church.

We experienced that the name of Jesus, and the Christian faith of the Founding Fathers, has all but been removed from the Old City in Philadelphia. The worldly influences, and commercialism were evident in the Old City; the selling of 'patriotic' flags, T-shirts, and banners, all brightly colored with red, white and blue. But, the true liberator of America, Jesus, and the cause of those men that fought for liberty were not evident at all! (Mt 24:10; Lk 4:18[KJV]; Jn 15:18,19; 1 Ti 4:1; 2 Ti 4:3,4).

On August 18, 2000, "Chief Justice Roy Moore" of Alabama shared a "poem" . . . at a "Ten Commandments Rally." These are excerpts from that poem:

"So with a firm reliance on Divine
Providence for protection,
They pledged their sacred honor
And sought His wise direction.

They lifted an appeal to God
for all the world to see,
And declared their independence
forever to be free.

I'm glad they're not here with us
to see the mess we're in,
How we've given up our righteousness
for a life of indulgent sin.

For when abortion isn't murder
and sodomy is deemed a right,
Then evil is now called good
and darkness is now called light.

But with man as his own master
we fail to count the cost,
Our precious freedoms vanish
and our liberty is lost."[302]

Today, "with man as his own master," even "believers" in Jesus Christ are leaving the faith of our forefathers and Founding Fathers. In March 2011, it was reported, "America (in) the last half century, (has) scrapped the Judeo-Christian worldview that has, from our founding, helped provide moral guidance, and exchanged it for 'anything goes' moral relativism . . . Historically, worldviews that have no place for God have led to deadly consequences."[303]

It was further noted, "Barna Research reports that only nine percent of Americans subscribe to a biblical worldview . . . Just 19 percent of born again Christians . . . think biblically . . . (The) Church . . . has become tolerant of a vast array of morally and spiritually dubious behaviors and philosophies."[304] (Mt 24:10,24; Ac 20:30,31; Gal 1:6,7; 2 Th 2:9-12; 1 Ti 4:1). It is apparent that many, even "believers" in Jesus, are turning away from the true Liberator, and the Word of God in these last days.

As we come to the end of "America Present," our forefathers, the Pilgrims left their homeland of England in order to freely worship God, according to their understanding of the Scriptures, and to escape from the hypocrisy of the Church of England. Today, true believers in Jesus in America may find themselves "in the same boat" as the Pilgrims.

It is interesting to note, that on February 23, 2009, we hung a framed painting in our living room, "The Embarkation of the Pilgrims," embarking from Holland to America. On February 26, 2009, after we had been fasting and praising the Lord Jesus, I was given some visions. In the first vision, I saw what appeared to be "the Mayflower," that the Pilgrims traveled on to America. On the main sail was a red cross. A long pencil represented the mast of the ship, and it was connected to the main sail at the top and the bottom. The Mayflower was leaving the eastern coastline of America heading out towards the northeast.

In the vision, my wife and I were in the Mayflower with Pilgrims, who had troubled faces. It was as if they had no place or direction to go to. Then I saw a vision of Jesus standing on the eastern, New England shore cooking fish over hot coals. He was waving the Pilgrims on that ship to come into landing there. An aerial vision followed of the town in Missouri, where my maternal grandparents lived all their lives together. Then I saw what appeared to be the inside of my wife's paternal grandmother's home.

The Lord Jesus then said, "Pilgrims left tyrannical England and then Holland, so they could worship and honor God, Jesus, freely without men's restrictions placed on them. Pilgrims are leaving America, because similar prohibitions and restrictions are being placed on them for honoring Jesus. So I am giving you the freedom to sail away to a place, where you will have freedom to worship God, and speak about Jesus freely and openly. Yet, the Pilgrims are troubled because they have discovered that they have no place to travel to (Ps 55:4-8; 12:14,16-22; Mt 19:29,30; Ac 4:18,19; 8:1).

"With (God's) pencil, you will write this in the book. Several of My disciples felt there was no place to go with Jesus after His death, and (some disciples) after His resurrection. They chose to go fishing again. But as Jesus was cooking fish on the shoreline, so He waved them in off the boat to have a place with Him. There are places in the United States that will worship Me freely, and speak about Me openly. I have called you to a new place on the east coast, just as I called the Pilgrims to anchor off Plymouth Rock (Hab 2:2,3; Mt 26:56; Jn 16:7; 21:3-14; Ac 20:29-31; 2 Pe 2:1,2).

"You will find refuge in a safe haven anchored in Christ Jesus. It is a place of understanding, a place of purity, a place of enjoyment, a place of freedom, a place in your hearts where God is taking you both, as you come with a repentant heart before the Lord. A place to embrace your mate like honeymooners, daily (Ps 107:29,30; Ecc 9:8; Mt 11:28-30; Ac 3:19,20; 2 Co 6:6; Heb 6:19,20).

"You remembered that your grandparents' hometown was filled with good smells, holy living and peace, because you found place with Me there in Jesus. Your wife found place with Me, a place of purity and holy living at her grandmother's home. As Pilgrims in a foreign land, you still have place with Me in America" (Mk 10:13-16; 2 Ti 4:17; 2 Pe 3:11,12). It is good to have a place near Jesus, as we now move into America's Future.

Will the American people turn to the faith of their forefathers, their Founding Fathers, and believing patriots, to the true Liberator, Jesus, as we move into the Future of this country? Or will America follow the prophetic utterance of the former President of the United States, George Washington, when he proclaimed at his first Inaugural address:

"The propitious smiles of heaven can never be expected on a nation, which disregards the eternal rules of order and right, which heaven itself has ordained!"[305]

[PART III]

★

AMERICA: FUTURE

THE STAR SPANGLED BANNER

★

"Oh, Thus be it ever when free men shall
stand Between there loved homes and the war's desolation;
Blest with victory and peace, May the Heav'n rescued land
Praise the Power that hath made and preserved us a nation!

Then conquer we must, when our cause it is just;
And this be our motto: 'In God is our trust!'
And the Star Spangled Banner in triumph shall wave
O'er the land of the free, and the home of the brave."[1]

(Verse 4)

. 15 .

AND A GREAT STORM AROSE

> "Thou shalt be visited of the Lord of hosts
> with thunder, and with earthquake, and great noise,
> with storm and tempest, and the flame
> of devouring fire."

What is in store for the United States of America in the future? Early in the morning of August 1, 2009, my wife received a vision from the Lord Jesus of an American flag furled up in the midst of dark clouds in the sky. There appeared to be some strength left in the furled flag, but other parts of the flag were hidden behind the clouds. It is significant to note, that in the painting, "The Embarkation of the Pilgrims," the sky is foreboding with dark clouds, when the Pilgrims left Holland, traveling to America.

That morning, the Lord Jesus said, "The United States is entering into a dark period in their history. As the tattered American flag withstood the bombing of Fort McHenry from the foreign nation, England (in 1814), so America is going to experience a period of bombing on her homeland from foreign nations. The skies will become darker in the days ahead. When this happens, look to the heavenlies, to Jesus, to bring His light into the dark places in America" (Lk 21:9,28; Jn 12:35,36; 2 Pe 1:19).

A dark storm, we believe, is coming to the United States and throughout the world. That storm, we believe will be used by Satan to establish a world government under his rule. In the book of Revelation, it is written that, "Men worshiped the dragon because he had given authority to the beast." In the Bible, "the dragon" is "called the devil, or Satan, who leads the whole world astray." In the last days, it is written that, "no one (can) buy or sell unless he had the mark, which is the name of the beast or the number of his name" (Lk 8:23,24; Rev 12:7-9; 13:4,16,17).

The Lord Jesus revealed to us, that in "the great tribulation," a world government and "World Church" will be established, which will include the United States. It will become a "police state" under "the dragon," Satan, where no one can buy or sell. America has been warned about a coming "storm." We are experiencing the rumblings of thunder already in the American economy (Mt 3:7; Mk 4:37,38; Rev 7:14; 13:11-15).

Warnings of a Coming Storm

On April 20, 2008, as I, (Mark) was sitting in a congregation during a Sunday service, I saw a vision of the earth covered by red paint. The Lord Jesus revealed to me, that this was like the logo of Sherwin Williams paint company, "Cover the Earth." Red paint was at the end of a paint brush, which was in the air next to the earth. Over one half of the earth was covered with red paint.

The Lord then said, "The Lord Jesus has covered the earth by His shed blood. America has been covered in the blood of Jesus since its founding, and those true believers in Jesus are still covered in His blood. But God is lifting His covering over the earth, because America, like other countries, has chosen other 'gods,' and not the true Lord Jesus Christ. You will see manifestations of the lifting of this covering in America." The following day, we discovered that in the logo for Sherwin Williams, red paint covered most of the earth, just like in the vision (Dt 29:18; Mt 26:28; Ro 4:7; Col 1:20; Rev 12:11).

In the morning of November 9, 2007, I saw a vision of a church during the Colonial times. There was a radio tower extending out from the church roof. The Lord then reminded me that Paul Revere warned the people that the British were coming, when lanterns were lit in a church tower. The Lord then disclosed, "Be like Paul Revere. He was a 'minute man.' When he saw the lanterns in the church, he rode off to warn the people 'in every middlesex, village and farm.' So when I call you to warn the people, that the United States will be attacked, be ready and alert!" (Isa 21:6-8; Eze 33:3; Mk 13:33).

The Lord revealed further on December 25, 1995, Christmas Day, that "The foreshadowing signs of the end-times are right before your eyes. Look at the world now! The financial conditions of most countries are desperately lacking. The European community is stepping up its plan to control those nations, financially. Look at your country, the government's debt is at phenomenally high figures. The government cannot make money fast enough to overcome the surmounting debt in America, a country in debt with itself (Pr 22:26; Hab 2:7; Mt 24:14).

"Deceit is increasing in the world. Politicians are more interested in getting re-elected, than in faithfully serving their country. Many of their forefathers did serve their country in the past. Deception will be disguised as a 'spirit of contentment,' when the world deals with troubled times ahead. This 'contentment' will be embraced by men and women in a desperately trying world. The world will look to man, and idolize a created being, Satan's plan from the beginning of time. But, My true gift to men and women in these last days is My Word, (is Jesus), who brings freedom from 'deceitful workmen,' who will bind themselves to the world, to the enemy" (Pr 11:18; Eze 13:10; 2 Co 11:13-15; 2 Th 2:3,9-11; 2 Ti 3:16,17; Rev 12:9[KJV]).

God's Judgments

Pastor David Wilkerson has shared about a dark storm coming to America in his messages at Times Square Church in New York City. Pastor Wilkerson disclosed in February 2007, "In recent weeks I have received prophecies from unknown but godly ministers . . . These shepherds are warning, 'A great disaster is coming upon us soon and suddenly. It will be so devastating, the world is going to shudder. Things will never be the same.' . . . A noted TV evangelist . . . said, God revealed to him that a sudden terrorist attack is coming soon to the United States, and that multitudes will be killed. A similar prophecy was given nationwide by another respected TV evangelist"[2] (Gen 19:12-17; Pr 6:15; Isa 45:7; 1 Pe 5:2; Rev 18:10).

Pastor Wilkerson shared further, "Terrorism is escalating . . . Iran and North Korea are racing to build nuclear arsenals, with Iran threatening to wipe Israel off the map . . . Any threat of U.N. sanctions is a joke . . . National security leaders are sending out alerts in the U.S. . . . Top security people are warning of a possible dirty bomb to be set off by terrorists . . . A dreadful day of reckoning is at the door, yet most people—including multitudes of Christians—don't want to talk . . . about it."[3]

Pastor Wilkerson said in a message on February 2009, "All over the world people are desperately searching for a safe place to hide their money. Multitudes are buying guns to protect their families for what they believe will be a dark time (ahead), . . . these include Bible-believing Christians . . . 'In the latter times some shall depart from the faith' . . . The love of many believers will grow cold or lukewarm. Others will lose their faith altogether and fall away from Christ" in the last days[4] (Joel 3:10; Mt 24:10-12; 1 Ti 4:1; Rev 3:16; 18:11-13).

In March 2009, Pastor Wilkerson sent out "An Urgent Message." He revealed that, "'An Earth—Shattering Calamity Is About To Happen. It Is Going To Be So Frightening, We Are All Going To Tremble—Even The Godliest Among Us' . . . For ten years I have been warning about a thousand fires coming to New York City . . . Major cities all across America will experience riots and blazing fires . . . There will be looting . . . We are under God's wrath . . . God is judging the raging sins of America and the nations. He is destroying the secular foundations . . . This is a righteous judgment—just as in the judgments of Sodom and in Noah's generation . . . I know it is not far off . . . I have unburdened my soul to you"[5] (Gen 6:13; 7:11,12; 19:24,25; Jer 50:32[KJV]; Rev 16:8,9; 20:9[b]).

Pastor Wilkerson also revealed in September 2008, "When darkness covers the earth—when men's hearts fail them with fear over all the dreadful things happening, . . . in the darkest hour, when things look hopeless, . . . in a world gone mad—when radical Islamics boast they have prevailed . . . Jesus Christ will rise up. And He will shine as a healing Sun, brighter than in all past generations . . . The devil knows the Scriptures, and he knows that a genuine, Holy Spirit-inspired revival of healing, . . . the last—day outpouring of the Spirit . . . is prophesied"[6] (Joel 2:28,29; Mal 4:2,3; Lk 21:26-28; 23:44; Ac 2:17,18).

In the book of Jeremiah, the Lord proclaimed, "I will pronounce my judgments on my people because of their wickedness in forsaking me." We understand through the Scriptures, that later in the book of Jeremiah, the Jewish people experienced famine, death, and the burning and destruction of the temple in Jerusalem. In the New Testament, Jesus declared that the temple of Jerusalem would again be destroyed, "every . . . stone . . . (would) be thrown down" for the Jewish people "were not willing" . . . "to gather" . . . "under" the Lordship of Jesus. We know that the temple was destroyed in 70 A.D. by Roman soldiers (Jer 1:16; 52:6-14; Lk 13:34; 21:6).

Also, it is written in the Scriptures that, "Sodom and Gomorrah and the surrounding towns gave themselves up to sexual immorality and perversion. They serve as an example of those who suffer the punishment of eternal fire." Almighty God judges peoples and nations throughout the Bible, who disobey His commandments, who do not listen to the warnings of His prophets, and who follow other "gods." America, we believe, has forsaken the founder of this country, our Lord Jesus, and, we believe that severe judgments are, and will come in these last days (Dt 11:7,16; 28:15-19; Jer 7:8-11,18-20; 52:13; Jude 7).

Our Lord Jesus has revealed to us, His warnings after we had fasted and praised the Lord on May 9, and September 25, 2008, and on August 6, and July 30, 2009. On May 9, my wife heard the words, "America is becoming sickly." That morning, I saw a vision of a picture we have in our Colonial room. A woman in this picture is mending a 13-star American flag. A man is sitting in a chair wearing a Revolutionary War officer's uniform. This man in the vision had an enlarged belly under his uniform. A vision followed of a Revolutionary War soldier in uniform walking through a pile of mud. Then I saw a vision of a hawk with the face of an owl.

The Lord then disclosed, "'America is becoming sickly,' because they, (men and women), are unwilling to exert themselves to proclaim righteousness and right living in the land. They would rather 'sit' down at their computers, 'sit' in front of their television sets, play their video games, and then come and serve the living God. They would rather 'sit' in their homes, than search for and attend a church where I am honored. They would rather 'sit' down on the job. America is a 'sick' nation, (whose people) have chosen to serve other 'gods,' fleshly pursuits, electronic devices in a 'sit down' way, a sickly way, rather than to (follow the Way) to serve their God in this country (Ps 1:1; Pr 6:6-11; 20:4; Ro 11:8; 1 Co 11:30; Rev 3:15-17).

"In the United States there will be a 'revolution' against their own people. There will be a revolution in America in which the police and the National Guard will not be able to quell. It will be like a 'civil war.' This country's own people will be fighting against each other in a battle for survival. In fact, there will be a time when the 'hawks' will be shooting down the 'doves' in America. America, like the owl, is choosing the night for its prey, the 'night owl,' instead of the day (to pray to the one true God) (Lev 11:13-18; Job 30:29; Mk 1:10; 13:12,13; Lk 21:9; Jn 3:19).

"The haunts in America will haunt their own people, because they would rather make 'gods' of themselves. Many follow their own selfish ways, rather than humble themselves, repent, and ask for forgiveness. You will see a war between 'truckers,' (truck drivers) in America, and American citizens. A war caused by the increase in fuel prices (2 Ch 7:14; Isa 34:11-15; Rev 18:2).

"America was ordained by God to fight the Revolutionary War against the tyrannical 'Great' Britain. Americans will, in the future, fight against themselves, because of their own tyranny against God in this country. Those who fought in the Revolutionary War would be walking through 'mud' in this country today. The 'mud,' the self-pride of men and women in the land of America today, is a reason that America will fall" (2 Ch 20:22,23; Isa 57:20; Ob 1-4; Lk 21:16; Ja 4:1,2; 2 Pe 2:22).

Early in the morning of September 25, my wife heard these words from the Lord Jesus, "Across the United States . . . I saw America fall like lightning." That morning I was given some visions from the Lord Jesus. In the first vision, I saw a kite like the one Ben Franklin reportedly flew in the air. A key was at the end of the kite. Lightning struck in the sky and went down through this key. A man holding the key appeared to be electrified. A vision followed of the burning of the city of Atlanta during the time of the Civil War. In the next vision, I saw red flags planted in the ground throughout the Midwestern states. Bulldozers and other large construction vehicles came to a halt in the Midwest.

A vision followed of a great conflagration, fighting among Americans throughout the United States. Then I saw believing Christians holding green flags, as they were moving in the air. A vision followed of the character, Charles Ingalls in one of the episodes from the *Little House on the Prairie*[7] television show. He was speaking in the pulpit to the congregation in their church. Then I saw a vision through a window pane of the Ingalls' house. The Ingalls' children were laughing and playing with each other in the vision, while Charles Ingalls and his wife were reading the Bible.

Finally, I saw a vision of myself about 18 years old in a colonial outfit wearing a three-cornered hat, standing on a large rock. The place that I was standing at appeared to be Boston, Massachusetts during the time period of the Revolutionary War. In the vision, my wife was standing next to the rock wearing a white bonnet and a colonial dress looking up at me. She appeared to be 18 years old. It appeared to me in the vision, that I was preaching and warning people, who were standing around the rock near us.

The Lord Jesus then disclosed, "'I saw Satan fall like lightning from heaven.' 'I saw America fall like lightning.' When lightning strikes, because the United States is not grounded in the Word of God, not grounded on the Rock, Jesus, it will fall, cities will fall. Some cities will burn for they have rejected the God of the Bible. Across the United States, Americans will suffer financial woes. America will be shut down over night. (America) will come to a 'stop.' America has been warned by prophets and believers in this country to turn back to the living God, to repent. Many will refuse to change, and there will be a great conflagration among the American people. Yet, there will be those who carry green flags, those who 'go' with Jesus in the spiritual realms, who will gain victories in villages, towns, and cities, just like (the character), Charles Ingalls preached about in one of the *Little House on the Prairie* (television) shows (Jer 37:8-10; Eze 33:9,11; Mt 7:26,27; Lk 10:18; Ro 2:4,7,8; Jude 20-23; Rev 18:10,17).

"Today, you rarely see families together reading the Bible and playing with one another. Families, today, are disunited from one another. Satan has pulled them apart through worldly devices, and other things, other 'gods.' You see that the fall in the family, is a fall in America (Mt 12:25,26; Ro 16:17; 1 Co 11:18).

"Believers, like yourselves, will be standing on the Rock, preaching to crowds to 'Turn to Jesus,' to repent, to turn from their wicked ways, to turn to the true God of heaven, (and) to not tolerate other 'gods.' The proud hearted Americans will fall, those who do not need God, those who have become their own 'gods.' Many believers in Jesus will not want to offend them, but I came to offend the unrighteousness, to offend evil, to offend Satan. It is right to offend wickedness, and stand on that 'Rock of Righteousness,' just like the patriot saints did during the Revolutionary War" (Isa 2:17,18; 26:4; 30:15; Jer 23:6; Mt 4:10; 9:11-13; 23:1-39; 24:10[KJV]; Lk 6:48; Ac 2:36-41).

Early in the morning on August 6, 2009, God revealed to me, Phyllis, the last verse in chapter 1 of the book of Job in the Bible. Job lost everything, but he did not blame God. He humbled himself, fell down to the ground, and worshiped God. The Lord showed me in the second chapter of Job, that three of his friends left their homes, places of comfort, and came to mourn with Job. Those three "friends" sat on the ground with Job for seven days and nights. Job's grief was so painful, that those "friends" did not say a word to him. The Lord revealed that He wants us to be able to leave our place of comfort, and be with those in need and in pain during the dark times ahead (Job 1:23; 2:11-13).

That morning, my wife and I observed a large hawk viciously digging into the body of a dove with its talons. We were looking at this from our Colonial room window. The hawk and dove were on our sidewalk about ten feet from us. When we rapped on our window to startle the hawk, the hawk glared at us in an arrogant manner. The dove was able to free itself from the talons of the hawk, and fly a short distance. The hawk then flew after the dove, attacking it with its talons again to kill the dove. It was an eerie scene.

God gave me, Mark, some visions that morning. In the first vision, I saw a Pony Express rider. He was riding speedily on a horse. As he was riding, I saw a train stopped on railroad tracks. Men wearing masks were robbing the people on that train. In the next vision, I saw my wife and me standing together on the earth looking up at the sun. The sun was blocked in an eclipse by a darkened moon. The earth was darkened like the nighttime. The sun was in close proximity to the earth with its hot fiery rays coming out towards the earth from around the moon. A vision followed of people running in fear in a major city.

Then I saw a vision of large trucks and cars stopped on the Golden Gate Bridge in San Francisco. The cars were backed up several miles. The Lord Jesus then reminded me of the earthquake that hit the Bay Bridge, the bridge that connects Oakland to San Francisco in California. The earthquake occurred during the baseball World Series in San Francisco. The Bay Bridge collapsed in different places, and many people died during that earthquake. A revelation followed of the first chapter of the book of Job, when Job was praying for his sons and daughters. Tragedies occurred that day in Job's life after he had prayed.

The Lord Jesus then shared, "As the Pony Express riders carried mail/messages throughout America, so God wants you to warn America about those who are robbers of the truth, enemies of God. In the last days, the sun will be darkened. There will be a darkness over the land, and the hot Son's rays will strike in wrath on the earth. Signs of birth pains occurred during the earthquake in San Francisco, a judgment against wickedness there. Just as you watched the World Series, you have and will hear about a 'series' of earthquakes in the 'world.' For God is judging this world for its blatant disdain towards Him and His Word (Isa 60:2; Joel 3:15; Mt 24:7,8; Jn 1:5; Ac 20:29-31; Ro 1:18).

"The 'hawkish' people in America and the world are, (and will be) destroying, killing Christians represented by the 'dove,' those who have the Holy Spirit. The 'hawks are attacking 'doves,' Christians. The Islamic terrorists are bent on destroying Christians and Jewish people. As you rapped on the window to startle the hawk, it glared at you. So the United States negotiates with Islamic terrorists, who glare like 'hawks,' unmercifully out for blood. America has become a 'dove' nation, not in the sense of being Christian, but in the sense of being weaker, cowardly, anti-Christian, antichrist. 'Hawkish' power, terrorists and bullies, will reign over a nation unwilling to stand up for righteousness (Dt 14:12,15; Pr 28:12[b],28; Lk 3:21,22; Jn 10:10[a]; Ac 9:1; Eph 6:13; 2 Ti 4:16,18; 1 Jn 2:18).

"In the last days, people will be eating and drinking like Job's sons and daughters, and tragedy will strike America and the world. God will send pestilence, plagues, and sicknesses like Job experienced, allowing Satan to have his way on the earth. For America and the world of nations are serving 'the god of this world,' rather than the one true God, Jesus. America will be restored when Jesus returns" (Job 1:12-19; Zec 14:6-9; Lk 17:27; 21:11; 2 Co 4:4[KJV]; Rev 15:1).

A Christian Holocaust

Our Lord Jesus has revealed to us judgments coming to America, a coming storm. We believe that true Christians in America will be despised and hated in the days ahead. We have reported in the "America: Present" section of our book, that already, many Americans, government "leaders" oppose God, the name of Jesus, and the Word of God. Our Lord Jesus shared that in the last days, "You will be handed over to be persecuted and put to death, and you will be hated by all nations because of me. At that time many will turn away from the faith and will betray and hate each other" (Mt 8:24; 24:9,10; Ac 4:18; 1 Jn 3:13).

The Lord Jesus disclosed further, "Brother will betray brother to death, and a father his child. Children will rebel against their parents and have them put to death. All men will hate you because of me . . . In fact, a time is coming when anyone who kills you will think he is offering a service to God." Our Lord has given us revelations of this happening in America and throughout the world in the future (Mk 13:12,13; Jn 16:2).

Throughout the past two milleniums, millions of true Christian believers and Jewish people have been murdered at different times. More recently, in some of the communist countries, and in some of the Middle East and African countries that are considered Muslim nations, Christians and Jews are being persecuted and killed today, which has been reported by numerous Christian organizations, and by the media at times. We believe it is just a matter of time before these acts of violence/murder will occur in the United States of America.

Still, we believe that our Lord Jesus will continue to make provision for His people in these last days. For God has said, "Never will I leave you; never will I forsake you." As we "abide in" Him, He will "abide in" us and protect us. For we believe there will be a mighty outpouring of the Holy Spirit on believers in our Lord Jesus during the last days; to heal deep wounds and pain, to perform "signs, wonders and miracles," and to "show" forth His "all surpassing power" and love to His own children. We believe He will eventually thwart the rising antichrist spirit in America and the world (Lk 10:33,34; Jn 14:23; 15:4[KJV]; Ac 2:17; 2 Co 4:7; 12:12; Heb 13:5; Rev 19:11-16).

Yet, we pray that we may "not shrink from death" in the last days, just like the soldiers during the Revolutionary War, who shed their blood for freedom, for liberty! We pray to stand "firm to the end," so we "will be saved." We pray to "be ready" when our Lord Jesus, "the Son of Man," gathers "his elect" to Himself in "the clouds." For we know that "the devil . . . is filled with fury because he knows that his time is short," and that "the dragon (is) enraged at . . . those who obey God's commandments and hold to the testimony of Jesus" (Mt 24:30,31,44; Mk 13:13; Col 1:20; Rev 12:11,12,17).

On July 30, 2009, the Lord Jesus gave me some visions. In the first vision, I saw a dark sky in the daytime. A tree was bent over by the wind, and then it righted itself up. There was a light shining on the tree in the midst of a dark storm. Then I saw a vision of Roman soldiers from the first century carrying shields. The soldiers were marching in formation down what appeared to be a major city street in New York City, today. A vision followed of the back side of a $1 dollar bill. The "eye" on the pyramid was pronounced on the dollar bill. That eye then turned into an "eye" of an evil monster, a beast.

Then I saw a vision of two middle-aged women wearing scarves bending over a baby. They were going to hide the baby by placing it in a basket. The Lord then reminded me of the Ten Boom family in the movie, *The Hiding Place*.[8] (During World War II the Ten Boom family placed a Jewish baby in a basket. Through an "underground" system in Holland, the Ten Boom family was able to hide many Jewish people and babies.) Finally, I saw a vision from the movie, *Fiddler on the Roof*,[9] when the Jewish people were being displaced from their homes, herded up in groups, and walked away, hopefully to find a refuge in other countries. (On May 26, 2008, I saw a vision of a picture we have hanging on a wall in our dining room. In that picture, a humble couple from Eastern Europe was planting crops in a dusty, "drought-ridden" area, where there was no sign of plant life. That couple, from years past, was praying together.)

The Lord Jesus revealed, "A great storm is coming. God will give true believers His light to see in the dark days ahead. The revived Roman Empire is infiltrating the United States at this time with a 'world consciousness.' The nations that are forming up a 'union,' will begin to take control of America, as the Romans had done in the past in Palestine/Israel (Da 2:41-43; Mt 8:24; 20:25; Jn 1:9; 12:35; Rev 17:8-14).

"In the last days the United States will become like a policed nation through a world 'union.' The 'eye' polices its people. 'Fix (your) eyes on Jesus.' Keep your eyes on the 'underground,' on

God's provision, not man's. Christians and Jews will be herded up by 'leaders' of the police state. It is coming to America. Jewish and Christian babies will need protection through the 'underground' (Ex 2:2; Job 24:4; Pr 3:7; 28:12[b]; Mt 18:10; Lk 16:15; 18:15-17; 1 Ti 6:17; Heb 12:2; Rev 13:14-17).

"Just as the Jews were rounded up in Eastern Europe, so will Christians be rounded up in the United States, and in other countries. They will be taken away from their homes, and their 'land.' Yet, God is rounding up His true believers to spare them from what is coming on the earth, a drought from the Word of God" (Am 8:11,12; Mk 10:29-31; Ac 8:1; 9:1,2; 1 Th 4:15-18). Received May 22, 2008.

On July 30, 2010, I saw a night vision of a desert area with wind blowing dry bushes and tumbleweeds. The Lord Jesus shared, "America has become like Egypt of old, choosing other 'gods,' choosing to kill their babies, choosing the world over the Hebrew God, Yeshua, Jesus. America, like (ancient) Egypt will suffer a major drought, for they have chosen the night, instead of the day, darkness instead of light. The land will become dry and barren, and I say, 'Let My People Go!' Let the Jewish people go to their homeland, Israel. Let My believers go from the clutches of the enemy, Satan, in America" (Gen 1:3-5; 41:53-57; Ex 1:15,22; 3:18; 5:1; Jer 17:8; Mt 24:7).

On September 6, 2007, I, Mark, saw a vision of the Empire State Building. There was an electric probe sticking out from the top of the building, and it appeared to be like a radio tower. That probe was electrified. I then saw a vision of the character, Ruby Bridges in the true story portrayed in the movie, *Ruby Bridges*.[10]

The Lord Jesus said, "God is giving you a warning for America. A time is coming when Christians will be abused and hated in America, similar to what Ruby Bridges experienced, (as revealed in the movie, *Ruby Bridges*.) In the last days, there will be such a hatred for Jesus, for Christianity, for the Christians that do not accept the Antichrist. The police will hate them too, and will not hold back mobs in the streets (ready to attack) Christians. Ruby Bridges endured her persecution with Jesus, and with her mother and father's support in Jesus. Ruby's mother shared (in the movie), 'Bless those who curse you. Pray for them, for they know not what they are doing.' Pray daily for your persecutors. As you do this, God will be with you and bless you. Help each other, when one is attacked by the enemy. Do not return 'evil for evil, or railing for railing,'" (but return a "blessing") (Job 1:9-11; Mt 5:44; Lk 6:27,28; 21:17; 23:34; 1 Pe 3:9[KJV]; Rev 12:17).

Another foreshadowing of coming Christian persecution in America took place in San Diego County, California. We have already reported an antichrist spirit growing rapidly across the United States. Chuck Norris, the actor, reported in an article on June 1, 2009, that "a California pastor and his wife (were) required by San Diego County officials to obtain a permit to hold a Bible study in their home." The pastor and his wife received a "citation claiming that (they) were guilty of 'unlawful use of land,' mandating them to 'stop religious assembly.'" After "hundreds of complaints, . . . officials . . . backed down from requiring (them) to obtain a permit . . . America's First Amendment rights are progressively being trampled."[11]

The New World Order

According to our Lord Jesus, "the great tribulation" will be an extremely dangerous time for Christians. Yet, how could this happen in "the home of the brave," and "the land of the free," the United States of America? We believe Satan has had a plan for years to regain America for himself, and to overthrow the one true liberator, Jesus Christ in this land. Author and former "high ranking government liaison" official, Gary Kah, sheds some interesting light on a "New World Order" coming to America and to the world in his book, *En Route to Global Occupation*[12] (Gen 3:1-5,14,15; Lk 4:5-8; Rev 7:14).

Gary Kah wrote, "More than ten thousand hours of research have led me to conclude that we are rapidly being pushed toward a one-world government by powerful Luciferic forces rooted in age-old secret societies, . . . (known) as the New World Order . . . Preparations (are) being made for the New World Order in the United States . . . This movement (has been) economic in nature, (and contains) a political dimension, (as well as a) . . . spiritual motivation . . . The relentless strategies employed by the prince of this world (are) to bring humanity under his rule"[13] (Ex 7:8; Isa 14:12[KJV]; Mt 4:8-11; Jn 14:30; Eph 6:11).

Freemasonry

Mr. Kah wrote further that, "An organization known as the Illuminati . . . was a secret Luciferic order founded . . . on 1 May 1776 by . . . a prominent Freemason, (just prior to the signing of the Declaration of Independence in Philadelphia) . . . Members had been initiated into the secret teachings of Lucifer, the supposed light-bearer, . . . according to the doctrines of illuminized Freemasonry . . . The Illuminati had been designed for one purpose . . . to create a New World Order . . . Initiates were . . . sworn to secrecy, taking bloody oaths . . . Illuminized Freemasonry, (were) European forces (that) began efforts to bring America's . . . banking system under their control . . . In 1913, the persistent efforts of illuminized Freemasonry . . . (ensured) European Illuminists a permanent role in America's finances . . . (through) the creation of the Federal Reserve System"[14] (Mt 5:33-37; 2 Co 11:14,15; 1 Ti 6:10; 2 Pe 2:1-3; Rev 2:24).

He revealed more, "One of the illuminized Freemasonry's secret symbols . . . was placed on the back of our dollar bill . . . This symbol was designed by Masonic interests and became the official reverse side of the Great Seal of the United States in 1782 . . . This Masonic symbol consists of a pyramid with an all-seeing eye of (the "gods") Osiris or Baal ... (Under the pyramid are Latin words meaning), 'The New World Order' ... Once the New World Order has been built and the one-world government is in place, the capstone will be joined to the rest of the pyramid ... The hierarchy of Freemasonry and the occult societies, resembling a multi-level pyramid structure, will ... be complete, with the Antichrist taking his seat of power atop of the pyramid"[15] (Ex 8:7,18; Ezc 13:20; Da 2:22; Lk 20:17; 2 Th 2:4,9; Rev 21:8).

Gary Kah reported that most "of its ... million-plus members in this country think of it as a noble and virtuous society, ... that Freemasonry is a Christian institution ... The history of Freemasonry ... was also the history of the secret societies ... of organized occultism—particularly in the Western world ... The occult teachings have been handed down from generation to generation, ... kept alive in the Western world by the secret societies ... Satan's plan (has been) to keep his priesthood and secret doctrines alive ... The central theme of Freemasonry is universality, an attempt to unite all the world's religions under one umbrella ... It conveniently demotes Jesus Christ from being the Son of God. ... Freemasonry subtly conditions its members to accept the false belief that all religions are pathways to the same God, rendering Christ's atonement on the cross ... meaningless"[16] (Ex 7:22; Mal 1:6-8; Mt 7:15-20; 26:63-66; Jn 14:6; Ac 4:12; 19:18,19; 20:29-31; 2 Co 11:13-15; 1 Jn 2:18,19; Rev 13:11,12; 16:13).

In a newsletter of October 2010, John Whitehead, President of "The Rutherford Institute," revealed information on the "all-seeing eye." He shared, "The emergence of a semi-police state ... seeks to track our every movement ....The government's growing arsenal of weapons and invasive technologies is being trained on the American people; satellites, so sophisticated ... can read a postage stamp lying on the ground from outer space ... Powerful computers with speech recognition technology ... enables the government to eavesdrop on phone calls ... The government ... is also edging closer and closer to requiring every citizen to carry a national ID card that will possess the most intimate information about us."[17]

John Whitehead further shared, "The National Security Agency (NSA) ... collects ... vast amounts of ... information (with) a computer system known as 'Aquaint,' which is then used to detect patterns and predict behavior ... The NSA (sends this information) to other intelligence agencies, which then share the data with the local police ... We are all increasingly being viewed and treated like enemies of the state."[18]

He reported, in a "2009 report issued by the Department of Homeland Security (DHS), (it) defines a right-wing extremist as individuals and groups 'that are mainly antigovernment, rejecting federal authority in favor of state or local authority,' ... a term it uses interchangeably with 'terrorist' ... It's midnight in America right now."[19] The "all-seeing eye" in America is truly becoming a reality, today.

World Organizations

The beliefs of Freemasonry has been moving upon "leaders" of the world towards the establishment of a world government. Gary Kah revealed further, "The World Constitution and Parliament Association (WCPA) was founded in 1959 in ... Colorado ... The WCPA's plan, which includes a ten region world government, ... calling for a new international monetary system, (has been) referred to as the 'New World Economic Order' ... The WCPA's leadership is (the) World Union, ... (an organization) joined with World Good-will—a creation of Lucis Trust—in 1961, ... (or Lucifer) Trust ... (It) is plugged into the highest levels of Freemasonry"[20] (Isa 14:12[KJV]; Da 7:20-25; Rev 17:12).

The "World Council of Churches, ... collaborating with (the WCPA) is (an) organization," ... Mr. Kah reported, that represents, "the leadership of most of the mainline Protestant church denominations in America and has privately been pushing for unification with the Church of Rome, (the Roman Catholic Church) . . . (This) organization is strongly influenced by Freemasonry . . . The Council has been . . . active in promoting interfaithism—the merging of all the world's major religions under one umbrella, . . . (which has been) necessary in order to bring humanity into a world government"[21] (2 Co 11:3,4; Gal 1:6-9).

Gary Kah declared further that, "The United Nations" represents almost all the nations of the world. Within the United Nations' structure are "the World Court, the U.N. peacekeeping forces, . . . the International Monetary Fund (IMF), the World Bank, (and) the World Health Organization (WHO)."[22] As the United States and other countries experience national and global debt; and as world hunger, natural disasters, earth quakes, famines, need for oil from Middle East countries, and wars both in the name of religions and for land access, as well as for self-defense, continue to accelerate, we believe Satan will set the stage for a world government under his rule (Zec 12:3; Mt 24:4-7; 2 Th 4:9-12; Rev 13:4).

United Nations

Today the United Nations is beginning to flex its muscles in order to gain more power and authority over the nations of this world, including the United States. It was reported in July 2009, that, "Already the United States is contributing more to the United Nations than any other country—22% of the U.N.'s regular budget—billions of dollars a year, (is) funding our own loss of sovereignty . . . Instead of America being sovereign, as she has been since July of 1776—she (may become subject) to the edicts of unelected and unaccountable bureaucrats at the U.N."[23]

It was reported further that, "George Washington . . . warned against entangling alliances with other countries, 'since history and experience prove that foreign influence is one of the most baneful foes of republican government' . . . The United Nations' 'Convention on the Elimination of All Forms of Discrimination Against Women (CEDAW),' . . . threatens traditional roles and undermines biblical moral standards. It promotes abortion, legalized prostitution, homosexuality, and more . . . (Our current) Secretary of State, . . . Hillary Clinton . . . supports it"[24] (Dt 29:12,13,18; Ps 139:13-16; Pr 29:3[b]; Mt 18:10; 1 Co 6:9,10).

In another report of August 2009, it was noted that, "a United Nations treaty supported by President Obama allows children to seek legal redress against their own parents . . . (with) more than 40 'fundamental rights' . . . (It is called) The Convention on the Rights of the Child . . . Under our Constitution . . . treaties become supreme law." If this treaty is ratified by the United States, "the government (would give children) . . . the ability to override every decision made by every parent . . . Christian schools that . . . teach that Christianity is the only true religion, (would be in opposition to) 'article 29' of the treaty . . . Children would have the right (to) . . . abortions without parental . . . consent"[25] (Dt 5:16; Mic 7:6; Mt 10:21; Mk 13:12; Col 3:20).

In addition, it was noted in a report in April 2009, about "The U.N. Law of the Sea Treaty." (President) Obama has promised to ratify this treaty, that would give corrupt foreign dictators total control over all the oceans and the minerals under them." In October 2010, it was revealed by Jay Sekulow, Chief Counsel for the American Center for Law and Justice, the "massive Organization for the Islamic Conference (OIC), the largest body of nations in the United Nations (U.N.), is pushing again to give *Islam* privileged status, and essentially criminalize Christianity . . .We are very concerned that our President (Obama) wants to placate the OIC."[26]

Globalism and President Obama

Satan, the master deceiver, "the prince of this world," we believe, is leading "the whole world astray," towards a global government. The United States, we believe, is "playing into the hands" of "the evil one." Our Lord Jesus said to His believing disciples, "You do not belong to the world, (for) I have chosen you out of the world. That is why the world hates you." As the United States draws closer to a submission to a world government, Christians will be disdained, hated, and despised more than ever, according to the Scriptures, as wickedness continues to flourish. However, as believers in Jesus, "We have an advocate with the Father, Jesus Christ, the righteous," who can help us, "because greater is he, (Jesus), that is in (me), than he that is in the world," the devil (Jn 12:31; 15:19; 1 Jn 2:1 [KJV]; 4:4[KJV]; Rev 12:9).

It was reported also by Phyllis Schlafly, President of Eagle Forum in April 2009, that, "America's independence and sovereignty are under attack from Barak Obama's plans to use treaties and other international agreements to force us to submit to one-world globalist rules . . . In April 2008, British Prime Minister Gordon Brown demanded that the United States reject our Declaration of Independence in favor of a 'Declaration of Interdependence.'" He said, "Americans must learn to think inter-continentally."[27]

England, the tyrannical nation of the past, that the United States declared their independence from over 200 years ago, has the audacity to "demand" that America give up their liberty and freedoms to "new global institutions" . . . It was further reported that, President "Obama went to Europe and declared himself a 'citizen of the world' before thousands . . . of cheering German socialists,"[28] deceptively pushing our country toward a New World Order!

It was noted also in July 2009, that, "America has (been moving) toward government control (over) your decisions more than ever before . . . Globalism is when your government . . . (gives) up (their) decision-making power . . . to international bodies like the United Nations." Evan Thomas of "Newsweek" shared, "Reagan was all about America. Obama is, 'We are above that now' . . . In a way, Obama is standing above the country, above the world. He's sort of God."[29] When a news reporter considers a created being, a "sort of God," we can surely see the signs of a coming Antichrist (Da 7:23-25; Mk 13:21-23; Ac 5:28,29; 12:22; 2 Jn 7).

In another report in June 2009, it was disclosed that in "President Barak Obama's April 6, (2009) speech in Turkey, . . . (he declared) that, "We (Americans) do not consider ourselves a Christian nation, or a Jewish nation." President Obama . . . "in an interview with France's Canal Plus, . . . (said) that America was one of the largest Muslim nations in the world . . . Congressman J. Randy Forbes, . . . (responded to President Obama's) statement, on the floor of the House of Representatives affirming America's Judeo—Christian heritage."[30]

In still another recent article by Jan Markell, founder and director of Olive Tree Ministries, Inc., she wrote, "We have now entered the most serious 'perilous times' (II Timothy 3:1) in history. President Obama's speech in Cairo was a total surrender to Islam and a drastic turn against one of our best allies, Israel . . . He sent . . . a dramatic message . . . that America respects Islam—even though they continue to be at war with us . . . In that speech, the president made it clear that America will stand with the Muslim world and (design) policies that will lead to Israel's destruction"[31] (Dt 32:16-18; 1 Co 10:20; Rev 9:20,21).

In addition, President Obama also supports "The Comprehensive Nuclear Test Ban Treaty." He "has pledged to push this through" for approval by government officials. This would mean "America's nuclear arsenal (would) be allowed to deteriorate until" we cannot protect our country, "and are defenseless against . . . regimes like Iran and North Korea."[32]

According to these reports, President Obama's decisions oppose our forefathers, our Founding Fathers, and the first President of the United States, George Washington's faith in the one true God, Jesus. He is opposing the Christian faith for another religion, another "god." For this reason, and many others, President Obama, we believe, is heading America to a "fiery" judgment. For in the Scriptures, Almighty God will judge a nation that turns its back on Him, and on the nation of Israel (Gen 12:1-3; Dt 32:20-25; Isa 13:11; 44:8; Lk 9:26; Jn 3:36).

Getting Ready for the Storm

In the Scriptures, our Lord Jesus warns that, "You also must be ready, because the Son of Man will come at an hour when you do not expect him." We are told to "keep watch," and be vigilant for Jesus' return. He says "to everyone: 'Watch'!" How do we 'watch' for His return? We believe that by spending time with Jesus in genuinely sorrowful repentance for the sin motives of our hearts, we can become "refined, purified and made spotless until the time of the end." In this way, we, His "bride," can watch for the Bridegroom's return by keeping our "oil" lamps "trimmed." Our Lord Jesus gave us some revelations on April 25, 2008, and on August 13, and 20, 2009, of coming storms, after we fasted and worshiped before Him (Da 11:35; Mt 24:42,44; 25:5-7; Mk 13:37; Ro 2:4; 2 Co 7:10; Rev 22:17).

On April 25, I saw a vision of dark, billowing storm clouds moving from the Atlantic Ocean to the western United States. Flashes of lightning and sounds of thunder were taking place in those clouds. Then I saw a huge figure of an old sage, a wizard with a cone-shaped hat on his head, hovering in the air over Washington, D.C. He was waving a wand back and forth over the city. In the next vision, I noticed that the people in Washington, D.C. were gazing up in the air. Their ears looked like the ears of Mr. Spock in the *Star Trek* series.

A vision followed of a young boy and girl in a modern-day shopping mall. They were sitting in the mouth of a gigantic crocodile. Then I observed the crocodile close his mouth with the children inside. He gave me a vision of Moses in the movie, *The Prince of Egypt*.³³ Moses was standing in front of a picture on a wall that displayed Hebrew babies being thrown into the Nile River. Crocodiles in the picture had their mouths open to eat the babies. Finally, I saw a daytime vision of very dark storm clouds that had the appearance of a large demonic figure. That figure was moving quickly over a city in America. The people in that vision were screaming and trying to run away from the dark clouds.

The Lord Jesus then shared, "There is a demonic principality, a wizard casting a spell over Washington, D.C., over the 'leaders' in that city. America has become like Egypt. They have chosen other 'gods.' They are unwilling to choose the Hebrew God, the God of Abraham, Isaac, and Jacob. For they are murdering the babies, throwing the unborn to the 'crocodiles' in America. They are like heathen nations, who sacrifice their infants in the fire to other 'gods.' This nation and its 'leaders' are under a spell contrived by Satan (Ex 1:22; 7:16,22,23; Lev 20:27[KJV]; Dt 18:10-12[KJV]; Isa 47:12; Ac 7:39-43; Eph 6:12[KJV]).

"The arrogance of men (and women) 'in their deceitful scheming,' in their 'lofty towers,' is coming down. For there is 'a day in store for all the proud and lofty' to 'be brought low.' Americans have 'their itching ears,' ears to hear what they 'want to hear.' Ears to listen to 'doctrines of devils,' and 'things taught by demons.' Just as the 'Twin Towers' fell with demonic figures seen in the smoke, in the dust of their fall, so this 'great' nation, this proud country will fall. You see the rumblings of it today" (Pr 16:18; Isa 2:12,15,17; Eph 4:14; 1 Ti 4:1[KJV]; 2 Ti 4:3).

On August 13, I saw a vision of a tattered American flag on a flagpole on our driveway, where we have a metal windmill. The wind was blowing on this flag in a rainstorm. The wind shifted from blowing to the right, to blowing the flag toward the left. The flagpole was falling over from the mighty wind. Then I saw my wife and me in rain gear, struggling together to prop up the pole with ropes attached to the pole and the ground. A vision followed of me opening up a scroll of parchment paper. On the top of that paper were the words, "Family Contract."

The Lord Jesus then revealed, "The Pilgrims, on their journey to America, almost lost the broken main mast on the ship, the Mayflower. Yet, they worked together to repair and restore it to its rightful position on the ship. So when the storms come, you will be working together to help America stand through them, just like the American flag was able to stand at Fort McHenry. (America's winds have changed from the right, righteous, to the left, leftist thinking) (Ecc 10:2; Mk 4:37[KJV]; 13:13; Ac 27:14,18,22-25).

"Just as the Pilgrims wrote and signed a covenant together, 'The Mayflower Compact' before landing in America, so you will be writing a covenant, a contract to be signed by your family members, so you can live and dwell together in peace amidst the coming storm" (Hab 2:2; Ro 12:18; 1 Co 10:11; 14:37).

On August 11, 2009, my wife heard these words early in the morning from our Lord Jesus, "America is under water." On August 20, I saw a vision of a Sword in the night sky around darkened clouds coming down to America. The Sword was held by the hand of Almighty God. That Sword was extending to the earth like a beam of light. The Lord was moving that beam into different areas of groups of people in the United States. Then I saw a vision of one cactus in the desert of the western United States. A vision followed of a stormy, gray, cloudy sky in the daytime, and then waves were crashing over America on the East Coast.

A vision followed of a lamp on a stand. In the next vision, I saw an evil face of a lion, followed by a larger, holy-looking lion swallowing the evil lion in his mouth. Then that holy lion spit out the evil lion, while evil cubs cowered away from the holy lion. Finally, I saw a vision of my wife and me playing the piano. Sitting on the right side on a piano bench, it appeared that I was moving my hands across the piano keys making thundering sounds. My wife sat on the left side of the bench, and she appeared to play soft, melodious sounds on the piano.

The Lord Jesus then said, "The night is coming, so be sure to take 'the Sword of the Spirit,' the Word of God in the last days. My 'Word is a lamp unto (your) feet, and a light unto (your) path.' Those who do not abide in My Word, in the Vine, in Jesus, will fall away from the faith. (They "will dwell in the parched places of the desert"), because of the famine coming, a famine of the Word of God (Ps 119:105[KJV]; Jer 17:6; Am 8:11,12; Mk 4:14-20; Jn 9:4; 15:5[KJV]; Eph 6:17).

"You must be willing to stand up for Jesus. 'Let your light shine before men,' as other believers will do throughout areas of America. For when 'the rains' fall, the 'winds' blow, and the 'flood' waters rise against America, you will be able to be My light standing together on the Rock; while most of 'America' will be 'under water,' under the rule of 'the evil one.' So 'stand firm then' and 'resist the devil,' who 'prowls around like a roaring lion looking for someone to devour,' especially Christians (Mt 5:16; 6:13; 7:24,25; Eph 6:14[a]; Ja 4:7; 1 Pe 5:8; 2 Pe 3:3-7).

"Spiritual warfare, (delivered through My true believers), is a must, and necessary 'against the wiles of the devil,' as the storms come to America. When you use 'the Word of God,' which is 'the Sword of the Spirit,' . . . 'the Lion of the Tribe of Judah' will 'destroy the devil's works,' and protect the ones who are in the 'light' (of God). Let the men lead in spiritual warfare before God amidst the thundering storms. Let the women follow their husband's lead in harmony, in humility, backing them up (against the opposition of the world)" (Jn 17:15; Eph 5:22-24; 6:11[KJV],17; 1 Pe 3:1-12; 1 Jn 3:8; Rev 5:5).

The Lord revealed further, "Only those who abide in Me can endure the opposition coming on the world. The world, you can see, is beginning to form an alliance against Me. They are betraying their Maker, as Judas betrayed Me. And there surely will be a 'last supper.' Look at the world today, you can see Satan taking his last stand. The battle lines are being set up for the greatest onslaught of mankind ever before seen. Be ever vigilant to hear the Word of God, for a time is coming when God's Words will be scarce throughout the land. It is yours to hear, and it is Mine to speak to listening ears, listening to the depth of God's love" (Isa 50:4,5; Lk 22:15,16; Jn 10:27; 13:21,27; 15:18,20,21; 2 Th 2:4,9; 2 Ti 4:2-4; Heb 12:2,3; Rev 16:14-16). Received April 14, 1997.

The Lord Jesus has revealed to us, and to other Christians, the coming storm to the United States of America, and to the world. He told us that His "coming" would be "soon." In three gospels, Matthew, Mark, and Luke, our Lord Jesus shared the signs of His "coming and of the end of the age" (Mt 24:3; Rev 22:20).

In previous chapters of "America: Past," we wrote about visions George Washington received at Valley Forge on the Revolutionary and Civil Wars. We will share about George Washington's vision of the future in our next chapter. As reported, George Washington strongly opposed foreign "alliances" and "influences." We will reveal some of the signs of our Lord Jesus' return for faithful followers of Jesus Christ, and His eventual judgment of America and the nations, who have opposed Him and opposed the nation of Israel.

16

WHAT WILL BE THE SIGN OF YOUR COMING?

"Proclaim this among the nations: Prepare for war! Rouse the warriors! Let all the fighting men draw near and attack. Beat your plowshares into swords and your pruning hooks into spears!"

Many times in our Bible studies, we examine and review the signs that Jesus spoke about before His return. One of the signs that we look at is in the gospel of Matthew, Chapter 24. Jesus declared, "You will hear of wars and rumors of wars . . . Nation will rise against nation, and kingdom against kingdom. There will be famines and earthquakes in various places. All these are the beginnings of birth pains" (Mt 24:3-8).

We often shared with our Bible study group, that many believers thought that Jesus would return after World War I, for nations all over the world were involved in that War. Yet, Jesus did not return after that War. After World War II, many believers thought that Jesus surely would return, since nations and kingdoms were at war. Still, Jesus did not return, for these were "the beginning of birth pains." It was not until after that War that the Scriptural conditions for the return of Jesus to the earth were now set to happen. For it was not until May 14, 1948, that the nation of Israel was re-established (Isa 66:7-10; Mk 13:7,8). (Message previously noted, and reiterated).

We believe that the prophetic fulfillment of Israel becoming a nation is key to Jesus' return. For we believe that "the fig tree," that Jesus shared about, as a sign of His return in the gospel of Matthew, represents Israel in the Bible. When Israel became a nation, "the fig tree('s) . . . leaves (came) out." Jesus said that Nathaniel was "a true Israelite," while he stood "under the fig tree." Then, Nathaniel said Jesus was "the Son of God; . . . the King of Israel." "Under the fig tree," is under Israel, under the "King of Israel." Then in the book of Hosea, Chapter 9, verse 10, the prophet shared, "When I found Israel, . . . it was like seeing the early fruit on the fig tree" (Hos 9:10; Mt 24:32-35; Jn 2:47-50).

So what does Israel have to do with America's future? We believe that America's support or rejection of the nation of Israel will reflect on the United States of America's future. For the Lord told Abraham, the Hebrew, "I will bless those who bless you, and whoever curses you I will curse." We believe that America has been blessed for allowing the Jewish people freedom to worship in this country and in Israel. We have blessed Abraham's descendants. Yet, in the later part of the twentieth century, and up to the present, the United States has wavered in their support of the nation of Israel (Gen 12:3; 14:13; Dt 30:4-7).

Let us look at our former General and President of the United States, George Washington, and his support of the Jewish people living freely in America. We will also share about his future vision of a war on America's soil. We believe that war has to do with America joining forces with Islamic nations, who are opposed to the existence of the nation of Israel.

George Washington

It was reported that at his inauguration in 1789, "George Washington placed his hand on a ... Bible, (and) opened to Genesis 49." That "chapter is a prophesy ... from ... Jacob, whose name was changed to Israel—to his twelve sons ... The choice of Scripture has often proved to be prophetic of a president's term of office." Some of "the chosen verses have ... reflected America's role in the plan of Bible prophesy"[34] (Gen 32:28; 49:1-28).

In that chapter of Genesis, Jacob blesses his son, Judah, and says, "Your brothers will praise you; ... You are a lion's cub, O Judah; ... The scepter will not depart from Judah, nor the ruler's staff, ... until he comes to whom it belongs and the obedience of the nations is his." We know from the Scriptures, that Jesus comes from the ancestral lines of Abraham, Isaac, Jacob, Judah, King David, and others. Jesus, according to the Word of God, is "the Lion of the tribe of Judah," who will come in the future against the enemies of Israel. George Washington, with his hand on the Bible, was swearing his oath as the first President of the United States, to the one, true God, Jesus, "the king of the Jews," to preserve America in the days ahead (Gen 49:8-12; Zec 14:2-5; Mt 1:1-3,6,16; 27:11; Rev 5:5).

At the outset of the Revolutionary War, General George Washington petitioned Congress to provide financial support for his Colonial Army. Many soldiers died at Valley Forge from the lack of food, clothing, arms, proper shelter, and from cold weather conditions. It was disclosed by Michael Evans, author and founder of the Jerusalem Prayer Team that, "A Jewish banker from Philadelphia ... gathered a gift of $1 million (from his fellow Jews) for the support of the American troops." Later, George Washington honored "the Jewish people" for their financial support during the War; (by prescribing that) on the back side "of the U.S. one-dollar bill" are "thirteen stars over the eagle's head that form the six-pointed Star of David. Around that is a cloud burst"[35] (1 Sa 2:30; Isa 40:31; 2 Co 8:2,3; Rev 22:16[b]).

It was further written by Mr. Evans, that "As president Washington welcomed the Jews as partners in building our new nation, . . . Washington and other founding fathers had called the Jews a friend and ally of our nation and seen the founding of America (comparable) . . . to the Jews' coming to possess their promised land . . . The final design of the Great Seal . . . of the United States" in the late 1700's, "included a pyramid (Egypt), eagle (protection), and rays of fire and a cloud (divine leadership). All were symbolic of the Red Sea experience of the children of Israel."[36] As we shared previously, the signers of the Declaration of Independence covenanted together with God, like the Israelites in the Old Testament, for freedom in their land (Ex 14:13-31; Jos 1:1-5; Ps 91:4).

On August 24, 2009, after we fasted and praised the Lord Jesus, He gave me a vision of the backside of a one-dollar bill. In the vision, I saw a pyramid without an "all-seeing eye" with a red, white, and blue covering over the capstone of the pyramid. There was an arrow pointing to the right, to the "Star of David" on the backside of the bill. The Lord Jesus then revealed, "The Lord oversees the wickedness from Egypt, the 'secret arts' of 'the evil one.' Those who bless Israel, represented by the 'Star of David,' will be blessed. So true Christians will be blessed for their support of the Jewish nation. The nation, America, will be cursed for its opposition to Israel" (Ex 7:11,22; Nu 24:8,9; Isa 9:7; 1 Jn 5:18).

This leads up to the vision George Washington had at Valley Forge, Pennsylvania concerning a third battle to take place on American soil at the end of times. As noted before, an "Anthony Sherman . . . was an officer with General George Washington at Valley Forge." Mr. Sherman revealed to "a Mr. Wesley Bradshaw" on "July (4), 1859, in Independence Square," the story about visions George Washington shared with him. Mr. Bradshaw's article on this matter "was reprinted in the *National Tribune* . . . for December, 1880."[37] It is significant to note, that we were writing about the visions that George Washington received on America's future on September 11, 2009, the anniversary of "9/11" (Joel 2:28; Ac 2:17).

The Vision of America's Future

This is what George Washington revealed, "I heard the mysterious voice saying, 'Son of the Republic, look and learn' . . . The dark, shadowy angel placed a trumpet to his mouth, and blew three distinct blasts; he sprinkled it upon Europe, Asia, and Africa . . . From each of these countries arose thick, black clouds that were soon joined into one . . . Throughout this mass there gleamed a dark red light by which I saw hordes of armed men, who, moving by with the cloud, marched by land and sailed by sea to America which country was enveloped in the volume of the cloud . . ."[38]

"I dimly saw these vast armies devastate the whole country and burn the villages, towns, and cities that I beheld springing up . . . My ears listened to the thundering of the cannon, clashing of swords, and shouts and cries of millions in mortal combat . . . The dark shadowy angel placed his trumpet once more to his mouth, and blew a long and fearful blast.[39]

"Instantly a light as of a thousand suns shone down from above me, and pierced and broke into fragments the dark cloud which enveloped America . . . The angel upon whose head still shone the word 'Union,' and who bore our national flag in one hand and a sword in the other, descended from the heavens attended by legions of white spirits. These . . . joined the inhabitants of America, who I perceived were well-nigh overcome, but who immediately taking courage again, closed up their broken ranks and renewed the battle.[40]

"The shadowy angel for the last time dipped water from the ocean and sprinkled it upon America . . . The dark cloud rolled back, together with the armies it had brought, leaving the inhabitants of the land victorious . . . Once more I beheld the villages, towns and cities springing up where I had seen them before . . ."[41]

"The bright angel . . . cried with a loud voice: 'While the stars remain, and the heavens send down dew upon the earth, so long shall the Union last.' And taking from his brow the crown on which blazoned the word 'Union,' he placed it upon the Standard while the people, kneeling down, said, 'Amen' . . . I at last saw nothing but the rising, curling vapor I had first beheld . . ."[42]

"The mysterious visitor, . . . said, 'Son of the Republic, what you have seen is thus interpreted: Three great perils will come upon the Republic. The most fearful is the third passing which the whole world united shall not prevail against her. Let every child of the Republic learn to live for his God, his land and the Union' . . . The vision vanished, and I . . . felt that I had seen a vision wherein had been shown to me the birth, progress, and destiny of the United States."[43]

Anthony Sherman said, "Such, my friends, were the words I heard from Washington's own lips, and America will do well to profit by them." It was reported that, the three battles that "George Washington saw all took place on American soil." In the third peril, "a red light accompanies these terrible invaders . . . They come by air (the cloud), land (perhaps via Canada) and sea. They devastate all of America . . . Just when all seems lost, divine intervention from heaven, angels and saints descend to assist the" Americans, "and win the final victory."[44]

It was further reported, that "A special warning (was) given by the Angel of the Union, . . . the guardian Angel of America, . . . to Americans, 'TO LIVE FOR HIS GOD, HIS LAND, AND UNION' . . . This is an indication that . . . the love of country, the respect for our constitution and our faith in God will be in great jeopardy. Already we find this to be the case."[45]

We have already revealed that the first two battles on American soil that George Washington saw, have been fulfilled in the Revolutionary and Civil Wars. The third battle involves the world of nations, including the United States of America. Almighty God allowed the Revolutionary War to take place, we believe, so that Americans could be free of a tyrannical government in England. He allowed the Civil War, we believe, primarily to set the African-American slaves free in this country. The third battle, we believe our God will allow, in order to judge this nation for its sins, for choosing other 'gods,' for its actions against Israel, and to set the American people free from Satan's hold over this country fostered through a strong, demonic antichrist spirit. How could this be possible? (Gen 27:29; Dt 11:16,17; 28:15; Jn 5:26,27; Ac 26:17,18; 1 Jn 2:18,19).

We believe the attacks on the World Trade Towers and the Pentagon by Islamic fundamentalists on September 11, 2001, were "the birth pains," and foreshadowing of the great battle coming to the United States by Islamic factions joined by world powers and communists countries. We believe this will be similar to the Battle of Armageddon in Israel that will occur in these last days (Mk 13:8; Jude 7; Rev 16:14-16).

We believe that Almighty God saw in George Washington, an honorable man of great faith in Jesus Christ, and therefore, he was given the privilege to receive the visions from heaven for America's future. As we reported previously, George Washington, like the prophet Daniel, was called by an angel, "Son." He was one of "the sons of God" under the Lord Jesus, to establish the Republic of the United States through the guidance of the Holy Spirit (Da 8:15-17; Jn 16:13; Ac 2:17).

Early in the morning on March 10, 2011, my wife heard these words from God, "Be willing to lay down your life for another." That morning, after we fasted and praised the Lord Jesus, He gave me visions. In the first vision, I saw the sun shining brightly. In the sun was the appearance of the head of Jesus, beaten and bruised with a 'crown' of thorns around his hair. Then I saw a silhouette of the head of George Washington.

The Lord Jesus shared, "The Son shines on those who will suffer for the kingdom of God. (Peter, James, John), many Christians martyrs, and Stephen, who suffered stoning, saw My glory shine. (Saul) called Paul suffered for My sake, and was blinded by a shining light. My disciples suffered, so that I (Jesus) might shine through them. 'For whoever wants to save his life will lose it, but whoever loses his life for My sake will find it' (Mt 16:25; 17:1,2; Jn 15:13; 19:5; Ac 7:55-60; 9:3-9; Rev 1:16).

"Former General George Washington suffered losses at Valley Forge. He suffered the loss of many soldiers, primarily from the lack of support from the so-called American 'leaders.' Men died from the lack of proper provisions; food, clothing, and shelter. (George Washington prayed to Almighty God for His help.) 'Be willing to lay down your life for another.' Light shone to George Washington 'as brilliant as of a thousand suns' in his visions at Valley Forge. It is through suffering for My sake, that the 'light' of God shines on you" (Isa 53:11; Eph 5:14; 1 Pe 4:12,13).

We have revealed already, how the United States of America was founded by our Lord Jesus through our forefathers and Founding Fathers. Like Abraham in the book of Genesis, who left his "country," his "people" and his "father's household" to "go to the land" our Lord would "show" him; so the Pilgrims and Puritans left their "country," their "people" and their "father's household," to go to the land of America through the guidance of Almighty God (Gen 12:1; Jn 16:13; Eph 2:19,20).

The Grand Union

Both America and Israel were founded by God, Almighty. Spiritually speaking, Abraham's descendants would establish a new nation, "descendants as numerous as the stars in the sky." Abraham's son, Isaac, blessed his son, Jacob, stating,

"May God give you of heaven's dew." By faith, we who believe in Jesus, are descendants of our Hebrew patriarchs. And for those in the United States of America, according to the vision of George Washington, "While the stars remain, and the heavens send down dew upon the earth, so long shall the Union last" (Gen 17:4,7; 22:17; Mt 1:1-3,16; Ac 7:8).

The United States was and will be united in "union" with one another and our Lord Jesus Christ, just like the nation of Israel will be in the millenium when Jesus reigns from Jerusalem over the whole earth. It is written, "I pastured the flock . . . and called . . . the other Union." For "such unity would be the result of the gracious leadership of the Good Shepherd."[46] General George Washington saw that, in those last days, "the bright angel" will take "from his brow the crown on which blazoned the word 'Union,'" and place "it upon the Standard while the people, kneeling down, said, 'Amen.'" For it is written that, "When the enemy shall come in like a flood, the Spirit of the Lord shall lift up a 'Standard' against him" (Isa 2:1-5; 59:19[KJV]; Zec 8:3; Eph 4:3-6; Rev 20:4[b]).

That "Standard" that the people kneel down to, we believe is Jesus. For it is written, "That at the name of Jesus every knee should bow, in heaven and on earth and under the earth." According to the Word of God, "In that day the Root of Jesse, (Jesus), will 'stand' as a banner for the peoples; the nations will rally to him." Thus, it is important for true believers in Jesus, prior to the great battle coming to America, "to live for his God, his land and the Union," by holding on to "the Standard" of righteousness, Jesus (Isa 11:10; 32:1; Mk 3:35; Php 2:10; Rev 16:14).

Judgments and War

On June 3, July 1, and December 28, 2010, after we fasted and praised the Lord Jesus, I was given some visions. On December 28, in the first vision, I was kneeling down at night and praying. Behind me were fires burning homes and stores in a town. Then I saw the character, Tavia in the movie, *Fiddler on the Roof*.[47] The scene was at the end of Part 1, when the Jewish village of Anatevka was burning from fires after his daughter's wedding ceremony. Tavia is angrily looking up to heaven with his hands open, as if saying, "Why, God?" A Russian militia was carrying out a pogrom, terrorizing his family, friends, and burning their stores and some homes.

A vision followed of a rapid swirling, moving around the earth. Then I saw thousands and thousands of dollars. The Lord Jesus revealed to me the visions George Washington received at Valley Forge of the third peril on American soil.

The Lord then disclosed, "The fires you saw will happen globally. My people have been mistreated in ungodly ways, and the nation of Israel has been terrorized by other nations. So I will send burning fires on the earth. As I wept over Jerusalem, because My people could not see My visitation then, so many believers in Jesus will be weeping and praying over America for not seeing Jesus in the midst of their catastrophe (1 Ch 21:1; Isa 22:4; Mt 24:19-24; Lk 19:41-44; Jude 7; Rev 8:6,7).

"Barak Obama has been prompted by 'the evil one,' to spend America out of existence as a sovereign nation. Enemy nations have propped up the economy through loans. America has become a debtor nation, dependent on other nations for its survival. The American people have broken away from George Washington's proclamation for this country to remain a sovereign nation. The vision he received at Valley Forge will take place, because Americans have forsaken Jesus as their Lord, and chosen the ways of their leader, Satan. Economically and spiritually, Americans will become bankrupt. This will usher in a global leader, the Antichrist, who will attempt to solve the world's problems after taking control over nations" (Dt 28:43,44; Mt 6:13; Lk 4:5-7; 2 Th 2:3,4,9-12; Rev 6:5,6; 13:16,17).

A weakened United States of America, we believe, will encounter another war. On July 1, I saw a vision of a large marijuana plant at the White House. A vision followed of a newspaper stand in what appeared to be New York City. The headlines proclaimed, "America Goes to War." A newspaper boy was shouting, "Read all about it!"

The Lord Jesus shared, "The so-called 'leaders' of the United States are being drugged by the enemy, Satan. Their liberal decision makers are making unholy, ungodly, unrighteous decisions apart from the Word of God, apart from the righteous decisions made by your Founding Fathers. Be ready for tribulation to strike America" (Mk 13:7,8,33,37; 1 Ti 1:9; 2 Pe 2:9,10).

As the American Armed Forces choose to accept unrighteous policies, the military will become weakened. On June 3, in the first vision, I saw what appeared to be a modern "F-14," American fighter jet, loaded with armament, missiles and guns, flying in the sky. A vision followed of the jet fighter spinning around in the air, and then spinning down to the ground in a "tail spin." In the next vision, I saw an American military soldier trying to shoot a gun, but the gun barrel was jammed. Then I saw another soldier holding a grenade, which exploded in his hand.

The Lord Jesus said, "It is a great travesty for the President of the United States to promote homosexuality in the military. The 'Commander-in-Chief' of the Armed forces follows the 'counsel' of the wicked one. George Washington, America's first Commander-in-Chief, would have considered today's decision for the military, (abhorrent). This country will fall militarily. America once was the head, militarily, but they will find themselves in a 'tail spin,' downwards. America's weaponry will jam and malfunction, because the military promotes sexual immorality, and the acceptance of another 'god,' Allah" (Dt 11:16,17; 28:15,25; 30:17,18; Ps 1:1; Ro 1:26-29; Jude 7).

Islam

Again, as revealed by our Lord Jesus, that "dark, shadowy angel," that George Washington saw, we believe was of Satan, who will be behind the killing of Americans "in mortal combat." Dark, demonic spirits forming "black clouds" joining from "Europe, Asia, and Africa" will move as "one" black cloud through "hordes of armed men," traveling by air, by land, and by sea. Those "armed men" forming "vast armies" under the guidance of the dark angel, Satan, and his demonic hordes, will "devastate the whole country," burning up "villages, towns and cities" in America. "Millions" of Americans will be fighting for their lives (Jer 52:13; Jn 3:19,20; 10:10[a]; 2 Co 11:14,15; Jude 7).

We have previously written that America will be under God's judgment, His "fire" for willfully disdaining the name of Jesus, for violating and opposing the Word of God, and for rejecting Jesus for other "gods." Pastor David Wilkerson, we reported before, revealed that in the upcoming days many cities will burn in America. Americans experienced some of that burning in Washington, D.C., and New York City on September 11, 2001, from Islamic fundamentalists, terrorists who were willing to sacrifice their lives to destroy symbolic places of strength in America, the World Trade Towers and the Pentagon, murdering over three thousand people[48] (Dt 11:16,17; Ps 2:2-12; Jn 8:16; 15:20,21; Ac 9:3-5; Heb 12:29; Jude 6).

Let's take a deeper look at the religion of the Islamic fundamentalists, growing in numbers in "Europe, Asia, and Africa." Mike Evans, author, reported that in the Old Testament, "Ishmael," the son of Abraham and Hagar, Sarah's "maid servant" from Egypt, "went on to be the father of the Arab race." Isaac was the son born from Abraham and Sarah, born "the son of promise" in the ultimate lineage of Jesus Christ. In the Muslims' book, "the Qur'an teaches that Ishmael, not Isaac, was Abraham's son of promise, and that he inherited the land and the title deed to Jerusalem"[49] (Gen 16:1-4,10-12; 17:15,16,21; 21:2,12; 22:18; Ro 9:7-9).

Mike Evans wrote further that, "The Bible begins and ends with the struggle between these two sons of Abraham. Today, their descendants are still in a Cain-and-Abel struggle for dominion . . . America is . . . the only nation today in alliance with both the historical brothers of prophesy—Ishmael and Isaac . . . Islamic fundamentalism is a religion that kills . . . (The) fundamentalists use religion to recruit . . . martyrs who are willing to kill themselves for the 'cause'" of worldwide Islamic domination[50] (Gen 4:6-12; 27:27-29,39,40; Jn 10:10[a]; 16:2).

Mike Evans reported, "The increase of rabid anti-Semitism in the Arab world . . . is now returning to Europe . . . The spirit that drove Hitler and Stalin is the same spirit that is driving terrorism today . . . It is the spirit of hatred, . . . hating Jews, . . . and then moves to hating Christians . . . As for America, (termed by Islamic fundamentalists as "Big Satan"), Islamic extremists . . . greatest hatred is our Christian majority and biblical principles by which we live our lives . . . America was attacked because of its unholy covenant with the descendants of . . . Ishmael—the Arab nations, (that are) heavily influenced by Islamic fundamentalist(s)"[51] (Ex 23:32,33; Mt 10:22; Mk 13:1,2; Jn 3:20; 15:18,19; Ac 18:2).

Michael Evans disclosed further, "America has promised something to Ishmael that it does not own—Israel's Bible land, including East Jerusalem . . . America has sold Israel out for oil . . . America is under a biblical curse"[52] (Ex 23:21; Nu 34:1-12; Dt 30:7; Zec 8:1-3; 12:7-9).

In October 2010, Alan Keyes, chairman of "Declaration Alliance," reported, "Islam is a doctrine of conquest, a massive political movement bent on world domination . . . (Islam) brutally suppress(es) the rights of others—so that it may achieve total government and social control! . . . Islam, therefore, contradicts the God-ordained standard of right that is the basis of liberty."[53]

Mr. Keyes further shared, "This falsely self-proclaimed 'religion of peace' seems most often to endanger political regimes. (Islam) brutally contradict(s) the most fundamental principles of the American public . . . Practitioners of Islamic terrorism

... slaughter innocents in their implacable jihad against infidels"[54] (Dt 5:17; Da 7:7,19-21; Rev 13:7).

African-American, Alan Keyes, disclosed his views on Barak Obama. "Obama proved his aversion to (the) truth, when recently quoting . . . the Declaration of Independence. He pointedly left out that our rights are endowed to us by our Creator God . . . He is the staunchest proponent of 'abortion rights' in American politics. And he has construed 'abortion rights' to include the 'right' to . . . murder, fully born infants if they are born alive"[55] (Gen 1:1,27,31; 2:1-3; Dt 5:17; Pr 17:15; Ro 1:25).

He further noted, "Barak Obama . . . proceeds, . . . wielding the power of the presidency . . . to fully implement his Marxist agenda . . . Obama sat under one of the most anti-white, anti-Semitic ministers in America for 20 years, one who supports (a) Nation of Islam, (who is a) ("black Muslim") leader . . . Mr. Obama is doing all he can to gin up animosity of Muslims toward Christians in America . . . The White House is taking every opportunity to promote Islam here and around the world . . . Barak Obama (is) the most tyrannical president ever"[56] (Ps 2:2; 161:2; Eph 6:12).

In October 2010, and January 2011, Jay Sekulow, Chief Counsel for the American Center for Law and Justice, reported on Islam. "We are seeing worldwide persecution of Christians as part of the radical Muslim mission to 'take the world for Islam' by purging Christianity from the face of the earth . . . If . . . Islamic extremists . . . have their way, we will see Sharia law—the astonishing brutal system governing Islam—operating in the courts of the United States"[57] (Mt 5:10,11; Jn 15:18).

It was further noted, "There's no religious liberty . . . under Islamic Sharia Law . . . As a Muslim, you're prohibited from renouncing your faith or converting to another religion . . . Criticizing Muhammad or the Koran—or even *Sharia* law itself—and you must die. 'Apostates' die too . . . Islam is intended to be the religion of all mankind—replacing

Christianity, Judaism, everything else... The storm clouds are gathering"[58] (Mt 24:9; Jn 16:2; Rev 2:10; 12:17).

Sandra Teplinsky, author of *Why Care About Israel?*, revealed that, "The United States has pressed persistently upon the Jewish nation to sacrifice more land,... to an enemy that cannot be appeased... Not unpredictably, when we refuse to let Israel, (termed by Islamic fanatics as "Little Satan"), quell terror on her own turf, it eventually made its way to American soil... To curse is to belittle—as in make tiny Israel even littler... Widespread devastation, treacherous weather aberrations and colossal accidents—including the... space shuttle crash... around Palestine, Texas—seemed to occur as America takes steps that endanger Israel... Those who claw ... at the apple of God's eye will experience His retribution"[59] (Dt 32:9,10; Pr 3:33; Zec 2:7-9; Mal 2:2).

In his book, *Eye to Eye*,[60] author and news reporter, William Koenig wrote, "President Bush and previous American president's... are accountable for: Dividing the land God gave to Abraham, Isaac and Jacob and their descendants... Israel's neighbors speak peace in English and war and destruction of Israel in Arabic... America is now experiencing the consequences (curses) of Middle East policies, which have been opposed to God's Word and to the preservation of His covenant land... The United States participation in Israel's destiny has been flawed when put in context of Holy Scripture."

He reported further, "The events of September 11, 2001, were a national wake-up call. (When) affirming a 'land for peace' approach, America can experience the further lifting of the Lord's protective hand"[61] (Gen 12:2,3; 15:18; Nu 34:1-12; Joel 3:2).

It was reported in a September 2009 newsletter, it has been said, "Islam is a 'religion of peace.'" Yet, "the Koran teaches Muslims to engage in 'holy war'... (There are) some 109 'war verses.'" Two of those verses are, "I will cast terror into the hearts of those who disbelieve. Therefore strike off their heads and strike off every fingertip of them (Koran 8:12);... (and) slay the idolaters wherever you find them, and take them captive and besiege them . . . (Koran 9:5)." It was revealed that, "Also allowed in Muslim culture is honor killing, . . . in which females who offend Muslim family honor are murdered." This type of killing has already occurred in the United States[62] (Lk 21:26; Jn 8:44; Rev 12:17; 20:4).

It was further reported in another newsletter of September 2009, that Islam is making its way into America. In "Dearborn, Michigan, . . . some 30 percent of the city's . . . residents are Muslim . . . In 2004, some Muslim residents of Dearborn held an anti-American, anti-Israel demonstration . . . Ayatollah . . . Khomeni . . . pictures . . . were displayed . . . The ultimate objective of Islamic extremists is to bring all nations under Muslim rule and into adherence with Sharia, Islam's code of law . . . The goal of jihadists, . . . is to Islamize America," according to a "counter-terrorism expert."[63]

It was noted further that Muslims "want to see Sharia law implemented . . . into the United States of America, . . . in education, . . . (in) law, in government, in finances," according to a former Muslim. Already there are reportedly, millions of "Muslims in Europe." It was also revealed that in a "Pew Forum . . . survey . . . in 2007, that 26 percent of American Muslims under age 30" believe that "suicide bomb attacks are justified."[64]

On June 11, September 10, 2009, and October 20, 2010, after we fasted and praised our Lord Jesus, He gave me some visions. On June 11, I saw a vision of a Ku Klux Klan, (KKK) member dressed in white, with a white hood over his head. Then I heard the word, "The Great Wizard." The Lord Jesus then said, "There is a reverse racism in the United States government. The 'leaders' in government, cabinet members, and the President are racing to the Muslims, to the Islamic religion. As the African-Americans, the 'negroes' were hated by the 'white' people, especially in the South, so true believers are undergoing a type of 'hatred' by those in government today. Many of those so-called 'leaders' are exalting Islam and despising Jesus, the Christ of the Bible," (through "the Great Wizard," Satan) (2 Ch 33:6[KJV]; Ps 22:7,8; Isa 19:3[KJV]; Lk 21:17; Jn 15:20,21; 1 Jn 2:22).

On September 10, He gave me some visions. In the first vision, I saw a man, which appeared to be President Obama, take a star off the Washington, D.C., Christmas tree at night, and put it in his pocket. Then I saw a vision of a dark, monster-like figure with tentacles. Those tentacles were moving in and out of windows, and squeezing the White House. A vision followed of faithful believers in Jesus bowing down before God, before Jesus, in humility, in reverence, and in honor. Then I saw a vision of thousands of Muslims bowing down before their "god," Allah.

In that vision, I observed a difference in bowing down before their "god." If a Muslim got up too soon from bowing down, or a Muslim felt within his conscience that he was not wanting to bow down to that "god," the Islamic fundamentalists would "weed" them out, and then beat them into submission. Another vision followed of what appeared to be a large lit up balloon like a mushroom cloud over an Arab city at night. As it moved in the air, it exploded over that city, and the fall out from the balloon, like a cloud, fell back on the city. Finally, I saw a vision from the air of railroad tracks. Then Harry Truman appeared to be on a caboose of a train during a "whistle stop" on what appeared to be his presidential campaign.

The Lord Jesus then said, "They, (President Obama and his White House cabinet and staff), are not like 'the wise men,' who sought and followed the Star in the sky looking for the coming King. They are not looking to the heavenlies. They are looking as to a tree, and idol, to the Islam religion, appeasing the Islamic peoples in the last days. (That administration) is squeezing Jesus out of America. Look for 'the Bright Morning Star,' . . . 'the star out of Jacob.' Look for the signs in the sky for My return. The wise men looked 'to things above, not on earthly things,' looking for Jesus . . . The fall out from their nuclear arsenal will fall back on Islam (Nu 24:17; Pr 16:18; Jer 10:1-5; Mt 2:1,2; Ac 8:1; Col 3:2; Rev 22:16[b]).

"The world stopped, a 'whistle' was blown in America when Harry Truman initiated and supported Israel becoming a nation. Through his actions, the prophetic words of the prophets were fulfilled in the re-gathering of exiles back to Israel. The nation of Israel was born in a day. Get ready for the greatest move of God across America through His remnant. Blow the 'whistle,' let it be known." The Lord said further, "When you see the devastation and destruction in America, you know the time is near. Be sober and alert, as the virgins were with their oil lamps ready to be trimmed. I want a man to speak up with eagerness about these last days" (Isa 6:8-10; 43:5,6; 66:7-10; Jer 31:10; Eze 37:21,22; Joel 2:28-32; Mt 25:1,4,7,10). Received September 20, 1999.

On October 20, I saw in the first vision, American fighter jets, whose pilots wore red and white striped helmets, with navy blue and white stars over the top of their helmets. The jets were flying rapidly in the direction of the Middle East. A vision followed of American naval ships, that appeared to be in the Persian Gulf, traveling speedily toward the Middle East.

In the next vision, I saw Barak Obama pulling up his pants. His legs appeared to be like skinny bird legs. Then I saw a toy rubber duck floating on water. Finally, I observed an aerial view over some cities like New York City. Bombs were exploding in isolated areas. Smoke was billowing up from the bomb targeted areas.

The Lord Jesus revealed, "There is about to be a great war in the Middle East. The United States will be involved in that war. When the United States militarily travels overseas to war, this country will be a 'sitting duck' for attacks by terrorist, Islamic factions. President, Barak Obama has no strength to support an attack on America. He is a 'lame duck' President, crippling the United States (2 Sa 3:1; Ps 147:10,11; La 1:6; Da 9:26[b]; Mt 24:6,7).

"He (Barak Obama) has forsaken the Holy God, who

founded this country. He has negotiated with the Islamic 'god.' This nation will reap destructive consequences from that 'god.' Barak Obama is and will terrorize the American people by negotiating with Islamic terrorists. He has forsaken the God of Israel, the Hebrew God of Abraham, Isaac, and Jacob, Jesus!" (Ex 4:5; 9:1; Dt 32:16-25; Lk 19:41-44; 23:3).

In February 2011, the Lord's message was confirmed. It was reported, "On an official visit to Indonesia in the wake of the Baghdad church bloodbath, (in which) al-Qaeda gunmen slaughtered 44 Christian worshippers, . . . even US President Barak Obama was undeterred from his consoling message that, 'Islam is a religion of peace . . . The United States will never be at war with Islam.'"[65]

The Lord disclosed that, "When a man is willing to stand up with Jesus against the devils, he helps a people, a nation, so they might no longer live in tyranny, in a slavery. When a man stands up against those who control and intimidate, he overcomes timidity. But if a man chooses timidity, to be accepted by those who intimidate him, he will receive false respect, a disrespect for submitting to the demons of intimidation" (Jn 12:42,43; Ac 4:13,18-20; 5:40-42; Eph 6:12,13; 2 Ti 1:7; 1 Pe 2:21-23). Received October 2, 1998.

So we see those Islamic "black clouds" are forming in the Middle East, in Europe, Asia, and Africa, and are joined with communist countries who have continuously supported Arab nations that have been fighting against Israel. The United States will be in a "red alert," seen as "a dark red light," of danger with their attempting to negotiate and appease Islamic terrorist countries, while wavering in their support of the nation of Israel. Eventually, America will find itself in a battle for its very existence as a nation. America will not be blessed, but cursed by God for not blessing Abraham's descendants, the Hebrews, the Jewish people. America will not be blessed, but cursed for siding with another "god" of hatred, Allah, instead of the God of love, Jesus (Gen 12:3; 14:13[a]; Ex 9:1; Ps 17:11,12; 55:4-11; Pr 29:10; Jn 15:9-17; Rev 6:4).

The Lord Almighty called His Hebrew people to His promised land, which was occupied by foreign nations. When the Hebrews entered the promised land, they encountered many battles, but the Lord God was with them to occupy His land for His purpose, to show the world that He was the One and Only, Sovereign God. The Hebrews were called to be obedient to God's commands, His decrees, to not follow after the "gods" of the nations occupying Canaan. Then they would be able to prosper, and live peacefully in the land of Israel (Gen 12:1-3; 13:14-17; 15:2; Ex 3:15; 4:5; Dt 28:1-15,63,64).

The God of Abraham, Isaac, and Jacob made a covenant with Abraham, the first Hebrew, to bless his seed, his descendants, future generations to live in the promised land. A king would be appointed by Almighty God, King David, to strengthen that covenant between God, and His chosen people. However, when the Hebrews became disobedient to His commands, and began serving other "gods" from other nations, they were dispersed throughout the world by "terrorist" countries (Gen 14:13; 17:1-8; 2 Sa 7:5-16; Jer 2:5-37; 11:1-17).

Yet, through the covenant God made with Abraham, Israel would be reestablished as a nation in May 1948. They would again fight battles with Arab and Islamic "terrorist" nations, to maintain their country for the protection of the Jewish people in their promised land (Isa 66:7-14).

In like manner, the Pilgrims and Puritans were called to a "new land," a "promised land," to America by the Hebrew God, the One and Only true Liberator, Yeshua, Jesus. Those men and women were willing to follow His commands, and not worship other "gods." The Pilgrims, Puritans, and early American colonists entered America, occupied by foreigners, Indians, and later the English "terrorists" (Gen 12:1-3; Jer 31:31-33; Mt 19:29; Lk 22:20).

The American people encountered many battles. Like Israel, they, our forefathers and Founding Fathers were in a covenant with Almighty God, established through their contracts; the Mayflower Compact, the Declaration of Independence, the

Constitution, and other state constitutions. Like Israel, the Lord Jesus would provide peace and prosperity to America, if they were obedient to follow His commands, and not worship other "gods" (Dt 28:1-5; 2 Co 3:6; Heb 9:15).

However, in the twentieth century, many of the American people began to despise the God of the Bible, Jesus, and exalted other "gods," demons. Because of their disobedience, we believe America will be invaded by foreign countries, by terrorists, just like the nation of Israel. When the American people are united together, and choose to follow the only God, the true Liberator, Jesus with the Father, and the Holy Spirit, then like Israel it will be restored and reestablished (Dt 28:15,25; Isa 11:9; Joel 3:9-11; Zec 14:2-9).

Recently, Rabbi Daniel Lapin of Toward Tradition shared, "Only two nations in history have been governed by constitutions, the ancient Israel and modern America...They are the two nations that are based on the biblical idea of covenant, contract constitutions...America has provided the most tranquil, haven of prosperity that Jews have enjoyed for 2000 years, and that's because America is a Christian nation"[66] (Dt 6:4; Lev 19:18; Jer 31:31-33; Mk 12:29-31; Lk 22:20).

Today, however, we see the Christian foundation in America, eroding rapidly. For we believe the "leaders" of the United States have broken faith with the covenant our forefathers and Founding Fathers made with Almighty God.

On March 17, 2011, after we fasted and praised the Lord Jesus, He gave me some visions. In the first vision, I saw a large white lollipop, which changed into a 1940s microphone. It appeared that former President Harry Truman was speaking into the microphone. Then I saw a modern microphone, and it appeared that Barak Obama was speaking into it. Finally, I observed a tornado spinning through the United States. On top of the tornado was a large chef's hat.

The Lord Jesus declared, "Through Harry Truman, Almighty God gave the Jewish people something 'sweet,' which was his support for the establishment of the nation of Israel. When the members of the United Nations granted Israel, a nation status, she, Israel, was attacked by neighboring Arab nations, and outnumbered by thousands to one. Yet, Israel won that war, for God was with her (Dt 28:8; Isa 66:7,8; Eze 39:27-29).

"Today, the 'President,' Barak Obama, is trying to divide the nation of Israel with disparaging and degrading remarks. Israel will be outnumbered in war by millions to one, globally and worldwide. The Israeli defense force is dedicated and ready to fight for their land. Again, Almighty God will intervene and help Israel win the victory in the very last days through the Messiah, Jesus. America will be in upheaval and turmoil for turning against the Jewish nation. For I will 'feed' them 'no peace.' For the American people do not want Jesus, 'the Prince of Peace,' and His Words" (Isa 9:6; 13:11; Eze 37:21,22; Zec 12:1-7; 14:2-9; Lk 2:14; Jn 14:27).

The Return of the Lord Jesus

We believe that close to that time when America is invaded, "the lawless one," the Antichrist will be ruling over the Revived Roman Empire, and the world. It will be during "the great tribulation," the last three-and-a-half years, "42 months," . . . "1260 days," . . . "for a time, times-and-a-half time" of a seven-year peace agreement with Israel. "The son of perdition" through "the dragon," Satan, will be making "war against . . . those who obey God's commandments and hold to the testimony of Jesus" (Da 9:26,27; 12:7[b]; 2 Th 2:8; 1 Jn 2:18; Rev 7:14[a]; 11:1-3; 12:9,14[b],17).

Through Satan, "the beast" will "make war against the saints . . . All who refuse to worship the . . . beast and his image . . . (will) be killed. We believe the United States of America will be included under the beast's "authority over every tribe, people, language and nation" (Rev 13:4-8,15; 14:9).

However, our Lord Jesus, who we believe, claimed the United States, as well as Israel for Himself, will not be overruled or outdone by Satan and his henchmen at the very last days. For George Washington saw "a light as of a thousand suns shone down from above (him), and . . . broke into fragments the dark cloud which enveloped America . . . The angel upon whose head still shone the word 'Union,' and who bore our national flag in one hand and a sword in the other, descended from the heavens attended by legions of white spirits. These immediately joined the inhabitants of America . . . The dark cloud rolled back, together with the armies it had brought, leaving the inhabitants of the land victorious."

About 3,000 years ago, when King David ruled over the nation of Israel, he received a similar revelation as George Washington. For in 2 Samuel, Chapter 22 it is written, "In my distress I called to the Lord; I called out to my God. From his temple he heard my voice; my cry came to his ears . . . He parted the heavens and came down; dark clouds (over America) were under his feet . . . Out of the brightness of his presence bolts of lightning blazed forth . . . He shot arrows and scattered the enemies, bolts of lightning and routed them . . . He rescued me from my powerful enemy, from my foes, who were too strong for me" (2 Sa 22:7,10,13,15,18.) King David was given a revelation of the last days, just like George Washington.

The prophet Zechariah was given a similar revelation concerning Israel. The Lord said, "I will gather all the nations to Jerusalem to fight against it . . . Then the Lord will go out and fight against those nations, as He fights in the day of battle . . . Then the Lord my God will come, and all the holy ones with Him . . . The Lord will be king over the whole earth. On that day there will be one Lord, and His name the only name," that name is Jesus! (Zec 14:2,3,5,9).

The apostle John, in the first century, also received a similar revelation. The Revived Roman Empire and the beast, we believe, "will make war against the Lamb, (Jesus)," whose "face was like the sun shining in all its brilliance, . . . but the Lamb will overcome them because he is Lord of lords and

King of kings—and with him will be his called, chosen and faithful followers," (deceased and raptured believers in Jesus). This revelation concerns "peoples, multitudes, nations, and languages," surely including the United States (Rev 1:16[b]; 17:12-15).

John further "saw heaven standing open and there before (him), was a white horse, whose rider is called Faithful and True. With justice he judges and makes war . . . His name is the Word of God, (Jesus). The armies of heaven were following him, riding on white horses and dressed in fine linen, white and clean;" ("white spirits," believers in Jesus and His angels). Out of his mouth comes a sharp sword . . . to strike down the nations. He will rule them with an iron scepter. He treads the winepress of the fury of the wrath of God Almighty" (Gen 28:10-15; Heb 1:14; Rev 19:11,13-15).

From the revelations in the Bible, and George Washington's vision of America's future, it appears that our Lord Jesus will descend from heaven and fight with His "holy ones," against the enemies of God in Israel, as well as in America. Then "the Lion of the tribe of Judah," Jesus, "the Root and the Offspring of David, and the bright Morning Star" will rule over the world (Zec 14:5[b]; Rev 5:5; 22:16).

Daniel in the Old Testament was given a revelation in the last days, "At that time Michael, the great prince who protects your people will arise." In the New Testament in the book of Revelation, "there was war in heaven. Michael and his angels fought against the dragon, . . . Satan, . . . and his angels . . . The great dragon . . . was not strong enough, and they lost their place in heaven." Could "the archangel Michael," who we believe will arise on behalf of Israel, arise on behalf of the American people at the end of time? We believe a mighty "guardian angel (over) America" will arise, just as it was seen by George Washington (Da 12:1; Ps 91:11-13; Jude 9[a]; Rev 12:7-9).

On September 14, 1997, I, Mark, saw a vision of the Liberty Bell ringing rapidly. It was as if there was a voice proclaiming, "Liberty, Liberty, Liberty." Then I saw a vision of sheaves of wheat waving in the air. The Lord said, "There is a wave of His Spirit over the land. The Spirit moving on the earth, moves like a wave, (in freedom and "liberty"). It will be like the people waving palm branches to Jesus on His way into Jerusalem for the preparation of His coming. For I am preparing My bride for My coming, (preparing for the "Bridegroom"). The banquet table must be prepared and ready for My return (Ex 29:24; Lev 23:11; Lk 4:18[KJV]; 14:16; Jn 12:13; Ac 17:28; Gal 5:1[KJV]; Rev 19:7-9; 22:17).

"As sheaves of wheat bowed down to Joseph (in his dream), so the whole world will bow down to the Light (of Jesus). So it will be at His coming, sheaves waving all over the land, all over the world to prepare for His return. People will be shouting, 'Hosanna in the Highest. Blessed is He who comes in the name of the Lord.'" The Lord revealed further, "My coming has been heralded by men and angels. See the revelation from heaven, a bright light in the skies that will blind all mankind. For the blindness is hidden in their hearts, it is their sins that blind men to the truth" (Gen 37:5-7; Ps 104:2; Isa 45:23; Mic 5:2; Mt 4:16; Mk 11:8-10; Lk 2:8-15; Jn 8:12; 12:40; Ac 1:10-12). Received December 9, 1996.

The Lord shared more, "There is a day coming, like a 'Day of Atonement,' a 'day of vengence,' when I will return to the earth, and atone for all sins of (men and women), for those who have rejected My Words and My Name to follow their own evil practices. You can see the signs unfolding very quickly in your lives, in the world. For as your sins are completely atoned for by the One who forgives your sins, Jesus Christ, the signs of My coming are surely becoming more evident" (Lev 23:26-28; Isa 61:2; Zec 12:10-14; 14:3; 1 Jn 4:10). Received September 30, 1998.

Signs of His Coming

When we moved to Whiteville, North Carolina in the summer of 1996, two hurricanes blew almost directly through Wilmington and Whiteville, North Carolina that year. The Lord Jesus revealed that, "The hurricane you experienced (in North Carolina) is a confirmation of the whirling upheaval that is beginning to take place in the United States." Yet, when the storms come, the Lord Jesus makes provision for His own people (Mk 4:36-41; Lk 21:25). Received September 15, 1999.

My husband and I were not prepared for the damaging winds of that hurricane. We, and the neighboring area, lost all of our electricity for over five days. By the second night, after the hurricane swept through our town, we were running low on water, the food in our refrigerator had defrosted, and we were cooking outside on a propane stove. Our supplies were dwindling. Yet, we continued to pray and praise our God during and after the storm. On the third day, we drove to the outskirts of the town and observed that the town was flooded with up to six to eight feet of water. The townspeople had evacuated earlier.

The next morning, the fourth day, we were running out of water, ice, and propane gas. We decided to drive to Wilmington that day, and fill our empty milk cartons with water. We went to a McDonald's fast-food restaurant, because the grocery stores had all been closed. While at McDonald's, a lady approached our car and asked, "Do you need water? I saw your husband with empty containers." My heart leaped for joy, "Oh, Yes!" She then said, "I'm here from South Carolina and many church groups from South Carolina are here to help. Do you need any ice?" she asked. "Oh, yes we do!" I exclaimed. "Do you need any propane gas?" she shared. "Well, yes we do!" I said. In three minutes, our Lord Jesus had supplied the only three things we had ventured out for, and I was overwhelmed with gratefulness to God (Eph 5:20; 1 Th 5:16-18).

A few weeks later, while I was standing at a checkout counter in a grocery store, I asked an elderly African-American woman, "How did you survive the hurricane?" The woman replied, "Well, we have a large family, and we rely on the summer produce of vegetables, fruits, and chickens, which we store in a large box-style freezer, in order to survive the winter. That freezer was brimming with all the foods from the hard efforts of my family. As a born-again Christian, I was losing faith, crying, and becoming deeply depressed, because all those foods were spoiling in that freezer.

"Then I had a wonderful idea of what I could do with all this food that was going to waste. Family members got together, aunts, uncles, cousins, and some men, who were standing around at the unemployment office, to help. We all rounded up charcoal grills, cooking utensils, paper plates, etc., and we cooked up all the meats and vegetables that had been in the freezer. Men who had been at the unemployment office drove trucks of the cooked meals to the local hospital and nursing home to feed the patients there. Then we took food to the schools, where many of the townspeople, who had been evacuated from their homes, were staying. Those people were suffering from being displaced from their homes after the hurricane. I felt so good about helping others."

While standing next to that woman, I realized that the Lord was showing us how closed our hearts were to others. For we were only concerned with our personal needs for survival. That woman chose to help many in the town of Whiteville with her own personal food items, turning a tragedy into a generous giving act on her part. We have been learning from that experience, to open our hearts more to others, so when hard times come, especially in the last days, we want to be ready to help. Almighty God, we believe, will make provision for His people at the end of the days (Lk 6:38; Ac 20:35; Ro 5:17; 2 Co 9:6-8).

Our Lord Jesus, when He spoke about the last days said, "There will be great earthquakes, famines and pestilence in various places, . . . and great signs from heaven . . . On the earth, nations will be in anguish and perplexity at the roaring and tossing of the sea . . . The heavenly bodies will be shaken . . . Stand up and lift up your heads, because your redemption is drawing near" (Lk 21:11,25-28).

Pastor David Wilkerson of World Challenge shared in messages in 2005, that "Multitudes are fearful as they watch incredible disasters unfold: hurricanes, earthquakes, tsunamis, mudslides, tornadoes . . . Massive hurricanes struck Florida, causing over $20 billion in damage and leaving multitudes homeless . . . Hurricanes Katrina and Rita destroyed a major American city . . . leaving thousands without homes . . . A tsunami struck in Asia, killing hundreds of thousands of people and leaving millions homeless . . . A massive earthquake struck Pakistan . . . killing over 70,000 people (and a) million (were) . . . left homeless."[67]

Pastor Wilkerson revealed further that, "International health organizations are warning of a deadly flu pandemic from a lethal strain of bird flu . . . If it mutates, it could kill 2 million people in the U.S."[68] Mike Evans reported that, "An entire continent, Africa, is suffering from drought, war, poverty, and plagues . . . New diseases such as AIDS and other sexually transmitted diseases are devastating nations. Viruses such as the West Nile and SARS have thrown many into panic."[69] The signs of the last days, that Jesus shared about, are revealed in three gospels of the New Testament (Mt 24; Lk 21; Mk 13). Those signs, those "birth pains," are increasing in intensity, today (Mt 24:8).

Look to the Heavenlies

On November 7, 1996, we saw two fighter jets fly over our house, and then fly off into the clouds. Shortly after that, they returned flying low to the ground just over our driveway. We believed the Lord Jesus was revealing a warning to us, that something big was going to happen in the days ahead. That day the Lord said, "Those planes symbolized a warfare formation, for there is great warfare now taking place in the heavenlies. For Satan 'knows that his time is short' on the earth. 'There will be great distress,' unheard of tribulation on the earth" (Mt 24:21; 1 Co 10:11; Eph 6:12; Rev 12:7-12[b]).

Then on July 15, 2009, after we fasted and praised the Lord Jesus, I received some visions. In the first vision, I saw the inside of the planetarium at the U.S. Naval Academy in Annapolis, Maryland. My wife and I had visited the Academy several years ago, and we had watched a star show in that planetarium. In the vision, the skyline in the planetarium changed from dusk, a magenta, purple hue into a nighttime darkness with twinkling stars. Then I saw a vision of a red flashing light moving around rapidly. Finally, I saw what appeared to be six "stealth" fighter jets in formation heading out from Israel, and a similar formation of "stealth" fighter jets leaving from the United States.

The Lord Jesus then said, "As you looked at the stars in the planetarium, so the 'wise men' followed the 'Star' in the sky searching for the coming of the King, Jesus. Look for the signs of My coming in the clouds. You will see things happen in the heavenlies before My return. This is not 'star gazing,' not astrology, which is of the devil, but this is looking into the heavens 'for your redemption draweth nigh,' for I am navigating you into the heavens (Isa 47:13-15; Mt 2:1,2[KJV]; Lk 21:27,28[KJV]).

"You have been given a 'Red alert' in the skies. When you see 'stealth' fighters, nations at war, you will know that My return is imminent! Warn the people! This is to be placed in the End time section of this book" (Eze 33:2,3; Lk 21:9,10; 1 Co 4:14; Rev 22:18).

Since the Lord spoke to us, we have been looking up in the sky, in the heavenlies for signs of His return. On July 25, 2009, while walking at our place of employment, we looked up into the sky, and my wife and I saw an image of a stealth fighter in the clouds.

On July 29, 2009, while we were driving on our way home from a trip to Philadelphia, we saw a long stretch of a beautiful blue and white silhouette in the sky, that appeared to be of the Old City in Jerusalem. A silhouette of the "Dome of the Rock" also appeared in the clouds. A minute or so later, the dome had toppled over. As we continued driving, it began to rain about forty minutes before we reached our home. A beautiful rainbow appeared in the sky, and it seemed to be following us all the way home. And then it disappeared! We sensed from that experience, that the presence of God was near us.

We believe the signs in the heavenlies are increasing with more frequent "birth pains," also with more unusual weather patterns and storms. The Son of Man's return in the clouds, we believe, is right at the door, for "this generation will certainly not pass away until all these things have happened" (Mt 24:8,10,30,34). Yet, as Jesus' return approaches, many will miss His coming! (1 Ti 4:1).

The Falling Away

Michael Evans revealed that, "The twentieth century witnessed a dramatic decline in membership in the mainline Protestant denominations . . . The last few decades have seen a departure from the historic faith . . . Many churches and entire denominations have abandoned biblical truth wholesale . . . I have seen this prophesied 'falling away' in my lifetime, and it is rapidly increasing . . . The culture . . . in the U.S. . . . has turned against God"[70] (Mt 24:10-13; 1 Ti 4:1,2; 2 Ti 4:3,4).

In 2008, Pastor David Wilkerson shared in a message, "A . . . Christian woman in Louisiana wrote" that her "five-year-old son stood up and said (at their church), 'I had a dream last night. Jesus told me He was coming soon' . . . Sadly, . . . Jesus' coming is seldom preached in churches anymore . . . (Many) churchgoers mock the possibility of Jesus' 'any time return.'

They scoff at the idea ... Many shepherds do not believe Christ is coming in their generation"[71] (2 Pe 2:1-3; 3:3-5; Rev 22:20).

It is written that, "In the last days scoffers will come ... They will say, 'Where is this coming He promised? Ever since our fathers died, everything goes on as it has since the beginning of creation'" (2 Pe 3:3,4). The Lord said, "Do not be one who says, 'Where is the promise of His coming?' For signs of His coming will be deep in your hearts, your souls, and your minds. All these signs; the riots, the earthquakes, the unusual weather changes, the destructive hurricanes, false 'gods,' the 'false Christs,' and the establishment of Israel as a nation, point to the signs of My coming. A door will open, and a trumpet call will herald My coming! (Isa 66:7,8; Mt 24:4,22,30-35; Lk 21:11,25,26; Rev 4:1).

"The time is coming when the whole world will be in poverty, poverty to the Word of God. For there is a movement in the land to hate Christ, to discredit what He has given this land, to credit man and his wisdom, and his acceptance of other 'gods.' For men are saying, 'See how prosperous this country is! We can do things our way, and God still blesses us.' But there is a day coming when My wrath will be unleashed upon a land, America, that has desecrated My Name and follows idols of man (Ps 10:4-7; Mk 13:13; Ro 1:25; 2 Ti 4:3,4; Rev 6:16,17; 19:15).

"Yet, the voice of God will be heard throughout the land. Thousands of souls will rise up and receive Jesus Christ, (the Messiah) into their hearts, so that their souls will be saved, eternally. The eyes of many Jews will be opened to see the Son of Man coming in the clouds. Weep for those who have committed themselves to their own needs, who never change their walk down the 'broad' road of 'destruction'" (Zec 12:10-13; 13:1,2; Mt 7:13; 24:14; Lk 23:28,29; Ro 10:8-13,17,18; Rev 1:7; 3:20). (Messages received from God on April 2, 1998, June 17, 1999, and December 25, 1999, Christmas Day).

On April 2, 2009, September 17, 2009, and July 23, 2010, after we fasted and praised the Lord Jesus, He shared some revelations with us. "The last days are like the days of

Jeremiah, the prophet, like the days of Noah and Lot. For the people have been warned time and time again by My servants, but they refuse to listen. Only a few are receiving the message today. For the people are '("eating and drinking"), buying and selling, . . . marrying and being given in marriage,' but they do not see that they live in these (end) times" (Jer 36 and 37; Mt 23:34-39; Lk 17:26-30). Received April 2, 2009.

On September 17, I was given some visions from God. In the first vision, I saw what appeared to be an old sage from times past, dressed in burlap, praying over a globe of the world. He appeared to be praying that the dark powers of the occult would move the people of the world to serve the devil. Then I saw what appeared to be the Lord Jesus' hands praying for the people in the world. He then held the world in His hands, and the world was split open. Inside the center of that world appeared to be a Revolutionary War cannon ball.

A vision followed of me and my wife in a school classroom teaching others about the Bible, and how believers in Jesus can prepare for the last days in America. Finally, I saw a black and white vision of myself, Mark, as a young man looking out of a window into the sky. The vision reminded me of the old original, black and white version of the movie, *The Christmas Carol*,[72] when the character, Ebenezer Scrooge was a young man, and he had been hurt in a relationship.

The Lord said, "The world, including the United States, has been hardened in their hearts by sin, by the one who leads them astray, the devil. George Washington was given a vision of America in 'mortal combat' with people from foreign nations. He heard the sound of the canon firing hardened canon balls. America will be paid back with an attack from the enemy due to their hardened hearts against the one true God. What is written in this book needs to be taught to the American people, believers and those willing to listen to you both (Jer 52:3; Mt 23:37,38; 24:2; 28:18-20; Ro 9:18; Heb 3:7-13; Rev 12:9).

"The emotional pain that the character, Ebenezer Scrooge suffered as a child, and as a young man, affected him later in life. He hoarded his money, was a 'scrooge,' cold to others, lived a life of a recluse, isolated, and had 'no room' for God in his life. The emotional pain, abuse that American people have suffered during their childhood has contributed to their choosing sinful lifestyles apart from God, and has affected the United States today (2 Sa 12:9,10; Isa 66:3[b]; Eze 18:20; Mt 18:6; Lk 2:6; Ro 1:22-25; 1 Ti 6:10).

"Many in leadership positions, in government, in education, in the private sector are hoarding their own paths to God, hoarding monies for their own personal and special interests; they are cold, acting as 'scrooge' to Christians, true believers in Jesus, and they have 'no room' for the one true God, living a reckless, recluse life style. Weep for the hidden pain that the so-called 'leaders' have suffered in (the United States of) America." In the last days, it is written, "Because of the increase of wickedness, the love of most will grow cold" (2 Sa 19:1; Ps 10:4; 126:6; Pr 25:20; 28:22; Mt 24:12; Jn 15:18,19; Ja 5:1-6).

On July 23, I was given more visions by God. In the first vision, I saw a tall weed that had the appearance of a cornstalk. Then I observed numbers of those weeds hovering over cornstalks. A vision followed of dry ground. Next, I saw men storing up food items and water in a red barn. Then I noticed that the barn door was closed, and people were outside knocking on the door.

In the next vision, I saw what appeared to be several people working in a modern warfare center that was hovering over the earth. The center had an evil presence. Finally, I was looking up at the bottom of an elevator that was dropping quickly to the ground. Under the elevator was blood dripping downward. It appeared to be an elevator at the Empire State Building.

The Lord Jesus revealed, "'Weeds' are being planted at night by Satan in these last days, over and around non-believers, and believers in Jesus, represented by the cornstalks. The 'weeds' of deceit are growing, as the drought of the Word of God is growing in America (Am 8:11,12; Mt 13:24-28,38,39; Mk 13:3).

"Those who store up the Word of God will be like Joseph in the Bible, who stored up grain in Egypt. Those who store provisions and water, 'living water,' will be prepared for the days ahead. However, many believers in Jesus, and non-believers will refuse to prepare themselves for the troubling days coming on earth. They will be shut out from God's 'barn,' His 'ark' (Gen 6:9-22; 7:16; 41:29-49; Lk 3:17; 17:26,27; Jn 4:10).

"Satan is now moving through certain men and women to take control over the world. Those (extremists) who destroyed the Twin Towers are planning an attack on the Empire State Building. New York City and America will experience a leveling, because the American people did not heed God's warnings" (Isa 2:12-18; 1 Co 10:6-12; 2 Th 2:9-12).

The Harvest is Plentiful

For true believers in Jesus Christ, the harvest of souls coming into the kingdom of God in the last days will be abundant. The Lord disclosed, "'Open your eyes,' so you can see 'the harvest is plentiful,' white, ready, and ripe, 'but the laborers are few.' Yours is to go into the field and bring in 'the harvest' in these last days. My laborers have sold everything they have, so that their work is totally for the kingdom of God. For he who 'loses his life for My sake will find it.' That is why your warfare ministry against Satan is crucial to God for opening doors in the harvest field (Mt 9:37[KJV]; 10:39; 13:39; Lk 18:22; Jn 4:35; 2 Co 10:4,5).

"Stay close together as helpmates in the field, just like (they did in the movie), *Places in the Heart*.[73] They brought the harvest in by never giving up (working) in the field together. Satan attacks my laborers, just like they did at the end of that movie. Yet, with love and fellowship together, they persevered and brought in the harvest. Persevere in the field of the 'blind,' the downtrodden, the abused, the mistreated, ("the poor, the crippled, the lame"), so you can produce a good crop, eternal life

(Lk 14:13; Ac 2:42-47; 5:32-35,41,42; Eph 2:21,22; Ja 4:7; 5:7-11; Rev 2:3). Received February 23, and March 12, 2002.

"There is a great quaking about to take place on the earth. The earth will quake and shutter at the things to come. That is why God is preparing you both to bear testimony to Jesus in these last days. The books God is writing through both of you, bear testimony to the truth. As My children, you are learning to renounce all evil practices from the present and the past. Yours is to stay focused on the King of your lives, Jesus! Do not be pulled away into devastation, but be willing to turn only to Jesus" (2 Sa 22:8; Joel 2:10; Mt 27:51[KJV]; 2 Co 4:2; 1 Ti 1:16,17; Heb 12:1,2; Rev 12:10,11). Received September 13, 2007.

On March 12, and September 3, 2009, after we fasted and praised the Lord Jesus, I was given some visions. On March 12, in the first vision, I saw the windmill in the movie, *Sarah Plain and Tall*.[74] Then I saw the character, Sarah, in that movie, calling out frantically for water. A vision followed of our red well pump. We were pumping water rapidly out of it, giving it out to people around us.

The Lord then said, "Many will be calling out for water in the last days. Calling out for the 'living water,' the Holy Spirit, the Comforter. You can already see a drought taking place in this country of the Word of God, a drought from salvation in Jesus. You are to pour out the 'living water,' I have given you, to others in the last days" (Am 8:11,12; Lk 21:17; Jn 4:10,14; 7:37-39).

While I, Mark, was at our place of employment on September 29, 2009, the Lord Jesus revealed to us how important the Word of God must be in the last days. A revelation was given of the Ten Boom sisters, Corrie and Betsy, in the movie *The Hiding Place*.[75] They desperately requested and received a Bible, when they were imprisoned for hiding Jews in their home. They hid their Bible from the German Nazi concentration guards, when they first arrived at the Ravensbruk Concentration Camp. God covered His Word, so they could feed on it in a lice-ridden, torturous, overly crowded, death-ridden, concentration camp where food was scarce. The Word sustained them through utterly deplorable living conditions (Ps 119:11; Mt 4:4; 5:6; Mk 4:14,20; Col 3:16).

On September 3, I was given some visions by God. In the first vision, I saw above the back door of our house, a metallic image of the side of a fish. It appeared to be like the fish symbol of the Christians in the first century. In the eye of the fish was a small cross. At our back door, my wife was welcoming people into our home. Then I saw a vision of our living room filling up with so much water, that one could swim in it. A vision followed of the worship DVD, *Given To Him*,[76] where dolphins were swimming off the southern coast of Israel.

Then I saw a vision of a silver pole outside in our backyard. It was like the pole in a fireman's quarters, standing up from the ground. At the top of the pole was a large man-made beehive. There were bird perches on that "hive," and blue birds were flying in and out of the "beehive." The birds from the vision appeared to be very active, checking out areas in the neighborhood. Finally, I saw a vision of my wife and me sliding down the fireman's pole, getting ready to put out a "fire."

The Lord Jesus then said, "In the last days, I have called you to be 'fishers of men' and women. Welcome the 'fish,' the people in your home seeking refuge. Like the prophet, Ezekiel, let the 'water' of the Holy Spirit rise up in your home through praise and worship, so believers and nonbelievers can be in the presence of God. You will be like fish swimming in the water, just like dolphins in the worship, DVD. The larger, stronger adult male dolphins, men, will be the protectors of the fellow believers, swimming on the outside. The adult female dolphins, women, will be on the inside taking care of 'the little ones,' the children, keeping fellow believers safe when they refuse to get the 'mark,' and refuse to worship the 'beast,' (and his image) in days ahead (1 Sa 30:1-3; 17-20; Eze 47:1-5; Mt 5:19; 18:10; Ac 10:44-46; Ro 16:3-5; 1 Co 11:3; Php 3:3; Tit 2:4,5; Rev 13:15; 14:9,10).

"Believers in Jesus will be like 'blue birds,' servants, 'busy as bees' at work, flying out as 'scouts,' and (coming) back home for protection. They will report on fellow believers, who are under 'fire,' under attack in the community by 'the evil one' in the last days. You both must be ready to help those under 'fire' in your community (1 Ki 20:40; Ecc 10:20[b]; Jn 13:14-17; Heb 11:24-26; 1 Jn 5:19; Jude 23).

"There will be a mighty 'underground' for believers in Jesus, for when 'the wicked rise to power, the people go into hiding.' Many will come to Jesus in those days realizing that the wicked are evil, are wrong. They will be part of the 'underground.' So your home must become like a 'Promised Land,' a shelter for the believers and sojourners. Your home must flow 'with milk and honey,' flowing with the sweetness of honey in the Lord, and flowing in the 'milk of the Word'" (Gen 50:24; Ex 3:8; Jos 2:4-6; Ps 19:8-10; 119:103; Pr 28:28[a]; Isa 58:7; Mt 13:39; Heb 5:12,13; 11:38; 1 Pe 2:2).

Pastor David Wilkerson in his book, *The Vision and Beyond*,[77] reported that "an army of true Jesus followers . . . will be part of an underground church that will be found preaching the return of Christ at the end of the age! They will be like a thorn in the side of the harlot church, and they will sting and sear the consciences of men by their devotion and spiritual power. Devil worshippers will be in open conflict with all these true Jesus followers. Only those living by true faith will be able to discern the 'spiritual wickedness' in high places" (Joel 2:1,2; 1 Co 12:7,10; 2 Co 12:7-9; Eph 6:12[KJV]; 1 Ti 4:1,2; 2 Pe 2:1-3).

We must be prepared spiritually for the Bridegroom's return, for His bride in these last days. Almighty God desires that we be "refined" from the sin motives of our hearts in repentance, so we can be "purified and made spotless," like "virgins" waiting to trim "their lamps" for Jesus' second coming. In the last chapter, we will reveal how our Father, "the gardener," desires that we grow up in His "garden" through the love of Jesus, and how He will make provision for us when "tribulation" strikes America (Da 11:35; Mt 25:1,7,10; Jn 15:1,2; Eph 4:15).

GOD BLESS AMERICA

"While the storm clouds gather far across the sea,
Let us swear allegiance to a land that's free,
Let us all be grateful for a land so fair,
As we raise our voices in a solemn prayer."

"God Bless America,
Land that I love,
Stand beside her, and guide her
Thru the night with a light from above.
From the mountains, to the prairies,
To the oceans, white with foam
God bless America, My home sweet home.
God bless America, My home sweet home."[78]

17

A SHELTER FROM THE STORM

"God is our refuge and strength, an ever-present help in trouble. Therefore we will not fear, though the earth give way and the mountains fall into the heart of the sea, though its waters roar and foam and the mountains quake with their surging."

Throughout this book, we have taken "whistle stops" on God's "train" at different places in the United States of America, passing through America's: Past, and Present, and ending up in America's Future. We have reported what we believe our Lord Jesus has revealed to us about the future of this country. The Lord has given us more direction on what we are and will be doing in these last days.

On September 24, 2009, after we fasted and worshipped the Lord Jesus, I received some visions from God. In the first vision, we had returned to the base of Mount Rushmore looking up at the carved heads of four presidents; George Washington, Thomas Jefferson, Abraham Lincoln, and Teddy Roosevelt. (We began this book at the base of Mount Rushmore, and we are in our last chapter revisiting that site in a vision). Then I saw a vision of an old parchment document with a ribbon tied around it, and I heard the words, "Magna Carta," and . . . "Declaration of Independence."

A vision followed of a newspaper boy at a newsstand in what appeared to be New York City. He was dressed in an outfit like those worn during World War II. The newspaper boy was shouting, "Extra, Extra. Read all about it!" On the headlines of the newspaper I saw these words, "America Struck Again on Own Soil"! Finally, I saw myself, Mark, brushing aside the newspaper.

Then the Lord Jesus revealed, "This country has not learned the lessons from the past, from statements to this nation from men of faith, who were carved in the mountain. Men and women today, are not referring to the original documents of your Founding Fathers. (The "Magna Carta," was a "charter" established in England in 1215, and literally meant a "great" charter. It limited the power and authority of the King of England, at that time "King John," by giving "certain civil and political liberties" and authority to the government, the Parliament, and the people of England. The principles in the Magna Carta were utilized by our Founding Fathers in helping to establish in part our form of a republican government in America)[79] (Pr 1:5; Da 9:6; Mt 23:34-39).

"In the Declaration of Independence, America declared its independence from a tyrannical monarch, (King George III), who chose not to limit his power and authority, (according to the "Magna Carta.") Though the Founding Fathers attempted to negotiate and appease the King of England, it was for naught. The King sent English troops to American soil to quell the 'rebellious' Americans, their enemies. In the same way today, government 'leaders' in America are trying to negotiate and appease Islamic (fundamentalists), which will come to naught. As England attacked America in the past, so America will again be attacked on American soil (Ps 108:12; Pr 19:19; 22:24-27; Jer 17:5; Gal 5:1).

"Do not get caught up in world events, for those things will happen in America, as they have in the past. But get caught up in the heavenlies with Jesus. Do not look to the things that are 'seen,' but look to the 'unseen,' the real working of the Holy Spirit in the United States to bring Americans, and others into the kingdom of God in the days ahead. America was founded on the 'Rock,' Jesus, as an independent nation, so as not to be dependent on other countries for its future prosperity. Today America's 'leaders' have placed this country's dependence on other countries for oil, and for its debt" (Hab 2:6-9; Lk 21:28; Jn 16:7-15; 1 Co 10:4; 2 Co 4:18).

On November 25, 1996, the Lord Jesus gave us a vision of an American flag drooping on a pole covered heavily with oil. The Lord said, "America is losing its strength by selling itself out. Oil is a key factor" (Gen 25:31-33; 2 Ki 4:7).

Farming in the Last Days

The Lord Jesus wants us to look to "the real working of the Holy Spirit" in the last days. One of the ways we can do that is to come into the garden of God, in which the Father is our "gardener." We can learn from the Lord Jesus about farming for souls. The Lord Jesus said, "Listen, and I will tell you a story. Many years ago, a farmer lived on his land, and planted crops so that he could provide food for his family. He had servants, tenants under his care, that helped him farm his crops. The farmer prayed to His God, and asked Him when the planting season would take place (Mt 6:9-11; 7:7,8; 21:33,34; Gal 6:9).

"God said, 'First plant seeds in the hearts of men and women under your care.' The farmer said, 'What kind of seeds can I plant?' The Lord replied, 'Only plant the good seeds, and throw out the bad seeds.' The farmer learned that only 'good seeds' were planted when he repented of the 'bad seeds' that had grown up in his heart. Those 'bad seeds' were planted when he gossiped about his servants, his tenants under his care, or when he gave them less wages than they deserved, or when he offended them publicly over wrong doing, rather than to speak to them privately (Mt 3:8-10; 13:24,25,38; 18:15; Mk 4:3-8; 2 Co 12:20; Ja 5:4; 1 Pe 1:23).

"In fact, the farmer repented over his 'bad seeds' of envious feelings towards two of his married tenants, who listened to God and always showed love to each other publicly. The farmer repented for his sins that had occurred over a long period of time. Afterwards, some said, 'The farmer was dead to this world.' Then the Lord said, 'The harvest is ripe. Harvest your good seeds.' The 'good seeds' began to bear fruit that would last. The farmer noticed that his tenants were happier, harvesting the crops, and multiplying 'seeds of joy.' 'Seeds of joy,' and 'seeds of love' sprouted up in the hearts of the servants, tenants (Joel 3:13; Mk 4:16; Lk 8:21; 10:39-42; Jn 12:24-26; 15:11,16,17; Col 3:14; Ja 3:14-16).

"The farmer loved the married couple more, after he repented and bore 'good seeds' of faithfulness and kindness to them. The farmer thanked His God, because He showed him how to plant 'good seeds' at the right time. The farmer's family was filled with love and happiness. He married a good wife, and they spread prosperity wherever the Lord would send them. So plant 'good seeds' of love publicly, showing kindness and patience to one another. 'I Am' the 'Farmer' who plants My seeds, My Words in your hearts. 'Produce fruit in keeping with repentance,' bearing the 'good seed,' the good fruit that will last forever in your lives, and in the lives of those under your care" (Pr 31:10,11; Mt 3:8; Mk 4:3,14,20; Jn 8:58; Ac 20:20; 1 Co 13:4; Gal 5:22; Eph 5:18; Heb 12:28; 1 Pe 5:2). Received July 25, 2000.

The Lord shared, "The riches of the glorious inheritance of the saints is seen through the eyes of the believers, who hear My Words, believe them, and put them into practice. It is like the farmer, who hears My Words and takes My Words and plants them in good soil, a noble soil, which is of a good heart. That soil has been freed from the entanglements of the world.

A Christian believer cannot sow 'good seed' daily, unless he has been freed from the world's ways of doing things (Mt 13:3,8; Lk 8:15,21; 9:23,24; Jn 15:19; Col 1:10-14; Heb 12:1).

"Television is a prime example of this, spending time viewing the world's ways. Commercials can subtly pull even the strongest believers away from the truth. Many believers spend much time watching Christian family programs. However, watching television takes away from time spent with God, and time spent in personal relationships. Your marriage is being established without advertisement, or time spent in front of the television. Your (marriage) is founded on 'the Rock' of truth, as you obey My Words and put them into practice, spending time together in your relationship" (Ps 119:57; Isa 26:4; Lk 4:5-7; 15:13,14; 2 Co 12:15; 1 Jn 2:15-17; Rev 12:9). Received September 29, 1999.

As revealed in our Introduction, in 1995, my wife saw a vision of a New England farm with a reddish-colored barn. Farmers were sowing seed, harvesting crops, and storing up their harvest. The Lord Jesus then said, "This is the end-time farming. Farming began in this country, and farming will become very valuable in the last days. For the farming of My seed, (the Word of God), 'shall not return unto Me void' . . . If you sow 'sparingly,' you will reap a sparse harvest. If you sow 'generously' to the kingdom of God, you will reap generously, souls" (Isa 55:10,11[KJV]; Zec 13:5; 2 Co 8:6; Gal 6:7-10).

On May 22, 2008, I saw a vision of my wife and me in our backyard garden. Then I saw a vision of the character, "Coach Grant Taylor" in the movie, *Facing the Giants*.[80] A "Mr. Bridges" was talking to that coach about "preparing for rain." The Lord said, "Be like the farmer, who prepared his fields, his garden for the coming rain. I want you to draw closer to each other, becoming more 'down to earth,' drawing nearer to God, nearer to the Word of God, closer to your family in your Father's garden, (where God's pruning takes place). 'Prepare for rain' from heaven, spiritually. That rain will fall on your garden, on your family. You have received much rain recently on your garden, (literally) but you are going to see a desert in the 'land' in the days ahead." (We planted a garden in our backyard in the spring of 2008) (1 Ki 18:1; Joel 2:23; Mt 5:5; 11:28-30; Jn 15:1,2; 2 Ti 4:2; Heb 10:22; Ja 5:7,17; 1 Pe 1:13).

God's Garden

The Lord Jesus instructed us to plant a garden of vegetables and herbs, so we could learn how to harvest crops, souls in the last days. He has used our garden for teaching us lessons in the days ahead. The Father's garden is where we grow up into Him, Christ Jesus, as He 'prunes' the 'dead branches' and 'dead things' from our hearts, so we can be set free from sin by the one and only true liberator, Jesus Christ. Our Lord has revealed to us His heart concerning His garden (Jn 8:34-36; 13:13,14; 15:1-8; Col 2:19).

On April 8, 2008, after having our garden area in our backyard plowed and tilled, my wife and I planted seeds and young plants in our garden. On April 11, the Lord Jesus gave me a vision of our plants in the garden with one weed sticking up in the center of the garden. The Lord said, "The 'gardener' is your Father. He is planting seeds in the 'garden' in your lives; seeds of kindness, seeds of compassion, seeds of love, and seeds of patience for your marriage, for your family, and for others. You are growing plants for the purposes of the kingdom of God (Isa 61:3[b]; 1 Co 3:6-8; Col 3:12-14).

"I want to weed out that which is not good in your garden; weeding out the attitudes that are not loving, that are accusing, that are negative, that are judging each other. Hoe, dig, uproot the old, and plant the new roots in love in your marriage, and at all times. A pruning of your hearts in repentance needs to take place, so that the fruit of repentance, the fruit of Jesus, (the fruits of the Spirit), may grow up in you. Take My 'garden' in you wherever you go. Water it with the Holy Spirit within yourselves, dig and hoe in the good soil that God has given you" (Jer 1:10; Mt 13:37-39; 15:13; Mk 4:14,20; Lk 3:8; 6:37; Jn 4:10; Gal 5:22,23; Eph 3:17).

On July 17, 2008, I saw a vision of a large onion growing in our garden. The Lord disclosed, "As you cut into this onion, into your past childhood experiences, Jesus helps you get to the source, to the pungent stench in your lives. That is the 'stench' of pride, an unwillingness to suffer the flesh, an elevation of self. You must be willing to examine that onion by peeling back the skin and cutting into the core of its bitter roots" (Nu 11:5; Isa 2:12; Jer 17:5; Heb 12:15; Ja 4:1-10).

On July 24, 2008, God gave me a vision of our small corn crop, which was eventually destroyed in our garden. We had a corn crop which consisted of just a few stalks of corn. The Lord Jesus revealed that our corn crop represented the 'corn crop' of the United States, eventually destroyed in the future. The Lord said, "The harvest in the United States will be coming down, the economy. The reason I, (Jesus), allowed your corn stalks to be destroyed was to reveal to you a greater destruction in the days ahead" (Pr 28:3; Isa 2:12-15; Joel 1:17[KJV]).

On June 26, 2008, I saw a vision of myself in North Carolina with my arms outstretched to heaven turning around in a rain shower in front of our car. Then I saw a vision of our address labels with oranges on them. A vision of a bag of oranges followed, sweet oranges that we had been buying at the grocery store. Then I saw a vision of our backyard garden. Our tomato plants were falling over close to the ground with newly formed green tomatoes growing on them. There was a tomato tied up to a tomato stake in the garden. Then a vision followed of a branch of a tree with two white linen ties wrapped around green tomatoes growing on a tomato plant, which was tied up to that branch.

The Lord Jesus revealed, "You have been called to be free in the Holy Spirit, as the 'rain' from heaven falls. You become free by bearing fruit through repentance before God, free from 'falling over,' tied to your past family ways. Your 'fruit' becomes sweeter, when you 'untie' yourself from your past.

You grow up in My garden, when you 'tie' up to Jesus. Your 'fruit' will come forth, and stand 'tied' up to His staff, His scepter from heaven, 'tied' up to the 'Branch' bearing 'fruit' that will last" (Gen 2:8,9; 49:10; Isa 58:6; Zec 3:8; 6:12; Jn 15:4,5,16; 2 Co 3:17; Gal 4:9).

On October 8, 2009, after we fasted and worshipped the Lord Jesus, I was given some visions. In the first vision, I saw the sword of Zorro from the former television program, *Zorro*,[81] cutting a "Z" in a chair. Then I saw a vision of apples in a bucket on the ground under one of our apple trees in our backyard near our garden. A "Z" was cut/carved in one of the apples. A vision followed of seeds within an apple core. Then I viewed a slice of an apple turning brown in color, and rotting.

The Lord shared, "In the last days, you must develop a 'z'eal for God. The character, Zorro, helped the poor, the oppressed, and downtrodden. Those that support 'Z'ion will be blessed, supporting the oppressed and downtrodden people of Israel, the 'apple of His eye.' God has planted the seeds of His Word in your hearts. But the seeds, the 'weeds' of the enemy were planted in your hearts by 'the evil one.' You must be willing to remove the core, the 'bad seeds' (Ps 82:3; 102:13; Zec 1:14; 2:7-12; Mt 7:17,18; 13:3,18,19,38,39; Jn 2:16,17; Ro 11:26; 12:11; Heb 12:22).

"Allow the Holy Spirit to dig deep into the core of your childhood memories to expose and remove the lies from 'the father of lies,' Satan.[82] One of those lies has been 'depending on flesh for your strength.' When you slice an apple, and let the sliced piece set awhile, the apple will become a brown color and eventually rot. If you sit awhile, and do not spend time with Jesus in prayer, worship, and His Word, your spiritual fruit will eventually rot" (Pr 20:4; 21:25; Jer 17:5; Joel 1:17[KJV]; Mt 18:3,4; Jn 8:44; 14:15-17).

The Lord declared further, "All your trials and tests are to condition you to grow as 'seeds', like in a garden. The Word of God, the 'seed,' takes root in good soil, so you can grow lasting fruits and vegetables in My 'garden.' When the winds blow and the rains fall, the winds and rains of opposition against your calling together, stand firm 'and produce a crop,' a 'hundred fold'" (Mt 7:24,25; Mk 4:3,14,20[KJV]; Ja 1:2-4; 1 Pe 4:12,13). Received August 10, 1999.

He disclosed, "Come and listen as I take you into My 'garden.' You see how well the vegetables grow; how the seed is planted in an orderly manner, and how rich the soil is. The soil becomes richer when My people become less, when they choose to 'come down to earth' from their lofty, self-protective 'walls.' You can become 'rich soil,' full of love and mercy, so that 'seedlings,' like offspring, spring up. The Holy Spirit fills you with His 'living water' to water the garden within your hearts, in order to break up clods of dirt that the Lord is removing. This is done with His loving hands, so that a 'wall of protection' is set around your heart, your 'garden' (Gen 2:15; Ezr 9:9[b]; Ps 25:6; Isa 2:12,15; 44:3,4; 49:16; Joel 1:17[a]; Lk 8:11,15; Jn 3:30; 7:37-39).

"At times the enemy tries to steal the 'seed' that God has planted in your soil. The enemy, Satan, strikes in the nighttime. As you become less in yourselves, My seed will be rooted deeper in the ground of your hearts, 'rooted and established in love,' so that nothing 'can separate you from the love of Christ.' Daily, do I 'garden' My people, who choose to repent from their sin (Mt 13:24,25; Lk 9:23-25; Jn 10:10[a]; Ro 8:35-39; Eph 3:17; Php 2:3-8).

"Sometimes heavy rainfalls come and winds blow against My 'seedlings,' My offspring. But the 'roots' of love are deep enough in Jesus, so that you return kindness, not hate when you are attacked by the winds and rains of others. Be willing to pull out those weeds and thorns, that can choke the words of love going forth. Help each other through love and forgiveness, and God's Son will shine on your 'garden,' that I have planted together in you as 'one'" (Pr 15:19; Mk 4:18,19; Lk 6:35,36; Ac 17:29[a]; Eph 4:14-16, 29-32; 5:14). Received March 2, 2001.

The Lord Jesus shared, "Come to the garden and see the beauty of the birds singing, the springs flowing, the butterflies flying. See the beauty of God all around you. You can become like Me, like birds freely singing, like springs freely flowing with 'living water,' like butterflies who have been freed out of their cocoons, and like the Israelites who were freed from their Egyptian bondage" (Ex 3:7-10; Ps 104:10-12; SS 2:12[KJV]; Isa 31:5[KJV]; 41:18; Jer 51:14[KJV]; Jn 7:38). Received June 4, 1999.

He added, "Cultivate patience in My 'garden of love.' What is patience? (It is like a vision I had of cotton growing in fields of the United States of America. It is soft, white, and fluffy. It is like a cushion filled with cotton, a pillow. The cushion takes a 'blow' when someone sits down on it. Yet, the cushion breathes out the 'blow'). Patience develops through receiving blows from others. It is the patience of Jesus within you. You have to practice patience" (Ro 2:4; Col 1:10,11; 1 Ti 1:16; Ja 5:7,8). Received February 16, 2009.

One of the forerunners, who was considered patient, "kind and generous" in cultivating gardens and orchards of apple trees was "John Chapman," who acquired the name "Johnny Appleseed." The Lord Jesus gave us the words, "Johnny Appleseed" on November 13, 2009. He was born in "Massachusetts" just prior to the Revolutionary War in "1774." Johnny Appleseed "introduced apple trees to large parts of Ohio, Indiana, and Illinois," and was a leader in displaying "the symbolic importance of apples." "He planted" gardens of apple trees, and "obtained the apple seeds free."[83]

But most of all, Johnny Appleseed spread the "seed," the Word of God wherever "he went." For "he was also a missionary for the Church of the New Jerusalem." Johnny Appleseed considered himself a "primitive Christian," who was "clad in coarse raiment," who "spread the . . . gospel ('news right fresh from heaven'), to the adults," who happened by his way.[84] Johnny Appleseed reportedly bore seed into "fruit that (would) last," which was a staple provision for the early colonists as he walked in the Father's "garden." We were informed that some of the trees that Johnny Appleseed planted are still alive today (Mt 3:4[KJV]; Mk 4:3,14,20; 16:15; Jn 15:1-4,16).

Before I, Phyllis, and my husband added this section about Johnny Appleseed to the book, I was preparing an "apple cake" from Stayman apples in preparation for Thanksgiving Day. My husband and I had picked these apples at a local apple orchard.

The Lord's Quilt

The Lord Jesus has been so patient with us, as we learn to grow up in His "garden." He has been patiently working with me, Phyllis, on a quilt representing this garden. From June 1995 through December 1998, we lived in Whiteville, North Carolina. We lived in the "Bible belt" area, and God was ever-present with us. At that time, the Lord placed it on my heart to begin making a quilt. When I began the quilt, I had no idea it would be a quilt for Jesus.

Slowly, each day and night, He would give me a word or revelations on something to place on the quilt. There were a few times, I actually received visions of floral material, and I knew I had to find material like it for the quilt. In the center of the quilt, I made a cross out of an old piece of "torn lace" from a curtain our daughter had given me. When I received a vision of certain material, I would find that material at a local fabric shop. On a white pillow case was embroidered the word, "His." As a border around the word, "His," in the quilt, I included a pink ribbon from my wedding gown.

From another fabric, I included a simple country church on the quilt. The Lord also had spoken of herbs being very important to me in the "End-times," like it was in the colonial times. There was a fabric that emphasized herbs, and I placed it on the quilt. The Lord Jesus gave me a Scripture that He wanted included on the quilt. "The Lord will guide you always; He will satisfy your needs in a sun-scorched land and will strengthen your frame. You will be like a well-watered garden, like a spring whose waters never fail" (Isa 58:11; Ro 16:5[a]; Heb 6:7[KJV]).

The Lord Jesus, I believe, desired this quilt for a future purpose, to give hope to families, especially in the "End-times" when things will seem hopeless, when hearts will be in despair. If we, like the Pilgrims and Puritans, spend our days in the Word of God for ourselves, our children, our families and neighbors, and embark on the basics of making a simple quilt, we believe Jesus will open up our eyes and hearts to see the abundant life in Him. For all those that will be suffering and lost, and for those filled with pain, He wants to draw them, adults and children, back to Himself, into His "garden"; to rest with Him, to sit at His feet, to learn from Him, and to just be in His presence. One of our favorite past hymns, *In the Garden*,[85] reveals this (Mt 4:4; 11:28-30; Mk 13:19,20; Lk 8:21;10:39; Jn 4:35; 6:44; 10:10[KJV]; 1 Jn 3:19).

In the Garden

"I come to the garden alone,
While the dew is still on the roses;
And the voice I hear, falling on my ear,
The Son of God discloses.

And He walks with me, and He talks with me,
And He tells me I am His own,
And the joy we share as we tarry there,
None other has ever known."

See Exhibits A and B, "The Lord's Quilt,"
at the end of this book.

God's Provision

When we are willing to abide with Jesus in our Father's "garden," He will make provision for us even in these last days. On March 10, 2008, my wife heard these words from the Lord Jesus, "Americans, how can they practically, make the transition?" The Lord then said, "In order to make a practical transition from having money, wealth, prosperity, to having it all taken away, to having nothing, no money, no wealth; one must be willing to give up their self-needs, their wants. They must be willing to sacrifice (Mt 10:9,10; Mk 10:21-31; Ro 12:1,2).

"Only allowing Jesus' love into your hearts, will you be able to make the transition. It is in entrusting that the Lord Jesus will make provisions, physical and spiritual, that you can make the transition from 'prosperity' to having nothing, 'but possessing everything' in Jesus. Spending time with Jesus will make the transition easier. A practical transition means a rethinking of how Americans, during colonial times, made the transition from not depending on their 'Mother country,' on England for provision, but trusting solely in God" (Pr 3:5,6; 29:25; Jn 21:15-17; Ac 4:13; Php 3:7-11).

One of those practical transitions occurred for us in August 1999. In December of 1998, we moved to Fredericksburg, Virginia. In Virginia, I, Phyllis, continued with intercessory prayer on behalf of certain individuals, that God would have me pray for during the day. One day, one of our daughters came by to see me at our house. She knew I loved to "can" vegetables in the summer time. Our daughter brought over twelve empty quart jars with lids, that she purchased at a yard sale. Though I wanted to "can" tomatoes and other vegetables immediately, the Lord was disciplining me to stay home close to Him in the Word of God to intercede on behalf of others. So the jars sat empty. Weeks went by, and I remained faithful to Him (Mk 4:18,19; Lk 10:39-42; Ro 8:27; 1 Ti 2:1).

One day in August 1999, my husband suggested we go out

and take a drive to George Washington's birthplace in Westmoreland County, Virginia. As we traveled that day, I noticed a huge field/garden near the road filled with ripened tomatoes. Then I said to my husband, "Please let's drive back there, and ask the owners if they will let us pick some tomatoes for canning." My husband said, "Okay." We drove up a gravel road to an old farmhouse. A man was standing out in the front yard. We asked him if we could pick some tomatoes and purchase them. That man shared, "I have just sold the entire field to someone else. The tomatoes are no longer mine."

But then he said, "How many did you want?" We replied, "About a bushel." He responded, "I'll tell you what. Go all the way down to the far end of the field, and pick out enough for a bushel, no charge!" The Lord was giving me my heart's desire. We picked about a bushel of tomatoes that afternoon. After returning home, I began to wash, peel, and cut out dark spots in the tomatoes. We threw away tomatoes that I knew would not be fit for canning. At the end of the canning process, the twelve jars our daughter had given us were filled to the brim. The tomatoes filled the twelve jars exactly. What an awesome God we serve, who daily makes provision for us! (2 Ki 4:3-7; Ps 37:4; Pr 31:15).

Provision from Israel for America

During five days in the summer of 1994, on July 28, 30, 31, and August 1, 2, while we were living in an apartment in a lower socio-economic area in Haifa, Israel, I, Phyllis, received visions, and personal words and revelations from our Lord Jesus regarding End-time provisions. In one vision, I saw a rainbow in the sky. Then I was given a vision of a gold bag with coffee being squeezed out of it. A vision followed of me, Phyllis, taking coffee out of a box on a table. A "coffee mate" non-dairy creamer was also on a table.

Later, I received a vision of herbs, one of which was

chamomile, and I heard the words, "Herbs better than verbs." Another vision followed of a loaf of bread on a floor. A pile of potatoes was in a flour sifter. A metal scoop was upside down in the vision, and a water pipe was shown to be plugged up.

On another day, I also received a vision of an aged, wrinkled, nervous, starving, and desperate man in a field. The man in the vision had lost all of his hair. He was looking over fields that had dried up, for all his crops were gone. Then I saw a salad placed on the far side of a table, while my husband and I were placing canned food items and non-perishables in a kitchen cabinet. There were jars full of sugar and flour in the cabinet. Another vision followed of a metal shower head attached to a sink faucet. Finally, I saw a vision of an angry man standing near fuel/gas pumps. The gas pumps were empty. The man in the vision appeared desperate. Then I heard the word, "Earthquake."

The Lord spoke to us about these visions and said, "The rainbow is a promise that I will not destroy all flesh. There is an earthquake coming, which will be loosed in the earth. America does not have enough strength to develop a monogamous relationship with itself and God. It cannot exist without committing 'adulteries' with other countries to survive. Banks are going to collapse in (America). The economic system as you know it will fall in America (Gen 9:8-16; Ps 106:35,36; Isa 2:12,15; Jer 3:6-9; Lk 21:11).

"The value of coffee and non-dairy creamers will be very high. Investing in herbs will be better than action (verbs). They will be useful like chamomile for teas and medicines, (and flavoring foods). Potatoes will be available, but rationed. Wheat and grain crops will be gone. The sweet things that you scooped up before will not be available. Collect bottles of fresh water, as it will be very valuable in the last days (Ex 17:1; Isa 3:1; Eze 4:16; Heb 6:7[KJV]; Rev 6:5,6).

"Due to the collapse in the economic system in America, those who find their value in things will be dying inside. They will be clothed in darkness. The fields of farmers' crops will be worthless. There will not be any money for the farmers. The farmers in the land will become economically bankrupt. You will have to put aside leafy vegetables for they will not be available. It will be important to store up non-perishables, flour and sugar, canned foods and vegetables (Gen 41:36; Pr 28:3; Joel 1:10,11; Lk 11:34; Jn 3:19).

"Fresh water will be scarce. Bathing will take place in sinks, rather than tubs and showers, and less frequently. America will not be able to survive without fuel, for they have not suffered such hardships in the past. The people in Israel have been used to hardships. They know how to survive in desperate situations" (Ps 63:1; Isa 41:17; Mt 24:21; Ac 14:22; Ja 5:17).

During those five days, the Lord revealed to me a list of items that will be important to have in the last days. Grocery items: rice, sugar, canned goods and meats, cooking oil, salt, pepper, spices, powdered milk, bottled water, baby formula, canned juices, vitamins and iron, flour, yeast, coffee, prune juice, peas, lentils, beans, honey, maple syrup, molasses, teas, potatoes, petroleum jelly and sulfur for salves, toiletries, toothpaste, deodorants, rubbing alcohol, hydrogen peroxide, medicines for colds, flu, and for vomiting and diarrhea, hot water bottles, soaps, antibacterial dish detergent, bandages, toilet paper, pain relievers, aspirin, brandy used for pain without the availability of penicillin, baby food, diapers, diaper rash medicines, shampoos, jars and lids for canning, laundry soap, scrub boards, oatmeal, paper for writing, pens and pencils, etc. (Pr 6:6-8; 10:5; 30:24).

Other items that will be important in the last days: chamber pots, dead bolt locks, batteries, radios, books, tape and CD players, tapes and CD's, buckets to collect water, fertilizer, lime, seeds/herbs, kerosene oil/kerosene lamps and wicks, gas containers filled with gasoline, blankets, pillows, warm socks and clothing, candles, matches, clothes lines and clothes pins, outside pots for outdoor cooking, farm utensils; hoes, shovels, axes, saws, nails, hammers, etc. Toys, games, books for children and adults, fishing and hunting gear, rifles, bullets, spices for curing meats, pine sol and items for cleaning, reading glasses, propane gas, and gas and charcoal grills, charcoal, pesticides for garden plants and trees, rodent traps, etc. (Pr 31:10-24; Eze 27:17-22; 1 Ti 6:19).

The Lord Jesus has also displayed His marvelous provision for the vehicles we have purchased in the past. One incident involved a Mazda station wagon that we sold before leaving for Israel in the summer of 1994. While in Israel, we received visions that we would be driving that car again. Following those visions in Israel, after we returned to the United States in October 1994, we believe that the Lord was telling us to repurchase the Mazda station wagon.

We drove our son's car over to the home of the man, who had purchased that vehicle. Amazingly, that man was willing to sell us back that car, after he had done some work on the wheels and brakes. What a blessing for us. The Lord Jesus helped us, by providing us a needed vehicle. Just as He made provision for us on our calling to Israel, so He will, we believe, make similar provision for His believers in these last days (Ps 46:1; 121:1,2; Jn 6:49-51; Ac 26:22).

Provision in the Last Days

Pastor David Wilkerson of World Challenge wrote on the importance of trusting Almighty God in the last days in his book, *The Vision and Beyond*.[86] He reported that, "It is not a time to hoard money, because it will not provide real security . . . The only security is in land . . . Every cent that is . . . given to God's work must be given with a purpose . . . Those who obey God's Word . . . will never have to beg for bread during the lean years. Those who see the hard times coming and prepare are wise . . . Don't buy anything unless it is needed. Avoid going into debt . . . Avoid piling up credit card bills" (2 Ki 4:7; Ecc 11:1,2; Da 12:3; Mk 4:20; Lk 6:38; 12:15-21).

Pastor Wilkerson wrote further, "God, in His love and

mercy, is allowing disasters to strike the earth to warn all who hear that Jesus is coming back, and that it's time to get ready . . . These labor pains will become more frequent and intense as we approach the last hour. There will be more famines, more pestilence, more earthquakes in more places, (but) . . . God has everything under control! . . . Everything that we now see happening has been clearly predicted in God's Word . . . Nature is controlled and limited by God[87] (Ps 65:7; 107:25,29; Pr 30:4; Mt 24:7,8; Mk 4:39-41; Lk 21:10,11,28).

"Even Satan is under control, as with Job . . . The devil's power is limited . . . Christians can put him to flight simply by resisting him through the Word and the blood of Christ . . . Satan . . . can persecute you . . . You can wind up penniless, having to pray for your very next meal . . . But, . . . no power in heaven or on earth can touch a man's . . . faith in Jesus Christ, no demon, no devil[88] (Job 1:8-12; 2:3-6; Ro 8:38,39; Ja 4:7; Rev 12:10,11,17).

"God's children . . . will never beg for bread, and He will supply every true need up to the very last minute of time . . . The future is also under His control, so we need not fear . . . He is still giving abundantly more than we can ask or think . . . The prepared Christian is going to face a time of sorrow and tribulation . . . Prepared Christians—wake up! Everything is under control and God is at work . . . The kingdom of God is coming. The kingdom of Satan is falling."[89] Our Lord Jesus will make provision for us in these last days through the one and only true Liberator, Jesus Christ! He will regain America for Himself (Ps 34:9; 37:25,26; Ro 14:1-4; Ro 13:11; Eph 3:20; Rev 20:1-3).

One other example of God's provision occurred in March 2004. In February 2004, the vehicle we were driving had high mileage, and was experiencing engine problems. The engine was cutting off at different times. We knew we had to trade in that car, or we might be left stranded somewhere. We phoned a car dealership in Leesburg, Virginia, which was about a forty minute drive from our home. The car salesman there informed us, they had a car reserved for us.

On the drive to that car dealership, our car engine was sputtering and cutting off at times. The Lord Jesus placed a beautiful rainbow in the sky during that drive. He revealed to us then, that He would help us find a car. When we arrived at the dealership, we found out that someone had just bought the car that had been reserved for us. We were very upset. There were no other cars at that dealership, that we were interested in, or could afford. We drove home discouraged, but the engine of our car did not cut off.

The next week, we drove to and from work without experiencing any engine problems. We phoned another car dealership in Warrenton, Virginia in March 2004. The owner of that dealership was a donor to the Youth Home where we worked at that time. While driving there, our car engine resumed its sputtering and cutting off. At the dealership, we were able to work with a Christian salesman. We purchased a used Ford Focus, which has been a most dependable car over the past years. The owner took off over $4000 from the listing price of the car.

Even recently, in August/September 2009, we received four new tires with balance and rotation on that Ford Focus at a Walmart at no extra cost for us. The tires were prorated on their computer system under their Warranty Protection Program. The Lord Jesus has faithfully provided us a reliable and dependable vehicle at a very reasonable cost. The Lord Jesus has been helping us learn "the secret of being content in any and every situation," for He never leaves us nor forsakes us! (Jn 12:36; Php 4:12; Heb 13:5[b]).

As we come to the end of this chapter, we were asked by our Lord Jesus to give a Eulogy for the United States of America.

The Eulogy of America

We are grateful for being born in a country, that was founded on the Rock, the Cornerstone, Jesus Christ through our forefathers, the Pilgrims and Puritans, and our Founding Fathers, who covenanted with one another and Almighty

God for the future of this nation. We are thankful that the direction, the moral compass, the Way, the simplicity, and the helm of America was under the guidance of the Holy Spirit, under the sovereignty of our Lord and Savior, Jesus (Ps 19:7; Da 4:25[b]; Jn 14:6; 16:13; Ac 4:32; 1 Co 10:4; 11:25,26; Eph 2:20; Col 3:15).

We are indebted to those Founding Fathers and patriots, who fought for true liberty, independence, and the freedom, privileges, and inalienable rights, we have received from past generations. Those rights are revealed in our founding documents, especially the Declaration of Independence and the Constitution of the United States of America. We have been blessed that our Lord Jesus was honored by men and women in public government facilities, in public schools, in the private sector, and in the medical profession; honoring the "sanctity of life," especially for the unborn (Ps 139:13-16; Jn 5:22,23; 2 Co 3:17[KJV]; 1 Ti 6:12).

We have been blessed that the Word of God, Scripture readings, prayer, and worship were the embodiment for the early settlers of this country in schools across the nation. They taught Christian moral values opposed to sexual immorality, fornication, incest, adultery, homosexual behavior, abortions, etc. We have been blessed that our school instructors taught the value of covenanted marriages between men and women, and the need to protect America's children from evil worldly influences (Mal 2:14-16; Jn 4:23,24; 1 Co 6:9,10,18-20; 2 Ti 3:16,17; 4:2; 1 Jn 2:14-17).

We are thankful for the wisdom of the justices of the United States Supreme Court, who called America a Christian nation; a nation in which we could pray and worship, read the Word of God publicly and privately, freely, and without our government's prohibition thereof (Ps 111:10; Mt 6:9-13; 10:7,8; Ro 12:1; 1 Ti 4:13; 1 Pe 4:16).

Yet, today we are writing this book to proclaim that America has lost that for which we were grateful, thankful, and blessed for in America. The American people have lost their true liberties, forsaking the one and only true God and Liberator from sin, our Lord Jesus through the decisions made by the so-called "leaders" in this country, primarily in over the last fifty years or so. America is on the "broad road" of "destruction" awaiting God's judgments for their blatant opposition to Jesus Christ and His Words (2 Ch 15:2; Jer 1:16; Mt 7:13; 10:39; Lk 9:25,26; Gal 4:9; 1 Ti 5:12).

Stand Firm to the End

We must daily seek to be in the presence of God during these last days, so we can be ready for His return. On October 1, 2009, after we fasted and praised our Lord Jesus, I was given some visions. In the first vision, I saw a court jester, jokester. The left side of his face was painted white, and his lips and eyes were painted red. The court jester was wearing a half-moon hat with bells at the top. He was laughing hilariously. When the court jester turned, the right side of his face was dark, black, and evil. Then the jester, jokester put on a black mask. The black mask covered a human face.

Finally, I saw a vision of a colonial picture in our living room. Near the base or bottom of the picture were my wife and I. She was a young girl, and I was a young boy. We wore colonial outfits, while we stood next to an apple tree. The tree was full of green leaves and apples. We were handing out apples to people who passed by us.

The Lord Jesus disclosed, "In the last days, the enemy, moving through people, will scoff, mock, joke, and laugh at Christians. Those in the media will make fun of Christians. Satan, 'disguised as an angel of light,' through his dark followers, will mock those who want to live righteous lives in Christ, Jesus. The Antichrist will be masked, disguised like 'an angel of light' providing resolutions to serious world problems. Inwardly, he will despise the one true God, Jesus, His Word and His followers (Ps 22:6,7; Da 7:20,21,25; Lk

6:25; Jn 15:18,19; 2 Co 11:14,15; 2 Th 2:3,4; 2 Pe 3:3; Rev 12:17).

"You are to bear fruit that will last from 'the tree of life,' from Jesus. It is 'the fruit of the Spirit' that comes through praise and worship. Bearing fruit comes also through time spent with Jesus in repentance and prayer, fruit for each other first, and fruit for others that will last through tribulation" (Mt 6:6; 21:16; Lk 3:8; Jn 15,16; Gal 5:22; Rev 2:7).

The Lord said further, "As the shepherds kept watch over their flocks by night, and were told of the coming of the Lord Jesus on earth, so be watchful again for the coming of the Lord Jesus. Keep your lamps lit, fixing your eyes on Jesus, 'the bright Morning Star,' and His Words about His return (5/22/99). Many of My people are trimming their sails in the storms, trimming their lamps, getting ready for My return in the third or fourth watch of the night. They are vessels willing to carry My message to a lost world. They are willing to get up in the middle of the night to make sure their oil lamps are lit. Their lamps will keep their households lit up in the last days (Mt 14:25; 24:42; 25:6,7; Lk 2:8-16; 12:39; 19:10; Ro 10:14,15; Heb 12:2; Rev 22:16-20). Received June 1, 1998.

"When everything looks dismal and bleak, look to Me. When your life seems to be in a shambles, look to Me. When you are holding on to the end of your rope, look to Me. When your life does not seem to be changing for the better, look to Me. When you encounter similar problems in your life over and over again, look to Me. When you look to Me, I will be with you. I will carry you through what appears to be the most trying and difficult times you have ever experienced. This will not be a time for giving up, but a time for holding on to endurance from Me (Dt 4:29-31; Ps 34:4,5; 105:4; Isa 17:7,8; 40:11; Lk 21:25-28; Jn 6:40; Heb 12:7).

"The Comforter, the Holy Spirit will help you endure suffering that is coming upon the earth, in preparation for My coming. It is only through the shedding of blood, that true love is offered to others in a dying world. This is a call to arms.

Let the 'arms' of the Lord strengthen you. Do not retreat from the battle lines, for the battle belongs to the Lord (Dt 33:27; 2 Ch 20:15,17; 32:7,8; Isa 41:10; Mt 3:3; Jn 14:16-18[KJV]; 2 Co 10:4; Heb 9:22). Received November 1, 1996.

"The flag of freedom still flies today. (My wife saw a vision of an American flag with thirteen stars). It is the flag of independence in the United States, representing the colonists' battle for freedom. There is a battle brewing to deliver those of God, to battle against the Antichrists, to destroy the seats of the enemy, to deliver the 'innocent ones,' the children (and the unborn), who were and are given 'millstones' from their families, burdens too heavy to bear. My children fight to the end! Don't give up the fight, for I am conditioning you for greater battles. Blessed is the nation who serves the Lord. Let your flag fly proudly. God's plan is that in these stormy trials, turn to Jesus!" (1 Sa 17:47; Ps 3:7,8; 24:8; 33:12; Isa 30:17; Mt 18:5-7,10; Mk 13:13; Ac 3:19,20; Gal 6:9; 1 Jn 2:18,19). Received June 10, 1998.

On October 22, 2009, and on January 3, 2008, after we fasted and praised the Lord Jesus, the Lord gave us some visions. On October 22, in the first vision, I saw the famous picture of the United States Marines placing the American flag on the Japanese island of Iwo Jima near the end of World War II. The flag was standing straight up, pointing up to heaven. A star was in the sky high above the flag. The Marines were raising up the flag towards heaven.

In the next vision, I, Mark, was standing near a white and red striped lighthouse, off, what appeared to be the New England coast. The vision appeared to take place in the late fall, while the sun was about to set on the horizon. In that vision, I am standing over a white guardrail looking out towards the ocean. My wife was standing on the beach below, and towards the right of me. We were dressed in coats and warm clothing. As the winds began to blow stronger, and the waves were becoming rougher, I waved my wife into the home at the base of that lighthouse.

A vision followed of dark, billowing clouds in the sky. Lightning was striking down from the clouds. Finally, I saw a vision of palm trees, like in Florida. The trees were blown over by the wind and rain.

The Lord Jesus then disclosed, "The battle ahead will be great, like the battle fought by the Marines at Iwo Jima. The Marines fought with valor and courage. They never gave up the fight. So be like Marines in the last days, working as a team fighting the enemy, the devil and his henchmen. Stand firm until the end. Reach up to the heavenlies, to 'the bright Morning Star,' for His guidance, His light in your house (Pr 24:6[a]; Joel 2:5; Mt 5:15; 10:22: Jn 8:12; Ac 7:56; Eph 6:13,14; Rev 22:16[b]).

"For the storms are coming. The winds are beginning to blow, and the waves will be crashing on America, blowing from the East Coast to the West. Come into My home to the warm crackling 'fire' of the Holy Spirit to be in a safe haven with Jesus. When you spend time with Jesus, He will keep you warm from the cold hearts of many in America, who have chosen to be in the world" (Pr 25:20; Mt 7:24,25; 11:28-30; 14:54; 24:12; Lk 3:16; Jn 14:23).

On January 3, I saw a vision of my wife and me looking at the hot rays of the sun. Then I was given an aerial view of a map of the thirteen original colonies next to the eastern coastline of the United States. In that vision, campfires were burning in each state. Then I saw arrows on that map pointing towards the west and across the United States.

The Lord then revealed, "(The Son) of God desires to warm us up, to warm/warn those living on the earth about the truth of the living God. My warming/warning is for both of you to take My Word with My fervor (hot) to a lost world, to a lost Church. Rest in the assurance that God will be warming you in the days ahead to take warm bread, ("the Bread of Life") to the lost, to the Church. This is My global warming/warning, to warm/warn the peoples on the earth, so that it can be a more comfortable place to live (1 Sa 21:6; Mt 3:7; Mk 16:15,16; Lk 19:10; Jn 6:48; Ac 20:31; Ro 12:11).

"My 'fires' will pass throughout the United States. Those

'fires' will move west, as the pioneers moved west and established 'new lands' in the United States. It will begin on the East Coast, where your (publisher), and local bookstores are located. It's about the books, about marriage and freedom. As scrolls were burned, (as revealed) in the Book of Acts, chapter 19, so there will be a burning of secular thinking in those campfires. Let that 'fire' of love be kindled, that 'fire' of compassion for each other, so you both can be a model of health and happiness to one another, and for those on the earth (in the last days)" (SS 8:6; Mk 9:49; Lk 12:49; Ac 19:18-20; 1 Th 5:19; 3 Jn 2).

God's Train

We have come to the last "train" station in this book. The Lord said, "The United States will be fractured in the days ahead. When all say, 'Peace, Peace,' the storms will come. Those that did not build their homes on the Rock, (Jesus, the Living Word of God) will fall, and not recover. Satan will attempt to deplete My saints' power, those that carry within themselves the fuel for the 'fire' that keeps My 'train' moving in the last days (Eze 13:10-12; Mt 7:26,27; 25:4; Mk 3:23-26; Lk 12:49; Rev 13:7).

"The Lord has a heavenly 'train' that picks up those that have been oppressed, deprived, persecuted, reviled as evil because of Me. I stand in line together with those getting on My 'train,' those who have given up their lives, their possessions, even their privacy; those chosen ones, who have died to the world's ways for the sake of God's kingdom (Ps 68:18; Mt 5:10-12; Lk 9:23-25; Jn 12:24-26; 1 Pe 2:9).

"Get on the train. It is moving to bring all the wounded soldiers in battle against Satan to their eternal rest. There is a 'light' at the end of the tunnel. The 'light' shines through the darkness. It penetrates through the tunnel, so you can reach the other side, to the opening, to freedom. Keep persevering with God, as He exposes the darkness to the light in your lives" (Mt 11:28; Jn 1:4,5; 3:21; Eph 4:8; 5:13,14; Gal 5:1). (The Lord gave us these "train" messages on September 9, 1999, March 22, 2000, and July 5, 2002).

Early in the morning on October 29, 2009, my wife heard these words, "Of the United States of America," and "What a rebellious nation." After we fasted and praised the Lord Jesus that morning, I received visions. In the first vision, I opened a children's picture storybook to a night scene in Israel. There were little children dressed up like shepherds looking up at the "Star" over the city of Bethlehem. Then I saw a little train in the child's storybook traveling over hills away from Bethlehem at night. It was like in the child's story of the train that "thought he could," and "knew he could" when he got over the mountain.

The Lord Jesus then revealed, "You must 'become like little children . . . to enter the kingdom of God.' Believers who get on God's 'train' must know that he or she can do it. They can make it in perilous times with Jesus Christ. 'Of the country of the United States of America,' they, (the American people), have become 'a rebellious nation.' For they, like the Israelites of old, have not been willing to see that the Messiah, Jesus is coming, which was revealed in the song, "While You Were Sleeping."[90] The American people are unwilling to 'become like little children,' for they are depending on their own ways, and not the God of heaven. Even many in the Church, (believers in Jesus), refuse to see the signs of My coming, for they have compromised with the world of sin. Be like little shepherds waiting eagerly for the King's return!" (Isa 6:1; 65:2-5[KJV]; Mt 18:2; 19:26; Lk 2:8-18; Php 4:13; 2 Pe 3:3-10; Rev 2:20-23).

WHILE YOU WERE SLEEPING

"Oh Bethlehem, what you have missed while you were sleeping.
For God became a man—And stepped into your world today.
Oh Bethlehem, you will go down in history—As a city with no room for its King.
While you were sleeping—While you were sleeping.

United States of America—Looks like another silent night.
As we're sung to sleep by philosophies—That save the trees and kill the children.
And while we're lying in the dark—There is a shout heard 'cross the eastern sky.
For the Bridegroom has returned—And has carried His bride away in the night.

America, what will we miss while we are sleeping—Will Jesus come again—And leave us slumbering where we lay.
America, will we go down in history—As a nation with no room for its King.
Will we be sleeping—Will we be sleeping.
United States of America—Looks like another silent night!"

We have hope, for we can take George Washington's vision of the future for America and know that our Lord Jesus will return soon, and the United States will once again be victorious under the Banner and Standard of Jesus Christ, the "True Liberator." Come ALL ABOARD His "train" in these last days!

It was proclaimed at the "Tea Party"[91] in September 2009, "So Americans wherever you are, all over this world; . . . If there are any patriots out there, I need you to stand up for America . . . I need you to stand up for liberty, and our freedom. Patriots stand up! Stand up! Stand up!"

There will be more stories to come on our journey with Jesus!

EPILOGUE

We have traversed through America's: Past, Present, and Future in this book through the guidance of the Holy Spirit with our Lord Jesus Christ. He has revealed more to us about this book and the book cover. On November 13, 2008, and August 24, 2009, after we fasted and worshiped before the Lord Jesus, He gave us some visions. On November 13, I saw the Empire State Building in New York City. The building was lit up from the ground floor to the top. The Lord then revealed, "You will shine light on this book from a place near the Empire State Building, Vantage Press" (Isa 60:1; Mt 5:16).

On August 24, I was given a vision of my wife and me taking pictures of the Amish and Mennonites' farmland in Lancaster County, Pennsylvania. The Lord Jesus then said, "That is where I want you to go to take pictures for the cover of this book." On August 27, 2009, my wife and I took a trip to Lancaster County, Pennsylvania, where many Amish and Mennonite families still live and farm the land there. We both took pictures that day of the farmland. We visited the Mennonite Information Center. As early as the 1600's through the 1700's, many Amish and Mennonites came to live in this area. They wanted to follow the true Jesus Christ and His teachings. They, like the Pilgrims and Puritans, suffered persecution in Europe before leaving to come to America. Today, especially in the Mennonite community, their life is centered in our Lord and Savior, Jesus Christ (Lk 9:23; Ac 2:42,44; Heb 6:7; 1 Pe 4:8).

On September 3, 2009, and August 13, 2009, after we fasted and praised the Lord Jesus, I was given more revelations. On September 3, I saw another vision of the cover of this book. On the right side of the vision, I saw a thirteen-star colonial American flag flying from the right to the left on a flagpole. In the background, there were green farmlands, like in Pennsylvania.

The center of the thirteen stars of the flag was somewhat transparent. Looking through the flag, I saw my wife and me with outstretched arms. Behind us were generations of American people also with outstretched arms. The generations appeared to be going all the way back to colonial times. The Lord said, "Today, and generations back, many Americans have stretched out their arms to God in thanks and gratefulness for the abundance of His provision in this country." He also shared, "As you are transparent in your book in Me, so be willing to be transparent to the world" (Dt 15:8; Ps 103:2-5; 136:1,25; Pr 31:20; Jn 1:47; Eph 4:15,25). Received October 29, 2009.

On August 13, I saw a vision of me, Mark, pulling out a book off our white mantle bookshelf that extends over our fireplace. There were about six hardback books with maroon covers standing up next to each other. Then I heard the words, "Breakneck speed." The Lord Jesus then disclosed, "My return is coming quickly, that is why I am moving you on these books at 'Breakneck speed.' The books need to go out to the public, whether or not they read and receive what God is revealing to them" (Eze 2:5; Hab 2:2,3; Rev 22:20). The Lord Jesus has helped us to write this book in a very timely manner.

FREEDOM PROCLAMATION

★ ★ ★

Hear Ye! Hear Ye! Proclaim liberty throughout the land of America to all its inhabitants, through Jesus, the true Liberator from sin!

We proclaim liberty:

For all who follow our forefathers, the Pilgrims and Puritans, and our Founding Fathers' faith in the Lord Jesus, the Rock and Cornerstone of this country; "proclaiming the good news that Jesus is the Christ."

For all who choose the one and only true God, the Father and His Son, Jesus, for there are no other "gods" before Him; proclaiming "freedom for the captives."

For all who dare to turn away from sin, and fleshly/worldly desires, and tyrannical "leaders" who oppose the Bible, the living Word of God; proclaiming "the kingdom of God."

For all who speak and pray in the Name of Jesus in public, in government, in schools, and in the private sector; proclaiming "His salvation day after day."

For all who boldly share the Scriptures on the evils of sin, sexual immorality, homosexuality, abortions, other "gods," antichrist spirits, etc.; proclaiming "justice to the nation."

For all who choose to become real Americans willing to "serve the living God" our Lord Jesus!

Proclaimed in the year of our Lord, 2010

NOTES

AMERICA: PAST

1. *Wikipedia, the free encyclopedia,* "Robert E. Lee," http://en.wikipedia.org/wiki/Robert_E._Lee.
2. *Historic Bethabara Park,* "The Moravian Story," http://www.bethabarapark.org/moravian/html.
3. *The History Place,* "American Revolution, The Mayflower Compact," http://www.historyplace.com/unitedstates/revolution/mayflower.html.
4. Jerry Wilkinson, "Influence of France on Florida,"p. 1 of 4, http://www.keys history.org/FL—Fla—Fr.html.
5. Mark Kirchberg and Phyllis Kirchberg, *The Great Cover-up: Living in the Shadow of a Lie, The Roman Catholic Church,* Vantage Press, Inc., New York, NY, 2009, pp. 45, 46.
6. Gary DeMar, *America's Heritage,* Coral Ridge Ministries, Fort Lauderdale, FL, 2002, p. 14.

    The First Charter of Virginia, (April 10, 1606), "The Laws of Nature and Nature's God," Lonang Library, 2003-2008, p. 2 of 10, http://www.lonang.com/exlibus/organic/1606-fcu.html.
7. Peter Marshall and David Manuel, *The Light and the Glory,* Fleming H. Revell, Grand Rapids, MI, 1977, pp. 80, 87, 96.
8. Ibid., p. 105.
9. Ibid.
10. Ibid., pp. 121, 134, 139, 144.
11. Gary DeMar, *America's Heritage,* Coral Ridge Ministries, Fort Lauderdale, FL, 2002, pp. 15, 16.

11. Kurt A. Grussendorf, Michael R. Lowman, and Brian S. Ashbaugh, *America Land I Love*, A Beka Book, Pensacola, FL, 1994, p. 28.
12. Peter Marshall and David Manuel, *The Light and the Glory*, Fleming H. Revell, Grand Rapids, MI, 1977, pp. 107-109.
13. Ibid., pp. 108, 109.
14. D. James Kennedy, *One Nation Under God*, DVD, Coral Ridge Ministries, Fort Lauderdale, FL, 2005.
15. Wright and Potter, *William Bradford*, "Of Plimoth Plantation," Boston, MA, 1901, http://smartandfinalisis.wordpress.com/2006/ll/22/thanksgiving-and-capitalism.
16. Gary DeMar, *America's Heritage*, Coral Ridge Ministries, Fort Lauderdale, FL, 2002, pp. 15-18.

    Peter Marshall and David Manuel, *The Light and the Glory*, Fleming H. Revell, Grand Rapids, MI, 1977, p. 113.

    Tom Freiling, *Reagan's God And Country*, Servant Publications, Ann Arbor, MI, 2000, pp. 55, 184
17. Peter Marshall and David Manuel, *The Light and the Glory*, Fleming H. Revell, Grand Rapids, MI, 1977, p. 151.
18. Tom Freiling, *Reagan's God And Country*, Servant Publications, Ann Arbor, MI, 2002, pp. 117,118.

    Peter Marshall and David Manuel, *The Light and the Glory*, Fleming H. Revell, Grand Rapids, MI, 1977, p. 120.

    D. James Kennedy, *One Nation Under God*, DVD, Coral Ridge Ministries, Fort Lauderdale, FL, 2005.
19. Rick Williams, "Thanksgiving and Capitalism," http://smartandfinalisis.word press.com/2006/ll/22/thanksgiving-and-capitalism.
20. Kurt A. Grussendorf, Michael R. Lowman, and Brian S. Ashbaugh, *America Land I Love*, A Beka Book, Pensacola, FL, 1994, p. 29.
21. Peter Marshall and David Manuel, *The Light and the Glory*, Fleming H. Revell, Grand Rapids, MI, 1977, pp. 126, 151.
22. Ibid., pp. 133-136.
23. Ibid., p. 139.

    Kurt A. Grussendorf, Michael R. Lowman, and Brian S. Ashbaugh, *America Land I Love*, A Beka Book, Pensacola, FL, 1994, p. 31.
24. Ibid., p. 518.

25. Mark Kirchberg and Phyllis Kirchberg, *The Profound Mystery: Marriage—The First Church,* Vantage Press, Inc., New York, NY, 2008.
26. Kurt A. Grussendorf, Michael R. Lowman, and Brian S. Ashbaugh, *America Land I Love,* A Beka Book, Pensacola, FL, 1994, p. 28.

    Peter Marshall and David Manuel, *The Light and the Glory,* Fleming H. Revell, Grand Rapids, MI, 1977, p. 148.
27. Ibid., p. 28.

    Ibid., pp. 108, 109.
28. Peter Marshall and David Manuel, *The Light and the Glory,* Fleming H. Revell, Grand Rapids, MI, 1977, pp. 150, 151.
29. Ibid., pp. 146, 169.
30. Ibid., pp. 168, 171, 175.
31. Ibid., p. 159.
32. D. James Kennedy, *One Nation Under God,* DVD, Coral Ridge Ministries, Fort Lauderdale, FL, 2005.
33. Davis Ross, Alden Vaughan, and John Duff, eds., *Colonial America: 1607-1763,* (New York: Thomas Y. Crowell Co., 1970), "John Winthrop and the Founding of New England," p. 25.
34. George McKenna, opening remarks from Edward Johnson, *Wonderful Working Providence of Sion's Savior in New England,* (1554), "The Puritan Origins of American Patriotism," http://books.google.com/books?id.

    Peter Marshall and David Manuel, *The Light and the Glory,* Fleming H. Revell, Grand Rapids, MI, 1977, pp. 163, 164.
35. D. James Kennedy, *One Nation Under God,* DVD, Coral Ridge Ministries, Fort Lauderdale, FL, 2005.
36. Peter Marshall and David Manuel, *The Light and the Glory,* Fleming H. Revell, Grand Rapids, MI, 1977, pp. 203, 204.

    The Works of Thomas Hooker at International Outreach, Inc., "The Christian's Two Chief Lessons," and "The Soul's Humiliation," http://jerel79.bizland.com/store/pagel.html.
37. Peter Marshall and David Manuel, *The Light and the Glory,* Fleming H. Revell, Grand Rapids, MI, 1977, pp. 247, 248.
38. Kurt A. Grussendorf, Michael R. Lowman, and Brian S. Ashbaugh, *America Land I Love,* A Beka Book, Pensacola, FL, 1994, pp. 52, 61.

39. Coral Ridge Ministries, *10 Truths about America's Christian Heritage*, Ft Lauderdale, FL, 2008, p. 69.

    New Hampshire Historical Society, "The First New Hampshire Teacher: John Legat," article, pp. 1, 2 of 3.

    J. Hammond Trumbull, ed., *The True-Blue Laws of Connecticut and New Haven*, 1876, http://www.quinnipiac.edu/other/abl/etext/true-blue/bluelaws.html.

40. Deborah Cariker, *Eclectic Homeschool Online, The New England Primer*, http://www.eclectichomeschool.org/reviews/individualreviews2.asp?revid=1282.

    D. James Kennedy and Jerry Newcombe, *What If Jesus Had Never Been Born?*, Thomas Nelson, Inc., Nashville, TN, 1994.

    Coral Ridge Ministries, 10 *Truths about America's Christian Heritage*, Fort Lauderdale, FL, 2008, p. 73.

    William Dix, *The Princeton University Library in the Eighteenth Century*, pp. 2, 5 of 105, http://infosharel.princeton.edu/rbsc.2/library/history/1755.

    Dave Miller, *Apologetics Press.org*, "Much Respect for the Quran—Not Much for the Bible"

    Benjamin Pierce (1833), *A History of Harvard University*, Cambridge, MA, (Brown, Shattuck, and Company).

    Franklin, Dexter, ed., (1916), *Documentary History of Yale University*, (New Haven, CT), Yale University Press.

41. Peter Marshall and David Manuel, *The Light and the Glory*, Fleming H. Revell, Grand Rapids, MI, 1977, pp. 171, 178, 179.
42. Ibid., p. 182.
43. Ibid., pp. 213, 214, 219, 220.
44. Ibid., p. 220.
45. Ibid., pp. 217, 221, 226, 228, 230.
46. Ibid., pp. 227, 228, 231.
47. Ibid., pp. 232, 233.
48. Ibid., pp. 235-238.
49. *American Exceptionalism*, "Origins: Exceptionalism and American Cultural Identity," (Edinburg & London: Edinburg University Press; Jackson, MS, University of Mississippi Press, 1998), p. 13 of 18, http://home.adm.unige.ch/~madsen/exceptionalism1.html.

50. *Hymns of Glorious Praise,* #494, "Battle Hymn of the Republic," Gospel Publishing House, Springfield, MO, 1969.
51. Ben Williamson, *U.S. Studies Online: The BAAS Postgraduate Journal,* "The Unutterable Entertainments of Paradise: The Landscape and Waste in the Fiction of David Foster Wallace," http://www.baas.ac.uk/resources/usstudiesonline/article.asp.

    Peter Marshall and David Manuel, *The Light and the Glory,* Fleming H. Revell, Grand Rapids, MI, 1977, pp. 175, 265.
52. *Hymns of Glorious Praise,* #493, "America, the Beautiful," Gospel Publishing House, Springfield, MO, 1969.
53. Tom Freiling, *Reagan's God and Country,* Servant Publications, Ann Arbor, MI, 2000, pp. 23, 24, 159.
54. Shane Idleman, *Good News Daily,* "Is America a Christian Nation?," www.good newsdaily.net/modules/news/article.php?
55. Gary DeMar, *America's Heritage,* Coral Ridge Ministries, Fort Lauderdale, FL, 2002, p. 21.
56. The Avalon Project: "Constitution of Delaware 1776," Yale Law School, http://avalonlaw.yale.edu/18thcentury/de0?.asp

    George Craik and Charles MacFarlane, "The Pictorial History of England During the Reign of George the Third," http://books. google.com/books?id.
57. Steve Lefemine, *No King But King Jesus!,* "Declarations and Evidences of Christian Faith," http://www.daveblackonline.com/nokingbutkingjesus.htm.

    Peter Marshall and David Manuel, *The Light and the Glory,* Fleming H. Revell, Grand Rapids, MI, 1977, p. 254.
58. Peter Marshall and David Manuel, *The Light and the Glory,* Fleming H. Revell, Grand Rapids, MI, 1977, pp. 256-260, 264, 265.

    American Exceptionalism, "Origins: Exceptionalism and American Cultural Identity,"(Edinburg & London: Edinburg University Press; Jackson, MS, University of Mississippi Press, 1998), p. 13 of 18, http://home.adm.unige.ch/~madsen/exceptionalisml.htm.
59. *Liberty! The American Revolution,* Video set, Vol. Two, "The Times that Try Men's Souls," Twin Cities Public Television, Inc., Burbank, CA, 1997.

60. Coral Ridge Ministries, *10 Truths about America's Christian Heritage,* Fort Lauderdale, FL, 2008, p. 25.
61. Tom Hooper, dir., *John Adams,* DVD series, Home Box Office Films, 2008.
62. William Wirt, *Sketches of the Life and Character of Patrick Henry (1836),* "Give Me Liberty or Give Me Death," speech, http://www.history.org/Almanack/life/politics/giveme.cfm.
63. Robert Stevenson, dir., *Johnny Tremain,* Disney Enterprises, Inc., Walt Disney Production, Burbank, CA, 1957.
64. *Hymns of Glorious Praise,* #494, "Battle Hymn of the Republic," Gospel Publishing House, Springfield, MO, 1969.
65. D. James Kennedy, *Coral Ridge Ministries,* CD, "The Faith of Washington," Fort Lauderdale, FL, 2005.
66. Ibid.
67. Ibid.
68. Ibid.
69. Ibid.
70. David Hogan, *Brownsville Revival: School of Ministry,* "Faith to Raise the Dead," Video series, Pensacola, FL, 1997.
71. *The Carpenters Company,* pamphlet, Philadelphia, PA, www.carpentershall.org.
72. Gary DeMar, *America's Heritage,* Coral Ridge Ministries, Fort Lauderdale, FL, 2002, p. 54.
73. *The Office of the Chaplain, United States House of Representatives,* "First Prayer of the Continental Congress," 1774, http://chaplain.house.gov/archives/continental.html.
74. D. James Kennedy, *One Nation Under God,* DVD, Coral Ridge Ministries, Fort Lauderdale, FL, 2005.
75. *America's Prayer Network,* "George Washington's Prayer for the United States of America," Washington, D.C.
76. *Independence National Historical Park, Pennsylvania,* "The Road to Nationhood," National Park Service, U.S. Department of the Interior, Philadelphia, PA, 2007.
77. D. James Kennedy, *One Nation Under God,* DVD, Coral Ridge Ministries, Fort Lauderdale, FL, 2005.
78. Peter Marshall and David Manuel, *The Light and the Glory,* Fleming H. Revell, Grand Rapids, MI, 1977, p. 267.
79. D. James Kennedy, *One Nation Under God,* DVD, Coral Ridge Ministries, Fort Lauderdale, FL, 2005.

80. Ibid., Peter Marshall and David Manuel, *The Light and the Glory,* Fleming H. Revell, Grand Rapids, MI, 1977, p. 303.
81. David Barton, *The Myth of Separation,* Wall Builders, Aledo, TX, Founding Fathers Quotations on Whether the United States was Founded as a Christian Nation, "Continental Congress."
82. Tom Freiling, *Reagan's God And Country,* Servant Publications, Ann Arbor, MI, 2000, pp. 171, 178.
83. Peter Marshall and David Manuel, *The Light and the Glory,* Fleming H. Revell, Grand Rapids, MI, 1977, pp. 303, 306.
84. Ibid., pp. 306, 307.
85. Coral Ridge Ministries, *10 Truths about America's Christian Heritage,* Fort Lauderdale, FL, 2008, p. 56.
86. D. James Kennedy, *One Nation Under God,* DVD, Fort Lauderdale, FL, 2005.
87. Ibid.
88. Ibid., "Early American Christian—University Fact," report.
89. D. James Kennedy, *One Nation Under God,* DVD, Fort Lauderdale, FL, 2005.
90. Tom Freiling, *Reagan's God And Country,* Servant Publications, Ann Arbor, MI, 2000, pp. 89, 90.
91. Michael Apted, dir., *Amazing Grace,* DVD, Bristol Bay Productions, Twentieth Century Fox, Home Entertainment, 2007.
92. Peter Marshall and David Manuel, *The Light and the Glory,* Fleming H. Revell, Grand Rapids, MI, 1977, p. 315.
93. Ibid., pp. 314, 314.
94. *mlive.com, Opinions & Columns Citizen Patriot,* "Founding documents do mention God," p. 3 of 5, scientist 2, http://blog.mlive.com/citpat_opinion/2007/11/founding_documents_do_mention.html.
95. Peter Marshall and David Manuel, *The Light and the Glory,* Fleming H. Revell, Grand Rapids, MI, 1977, pp. 321, 322.
96. Scholastic, Dear America, *The Winter of Red Snow,* video, Scholastic Entertainment, Inc., 1999.
97. Ibid.
98. Peter Marshall and David Manuel, *The Light and the Glory,* Fleming H. Revell, Grand Rapids, MI, 1977, pp. 322, 324.
99. Tom Freiling, *Reagan's God And Country,* Servant Publications, Ann Arbor, MI, 2000, p. 184.

100. D. James Kennedy, *One Nation Under God,* DVD, Coral Ridge Ministries, Fort Lauderdale, FL, 2005.
101. Peter Marshall and David Manuel, *The Light and the Glory,* Fleming H. Revell, Grand Rapids, MI, 1977, p. 326.
102. End-Time Handmaidens and Servants International, "Washington's Vision," Jasper, AR.
103. Kenneth Barker, ed., *The NIV Study Bible,* "Introduction: Ezekiel," Zondervan Publishing House, Grand Rapids, MI, 1995, p. 1595.
104. *Hymns of Glorious Praise,* #167, "Onward Christian Soldiers," Gospel Publishing House, Springfield, MO, 1969.
105. Ibid.
106. *Historic Bethabara Park,* "The Moravian Story," p. 3 of 7, http://www.bethabaraPark.org/moravian.htm.
107. Peter Marshall and David Manuel, *The Light and the Glory,* Fleming H. Revell, Grand Rapids, MI, 1977, pp. 332, 339.
108. *America's Prayer Network,* "George Washington's Prayer for the United States of America," Washington, D.C.
109. D. James Kennedy, *One Nation Under God,* DVD, Coral Ridge Ministries, Fort Lauderdale, FL, 2005.
110. *Independence National Historical Park,* "Independence," brochure, Philadelphia, PA.
111. David Limbaugh, reviewed by Sandra Alexander, *Persecution: How Liberals Are Raging War Against Christianity,* August 2004, http://www.intellectualconserva-tive.com/article3730.html.
112. Coral Ridge Ministries, *10 Truths about America's Christian Heritage,* Fort Lauderdale, FL, 2008, p. 56.
113. D. James Kennedy, *One Nation Under God,* DVD, Coral Ridge Ministries, Fort Lauderdale, FL, 2005.
114. Ibid.
115. Ibid., Coral Ridge Ministries, *10 Truths about America's Christian Heritage,* Fort Lauderdale, FL, 2008, p. 83.
116. *Coral Ridge Ministries,* newsletter, "The Attack on America's Christian Heritage," Fort Lauderdale, FL, July 18, 2008.
117. Ed Smith, *Beyond Tolerable Recovery,* Alathia Publishing, Campbellsville, KY 2000.
118. D. James Kennedy, *One Nation Under God,* DVD, Coral Ridge Ministries, Fort Lauderdale, FL, 2005.

119. Peter Marshall and David Manuel, *The Light and the Glory*, Fleming H. Revell, Grand Rapids, MI, 1977, pp. 346, 347.
120. *The Bill of Rights, Foundation for Moral Law,* "The First Ten Amendments to the Constitution of the United States."
121. Tom Freiling, *Reagan's God And Country,* Servant Publications, Ann Arbor, MI, 2002, pp. 130, 131, 133.
122. David Limbaugh, reviewed by Sandra Alexander, *Persecution: How Liberals Are Waging War Against Christianity,* August 2004, http://www.intellectualconserva-tive.com/article3730.html.
123. D. James Kennedy, "The Real Thomas Jefferson," CD, Coral Ridge Ministries, Fort Lauderdale, FL, 2002.
124. D. James Kennedy, *One Nation Under God,* DVD, Coral Ridge Ministries, Fort Lauderdale, FL, 2005.
125. D. James Kennedy, "The Real Thomas Jefferson," CD, Coral Ridge Ministries, Fort Lauderdale, FL, 2002.
126. *Hymns of Glorious Praise,* #494, "Battle Hymn of the Republic," Gospel Publishing House, Springfield, MO, 1969.
127. D. James Kennedy, *One Nation Under God,* DVD, Coral Ridge Ministries, Fort Lauderdale, FL, 2005.
128. Kurt A. Grussendorf, Michael R. Lowman, and Brian S. Ashbaugh, *America Land I Love,* A Beka Book, Pensacola, FL, 1994, p. 118.
129. Ibid.
130. Coral Ridge Ministries, *Impact,* news report, Fort Lauderdale, FL, November 2008, p.1.
131. David Limbaugh, reviewed by Sandra Alexander, *Persecution: How Liberals Are Waging War Against Christianity,* August 2004, http://www.intellectualconserva-tive.com/article3730.html.
132. Kurt A. Grussendorf, Michael R. Lowman, and Brian S. Ashbaugh, *America Land I Love,* A Beka Book, Pensacola, FL, 1994, p. 124.
133. Michael D. Evans, newsletter, *Jerusalem Prayer Team,* Bedford, TX, September 20, 2008.
134. Ibid.
135. *Wikipedia, the free encyclopedia,* "George Washington and slavery," pp. 1-3 of 4, http://en.wikipedia.org/wiki/George_Washington_and_slavery.

136. Edward Zwick, dir., *Glory,* "America," song, Columbia Pictures Home Video, Burbank, CA, 1989.
137. Larry Rice, "What Can I Do?," http://www.christianparents.com/whatudo.htm.
138. Jennifer Cassidy, newsletter, *Coral Ridge Ministries,* Fort Lauderdale, FL, July 3, 2008.
139. *Editorial Staff,* "America's Christian Rulers: John Quincy Adams—The Fore-Runner," http://forerunner.com/forerunner/X0205 John_Quincy_Adams.html.
140. Dave Miller, *Apologetics Press,* "Much Respect for the Quran—Not Much for the Bible," 2005, http://www.apologeticspress.org/articles/302.
141. Kurt A. Grussendorf, Michael R. Lowman, and Brian S. Ashbaugh, *America Land I Love,* A Beka Book, Pensacola, FL, 1994, pp. 218, 220.
142. Ibid., p. 218.
143. Dave Miller, *Apologetics Press,* "Much Respect for the Quran—Not Much for the Bible," 2005, http://www.apologeticpress.org/articles/302.
144. Coral Ridge Ministries, *10 Truths about America's Christian Heritage,* Fort Lauderdale, FL, 2008, p. 70.
145. Randy McNutt, *The Cincinnati Enquirer,* "Oxford pays tribute to 'McGuffey Reader' writer," http://www.enquirer.com/editions/2000/09/21/loc_oxford_pays_tribute.html.
146. *The People v. Ruggles,* David Barton, "The Myth of Separation," http://candst.tripod.com/case03.htm.
147. *Vidal v. Girard's Executors,* "No Schools Without Christ," Supreme Court of the United States, 1844 Term, http://vftonline.org/Test Oath/Vidal.htm.
148. *Wikipedia, the free encyclopedia,* "Second Great Awakening," pp. 1-3 of 5, http://en.wikipedia.org/wiki/Second_Great_Awakening.
149. *Forgotten Word Ministries,* "The Circuit Riders and the spread of Early Methodism," pp. 1-3 of 3, http://forgottenword.org/circuitriders.html.
150. *End-Time Handmaidens and Servants International,* "Washington's Vision," Jasper, AR.
151. Franco Zeffirelli, dir., *Jesus of Nazareth,* video series, LIVE Entertainment Inc., 1992.

NOTES

152. *Wikipedia, the free encyclopedia,* "Harriet Tubman," pp. 1, 4, 5 of 19, http://en.wikipedia.org/wiki/Harriet_Tubman.
153. Ibid.
154. Kurt A. Grussendorf, Michael R. Lowman, and Brian S. Ashbaugh, *America Land I Love,* A Beka Book, Pensacola, FL, 1994, p. 221.
155. *negrospirituals.com,* "Go Down Moses (First version)," http://www.negrospirituals.com/news-song/go_down_moses1.htm.
156. *negrospirituals.com,* "Free At Last," http://www.negrospirituals.com/news-song/free_at_last.htm.
157. Coral Ridge Ministries, *10 Truths about America's Christian Heritage,* Fort Lauderdale, FL, 2008, p. 92.
    Jennifer Cassidy, newsletter, Coral Ridge Ministries, Fort Lauderdale, FL, July 2010.
158. *The Wit and Wisdom of Abraham Lincoln,* Fleming H. Revell Company, Old Tappan, NJ, 1965, p. 8.
159. Ibid., pp. 9,10.
160. David Limbaugh, reviewed by Sandra Alexander, *Persecution: How Liberals Are Waging War Against Christianity,* August 2004, http://www.intellectualconservative.com/article3730.html.
161. *The Wit and Wisdom of Abraham Lincoln,* Fleming H. Revell Company, Old Tappan, NJ, 1965, pp. 10, 11.
162. Victoria Neufeldt, ed., *Webster's New World Dictionary: Third College Edition,* "Emancipation Proclamation," Prentice Hall, New York, NY, 1994, p. 442.
163. Coral Ridge Ministries, *10 Truths about America's Christian Heritage,* Fort Lauderdale, FL, 2008, p. 93.
164. Abraham Lincoln, *Proclamation for National Day of Humiliation, Fasting, and Prayer,* March 13, 1863.
165. Tom Freiling, *Reagan's God And Country,* Servant Publications, Ann Arbor, MI, 2002, pp. 10, 11, 89, 118, 124.
166. Ibid., p. 183.
167. D. James Kennedy, "Was Abraham Lincoln a Christian?," CD, *Coral Ridge Ministries,* Fort Lauderdale, FL, 1995.
168. *The Wit and Wisdom of Abraham Lincoln,* Fleming H. Revell Company, Old Tappan, NJ, 1965.
169. Edward Zwick, dir., *Glory,* Columbia Pictures Home Video, Burbank, CA, 1989.

170. *The Tennessee Encyclopedia of History and Culture,* "United States Commission," pp. 1, 2 of 2, http://tennesseeencyclopedia.net/imagegallery.php?
171. Kurt A. Grussendorf, Michael R. Lowman, and Brian S. Ashbaugh, *America Land I Love,* A Beka Book, Pensacola, FL, 1994, pp. 293, 294.
172. Hong Min Zou, artist, "Resurrection Morn."
173. Jay Rogers, "American Abolitionism," April 2008, http://fore-runner.com/fore-runner/X0214_Phillis_Wheatley.html.
174. Ibid.
175. James Dobson, *Focus on the Family,* newsletter, "Focus on the Family Action," Colorado Springs, CO, October 2008.
176. Ibid.
177. Euzhan Palsy, dir., *Ruby Bridges,* DVD, Buena Vista Home Entertainment Inc., Burbank, CA, 2004.
178. Victoria Neufeldt, *Webster's New World Dictionary: Third College Edition,* "Roosevelt, Theodore," Prentice Hall, New York, NY, 1994, p. 1165.
179. Coral Ridge Ministries, *10 Truths about America's Christian Heritage,* Fort Lauderdale, FL, 2008, p. 46.
180. Victoria Neufeldt, ed., *Webster's New World Dictionary: Third College Edition,* "Wilson (Thomas) Woodrow," Prentice Hall, New York, NY, 1994, p. 1529.
181. *Coral Ridge Ministries,* news report, "The Attacks on America's Christian Heritage," Fort Lauderdale, FL, received July 18, 2008.
182. William F. Claxton, dir., *Little House on the Prairie,* television series, "Harriet's Happenings," approx. 1979-1980.
183. Laura Ingalls Wilder, *Little House on the Prairie,* Harper Collins Publishers Inc., New York, NY, 1935, Trophy edition, 1971.
184. William F. Claxton, dir., *Little House on the Prairie,* television series, "Harriet's Happenings," approx. 1979-1980.
185. Robert Stevenson, dir., *Old Yeller,* DVD, (2004), Walt Disney Production, Buena Vista Home Entertainment, Inc., 1957.
186. William F. Claxton and Michael Landon, dirs., *Little House on the Prairie,* NBC Production, 1974, Good Times Home Video, 1989.
187. Rosalie Slater, "The Principle Approach: an Intriguing Method of Education from America's Past," Appendix, November 1981.

NOTES

188. *Wikipedia: the free encyclopedia,* "The Third Great Awakening," http://en.wikipedia.org/wiki/Third_Great_Awakening.
189. *Christian History & Biography,* "The Time for Prayer: The Third Great Awakening," July 1, 1989, http://www.ctlibrary.com/ch/1989/issue23/2332.html.
190. *Wikipedia: the free encyclopedia,* "Dwight L. Moody," http://en.wikipedia.org/wiki/Dwight_L._Moody.
191. Ibid.
192. Ibid.
193. J. Wilbur Chapman, "The Life & Work of Dwight Lyman Moody," http://www.biblebelievers.com/moody/19.html.
194. *Wikipedia: the free encyclopedia,* "The Third Great Awakening," http://en.wikipedia.org/wiki/Third_Great_Awakening.

    Christian History & Biography, "The Time for Prayer: The Third Great Awakening," May 1, 1989, http://www.ctlibrary.com/ch/1989/issue23/2332.html.

    Wikipedia: the free encyclopedia, "Dwight L. Moody," http://en.wikipedia.org/wiki/Dwight_L._Moody.
195. *Children's Ministries Institute,* "Teaching Children Effectively," student manual, Warrenton, MO, 1996.
196. Robert Liardon, *God's Generals,* Whitaker House, New Kensington, PA, 1996, pp. 140, 141.
197. Ibid., pp. 109, 133, 141-143, 156, 157.
198. Ibid., pp. 140, 147, 148, 150, 151.
199. Ibid., pp. 151, 154.
200. Ibid., pp. 154, 155.
201. Ibid., pp. 139, 144, 161-163.
202. Rodney Howard-Browne, *There Is a River,* Praise song, Revival, Oxon Hill, MD, February 1994.
203. *Church Of The Holy Trinity v. United States,* 132 U. S. 457 (1897), "U.S. Supreme Court," http://supreme.justia.com/us/143/457/case.html.
204. Ibid.
205. *U.S. v. MACINTOSH,* 283 U.S. 605 (1931), "U. S. Supreme Court," Find Law/ Cases and Codes, http://caselaw.lp.fmdlaw.com/cgi-bin/getcase.pl?const.
206. Coral Ridge Ministries, *10 Truths about America's Christian Heritage,* Fort Lauderdale, FL, 2008, pp. 100, 102.

207. Ramon Arias, "It's Insane to want religion out of politics," http://culturallegacy.org/templates/System/details.asp?id.
208. Ibid.
209. Ibid.
210. Kurt A. Grussendorf, Michael R. Lowman, and Brian S. Ashbaugh, *America Land I Love*, A Beka Book, Pensacola, FL, 1994, p. 410.
211. Vision Forum Ministries, *The League of Grateful Sons*, DVD, San Antonio, TX, 2005.
212. Victoria Neufeldt, ed., *Webster's New World Dictionary: Third College Edition*, "Truman, Harry S.," Prentice Hall, New York, NY, 1994, p. 1435.
213. Thomas Ice, "Happy Birthday Israel," Internet article.
214. Ibid.
215. Ibid., Thomas Ice, "Lovers of Zion: A Brief History of Christian Zionism," http://www.zionism-israel.com/christian_Zionism/Christian_Zionism_History_ice.html.
216. Ibid.
217. Joseph Andrews, "Revolutionary Jews and the Bunker Hill bridge," pp. 1, 2 of 2, http://www.kulana.org/usa/revolutionary.php.
218. Ibid.
219. [2163] Woodrow Wilson, *New York Times*, "Rabbi Wise & The Armenian Mandate," November 6, 2007, http://armenians-1915.blogspot.com/2007/11/2163-woodrow-wilson-rabbi-wise-armenian.
220. Victoria Neufeldt, ed., *Webster's New World Dictionary: Third College Edition*, "Eisenhower, Dwight David," Prentice Hall, New York, NY, 1994, p. 435.
221. Coral Ridge Ministries, DVD, *The Christian Roots of America*, Fort Lauderdale, FL, 2010.
222. Ibid., Coral Ridge Ministries, *10 Truths About America's Christian Heritage*, Fort Lauderdale, FL, 2008, pp. 89, 93.
223. *Wikipedia: the free enyclopedia*, "Everson v. Board of Education, " 1947.
224. Mark Kirchberg and Phyllis Kirchberg, *The Profound Mystery: Marriage—The First Church*, Vantage Press, Inc., New York, NY, 2008, pp. 280-282.
225. Coral Ridge Ministries, DVD, *Code Red for America*, Fort Lauderdale, FL, 2010.
226. American Bible Society, *Record Magazine*, New York, NY, Spring 2011, p. 17.

AMERICA: PRESENT

1. *Hymns of Glorious Praise,* #498, "God Save America," Gospel Publishing House, Springfield, MO, 1969.
2. Daniel Scuhugwrensky, ed., *History of Education: Selected Moments of the 20th Century,* "Engel v. Vitale,"(1962), http://www.oise.utoronto.ca/research/edu20/moments/1962engel.html.
3. Ibid.
4. U.S. *Supreme Court,* "School Dist. of Abington Tp. v. Schem," pp. 374 U.S. 203 (1963), http://supreme.justia.com/us/374/203/case.html.
5. Ibid.
6. Ibid.
7. Ibid.
8. Ibid.
9. David Limbaugh, reviewed by Sandra Alexander, *Persecution: How Liberals Are Waging War Against Christianity,* August 22, 2004, http://www.intellectualconser-vative.com/article3730.html.
10. Alan Keyes, newsletter, *Declaration Alliance,* Houston, TX, received May 31, 2007.
11. Coral Ridge Ministries, *10 Truths about America's Christian Heritage,* Fort Lauderdale, FL, 2008, p. 44.
12. *Wikipedia, the free encyclopedia,* "Fourth Great Awakening," pp. 1 of 2, http://en.wikipedia.org/wiki/Fourth_Great_Awakening.
13. Ibid.
14. *Wikipedia, the free encyclopedia,* "Jesus movement," pp. 1 of 7, http://en.wikipedia.org/wiki/Jesus_movement.
15. Ibid.
16. David Di Sabinto, *The Jesus People Movement,* 2004, http://www.jesuspeoplemovement.com/home.html.
17. Victoria Neufeldt, ed., *Webster's New World Dictionary: Third College Edition,* "Reagan, Ronald (Wilson)," Prentice Hall, New York, NY, 1994, p. 1118.
18. Tom Freiling, *Reagan's God And Country,* Servant Publications, Ann Arbor, MI, 2000, pp. 10, 19, 35, 36.
19. Ibid., pp. 23, 125, 145, 147, 153.
20. Ibid., pp. 24, 33, 37, 40.

21. Ibid., pp. 37, 38.
22. Ibid., pp. 133, 187, 192, 193.
23. Ibid., pp. 21-23.
24. Ibid., pp. 45, 149, 150.
25. Ibid., pp. 142-144.
26. D. James Kennedy, DVD, *One Nation Under God*, Coral Ridge Ministries, Fort Lauderdale, FL, 2005.
27. Alan Sears, newsletter, *Alliance Defense Fund*, "The ACLU vs. America," Scottsdale, AZ, received March 1, 2008.
28. Ibid.
29. David Wilkerson, *Times Square Church Pulpit Series*, "The Only Hope in The Coming Storm," New York, NY, March 3, 1998.
30. David Wilkerson, *World Challenge Pulpit Series*, "Steadfast and Confident To The End," New York, NY, May 12, 2008.

    David Wilkerson, *World Challenge Pulpit Series*, "A Fresh Outpouring Of the Holy Spirit,"September 15, 2008.
31. Jennifer Cassidy, newsletter, *Coral Ridge Ministries*, Fort Lauderdale, FL, December 29, 2008.
32. Coral Ridge Ministries, *10 Truths about Christians and Politics*, Fort Lauderdale, FL, 2008, pp. 29, 31, 34, 45.
33. Bob Russell, *Billy Graham's Prayer For Our Nation*, Snopes.com, http://www.snopes.com/politics/soapbox/prayernation.asp, collected via e-mail, November 2008.
34. James Dobson, *Focus on the Family*, "Family News," Colorado Springs, CO, March 2008.
35. Ibid.
36. Ibid.
37. Coral Ridge Ministries, newsletter, *Impact*, "New Documentary Answers: Christ-Bashing Media," Fort Lauderdale, FL, December 2008.
38. Ibid., D. James Kennedy with Jerry Newcombe, "Dr. Kennedy: Lighting Candles Is Best Answer to Media Bias," December 2007.
39. Ibid.
40. Coral Ridge Ministries, *Fact Sheet*, "Hate Crimes' Laws: A Grave Threat to Your Religious Freedom," Fort Lauderdale, FL, received 2008.

NOTES

41. Brian Fisher, newsletter, *Coral Ridge Ministries*, Fort Lauderdale, FL, March 29, 2007.
42. David Limbaugh, reviewed by Sandra Alexander, *Persecution: How Liberals Are Waging War Against Christianity*, August 22, 2004, http://www.intellectualconservative.com/article3730.html.
43. Roy Moore, newsletter, *Foundation for Moral Law*, Montgomery, AL, received September 21, 2008.
44. Michael Reagan, newsletters, *National Committee for Faith & Family*, Washington, D.C., received June 6, 2007, and August 12, 2008.
45. Liberty Counsel, *Fact Sheet*, "Some Amazing Facts about America's 'Enemy Within,'" Orlando, FL, received September 23, 2008.
46. Ramon Arias, "It's Insane to want religion out of politics," https://culturallegacy.org/templates/System/details.asp?id.
47. David Wilkerson, *Times Square Church Pulpit Series*, "The Dethroning of Christ in America!," New York, NY, April 20, 1998.
48. Ibid.
49. David Wilkerson, *Times Square Church Pulpit Series*, "The Only Hope in The Coming Storm," New York, NY, March 30, 1998.
50. David Wilkerson, *World Challenge Pulpit Series*, "Seeking the Face of God," New York, NY, November 7, 2005.
51. David Wilkerson, *World Challenge Pulpit Series*, "God Has Not Passed You By," New York, NY, February 27, 2006.
52. David Wilkerson, *World Challenge Pulpit Series*, "Trusting God in the Face of Impossibilities," New York, NY, January 7, 2008,

    David Wilkerson, *World Challenge Pulpit Series*, "The Last Revival," January 28, 2008.
53. Ibid.
54. David Wilkerson, *World Challenge Pulpit Series*, "Steadfast and Confident To The End," New York, NY, May 12, 2008.

    David Wilkerson, *World Challenge Pulpit Series*, "The High Cost of Mercy," August 4, 2008.

55. Ibid., "Steadfast and Confident To The End."
56. David Wilkerson, *Times Square Church Pulpit Series,* "The Only Hope in The Coming Storm," New York, NY, March 30, 1998.
57. Nina Totenberg, "Supreme Court Ends Death Penalty for Juveniles," http://www.npr.org/templates/story/story.php.
58. *Office of Juvenile Justice and Delinquency Prevention,* brochure, "Parents' Guide to Gangs," Washington, D.C., received April 1, 2008.
59. James Dobson, *Focus on the Family,* "Family Newsletter," Colorado Springs, CO, October 2006.
60. Ibid.
61. Kamal Saleem, *Jewish Voice Today,* "What is Written on the Dome of the Rock about Jesus?," Phoenix, AZ, March/April 2008, p. 17.
62. Gary Kreep, newsletter, *United States Justice Foundation,* Houston, TX, received 2008.
63. Ibid.
64. David Wilkerson, *World Challenge Pulpit Series,* "The Wrath of Satan Shall Praise God," New York, NY, September 11, 2006.
65. Ibid.
66. *Coral Ridge Ministries,* Fact report, "All The President's Men & Women," Fort Lauderdale, FL, 2009.
67. Rich Hobson, and Roy Moore, newsletter, *Foundation for Moral Law,* Montgomery, AL, received March 12, 2008.
68. Ibid.
69. *American Bible Society,* "Good News," Vol. 17, No, 2, New York, NY, February/March 2009.
70. James Dobson, *Focus on the Family,* "Family News From Focus on the Family," Colorado Springs, CO, January 2008.
71. James Dobson, *Focus on the Family,* "Focus on the Family Action," newsletter, Colorado Springs, CO, May 2007.
72. Coral Ridge Ministries, *10 Truths about Abortion,* DVD, Fort Lauderdale, FL, 2007.
73. Ibid.
74. Coral Ridge Ministries, *10 Truths about Abortion,* Fort Lauderdale, FL, 2007, pp. 22, 23.

NOTES

75. *Touro Law Center*, "Roe v. Wade," 1995-2009, pp. 1, 2 of 29, http://www.tourolaw.edu/patch/Roe.
76. *Wikipedia, the free encyclopedia*, "Roe v. Wade," pp. 3, 4 of 18, http://en.wikipedia.org/wiki/Roe_v._Wade.
77. Ibid., pp. 4, 5 of 18.
78. Ibid., pp. 5, 6 of 18.
79. Ibid., p. 6 of 18.
80. Ibid., pp. 2, 3 of 18.
81. Coral Ridge Ministries, *10 Truths about Abortion*, DVD and booklet, Fort Lauderdale, FL, 2007, pp. 32, 64, 65.
82. Ibid., DVD.
83. "Doe v. Bolton," pp. 1-3 of 6, http://law.jrank.org/pages/13300/Doe-v-Bolton.html.
84. Ibid., p. 3 of 6.
85. Ibid., pp. 3, 4 of 6.
86. Ibid., p. 4 of 6.
87. Coral Ridge Ministries, *10 Truths about Abortion*, DVD, Fort Lauderdale, FL, 2007.
88. Ibid.
89. Coral Ridge Ministries, *10 Truths about Abortion*, Fort Lauderdale, FL, 2007, pp. 33, 36.
90. Coral Ridge Ministries, *10 Truths about Abortion*, DVD, Fort Lauderdale, FL, 2007.
91. Tom Freiling, *Reagan's God And Country*, Servant Publications, Ann Arbor, MI, 2000, pp. 26, 82, 83.
92. Ibid., pp. 83, 84, 86, 87.
93. James Dobson, *Focus on the Family*, "Family News from Focus on the Family," Colorado Springs, CO, January 2008.
94. David Wilkerson, *Times Square Church Pulpit Series*, "The Only Hope in The Coming Storm," New York, NY, March 30, 1998.

    David Wilkerson, *World Challenge Pulpit Series*, "These Times Demand Special Trust," December 17, 2007.
95. Coral Ridge Ministries, *10 Truths about Abortion*, DVD, Fort Lauderdale, FL, 2007.
96. Ibid., booklet, pp. 13, 14.
97. David Wilkerson, *America's Last Call*, Wilkerson Trust Publications, Lindale, TX, 2008, pp. 46, 47.

98. Ibid., p. 45.
99. Coral Ridge Ministries, *10 Truths about Abortion,* DVD and booklet, Fort Lauderdale, FL, 2007, p. 26.
100. James Dobson, *Focus on the Family,* "Family News from Focus on the Family," Colorado Springs, CO, January 2008.
101. Ibid.
102. Rob Schenck, *Word Alive Church,* "Calibrating the Soul of Man," CD, Manassas, VA, June 3, 2007.
103. Don Swarthout, *Christians Reviving America's Values (CRAVE),* "Exposing the ACLU," Fact report, Lexington, KY, received 2008.
104. *American Center for Law & Justice,* newsletter, "The Untold Story," Washington, D.C., received May 27, 2007.
105. Coral Ridge Ministries, *10 Truths about Abortion,* Fort Lauderdale, FL, 2007, p. 43, newsletter, *Impact,* January 2009.
106. Dana Cody, newsletter, *Life Legal Defense Foundation,* Napa, CA, received June 8, 2007.
107. *American Center for Law & Justice,* newsletter, "The Untold Story," Washington, D.C., received May 27, 2007.
108. Coral Ridge Ministries, *Fact report,* "It Stops Now," Fort Lauderdale, FL, February 21, 2009.
109. Ibid.

    Jennifer Cassidy, newsletter, Coral Ridge Ministries, Fort Lauderdale, FL, January 13, 2011.
110. Coral Ridge Ministries, *Pastors, Pulpits, & Politics: Christian Rules of Engagement,* DVD, Fort Lauderdale, FL, 2008.
111. James Dobson, *Focus on the Family,* "Focus on the Family Action," newsletter, Colorado Springs, CO, May 2007.
112. *Coral Ridge Ministries,* newsletter, "The Terrible Truth about the Freedom of Choice Act," Fort Lauderdale, FL, received January 17, 2009.
113. Coral Ridge Ministries, news report, *Impact,* January 2009, and newsletter, "The fight for life just got hotter," Fort Lauderdale, FL, February 9, 2009.
114. Coral Ridge Ministries, DVD, *Freedom to Kill: Unlimited Abortion at your Expense,* Fort Lauderdale, FL, 2009.
115. Tom Freiling, *Reagan's God And Country,* Servant Publications, Ann Arbor, MI, 2000, pp. 151-152.

116. Malcolm Hedding, newsletter, *International Christian Embassy Jerusalem*, January 2009.
117. Ibid.
118. David Wilkerson, *Times Square Church Pulpit Series*, "The Only Hope in The Coming Storm," March 30, 1998.

    David Wilkerson, *World Challenge Pulpit Series*, "A Fresh Outpouring of the Holy Spirit," New York, NY, September 15, 2008.
119. Ibid., "That Dreadful Day No One Wants to Talk About," February 5, 2007.
120. Ibid., "In One Hour, Everything is Going to Change," September 3, 2007.
121. Mark Kirchberg and Phyllis Kirchberg, *The Great Cover-up: Living in the Shadow of a Lie, The Roman Catholic Church*, Vantage Press, Inc., New York, NY, 2009.
122. David Wilkerson, *World Challenge Pulpit Series*, "God Has Not Passed You By," New York, NY, February 27, 2006.
123. Alex Kendrick, dir., *Fireproof*, DVD, Sherwood Pictures, Affirm Films, Albany, GA, 2009.
124. Tom Freiling, *Reagan's God And Country*, Servants Publications, Ann Arbor, MI, 2000, pp. 110, 112, 114.
125. Dawson McAllister, newsletter, Spring Hill, TN, received June 23, 2007.
126. Don Swarthout, *Christians Reviving American's Values (CRAVE)*, Fact sheet, Lexington, KY, received 2008.
127. Alan Sears, newsletter, *Alliance Defense Fund*, "The ACLU vs. America," Scottsdale, AZ, September 27, 2008.
128. Mark Kirchberg and Phyllis Kirchberg, *The Profound Mystery: Marriage—The First Church*, Vantage Press, Inc., New York, NY, 2008, Chapters 11-13.
129. *The Proceedings of the Old Bailey*, "Homosexuality: Gay and Lesbian Subcultures," http://www.oldbaileyonline.org/static/Gay.isp.
130. *Wikipedia, the free encyclopedia*, "Lawrence v. Texas,"pp. 2, 3 of 13, http://en.wikipedia.org/wiki/Lawrence_v._Texas.
131. *Wikipedia, the free encyclopedia*, "Bowers v. Hardwick,"pp. 1, 2 of 5, http://en.wikipedia.org/wiki/Bowers_v._Hardwick.
132. Ibid., p. 3 of 5.

133. Ibid., p. 4 of 5.
134. *Wikipedia, the free encyclopedia,* "Lawrence v. Texas," p. 1 of 13, http://en.wikipedia.org/wiki/Lawrence_v._Texas.
135. Ibid., p. 4 of 13.
136. Ibid., p. 5 of 13.
137. Ibid., pp. 6, 7 of 13.
138. Tom Minnery, letter, *Focus on the Family,* Colorado Springs, CO, received April 18, 2008.
139. Peter Marshall and David Manuel, *The Light and the Glory,* Fleming H. Revell, Grand Rapids, MI, 1977, pp. 354, 355.
140. Ibid., pp. 356-359.
141. D. James Kennedy and Jerry Newcombe, news report, *Impact,* "Lighting Candles Is Best Answer to Media Bias," Coral Ridge Ministries, Fort Lauderdale, FL, December 12, 2007.

   Jennifer Cassidy, newsletter, Coral Ridge Ministries, Fort Lauderdale, FL, July 1, 2010.
142. David Wilkerson, *Times Square Church Pulpit Series,* "The Only Hope in The Coming Storm," New York, NY, March 30, 1998.
143. David Wilkerson, *World Challenge Pulpit Series,* "The Unhindered Gospel," New York, NY, September 5, 2005.
144. David Wilkerson, *World Challenge Pulpit Series,* "The Great and Final Apostasy," October 2, 2006.

   David Wilkerson, *World Challenge Pulpit Series,* "When God Sets His Heart on You," New York, NY, December 25, 2006.
145. Brian Fisher, newsletter, *Coral Ridge Ministries,* Fort Lauderdale, FL, March 29, 2007.
146. Michael Evans, *Jerusalem Prayer Team,* "Jerusalem Urgent Gram," Phoenix, AZ, May 1, 2006.
147. *Wikipedia, the free encyclopedia,* "Boy Scouts of America v. Dale," p. 2 of 5, http://en.wikipedia.org/wiki/Boy_Scouts_of_America_v._Dale.
148. Ibid., pp. 1, 2 of 5.
149. Mathew Staver, newsletter, *Liberty Counsel,* Orlando, FL, received September 23, 2008.
150. Ibid.
151. Don Swarthout, newsletter, *Christians Reviving America's Values (CRAVE),* "CRAVE: Exposing the ACLU," Washington, D.C., received 2008.

NOTES

152. Mike Stobbe, *Associated Press*, "CDC Understated number of new HIV infections in US," August 2, 2008, http://hosted.ap.org/dynamic/stories/M/MED_HIV_INFECTIONS.
153. Ibid.
154. *Wikipedia, the free encyclopedia*, "Lawrence v. Texas," p. 8 of 13, http://en.wikipedia.org/wiki/Lawrence_v._Texas.
155. Louis Sheldon, newsletter, *Traditional Values Coalition*, Washington, D.C., received June 5, 2007.
156. Jennifer Cassidy, newsletter, *Coral Ridge Ministries*, Fort Lauderdale, FL, September 16, 2008.
157. Rick Santorium, newsletter, *National Organization for Marriage*, Princeton, NJ, October 2008.
158. Ibid.
159. James Dobson, *Focus on the Family*, "Family News from Focus on the Family," Colorado Springs, CO, June 2008.
160. Jennifer Cassidy, newsletter, *Coral Ridge Ministries*, Fort Lauderdale, FL, March 9, 2009.
161. David Bossie, newsletter, *Citizens United*, "Hype: The Obama Effect," Washington, D.C., received September 2, 2008.
162. Mark Kirchberg and Phyllis Kirchberg, *The Profound Mystery: Marriage—The First Church*, Vantage Press, Inc., New York, NY, 2008, pp. 194, 195.
163. John Aman, *10 Truths about Hate Crime Laws*, Coral Ridge Ministries, Fort Lauderdale, FL, 2008, pp. 16, 17.
164. Ibid., p. 16.
165. *Focus on the Family*, newsletter, "Media Coverage of Love Won Out," Colorado Springs, CO, 2007.
166. David Limbaugh, reviewed by Sandra Alexander, *Persecution: How Liberals Are Waging War Against Christianity*, August 22, 2004, http://www.intellectualconservative.com/article3730.html.
167. Ibid.
168. Brian Fisher, newsletter, *Coral Ridge Ministries*, Fort Lauderdale, FL, May 2007.
169. James Dobson, *Focus on the Family*, newsletter, "Focus on the Family Action," Colorado Springs, CO, October 2008.
170. David Wilkerson, *World Challenge Pulpit Series*, "The Private War Of a Saint," New York, NY, October 15, 2007.

171. Louis Sheldon, newsletter, *Traditional Values Coalition*, Washington, D.C., received June 5, 2007.
172. Don Swarthout, newsletter, *Christians Reviving America's Values (CRAVE)*, Lexington, KY, received 2008.
173. *Concerned Women for America*, "National Impact Survey of the Radical Homosexual Agenda on Virginia Public Schools," Washington, D.C., received May 8, 2003.
174. Alan Sears, newsletter, *Alliance Defense Fund*, "Taking Away Parents' Rights," Scottsdale, AZ, received February 3, 2009.
175. Ibid.
176. Ibid.
177. Alan Sears, newsletter, *Alliance Defense Fund*, "Homosexual Agenda: Taking Away Parents' Rights," Scottsdale, AZ, received October 1, 2007.
178. Brian Fisher, newsletter, *Coral Ridge Ministries*, Fort Lauderdale, FL, May 2007.
179. Mel Gibson, dir., *The Passion of the Christ*, Icon Productions, 2004.
180. Norman Foster, dir., *The Complete Davy Crockett Televised Series*, 1954, 1955, Walt Disney Treasuries, http://www.amazon.com/exec/obidos/tg/detail.
181. Tom Freiling, *Reagan's God And Country*, Servant Publications, Ann Arbor, MI, 2000, p. 173.
182. Ibid., pp. 173, 174.
183. Ibid., pp. 168, 169.
184. Brian Fisher, newsletter, *Coral Ridge Ministries*, Fort Lauderdale, FL, October 2007.
185. Don Swarthout, *Christians Reviving America's Values*, Washington, D.C., received 2008.
186. James Dobson, *Focus on the Family*, "Family News From Dr. James Dobson," Colorado Springs, CO, June 2008.
187. Mark Kirchberg and Phyllis Kirchberg, *The Great Cover-up: Living in the Shadow of a Lie, The Roman Catholic Church*, Vantage Press, Inc., New York, NY, 2009.
188. Jennifer Cassidy, newsletter, *Coral Ridge Ministries*, Fort Lauderdale, FL, April 28, 2009.
189. Barbara Wheeler, newsletter, *America's Prayer Network*, Washington, D.C., received May 5, 2007.

190. Roy Moore, newsletter, *Foundation for Moral Law,* "From the Desk of Judge Roy Moore," Montgomery, AL, received September 21, 2008.
191. Martin Mawyer, news report, "Islamic Programs and Activity in America's Public Grade Schools and Universities," Forest, VA, received April 24, 2008.
192. Ibid.
193. Ibid.
194. Ibid.
195. Barbara Wheeler, newsletter, *America's Prayer Network,* Washington, D.C., received May 5, 2007.
196. Jennifer Cassidy, newsletter, *Coral Ridge Ministries,* Fort Lauderdale, FL, April 28, 2009.
197. David Limbaugh, reviewed by Sandra Alexander, *Persecution: How Liberals Are Waging War Against Christianity,* August 22, 2004, http://www.intellectualconservative.com/article3730.html.
198. Brittany McComb, newsletter, *The Rutherford Institute,* Charlottesville, VA, received April 2007.
199. Philip Jauregi, newsletter, *Judicial Action Group,* "Why are judges who share our Founding Fathers' beliefs ostracized, while liberal judges are free to remove God from public life?," Washington, D.C., received January 17, 2008.
200. Brian Fisher, newsletter, *Coral Ridge Ministries,* Fort Lauderdale, FL, May 2007.
201. Coral Ridge Ministries, news report, *Impact,* Fort Lauderdale, FL, April 2008.
202. Ibid., May 2008.
203. Yahoo! Answers, "Darwin's deathbed confession... is it true," http://answers.yahoo.com/question/index?qid, pp. 2, 3 of 5.
204. Coral Ridge Ministries, news report, *Impact,* Fort Lauderdale, FL, April 2008.
205. Martin Mawyer, news report, "Islamic Program and Activity in America's Public Grade Schools and Universities," Forest, VA, received April 24, 2008.
206. David Limbaugh, reviewed by Sandra Alexander, *Persecution: How Liberals Are Waging War Against Christianity,"* August 22, 2004, http://www.intellectualconservative.com/article3730.html.

207. David Wilkerson, *World Challenge Pulpit Series*, "The Great and Final Apostasy," New York, NY, October 2, 2006.
208. David Wilkerson, *World Challenge Pulpit Series*, "The High Cost of Mercy," New York, NY, August 4, 2006.
209. Barbara Wheeler, *America's Prayer Network*, "History of the School Prayer Battle," Washington, D.C., received May 5, 2007.
210. David Wilkerson, *World Challenge Pulpit Series*, "In One Hour, Everything Is Going to Change," New York, NY, September 3, 2007.
211. *Wikipedia, the free encyclopedia*, "Amish_school_shooting," October 2, 2006, http://en.wikipedia.org/wiki/Amish school shooting.
212. *Wikipedia, the free encyclopedia*, "Platte Canyon High School shooting," September 27, 2006, http://en.wikipedia.org/wiki/Platte_Canyon_High_School_shooting.
213. *Wikipedia, the free encyclopedia*, "Weston High School shooting," September 29, 2006, http://en.wikipedia.org/wiki/Weston_High_School_shooting.
214. Deb Riechman, *Associated Press*, "Bush Visits School Devastated by Twister," March 3, 2007, http://hosted.ap.org/dynamic stories/B/BUSH_TORNADOES.
215. *Associated Press*, "NIU Gunman Stopped Taking Medication," February 15, 2008, http://old.isp.com/members/home.pl.
216. Gary Strauss and William Welch, *USA Today*, "Virginia Tech mourns those lost as details emerge about killer," April 18, 2007.
217. Gordon Klingenschmitt, newsletter, *Declaration Alliance*, Houston, TX, received October 6, 2008.

    Gordon Klingenschmitt, newsletter, *Declaration Alliance*, Houston, TX, received February 25, 2009.
218. Council Nedd, II, newsletter, *In God We Trust*, "Does America Hate God?," Washington, D.C., received April 22, 2009.
219. Ibid.
220. David Wilkerson, *World Challenge Pulpit Series*, "The Wrath of Satan Shall Praise God," New York, NY, September 11, 2006.
221. Gordon Klingenschmitt, newsletter, *Declaration Alliance*, Houston, TX, received February 25, 2009.

222. Ibid.
223. Gordon Klingenschmitt, newsletter, *Declaration Alliance*, "Chaplain ousted from Navy for praying 'in Jesus' name,'" Houston, TX, received 2008.
224. Ibid.
225. Rob Schenck, newsletter, *Faith and Action*, Washington, D.C., received 2007.

   Coral Ridge Ministries, news report, *Impact*, "Pentagon Prayer Snub Exposes America's Spiritual Drift," Fort Lauderdale, FL, July 2010.
226. Jennifer Cassidy, newsletter, *Coral Ridge Ministries*, "Christian Alert," Fort Lauderdale, FL, May 7, 2009.
227. Ibid.
228. James Dobson, newsletter, *Focus on the Family*, "Focus on the Family Action," Colorado Springs, CO, May 2007.
229. *Hymns of Glorious Praise*, #494, "Battle Hymn of the Republic," Gospel Publishing House, Springfield, MO, 1969.
230. Mark Kirchberg and Phyllis Kirchberg, *The Profound Mystery: Marriage—The First Church*, Vantage Press, Inc., New York, NY, 2008.
231. James Daly, newsletter, *Focus on the Family*, "Telling the truth about marriage protects and preserves God's plan for the family," Colorado Springs, CO, November 2006.
232. Ibid.
233. James Dobson and James Daly, newsletter, *Focus on the Family*, "Family News from Dr. James Dobson," Colorado Springs, CO, May 2008.
234. James Dobson, newsletter, *Focus on the Family*, Colorado Springs, CO, November 19, 2007.
235. Ibid.
236. Ibid.
237. Jennifer Cassidy, newsletter, *Coral Ridge Ministries*, Fort Lauderdale, FL, June 2009.
238. James Dobson, newsletter, *Focus on the Family*, "Family News from Dr. James Dobson," Colorado Springs, CO, October 2006.
239. Alan Keyes, newsletter, *Declaration Alliance*, Houston, TX, April 5, 2007.

240. Coral Ridge Ministries, news report, *Impact,* Fort Lauderdale, FL, June 2009.

   Jennifer Cassidy, newsletter, *Coral Ridge Ministries,* Fort Lauderdale, FL, November 2010.
241. Stephen Kendrick and Alex Kendrick, *The Love Dare,* B&H Publishing Group, Nashville, TN, 2008, p. 113.
242. Rob Schenck, *Word Alive Church,* "Calibrating the Soul of Man," Manassas, VA, June 3, 2007.
243. Ibid.
244. Exploration Films, *Given to Him: The Worship DVD,* Monument, CO, 2004.
245. J. Wilbur Chapman, *The Life & Work Of Dwight Lyman Moody,* "Mr. Moody as an Evangelist," http://www.biblebelievers.com/moody/19.html.
246. Ibid.
247. Mark Kirchberg and Phyllis Kirchberg, *The Profound Mystery: Marriage—The First Church,* Vantage Press, Inc., New York, NY, 2008, pp. 211-213.
248. Alex Kendrick, dir., *Fireproof,* DVD, Sherwood Pictures, Affirm Films, Albany, GA, 2009.
249. Stephen Kendrick and Alex Kendrick, *The Love Dare,* B&H Publishing Group, Nashville, TN, 2008, p. 199.
250. Alex Kendrick, dir., *Fireproof,* DVD, Sherwood Pictures, Affirm Films, Albany, GA, 2009.
251. Joseph Sargent, dir., *Miss Rose White,* video, Hallmark Home Entertainment, 1991.
252. Tom Hooper, dir., *John Adams,* DVD series, Home Box Office, Inc., 2008.
253. *Wikipedia, the free encyclopedia,* "The Honeymooners," 1955, 1956, http://en.wikipedia.org/wiki/The_Honeymooners.
254. Michael Apted, dir., *Amazing Grace,* DVD, Bristol Bay Productions, Twentieth Century Fox Home Entertainment, 2007.
255. The History Channel, *Dogfights,* DVD series, A & E Television Networks, 2007, 2008.
256. David Wilkerson, *Times Square Church Pulpit Series,* "The Only Hope in The Coming Storm," New York, NY, March 30, 1998.

257. David Wilkerson, *America's Last Call: On the Brink of a Financial Holocaust*, Wilkerson Trust Publications, Lindale, TX, 1998, pp. 11, 13, 19, 22.
258. Ibid., pp. 24, 29.
259. David Wilkerson, *World Challenge Pulpit Series*, "The Private War Of a Saint," New York, NY, October 15, 2007.
260. Ibid., "The Dreadful Day No One Wants to Talk About," February 5, 2007.
261. David Wilkerson, *America's Last Call: On the Brink of a Financial Holocaust*, Wilkerson Trust Publications, Lindale, TX, 1998, pp. 69, 77, 102.
262. Ibid., pp. 105, 106, 110.
263. Ibid., pp. 110, 111, 113, 114.
264. David Wilkerson, *World Challenge Pulpit Series*, "These Times Demand Special Trust," New York, NY, December 17, 2007.
265. James Dobson, *Focus on the Family*, "Family News from Focus on the Family," Colorado Springs, CO, December 2008.
266. David Wilkerson, *World Challenge Pulpit Series*, "God's People Will Not Be Ashamed in the Time of Calamity," New York, NY, December 8, 2008.
267. Ibid., "What It Means to Live By One's Faith," February 9, 2009.
268. Ibid., "The Most Important Issue of This Hour," May 12, 2008.
269. *Associated Press*, "Many states appear to be in recession," April 25, 2008, http://old.isp.com/members/home.pl.
270. *Associated Press*, "Consumer prices rise at double expected rate," August 14, 2008, http://www.msnbc.msn.com/id.
271. Julie Davis, *Associated Press*, "House Ignores Bush, Rejects $700 B bailout bill," September 29, 2009, http://hosted.ap.org/dynamicstories/FINANCIAL_MELTDOWN.
272. *Associated Press*, "Dow plunges 800 points amid global sell-off," October 6, 2008, http://old.isp.com/members/home.pl.
273. Jeannine Aversa, *Associated Press*, "Dow plunges 733 on new disheartening economic data," October 15, 2008, http://hosted.ap.org/dynamicstories/FINANCIAL_MELTDOWN

274. *Associated Press,* "Dow industrials fall below 7,000," March 2, 2009, http://old.isp.com/members/home.pl.
275. *Associated Press,* "6.1 million getting jobless benefits," April 6, 2009, http://old.isp.com/members/home.pl.
276. David Wilkerson, *World Challenge Pulpit Series,* "In One Hour Everything Is Going to Change," New York, NY, September 3, 2007.
277. D. James Kennedy, *The Mortgaging of America,* Coral Ridge Ministries, Fort Lauderdale, FL, 2009, pp. 8, 45.
278. Ibid., pp. 46, 49.
279. Ibid., pp. 41, 52, 53.
280. Ibid., pp. 54, 68.
281. D. James Kennedy, news report commentary, *Impact,* "Taking the Strain Out of Finances," Coral Ridge Ministries, Fort Lauderdale, FL, June 2009.
282. D. James Kennedy, *D. James Kennedy Archives,* "The Truth is Undeniable: God Blesses Givers," Coral Ridge Ministries, Fort Lauderdale, FL, received April 6, 2009.
283. D. James Kennedy, *One Nation Under God,* DVD, Coral Ridge Ministries, Fort Lauderdale, FL, 2005.
284. Coral Ridge Ministries, news report, *Impact,* "Spending Bill: Needed 'Jolt' or 'Generational Theft'?," Fort Lauderdale, FL, March 2009.
285. James Dobson, *Focus on the Family,* "Family News From Focus on the Family," Colorado Springs, CO, December 2008.
286. Jennifer Cassidy, newsletter, *Coral Ridge Ministries,* Fort Lauderdale, FL, February 26, 2009.
287. James Dobson, *Focus on the Family,* "Family News From Focus on the Family," Colorado Springs, CO, April 2008.
288. Ibid.
289. Jennifer Cassidy, newsletter, *Coral Ridge Ministries,* Fort Lauderdale, FL, February 2011.

   Coral Ridge Ministries, news report, "Bold Faith for America's Future," received December 6, 2010.
290. Kenneth Barker, ed., *The NIV Study Bible,* Zondervan Publishing House, Grand Rapids, MI, 1995, p. 1997, (Note: Lk 3:12).
291. *Associated Press,* "Protestors throw tea bags over White House fence," April 15, 2009, http://www.poconorecord.com/apps/pbcs.dll/article.

292. *nj.com, New Jersey Real—Time News*, "Thousands take part in 'tea party' protest against high taxes in Morristown," July 4, 2009, http://www.com/news/index.ssf/2009/07.
293. Michael van der Galien, *Poli Gazette*, "Anti-Obama case: Protestors Take the Streets, Democrats Panic," July 18, 2009, http://www.poligazette.com/2009/07/18.
294. Pritchett Cotten, dir., *Tea Party: The Documentary Film*, DVD, Ground Floor, LLC., 2009.
295. Robert Stevenson, dir., *Johnny Tremain*, Disney Enterprises, Inc., Walt Disney Production, Burbank, CA, 1957.
296. David Wilkerson, *World Challenge Pulpit Series*, "A Fresh Outpouring Of the Holy Spirit," New York, NY, September 15, 2008.
297. Jennifer Cassidy, newsletter, *Coral Ridge Ministries*, Fort Lauderdale, FL, August 2010.
298. Tom Stewart, "The Church of Philadelphia Hall of Fame," p. 1 of 19, http://www.whatsaiththescripture.com/Fellowship/Church.Philad.Hall.of.Fame.html.
299. *Experience Shift*, "Founding Fathers," July 3, 2009, http://www.experienceshift.blogspot.com/2009/07/founding-fathers.html.
300. Ibid.
301. D. James Kennedy, *One Nation Under God*, DVD, Coral Ridge Ministries, Fort Lauderdale, FL, 2005.
302. Sam Kastensmidt, *End-Time Handmaidens & Servants Magazine*, "Our American Birthright," Jasper, AR, March 2004.
303. Coral Ridge Ministries, news report, *Impact*, "Faulty Worldview Explains 'Don't Ask, Don't Tell' Repeal, Much Else," Fort Lauderdale, FL, March 2011.
304. Ibid.
305. Coral Ridge Ministries, DVD, *10 Truths about America's Christian Heritage*, Fort Lauderdale, FL, 2008.

AMERICA: FUTURE

1. *Hymns of Glorious Praise*, #497, "The Star Spangled Banner," Gospel Publishing House, Springfield, MO, 1969.
2. David Wilkerson, *World Challenge Pulpit Series*, "That Dreadful Day No One Wants to Talk About," New York, NY, February 5, 2007.

3. Ibid.
4. David Wilkerson, *World Challenge Pulpit Series,* "What It Means to Live By One's Faith," New York, NY, February 9, 2009.
5. David Wilkerson, *World Challenge, Inc.,* "An Urgent Message," Lindale, TX, March 23, 2009.
6. David Wilkerson, *World Challenge Pulpit Series,* "A Fresh Outpouring Of the Holy Spirit," New York, NY, September 15, 2008.
7. William F. Claxton, dir. *Little House on the Prairie,* "Harriet's Happenings," NBC Production, approx. 1979-1980.
8. James F. Collier, dir., video, *The Hiding Place,* World Wide Pictures, Inc., 1975.
9. Norman Jewison, dir., video, *Fiddler on the Roof,* Mirish Productions, Inc., 1971.
10. Euzhan Palcy, dir., DVD, *Ruby Bridges,* The Wonderful World of Disney, Buena Vista Home Entertainment, 2004.
11. Chuck Norris, *Jewish Voice Today,* "Got Your Permit to Study the Bible?," Vol. 43, Number 4, Phoenix, AZ, September/October 2009.
12. Gary Kah, *En Route to Global Occupation,* Huntington House Publishers, Lafayette, LA, 1992.
13. Ibid., pp. 6,7.
14. Ibid., pp. 24, 25, 28, 29.
15. Ibid., p. 34.
16. Ibid., pp. 91, 95, 99, 125, 127, 136.
17. John Whitehead, newsletter, *The Rutherford Institute,* Charlottesville, VA, received October 30, 2010.
18. Ibid.
19. Ibid.
20. Gary Kah, *En Route to Global Occupation,* Huntington House Publishers, Lafayette, LA, 1992, pp.77, 79, 83.
21. Ibid., pp. 84, 109.
22. Ibid., p. 142.
23. Jennifer Cassidy, newsletter, *Coral Ridge Ministries,* Fort Lauderdale, FL, July 21, 2009.
24. *Coral Ridge Ministries,* news report, "America's Rush to Destruction," Fort Lauderdale, FL, 2009.

25. Jennifer Cassidy, newsletter, *Coral Ridge Ministries,* Fort Lauderdale, FL, August 2009.
26. Phyllis Schlafly, newsletter, *Eagle Forum,* Alton, IL, received April 2009.

    Jay Sekulow, newsletter, *American Center for Law & Justice,* Washington, D.C., received October 25, 2010.
27. Phyllis Schlafly, newsletter, *Eagle Forum,* Alton, IL, received April 2009.
28. Ibid.
29. Jennifer Cassidy, newsletter, *Coral Ridge Ministries,* Fort Lauderdale, FL, July 21, 2009.
30. *Let Freedom Ring, Inc.,* news, "Our Judeo-Christian Nation," June 29, 2009, http://www.letfreedomringusa.com/news/read.
31. Jan Markell, *Jewish Voice Today,* "Why Perilous Times Are Now in Overdrive," Vol. 43, Number 4, Phoenix, AZ, September/October 2009.
32. Phyllis Schlafly, newsletter, *Eagle Forum,* Alton, IL, received April 2009.
33. Brenda Chapman, Steve Hickner, and Simon Wells, dirs., VHS, *The Prince of Egypt,* Dream Works Home Entertainment, 1999.
34. Michael Evans, *The American Prophecies,* Time Warner Book Group, New York, NY, 2004, pp. 1, 2.
35. Ibid., p 42.
36. Ibid., pp. 43, 45.
37. *End-Time Handmaidens, Inc.,* "Washington's Vision," Engeltal, AR.
38. Ibid.
39. Ibid.
40. Ibid.
41. Ibid.
42. Ibid.
43. Ibid.
44. Ibid.
45. Ibid.
46. Kenneth Barker, ed., *The NIV Study Bible,* Zondervan Publishing House Grand Rapids, MI, 1984, p. 1838, (Note Zec 11:7).

47. Norman Jewison, dir., *Fiddler on the Roof*, The Mirisch Production Company, video, 1971.
48. Jennifer Cassidy, newsletter, *Coral Ridge Ministries*, Fort Lauderdale, FL, September 2009.
49. Michael Evans, *The American Prophecies*, Time Warner Book Group, New York, NY, 2004, p. 16.
50. Ibid., pp. 16, 18.
51. Ibid., pp. 22-24, 27.
52. Ibid., pp. 27, 214, 245.
53. Alan Keyes, newsletter, *Declaration Alliance*, Houston, TX, received October 30, 2010.
54. Ibid.
55. Ibid.
56. Alan Keyes, newsletter, *Conservative Majority PAC*, Houston, TX, received October 19, 2010.
57. Jay Sekulow, newsletter, *American Center for Law & Justice*, Washington, D.C., received October 25, 2010, and January 15, 2011.
58. Ibid., news report, received January 15, 2011.
59. Sandra Teplinsky, *Why Care about Israel?*, Chosen Books, Grand Rapids, MI, 2007, p. 49.
60. William Koenig, *Eye to Eye*, About Him Publishing, Alexandria, VA, 2008, pp. x, xi.
61. Ibid., p. xxi.
62. Jennifer Cassidy, newsletter, *Coral Ridge Ministries*, Fort Lauderdale, FL, September 2009.
63. Coral Ridge Ministries, newsletter, *Impact*, "New TV Special/Looks at Radical Islam," Fort Lauderdale, FL, September 2009.
64. Ibid.
65. David Parsons, news report, "Word from Jerusalem," Murfreesboro, TN, February 2011.
66. Coral Ridge Ministries, DVD, *One Nation Under God*, Fort Lauderdale, FL, 2005.
67. David Wilkerson, *Times Square Church Pulpit Series*, "It's Harvest Time," New York, NY, May 2, 2005.

David Wilkerson, *World Challenge Pulpit Series*, "A Christian's Response to Calamities," New York, NY, November 28, 2005.

68. Ibid.
69. Michael Evans, *The American Prophecies*, Time Warner Book Group, New York, NY, 2004, p. 31.
70. Ibid., pp. 30, 32.
71. David Wilkerson, *World Challenge Pulpit Series*, "Getting Ready for the Coming of the Lord," New York, NY, February 18, 2008.
72. Brian Desmond, dir., *The Christmas Carol*, (original B&W version), 1951.
73. Robert Benton, dir., *Places in the Heart*, TriStar Pictures, 1984.
74. Glenn Jordan, dir., *Sarah Plain and Tall*, Hallmark Home Entertainment, 1990.
75. James F. Collier, dir., *The Hiding Place*, World Wide Pictures Home Video, 1975.
76. Exploration Films, *The Worship DVD, Given to Him*, A Reel Productions, 2004.
77. David Wilkerson, *The Vision and Beyond*, World Challenge Publications, Lindale, TX, 2003, p. 53.
78. Irving Berlin, *Trustees of the God Bless America Fund*, "God Bless America," 1965, 1966, http://www.scoutsongs.com/lyrics/godblessamerica.html.
79. Victoria Neufeldt, ed., *Webster's New World Dictionary, Third College Edition*, "Magna Carta," Prentice Hall, New York, NY, 1994, p. 812.
80. Alex Kendrick, dir., DVD, *Facing the Giants*, Sherwood Baptist Church, Albany, GA, 2006.
81. *Wikipedia, the free encyclopedia*, "Zorro," Walt Disney Productions TV series, 1957 through 1961, http://en.wikipedia.org/wiki/Zorro (1957 TV series).
82. Ed Smith, *Beyond Tolerable Recovery*, Alathia Publishing, Campbellsville, KY, 2000, pp. 39-57.
83. *Wikipedia, the free encyclopedia*, "Johnny Appleseed," http://en.wikipedia.org/wiki/Johnny_Appleseed.
84. Ibid.
85. *Hymns of Glorious Praise*, #304, "In the Garden," Gospel Publishing House, Springfield, MO, 1969.
86. David Wilkerson, *The Vision and Beyond*, World Challenge Publications, Lindale, TX, 2003, pp. 24, 25.

87. Ibid., pp. 122, 124.
88. Ibid., p. 125.
89. Ibid., pp. 126-128.
90. Mark Hall, Casting Crowns, CD, *Peace on Earth,* "While You were Sleeping," EMT CMG Publishing, Nashville, TN, 2008.
91. Pritchett Cotton, dir., *Tea Party: The Documentary Film,* DVD, Ground Floor, LLC., 2009.

The Lord's Quilt

Exhibit: A

The Lord's Quilt

Exhibit: B